R. Gupta's®

NCC

National Cadet Corps

ARMY WING

Covers both Common & Special Subjects

Including

Previous Papers & Solved Questions

RAMESH PUBLISHING HOUSE, NEW DELHI

Published by:

O.P. Gupta *for* Ramesh Publishing House

Admin. Office:

12-H, New Daryaganj Road, Opp. Officers' Mess,
New Delhi-110002 ✆ 23275224, 23245124

✦ **E-mail:** info@rameshpublishinghouse.com

✦ **For Online Shopping:** www.rameshpublishinghouse.com

Showroom:

- Balaji Market, Nai Sarak, Delhi-6 ✆ 23253720, 23282525
- 4457, Nai Sarak, Delhi-6, ✆ 23918938

Book Code: R-2126

3rd Edition: February, 2025

ISBN: 978-81-948811-1-7

Price: ₹ 280

Printed at: Deepak Offset, Delhi

Preface

Most of our young school and college students join the NCC while pursuing their course of education at their respective institutions. While joining the NCC they dedicate an important part of their educational period for a greater cause. NCC activities are not just for fun and games, these are for the overall development of better people and a better society. In other words, it is a service to the nation. The time devoted to NCC training is never wasted but is used in a better way and more meaningful manner for the society and the country.

The NCC training not only makes you more disciplined and responsible in life but it also helps you develop your personality and character traits. There is no dearth of knowledge and application of the educational subjects in it. Various social and science subjects are put to use in this training in different aspects of life. It also involves physical, arms, field craft, self-defence, and adventure training along with many more activities to make the cadets more confident and fully competent to tackle any eventuality and challenges in life with success.

All these things require some valuable time of the cadets who also have to study their academic subjects in detail. The present book has been published with the aim to save some precious time of the cadets by providing most of the reading material in a very concise and easy manner for a quick grasp.

It is the dream of every NCC cadet to join the Defence Services. Special chapters like The Armed Forces and Military History, A Career in Defence Services, Services Tests & Interviews, and Leadership & Personality Development are incorporated in the book to guide the cadets in this direction.

It is sincerely believed that this book will immensely help the readers become good cadets, and in future—good soldiers, good officers, and above all—good citizens and good leaders of India.

The book is published in the best interests of NCC cadets with extensive study and research on the subject from existing literature and Internet. Absolute originality is not claimed regarding the contents of the book as whatever we read and observe, influences our writing and expression one way or the other.

We express our deep gratitude to all those who have directly or indirectly contributed in the making of this book.

— Publisher

Contents

❑❑❑

NCC

NATIONAL CADET CORPS

ARMY WING

PREVIOUS PAPERS

NCC-A Certificate Previous Paper

PART I

COMMON SUBJECT

Q.1. What does 'Lotus' represent in the NCC flag?

Ans. The seventeen lotuses represent 17 State Directorates.

Q.2. In vishram position, what is the distance between the feet?

Ans. 12″.

Q.3. Give any two advantages of cycle expedition.

Ans. It develops stamina and endurance.

Q.4. Name the insects which are the carriers of the germs of Malaria, Dengue and Filariasis.

Ans.
- Malaria – Female Anopheles Mosquito
- Dengue – Aedes Aegypti Mosquito
- Filariasis – Culex Fatigans Mosquito

Q.5. Name the factors mainly responsible for air-pollution.

Ans. Smoke and Dust.

Q.6. What is the procedure of Ground Arms (Bhumi Shastr)? Explain it.

Ans. Ground Arms:

- **Command :** Bhumi Shastr-ek (Ground arms one) : Keep the upper body straight but inclined forward and bend down by bending and opening the knees keeping the heels together, lay the rifle gently on the ground at the right side, magazine to the right, muzzle pointing straight to the front, right hand in line with the toe of the boot.
- **Command :** Squad Do (Squad two) : Release the rifle with the right hand and resume the position of attention.

Q.7. Mention the laws of aiming.

Ans. Correct aim is essential for a successful shot. The rules of aiming are:

(i) Focus the target at the centre with the eye and the foresight.

(ii) Hold the rifle properly.

(iii) Close the left eye and focus the foresight.

(iv) See the foresight through the backsight 'U'.

Q.8. For creating a sense of adventure and to develop confidence and courage in the NCC cadets, what type of activities are organised? Name any four of these activities.

Ans. Mountaineering, Trekking, Cycle Expedition and Motorcycle Expedition, Horse Riding.

Q.9. Which century marks the beginning of the modern period of India? How did the country face its struggle with the enemy?

Ans. 18th Century. The Indian Independence Movement encompassed activities and ideas aiming to end the East India Company rule (1757-1858) and the British Indian Empire (1858-1947) in the Indian subcontinent. The movement spanned a total of 190 years (1757-1947). The early part of the 20th century saw a more radical approach towards political self-rule proposed by leaders such as the Lal, Bal, Pal and Aurobindo Ghosh. Nationalists like Netaji Subhash Chandra Bose and Bhagat Singh preached armed rebellion to achieve self-rule. The last stages of the self-rule struggle from the 1920 onwards saw Congress adopt Gandhi's policy of non-violence and civil resistance, and several other campaigns which finally brought the curtains down on the British rule in India in 1947. India's freedom struggle has been able to unite the entire country irrespective of caste, creed, religion, ethnicity, language, age, gender or any other differences and fight for their independence unitedly as one nation.

Q.10. What is the meaning of 'Depletion' in the context of environment? Give its two causes.

Ans. Depletion means thinning of environmental resources. Main causes of depletion are overuse and pollution.

Q.11. What is the sequence of firing a shot?

Ans. (i) **Aiming Position :** On taking the aim, the firer must take the first pressure.

(ii) **Breathing :** Just before taking an aim, breathing must be gently restrained. It is important to coordinate so that when the foresight comes to the point of aim, the breath is partially exhaled.

(iii) **Firing :** Immediately on 'correct aim' the second pressure will be taken and shot fired. For a second or two after firing, there should be no relaxation of the hold or movement of trigger finger or head.

(iv) **Follow Through :** The hold and aim must be maintained until the bullet has left the barrel. Better still, fire should follow through until the bullet has reached the target.

Q.12. List any six man-made disasters.

Ans. Accidents, Industrial Mishaps, Fire, Forest Fire, Contamination, Terrorist Activities.

Q.13. What do you understand about sizing and forming of squad?

Ans. Sizing and Forming

- **Command :** Lamba Dahine, Chhota Baen, ek line men–Kadvar (tallest on the right, shortest the left in single rank-size) : The whole squad turns right, counts a pause and then sort themselves out by size remaining at attention facing the instructor in one single line.

- **Command :** Squad dahine se ginti kar (Squad count from right) : The squad numbers from the right to left.
- **Command :** Visham Cadet ek qadam aage, Sam cadet ek qadam pichhe chal : (Odd numbers one pace forward even numbers one pace step back march) : All follow command.
- **Command :** Dahina cadet khara rahe. Visham cadet dahine, sam cadet baen, line dahine aur baen mur (stand fast the right hand man, odd numbers to the right, even numbers to the left, ranks right and left turn) : All turn as ordered except the right hand man who remains facing the front. The squad then forms three ranks with even numbers following behind the odd number. On halting in position, each man turns to his front, takes up his own dressing and remains at attention.
- **Command :** Teen line banao, tez chal (Form up in three ranks quick march): The cadets position themselves in three ranks, front, centre and rear with 30 inches between ranks and an interval of one arm's length between two cadets.

Q.14. How can youth be helpful in preventing the spread of HIV?

Ans. Youth can educate general public by spreading the following information:

(i) Being in a mutually faithful sexual relationship.

(ii) Correct and consistent use of condoms for every sexual act.

(iii) Checking all the blood and blood-products for HIV infection before transfusion.

(iv) Avoiding sharing needles and syringes for injecting drugs.

(v) Preventing mother to child transmission of HIV infection.

Q.15. Name any six equipments used for rock climbing. How can they be utilized?

Ans. Rock Climbing Equipment: A wide range of equipment is used during Rock Climbing. They are as follows:

- **Rope and Webbing**

  (i) **Dynamic Ropes:** These are designed to absorb the energy of a falling climber, and are usually used as Belaying ropes. When a climber falls, the rope stretches, reducing the maximum force experienced by the climber, their belayer.

  (ii) **Low Elongation Ropes:** Ropes which stretch much less, and are usually used in anchoring systems.
- **Carabineers:** Carabineers are metal loops with spring-loaded Gates used as connectors and they are primarily made from steel.
- **Quick Draws:** Quick draws are used by climbers to connect ropes to bolt anchors, allowing the rope to move through the anchoring system with minimal friction.
- **Harnesses:** A harness is a system used for connecting the rope to the climber. There are two loops at the front of the harness where the

climber ties into the rope at the working end using a figure eight knot. Most harnesses used in climbing are pre-constructed and are worn around the pelvis and hips.

- **Belay Devices:** Belay devices are mechanical friction brake devices used to control a rope when belaying. Their main purpose is to allow the rope to be locked off with minimal effort to arrest a climber's fall.
- **Rappel Devices (Descenders):** These devices are friction brakes which are designed for descending ropes.
- **Ascenders:** Ascenders are mechanical devices for ascending on a rope.
- **Helmet:** The climbing helmet is a piece of safety equipment that primarily protects the skull against falling debris.
- **Climbing Shoes:** Specifically designed foot wear is usually worn for climbing to increase the grip of the foot on a climbing wall or rock face.
- **Belay Gloves:** Belay gloves are constructed from either leather or a synthetic substitute. They typically have heat resistant padding on the palm and fingers.

Q.16. Compare any six characteristics of Rifle ·22 No. II MK IV BA with Rifle ·22 Deluxe BA.

Ans. Comparison of Characteristics of Rifle .22 No II MK IV BA and Rifle .22 Deluxe BA

Characteristics	Rifle .22 No II MK IV BA	Rifle .22 Deluxe BA
* Length	45"	43"
* Weight	8 Lbs 10½ OZ	6 LBs 2 OZ
* Magazine Capacity	10 rounds	05 rounds
* Muzzle Velocity	2700 per sec	2700 per sec
* Grooves in the Barrel	06	06
* Effective Range	25 yds	25 yds
* Max Range	1700 yds at 33 angle	1700 yds at 33 angle
* Calibre	.22"	.22"
* Ammunition	.22"	.22"
* Rate of fire :		
(i) Normal	5 rounds per minute	5 rounds per minute
(ii) Rapid	10-15 Rds per minute	10-15 rounds/minute

Q.17. Identify the measures that can be taken to improve the character of a citizen. Also explain them.

Ans. Some of the traits if followed religiously can help to improve character. These are :

(i) Initiative; (ii) Courage; (iii) Decisiveness;
(iv) Enthusiasm; (v) Morality; (vi) Loyalty;
(vii) Justice; (viii) Patriotism; and (ix) Sense of Duty.

Some distinguishing qualities which if demonstrated in regular activities, help a person to earn the respect, confidence, willing obedience and loyal co-operation of his subordinates. These are :

- **Alertness :** Alertness of mind is what helps a person to pick up the opportunities at the right time and exploit the situation to his own advantage.
- **Bearing :** It is creation of favourable impression, upright carriage and appearance, alertness and energy in actions and movements, and high personal conduct at all times. Appearance and manner must show competence and confidence.
- **Courage :** It is a mental quality that enables a man to accept responsibility and act correctly in a threatening situation with calmness and firmness; requires moral and physical courage.
- **Decisiveness :** It is the ability to take decision promptly and announce them in a clear and forceful manner.
- **Dependability :** It is proper performance of duty and carrying out actively, intelligently and willingly the orders of superiors.
- **Endurance :** It is mental and physical stamina measured by the ability to withstand pain, fatigue, stress and hardship.
- **Enthusiasm :** It is the display of sincere interest and zeal in performance of duties.
- **Initiative :** It is to do what is to be done even in the absence of orders and to avoid inactivity.
- **Integrity :** It is the uprightness of character, soundness of moral principles, quality of absolute truthfulness and honesty.
- **Judgement :** It is the quality of logically weighing facts on which to make sound decisions.
- **Justice :** It is the quality of being impartial and consistent.
- **Knowledge :** A leader must have sound knowledge than the men he commands.
- **Loyalty :** It is the quality of faithfulness to country, your seniors and colleagues.
- **Sense of Humour :** It is the ability to remain cheerful under stress.
- **Tact :** It is the ability to deal with others without offending anyone.
- **Unselfishness :** It is the quality of refraining from own comfort and personal advancement at the expense of others.

Some other important leadership traits are listed below:

(i) Truthfulness (ii) Self-confidence (iii) Maturity
(iv) Esprit-de-corps (v) Humility and Sympathy (vi) Patience

PART II

SPECIAL SUBJECT – ARMY

Q.18. Name any four tasks which army engineers provide to the army.

Ans. The various tasks performed by Army Field Engineers are:

(i) Laying of mine fields
(ii) Breaching of mine fields
(iii) Construction of field defences
(iv) Construction of tracks in mountains
(v) Construction/maintenance of border roads
(vi) Water supply to troops in the field, especially in deserts
(vii) Construction of Helipads where ever required
(viii) In Counter Insurgency Operation : 1. Detection, neutralisation and removal of IEDs and explosives. 2. Road opening etc for all type of traffic
(ix) Maintenance of essential services

Q.19. Name any four officers of Armed Forces who have been awarded 'Param Vir Chakra'.

Ans. Captain Vikram Batra, Lt. Manoj Kumar Pandey, Major Somnath Sharma, Major Shaitan Singh.

Q.20. Answer the following:

(a) What are grid lines? State their purpose.

(b) How many types of slopes are there?

(c) How many types of North are there?

Ans. (a) A military map is covered with a network of purple lines, some running North and South and other West and East. These form a series of small squares all over the map. These lines are known as Grid Lines. The purpose of Grid Lines is to make possible giving and reading Grid References and to facilitate measurement of bearings.

(b) The natural rise and fall between two permanent places on the surface of the Earth is called slope.

It is of two types:

1. Regular slope 2. Irregular slope

In regular slope the pattern of rise and fall of land is equal. It is further of two types:

1. Uniform gentle slope 2. Uniform steep slope

In irregular slope, the pattern of rise and fall of land is not equal. It is also of two types :

1. Concave slope : When the slope of the bottom part of the hill is broad and gentle and the slope of the top of the hill is comparatively narrow and steep, it is called concave slope.

2. **Convex slope :** When the slope of the bottom of the hill is narrow and steep and slope of the top of the hill is comparatively broad and gentle, it is called convex slope.

(c) Various types of North are:

(i) **True North :** The direction of North pole from the observer.

(ii) **Magnetic North :** It is the point to which an accurate compass needle points, when freely suspended.

(iii) **Grid North :** It is the direction to which the North South grid lines on a map point.

Q.21. What is the basis of Battle Craft? Also describe its subject.

Ans. Battle craft is nothing but set of drills which are essential for conduct of successful operations in the battle field. These battle drills are very useful in tackling minor tactical problems. They save time, ensure rapid action and avoid confusion. Knowledge of field signals and section and platoon formations, however, is essential in the execution of various battle drills. Battle Craft includes the following subjects:

(a) Field Signals
(b) Section Formations
(c) Fire control orders
(d) Fire and move
(e) Section battle drills

Q.22. List the types of satellites and explain their functions.

Ans. Types of Satellites:

(a) **Wheather Satellite:** The weather satellite is a type of satellite that is primarily used to monitor the weather and climate of the Earth. Satellites can be polar orbiting, covering the entire Earth asynchronously, or geostationary, hovering over the same spot on the equator.

(b) **Scientific Satellite:** Scientific research satellites provide meteorological information, land survey data (e.g. remote sensing), Amateur (HAM) Radio, and other different scientific research applications such as earth science, marine science, and atmospheric research.

(c) **Communication Satellite:** A communication satellite is an artificial satellite that relays and amplifies radio telecommunications signals via a transponder; it creates a communication channel between a source transmitter and a receiver at different locations on Earth. Communications satellites are used for television, telephone, radio, internet, and military applications. There are over 2,000 communications satellites in Earth's orbit, used by both private and government organizations.

(d) **Navigation Satellite:** A satellite navigation or satnav system is a system that uses satellites to provide autonomous geo-spatial positioning. It allows small electronic receivers to determine their location (longitude, latitude, and altitude/elevation) to high precision (within a few metres) using time signals transmitted along a line of sight by radio from satellites. A satellite navigation system with global coverage may be termed a global navigation satellite system (GNSS).

(e) **Military Satellite:** A military satellite is an artificial satellite used for a military purpose. The most common missions are intelligence gathering, navigation and military communications. The first military satellites were photographic reconnaissance missions.

Q.23. What is Compass Error? Which system has replaced this old instrument?

Ans. **Compass Error:** Sometimes due to the presence of impurities in the material of which a compass is made or other reasons, the magnetic needle may not point toward the magnetic NORTH but a little to the EAST or WEST of it. This deviation of the magnetic needle in the compass from the magnetic NORTH is termed compass error.

Global Positioning System: Global Positioning System (GPS) refers to a system of satellites and receivers that allows people and devices to pin point their precise location on the earth. The first GPS satellite was launched in 1974. GPS is funded and controlled by the United States, Department of Defence. Present technology provides very handy and accurate navigation.

Q.24. Name the different types of section formations. What are the basic factors required for a section formation?

Ans. The different types of section formations are:

1. Single File
2. File Formation
3. Diamond Formation
4. Arrow Head Formation
5. Spear Head Formation
6. Extended Line Formation

The different sections have to be divided into several formations or shapes in certain conditions.

It basically depends upon the conditions of soldiers on land, firing from the enemy's side, excessive firing from the counter part, and the control of section commander over the section, etc.

In a Section Formation, the distance between the two soldiers should at least be 15-25 yds. They should not move in a line but should spread in a zig-zag manner.

❖ ❖ ❖

NCC-B Certificate Previous Paper

PART I

COMMON SUBJECT

Q.1. Which traits does 'drill' inculcate in a cadet?

Ans. Smartness, Steadiness and Coordination.

Q.2. What all is included in hospital or bio-medical waste?

Ans. Hospital waste is generated during the diagnosis, treatment, or immunization of human beings or animals or in research activities in these fields or in the production or biological testing. It may include Soiled Waste, Disposables, Anatomical Waste, Discarded Medicines and Chemical Wastes.

Q.3. How are air-conditioners responsible for depletion of the ozone layer?

Ans. Gases called Chlorofluorocarbons (CFCs), used in airconditioners, refrigerators and many aerosol sprays are rapidly destroying the ozone layer in the atmosphere.

Q.4. Write about any two current objectives of our nation.

Ans. (i) Self sufficiency in nuclear-power.

(ii) Availability of reliable power supply for farming and industries.

(iii) Production of goods for world markets.

(iv) Balancing growth in both public and private sector.

(v) Modernization of villages, linking with roads and provision of electricity to all villages.

Q.5. What is the importance of moral values in an individual's life?

Ans. 'Values' means a standard of behaviour and 'Ethics' means a set of moral principles that govern a person's behaviour. A person of values excels others in all fields. The values and ethics which drive a person may be inherited from the society they live in, *i.e.* from the people around them and to a large extent the family they hail from.

To develop into a good leader, a person needs certain values in him or one can say he must possess distinctive ethics in his life.

A leader may be intelligent, knowledgeable and hard-working, but unless he is driven by a set of values which are morally acceptable, he cannot be a good leader. Generally, a group in particular and its work and achievements as a whole are judged by the values and the behaviour and good manners of its leader.

Q.6. "In 1942, a mass civil disobedience movement was launched. It was followed by large-scale violence directed at railway stations, telegraph

offices, government buildings, other emblems and institutions of colonial rule."

(a) Identify the movement explained in the above passage.

(b) Under whose leadership was this movement started?

(c) According to the government, who was responsible for these acts of violence?

Ans. (a) Quit India Movement

(b) M.K. Gandhi

(c) M.K. Gandhi

Q.7. Why is drill an important part of a cadet's life? State any three reasons.

Ans. NCC cadets are trained for obedience, smartness, proper dressing, self-defensiveness, unity, discipline for gaining state of physical and mental balance. The training, which includes all these aspects is called "Drill".

Reasons of importance:

(i) To create self confidence

(ii) To inculcate a sense of discipline

(iii) To improve bearing, smartness in appearance and turn out

(iv) To develop the quality of immediate and implicit obedience to orders.

Q.8. Which technique should a firer adopt to maintain a stable position while shooting?

Ans. For a stable lying position, the firer should lie as if fixed to the ground with:

(i) Body slanting to the left from the line of the target and legs opened wide apart.

(ii) Lie on the ground in such manner to form a horizontal triangle by the three points where the chest leaves the ground, the left elbow and the right elbow.

(iii) A vertical triangle, as viewed from the front of firer, formed by the forearms, the base being the ground between elbows.

(iv) The shoulders should be level.

(v) The right hand is bedded in providing steadiness and the forefinger to be actually on the trigger.

(vi) The left hand acts as support to the forward part of the rifle.

(vii) The butt plate should be bedded into the shoulder.

(viii) The weight of the head should press the chin downwards and to the right against the butt.

(ix) Aim correctly and then hold breath while pressing the trigger firmly.

Q.9. Identify any three elements that cause fire. Briefly explain these elements.

Ans. Fire is the outcome of either heating or over heating of a combustible substance to the required temperature or igniting an inflammable material. The following three elements are essential for creation of fire and its continuation:

(a) Oxygen.

(b) Sufficient heat to raise the temperature of fuel to its burning point or ignition temperature.

(c) Combustible or burnable material (Solid, Liquid or Gas).

The three things or conditions that are necessary to start a fire—fuel (Combustible Material), oxygen (Air) and sufficient Heat to raise the temperature of the fuel to its burning point—should not be present at the same place and time to prevent out break of any type of fire.

Q.10. Weapons have always been considered dangerous for society, but they are also used for the maintenance of law and order and for border security. Give your views regarding the same.

Ans. It is true, weapons have always been considered dangerous for society but only if they are in the hands of persons incompetent to handle them such as children, insane persons or criminals. A weapon in the hands of such a person may lead to injury, accident, crime and even murder. On the other hand weapons are used for maintenance of law and order and for border security. If a police officer is without a weapon how will he prevent a crime by an armed criminal? Our armed forces protect our borders from the enemy. If they are without arms how will they counter-attack the enemy who is well-armed? Arms are also used for self-defence by many people. Hence, arms are not always dangerous, they are also used for safety and protection of life and property and protect the borders of the country as well.

Q.11. How can we maintain our personal hygiene? Give three methods for the same.

Ans. Personal hygiene involves those practices performed by an individual to care for one's bodily health and well being, through cleanliness. Maintenance of personal hygiene is very important in preventing disease. It deals with the practices that help in the maintenance and promotion of a person's health. Personal hygiene habits such as washing hands and brushing teeth will keep bacteria, viruses and illness at bay. There are mental and physical benefits. Practicing good body hygiene helps you feel good about yourself. Main components of personal hygiene are:

(i) Bathing, keeping the skin clean and in healthy condition is essential for good health. Wash your body regularly. Your body is constantly shedding skin. That skin needs to come off. Otherwise, It will cake up and cause illnesses.

(ii) Brush your teeth twice a day. Brushing minimizes the accumulation of bacteria in mouth which can cause tooth decay and gum diseases.

(iii) Keeping finger and toe nails trimmed and in good shape will prevent problems such as hang nails and infected nail beds. Feet that are clean and dry are less likely to contact Athlete's foot.

Q.12. What do you understand by psychoactive drugs? List down the main types of drugs that affect the central nervous system.

Ans. A 'Drug' is any substance (other than food that provides nutritional support) that, when inhaled, injected, smoked, consumed, absorbed via a patch on the skin, or dissolved under the tongue causes a physiological change in the body. They act on the brain and can change the way a person thinks, feels or behaves. 'Drug Addiction' is one of the most serious problems facing the world. Drug trafficking and drug abuse are considered as a greater problem than drug consumption.

Types of drugs: There are three main types of drugs affecting the central nervous system:

(i) **Depressants:** Depressants are drugs that slow down the function of the central nervous system. Example includes Alcohol, Cannabis, Hashish, etc.

(ii) **Stimulants:** Stimulants acts on the central nervous system to speed up the messages to and from the brain. They make the user feel more awake, alert or confident. Stimulants increase heart rate, body temperature and blood pressure. Other effects include craving, stretched pupils, talkativeness, agitation and sleep disturbance. Mild stimulants include Caffeine in coffee, Nicotine in tobacco, Ephedrine in medicines for cough, asthma etc.

(iii) **Hallucinogents:** Hallucinogens affect awareness. People who have taken them may believe they see, hear, and notice things that are not really there. Example includes Dhatura, Ketamine etc.

Q.13. Describe the procedure followed for ceremonial drill. What compliments are given to dignitaries?

Ans. In the NCC, the Ceremonial Drills are organised time to time and also at the culmination of the cadet's training. The Ceremonial Drill may be arranged for various dignitaries and VIPs.

National salute is given to the President of India and the Governors of the various states within their own jurisdiction. General salute is given to dignitaries of the rank of Major General and above. All other dignitaries are only given Salami Shastra (Present Arms).

The Ceremonial Parade is conducted in the following manner:

The VIP on arrival will be received by the Senior Officer serving with the NCC present and taken to the saluting base. The Parade Commander on seeing the VIP alighting from the car will order 'Parade Savdhan'. After VIP has come to the dais and is ready to take the salute, the Parade Commander will give the following words of command:

(i) Parade General Salute Degi
General Salute Salami Shastra.
Or
Parade Rashtriya Salute Degi
Rashtriya Salute Salami Shastra.
Or
Parade Salami Degi-Salami Shastra.

(ii) Parade Bazu Shastra.

The Parade Commander marches up smartly to the saluting base and reports to the VIP 'No. 1 Bn Parade Apke Nirikshan Ke Liye Hazir Hai Sriman/Srimati Ji'. After the VIPs permission has been obtained to let the parade stand-at-ease and prior to commencement of the inspection, Parade Commander gives the word of command 'Number one company Khara rahe, Baqui Vishram'. After the inspection is finished and the VIP has turned to the saluting dais, the following words of command will be given for the march past:

(i) Parade Savdhan
(ii) Parade Nikat Line Chal
(iii) Bagal shastra
(iv) Parade kooch kalam men manch se guzregi No ---- Aage.
(v) Parade tin-O-tin kalam men dahine mur

Word of command by respective company Commander in their own turn for the march past. 'Number one Company Baen se tez chal'. At the first flag (6 paces of the saluting base) each company commander will give the following words of command, 'Company Dahine Dekh'. After the company has gone past the saluting base (indicated by the next flag) his word of command will be 'Company Samne Dekh'. When the parade returns to the inspection line, each company will be given word of Command 'Company Tham'. This will follow the command:

(i) 'Number one company aage barhegi baen mur', and will then remain at Savdhan.
(ii) The entire parade will be made to stand-at-ease by the Parade Commander by giving command 'Parade Vishram'.

In case the parade is to advance in view order, the following word of command will be given by the Parade Commander:

(i) Parade Savdhan
(ii) Parade Madhya Se-saj
(iii) Parade Samne Dekh
(iv) Parade samiksha karan men Madhya se tez chal

The parade will automatically halt after taking 15 paces. The halt must coincide with stopping of music in case the band is in attendance. Compliment will be paid again accordingly to the status of the VIP. After this stage, stand-at-ease (Vishram). In case the parade is not required to advance in review order, the parade commander will give the words of command 'Vishram' when the entire parade has reached the inspection line and has been turned to the front. When the VIP leaves the Parade ground, the Parade Commander marches off the cadets.

Q.14. What are the dimensions of self-awareness? Explain any four of these dimensions.

Ans. Dimensions of Self Awareness

Self awareness involves knowing ourselves and our personality, and accepting oneself inspite of our imperfection. It includes all aspects of our selves—our thoughts, emotions, like, dislikes, strengths, and weakness, knowledge the fact that though I am imperfect, but still I like myself since I am a good human being and possess many qualities. It acknowledges the fact that I may be imperfect, but still I like myself since I am a good human being and possess many qualities. To have complete self awareness one needs to concentrate on two aspects the first being how we perceive ourselves our strengths, weaknesses, abilities etc. and secondly how others perceive us. Both the views together give a person a complete picture about one self. Every person perceives oneself in three aspects as:

(i) The perceive self - the way we see that part of ourselves.
(ii) The real self - the way we truly are.
(iii) The ideal self - the way we would like to be in that area.

Unhappiness and poor adjustments in persons are mainly because of discrepancies between the perceived and the real or ideal self. These unhappiness and poor adjustments are due to misperceptions of self which thereby leads to discontentment. Many people limit their self awareness to their bio-data which is usually things known by everybody. However at a deeper level there is so much inside each one of us that it has many dimensions:

(i) **Self Realization:** Self-realization is the ultimate of self-awareness when one realizes oneself and the requirement of their existence in the world.

(ii) **Self Knowledge or Self Exploration:** This is a process through which we undo or explore ourselves. This exploration and understanding and knowledge about three important areas Physical self-knowledge about our own body, Social self-knowledge about how we relate and interact with society; whether we are social, extroverts or introverts; helping nature; empathetic, etc. Inner self - Knowledge about our goals, dreams, aspirations, secrets, fears, etc.

(iii) **Self Confidence:** Self-confidence builds in from self-esteem and this is possible only when one is completely aware about ones abilities and limits. Success, appreciation, care, love etc. are factors that boost up the self-confidence.

(iv) **Self Talk:** These automatic thoughts can be positive or negative. Some of our self talk comes from logic and reason. Other self talk may arise from misconceptions that we create because of lack of information. This is the endless talks and conversations that runs through our minds through the day. This is also a strategy for raising ones' self-confidence if one practices positive thinking.

Q.15. What is the aim of obstacle training course? What safety measures are used during the training of NCC cadets?

Ans. The training in crossing the obstacles/barriers by NCC cadets is a very important aspect of NCC syllabus. The obstacle course training not only makes the cadets physically strong but also develops a very high degree of confidence and develops the qualities of patience and courage to face all types of challenges and barriers in life.

Safety Measures: Following safety measures must be ensured during the conduct of Obstacle Course training to cadets:

- Suitable and physically fit cadets only to be selected.
- Training to be given first in PT dress, later on with packs and weapon.
- Emphasis to be given on closing of individual timings and later team timings.
- Wet and slippery obstacles and area to be avoided.
- Obstacles to be done under supervision of qualified instructors and correct technique only to be used.
- Arrangement of first aid to be ensured.

PART II
SPECIAL SUBJECT - ARMY

Q.16. Define Grid lines.

Ans. A military map is covered with a network of purple lines, some running North and South and other West and East. These form a series of small squares all over the map. These lines are known as Grid Lines.

Q.17. What is Wi-Fi?

Ans. Wi-Fi is a wireless local area network that enables portable computing devices to connect easily to the Internet. Wi-Fi has become the de facto standard for access in private homes, within offices, and at public hotspots. Cellular data service offers coverage within a range of 10-15 miles from the nearest cell site.

Q.18. Which methods are used to find one's own position on the map?

Ans. Methods of Finding Own Position on Map:

(i) By resection method or Compass method

(ii) By inspection method.

Q.19. State any four items required for search operation by the navigation party.

Ans. Items required by Navigation Party:

(i) Set compass as per bounds

(ii) Luminous stick

(iii) White cloth

(iv) Marching chart

(v) White lime/chalk

(vi) Stone pebbles for measuring steps

(vii) Frosted torch

Q.20. Give any two advantages of line communication.

Ans. Advantages of line communication:

(i) Reliable and practically free from electrical interference.

(ii) Relatively secure.

(iii) Number of circuits and message carrying capacity is more but limited only by availability of material and manpower.

Q.21. What do you understand by field formations? Name the categories of field formations.

Ans. Field formation:

The different sections have to be divided into several formations or shapes in certain conditions.

It basically depends upon the conditions of soldiers on land, firing from the enemy's side, excessive firing from the counter part, and the control of section commander over the section, etc.

In a Section Formation, the distance between the two soldiers should at least be 15-25 yds. They should not move in a line but should spread in a zig-zag manner.

The common Field formations are mentioned below:

1. Single File
2. File Formation

3. Diamond Formation
4. Arrow Head Formation
5. Spear Head Formation
6. Extended Line Formation

Platoon Formation:

A platoon may have the following formations:

1. One up Formation
2. Two up Formation

Q.22. Give reason why the 30 mm automatic grenade launcher is a flexible weapon.

Ans. It can be mounted on a vehicle or helicopter. It can fire in low angle as well as in high angle. It has crest clearance capability. Flexibility is mainly due to:

(i) Controlled Elevation – 67 degrees
(ii) Controlled Depression – 14 degrees
(iii) Free Traverse – 260 degrees

Q.23. Write a short note on "Kargil Conflict".

Ans. In mid-1999 Pakistani paramilitary forces and Kashmiri insurgents captured deserted, but strategic, Himalayan heights in the Kargil district of India. These had been vacated by the Indian army during the onset of the inhospitable winter and were supposed to be reoccupied in spring. Once the scale of the Pakistani incursion was realised, the Indian Army quickly mobilised about 200,000 troops and Operation Meghdoot was launched.

The Battle of Tololing, among other assaults, slowly tilted the combat in India's favour. Nevertheless, some of the posts put up a stiff resistance, including Tiger Hill (Point 5140) that fell only later in the war. The Indian Army mounted some direct frontal ground assaults which were slow and took a heavy toll given the steep ascent that had to be made on peaks as high as 18,000 feet (5,500 m). Two months into the conflict, Indian troops had slowly retaken most of the ridges they had lost.

The Indian Army launched its final attacks in the last week of July; as soon as the Drass subsector had been cleared of Pakistani forces, the fighting ceased on 26 July. 26 July has since been marked as Kargil Vijay Diwas in India.

Q.24. What is the need of field signals? Explain the various field signals used by day and night.

Ans. Field signals are alternate means of giving orders and to control troops when voice control is not possible. Control over troops deployed can be done better by field signals than by voice control. There are various occasions when voice control is not possible. They are:

(a) Battle noises.
(b) Need for silence.
(c) Intervening distances are too large.

Field Signals By Day: Some of the visual signals used during the day are flags and mercury coated mirrors. Flags are very effectively used by Navy on board a ship.

(a) Flags: (Red, Green and White flags)
(b) Mercury coated mirrors
(c) Smoke
(d) Miscellaneous: Various signals can be improvised and pre-arranged as under:
    (i) Clothes superficially hung out to dry.
    (ii) Hurricane lamp, kept in the window.
    (iii) Flashing of torch is used as Morse Code.
    (iv) Applying various colours/signs on forehead and arms.

Field Signals By Night: Some of the field signals that can be used at night are:

(a) Pre decided signals on a walkie talkie.
(b) Click by fingers.
(c) Clicks by using tongue.
(d) Whistle by the mouth.
(e) Use of rope.
(f) Use of colour light.
(g) Use of blacked out torch.
(h) Firing of weapon.

❖ ❖ ❖

NCC-C Certificate Previous Paper

COMMON SUBJECT

DRILL

Q.1. What is the Aim of Drill?

Ans. (i) Create self confidence
(ii) To inculcate a sense of discipline
(iii) Improve bearing, smartness in appearance and turn out
(iv) To develop the quality of immediate and implicit obedience to orders.

Q.2. Fill in the Blanks :

(i) ___________ steps are taken in Khuli Line Chal.
(ii) Only ___________ step(s) are allowed forward & backwards.
(iii) Distance between two heels in Vishram position is ___________.
(iv) On the word of command 'Parade Par' thamm after ___________.
(v) Length of step in double march is ___________.

Ans. (i) 1½ (ii) One (iii) 12" (iv) 15 paces (v) 40".

Q.3. Fill in the blanks :

(i) In Adha Dahine Mur the squad turns ___________ degree.
(ii) In Tez Chal the distance between two cadets is ___________ inch.
(iii) In Dahine Saj, the squad takes a step forward by ___________ inch.
(iv) Angle between toes in Savdhan position is ___________ degree.
(v) In Pichhe Mur the squad turns ___________ degree.

Ans. (i) 45 (ii) 45 (iii) 15
(iv) 30 (v) 180

Q.4. What are the points to be observed while 'Saluting'?

Ans. (i) Bring the right hand by smart circular motion keeping all the fingers clenched together and the palm completely open, fingers, wrist and elbow in a straight line.
(ii) The top of forefinger will remain near the centre of the right eye brow.
(iii) Keep the hand in the position for the definite pause.
(iv) Cut down the hand smartly by the shortest possible route and take up the 'Savdhan' position.

Q.5. Who are entitled for National Salute?

Ans. (i) National Flag
(ii) President of India
(iii) Governor of State

Q.6 What are the points to be seen in 'Savdhan' Position?

Ans. (i) Body erect, perfectly still but not stiff.

(ii) Head up.

(iii) Eyes looking straight at the front of one's own height and still.

(iv) Chin vertical, neck straight and filling the collar.

(v) Shoulder square and forced downwards.

(vi) Chest up.

(vii) Hands fixed with body behind the seam of the trousers, elbow straight, fingers making loose half fist and the thumb towards the front.

(viii) Weight of the body on both the legs and knees straight.

(ix) Heels together making an angle of 30 degree at the front.

WEAPON TRAINING

Q.7. What is the sequence of action while firing a shot?

Ans. (i) **Aiming Position :** On taking the aim, the firer must take the first pressure.

(ii) **Breathing :** Just before taking an aim, breathing must be gently restrained. It is important to coordinate so that when the foresight comes to the point of aim, the breath is partially exhaled.

(iii) **Firing :** Immediately on 'correct aim' the second pressure will be taken and shot fired. For a second or two after firing, there should be no relaxation of the hold or movement of trigger finger or head.

(iv) **Follow Through :** The hold and aim must be maintained until the bullet has left the barrel. Better still, fire should follow through until the bullet has reached the target.

Q.8. Define laws of aiming?

Ans. (i) Focus the target so that a clear picture is formed on the retina of the eye and get the true centre of the target. Then with the eye focus to the foresight.

(ii) Hold the rifle properly and keep it upright.

(iii) Close the left eye and focus the foresight.

(iv) See the foresight through the backsight 'U'. The foresight should be seen right in the centre of the U. The tip of the foresight must be aligned in the centre and in level with the shoulder of the U.

Q.9. What are the qualities of a good firer?

Ans. (i) Good Aiming

(ii) Good Holding

(iii) Good Trigger Operation

Q.10. What is the difference between 'Loading a Rifle' and 'Charging the Magazine'?

Ans. A rifle is loaded when there is a round in the chamber. Charging the magazine means that all the rounds are in the magazine itself.

Q.11. Fill in the blanks :

(i) The size of Flannelette for cleaning is __________.

(ii) Magazine capacity of 7.62 mm SLR is __________ rounds.

(iii) __________ pressures will be found on pressing of a 7.62 mm SLR.

(iv) The weight of magazine alone is __________ Ozs.

(v) The capacity of SLR magazine is __________.

Ans. (i) 4"×2" (ii) 20 (iii) Two (iv) 9 (v) 20 rounds.

Q.12. What are the main parts of SLR?

Ans.

(i) Butt	(ii) Pistol Grip	(iii) Trigger Guard
(iv) Trigger	(v) Magazine	(vi) Hand Guard
(vii) Carrying Handle	(viii) Barrel	(ix) Gas Plug
(x) Foresight Protector	(xi) Piston	(xii) Breech Block
(xiii) Ejection Slot	(xiv) Body Cover	

Q.13. Write True (T) or False (F) :

(i) 7.62 mm LMG can be stripped in five groups.

(ii) There are six grooves in 7.62 mm SLR.

(iii) Magazine capacity of Pt 22 Rifle is 10 rounds.

(iv) The Caliber of Pt 22 Rifle is 0.22 mm.

(v) The effective range of Pt 22 Rifle is 25 yards.

Ans. (i) True (ii) True (iii) False (iv) True (v) True.

NATIONAL INTEGRATION

Q.14. What are the current objectives of India?

Ans. (i) Self sufficiency in nuclear-power.

(ii) Availability of reliable power supply for farming and industries.

(iii) Production of goods for world markets.

(iv) Balancing growth in both public and private sector.

(v) Modernization of villages, linking with roads and provision of electricity to all villages.

Q.15. Why is national integration important for progress of any nation?

Ans. It is important for the following :

(i) Maintenance of sovereignty and territorial integrity of the nation.

(ii) Maintenance of peace and harmony.

(iii) Growth and development of the nation.

(iv) Eradication of poverty and illiteracy.

(v) Internal security and law & order.

(vi) Culture and religious development.

(vii) Economic and industrial growth.

(viii) Attract foreign investment and increase import and export.

(ix) Exchange of technological know-how and culture.

(x) Dignity and self-respect as a nation.
(xi) Welfare and well-being of the people.
(xii) Foreign relations and better standing among the nations of the world.

Q.16. Write True or False.

(i) The policy of 'Sulah-e-kul' (peace with all) was adopted by Akbar.
(ii) Influence of New 'Gods' and new methods of worship was brought to India by the Dravidians.
(iii) The British in India followed a policy of divide and multiply.
(iv) Jesus Christ was born in 4 BC in Judaea.
(v) Gautam Buddha was the son of Indian Prince Suddhodan.

Ans. (i) True (ii) False (iii) False (iv) False (v) True.

Q.17. Youth can contribute for nation building at personal level by saying 'no' to what all social evils?

Ans. (i) Drugs
(ii) Dowry
(iii) Illicit sexual relations
(iv) Antisocial activities in thought and action
(v) Exploitation of underprivileged in society
(vi) Use of child labour
(vii) Unfair means during exams
(viii) Accepting and offering bribe in all forms.

LEADERSHIP

Q.18. What are Leadership traits?

Ans. These are :

(i) Alertness (ii) Bearing (iii) Courage
(iv) Decisiveness (v) Dependability (vi) Endurance
(vii) Initiative (viii) Integrity (ix) Judgement
(x) Justice (xi) Knowledge (xii) Loyalty
(xiii) Sense of humour (xiv) Tact (xv) Selflessness

Q.19. List out important values of a good and successful leader?

Ans. These are :

(i) **Honesty** : not to steal, cheat or lie.
(ii) **Integrity** : uprightness.
(iii) **Purity** : no duplicity, insincerity in thought, word or deed.
(iv) **Discipline** : behaviour according to essential rules and norms which is self-imposed.
(v) **Selflessness** : unselfishness, rising above selfish or self-centered individualism, self-sacrifice.

(vi) **Loyalty** : true, faithful to duty, love or obligation to person institution, faithful in allegiance to the nation or mother country.
(vii) **Fairness** : being impartial, giving right decision.
(viii) **Equality** : treat everyone equally.
(ix) **Trust** : firm belief in the reliability, ability, strength of someone or something.
(x) **Support** : giving help, encouragement, or approval.
(xi) **Respect** : a feeling of admiration for someone because of their qualities.

Q.20. Define two elements of perception?

Ans. (i) Perception is a process of selection or screening which prevents us from processing irrelevant or disruptive information, and

(ii) There is organization of stimuli implying that the information that is processed has to be ordered and classified in some logical manner which permits us to assign meaning to the stimuli situations.

Q.21. Who is a Leader?

Ans. A leader is one who influences men and material to win the goal.

Q.22. What are the types of leaders?

Ans. (i) Born Leaders (ii) Trained leaders (iii) Assumed leaders.

Q.23. Define Duty?

Ans. Duty may be defined as moral or legal obligations and a binding force of what is right and good behaviour towards superiors, colleagues and subordinates.

Q.24. What are the duties of a good citizen?

Ans. (i) To be loyal and owe allegiance to the State.

(ii) To be patriot and work for preservation of the independence of the country.

(iii) To put service before self.

(iv) To have good sense of duty.

(v) To care and protect the government property.

(vi) To have high character.

(vii) To consider rights of other citizens as important as one's own rights.

DISASTER MANAGEMENT

Q.25. Define disaster?

Ans. Disaster denotes any odd event natural or man-made which brings about immense misery to a region and it becomes difficult to cope up with the situation through local resources. There are two types of disasters i.e. Natural and Man-made.

Q.26. What are different natural disasters?

Ans. (i) **Wind Related:** Storm, Cyclone, Tornado, Storm surge and Tidal waves.

(ii) **Water Related:** Flood, Cloudburst, Flash flood, Excessive rains and Drought.

(iii) **Earth Related:** Earthquake, Tsunamis, Avalanches, Landslides and Volcanic eruptions.

Q.27. What are different man-made disasters?

Ans. (i) **Accidents:** Road, Rail, Air, Sea and Building collapse.

(ii) **Industrial Mishaps:** Gas Leak, explosion, sabotage and safety breach.

(iii) **Fire:** Building, Coal and Oil.

(iv) **Forest Fire:** In tropical countries forest fires are often man-made.

(v) **Contamination/Poisoning:** Food, water, illicit-liquor and epidemics.

(vi) **Terrorist Activities:** Bomb blasts and mass killings.

(vii) **Ecological:** Pollution (air, water, noise), soil degradation, loss of biodiversity, global warming, sea level rise, toxic wastes and nuclear accidents.

(viii) **Warfare:** Conventional, chemical and nuclear.

SOCIAL SERVICE

Q.28. What are the various types of social services?

Ans. (i) Education.

(ii) Family welfare, Medical care, Family planning and Nutrition.

(iii) Provision of Water and Cooking fuel, Roads, Electricity and Sanitation.

(iv) Old age support systems.

(v) Employment.

(vi) Social assistance, Social security, Care & protection.

(vii) Housing and Rehabilitation.

(viii) Recreation, Sports and Social activities.

Q.29. What are various arguments in favour of Reservation Policy?

Ans. (i) Social diversity is desirable in campuses and work places. It can bring out hidden talent of society.

(ii) One way to do it is to provide relaxed entry criteria for under-privileged groups.

(iii) Hardship faced by those in general category is due to shortage of seats in professional colleges and shortage of employment opportunities and not due to reservation.

Q.30. What are various points against reservation policy?

Ans. (i) Economic conditions should be the basis for reservation.

(ii) Reservation decisions are taken keeping political interests in mind.

(iii) Allocation of quotas on the basis of caste is a form of racial discrimination and thus contrary to right to equality.
(iv) Merit is severely compromised by reserving seats for certain caste-based communities.
(v) Caste system is being kept alive by reservation policy.

Q.31. Define family planning?

Ans. Family planning is defined as the voluntary, responsible decision made by individual and couples as to the desired family size and timing of birth.

Q.32. What are the various methods of family planning?

Ans. (i) Vasectomy
(ii) Tubectomy
(iii) Condoms
(iv) Oral pills

Q.33. Define HIV?

Ans. HIV (Human Immuno-deficiency Virus) is a virus that gradually destroys the human body's immune system.

Q.34. What are the roles of Cadets towards society?

Ans. (i) Develop a sense of loyality to the community to which one belongs.
(ii) Work towards national integration and develop loyality to the nation.
(iii) Actively participate in the development plans of the nation either by directly involving oneself or by propagating the ideas of development and by helping others in participating in the development process.

HYGIENE AND SANITATION

Q.35. What is hygiene?

Ans. Hygiene is the science which deals with the principles of promoting health—personal and public.

Q.36. What is sanitation?

Ans. Sanitation is the art of keeping ourselves and surroundings neat and clean.

Q.37. What is personal hygiene?

Ans. (i) Cleanliness of hair (ii) Cleanliness of body and skin
(iii) Cleanliness of nails (iv) Cleanliness of clothes
(v) Cleanliness of teeth.

Q.38. What are various methods to purify water?

Ans. (i) Sedimentation (ii) Filtration (iii) Sterilization
(iv) Chlorination (v) Boiling.

Q.39. What are types of latrines?

Ans. (i) Water carriage System (ii) Aqua privy (iii) Removal System
(iv) Deep Trench Latrine (v) Shallow Trench Latrine

Q.40. What are preventive measures for Malaria?

Ans. (i) DDT Spray
(ii) Use of mosquito nets
(iii) Use of mosquito repellents
(iv) Wearing fully covered dress
(v) Avoid stagnant water near living area
(vi) Spray kerosene oil in stagnant drainage water.

Q.41. What is the importance of Sanitation?

Ans. Health of a community depends on the sanitation. Under sanitation the cleanliness of the physical surroundings, habits of the people, quality of food, water and air is taken care of.

ADVENTURE ACTIVITIES

Q.42. What are the various land base adventure activities?

Ans. (i) Mountaineering
(ii) Mountaineering Expeditions
(iii) All India Treks
(iv) Cycle and Motor Cycle Expeditions.

Q.43. What do you understand by adventure training?

Ans. The training given to the cadets/youth by the NCC to develop the quality of leadership, self-confidence, determination and feelings of team spirit.

ENVIRONMENT AND ECOLOGY

Q.44. What is green house effect?

Ans. It is the effect arising due to increased carbon dioxide content, increase in global temperature and depletion of ozone layer due to chloro-fluorocarbons used. It poses the greatest threat to the very existence and survival of human beings and flora and fauna around the globe.

Q.45. What are the effects of environmental degradation?

Ans. (i) Global Warming
(ii) Acid Rain
(iii) Depletion of Ozone Layer.

Q.46. What is the role of NCC cadets towards environmental degradation?

Ans. NCC cadets can take following actions to curb environmental degradation:
(i) Tree plantation
(ii) Guiding and motivating people
(iii) Water conservation
(iv) Disposal of waste
(v) Educating the people.

SPECIAL SUBJECT – ARMY

THE ARMED FORCES

Q.47. What are the names of various Army Commands?

Ans. Northern Command, Western Command, Central Command, Southern Command, South Western Command, Eastern Command, Training Command.

Q.48. Name the fighting Arms?

Ans. (i) Armoury (ii) Infantry (iii) Mechanized infantry.

SELF-DEFENCE

Q.49. What precautions should be taken by boys and girl cadets so that their conduct is never questionable?

Ans. These are as under :

(i) Realize their responsibilities and become role model for the youth.
(ii) Keep away from drugs, alcohol and tobacco.
(iii) Must keep good company.
(iv) Develop healthy hobbies like reading, music, painting, gardening etc.
(v) Never waste time.

Q.50. What should be the general behaviour of NCC cadets?

Ans. It should be as under :

(i) They should be strictly disciplined, peaceful, friendly and co-operative.
(ii) Have a sense of healthy competitiveness and remain free of jealousy.
(iii) Maintain positive attitude and have mutual respect.
(iv) Boys should never indulge in eve teasing.
(v) All must behave elegantly.

MAP READING

Q.51. What is a Map?

Ans. Map is proportionate representation of a piece of ground with all its natural and man made features shown by some conventional signs.

Q.52. What are the uses of Map?

Ans. (i) To find own position.
(ii) To determine direction from one object to another.
(iii) To locate various features of ground.
(iv) To plan moves during war.

Q.53. Name the main parts of a Compass.

Ans. (i) Thumb Ring (ii) Lid (iii) Window
(iv) Tongue (v) Lubber Line (vi) Direction mark
(vii) Prism.

Q.54. What are cardinal points and kinds of North?

Ans. (i) North (ii) South (iii) East (iv) West

Kinds of North are : True North, Magnetic North and Grid North.

Q.55. Draw the following conventional signs?

(i) Streams (ii) Temple (iii) Tube well (iv) Mosque (v) Fort.

Ans. (i)  (ii)  (iii)  (iv)  (v) 

Q.56. What are the uses of Compass?

Ans. (i) To find the North

(ii) To set the map

(iii) Measure magnetic bearing

(iv) During Night March.

FIELD CRAFT AND BATTLE CRAFT

Q.57. Define Field craft?

Ans. Field Craft is an art of using the ground and the weapons available to the best of one's own advantages.

Q.58. What subjects are included in Field craft?

Ans. (i) Description of Ground

(ii) Observation and concealment

(iii) Judging distance

(iv) Recognition and description of targets

(v) Movement with and without Arms.

Q.59. What are the various type of grounds, explain?

Ans. (i) **Broken Ground :** It is uneven and is generally interspersed with nullahs, bumps and field in the ground. It is suitable for movement of infantry and hinders observation of activities.

(ii) **Flat and Open Ground :** It is an even ground with little cover *e.g.* bushes, hedges and similar foliage. It is not suitable for movement of Infantry by day.

(iii) **High Ground :** Ground far above the general level of the area *e.g.* hill. It facilitates domination of area around it by observation or fire or both.

(iv) **Dead Ground :** Ground that is hidden from an observer's view. It can not be covered by fire.

Q.60. What are the various methods of judging distance?

Ans. (i) Unit of measure (ii) Appearance method

(iii) Section average (iv) Key ranges

(v) Halving (vi) Bracketing

Q.61. What is the sequence of indicating targets?

Ans. The easy way to remember this sequence is to remember the word 'GRAD'. The sequence is as follows:

(i) Designation of **G**roup
(ii) **R**ange
(iii) **A**id
(iv) **D**escription.

Q.62. What are the various methods of communication?

Ans. (i) Sign Language
(ii) Voice Medium
(iii) Written script
(iv) Runners and message bearers
(v) Line and cable
(vi) Wireless.

INFANTRY WEAPONS AND EQUIPMENTS

Q.63. Fill up the blanks :

(i) Effective range of 7.62 mm SLR is ________ mtr.

(ii) Rapid range of fire of LMG is __________ per minute.

(iii) Expand SMC ____________________.

(iv) LMG can be stripped into _________ main groups.

(v) No. of groves in 7.62 mm SLR is _________.

Ans. (i) 275
(ii) 3 Magazines
(iii) Sten Machine Carbine
(iv) five
(v) six

Q.64. Answer the following :

(i) What is the calibre of Rif 7.62 mm SLR?

Ans. 7.62 mm.

(ii) What is the weight of Rif 7.62 mm SLR with fully loaded magazine?

Ans. 5.1 Kg.

(iii) What is the Effective Range of Rif 7.62 mm SLR?

Ans. 275 meters.

(iv) How many rounds are loaded in Rif 7.62 mm SLR?

Ans. 20 rounds.

(v) What is the full name of Rif 7.62 mm SLR?

Ans. 7.62 mm self loading rifle.

Q.65. Write main articles for cleaning the Rif 7.62 mm SLR?

Ans. (i) Pull through
(ii) Oil bottle
(iii) Combination tool
(iv) Gas regulator key
(v) Screw driver
(vi) Cylinder/Chamber cleaning brush
(vii) Rifle cleaning brush
(viii) Graphite grease tube
(ix) Flannelette/Chindi.

MILITARY HISTORY

Q.66. Write a short note on battle of Haldighati in about 50 words.

Ans. Battle of Haldighati was fought between Rajputs and Mughal Army in 1576. It was fought between 20,000 Rajputs and 80,000 Mughal army. The battle was fierce but indecisive. Maharana Pratap was saved by his estranged brother however his famous loyal horse Chetak died while saving the life of Maharana Pratap.

Q.67. Answer the following :

(i) During which period did Akbar rule Mughal Empire?

(ii) Who was The Chief of the Indian Army during Indo-Pak War of 1971?

(iii) Which was the 'fourth war' fought between India and Pakistan?

Ans. (i) 15 Oct 1542 - 27 Oct 1605

(ii) Gen Sam Manekshaw (later FM).

(iii) The Kargil War.

Q.68. Fill in the blanks :

(i) The first Indian Chief of Staff was ....

(ii) Over .... Pakistanis were taken as POW in 1971 war.

(iii) .... was the first recipient of Param Vir Chakra.

(iv) Pakistan's Lt. General .... signed the Instrument of surrender in 1971 War.

Ans. (i) Field Marshal K.M. Cariappa (ii) 90,000

(iii) Major Som Nath Sharma (iv) A.A.K. Niazi

Q.69. Mark True (T) or False (F).

(i) Second Lt. Arun Khetarpal martyred in the 1971 Indo-Pak War.

(ii) Major Shaitan Singh martyred in the 1962 Indo-China War.

Ans. (i) True (ii) True

Q.70. Write the correct names of War Heroes.

Captain ....(i)....................., Lieutenant ....(ii)................. Grenedier .... (iii)................., and Rifleman ....(iv)................. have been awarded the Param Vir Chakra for their gallantary services during the Kargil War.

Ans. (i) Vikram Batra (ii) Manoj Kumar Pandey

(iii) Yogendra Singh Yadav (iv) Sanjay Kumar

❖ ❖ ❖

राकैको
NCC

एकता और अनुशासन

NCC

NATIONAL CADET CORPS

ARMY WING

STUDY MATERIAL

(2126) NCC (Army Wing)—3

CHAPTER

1 NCC : At a Glance

Introduction to NCC

The National Cadet Corps (NCC) is the Indian military cadet corps with its head quarters at New Delhi. It is a voluntary organization which recruits cadets from high schools, colleges and universities all over India. The cadets are given basic military training in small arms and parades. The officers and cadets have no liability for active military service once they complete their course but are given preference over normal candidates during selections based on the achievements in the Corps.

HISTORY OF NCC

National Cadet Corps is a Tri-Services Organization, comprising the Army, Navy and Air Force, engaged in grooming the youth of the country into disciplined and patriotic citizens.

The origin of NCC can be traced back to the 'University Corps', which was created under the Indian Defence Act 1917, with the object to make up the shortage of the Army. In 1920, when the Indian Territorial Act was passed, the 'University Corps' was replaced by the University Training Corps (UTC). The aim was to raise the status of the UTC and make it more attractive to the youth. The UTC officers and cadets dressed like the army. It was a significant step towards the Indianisation of armed forces. In 1942, the UTC was re-christened as the 'University Officers Training Corps' (UOTC).

During World War II, the UOTC never came up to the expectations set by the British. This led to the idea that some better schemes should be formed, which could train more young men in a better way, even during peace times.

After the Independence, a committee headed by Pandit HN Kunzru recommended a cadet organization to be established in schools and colleges at a national level. The National Cadet Corps Act (XXXI Act) was passed and on 15 July, 1948 the National Cadet Corps came into existence.

The Girls Division of NCC was raised in July, 1949. The Air Wing was raised on 01 April, 1950 and the Naval Wing in July, 1952, thus representing all the three services in the Corps.

During the 1965 and 1971 wars with Pakistan, NCC cadets were the second line of defence. They organised camps to assist the ordinance factories, supplying arms and ammunition to the front, and also were used as patrol parties to capture the enemy paratroopers. The NCC cadets also worked hand in hand with the Civil Defence authorities and actively took part in rescue work and traffic control.

After the 1965 and 1971 Indo-Pak wars the NCC syllabus was revised. Rather than just being the second line of defence, NCC syllabus laid a greater stress on developing qualities of Leadership and Officers-Like-Qualities. The military training which the NCC cadets received was reduced and greater importance was given to other areas like social service and youth-management.

The Corps started in a small way with 32,500 Senior Division and 1,35,000 Junior Division cadets. It has grown exponentially since then and the authorized cadet strength has now reached 13.47 lakhs. While this figure by itself is quite substantial, it covers only approximately 3.5% of the eligible student population. These 17 directorates are divided in total of 837 units. There are a total of 20390 institutions which includes 2809 Shools, 1744 Inter-colleges and 5837 Colleges. Wing-wise distribution of enrolled cadet strength as on March 31, 2023 is as under:

Wing	*Boys*	*Girls*	*Total*	*Percentage*
Army	777161	466052	1243213	87.88
Navy	64129	27404	91533	6.47
Air	53107	26900	80007	5.65
Total	**894397**	**520356**	**1414753**	**100%**

Motto of NCC

Unity and Discipline (Ekta aur Anushasan)

Vision of NCC

Empower volunteer youth to become potential leaders and responsible citizens of the country.

Mission of NCC

To develop leadership and character qualities, mould discipline and nurture social integration and cohesion through multi-faceted programs conducted in a military environment.

DG's four Cardinal Principles of Discipline

1. Obey with a smile
2. Be Punctual
3. Work hard and without fuss
4. Make no excuses and tell no lies

Aims of NCC

1. To develop character, camaraderie, discipline, secular outlook, spirit of adventure and ideals of selfless service amongst the youth.
2. To create a human resource pool of organized, trained and motivated youth to provide leadership in all walks of life and be always available for the service of the nation.
3. To provide a suitable environment to motivate the youth to take up a career in the Armed Forces.

Objectives of NCC

The objectives of the NCC are:

1. Reach out to the maximum youth through various institutions.
2. Make NCC as an important part of the society.
3. Teach positive thinking and attitude to the youth.
4. Become a main source of National Integration by making NCC as one of the greatest and strong united forces of our nation irrespective of any caste, creed, religion or region.

NCC SONG

Hum Sab Bharatiya Hain, Hum Sab Bharatiya Hain.
Apni Manzil Ek Hai, Ha, Ha, Ha, Ek Hai, Ho, Ho, Ho, Ek Hai.
Hum Sab Bharatiya Hain, Hum Sab Bharatiya Hain.
Kashmir Ki Dharti Rani Hai, Sartaj Himalaya Hai,
Sadiyon Se Hamne Isko Apne Khoon Se Pala Hai.
Desh Ki Raksha Ki Khatir Hum Shamshir Utha Lenge,
Hum Shamshir Utha Lenge.
Bikhre-Bikhre Tarey Hain Hum, Lekin Jhilmil Ek Hai,
Ha, Ha, Ha Ek Hai, Ho, Ho, Ho, Ek Hai.
Hum Sab Bharatiya Hain, Hum Sab Bharatiya Hain.
Mandir Gurudware Bhi Hain Yahan Aur Masjid Bhi Hai Yahan,
Girja Ka Hai Ghadiyal Kahin, Mullah Ki Kahin Hai Ajaan.
Ek Hi Apna Ram Hai, Ek Hi Allah Taala Hai, Ek Hi Allah Taala Hai.
Rang Birange Deepak Hain Hum, Lekin Jagmag Ek Hai.
Ha, Ha, Ha Ek Hai, Ho, Ho, Ho, Ek Hai.
Hum Sab Bharatiya Hain, Hum Sab Bharatiya Hain.

Oath

"I do hereby solemnly promise that I will serve my motherland most truly and loyally and that, I will abide by the rules and regulations of the National Cadet

Corps. Further under the command and control of my commanding officer I will participate in every camp most sincerely and wholeheartedly".

Pledge

We, the cadets of the National Cadet Corps, do solemnly pledge that we shall always uphold the unity of India. We resolve to be disciplined and responsible citizen of our nation. We shall undertake positive community service in the spirit of selflessness and concern for our fellow beings.

NCC Flag

NCC Flag contains NCC Crest in gold in the middle, with the letters "NCC" encircled by a wreath of seventeen lotuses with a background in Red, Blue and Light blue. Red depicts the Army, Deep Blue depicts the Navy and Light Blue depicts the Air Force. The seventeen lotuses represent the 17 State Directorates. "Ekta aur Anushasan" (Unity and Discipline) is written at the bottom of the NCC Flag.

Who is a Cadet?

The term Cadet stands for "trainee". It is generally used as a military term. Cadets are the integral part of NCC and they are divided into two divisions i.e. SD/SW and JD/JW. SD/SW represents cadets from colleges and universities whereas JD/JW represents cadets only from schools. Any volunteer citizen of India or Nepal who is of good character and on the roll of a school or college; fulfilling the age, medical and other criteria can be enrolled into NCC as a cadet. He/she has to undergo the stipulated training; both at his/her institution as well as at a training camp. He/she is called a cadet of NCC.

Advantages of Being a Cadet

The advantages of being an NCC cadet are manifold. NCC as an organization plays an active role in shaping the character and outlook of the cadet through its training and strict day-to-day schedule. An NCC cadet wearing a uniform and seen around is envy to the society especially youth. The main advantages of being an NCC cadet are enumerated below:

1. Being part of 13-lakhs strong and the largest youth organization in the world.
2. Wear the uniform and lead a life style akin to military.
3. Being moulded into a disciplined and motivated youth.
4. Opportunity to attend NCC camps like ATC, CATC, NIC, COC etc.

5. Chance to take part in disaster relief tasks.
6. Opportunity to take part in social awareness programs.
7. Opportunity to visit foreign countries as part of YEP.
8. Preference in higher studies.
9. Getting incentives and scholarships.
10. Preference for joining armed forces and other forces.

Duties and Responsibilities of Cadets

NCC is the largest youth organization in the world with an enrolled strength of more than 13 lakh Cadets. The aim of NCC is to train the young boys and girls to be better citizens and future leaders of our great country in all walks of life, including defence forces. NCC strives to be and is one of the strongest unifying forces of our nation, bringing together the youth hailing from different parts of our country and moulding them into united, secular and disciplined citizens of our nation.

An NCC cadet once enrolled has certain duties and responsibilities unlike his/her peers in the institution. The duties and responsibilities are towards nation, society at large, his/her institution, NCC organization and to his/her fellow cadets too, and he/she must maintain a conduct expected of a trained youth leader of the country.

Duties:

Duties of NCC cadets during parades and camps are as under:

1. Self-discipline is the most basic trait of an NCC Cadet.
2. He/she has to be punctual during parade and roll call.
3. Attend all NCC parades regularly without fail.
4. Extend complete cooperation to the seniors.
5. Participate in the teamwork.
6. Pursue the adventure activities.
7. Take part in the cultural activities organized by NCC.
8. Every cadet should participate in camp activities with complete enthusiasm.
9. Obeying the orders of higher ranks is yet another important duty of an NCC Cadet.
10. Always take proper haircut and wear clean and correct pattern of uniform. Polishing of shoes, ironing of uniforms and wearing of beret in correct manner should be followed.

Responsibilities:

An NCC cadet by the very fact of being an active cadet has to shoulder extra responsibilities unlike his/her fellow classmates who are not members of NCC. His/

her responsibilities are nowhere written but obligatory as an outcome of his training. Thus, he or she fulfils the main aims of NCC i.e., becoming a potential leader with character qualities and a responsible citizen.

He/she has separate responsibilities to his/her NCC unit, organization, his/her institution, society at large and to the country. That includes active participation in social awareness initiatives, environmental issues, disaster relief, adventure and sports activities and other nation building efforts. It doesn't end with his/her NCC training at his/her institution, but has to be carried forward to all the fields where he/she is going to be engaged in the future too. Thus, with passage of time, country would have had past NCC cadets occupying leadership positions in all walks of life espousing the noble values and objectives of NCC.

Conduct by NCC Cadets

A trainee or a trained cadet of NCC is expected to conduct himself/herself in a manner befitting the noble values championed by NCC. It is expected both at on and off parades or when he/she is not under supervision too; in short in his/her entire life. A cadet must imbibe the spirit of NCC i.e., a Youth leader and responsible citizen in any walk of life. He/she should be a witness to the high ideals of NCC and a role model for rest of the society.

The young generation of today is the future leaders of India. The NCC cadets of today should endeavour to be good citizens of tomorrow and motivate others to emulate them. NCC cadets should understand their duties completely so that both, the nation as well as the society benefit from them.

Enrolment in NCC

Induction into the NCC is on a voluntary basis and students–both boys/girls–can join at the age of 13 years in Junior Division (JD)/Junior Wing (JW) (generally class VIII to X and in Senior Division (SD)/Senior Wing (SW) from 11th class onwards).

Eligibility for Enrolment as Cadet:

1. Should be a citizen of India or a subject of Nepal.
2. Should be on the roll of the school or college which has an NCC unit or part thereof.
3. The cadet should be within the age as mentioned below:
   (i) **Junior Division:** Not less than 13 years and below 18 years and 6 months.
   (ii) **Senior Division:** Should be below 26 years.

Cadets Commandments

Director General, NCC has given out a list of 'Cadets Commandments' for all NCC cadets to follow in their life. They are given below:

1. I will ensure construction of toilet in my house and motivate at least 10 persons for the same.
2. I will be an 'Aadhar' Indian and would motivate 10 more persons to be one.
3. I will donate blood at least once every year.
4. I will make only digital transactions wherever possible and motivate others for the same.
5. I will plant minimum two trees in a year and care for the same.
6. I will obtain my Voter and PAN Card once I cross 18 years of age.
7. I will ensure garbage segregation in my house and within 100 metre of my neighbourhood.
8. I will undertake 100 hours of shramdaan for social service every year.
9. I will help physically-challenged persons to live their dreams.
10. I will be a role model for gender sensitivity, secular outlook and spirit of nationalism without any regional bias.
11. I will rush to help any accident victim.
12. I will always uphold motto of NCC - 'Unity and Discipline'. I will be equally disciplined when not under observation.

NCC ORGANISATION

At the Headquarters level, this organization is headed by an officer of the rank of Lieutenant General. He is the Director General of the NCC. Two other officers of the rank of Major General, five Brigadier level officers and other civil officials assist him. The Headquarters is located in New Delhi. There are 17 Directorates located in the state capitals headed by an officer of the rank of a Brigadier from the three Services.

Depending upon the size of the state and growth of NCC in the state, Directorates have up to 14 Group Headquarters under them through which they exercise their command and control of the organisation in the state. Each group is headed by an officer of the rank of Colonel or equivalent known as Group Commander. Each NCC Group Headquarters control 5-7 units (Bns) commanded by Lt. Colonel/Major or equivalent. Each Battalion consists of companies which are commanded by the Associate NCC Officer (ANO) of the rank of lieutenant to major.

In all, there are 96 Group Headquarters in the country who exercise control over a network of 684 Army Wing Units (including technical and girls unit), 69 Naval Wing Units and 61 Air Squadrons.

There are two very important institutions which give training to the NCC officers

1. Officers Training School, Kamptee (Maharashtra).
2. NCC College for Women, Gwalior (Madhya Pradesh)

Both these institutions work under Director General NCC.

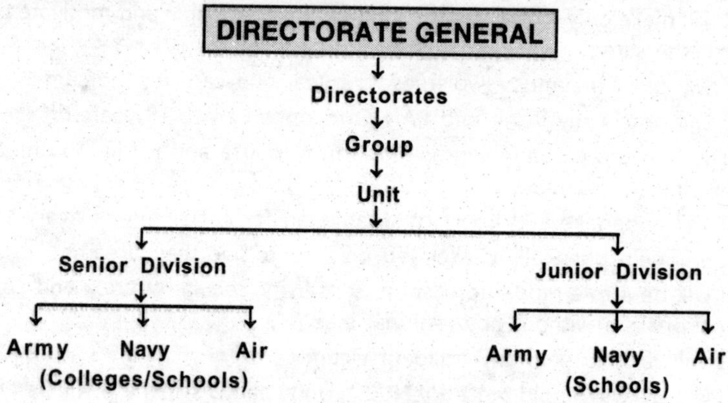

Organizational Structure

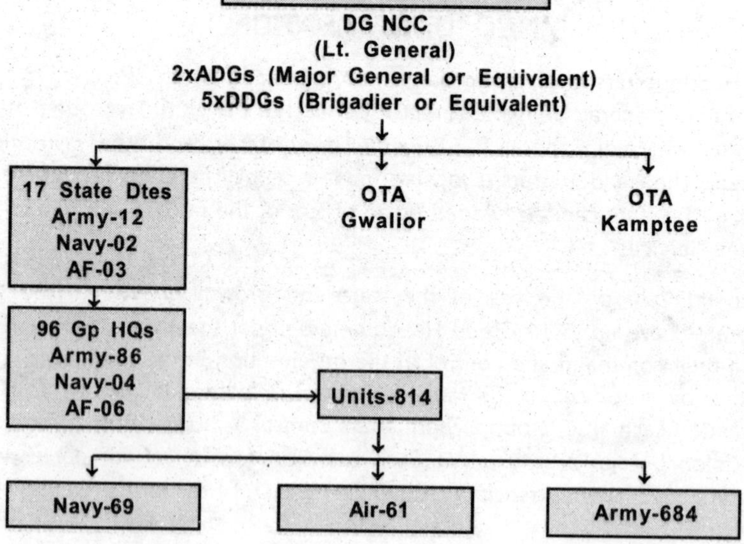

SKELETON OF NCC ADMINISTRATION

MINISTRY OF DEFENCE

↓

Director General NCC
Headquarters : New Delhi

↓

Addl. Director General (ADGs)
Headquarters : State Capital/Big City

↓

Deputy Director General NCC
Headquarters : Either the Capital of the State or the Big City of the State

↓

Group Commander NCC
(Colonel/Equivalent)
Headquarters : Big Cities of the Province

↓

Battalion Commander
(Lt. Colonel)
Headquarters : Different Cities/Towns

↓

Company/Platoon Commander
(Officer of NCC from 2nd Lieutenant to Major rank)
Headquarters : Different Schools/Colleges.

DIRECTORATES OF NCC IN INDIA

- Andhra Pradesh & Telangana
- Bihar & Jharkhand
- Delhi
- Gujarat, Dadra & Nagar Haveli
- Jammu & Kashmir
- Karnataka & Goa
- Kerala & Lakshadweep
- Maharashtra
- Madhya Pradesh & Chhattisgarh
- Odisha
- North East Region (Arunachal Pradesh, Assam, Manipur, Meghalaya, Mizoram, Nagaland & Tripura)
- Punjab, Haryana, Himachal Pradesh and Chandigarh
- Rajasthan
- Tamil Nadu, Puducherry, Andaman & Nicobar
- Uttar Pradesh
- Uttarakhand
- West Bengal & Sikkim

NCC TRAINING

Training in NCC instils qualities like nationalism, patriotism, discipline, team spirit, esprit-de-corps, leadership and self-confidence and promotes overall personality development. NCC gives a tremendous opportunity to one and all for betterment, irrespective of caste, creed, religion or economic status. Based on the aims of NCC, the organisation has laid down training syllabi for the cadets.

The syllabi for the Junior Division cadets cover a period of two years and for Senior Division cadets the period of three years. Except for minor variations, the syllabi for each Division is similar for both Boy and Girl cadets. The training year matches the academic and financial years i.e., 01 April to 31 March. Training schedules planned for cadets ensure that the optimum benefits of the organisation reach maximum number of cadets.

On successful completion of the laid down syllabi, cadets of Junior Division are eligible for 'A' certificate examination and cadets of Senior Division for 'B' & 'C' certificate examinations. The cadets who have completed requisite number of periods and camps during their training are eligible for examination.

NCC training can be classified in two types—Training 'A' and Training 'B'.

ACTIVITIES OF TRAINING 'A'

The training activities of Training 'A' can be broadly classified under the following heads:

1. Institutional Training
2. Camp Training
3. Attachment Training (Service Units)
4. Air Wing Training
5. Social Service and Community Development
6. Youth Exchange Programme

Institutional Training

This training is mostly carried out in schools and colleges by the cadets. In addition, depending upon the type of wing, basic knowledge of that service is imparted to the cadets e.g. gliding and powered flying for Air Wing cadets and boat pulling and sailing for Naval Wing cadets. Common syllabus consists of 70% and special to services subjects 30% of the entire syllabus.

Camp Training

Camp training constitutes the most important part of NCC training. Every cadet in the NCC is expected to attend at least two camps during one's tenure to complete the Training Syllabi. Therefore, nearly 50 per cent of the enrolled strength gets this opportunity every year. In camps, the young cadets get the thrill and joy of outdoor and community living as they are made to live under canvas/camp conditions and also follow a rugged but interesting routine. Camps also help in developing camaraderie, teamwork, leadership qualities, self-confidence, self-reliance and dignity of labour among cadets. This contributes greatly towards promoting national integration. The various camps conducted by the NCC are as follows :

(a) Annual Training Camps (ATC) : These are held within the State under the aegis of respective NCC Directorates. The camps are of 12 days for senior boys/girls and 10 days duration for junior boys/girls. 50% of the enrolled strength undergoes the camps.

Rationale:

- The Annual Training Camp is an exciting and essential element of NCC. Activities at the camp will help students develop qualities like social service, team spirit, challenge, leadership, discipline, self-confidence, widen horizon, develop ambition to do creative work, enhance personal and social development, learn how to overcome adversity, civil defence & self-defence, other new and exciting experiences.
- The Training Camp will make the students become more aware that they are part of a greater ecosystem and are not as bound by social customs and norms. In essence, students will be true to themselves and more able to see others as people regardless of class, colour and creed.
- Camp activities will lead students to self-reliance, self-confidence, national spirit and leadership, and will enhance the NCC aims of developing character, comradeship, discipline, secular outlook, spirit of adventure and the ideals of selfless service among the youth of the country.
- The Training Camp will let students live in the camp with a social environment and help teachers observe and understand their students' development in terms of personal aspirations, psychological behaviours and social skills. It will also allow students to appreciate their environment and natural surroundings and provide opportunities for students to be independent and exercise self-discipline.
- The Annual Training Camp is the culmination of NCC training which instils and stimulates in youths an urge for excellence and inculcates a spirit of adventure and outdoor activities.

Objectives:

- Attendance of ATC is a mandatory requirement before the cadet is eligible for 'A' and 'B' Certificate in case JD/JW and SD/SW respectively.

- ATC is conducted for a duration of 10 days in the second year of JD/JW and SD/SW to provide outdoor practical training.
- General activities covered during the ATC are as under:
  - ✦ Physical fitness to include PT, Yoga, Games, Obstacle Training, Drill
  - ✦ Weapon Training and Firing.
  - ✦ Map Reading
  - ✦ Field Craft and Battle Craft
  - ✦ Personality Development
  - ✦ National Integration and Social Awareness
  - ✦ Cultural Activities
  - ✦ Lectures on Civil Affairs, Social Awareness and Community Development, Health and Hygiene and Environment Issues
- Cadets will be tested for practical training during the camp as under:
  - ✦ Drill
  - ✦ Weapon Training
  - ✦ Firing
  - ✦ Obstacle Training
  - ✦ Map Reading
  - ✦ Field Craft and Battle Craft
- ATC will be conducted under the aegis of the unit affiliated to the school/ college.
- ATC will be conducted during the period from August to February by the ANO and Cadets keeping in view the availability of cadets as per their academic/curricular schedule.

(b) Centrally Organised Camps (COC) : These camps are of an all India nature and are planned by HQ DGNCC in consultation with the Directorates nominated to conduct them. Selected cadets, as per the vacancies allotted to each Directorate, participate in these camps. The following types of centrally organised camps are conducted :

(i) **Leadership Camps (LC) :** These camps are conducted on an all India basis. There are four Advance Leadership Camps (ALC), one each for SD, JD, SD Naval Wing boys and SW Girls. Three Basic Leadership Camps are held, one each for SD boys, SW and JW Girls.

(ii) **Vayu Sainik Camp (VSC) :** This Centrally Organised Camp is organised for Air Wing Cadets. It is generally conducted in the month of October.

(iii) **Nau Sainik Camp (NSC) :** This Centrally organised Naval Camp is conducted annually for selected Naval Wing Cadets. Boat pulling, regatta and sailing competitions are the main attractions of this camp. It is conducted during the months of Oct/Nov.

(iv) **Rock Climbing Camps (RCC) :** Eight rock climbing camps are held each year to expose the cadets to the basics of rock climbing and to inculcate spirit of adventure.

(v) **National Integration Camps (NIC) :** These camps are conducted on an all India basis and help bridge the cultural gap among various states of India. In addition, NCC conducts NICs at remote and forward areas to promote national integration. Special NICs are being conducted regularly at Leh, Srinagar, North Eastern Region and at Port Blair.

(vi) **Thal Sainik Camp (TSC) :** Two TSCs are conducted at RD Parade ground, Delhi Cantt every year i.e., one for SD/JD boys and other for SW/JW girls. Points scored by NCC Dtes during various competitions held during the camp contribute towards Republic Day Banner.

(vii) **Republic Day Camp (RDC) and Prime Minister's Rally :** Republic Day Camp is a prestigious camp inaugurated by the Vice President of India and visited by Defence Minister, Minister of State for Defence, Chief Minister of Delhi, the three Service Chiefs and other dignitaries. During the Camp, a Horse Show and three Cultural Programmes are held wherein important dignitaries are invited as Chief Guests. The camp culminates in the Prime Minister's Rally on 27 January every year which showcases all the activities of NCC.

(c) Adventure Training: To inculcate a spirit of adventure and teamwork, NCC cadets undergo various adventure activities such as parajumps, parasailing, trekking, mountaineering and sailing expeditions.

(d) Attachment Camps: To give the cadets exposure to interact with Regular Army, Navy and Air Force units, attachment camps are conducted, where cadets are attached with these units. To motivate cadets to join the Armed Forces attachment of cadets with Indian Military Academy is also conducted.

Attachment Training

NCC cadets are given an opportunity to live and work in regular service units in the form of Attachment Training. Allocation of vacancies for attachment to various Army Command HQs is done by the Army HQs. Every year a large number of officers and cadets are attached with various Army units. This includes cadets who are attached with various Centres/Depots where lady officers are posted. The attachment training is for approx 15 days duration.

Attachment Military Hospitals : A large number of Senior Wing Girl cadets are attached with various Military Hospitals every year.

IMA Attachment : Many cadets are attached with IMA for training every year.

ATT OTA : Many SW girl cadets are attached with OTA, Chennai for training every year.

Air Wing Training

NCC Air Wing was established in 1950. The major objective of the Air Wing training is to create interest amongst the youth of the country in aviation activites. In the flying Sqns, besides normal training, cadets are imparted training in Gliding/ Microlite activities. The cadets are imparted basic theoretical knowledge in aviation subjects like aerodynamics, navigation, airmanship, meteorology and aero engine. The following practical training is also imparted:

(i) **Gliding :** Gliding is the most appropriate and economic way of bringing aviation within the reach of a large number of cadets.

(ii) **Microlite Flying :** Microlite Flying has been introduced in NCC as an adventure activity with a view to give air experience/training to the NCC Cadets (SD/SW) of Air Wing.

(iii) **Aeromodelling :** Aeromodelling is the best way to demonstrate and understand how the forces of aerodynamics work on a flying wing (aerofoil). It is a vital link between the theory and practical flying training. It is divided into two general categories of static and dynamic aeromodelling. In static aeromodelling, non-flying type aeromodels are made to a specific similar scale of the actual aeroplanes.

In dynamic aeromodelling, the aeroplanes are made to fly with the help of small engine fixed on it or without it depending on whether the aeromodeller wants to display his skill on a power model or a gliding model. In any case, both types involve controlling through radio control. There is another type of non-control dynamic aeromodelling, where a powered aeromodel attached to a string is made to perform various manoeuvres.

(iv) **Attachment Training :** The main aim of the Attachment Training is to familiarize Air Wing NCC Officers and Cadets about working of Air Force Stations/Estts. During their training, intensive training on air subjects is given to the cadets.

(v) **Courses :** Every year one Pre-commission and one Refresher course for senior Division NCC Officers and two Pre-commission and two Refresher courses for Junior Division NCC Officers are conducted.

Social Service and Community Development

NCC has adopted community development activities with the aim of imbibing amongst cadets selfless service to the community, dignity of labour, importance of self help, need to protect the environment and to assist weaker sections of the society in their upliftment. This was envisaged through programmes involving adult education, tree plantation, blood donation, visit to old age homes, slum clearance, village upliftment and various other social schemes. Some of the major activities of NCC cadets are:

(i) **Tree Plantation** : NCC cadets plant saplings and look after them in conjunction with the concerned State Departments.

(ii) **Blood Donation** : Cadets donate blood as voluntary service whenever needed by a Hospital/Red Cross.

(iii) **Old Age Homes** : Old Age Homes in the country are patronised and regularly visited by NCC cadets.

(iv) **Adult Education** : NCC cadets visit remote areas, villages and underdeveloped areas to emphasise the need for education and to assist in the conduct of the Adult Education Programmes.

(v) **Community Work** : Cadets of NCC participate in the rural and urban community project and other development works like village track improvement, cleaning of streets and ponds, sanitation drives etc.

(vi) **Disaster Relief** : NCC has always extended its helping hand during natural disasters and other calamities and accidents. Over the years, NCC cadets have rendered outstanding service during floods, earthquakes, cyclones, tragic train accidents and provided the healing touch to people in riot affected areas.

(vii) **Anti Leprosy Drive** : NCC Cadets have launched anti-leprosy drive throughout the country and are helping various voluntary Government Organisations.

(viii) **AIDS Awareness Programme** : NCC participates actively in the AIDS awareness programme and is working alongwith UNAIDS and DG AFMS in carrying out AIDS Awareness Programmes throughout the country.

(ix) **Cancer Awareness Programme** : NCC Cadets actively participate in Cancer Awareness Programmes organized at various cities.

Youth Exchange Programme (YEP)

The aim of YEP is a country to country exchange of cadets belonging to NCC/equivalent Govt/Youth Organisations of friendly countries and participation in NCC activities of the host country to create an increased awareness among participants and appreciation of each others socio-economic and cultural realities. The exchange programme acts as the 'third tier of diplomacy' by supplementing the efforts of our diplomats and leaders in building bonds with other friendly nations.

ACTIVITIES OF TRAINING 'B'

Training 'B' is mainly responsible for the following :

1. Conduct of Republic Day Camp.
2. Conduct of courses at OTA Kamptee and OTA Gwalior.
3. Policy with regard to issue of Directive and conduct of Certificate Examination of Senior and Junior Divisions/Wings.

4. Participation of NCC Team in All India G.V. Mavlankar Shooting Championship (AIGVMSC) and National Rifle Association of India Shooting Championship.
5. NCC Special Entry Scheme SSC(NT) at OTA Chennai.
6. Remount & Veterinary (R&V) Units.
7. Courses at National Civil Defence College.
8. Naval Training.
9. Adventure Training.

Annual Republic Day Camp

The Annual Republic Day Camp (RDC) is held at Garrison Parade Ground, Delhi Cantt every year from 01 to 29 January. A large number of selected NCC cadets from all States and Union Territories attend the Camp. This camp represents all parts of India and is in fact a 'Mini India' in itself. The Camp is normally inaugurated by the Vice President of India and culminates with the Prime Minister's Rally on 27 January.

OTA Kamptee

The NCC OTS was established on 01 March, 1957 but was formally inaugurated on 06 May, 1957 by the then Dy Defence Minister Sardar Surjit Singh Majithia. A Girls' Wing for pre-commission training for lady officers was added to the School in August 1959. It was later shifted to Gwalior in April 1965 and is known as WOTS. The NCC Academy at Purandhar, which was established in September 1961, was closed down on 31 March 1979 and merged with the School.

NCC OTA Gwalior

The Girls Wing for pre-commission training for Lady ANOs which was shifted to Gwalior in April 1965 is presently known as OTA, Gwalior, which is a premier women officer training institution. The courses are conducted for the lady ANOs/ WTLO's. During the lean periods, rock climbing courses are conducted for the cadets in the month of January/February. Selected NCC girl cadets are also given coaching for SSB.

Directive for Certificate Examination

This scheme was introduced in 1997. 'C' certificate holders of all wings are exempted from written examination for entry into SSC (NT) courses at OTA Chennai.

SSB Screening Courses

Two SSB Screening Courses for SD and SW cadets are conducted at OTA Kamptee at Gwalior every year.

Remount & Veterinary (R&V) Units

The NCC has R&V Units affiliated to Agriculture Universities to give equestrian training to boy and girl cadets in addition to basic military training. NCC has one R&V Regiment at Hyderabad and elevan R&V Squadrons, one each at Mhow, Bhubaneshwar, Jabalpur, Guwahati, Ludhiana, Chennai, Bikaner, Trichur, Mathura, Pantnagar and Delhi.

During the Republic Day Camp every year, the NCC Horse Show and various equestrian competitions are held in order to adjudge the Best Rider amongst the boy and girl cadets of R&V Units. The basic aim of the Competition is to promote a sense of participation, equestrian skill and mastery in horsemanship.

Naval Wing Activities

There are 69 Naval Units covering all the States and Union Territories. The institutionalized syllabus is completed in 300 periods over two years for JD cadets and 360 periods over three years for SD cadets.

Officers and Cadets Training : The following training is imparted :

(i) **Sea Training :** 145 NCC Naval (SD) cadets and nine ANOs from all Dtes are imparted training at Mumbai and Visakhapatnam for a period of twelve days during Dec-Jan every year. During their training, intensive training in Naval subjects like Seamanship, Navigation, Communication, Gunnery, Damage control and Ship safety are imparted to the Naval cadets.

(ii) **Sea Attachment :** 150 NCC Naval SD cadets and 10 ANOs are attached to various Naval Ships/Establishments at Mumbai and Kochi for a period of 12 days during May/June every year. This also gives the cadets opportunity to undergo an intensive training in Naval activities.

(iii) **Naval Attachment :** This has been started since 2001, having been approved by NHQ. 25 SD cadets from all Dtes are attached every year for 12 days in Dec/Jan at the Naval Academy, INS Mandovi, Goa.

(iv) **Coast Guard Sea Sortie :** Two coast guard sea sorties of one week duration each are conducted off Kerala Coast. Six SD cadets embark ship in each trip. Port of embarkation/disembarkation is Kochi.

(v) **Foreign Cruise-Naval :** Every year 20 SD cadets and two PI Staff are selected for foreign cruise which is organised on board ships of the 1st Training Squadron of the Indian Navy during Mar/April & Sep/Oct. Foreign Cruise gives the cadets an exposure of open seas for a longer duration and also an opportunity to interact with foreign nationals.

(vi) **Foreign Cruise-Coast Guard :** This has commenced since 2001. The Govt has approved six NCC Naval cadets to proceed onboard Coast Guard ships. Unlike Naval ships which go on a cruise twice in a year, there is no regularity in the case of Coast Guard ships.

(vii) **Nau Sainik Camp :** Every year a combined Nau Sainik Camp is held at Visakhapatnam for a period of 12 days during Oct/Nov. 386 SD and 204 SW cadets participate in the camp. Apart from the camp training, Non-RD Banner competitions like Semaphore, and Cultural competitions are conducted. RD Banner competitions namely Boat Pulling, Sailing, Ship Modelling, Firing and Line Area are also conducted during this camp.

(viii) **Advance Leadership Camp (ALC) :** Every year ALC with Naval bias is conducted at Thoothukudi (Tuticorin) during May/June for a period of 12 days where in 150 SD cadets from all Dtes attend the camp. Beside visiting the Naval and Coast Guard ship/installations, cadets carry out Adventure training, Security exercises, and also take part in Best Cadet, Firing, Seamanship, Communications and Navigation competitions.

(ix) **Naval Technical Camp :** The National level Technical Camp is organised every year for 125 cadets belonging to Engineering colleges of Chennai in two phases during May/June.

Naval Adventure Activities

(i) **Scuba Diving :** Diving has gained popularity amongst NCC cadets. Scuba Diving courses are being conducted at Kochi, Vizag, Mumbai and Delhi with complete assistance from the Naval Diving Teams located at these stations.

(ii) **Sailing Expedition :** Sailing Expedition is an interesting feature of the Naval Training. Each NCC Dte plans and executes at least one sailing expedition during a year. During Sailing Expedition, the cadets get practical training in Boat Pulling and Sailing. They face and overcome the hazards of changes in weather conditions and changing moods of rivers/sea.

(iii) **Wind Surfing and Kayaking :** 85 Wind Surfers and 101 Kayaks have been allotted to Naval Units and cadets participate in these activities on a regular basis in their units.

All India NCC Yachting Regatta

NCC Yachting Regatta in enterprise class boats is held every year in the month of January at INS Chilka. 48 SD and 48 SW cadets from all the State Dtes attend it. Cadets get an opportunity to test their sailing skills during these competitions.

Adventure Training and Sports

NCC Cadets from all over India participate in various championship and sports activities such as shooting, football, hockey and many other types of activities of state and national level. Some of them are :

(i) **Mountaineering Courses :** There are three premier mountaineering institutes for training i.e., Nehru Institute of Mountaineering, Uttarkashi Himalayan Mountaineering Institute, Darjeeling and Directorate of Mountaineering & Allied Sports, Manali.

(ii) **Mountaineering Expeditions :** NCC has been conducting two Mountaineering Expeditions every year, one for the Senior Division boy cadets and the other for Senior Wing girl cadets.

(iii) **Trekking Expeditions :** Ten All India Treks i.e., three for girls and seven for boys are conducted every year and a total of 12,000 cadets take part in it.

(iv) **Cycle/Motor Cycle Expeditions :** These expeditions are organized both at the National and State Directorate level.

(v) **Parachute Sailing :** The State Directorates conduct Parasail training every year.

(vi) **Para Courses :** Every year, Army HQ releases 80 vacancies for Para Basic Course. These are generally distributed to 40 Senior Division and 40 Senior Wing cadets from all over the country. This course is conducted at Agra.

(vii) **Slithering :** Every year, slithering training is conducted for NCC cadets.

(viii) **Desert Safari :** Rajasthan Directorate conducts a Camel Safari every year in the month of November. About 20 SD cadets take part along with foreign cadets who come for Youth in Exchange Programme (YEP).

(ix) **White Water Rafting :** White Water Rafting Node has been established at Raiwala (Haridwar).

NCC SYLLABUS

The syllabus includes common subjects for all three wings and specialized subjects with respect to Army, Navy and Air Force. The common subjects comprise of approximately 70% and specialized subject 30% of the curriculum.

In addition to this syllabus, cadets attend one Annual Training Camp in the second year of junior and senior division to be eligible to appear in Part 'A' and Part 'B' certificate examination.

Cadets willing to pursue Part 'C' Certificate will have to attend the third year senior division in their colleges.

CONDUCT OF NCC CERTIFICATE EXAMINATION

The NCC Certificate Examinations are conducted in March-April every year.

There are three types of certificates NCC cadets can secure: 'A', 'B' and 'C'. You will be eligible for the 'A' certificate after you have spent 1-2 years in the Junior Division (school-level) and attended one training camp. For the 'B' certificate, you should have attended at least 75 per cent classes in the Senior Division (in college) and one training camp. The most coveted is the 'C' certificate. To be eligible for this exam, you should be a 'B' certificate-holder, in your third year at college and should have attended at least one outdoor camp and one national integration camp or Republic Day parade or any other outdoor activity organized by the Directorate of the NCC. A 'C' certificate-holder has many advantages when it comes to the selection process in the armed forces.

Detailed Eligibility Conditions for Certificate Examinations : The detailed eligibility conditions for various NCC Certificates are as under :

Certificate 'A'

(i) The candidate must have attended a minimum of 75% of total training periods laid down in the syllabus for the first and second years of Junior Division/Wing NCC (All Wings).

(ii) Break in the NCC Service of the cadets prior to his appearing in the examination should not exceed more that 12 months at one time.

(iii) The candidate must have attended one ATC.

Certificate 'B'

(i) The cadet must have attended a minimum of 75% of total training periods laid down in the syllabus for the first and second years of Senior Division/Wing of NCC (All Wings).

(ii) Break in the NCC Service of the cadets prior to his appearing in the examination should not exceed more than 12 months at one time.

(iii) The candidate must have attended one ATC.

(iv) Cadets possessing 'A' certificate will be awarded 10 bonus marks.

(v) An Air Wing Cadet must do a minimum of 10 Glide Launches.

Certificate 'C'

(i) The candidate must be in possession of Certificate 'B'.

(ii) The cadet must be in the third year of SD/SW NCC Training.

(iii) The cadet must have attended a minimum of 75% of the periods of 3rd year syllabus during the academic session.

(iv) Break in the NCC Service of the SD/SW cadet prior to appearing in the exam should not exceed more than 18 months at one time.

(v) The cadet must have attended one ATC and one of the following :

- Annual Training Camp (This is in addition to one mentioned above).
- RD Camp at Delhi (RDC).
- Centrally Organised Camp (COC).
- Para Training Camp (PTC).
- National Integration Camp (NIC) (When applicable for SD/SW cadets).
- All India Trekking Expedition (DGNCC Organised).
- All India Mountaineering Expedition (DGNCC Organised).
- Attachment Training with Army Unit, Air Force Station and Naval Base.
- Sailing expedition with actual sailing exceeding 10 days duly approved by DGNCC.
- Attended Adventure Courses like Mountaineering Water Skiing, Snow and Ice Course.
- Any cadet participating in NRAI matches as part of DG NCC team.
- Special Services Camps (Essentially with 50% service training).
- Successfully done Scuba Diving Course.
- Attended Youth Exchange Programme.
- Foreign Cruise (Navy).

Grading

A cadet has to obtain minimum 45% marks in each paper and 50% marks in the aggregate to pass the examination. Grading based on total marks obtained will be awarded as follows :

(i) Grading 'A' - Cadets obtaining 80% marks or above.

(ii) Grading 'B' - Cadets obtaining 65% marks and above but below 80%.

(iii) Grading 'C' - Cadets obtaining 50% marks and above but below 65%.

(iv) Fail - Cadets obtaining less then 45% marks in any paper or less than 50% in the aggregate.

NCC UNIFORM

Army cadets wear khaki uniform. Naval cadets wear white uniform of Navy. Air Force cadets wear light blue and grey (LBG) uniform. The uniform is compulsory on all the occasions.

Cadets from SD boys Army wing wear khaki full sleeve shirt and trousers and cadets from JD wear khaki shirt and khaki shorts. Girl cadets from SW & JW both wear khaki full sleeve shirt and trousers. Cadets from SD boys Naval wing wear white half sleeve shirt and white trousers and JD boys wear half sleeve white shirt and white shorts. Girls from Naval wing SW & JW wear white half sleeve shirt and trousers.

Cadets from SD boys Air wing wear light blue half sleeve shirts and trousers and JD cadets wear light blue half sleeve shirts and trousers. Girls from SW and JW wear light blue half sleeve shirts and trousers.

In addition to these SW & JW girl cadets wear white salwar and kamiz during activities other than parade. A green beret is compulsory for all the cadets except Sikh cadets who wear a green turban. For physical training, cadets wear brown canvas shoes and for drills black leather shoes called D.M.S. (Drill March Shoes). Woollen vests are compulsory in cold areas whose colour is—khaki for army, dark blue for navy, and black for air.

PROMOTION OF NCC CADETS

First of all, students are recruited as cadets. In due course, they are promoted gradually. There are certain terms and conditions for such promotions. The terms and conditions for each post are given as under :

- **Lance Corporal**
  1. He/She must have got minimum training of three months in NCC.
  2. He/She must have been present at least 75% times in the parade.
  3. He/She must have passed the test of drill and map reading.
- **Corporal**
  1. He/She must have been on the post of Lance Corporal for six months.
  2. He/She must have passed the test of Weapon Training (WT).
- **Sergeant**
  1. He/She must have been on the post of corporal for six months.
  2. He/She must be the cadet of Second Year in NCC.

- **Under Officer**

  He/She must have been on the post of sergeant for six months and have passed the 'B' certificate.

- **Senior Under Officer**

  He/She must have been on the post of under officer at least for six months.

AIM & ADVANTAGES OF NCC TRAINING

Main Aim of NCC—True Youth Development

NCC is a youth organization, open to students of academic institutions. The NCC has undergone many changes i.e., from a purely military oriented organization it has changed to a true youth development organization spread over in all States of the Country in the true spirit of its motto 'unity and discipline'.

Today, the NCC offers a wide spectrum of activities classified into five main areas. Institutional training is paramount amongst these and it includes conduct of Annual Training Camps. Flying, Sea Training and Familiarization Training with various Services institutes like Indian Military Academy at Dehradun and Officers Training School at Chennai. Community Development is another area in which cadets have set an example by involving in various activities viz. adult literacy, anti-drug, anti-leprosy campaigns, planting of trees to conserve ecology etc.

Of late, the scope of adventure and sports activity has been enlarged bringing in its ambit events like parasailing, scuba-diving, car and motorcycle rallies and expeditions designed to explore the national heritage of India, beside the conventional activities like mountaineering.

Youth Exchange Programmes (YEP)

Youth Exchange Programmes between NCC of India and youth organizations of other countries are undertaken yearly. The Exchange Programme includes mutual visits up to 24 days in which cadets undertake billeting families, community work projects, educational activities etc. These projects develop mutual respect, adaptability, self-discipline, cross-cultural learning and above all, love for one's country. India has Youth Exchange Programme with Australia, Bangladesh, Bhutan, Canada, Maldives, Nepal, Singapore, Sri Lanka, United Kingdom and Vietnam. These programmes give the youth of our nation an enhanced understanding of the international environment and help them to become effective leaders in the future.

Advantages of NCC Training

There are several advantages of undertaking an NCC training, such as :

1. NCC Cadets develop qualities like social service, team spirit, leadership, discipline and self-confidence.

2. NCC camps are held at different places in the country hence cadets get opportunity to visit important historical and industrial places and social centres and widen their horizon and develop ambition to do creative work.
3. NCC cadets are taught civil defence and self-defence. Due to this cadets develop national spirit and confidence.
4. NCC cadets are attached with army units every year so that they get acquainted with the army life.
5. NCC cadets are trained for parachute jumps and mountaineering so that they develop capacity to do courageous work.
6. Selected cadets are sent to foreign countries every year for YEP.
7. 32 seats are reserved per course in the IMA for cadets who have passed NCC 'C' certificate examination. NCC cadets having 50% aggregate marks in graduation with minimum 'B' grade in 'C' certificate examination are eligible for short service commission (NCC special entry scheme) without qualifying CDS written examination. They can face direct SSB interview.
8. NCC trained cadets are given preference in recruitment of armed forces.
9. Many industries give priority in jobs to NCC trained cadets.
10. Central and State Governments also give priority in jobs to NCC cadets.
11. Priority is given to NCC trained students by Universities in B.Ed, MA, MSc admission and hostel.
12. NCC trained students are given priority in recruitment in Central Reserve Police Force (CRPF) and Border Security Force (BSF) etc.
13. NCC cadets are given refreshment on every parade and are given washing allowance for uniform.
14. NCC cadets are given facility to purchase goods from military canteen.
15. In case of death or becoming permanently handicapped of an NCC cadet during NCC activities, financial assistance is given by Cadets Welfare Society (CWS).

The Aims and Financial Assistance provided by Cadets Welfare Society (CWS)

The present aims of Cadets Welfare Society are :

1. To give financial assistance to cadets NOK/nominee in case of a demise during NCC activity.
2. To give financial relief to cadets on sustaining injury/disability during NCC activity.
3. To grant scholarships to academically brilliant students.
4. To grant Best and 2nd Best Cadet awards at Group level.

5. To conduct sports and adventure activities which cannot be funded by Public Funds.

Financial Assistance/Relief: The Society grants financial assistance and relief, as under, to cadets who sustain injury or death during NCC-related activity as well as for sports and adventure activities.

NCC-Related Activities	Death Cases	Permanent Disability	Temporary Disability
High Risk	₹ 5,00,000/-	Upto ₹ 4,00,000/-	Upto ₹ 1,75,000/-
Other Activities	₹ 4,50,000/-	Upto ₹ 3,50,000/-	Upto ₹ 1,75,000/-

HONOURS AND AWARDS

1. The NCC was introduced with the vision to provide secular, united and disciplined citizens for the future India. With the passage of time, the NCC personnel achieved historic feats and did exceptional acts, which needed to be commended and elevated at the national level. For this purpose, the following awards were instituted in order to not only provide recognition to NCC personnel but also to motivate others to emulate.
   - Raksha Mantri's Padak : Awarded by Defence Minister
   - Raksha Mantri's Prashansa Patra : Awarded by Defence Minister
   - Raksha Sachiv's Prashansa Patra : Awarded by the Defence Secretary
   - Mahanideshak's Prashansa Patra : Awarded by the DG NCC
2. While the Defence Secretary's Prashansa Patra and the DG NCC's Prashansa Patras were instituted in 1984, the Raksha Mantri's Padak and Raksha Mantri's Prashansa Patras were started in 1989.
3. The following category of NCC Personnel are eligible for these awards:
   - NCC Whole Time Officers
   - Associate NCC Officers (ANOs)
   - Under Officer Instructors & Sergeant Major Instructors
   - NCC Cadets (both boys and girls)
4. These awards are given to individuals who perform exceptional acts involving courage, devotion to duty and any contribution of lasting value to the organization and the one which brings glory and fame to the NCC. The highest award is Raksha Mantri's Padak. These awards are announced on the NCC Day which falls on the last Sunday of the month of November, every year, and are given by the Hon'ble Defence Minister during his/her visit to the Republic Day NCC Camp.

INCENTIVES FOR NCC CADETS BY CENTRAL AND STATE GOVTS

Apart from training and preparing the youth for future challenges in NCC, cadets are given various benefits in terms of job opportunities and scholarships. Some of them are:

1. Vacancies reserved for commission in Defence Forces for NCC 'C' Certificate	Army 64 per year—Indian Military Academy (IMA), Dehradun through UPSC and Service Selection Board (SSB) Interview. 100 per year—in Officers Training Academy (OTA), Chennai for Short Service Commission Non-Technical No UPSC Exam, only SSB. Navy-6 per Course. No UPSC Exam, only Naval SSB. IAF—10% in all courses including Flying Training courses. No UPSC Exam, only Air Force SSB.
2. For ORs, Sailors, Airmen	5 to 10% bonus marks awarded for recruitment.
3. Para Military Forces	2 to 10 bonus marks awarded for recruitment.
4. Department of Telecommunication	Bonus marks awarded for recruitment.
5. CRPF	NCC Cadets holding a degree are eligible for recruitment to gazetted post.
6. National Cadet Corps	Civilian Gliding Instructors/Girl Cadet Instructors and NCC WTLOs.
7. State Governments	Preference in State Services in certain States.
8. Industry	Some Industries give preference to NCC 'C' Certificate holders for various jobs.

Scholarship Scheme

150 Scholarships to JD/JW and 100 scholarships to SD/SW of ₹ 2000/- each are awarded annually to meritorious NCC Cadets who have undergone two years training with minimum 60% attendance.

1. JD/JW - 10th pass with minimum 70% marks in aggregate.
2. SD/SW - 10+2 or Pre-Degree/Pre-University/Diploma in Polytechnic, with 70% in aggregate of Science stream & 60% of Arts/Commerce stream.

❖ ❖ ❖

CHAPTER

2 Drill & Commands

DRILL

NCC cadets are trained for obedience, smartness, proper dressing, self-defensiveness, unity, discipline for gaining state of physical and mental balance. The training, which includes all these aspects is called "Drill". A cadet should take care of the points given below :-

1. Uniform should be tidy, starched and ironed.
2. Shirt and Pants should be properly stitched and buttoned.
3. Buttons should be of similar colour, texture and size.
4. Uniform should be neither too loose, nor too tight.
5. Shoes should be well-polished and laces properly tied.
6. Belt should be properly tightened with the pants.
7. Belt should be polished and its metallic part should be brass-polished.
8. Hair should be short and neat.
9. Shaving for boys is a must before Drill.
10. Caps should be properly placed on head.

WORDS OF COMMANDS

Words of commands symbolises certain commands for Drill. It has two parts :

1. Cautionary 2. Executive

For example : Get on parade, right turn, here "Get on parade" is a cautionary and "right turn" is executive word of command. A good parade command should take care of the following points :

(i) Words of commands should be loud and clear.

(ii) Cautionary words of command should be in a normal pitch and "executive" words of commands should be in high pitched voice.

(iii) Cautionary words of command should be narrated in a dragged manner while executive words of command should be narrated frequently.

(iv) There should be a pause between the two words of commands.

POSITIONS & COMMANDS

Command : Squad Savdhan (Squad Attention)

The position of 'Savdhan' is a basic movement of drill. Place heels together and in line, feet turned out equally forming an angle of 30 degrees, knees straight without stiffness, hips level and drawn back slightly, body erect and resting equally on hips, chest lifted and arched shoulders square, falling equally and neck filling the collar properly. Keep arms hanging straight down without stiffness so that the thumbs are immediately behind the seams of the trouser, back of the hand outwards, hands closed (not clenched) and thumbs straight to the front. Keep head erect and square to the front, chin vertical and eyes straight to the front. Keep weight of the body resting equally on the heels and the toe of the feet. Bring heels together with extreme sharpness by lifting the left foot six inches from the ground and placing it flat and very firm besides the right, avoid stamping of foot. All drill movements commence after getting into Savdhan position, also while speaking to or being addressed by a superior officer, a cadet should stand in Savdhan.

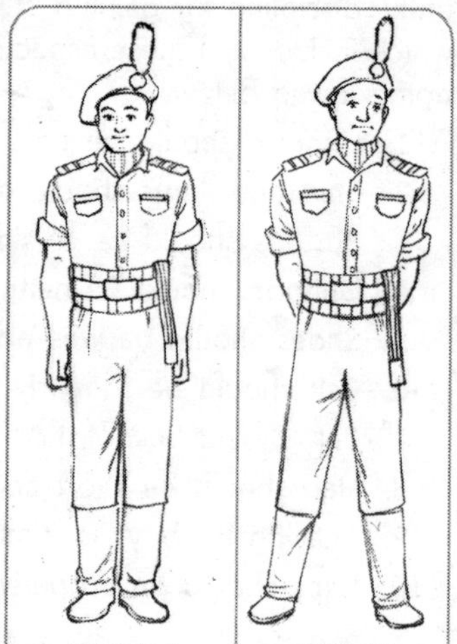

SAVDHAN VISHRAM

Command : Vishram (Stand at Ease)

Take left foot 12 inches to the left; place the weight of the body on both feet. While doing the movement raise the foot 6 inches from the ground. Simultaneously both the hands will be taken behind the back, through shortest route, the right hand over the left with open palms facing outwards and thumbs interlocked.

Command : Aram Se (Stand Easy)

Relax the limbs, body and head without moving the feet. On the cautionary word of command 'Squad', assume correct position of stand-at-ease by an upward snappy jerk of the body. Talking, turning the head, slouching and using a handkerchief is not permitted.

Turning Command : Dahine Mur (Right Turn)

In all turns, keep the weight of the body on the forward foot. Turning both knees straight, turn 90 degrees right on the right heel and left toe, raising the right toe and left heel, in doing so keep weight of the body on the right foot. Bring the left foot into the right by lifting the foot 6 inches clear of the ground.

Turning Command : Pichhe Mur (About Turn)

Turn 180 degrees, bracing the legs and maintaining the balance by locking the thighs together. The about turn is always made right about.

Inclining Command : Adha Dahine/Baen Mur (Half Right/Left Turn)

In inclining (adha dahine or adha baen mur), the movement is the same as in Turning except that the individual or squad turns through 45 degrees only in place of 90 or 180 degrees.

SIZING AND FORMING

Sizing and Forming

- **Command : Lamba Dahine, Chhota Baen, ek line men—Kadvar** (tallest on the right, shortest the left in single rank-size) : The whole squad turns right, counts a pause and then sort themselves out by size remaining at attention facing the instructor in one single line.
- **Command : Squad dahine se ginti kar** (Squad count from right) : The squad numbers from the right to left.
- **Command : Visham Cadet ek qadam aage, Sam cadet ek qadam pichhe chal :** (Odd numbers one pace forward even numbers one pace step back march) : All follow command.
- **Command : Dahina cadet khara rahe. Visham cadet dahine, sam cadet baen, line dahine aur baen mur** (stand fast the right hand man, odd numbers to the right, even numbers to the left, ranks right and left turn) : All turn as ordered except the right hand man who remains facing the front. The squad then forms three ranks with even numbers following behind the odd number. On halting in position, each man turns to his front, takes up his own dressing and remains at attention.
- **Command : Teen line banao, tez chal** (Form up in three ranks quick march): The cadets position themselves in three ranks, front, centre and rear with 30 inches between ranks and an interval of one arm's length between two cadets.

Numbering

Each cadet keeps head and eyes steady to the front. The front rank of the squad will number off sharply from right to left, the right hand cadet calling out 'one' the next 'two' and so on. Cadets in the centre and rear ranks take the number of the front.

Open Order March

- **Command : Khuli line-chal** : For inspection and squad drill it is necessary for the squad to be in 'Open Order' *i.e.* the front rank and rear rank take one and half paces forward and to the rear respectively while centre rank stands fast at his place. The front rank shoot the right foot forward one full step and left foot one short step and lift right to bring the two feet together, arms to sides throughout. The rear rank conforms to similar movement to the rear. The centre rank doesn't move at all.

* **Command : Dahine Saj (Right Dress)** : In this command the right hand man stands fast, squad takes a short sharp pace 15 inches forward with left foot, count regulation pause (40 movements to the minute), turn head and eyes to the right (Except the right hand man of each rank). Men in the front rank only will extend the right arm first clenched, back of the hand uppermost knuckles touching the shoulder seam of the man on the right, count a regulation pause, each individual then dresses by taking short quick steps until he can just see the lower part of the face of the man two places away from him. The right hand man of the centre and rear rank, places himself 30 inches from the rank in front, each individual of these ranks covering off correctly by glancing out of the corner of his eye. The turning of the head and eyes should not be a casual glance but a deliberate movement by cadets.

SALUTING

Salute to the Front

* **Command : Ginti se salute, Samne salute ek** (Saluting by number, salute to the front-one) **:** The right arm kept straight, raised sideways until it is horizontal, palm of the hand to the front, fingers extending, thumb close to the forefinger.

SALUTE TO THE FRONT

* **Command : Squad do (Squad two) :** Keeping the upper arm still, hand and wrist straight, bend elbow until the forefinger tip on the right hand is one inch above the right eye. Keep upper arm horizontal and at the right angles to the side, forearm, wrist and fingers all in one straight line and palm of the hand vertical.
* **Command : Squad teen (Squad three) :** Return to position of attention cut the shortest way to the side by dropping the elbow to the front, fingers curled up on the way down. When judging the time, the hand will remain at the position of the salute for a regulation pause.
* **Command : Samne Salute (Salute to the front) :** Avoid saluting movement before actual halt and avoid speaking before completing the final movement.

Salute to the Flank

* **Command : Dahine ko Salute (Salute to the right) :** Cadet takes his position of the salute to the front. He turns his head, eyes square off to the right and without upsetting position of the right arm, wrist or hand, shifts the head so that right eye can just look along the palm of the hand. The cadet either looks along his own height or into the eyes of the officer he is saluting.
* **Command : Baen ko Salute :** All action are same except that cadet turns his/her head to the left.

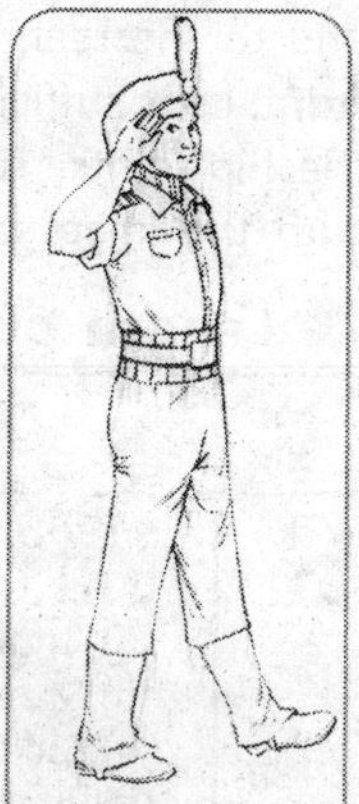

DAHINE KO SALUTE

Getting on Parade

Squad forms up in three ranks, on the end of the parade ground facing in the direction, to be on parade. The right guide or right hand man acts as right marker.

* **Command : Dahine (Right) :** On this command come properly to ease.
* **Command : Darshak (Marker) :** The right marker comes to attention, marches in quick time 15 paces straight to his front halts and stands at ease.
* **Command : Parade-Par (Get on Parade) :** Marker and squad come to attention. The squad marches forward to their front, halt on the 15th pace, dress automatically, look to the front and stand at ease, a regulation pause will be made between each movement.

BAEN KO SALUTE

Dismissing

* **Command : Visarjan (Dismiss) :** Turn to the right, salute, (If an officer/JCO is present on parade) pause and then step off. When marching independently, keep in step until clear of the parade ground.

Falling Out

* **Command : Line Tor (Fall out) :** It does not signify the end of the parade, but only a break in it. Salute is not given. Cadets fall out but do not leave the vicinity of their place of parade or line of march.

MARCHING

In marching, maintain position of attention and remain well balanced. Swing naturally from the shoulder, hands reaching as high as shoulder level in front and/to the rear. Hand kept closed and fingers slightly clenched always to the front. Legs sufficiently bent at the knee, swung forward freely and naturally from the hip joints. The foot should be carried to the front, placed on the ground with the knee straight.

Length of Pace and Time of Marching

Sr. No.	Movement	Length of pace in inches	Paces in a minute	Distance in yards
1.	Slow time	30	70	
2.	Quick time	30	120	100
	(i) Step out	33		
	(ii) Step short	21		
	(iii) Side step	12		
3.	Double time	40	180	200

Quick March

* **Command : Tez Chal (Quick March) :** March from the position of attention with the band, give the word of command on successive beats of paces *i.e.* 'Quick' on the left foot, 'March' on the right foot. On the command 'chal' (March) step off a full pace with the left foot and swing the right arm.

Slow March

* **Command : Aage Barh (Slow March) :** Move your left leg forward balancing on the right foot. Move left leg till it reaches right foot, maintaining balance on right foot, move the left leg further ahead and place left foot on ground. The distance of one pace is 30 inch. Similarly put the right foot ahead and halt. Hands will remain by the side of the body as in attention position.

Halt

* **Command : Squad-tham (Squad halt) :** This command is given when right foot passes the left. Check the forward movement as the right foot comes to the ground. Complete a short pace of 15 inches with the left foot, bend the right knee and bring the right foot in sharply to the left and assume the position of attention.

TURNING ON THE MARCH AND WHEELING

Turning on the March

* **Command : Ginti se Murna-baen Mur-ek (Turning by numbers, left turn one) :** The cadet will freeze with the left foot forward flat on the ground, the right foot 30 inches to the rear, heel raised; both legs braced, body balanced evenly between them, right arm swung forward and left arm swung back.

* **Command : Squad Do (Squad two) :** Bring both arms to the side, bend the right knee, foot raised with the toe at least six inches clear of the ground.
* **Command : Squad Teen (Squad three) :** Straighten the right knee towards new direction. As the foot comes to the ground, shoot the left foot forward 15 inches, hands still on the sides, body in attention position shoulder back.
* **Command : Squad Aage Barh (Squad forward) :** Lead on in quick time with the left foot, swinging the arms.
* **Command : Qadam Tolkar Murna, Baen Mur (Turning by balance step, left turn) :** Check the pace with the left foot, cut the hands to the sides, bend the right knee, force the body round to the new direction and as the right foot comes to the ground, shoot the left forward, 'Squad forward', lead on in quick time with the left foot, swinging the arms.
* **Command : Ginti Se Pichhe Murna, Pichhe Mur Ek (Turning about by numbers, about turn one) :** Complete the pace with the left foot, take half pace with the right foot and freeze with the left arm forward, right arm back and left heel off the ground.
* **Command : Sqaud Do (Squad two) :** Cut the arms to the sides, turn right, bend the left knee to adopt position of attention.
* **Command : Squad Teen (Squad three) :** Again turn right parading on the left foot and bend the right knee to adopt the attention position.
* **Command : Squad Char (Squad four) :** Mark time, once pace with the left foot and resume position of attention.
* **Command : Squad Aage Barh (Squad forward) :** Step off with the right foot and continue marching.

Wheeling

* **Command : Dahine/Baen Ghoom (Right/left wheel) :** This command is used when marching in single file or in threes, the inner man wheels on the circumference of a circle four feet in diameter and changes direction through 90 degrees, speed governed by the ability of the outside man to keep pace by stepping out. The inner man adjusts and shortens his pace accordingly.

SALUTING ON THE MARCH

Saluting to the Flank

* **Command : Ginti Se Salute-danine Salute Ek (Saluting by numbers salute to the right one) :** The commands is given as left foot touches the ground. Complete next pace with the right foot forward, heel on the ground, toe raised, arms at the maximum extent of the swing, shoot the left foot

forward, complete the next pace with left foot, heel on the ground, toe raised, bring the right arm smartly to the position of the salute, turn the head and eyes to the right, cut the left hand to the side. As the left foot comes to the ground, the squad shouts 'Up'.

- **Command : Squad Do (Squad two) :** Keep left arm still to the side maintain correct position of salute without swinging the shoulder, complete the next pace with the right foot and shout 'two'. The order 'two', 'three', 'four' and 'five' may be given in quick succession, one pace being taken on each, and the appropriate number shouted each time.
- **Command : Squad Chhe (Squad six) :** Complete the pace with the right foot. As the heel touches the ground, turn the head and eyes to the front, cut the right hand away to the side and shout 'Down'.
- **Command : Squad Saat (Squad seven) :** Continue marching in quick time, swing the arms and shout 'Swing' on the first pace.
- **Command : Saluting Dahine-ko salute-Salute (Salute to the right-Salute) :** Given as the left foot comes to the ground. Come up to the salute the next time the left foot, touches the ground and cut the hand away on the sixth pace (right foot) (Cadets will continue to call out each time).

Salute while Passing an Officer

While passing an officer, salute on the third pace before reaching him and lower the hand on the third pace after passing him. During the salute look at the officer full in the face.

Saluting to the Front

The word of command given as the right foot passes the left, is as for the halt. Halt, salute to the front, wait for regulation pause, salute to the front again, pause, turn about, pause and lead off in quick time.

Eyes Right and Left

- **Command : Dahine Dekh (Eyes right) :** A formed body requiring to pay a compliment to a flank will receive the order to march by the desired flank. The guide will look to his front in order to keep direction. All officers, in command will salute, the remainder will turn their heads. The word of command given as the left foot touches the ground in quick time and every one looks right when the left foot next comes to the ground.
- **Command : Samne Dekh (Eyes front) :** This command is given in a similar manner.

SIDE PACE, PACE FORWARD AND TO THE REAR

Side Pace

* **Command : Dahine Ya Baen Bazu Chal, Ya Qadam Dahine Ya Baen Bazu Chal (Right or left close march) :** The side pace (12 inches) is used to move the squad not more than 12 paces to a flank. Carry right foot to a distance of 12 inches, close left foot to it by bending left knee and completing the pace in double time. Shoulders square, direction straight to the flank and uniform pause after each pace.

Pace Forward and to the Rear

* **Command : Pace Forward and to the Rear :** Left foot shot forward or rear to the required distance. If more than one pace, adopt normal marching, stepping a full pace of 30 inches. Maximum number of paces ordered to step forward or rear will be three.

MARKING TIME

Marking Time

Maintain position of attention. Marking time is done in the same cadence as marching.

To Quick Mark Time from Halt

* **Command : Tez Qadam Tal (Quick mark time) :** Raise the left knee and top of the thigh parallel with the ground, lower leg perpendicular, foot at natural angle, straighten leg again directly, and resume the position of attention, bend and straighten the right knee in a similar manner, body erect, shoulders square to the front and arms to the sides.

Halt

* **Command : Tham (Halt) :** Bring the right foot down sharply and firmly to resume the position of attention.

To Mark Time from Quick Marching

* **Command : Qadam Tal (Mark time) :** The command is given with cautionary word well drawn out and executed as the left passes the right. Take short pace of 15 inches with right foot and begin the marking time with the left foot.
* **Command : Aage Barh (Forward) :** To move forward when quick marking time, the word of command is given as the left foot is being raised. Right foot comes to ground, shoot left foot forward and resume marching.

Changing Step

Changing step in quick time by numbers.

- **Command : Qadam Badalna Ek** (Changing step-one given as the right foot reaches the ground) **:** Complete pace with left foot so that the left foot is flat on the ground and 30 inches in front of the right foot. The right arm is raised in front, and the left arm in rear of the body.
- **Command : Squad Do (Squad two) :** Bend the left foot forward placing flat on the ground with the hollow in the heel of the left foot and the arms are cut to the sides.
- **Command : Squad Teen (Squad three) :** Shoot the left foot forward placing the heel of the left foot on the ground 30 inches in front of the right foot.

DRILL WITH ARMS

Attention, Stand at Ease and Stand Easy

- **Command : Savdhan (Attention) :** The normal position of attention is maintained except that the right hand will hold the rifle with magazine to the front at the right side, thumb on the left of the rifle, butt of the rifle flat on the ground, toe of the butt in line with the toe cap of the boot.
- **Command : Visharam (Stand-at-Ease) :** Place the left leg to the left so that the feet are about 12 inches apart, keep the left arm to the side, force the rifle straight out to the front by keeping the right arm straight.
- **Command : Aram Se (Stand Easy) :** Force the right hand to the nose cap of the rifle, the fingers and the thumb curling round the rifle, bend the right arm so that the angle of the rifle is not altered.

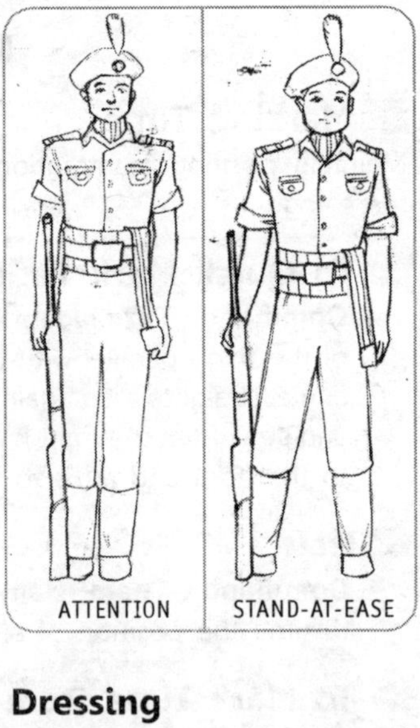

Getting on Parade with Rifle and Dressing

- **Getting on Parade :** When getting on parade with rifle, the rifle is carried out at 'Tol Shastra' (short trail). As soon as the squad halts, the butt is placed noiselessly on the ground in the correct position of attention.
- **Sajna (Dressing) :** In dressing, the front rank raises the left arm instead of the right arm and the rifle is again raised to the position of short trail when moving.
- **Dismissing and Falling Out :** The procedure will be as for Foot Drill, but rifles will be shouldered before the squad is dismissed.

Ground Arms

* **Command : Bhumi Shastr–ek (Ground arms one) :** Keep the upper body straight but inclined forward and bend down by bending and opening the knees keeping the heels together, lay the rifle gently on the ground at the right side, magazine to the right, muzzle pointing straight to the front, right hand in line with the toe of the boot.
* **Command : Squad Do (Squad two) :** Release the rifle with the right hand and resume the position of attention.

Take Up Arms

* **Command : Uthao Shastr–ek (Take up arms one) :** Bend down as in the first movement of the ground arms, seize the rifle with the right hand in the original position by the right toe, raise the muzzle sufficiently to put the thumb and fingers between the rifle and the ground.
* **Command : Squad Do (Squad Two) :** Resume the position of attention and bring the rifle to its correct position at order.

BAGAL SHASTRA

Shoulder Arms

* **Command : Bagal Shastra–ek (Shoulder arms one) :** Throw the rifle perpendicularly up the right side in the first movement, the left arm comes across the body to seize the rifle in line with the waist belt on the hand guard and right hand on the pistol grip simultaneously with forefinger from outside and thumb from inside. Barrel resting in the hollow of the right shoulder.
* **Command : Squad Do (Squad Two) :** Cut the left hand to the side in attention position.

Order Arms

* **Command : Bazu Shastra–ek (Order arms one) :** Hold the barrel below the bayonet stand with left hand.
* **Command : Squad Do :** Drop the rifle with help of left hand till the butt is one inch from the ground and with the right hand, hold the rifle on the hand guard simultaneously.
* **Command : Squade Teen :** Cut left hand in attention position and drop butt of the rifle on ground.

Present Arms

* **Command : Salami Shastra–ek :** Throw the rifle upwards with the right hand, catching it with the left hand at the point of balance, thumb of the

left hand in the hollow of the right shoulder and the right hand at the small of the butt, thumb to the left, elbow to the rear.

- **Command : Squad Do :** Bring the rifle to a perpendicular position in front of the centre of the body. Striking left hand on the side of rifle and hold small of the butt with right hand simultaneously.
- **Command : Squad Teen :** Tilting the rifle with the left hand, bring the rifle down, perpendicularly in front of and about three inches from the centre of the body. Right hand to hit the magazine. Holding the rifle at the full extent of the right arm, fingers together, slanting downwards meet it smartly with the left hand immediately behind the backsight in the line with waist belt, outside the selling thumb pointing upwards to the muzzle and on the left of the rifle, at the same time place the hollow of the right foot against the left heel, both knees straight. The weight of the rifle to be supported by the left hand.

SALAMI SHASTRA

Order from Present

- **Command : Baju shastra–ek :** Hold pistol grip with right hand and simultaneously lift right foot and place it with left foot as in attention position.
- **Command : Squad Do :** Carry the rifle to right side and seize it with right hand at the pistol grip.
- **Command : Squad Teen :** Cut left hand to attention position.

Saluting with Arms at the Shoulder

- **At the Halt :** For saluting with the rifle at the shoulder take the left hand across the body, forearm parallel to the ground. Strike the hand guard with palm of the hand so that the knuckle of the thumb is parallel to the outer edge of the handguard, fingers and thumb together and extended, back of the hand to the front and elbow forced into the body. After a regulation pause the left hand will be cut to the side.
- **On the March :** The salute will be carried out in the manner as explained above. Simultaneously turning the head and the eyes towards the officer, looking him fully in the face. The salute will be given on the third pace before reaching the officer and hand cut away and head turned to the front on the third pace after passing him.

Short/Long Trail from The Order

- **Command : Samtol Shastra (Short Trail) :** Slightly bend the right arm to raise the butt of the rifle about one inch from the ground. The butt is placed noiselessly on the ground in the correct position of attention as soon as the movement is completed. The short trail is normally carried out when getting on parade with rifle and when stepping forward and to the flanks and during dressing.
- **Command : Tol Shastra (Trail Arms) :** With the flick of the wrist throw the nozzle forward and downwards, catching rifle at the point of balance, back of the hand to the right, arm straight so that the rifle is horizontal, muzzle pointing to the front and magazine underneath.
- **Command : Bazu Shastra (Order Arms) :** With the right hand, force the butt to the ground and raise the muzzle to assume the correct position of the order.

Examine from the Order

- **Command : Janch Shastra (Examine Arms) :** Bend the left knee, placing the front of the foot on the ground about 16 inches to the left front and force the muzzle downwards with the left hand keeping the arm slightly bent so that the rifle is in front of the right thigh. Cocking the rifle and applying holding opening catch with left hand place the right thumb in the charge guide with the nail upper-most and at an angle to reflect and light up the barrel, fingers together on the right of the rifle and extending towards the ground.
- **Command : Chal-wale Purze Aage Kar :** Pull back and release the cocking handle and on order, press the trigger and bring back the weapon as in attention position.

The Order from the Examine

- **Command : Bazu Shastra-ek (Order Arms One) :** Strike the rifle with the right hand in the same place as that held at the order, finger and thumb curled round the rifle, forearm and elbow on the stock, bend the left knee to close the heels.
- **Command : Squad Do (Squad Two) :** Pull the rifle down to the right side striking it with the left hand just below the nosecap as for the second movement of the order from the slope.
- **Command : Squad Teen (Squad Three) :** Cut the left hand away as in the third movement of the order from the slope.

CEREMONIAL DRILL

In the NCC, the Ceremonial Drills are organised time to time and also at the culmination of the cadet's training. The Ceremonial Drill may be arranged for various dignitaries and VIPs.

National salute is given to the President of India and the Governors of the various states within their own jurisdiction. General salute is given to dignitaries of the rank of Major General and above. All other dignitaries are only given Salami Shastra (Present Arms).

The Ceremonial Parade is conducted in the following manner :

The VIP on arrival will be received by the Senior Officer serving with the NCC present and taken to the saluting base. The Parade Commander on seeing the VIP alighting from the car will order 'Parade Savdhan'. After VIP has come to the dais and is ready to take the salute, the Parade Commander will give the following words of command :

(i) Parade General Salute Degi General Salute Salami Shastra. Or Parade Rashtriya Salute Degi Rashtriya Salute Salami Shastra.

Or

Parade Salami Degi-Salami Shastra.

(ii) Parade Bazu Shastra.

The Parade Commander marches up smartly to the saluting base and reports to the VIP, 'No. 1 Bn Parade Apke Nirikshan Ke Liye Hazir Hai Sriman/Srimati Ji'. After the VIPs permission has been obtained to let the parade stand-at-ease and prior to commencement of the inspection, Parade Commander gives the word of command 'Number one company Khara rahe, Baqui Vishram'. After the inspection is finished and the VIP has turned to the saluting dais, the following words of command will be given for the march past :

(i) Parade Savdhan
(ii) Parade Nikat Line Chal
(iii) Bagal shastra
(iv) Parade kooch kalam men manch se guzregi No. ---- Aage.
(v) Parade tin-O-tin kalam men dahine mur

Word of command by respective company Commander in their own turn for the march past. 'Number one Company Baen se tez chal'. At the first flag (6 paces of the saluting base) each company commander will give the following words of command, 'Company Dahine Dekh'. After the company has gone past the saluting base (indicated by the next flag) his word of command will be 'Company Samne Dekh'. When the parade returns to the inspection line, each company will be given word of Command 'Company Tham'. This will follow the command :

(i) 'Number one company aage barhegi baen mur', and will then remain at Savdhan.
(ii) The entire parade will be made to stand-at-ease by the Parade Commander by giving the command: 'Parade Vishram'.

In case the parade is to advance in view order, the following word of command will be given by the Parade Commander :

(i) Parade Savdhan

(ii) Parade Madhya Se-saj

(iii) Parade Samne Dekh

(iv) Parade Samiksha karan men Madhya se Tez chal

The parade will automatically halt after taking 15 paces. The halt must coincide with stopping of music in case the band is in attendance. Compliment will be paid again accordingly to the status of the VIP. After this stage, stand-at-ease (Vishram). In case the parade is not required to advance in review order, the parade commander will give the words of command 'Vishram' when the entire parade has reached the inspection line and has been turned to the front. When the VIP leaves the Parade ground, the Parade Commander marches off the cadets.

GUARD MOUNTING

Guard mounting requires Guard Commander, Assistant Guard Commander and six cadets. Personnel detailed will be turned out by guard mounting NCO on the previous evening for guard practice. The Guard Commander will fall in the Guard 15 minutes before the appointment time for Guard and complete the adjustments before the guard mounting. NCO falls in the Guard in two ranks. The Guard commander will be on the right and assistant guard commander on the left of the front rank.

The Guard mounting NCO will be 12 paces away from the guard. He will fall in the Guard and inspect as under :

(i) **Guard-Parade Par :** On this command the guard will come to attention, step off and fall in the open order, twelve paces away from the guard mounting NCO and stand at ease in succession from the right.

(ii) **Guard Savdhan :** On this command Guard will come to attention.

(iii) **Guard Dahine Saj :** The Guard commander will turn to his right and march out five paces, halt, turn about, dress the front rank. He will then dress the rear rank and give command 'SAMNE-DEKH' and return to his original position.

(iv) **Guard-Bagal Shastra :** On this command Guard will do shoulder arms.

(v) The Guard Mounting NCO will then report to the orderly officer.

(vi) **Guard Nirikshan Ke Liye Hazir Hai :** The guard mounting NCO will then fall in on the right of the guard six paces away from the guard commander.

The Orderly Officer will take over, inspect and mount the guard as under :

(i) **Guard-bazu-Shastra :** The orderly officer will inspect the guard and come back to his orginal position.

(ii) **Guard Nirikshan Ke Liye Janch Shastra :** The guard will take the position to examine arms. The orderly officer then inspects the arms commencing from the Guard Commander. After he completes the first person and moves to the second, the guard commander will fall out and accompany the orderly officer. After inspection the orderly officer will return to his original position and the guard commander to his position.

(iii) **Guard-Bolt Chalao :** Guard will Ease spring and close the bolt.

(iv) **Guard-Bazu Shastra :** Guard will order arms.

(v) **Number...Samne Ki line-stick orderly-stick orderly Line Tor :** The stick orderly called out by the orderly officer will take a step forward, shoulder arms, turn to the right, quick march and fall in on right of the guard mounting NCO.

(vi) **Guard-Bagal Shastra :** Guard will shoulder arms.

(vii) **Guard—Apni Duty Ke Liye Dahine Se-Tez Chal :** The Guard marches off. The Guard Commander gives 'Dahine Dekh' to the orderly officer and then moves to take over from the old guard.

Guard Room Procedure

When the sentry sees the new guard approaching him, he will turn out the old guard. The new guard halts at the appointed place. The old guard commander will 'fall in' his guard fifteen paces in front of the new guard. The old guard will present arms and the new guard will return the compliment. Both guards will in succession order arms and stand at ease. The first relief of the new guard will then take over duties from the old guard sentry. The assistant guard commander of the old guard will post the new sentry. He will bring the relieved sentry and fall in with the rest of the guard. The old guard will move off for dismissal. The new guard will give present arms and then old guard will return the compliment with 'Dahine Dekh' (Eyes right).

Guard of Honour

Guard of Honour is provided by National Cadet Corps Senior Division Units only to the dignitaries listed below. The other dignitaries specially invited as guests of honour to the NCC functions or to visit NCC Units in camps may on special occasion are given guard of honour only with the prior concurrence of the Dy DG National Cadet Corps of the States concerned.

The guard of honour is given to the following:

(i) The President, Vice President and the Prime Minister

(ii) The Governors of states and Lt Governor/Chief Commissioners of Union Territories
(iii) The Defence Minister/Minister in the Ministry of Defence/Deputy Defence Minister
(iv) The Chief Minister of State
(v) The Chief of Army/Naval/Air Staff
(vi) The Defence Secretary
(vii) The General Officer Commanding-in-Chief of the command in which the Unit is located (Army Wing Units only)
(viii) The Flag officer Commanding-in-Chief within their commands (Naval Wing units only)
(ix) The Air Officer Commanding-in-Chief, within their commands (Air Wing Units only)
(x) The Vice chief of Army/Naval/Air Staff
(xi) The Dignitaries addressing the convocation of a University
(xii) Chancellor of a University (where Governor of the State is not the Chancellor)
(xiii) Pro-Chancellor/Vice Chancellor of a University when attending important university functions as Chief guest in their University
(xiv) Director General NCC

Strength

The strength of the Guard of Honour will be as follows :

(i) 150 rank and file for the President (in 3 equal divisions).
(ii) 100 rank and file for the Vice President and Prime Minister (in 2 equal divisions).

Compliments

(i) **Rashtriya Salute :** The President and the Governors within their own states.
(ii) **General Salute :** Other dignitaries of the rank of Major General and above.
(iii) **Salami Shastra :** Given to all other VIPs.

Procedure

(i) Guard will form up in two ranks of 24 cadets each with a distance of 4 paces between the front and the rear ranks. The officers of the Guard and the JCO carrying the colour will be two paces in front of the front ranks. The guard commander will be 8 paces in front of the centre of the front rank. The distance between cadets will be 24 inches.
(ii) The band will form up on the right flank in line with the guard and 7 paces from the right guard of the guard.
(iii) There will always be two ADCs who will stand on either side of the dais, 2 paces on the right and left of its front edge.

(iv) The conducting officer who receives the VIP and conducts him to the saluting base will, after conducting the VIP to the dais, positions himself in the centre and rear of the dais and 3 paces, from it.

Inspection

The following procedure for the inspection is observed :

(i) The guard commander will march forward and report to the VIP. He will do so in suitably loud voice. The report will be in Hindi like : 'Guard (Name of Unit) Samman Guard Nirikshan Ke Lie Hazir Hai Shriman/Shrimati Ji'.

(ii) The VIP will come down from the dais and the Guard Commander will conduct him/her moving on the VIP's left. On reaching the right hand man of the band, Right Guide of the Guard of Honour, the Guard Commander will move to the VIP's right and in line with him.

(iii) The ADCs will not march in front of the VIP except in the case of the President of India.

(iv) The band will not turn their heads and eyes toward the VIP during the inspection of the band but will look straight to the front.

(v) During inspection, all ranks of the Guard will turn their heads and eyes towards the VIP and will look at him, taking time from the first beat of the drum. As the VIP moves on, all ranks of the Guard will also move their heads and eyes looking at him all the time. The band will stop playing as soon as the VIP has finished the inspection and the Guard taking the time from the last note of the music will turn their heads and eyes to the front.

(vi) The VIP will be conducted by the Guard Commander towards the conducting officer. The Guard Commander will then salute the VIP. The Guard Commander must be prepared to shake hands with the VIP, should the latter offer to do so.

Dismiss

The Guard Commander will return to his post and after the VIP has proceeded some distance away from the Guard of Honour, he may then stand the Guard of Honour, 'At Ease' (Vishram). The Guard will however, not march off or 'Stand Easy' (Aaram Se) till the VIP for whom it is mounted, has left the place of the Guard.

❖ ❖ ❖

CHAPTER 3

Weapon Training & Infantry Weapons

Shooting at the firing ranges helps a cadet master this as a sport and also to learn handling of a weapon for self-protection. The art of shooting teaches you precision, accuracy, co-ordination of body movements, patience and confidence which all help make you a better person in public life.

The below mentioned Rifles are being used in Weapon Training these days:

(a) Rifle 0.303" Bore (b) Rifle 0.22" Bore

MAIN PARTS OF A RIFLE

1. Stock
2. Heel
3. Recoil Pad
4. Toe
5. Comb
6. Receiver
7. Bolt
8. Ejection Port
9. Operating Handle
10. Extractor
11. Rear Sight
12. Checkering
13. Front Sight
14. Muzzle
15. Magazine Cap
16. Fore-End
17. Grip
18. Magazine Loading Port
19. Carrier Release
20. Trigger
21. Trigger Guard
22. Safety Switch
23. Magazine (Inside-fore end)

A rifle contains certain "numbers" on particular parts:

1. On Barrel
2. Near the Fore Sight
3. On the sling chain
4. Near the Rear Sight
5. On the Bolt lever
6. On the Magazine
7. On the Butt plate

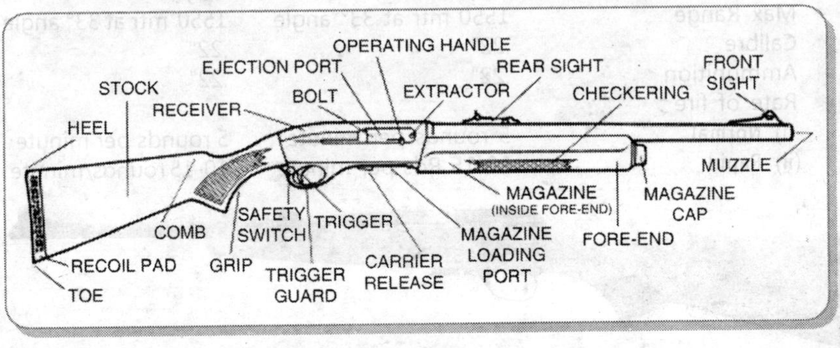

CHARACTERISTICS OF 0.303" BORE RIFLE

* Length along with the bayonet – 5 feet 1½ inches
* Weight along with the bayonet – 9 pounds 11½ ounce
* Length without the bayonet – 3 feet 8½ inches
* Weight without the bayonet – 8 pounds ½ ounce
* Minimum Range – 200 yards
* Maximum Range – 2000 yards
* Effective Range – 300 yards
* Muzzle Velocity – 2400 feet per second
* Capacity of Magazine – 10 rounds
* Normal Rate of fire – 5 rounds per minute
* Fast-Rate of fire – 15 rounds per minute
* Ammunition – 0.303"
* Calibre – 0.303"

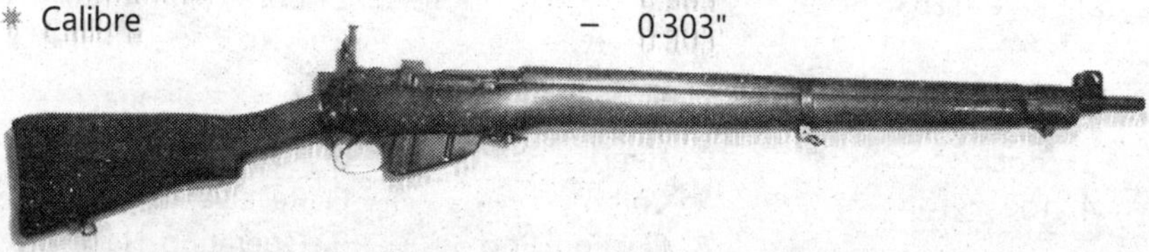

CHARACTERISTICS OF .22" BORE RIFLE

Characteristics	***Rifle .22 No II MK IV BA***	***Rifle .22 Deluxe BA***
* Length	45"	43"
* Weight	3.93 kg	2.78 kg
* Magazine Capacity	10 rounds	05 rounds
* Muzzle Velocity	2700 per sec	2700 per sec
* Grooves in the Barrel	06 RH	06 RH
* Effective Range	25 yds	25 yds
* Max Range	1550 mtr at 33° angle	1550 mtr at 33° angle
* Calibre	.22"	.22"
* Ammunition	.22"	.22"
* Rate of fire :		
(i) Normal	5 rounds per minute	5 rounds per minute
(ii) Rapid	10-15 Rds per minute	10-15 rounds/minute

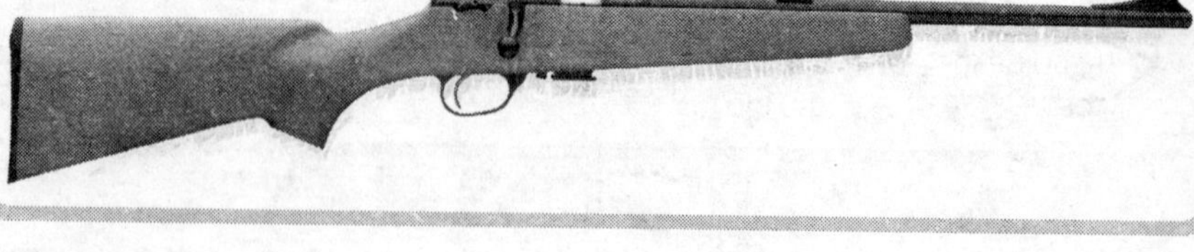

Safety Precautions

(i) Push forward the safety catch by raising and drawing back the bolt knob.
(ii) Examine the chamber and the magazine to be clear.
(iii) Push the bolt knob forward and then down.
(iv) Press the trigger and apply the safety catch.
(v) Check the drill cartridges to ensure that there is no live ammunition.

Stripping Rifle

(i) Check that the number on the left side of the body corresponds with the number on the back side of the lever of the bolt.
(ii) Remove the bolt raising the leaf backsight and pushing forward the safety catch.
(iii) Keep the left hand under the magazine with the middle finger on the restraining catch.
(iv) Withdraw the bolt to the rear, turning the bolt head upwards and fold back the backsight.
(v) Press the magazine catch upwards and take out the magazine.

Assembling Rifle

(i) Check the magazine and ensure that the magazine number is the same as that of the rifle.
(ii) Insert the magazine at its place and press it.
(iii) Ensure that the magazine is fixed in its place.
(iv) Insert the bolt by holding bolt lever with right hand and rifle with the left.
(v) Push forward the bolt until it touches in the charger guide and turn the bolt head towards right till the click sound is heard.
(vi) Push forward, press the trigger and apply the safety catch.
(vii) Set the sight by pressing the thumb spring.

Points to Remember:

(i) Bolt head to be fully tight.
(ii) Bolt head and guide rib as well as cocking piece and steel lug to be in a line.
(iii) Number of the bolt should tally with that of the rifle.
(iv) Safety catch must be applied.

Care & Cleaning Rifle

For efficient operation rifle must be cleaned regularly. For cleaning, strip the rifle, open the butt trap, remove the pull through and the oil bottle for cleaning. Items required for cleaning are:

(i) Pull through
(ii) Wire guage (2.5" × 1.5")
(iii) Oil
(iv) Flannel (4" × 2")
(v) Flannel for oil (4" × 1.5")

Open the rifle and clean in this sequence :

(i) Barrel (ii) Chamber (iii) Bolt
(iv) Magazine (v) Bayonet & Scabbard

LOADING AND UNLOADING

Loading

Clean and load the ammunition one by one when ordered. Also clean the charger prior to loading. Do it in a clear and confident manner. The steps to load in a lying position are :

(i) Take a long pace forward with the left foot and pass the rifle into left hand.
(ii) Place the right hand on to the ground.
(iii) Push the rifle forward and lower to the ground.
(iv) Extend the left arm to the front and legs well apart.
(v) Load the rifle.

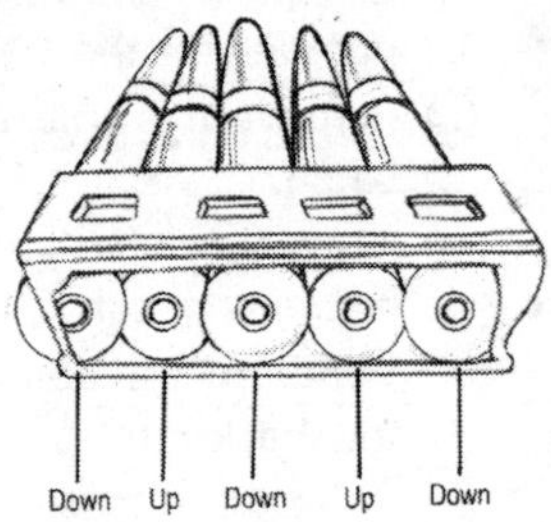

Unloading

(i) Unload the rifle.
(ii) Place the right hand on the ground.
(iii) Draw up the left hand.
(iv) Stand up quickly.

POSITION AND HOLD

There are mainly four types of firing positions :

(i) The standing position (ii) The sitting position
(iii) The Kneeling position (iv) The Lying position

The three basic needs of good shooting are :

(i) Comfortable position and firm hold.
(ii) Correct aim.
(iii) The aim is not disturbed when trigger is pressed.

Position and Hold

For a stable lying position, the firer should lie as if fixed to the ground with:

(i) Body slanting to the left from the line of the target and legs opened wide apart.
(ii) Lie on the ground in such manner to form a horizontal triangle by the three points where the chest leaves the ground, the left elbow and the right elbow.

(iii) A vertical triangle, as viewed from the front of firer, formed by the forearms, the base being the ground between elbows.
(iv) The shoulders should be level.
(v) The right hand is bedded in providing steadiness and the forefinger to be actually on the trigger.
(vi) The left hand acts as support to the forward part of the rifle.
(vii) The butt plate should be bedded into the shoulder.
(viii) The weight of the head should press the chin downwards and to the right against the butt.
(ix) Aim correctly and then hold breath while pressing the trigger firmly.

AIMING

Correct aim is essential for a successful shot. The rules of aiming are :
(i) Focus the target at the centre with the eye and the foresight.
(ii) Hold the rifle properly.
(iii) Close the left eye and focus the foresight.
(iv) See the foresight through the backsight 'U'.

TRIGGER CONTROL

For accurate shooting, trigger operation without disturbing the aim is a must. To achieve this do the following practices :
(i) Practise independent action of the index finger.
(ii) Practise further muscular control of the hand.
(iii) Practise to develop co-ordination between the right eye, brain and right hand index finger.
(iv) Practise to introduce an element of 'holding' and the co-ordination between right eye, brain and right index finger.
(v) Practise to perfect the element of 'holding' and the co-ordination between right eye, brain and right hand index finger.

Limber up: It is a sort of rehearsal or warm up before actual firing practice.

Firing a Shot
(i) Before shooting a firer must be fully determined that it is going to be a perfect shot.
(ii) As soon as the correct holding is achieved, not more than five seconds should be taken to fire a shot.

(iii) As the 'range' is given the fierer should adjust his sights and wait for indication of the target.
(iv) On coming into the aim, the firer should take the first pressure.
(v) Just before taking an aim, breathing should be gently restrained.
(vi) Immediately on 'correct aim' the second pressure should be taken and shot fired.
(vii) The hold and aim should be maintained until the bullet has left the barrel.
(viii) The firer should declare if the aim at the time of firing is not correct *e.g.* left, right, high or low.
(ix) Immediately after follow through or declaration, reloading at the shoulder should be carried out.
(x) Having reloaded the firer should realign his sights on the target.

SAFETY PRECAUTIONS

(i) A red flag displayed on the butt indicates that no firing should take place.
(ii) If firing is suspected during the practice, weapons will be placed on the ground and the firer will stand clear.
(iii) During inspection, loading, and unloading, all the rifles must point towards the target.
(iv) On the command 'Nirikshan Ke Liye Janch Shastra' (Examine Arms), rifles will be held parallel to the ground and pointing in the direction of the target.
(v) No one will go to the targets until all weapons have been unloaded, inspected and permission to go has been given by the officer-in-charge.

RANGE PROCEDURE

The following is the normal procedure on the firing points :
(i) On the order of Detail Advance 'Aage Barh' the first detail will take position on the firing point.
(ii) On the lowering of the red flag at the butt, the officer gives the order of 'Detail Advance'.
(iii) The coaches check up their positions and correct them if needed, and give the word of command 'Limber Up'.
(iv) The officer will then give the order to load and carry on.
(v) The firing will start only after getting orders from officer-in-charge, firing.
(vi) On completion of fire, the firers must raise their right hand up, keeping the elbow on the ground.
(vii) Officer-in-charge will give the word of command 'Khali Kar' when all have finished. On this the firers will take their rifles onto their shoulders and move the bolt twice, press the trigger and stand up.

(viii) The officer-in-charge will give the command 'Detail Report', on this the firers would report 'Number ek rifle theek, do theek, teen theek and so on. The report will be from left to right.

(ix) The details are changed by word of command and the new detail which has been waiting comes up while another detail forms up behind.

(x) Before the firers leave the range they will have a further weapon inspection. Each firer must ensure that he/she has no live ammunition with him/her.

MPI & ELEVATION

Mean Point of Impact (MPI)

The central point of area covered by the group of rounds fired with consistent aim and held at the same aiming mark is called MPI.

Elevation

When during firing it is found that the elevation of the barrel is not correct *i.e.* when the rifle is fired correctly with correct aim, the shot goes high or low instead of hitting at the point of aim. It will be necessary to readjust the setting of backsight.

Alteration of Sight

The amount of alteration needed may be found from the following table which shows the change of MPI when the sight is altered by 100 yards.

Range Target	Rise or drop of MPI on Target
200 Yards	6 inches
300 Yards	12 inches

Range Target	Rise or drop of MPI on Target
400 Yards	18 inches
500 Yards	24 inches

An alteration of 50 yards in the sight will bring half the effect shown above. 200 yards will double it on the target.

GROUP AND SNAP SHOOTING

The Group MPI

During training the group implies five consecutive well-fired shots, fired with consistent aim at the same aiming mark. The central point of impact is called the Mean Point of Impact (MPI) of the group.

Grouping Capacity

Firers are classified into certain grouping capacities and measured at a range of 100 yards. These capacities are represented by the diameter of the circles *e.g.* 2 inches, 4 inches and so on. The diameter of a circle containing all five shots fired by a cadet to the best of his ability is known as his grouping capacity.

Group Fire

In group fire, a cadet has to make a group, from the distance of 25 yards by keeping five bullets close to each other on a target of 1′ × 1′.

While measuring the group, the distance between the two bullets is measured in centimeters. According to the size of the group, marks are distributed. The distribution is given below. Maximum marks are 40.

1.	Group of 2.5 cm or less	40 Marks
2.	Group of 3.5 cm	32 Marks
3.	Group of 4.0 cm	28 Marks
4.	Group of 3.0 cm	36 Marks
5.	Group of 4.5 cm	24 Marks
6.	Group of 5.0 cm	20 Marks
7.	Group of 5.5 cm	16 Marks
8.	Group of 6.0 cm	12 Marks
9.	Group of 6.5 cm	08 Marks
10.	Group of 7.0 cm	04 Marks

A cadet should take care of this thing that all the five bullets should be fired on the same target, where the first bullet was fired. He/She should keep firm his/her hand on the same destination till all the bullets are fired.

Application Fire

In this firing too, a cadet is supposed to fire at a distance of 25 yards, firing five bullets on 1' × 1' target. It has maximum 40 marks. Firing at separate circles in target gives different marks.

For example - Fire at "Bull" gives 8 marks.
"Inner" gives 6 marks.
"Magpie" gives 4 marks.
"Outer" gives 2 marks, etc.

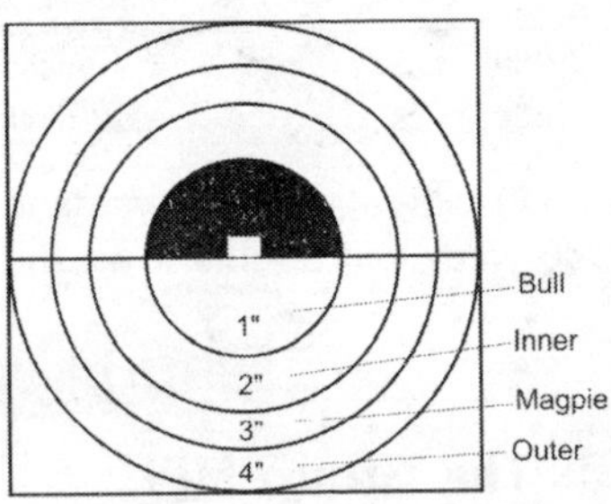

For achieving maximum marks one should fire all the five bullets on "Bull".

Snap Shooting

The snap shooting should be fired to defeat the time factor. It should be done on miniature range. Before one is made to fire he/she should be given enough practice.

Practice firing is done at figure targets 11, 12 and snap shooting at ranges 100, 200 and 300 yards. For firing on miniature range representative figure targets are used and the time progressively reduced from 7 to 4 seconds. The size of the targets is also reduced. Accuracy before speed is insisted upon.

In this shooting, all the five bullets are supposed to be fired at "Figure Target 11 at a distance of 25 yards. Each hit is entitled with 10 marks. Maximum marks in this shooting are 50.

Continuous Snap Shooting

This is to take on the targets as they appear. In this case, having shot one target, firer must at once shoot another, firing continuously and methodically as long as target remains.

Advance Shooting Competition

The advance shooting is held at "National Rifle Association of India" (NRAI) Target. This target has five "Bulls". In this competition a cadet is supposed to fire at a distance of 25 yards, but, from three different positions.

(i) **Lying Position:** In this position, first of all, the cadet will fire five bullets for "sight setting". After this he/she will set his/her sight, according to the bullets fired on the target. Then the cadet will again fire five bullets, so that each bullet hits their respective bulls.

(ii) **Kneeling Position:** In this position, the cadet will fire five bullets and adjust his/her sight. After that, he/she will take the kneeling position and will fire 10 bullets in such a way that each bull takes 2 bullets.

(iii) **Standing Position:** In this position, 5 bullets are fired on the target while standing, after the sight is adjusted, 10 bullets will be fired in such a way that each bull gets two bullets.

Therefore, in "Advance Shooting" each position requires '5' bullets for "Sight Setting" and 25 bullets more for firing are made available. Each "hit" gives a mark-status. Maximum marks in this shooting are 25.

SHORT RANGE FIRING (.22 RIFLE)

No.	Practice	Target	Range in	Round	Instructions	Scoring
1.	Deliberate	1Ft (1'×1')	25 yards	10	(i) Position lying supported (ii) One practice of 5 rds	Bull & Inner-3 points Magpie-2 points Outer-1 points HPs-15 points

LONG/SHORT RANGE FIRING (7.62 MM RIFLE)

No.	Practice	Target	Range in	Round	Instructions	Scoring
1.	Deliberate	4'×4'/ 1'×1'	100/ 25 yards	5	(i) Position lying supported (ii) Position lying supported	Bull & Inner-3 points Magpie-2 points Outer-1 points HPs-15 points Bull & Inner-3 points Magpie-2 points Outer-1 points HPs-15 points

INFANTRY WEAPONS & EQUIPMENTS

5.56 MM INSAS RIFLE

Characteristics

* Calibre	– 5.56 mm
* Length of Rifle without bayonet	– 960 mm
* Length of Rifle with bayonet	– 1110 mm
* Length of Barrel	– 464 mm
* **Weight**	
(i) Fixed butt with empty magazine	– 4.018 kg
(ii) Fixed butt with loaded magazine	– 4.368 kg
(iii) Empty magazine	– 90 gms
(iv) Full magazine	– 350 gm
(v) Bayonet	– 305 gm
* Effective Range	– 400 mtr
* Sight Radius	– 470 mm
* Muzzle velocity	– 900 m/s
* System of operation	– Gas Operation
* Penetration	– 3 mm at 700 m
* Mode of fire	– Single shot & 3 rounds burst (TRB)
* **Rate of Fire**	
(i) Normal	– 60 rounds/min
(ii) TRB	– 90 rounds/min
(iii) Intense	– 150 rounds/min
(iv) Cyclic	– 600 to 650 rounds/min
* **Ammunition**	
(i) Ball Round	(ii) Tracer Round
(iii) Blank Round	(iv) HD Cartridge

SELF LOADING RIFLE (7.62 MM SLR)

SLR is the basic weapon of the soldiers. These days, it is being provided for practice to NCC cadets also.

Characteristics of SLR

* Calibre	–	7.62 mm
* Length	–	45 inches
* Length of the Barrel	–	21 inches
* Weight	–	4.4 kg
* Capacity of the Magazine	–	20 rounds
* Range on-duty	–	300 yards
* Muzzle velocity	–	2700 ft. per/second
* Normal rate of firing	–	20 rounds per minute
* Rate of rapid firing	–	60 rounds per minute
* System of Operation	–	Gas operation

Parts of SLR

1. Butt
2. Pistol grip
3. Trigger guard
4. Magazine
5. Carrying handle
6. Hand guard
7. Sling Carrier
8. Barrel
9. Gas plug
10. Foresight protector
11. Piston
12. Ejection slot
13. Body cover
14. Backsight leaf
15. Ejector

LIGHT MACHINE GUN (LMG)

LMG is the basic weapon of the army. LMG can fire several rounds at one time. It is of four types.

1. Mark 1
2. Mark 2
3. Mark 3, and
4. Mark 4

It can do splash firing.

Characteristics of LMG

Characteristics	*Mark 1, 2 (0.303")*	*Mark 3, 4 (7.62 mm)*
* Weight of the gun	23 pounds	19 pounds
* Weight of the empty barrel	6.5 pounds	4.5 pounds
* Weight of the empty magazine	17 ounce	
* Weight of full magazine	2.75 pounds	
* Capacity of magazine	30 rounds	
* No. of rounds to be filled	28 rounds	
* Range on-duty	500 yards	
* Muzzle velocity	2700 ft. per second	
* Types of firing	Single shot & Automatic shot	
Slow fire rate	28 rounds per minute	
* Rapid fire rate	84 rounds per minute	

Parts of LMG

1. Butt plate
2. Butt plate buffer spring
3. Butt handle
4. Tripod mounting
5. Butt strap
6. Recoil spring
7. Piston buffer spring
8. Body locking pin
9. Recoll spring pushrod
10. Sheer
11. Change lever
12. Trigger spring
13. Trigger
14. Piston grip
15. Bolt
16. Magazine catch
17. Breech block
18. Piston post
19. Magazine
20. Spring
21. Follower
22. Magazine opening cover
23. Chamber
24. Extractor
25. Carrying handle
26. Barrel carrier
27. Barrel
28. Gas block
29. Foresight
30. Flash eliminator
31. Gas band
32. Gas regulator
33. Bipod mount
34. Piston
35. Tripod Mounting Pin
36. Gas Cylinder

STEN MACHINE CARBINE (STEN GUN)

A Sten Gun OR Sten Machine Carbine is an automatic weapon. It does splash firing. This is the weapon used in CQB (Close Quarter Battle). It is of many type such as—

1. Mark 1   2. Mark 2   3. Mark 3   4. Mark 4, and   5. Mark 6

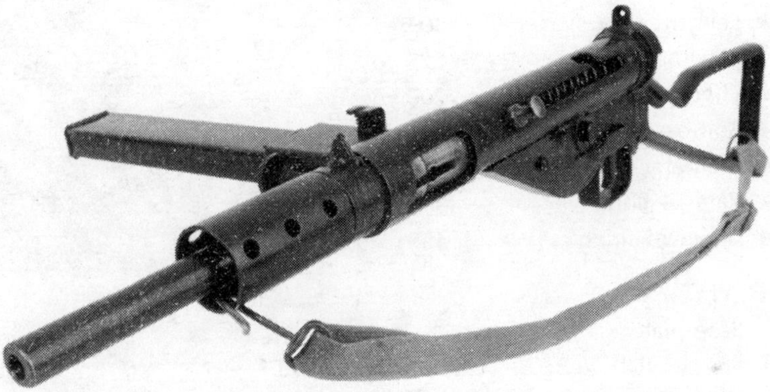

Characteristics of Sten Gun

* Weight	–	6.5 Pounds or 2.9 kg
* Diameter of the Barrel	–	9 mm
* Maximum Range	–	100 yds.
* Range on-duty	–	30 yds.
* Muzzle velocity	–	1200 ft. per second
* Capacity of the magazine	–	30 rounde

Parts

1. Butt
2. Cap
3. Recoil spring housing
4. Recoil spring
5. Cocking handle
6. Breech block
7. Barrel
8. Magazine housing
9. Magazine catch
10. Body
11. Change lever
12. Magazine
13. Platform
14. Spring
15. Bottom plate

2" MORTAR OR 51 MM MORTAR

2" Mortar is the artillery of the platoon head quarters. Variety of bombs such as—super explosive bomb, smoke bomb, signal bomb or parachute bombs are fired through 2" mortar.

Characteristics

* Weight – 12 Pounds
* Length – 19.9"
* Maximum range – 525 yds.
* Effective range – 200 yds.
* Bombardment range – 8 yds.
* Diameter of the barrel – 2 inches
* Rate of firing – 3-4 bombs per min.
* Angle of firing – 45° to 90°

Parts

1. Base plate
2. Fixing screw
3. Firing pin
4. Barrel catch
5. Steel pad
6. Barrel hand
7. Firing pin spring
8. Barrel thread
9. Direction mark
10. Guard muzzle cover

H.E. GRENADE

H.E. Grenade is a light weapon. For the purpose of attack, it is thrown on the enemies with the help of G.F. Rifle. It is of three types:

1. For the purpose of "Training".
2. For the purpose of "Drill practice"
3. For the purpose of "Service"

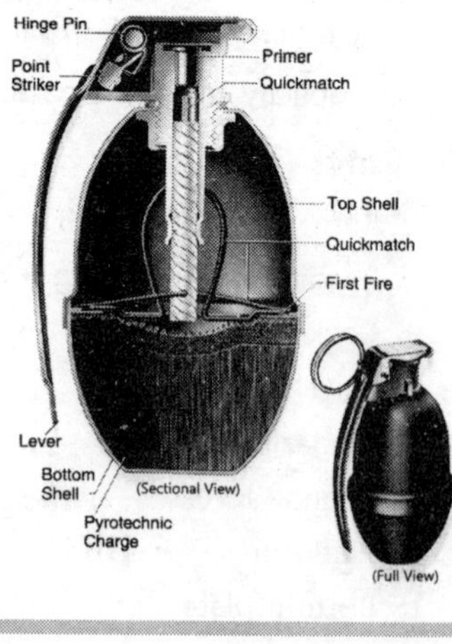

Characteristics

* Weight - 1 Pound, 10.5 Ounce
* Effective Range - 9 yds (diameter)
* Danger Zone - 300 yds (diameter)

Time for Explosion

1. Hand Grenade - 4 sec.
2. Rifle Grenade - 7 sec.

Parts

1. Base plug
2. Safety pin
3. Striker nipple
4. Body
5. Filling screw
6. Center sleeve
7. Side sleeve
8. Detonator sleeve
9. Detonator safety fuse

PISTOL

Pistol is the basic weapon used in an encounter. It has small barrel, hence, it can be used for firing in any direction. Officers in different forces keep pistols for self-defence.

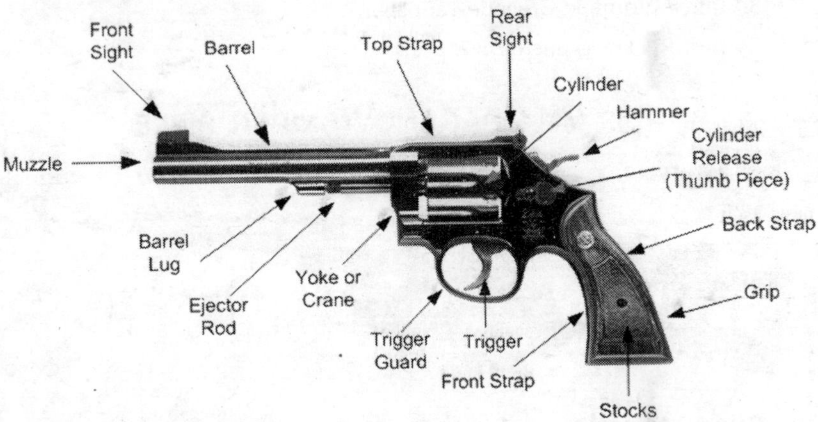

Characteristics

* Name of the weapon – 0.38 Pistol
* Length – 9.5"
* Bore – 0.38"
* No. of chambers – 6
* Weight – 1 Pound, 11 Ounce

Parts

1. Muzzle
2. Front sight
3. Barrel
4. Top Strap
5. Rear sight
6. Cylinder
7. Hammer
8. Cylinder Release
9. Back Strap
10. Grip
11. Stocks
12. Front Strap
13. Trigger
14. Trigger Guard
15. Yoke or Crane
16. Ejector Rod
17. Barrel Lug

Precautions while Handling a Pistol

1. Always consider a "Pistol" as loaded whether in use or not.
2. Always keep the barrel towards the target.
3. Naver play with pistol for fun.
4. Never give or take pistol without checking properly.
5. Never go so close to the enemy that he snatches your pistol.

TYPES OF INFANTRY COMPANY SUPPORT WEAPONS

1. 7.62 mm Dragunov Sniper Rifle
2. 7.62 mm Medium Machine Gun
3. 30 mm Automatic Grenade Launcher
4. 84 mm Rocket Launcher

7.62 MM DRAGUNOV SNIPER RIFLE

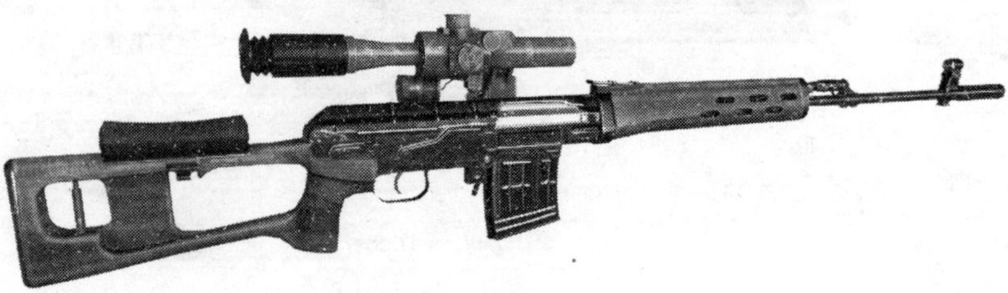

Characteristics

✱ Caliber	7.62 mm
✱ Range	800 Mtr.
✱ Range with telescope sight	1300 Mtr
✱ Weight	4.3 kg
✱ Magazine capacity	10 Rounds

✱ Ammunition fired

(i) Armour Piercing

(ii) Sniper Balls

(iii) Steel Core

(iv) Tracer

(v) Incendiary

7.62 MM MEDIUM MACHINE GUN

Characteristics

✱ Weight	
(i) Gun	14.2 kg
(ii) Tripod	10.2 kg
✱ Effective Battle Range	1800 m
✱ Traverse	360 degree
✱ No. of rounds in belt	235 Rounds
✱ Rate of Fire	
(i) Normal	100 round per min
(ii) Rapid	200 round per min
(iii) Cyclic	500-1000 rounds per min (Adjustable by setting of gas regulator)
✱ Length of Service Burst	20 rounds
✱ Sustained Fire	Being air-cooled can maintain normal rate of fire indefinitely. However barrel should be changed after firing four belts.
✱ Beaten Zone	
Range	**Beaten Zone**
(i) 560 m	110 m × 1 m
(ii) 600 m	100 m × 1 m
(iii) 1200 m	65 m × 3 m
(iv) 1800 m	50 m × 4 m
✱ Trajectory	When this sight is fixed up to 600 m bullets do not rise above 1.2 m (4 ft.)
✱ Night Firing	It is possible to fire the gun at night using passive night sight.

30 MM AUTOMATIC GRENADE LAUNCHER

Characteristics

✷ Weight	
(i) Launcher	18 kg
(ii) Mount	12 kg
(iii) Sight	1 kg (without case); 3.5 kg (with case)
(iv) Gun Box	14.5 kg (with 29 grenades in one belt)
(v) Sight with case	3.5 kg
✷ Range	800 to 1700 m (With and without sight)
✷ Rate of Fire	
(i) Normal	50 grenades/Min
(ii) Rapid	100 grenades/Min
(iii) Cyclic	350 to 400 grenades/Min
✷ Flexibility	It can be mounted on a vehicle or helicopter. It can fire in low angle as well as in high angle. It has crest clearance capability. Flexibility is mainly due to:
(i) Controlled Elevation	67 degrees
(ii) Controlled Depression	14 degrees
(iii) Free Traverse	260 degrees
✷ Effect of Fire	It fires a fragmentation type of grenade which can be fired in a single shot or burst mode. The killing area of a grenade is 7 m all around from the point of burst.
✷ Limitations	It has the following limitations:

(i) Due to sustained fire small parts get damaged.
(ii) Barrel needs to be cooled after firing 80 to 90 grenades.
(iii) It gives out flash and blast on firing.

84 MM ROCKET LAUNCHER

Characteristics

✱ Caliber	84 mm
✱ Weight	16 kg with mount and telescopic sight
✱ Length	1065 mm
✱ Traverse	No traverse of its own
✱ Range	
(i) Heat	400 m (moving targets) 500 m (stationary targets)
(ii) HE	1000 m (killing area 10 m)
(iii) Smoke	1300 m (width 15 m)
(iv) Illumination	2100 m (area of 400-500 m diameter for 30 seconds)
✱ Rate of fire	Maximum sustained 06 rounds per minute
✱ Types of ammunition	Heat, HE, Smoke, Illumination
✱ Armour Penetration	400 mm (Heat)
✱ Back Blast Area	15 m

INFANTRY BATTALION SUPPORT WEAPONS : 81 MM MORTARS

Characteristics

✱ Caliber	81 mm
✱ Weight	40.6 kg (without sight) 4.7 kg (sight without case)
✱ Range	
(i) Minimum	68 mts (from safety point of view 90 m)
(ii) Maximum	5200 m
✱ Rate of Fire (per minute)	
(i) Slow	6-8 rounds
(ii) Normal	9-11 rounds
(iii) Rapid	12-20 rounds
✱ Muzzle Velocity	305 m/sec (maximum)
✱ Elevation Limit	45 degrees to 85 degrees (g)
✱ Safety Distance	Flanking 200 m, Overhead 250 m

ANTI TANK GUIDED MISSILE (ATGM)

Characteristics

✱ Minimum Range	75 m
✱ Maximum Range	2500 m
✱ Rate of Fire	03 missiles per minute
✱ Hit Probability	90% to 96%
✱ Accuracy	60 cm around point of aim, at maximum range
✱ Generation	Second
✱ Launcher Mount	
(i) Traverse	360 degrees
(ii) Elevation	8 degrees + 20 degrees
(iii) Magnification	10 times
✱ Guidance	Semi atuomatic optically tracked Wire guided
✱ Penetration	At 90 degrees angle of impact 460 mm At 60 degrees angle of impact 230 mm

❖ ❖ ❖

CHAPTER

4 National Integration

UNITY IN DIVERSITY

India is a Sovereign, Socialist, Secular, Democratic and Republic country with diversity in caste, religion, customs and traditions where people from different ethnological groups speak different languages or dialects, follow different rituals in daily life and work together harmoniously. In spite of diversity in physical features and social systems, there is unity in India. It is held together by many bonds like territory, language, culture and economic inter-dependence etc. Unfortunately India's history is replete with examples that illustrate the setbacks suffered by us because of our disunity. Mohammad Ghori was able to set his foot on Indian soil because of internal friction and disunity between two Indian rulers. The British too followed the policy of 'Divide and Rule' and enslaved India, because they could disunite Indians easily. It is rightly said, "United we stand divided we fall".

National Unity

National unity is quite essential for communal peace and harmony. We can enjoy peace and security only if there is a mutual trust and goodwill among all the sects of people of the country. No progress can be made in any field, including the field of art and literature, science and cultural advancement and economic well-being if disruptive tendencies and divisive forces are around to tear apart the very fabric of national life. Also, we can play an effective role in the international arena if we can set our own house in order first. Our unity is our strength.

Hindrances in National Unity

Some of the hindrances in National Unity are :

1. **Language :** Blind love towards one's own language and negative feeling towards others is a major hindrance to unity. A language, instead of dividing, should be a unifying force. Alongwith regional languages one national language should be fully developed. Languages of different states should be encouraged in the educational institutions. A common national language, acceptable to all, can bring the linguistic unity in India.
2. **Casteism :** It is seen everywhere in society and almost in all walks of life. The feeling of belonging to an upper caste and hatred for the lower caste

is not only an offence against mankind it is a threat to India's unity. The system of casteism and untouchability would eat into the very vitals of a society. Casteism should be tackled with an iron hand. There should be no communal or special constituents. The minority communities should be given their due share of advancement and communal favouritism should be sternly dealt with. Every Indian should be treated equal irrespective of his caste and creed.

3. **Illiteracy :** Education makes a man civilized. In India about half of the total population is illiterate. An illiterate person cannot understand what is good or bad for himself or his country. Literacy is an important ingredient for unity. The pattern of education should be so oriented that it encourages love, brotherhood and unity amongst various communities. There could be exchange of teachers from one state to another and there should be no bar on the students of one state for admission into the universities of other states. It would help cement the bonds of unity which is an essence of any nation. A common education system of India will greatly help in this.
4. **Communalism :** It is the discriminatory feeling of an individual against another on the basis of religion or creed. This also endangers the unity of our country. Fundamentalism is the greatest challenge to India's unity. This has to be sternly dealt with. The politicians who encourage provincialism and regionalism should be debarred from elections as members of legislative bodies. All citizens should regard themselves as Indians first and build unity between different sections of our society. Think India as a larger community.
5. **Regionalism :** India is quite a vast country where various regional diversities exist. The feeling of loyalty towards one's own state or region first is also a major hindrance in unity. People from different parts of the diversified India should meet under a common wing of national consciousness, forgetting the regional differences, sharing the feelings of togetherness and realise the proud feeling in themselves of being part and parcel of a common Indian diaspora. A common Indian subcontinent should be conceived irrespective of region of diversities.
6. **Extremism :** The extremist movements going on in different parts of the country are yet another challenge to national integration. These movements quite often use violence, create fear in public life, cause loss of lives of government personnel and people and destroy public property. Mostly the youth participate in such movements. The basic reason for taking up arms by the youth is the continuing state of socio-economic deprivations. Moreover, the day-to-day humiliation, denial of justice, human rights violations, various kinds of exploitation and political marginalization prompt them to join the extremist activities which have been threat to law and order and peaceful living of the people residing in the affected areas.

7. **Social Disparity :** Social disparity among the people of different communities, castes and sometime within the community and caste causes tension and imbalance among the people. Social disparity poses great threat to national integration.

NATIONAL INTEGRATION

National integration means a feeling of togetherness and unity among the people of country. It also means an atmosphere in which all citizens, irrespective of their caste, religion and region live together peacefully. It refers to integration in all respects, social, political, economic and emotional. In an integrated country people share common goals. They all work together and co-operate with each other for the prosperity of the nation.

National integration means that though we belong to different castes, religions and regions and speak different languages, India is a secular democratic country and that we are all one. This kind of integration is very important in the building of a strong and prosperous nation. A unique feature of our country is that all the major religions of the world are practised here. There are also great varieties in costumes, food habits, and social customs. Geographically our land is diverse and there are amazing differences in climate.

Despite all these differences India is a single political entity, every part of which is governed under the same Constitution. The need for national integration was never felt before as it is felt today. The complex atmosphere and the worsening law and order situation in the country have led to the necessity of national integration.

National integration is very important for the progress of any nation and for :

(i) Maintenance of peace and harmony.
(ii) Dignity and self-respect as a nation.
(iii) Growth and development of the nation.
(iv) Welfare and well-being of the people.
(v) Internal security and law and order.
(vi) Maintenance of sovereignty and territorial integrity of the nation.
(vii) Cultural and religious development.
(viii) Exchange of technological know-how and culture.
(ix) Economic and industrial growth.
(x) Eradication of poverty and illiteracy.
(xi) Foreign relations and better standing among the nations of the world.
(xii) Attracting foreign investment and increase import and export.

Essence of National Integration

National integration is an emotional and spiritual bond which binds all of Indians irrespective of caste, creed, colour, race, religion and region. In reality, it is the common ideal whose intensity in the passions of the people, determines our 'real strength'. Emotional integration of the country connotes a firm conviction on the part of the individual that there exists a stake for him or her in the well-being of the Nation. In short, being a good citizen of the country in its true sense is what National Integration is all about. In fact, National Integration and Nation Building are synonymous.

It is the duty of each and every citizen of our country to strive to achieve unity in spite of diversity and further maintain that. We must remember that there should be no divisions between different parts of the country. There is only one India of which we all Indians are inheritors. We are Indian first and Indians last. The unity in diversity of which we are proud of can only be maintained if we have the understanding and respect for each other's religion, customs and traditions.

Opportunities for National Integration

The following opportunities must be exploited at all times to ensure National Integration :

1. **Defence Forces & Central Police/Other Organisations :** These organisations provide us with an opportunity to maintain National Integrity at all times since, these are all India based organisations and consist of personnel from the whole country, working, eating, living and fighting together for the integrity of the country.
2. **National Level Games :** Games like the Olympics, Asiad, Commonwealth etc., provide an excellent opportunity to foment National Integration since players/athletes from all over the country participate as 'one team' – forgetting their regional/other differences/considerations.
3. **NCC :** NCC is an excellent organisation which propagates and maintains National Integration in all aspects of training the youth through National Integration Camps, Adventure Camps and the RDC.

Relevance of NCC in Unifying India

NCC inculcates awareness amongst cadets about the diverse heritage of our country and fosters national integration despite linguistic, cultural, religious and geographical barriers. It helps cadets gain experience to live together, co-operate with each other and work in harmony with cadets of other states whom they have not known before, thus helping in strengthening unity as under :

1. **Ethics and Social Values :** These values are very important in day-to-day activities on the ground and are the essentials of personality. NCC helps to cultivate these values through which the spirit of unity and value of personal sacrifice are ignited in the minds of cadets.

2. **Cultural and Traditional Values :** India has diverse groups which have been divided on grounds of religion, caste, creed and language. NCC organises various camps and group activities where ample opportunity is given to the cadets to closely watch the cultural and traditional shows of other regions. It provides the cadets with an opportunity to appreciate each other's uniqueness and cultivate friendship amongst them.
3. **Discipline and Patriotism :** An NCC cadet is trained to give selfless service to society and be available anytime for national cause. NCC can be described as the nation's disciplined, trained and motivated young force available for national service to provide assistance in various places as well as provide future leadership and participation in all walks of life. The spirit of discipline and patriotism is inculcated in the cadets from the very beginning.

CONTRIBUTION OF YOUTH IN NATION BUILDING

Youth is the backbone, hope of the future, potent tools of national integration and reckonable force to shape the destiny of the nation. The youth can play a leading role in bringing together the people of different states and religions with a view to integrating them emotionally, culturally and geographically.

To contribute individually for nation building youth should:

(i) Be good human being by imbibing Oriental value system.
(ii) Help the friends & colleagues from unprivileged section of society.
(iii) Improve personal talent, innovate and enhance their usefulness for society and nation.
(iv) Discourage corruption in every form and manifestation in society.
(v) Participate in sports, yoga and improve personal health.
(vi) Use national/natural resources like, energy in all forms, communication spectrum, water resources etc with due austerity and discourage its misuse by others.
(vii) Develop secular outlook and tolerance for all sections of society.
(viii) Extend willing help to civil administration during natural and man-made disasters.
(ix) Learn healthy politics during college and university days.

Things to say 'No' to contribute for Nation Building

Youth can contribute for nation building at personal level by saying 'no' to under-mentioned social evils :

(i) Drugs;
(ii) Dowry;
(iii) Illicit sexual relations;
(iv) Antisocial activities in thought and action;
(v) Exploitation of underprivileged in society;

(vi) Use of child labour;
(vii) Unfair means during exams; and
(viii) Accepting and offering bribe in all forms.

Things to say 'Yes' to contribute for Nation Building

Youth can contribute for nation building at personal level by saying 'yes' to under-mentioned good personal habits :

(i) Avoid rash driving of vehicles.
(ii) Carry driving license and wear helmet always while driving 2-wheelers.
(iii) Follow road etiquettes and road safety norms explicitly.
(iv) Don't use mobile phone while driving and avoid overspeeding.
(v) Extend willing help during natural and man-made disasters.
(vi) Organise traffic control during accidents.
(vii) Plant trees on special occasions like birth of child, birthday & anniversaries etc and prevent extravaganza by all means.
(viii) Help and look after aging parents, relatives and neighbours.
(ix) Groom & nurture your children so that they become responsible citizens of the nation.
(x) As responsible citizens, employees, entrepreneurs & Govt servants, ensure punctuality, excellence, simple living and high thinking.
(xi) Help your colleagues from under-privileged section of society.

Hindrance Removal Methods

The process of creating and strengthening the feeling of National Unity is called National Integration. The methods to remove hindrances to it are :

(i) The education system should be improved and the students should be taught the lesson of secularism, toleration and mutual respect.
(ii) The illiteracy should be eradicated as early as possible.
(iii) The economic disparity should be narrowed.
(iv) The political parties should not be formed on the basis of religion.
(v) Every citizen should be taught to respect the National language, the National Flag, the National song and participate in National festivals.
(vi) We should keep the neighbourhood clean and beautiful.
(vii) To develop ideal citizenship.
(viii) To promote social equality.
(ix) To arrange National Integration camps.

The Aims of National Integration Camps are :

(i) Create awareness amongst the youth of diverse cultural heritage of our country.

(ii) To foster national integration despite cultural, religious, geographical and environmental barriers.

(iii) To gain experience, to live, co-operate and work in harmony with cadets of other states whom they have not known before.

(iv) To help in personal growth of cadets.

The Factors which Lead to the Growth of Indian Nationalism are :

(i) Religions, social and cultural renaissance.

(ii) Influence of western education and literature.

(iii) Influence of modern means of transport and communication.

(iv) Influence of Indian press and literature.

The Geographical Factors which Influence the Defence of India are :

(i) The Himalayas in the North of India.

(ii) Deserts on western borders.

(iii) The Arabian sea in the west coast of India.

(iv) South Indian Ocean.

(v) The Bay of Bengal in the east.

(vi) Plains of Punjab.

Nation State, National Interest and Objectives

Nation State can be defined as a country which has 'essential elements' of population, territory, sovereignty and Government.

The national interests of a Nation are as under:

(i) **Sovereignty :** Foremost interest of the nation is to be autonomous and remain independent.

(ii) **Integrity :** The nation should be full, indivisible and have a well-defined territory.

(iii) **Unity :** The nation should be a secular union of states with political power belonging to a central confederate authority, with united and undivided goals without factional, sectarian or fanatical prejudices. It should be tolerant towards caste, colour, creed, religion and language of each other.

(iv) **Security :** The nation must ensure safety, territorial integrity and protection of the state against external threat or subversion.

The Important Objectives and Directive Principles of State Policy :

(i) Education to all.

(ii) Equal justice to all.

(iii) Adequate means of livelihood to all citizens.

(iv) Equal pay for equal work for both men and women.

(v) Provision of maternity relief.
(vi) Promotion of cottage industries.
(vii) Participation of workers and labourers in labour law.
(viii) Improvement of public health.
(ix) Prohibition of intoxicating drinks and drugs.
(x) To have uniform code of law irrespective of caste, creed, colour or religion.
(xi) To ensure and protect a social order which stands for the welfare of the people.
(xii) Promotion of educational and economic interests of weaker sections of the people.
(xiii) Separation of judiciary from the executive.
(xiv) Protection and improvement in environment, forests and wild-life.
(xv) Organise agriculture and animal husbandry on modern and scientific lines.
(xvi) Protection of national monuments.

CITIZEN

A member of the community who owes allegiance to the state and who enjoys protection and the rights granted by the constitution of the country is called as a 'citizen'.

The ways in which the citizenship of India can be acquired :

(i) **By Birth :** Persons born in India are Indian citizens.
(ii) **By Descent :** Children born of Indian citizens living in foreign countries acquire Indian citizenship.
(iii) **Immigration :** Immigrants from Pakistan at the time of partition.
(iv) **Registration :** By registration and living in India for a period of 5 years.
(v) **Nationalization :** A person who applies for citizenship, by fulfilling certain conditions like residence, appointment in service of the state, purchase of land or marriage with an Indian citizen if the govt. of India gives a certificate to that effect.

Five Duties of a Citizen

(i) To abide by the constitution and respect its ideals and institutions.
(ii) To protect and upheld the sovereignty, unity and integrity of India.
(iii) To defend the country and render national service when called upon to do so.
(iv) To promote harmony and the spirit of common brotherhood amongst all the people of the country.
(v) To safeguard public property and abjure violence.

Images & Slogans on NATIONAL INTEGRATION

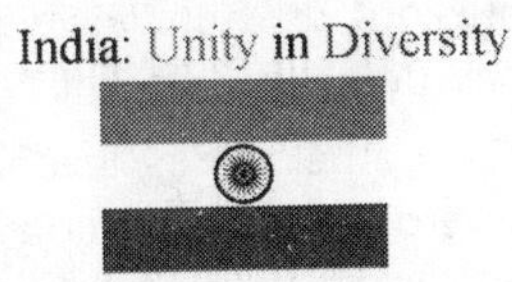

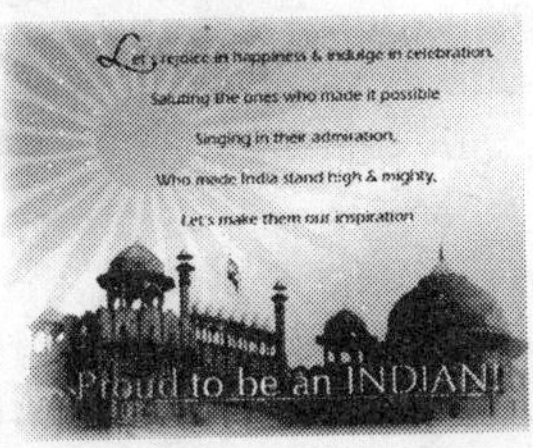

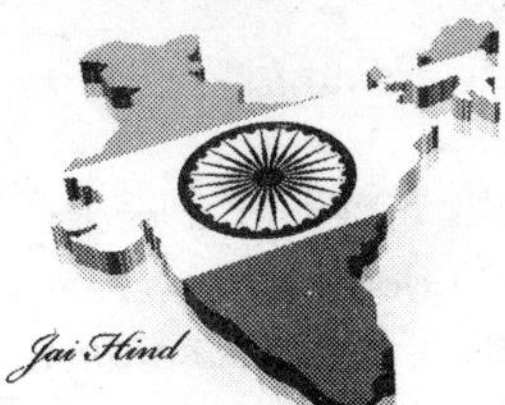

❖ ❖ ❖

CHAPTER

5

Leadership & Personality Development

Leadership

Leadership is the ability to build up confidence and zeal among people and to create an urge in them to be led. To be a successful leader one must possess foresight, drive, initiative, self-confidence and personal integrity. Different situations may demand different types of leaderships.

In other words, leadership is the act of influencing other people to cooperate towards some common goals which they come to find desirable. This act is performed by a very few in a society.

Leadership is a dynamic process that caters to the needs of the members of the group. Further, it emerges in the interaction of individuals with one another. Without right leadership, no home, community, organisation, discipline, institution, profession and finally nation can move on the path of progress. It means that the welfare as well as progress of society or a profession depends upon qualitative leadership. Therefore, the leader is said to "give the lead" if he makes acceptable suggestions, shows the right path, acts as a model for others, give commands, which are respected and carried out.

In all the cases, what a leader does affect others more than himself or herself. Without the cooperation of his followers, no leader can retain his position and prestige for a long duration. He may rule as a dictator for some time but his future certainly will be in dark. Therefore, he should not adopt dictatorial attitude.

Nature and Characteristics of Leadership

The nature and characteristics of leadership are stated below :

1. Leadership is a personal quality.
2. It exists only with followers. It is implied that if there are no followers, there is no leadership.
3. It is the willingness of people to follow that makes a person a leader.
4. Leadership is a process of influence. It means that a good leader will always strive to influence the behaviour, attitude and beliefs of his subordinates.
5. It exists only for the realization of common goals.

6. It involves readiness to accept complete responsibility in all situations.
7. Leadership is the function of stimulating the followers to strive willingly to attain objectives of the profession/group.
8. Leadership styles do change under different circumstances.
9. Leadership is neither bossism nor synonymous with management.

TYPES OF LEADERSHIP

A leader is a person who excels the average members of his group in intelligence, scholarship, dependability in exercising responsibility, activity and social participation. Successful leaders have some inborn characteristics as well as developed by their experience, such as integrity, moral courage, confidence, correct judgement and a highly developed sense of responsibility.

Leadership Styles

There are broadly three ideal leadership styles :

1. **Autocratic Leadership Style :** In this leadership style, all policies and procedures are determined by the leader.
2. **Democratic Leadership Style :** In this leadership style, policies are matter of a group decision and discussion with active encouragement and assistance by the leaders.
3. **Laissez Faire Leadership Style :** In this leadership style, leader plays a rather passive role in social participation and leaves complete freedom for group or individual decisions in relation to group activity and procedure.

QUALITIES OF A LEADER

Progress in any field depends upon the quality of professional leadership available. When any leader is striving to promote his profession, he is promoting himself directly or indirectly. Directly, he is gaining stature and social recognition, and indirectly, he gets the gains of profession through work. Leadership is not a quality which can be bestowed upon any person. One does not become a leader by accident. The responsibility of leadership comes on the shoulders of one who has his background of experience and training coupled with vital personal qualities, because these all add to the professional competence of the leader. One thing is certain that there are certain qualities which distinguish a leader from other individuals around.

In general, the qualities that make the individual a leader can be mentioned, such as confidence, diligence, courage, will power and determination, foresightedness, mental alertness, logical reasoning and decision making, sense of morality and a strict code of ethics, disciplinarianism and dynamism. Though the qualities of a leader are innumerable yet the word "LEADERSHIP" itself contains the qualities of a great successful leader. Each letter of "leadership" can be abbreviated in the following manner:

L : Loyalty
E : Enthusiasm, Endurance, Engaging Personality
A : Alertness, Adjustment, Ability to Coordinate Activities
D : Discipline, Dutifulness, Dependability, Desire to Help others
E : Energetic, Earnestness
R : Reliability, Right-thinking and Right Judgement
S : Sincerity, Sympathy, Self Control, Sacrifice, Super Motor Capacity
H : Health, Honey-tongue, Humour
I : Intelligence, Industriousness, Impartiality, Interest in Teaching
P : Patience, Perseverance, Personality, Physical Skill, Public Relations.

In addition to the above stated qualities a few qualities such as knowledge of one's growth and development, moral character, competence in writing and oral language, tactfulness, friendliness, tolerance and good temperaments would add extra strength to the popularity of one's leadership.

In brief, leaders must be dynamic too. They should be able to theorize, analyze, organize, improvise, deputize, harmonize, supervise and if need be–compromise. Such qualities would enable them to handle human beings in competitive situations, build up their esteem and prestige in the society and shape the destiny of their followers.

LEADERSHIP TRAITS

These are distinguishing qualities which if demonstrated in regular activities, help the leader to earn the respect, confidence, willing obedience and loyal co-operation of his subordinates. These are :

- **Alertness :** Alertness of mind is what helps a person to pick up the opportunities at the right time and exploit the situation to his own advantage.
- **Bearing :** It is creation of favourable impression, upright carriage and appearance, alertness and energy in actions and movements, and high personal conduct at all times. Appearance and manner must show competence and confidence.
- **Courage :** It is a mental quality that enables a man to accept responsibility and act correctly in a threatening situation with calmness and firmness; requires moral and physical courage.
- **Decisiveness :** It is the ability to take decision promptly and announce them in a clear and forceful manner.
- **Dependability :** It is proper performance of duty and carrying out actively, intelligently and willingly the orders of superiors.

- **Endurance :** It is mental and physical stamina measured by the ability to withstand pain, fatigue, stress and hardship.
- **Enthusiasm :** It is the display of sincere interest and zeal in performance of duties.
- **Initiative :** It is to do what is to be done even in the absence of orders and to avoid inactivity.
- **Integrity :** It is the uprightness of character, soundness of moral principles, quality of absolute truthfulness and honesty.
- **Judgement :** It is the quality of logically weighing facts on which to make sound decisions.
- **Justice :** It is the quality of being impartial and consistent.
- **Knowledge :** A leader must have sound knowledge than the men he commands.
- **Loyalty :** It is the quality of faithfulness to country, one's seniors and colleagues.
- **Sense of Humour :** It is the ability to remain cheerful under stress.
- **Tact :** It is the ability to deal with others without offending anyone.
- **Unselfishness :** It is the quality of refraining from own comfort and personal advancement at the expense of others.

Some other important leadership traits are listed below :

(i) Truthfulness (ii) Self-confidence (iii) Maturity
(iv) Esprit-de-corps (v) Humility and Sympathy (vi) Patience

PERSONALITY & CHARACTER DEVELOPMENT

Personality Development means enhancing and grooming one's outer and inner self to bring about a positive change to your life which includes boosting one's confidence, improving communication and language speaking abilities, widening one's scope of knowledge, developing certain hobbies or skills, learning fine etiquettes and manners, adding style and grace to the way one looks, talks and walks and overall imbibing oneself with positivity, liveliness and peace.

Personality

Personality is the characteristics and patterns of feelings, thoughts, and behaviours, which make a person exceptional, one of a kind and exclusive to his or herself. Positive personality factors are extremely important in day-to-day life. Often the wrong kind of personality proves disastrous and causes undesirable situations or in the least tensions and worries in organisations. Some people arouse hostility and aggression in their associates while others invoke sympathy and supportive responses because of their personality features. Some people tolerate severely stressful situations, while tensions and similar circumstances swamp others.

Character

A person of character would have some characteristics inborn as well as developed by experience and judgement such as integrity, moral courage, confidence, justice and highly developed sense of responsibility. A person of a good character excels over others in certain qualities. A good character comprise virtues of having certain qualities of character more pronounced than others. The qualities of a good character bring magnetism in one's personality which comes from a proper adjustment of the many qualities of head and heart such as knowledge, tact, friendship and co-operation.

How to Develop the Personality

Some people at work and in our daily life always appear to be self-confident and on top of the world. Everything seems to go right for these people. These people are not born with such qualities but there are lots of inputs and efforts behind their personality. Some of the important qualities which an individual should develop in personality are :

(i) **Judgement :** Understand the situation from others' point of view, setting aside personal interests and opinion helps in taking appropriate decision that benefits all.

(ii) **Mirroring :** Understand the body language of ideal people and make it a part of your attitude.

(iii) **Be Cheerful and Nice :** Always make sincere efforts to raise others spirits.

(iv) **Be Sincere and Trustworthy :** Make others feel that whenever they need your help you will always be there to help.

(v) **Provide Compelling Ideas :** Justify how your ideas and suggestions could be the most effective techniques to implement.

(vi) **Conviction :** This is a very important thing while persuading anyone. People are self-centered and they always put their own ideas and well-being before others. Your own conviction in convincing others is essential.

(vii) **Positive Attitude :** This leads to the confidence of the individuals. So whatever the situation may be, one should always try to be positive in thinking and attitude.

(viii) **Leadership Skills :** Leadership is the quality of influencing the activities of an individual or a group towards the achievement of a goal in a given situation.

(ix) **Communication Skills :** An effective communication skill is necessary to achieve success. A good communication skill is essential to influence others.

USEFUL TIPS FOR PERSONALITY DEVELOPMENT

A cadet must develop his personality in every possible manner. Everyone can improve his personality with the help of the following useful tips:

* Honestly analyze the traits of your personality and character.
* Enlist your bad habits and try to get rid of them.
* Listen to everyone patiently, even if their ideas are baseless or not of your interest.
* During conversation, do not keep talking about yourself too much.
* Keep your morale high in case of defeat and be more polite on being victorious.
* Solve your problems in a creative way. Try your best not to let these spoil your relations with your friends.
* Independent thinking and freedom to work is the only source of progress and welfare.
* Positive attitude is of great importance in our personality. Nobody likes people who have narrow outlook. In life, only that person is considered well-behaved who has positive and healthy bend of mind.
* The real beauty of man lies not in his physical appearance but in his work and good qualities. That is why it is important that we improve mental outlook to develop our personality.
* Keep improving your physical appearance also as it is the first thing anyone notices about you, even before you speak and work.
* Every individual should develop the ability to adjust with others, because basically man is a social animal, so one can not survive by living alone.
* You should respect and appreciate others but do not try to copycat them. You cannot, in fact. Instead, focus on your good traits and enhance them.
* Have a close analysis of your own behaviour. If you are young, your friends should like you and more should befriend you. If not, there is a flaw in your behaviour. Either you are too shy or unfriendly or too rude with others. If you realize it, improve it.
* Your attitude should be broad, confident, respectful and ready-to-take-criticism. But if not, you will remain in your own world, thinking, why others do not accept you.
* A negative reply with a smile is far more effective than a rude positive answer. Smiles help us communicate better, keep smiling.
* Observe and improve your sitting and walking postures.
* Inculcate healthy eating, living and sleeping habits.
* Develop good reading habits, viewing news channels and debates and analyse them yourself.
* Develop habits of discussing on various topics and practise giving lectures before friends and family members.

* Some people often have a favourite sentence which they repeat frequently. One should try and get rid of such a habit.
* Improve your knowledge of English and practise good conversation with your friends.
* Listen with utmost care to your critics and improve yourself.
* Develop good listening and comprehending skills.
* Improve your memory and concentration of mind.
* Start doing everything in a planned manner.
* Form a group of friends and organise help, relief and charity works.
* Interact with different types of people and know their views.
* Organise some small and big activities.
* Try to solve small and big problems at home and around.
* Start participating in different social activities.
* Start doing some voluntary social work.
* Start playing some indoor and outdoor games.
* Start doing physical exercise and yoga daily.
* Observe the personality, mannerism and good habits of the people you like and admire and keep improving yourself.

Remember, we are individuals and each individual has his/her own unique personality. One can lack in some but can be good at some. Try to better the good ones and inculcate the ones which you don't have. Bring out a lovely personality and make your presence felt everywhere.

If you take care of these small but very useful tips, you will be able to develop an impressive and influential personality abundant in Officers Like Qualities (OLQs).

MORAL VALUES AND CHARACTER TRAITS

'Morals' describe what is right and wrong, whereas 'values' explain important behaviour and beliefs of a person or group. Moral values comprise of qualities relating to character and behaviour which makes a person's personality. Moral values are the aggregate of qualities like truthfulness, honour, honesty, loyalty, kindness, reliability and sense of responsibility towards others and to the society. Good moral values allow a person to make the right decisions and improve one's interaction with other people.

Moral Values

Moral values consist of acts, well and honourably performed. Our habits, behaviour and conduct are reflections of our values. An NCC cadet must conduct himself/

herself such that his/her personal habits are not open to criticism. Tendencies toward selfishness and self-indulgence in luxuries are to be avoided strictly. As per Greek philosopher, Plato, there are four cardinal virtues or human values. They are:

(i) Prudence - To make right decision.

(ii) Courage - To stay course and resist temptation of all kind.

(iii) Self-control - To subordinate passion, emotion and feelings to the spirit and fulfill mission at hand.

(iv) Justice - To give every individual his due.

Character Traits

What is Character?

Each individual is a bundle of virtues and weaknesses, of head and heart. The resulting individuality of a person, from this balance sheet of good and bad qualities is his character; it is reflected in his conduct.

Character traits are all the aspects of a person's behaviour and attitude that makes up a person's personality. It is the proudest possession of any person. Character is not inborn, but developed over period of time.

There are certain character qualities which have been listed below and their observance will go a long way in day to day interaction with others:

(i) **Speak Truth:** The consequences of speaking a lie are enormous and cannot be taken back. Hence speak truth always.

(ii) **Be Honest:** It means total honesty in thought, word and behaviour.

(iii) **Keep Your Word:** Always keep the word once given. You will be recognised for this and will gain respect for the same.

(iv) **Own Up Your Mistake:** Have the moral courage to admit to mistakes, however unpleasant the results.

(v) **Be Your Own Judge:** Be honest even when not under supervision.

(vi) **Do Not Seek Cheap Popularity:** A person of character is always loved for his qualities of honesty, self-sacrifice and attention to duty.

(vii) **Resist Temptation:** Temporary gain leads to long term pain. Hence, a person should not be attracted towards immediate pleasure and control his mind from all kinds of temptations by keeping in view his future life.

(viii) **Set an Example:** By doing this one inspires others to act like self. You should not do things which you do not expect others to do.

(ix) **Sense of Responsibility:** Take responsibility for your actions.

(x) **Self Sacrifice:** Interests of others and the society above always one's own are always appreciated.

(xi) **Be Impartial:** Be just and impartial in all your dealings with others. You should not show favouritism.

(xii) **Discipline:** One's personal discipline must be of highest standards and it should be followed strictly.

(xiii) **Do Your Duty:** It means to carry out duties even when you disagree with others or when conditions are difficult. It also implies doing one's best without looking for reward or recognition.

How to Improve Character

Some of the leadership traits if followed religiously can help to improve character. These are:

(i) Initiative
(ii) Courage
(iii) Decisiveness
(iv) Enthusiasm
(v) Morality
(vi) Loyalty
(vii) Justice
(viii) Patriotism
(ix) Sense of Duty.

Role of NCC in Personality & Character Development

NCC helps in developing the overall personality of cadets through various activities such as :

(i) **Drill :** Active participation in drill helps cadets keep correct posture. They will walk more confidently than others. A good physique is an integral part of a good personality.

(ii) **Interaction of Cadets in Camps :** An NCC cadet gets many good opportunities to interact with cadets from different parts of the country. Camps groom their personality. Here cadets from different states exchange information of each others' culture and traditions. Thus they learn about the diverse culture of the nation. They become friends resulting in the development of comradeship and personality.

(iii) **Competitions :** Various competitions held in camps, drill and performing cultural programmes, develop sportsmanship and team spirit among the cadets.

(iv) **Sports & Adventure Activities :** Sports and Adventure are important for youth as they teach them a number of useful lessons on comradeship, healthy competition, courage to face challenges, art of leadership, team work, grit and determination.

Values and Ethics

Leadership is an important feature of every sphere of human activity, whether at play, work or at war. In fact, wherever there are two or more people functioning together, there is a need for a leader. To develop into a good leader, a person needs certain values in him or one can say he must possess distinctive ethics in his life.

'Values' means a standard of behaviour and 'Ethics' means a set of moral principles that govern a person's behaviour. A person of values excels others in all fields. The values and ethics which drive a person may be inherited from the society they live in, *i.e.* from the people around them and to a large extent the family they hail from.

A leader may be intelligent, knowledgeable and hard-working, but unless he is driven by a set of values which are morally acceptable, he cannot be a good leader. Generally, a group in particular and its work and achievements as a whole are judged by the values and the behaviour and good manners of its leader.

Important Values

A person who practises good human values and follows a principled code of ethics will essentially stand out as a good leader. A few important values in day-to-day life are :

(i) **Honesty** - not to lie, cheat or steal
(ii) **Integrity** - uprightness
(iii) **Purity** - no duplicity, insincerity in thought, words or deeds
(iv) **Discipline** - behaviour according to rules and norms
(v) **Selflessness** - unselfishness, rising above individualism, self-sacrifice
(vi) **Loyalty** - true, faithful to duty, love or obligation
(vii) **Fairness** - being impartial, taking right decision
(viii) **Equality** - treating everyone equally
(ix) **Trust** - firm belief in the reliability, ability, strength of someone
(x) **Support** - giving help, encouragement, or approval
(xi) **Respect** - a feeling of regard for someone

HONOUR CODE CONCEPT

The honour code concept has been introduced with an aim to foster the vital ingredients of a character amongst NCC cadets. In our country, good character has been the mainstay of our existence. The growing consumerism and societal pressure at times divert the youth towards easier wrong than the harder right. The honour code concept is an effective system to ensure character development in an organisation.

The character qualities which are being fostered are given below:

(i) Respect (ii) Integrity (iii) Character
(iv) Discipline (v) Moral courage (vi) Comradeship.

The Honour Code

The directions of the honour code are:

(i) You shall not lie, steal, cheat or tolerate those who do so.
(ii) You shall not do anything selfish or mean including letting down a fellow cadet for self-interest.

(iii) You shall not, by any actions bring the name of your institution to disgrace.
(iv) You shall accept voluntarily your responsibility for any violation of this code.

Tenets of Honour Code

Tenets of Honour Code are given below:

(i) Good conduct to enhance your own self-respect, honour and image of institution.
(ii) Give priority to group interest over personal interest.
(iii) Stand up for what is right and accept responsibility.
(iv) Answer questions fully and truthfully to the honour code committee even if it results in action against you or your friends.
(v) Own up to the committee any breach of discipline or honour code, whether intentional or unintentional.
(vi) Give all help and encouragement to fellow cadets who are weak.
(vii) Participate in all competitions and sports in the true spirit of sportsmanship.
(viii) Accept defeat with grace and victory with humility.
(ix) Treat all fellow cadets with love and affection.
(x) Be secular, truthful, honest and straight forward in your dealings.

SKILL DEVELOPMENT

To live a meaningful and successful life every person must have some skills. A skill can be defined as expertise, knowledge or authority over some subject, work or activity, etc.

Types of Skills

Various types of skills are :

(i) **Literacy Skills :** Reading, writing, computing and arithmetic skills.
(ii) **Language Skills :** Communicating using a language in reading, writing and speech.
(iii) **Functional Skills :** Using ATM, Telephone, Calculator, Computer, Filling up bank forms to deposit or withdraw money, able to read map, booking railway tickets, fix a fused bulb or leaky tap, cycle chain etc.
(iv) **Vocational Skills :** Enhancing livelihood opportunities–carpentry, electrician, tailoring. Making handicrafts, fisheries etc.
(v) **Sports Skills :** Capable of playing on the field as part of a team or as a single player.
(vi) **Cultural Skills :** Capacity to lighten the spirits of the group one belongs to with activities that can break the monotony by jokes, songs, dance, energizers etc.

(vii) **Life Skills :** Self-awareness, empathy, creative thinking, critical thinking, effective communication, interpersonal relationship, decison making and problem solving, coping with stress, coping with emotions.

Life Skills

"Life Skills are abilities for adopting positive behaviour that enable individuals to deal effectively with the demands and challenges of everyday life" –WHO.

Life Skills are acquired through practice and patience. A skilled person uses less time, energy and resources to do a job and produces quality results. Enhancing Life Skills enables us to adapt to situations and people and helps us to lead a healthy and positive life.

There are ten core Life skills which help in enhancing the personality of an individual. They are as follows :

(i) **Self Awareness :** It is recognition of self, our character, our strengths and weaknesses, desires, likes and dislikes, and skills. Being aware of the good points about oneself helps young people build a sense of self-esteem and self-confidence. Being aware of their weaknesses will make young people be willing to learn more. This also helps them utilize the opportunities available to them in relation to their abilities. Self-awareness is necessary for developing a positive attitude towards life.

(ii) **Empathy :** It is the ability to be sensitive to another person's situation, to understand his/her concerns, worries, fears and needs and how they feel. Empathy works wonders when we apply it to our relationships - with our loved ones, classmates, parents, friends, cousins and colleagues. It helps us move closer to solutions, to resolve conflicts, and enhance our quality of life.

(iii) **Critical Thinking :** It is the ability to analyze information and experience in an objective manner. It can help us recognize and assess the factors that influence our attitude and behaviour, such as media and peer pressure influences.

(iv) **Creative Thinking :** Creativity is the ability to generate new ideas by combining, changing, or reapplying existing ideas. It helps us to look beyond our direct experience, and to respond adaptively and with flexibility to situations in our daily lives.

(v) **Problem Solving Skills :** They enable us to deal with problems in our lives in a constructive manner. The process of problem solving involves various steps. They are identifying the problem, exploring the available alternative and deciding on the best possible solution.

(vi) **Decision Making** : Decision making is to choose from the varied options based on the existing knowledge of the topic under consideration keeping in mind the positive or negative consequences of each of the option.

(vii) **Interpersonal Relationship :** Ability to establish positive relationships helps us to relate in positive ways with the people we interact with. This means being able to make and maintain friendly relationships, which can be of great importance to our mental and social well being. It may also mean being able to end relationships constructively. Positive relationships help in the growth of the individuals involved.

(viii) **Effective Communication :** It is the ability to express, verbally through spoken or written language and non-verbally through gestures and body movements, in ways that are culturally acceptable.

(ix) **Coping with Emotions :** Being aware of the predominant emotion that preoccupies the mind at any point of time, knowing how emotions influence behaviour, and being able to respond to emotions appropriately.

(x) **Coping with Stress :** It means recognizing the source of stress in our lives, recognizing how this affects us physically and emotionally, and acting in ways that help us control our levels of stress, by changing our environment or lifestyle and learning how to relax.

SELF AWARENESS

Self-awareness is the concept that one exists as an individual, separate from other people, with private thoughts. It is a personal understanding of the core of one's own identity. Self-awareness includes self-recognition, character, strengths, weaknesses, desires and dislikes. The dimensions of self-awareness are self-realization, self-knowledge or self-exploration, self-confidence, self-talk, self-motivation, self-esteem, self-image, self-control, self-purpose, individuality and uniqueness, personality, values, attitude, and character.

Self-awareness involves knowing ourselves and our personality, and accepting ourself in spite of our imperfection. It includes all aspects of ourselves—our thoughts, emotions, likes, dislikes, strengths, weaknesses, fears, fantasies, ambitions, values, priorities, goals, desires, needs, etc. It acknowledges the fact that I may be imperfect, but still I like myself since I am a good human being and possess many qualities. To have complete self awareness one needs to concentrate on two aspects—the first being how we perceive ourselves—our strengths, weakness, abilities etc, and secondly, how others perceive us. Both the views together give a person a complete picture about oneself.

SELF EXPLORATION THROUGH SWOT ANALYSIS

An interesting way to become self aware is the use of SWOT analysis. SWOT analysis focuses on the internal and external environments, examining strengths and weaknesses in the internal environment and opportunities and threats in the external environment. The table ahead will give you a clear understanding:

• **INTERNAL**	Your **S**trengths	Your **W**eaknesses
• **EXTERNAL**	**O**pportunities in Your Career Field	**T**hreats in Your Career Field

MINDSET

Mindset is something which constantly carries on in a person's mind. It is an attitude towards someone or something. It can form a permanent impression on the mind and is very difficult to change. At times it can develop into a negative attitude leading to disaster. Your mindset is the sum of your knowledge, including beliefs and thoughts about the world and yourself in it. It is your filter for information you get in and put out. It determines how you receive and react to information. It's often used for a specific part in your life, as in the mindset of an entrepreneur or the growth mindset.

How to Change Your Mindset

(i) Find Your Inner Voice
(ii) Protect Your Mindset
(iii) Examine Your Current Beliefs
(iv) Redefine What Failure Means
(v) Put an End to Perfectionism
(vi) Get the Best Information Only
(vii) Let Go of Comparisons
(viii) Look at the Evidence
(ix) Role Model the Best People

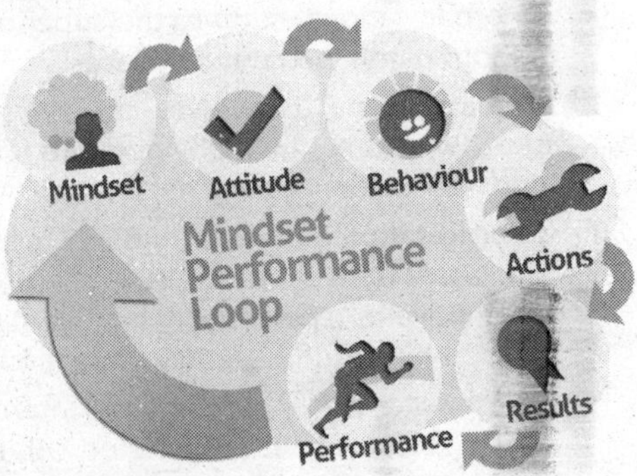

(x) Stop Worrying About What People Think
(xi) Shape Your Mindset with Vision and Goals.

Developing the right mindset is really crucial to succeed in anything. Work to make changes in the mindset areas that are acting as the roadblocks to your success.

MOTIVATION

Motivation is the process by which one is inspired to act in the desired manner with the help of catalytic persuasion. It is the application of will power and is expressed commonly as a desire, wish, need, preference, want or striving. It is an act of inspiring men to do their jobs.

The various means of motivation are:

(i) Integrating as far as possible the personal needs of the men with the needs of the organization.

(ii) Providing opportunity, where practicable, for individuals to participate in establishing goals and standards of performance. Such participation fosters ready acceptance of objective.

(iii) The leader himself setting a personal example of optimum performance. In doing everything, it is better to check up one's conduct and to act on lines laid down by sages :

"You, who are a leader of men, must set the example"–BHAGVAD GITA."

PERCEPTION

The process of perception may be defined as a complicated interaction of selection, organization, and interpretation of stimuli.

Perception involves five sub-processes—stimulus, registration, interception, feedback and consequence.

(i) **Stimulation :** Perception initiates with the presence of a stimulus situation. In organisational setting, the superior forms the stimulus situation for the subordinate's perceptual process.

(ii) **Registration :** It involves the physiological mechanism including both sensory and neutral. Obviously an individual's physiological ability to hear and see influences his perception.

(iii) **Interpretation :** It is a highly crucial sub-process. Other psychological processes assist in perceptual interpretation. For instance, in work settings, his motivation, personality and learning process determines an individual's interpretation of a stimulus situation.

(iv) **Feedback :** It is important for interpreting the perceptual event data. In work settings, the psychological feedback that is likely to affect a subordinate's perception may be in the form of a variation in the behaviour of superior.

(v) **Consequence :** Perception ends in reaction or response, which may be in the overt or covert form. As a consequence of perception, an individual responds to work demands. These sub-processes indicate the complexity of perception.

COMMUNICATION

Communication is sharing ideas, opinions, thoughts, feelings and understanding through speech, writing, gestures or symbols between two or more persons. We are communicating all the time with others.

Basics of Communication

Communication is conveying a message - verbally, written or through the use of signs. If we do not talk with others, then they will not know what we are thinking and they will not be able to understand us. One will feel terribly lonely this way.

For some people, it is the problem of not knowing how to communicate. For others, it may be that they are too afraid to talk about their problems, share their views, and let others know what is going on in their mind.

In fact, without communication, our relationships with others are likely to be dominated by suspicion, guess work, misunderstandings and false assumptions. Empathy creates wonderful results only when we are willing to let others know how we feel.

Lack of communication breeds problems in our relationships. We tend to assume that others know what we want or how we feel. Then when they do not react as we expect they should, we get upset. We expect people to understand us. The truth is they do not understand us, if we choose to believe that ideas can get across at the unspoken level! All too often, the communication between us and our loved ones, is merely functional - out of necessity. We waste many opportunities to enhance our understanding of each other and improve our relationship.

Effective Communication

Effective Communication involves:

- **Verbal Communication :** One person talks and the others listen to be able to react. The conversation can be informative, in the form of questions, a negotiation, and statement or open ended questions, instruction, etc. And the situation can be formal or informal. In relationships, communication is usually informal. Speech problem, too long sentences, mumbling, speaking too softly, hearing problems, listeners interrupting the speaker, loud external noises, etc. all hamper proper communication.
- **Non-Verbal Communication :** Non verbal communication is that gives meaning to what is said and may communicate both appreciation and rejection. It includes such things as tone of voice, a nod of head, using silence, frowning, smiling, body posture, touch, shaking of the head to communicate approval or disapproval, lifting of the eyebrows to show surprise, distance between persons, playing with something in hand instead of focusing. Make use of body language to communicate effectively. Ensure that you appreciate others through body language. React to what others say by nodding, smiling and generally showing you are listening.
- **Listening :** During communication, one person talks and other people listen. The listeners must give attention to all that is said, without interrupting the speaker and react later in a relevant manner. Many people may listen but only few know what the full message is. Some people react to when only half is said. There are people who listen selectively, who miss much of the message and only focus on points relevant to them. Sometime we

do not listen to our friends and other people; sometimes they do not listen to us. In either situation, there will be a problem in communication and understanding.

Always Communicate Tactfully

T - Think before you speak
A - Assertive communication
C - Clarity of thoughts and content
T - Tone and pitch of voice
F - Focus on interests, needs of the listener
U - Uncover hidden feelings
L - Listen for feedback

Effective Talking

* **Voice Quality :** A good voice quality means vocal expressions that vary in pitch, change in delivery speed and alternate in volume.
* **Talking Style :** Talking style refers to a set of behaviours of an individual that give uniqueness to that person.
* **Vocabulary :** Vocabulary is a critical factor for good talking. The larger the vocabulary, the better is the talking.
* **Adaptation :** Adaptation means to select the right words and use the right voice pitch, speed, volume and style for the intended listener.

Effective Listening

Important points for effective listening :

(i) Show interest in the speaker.
(ii) Exercise mental discipline and concentrate.
(iii) Never be distracted.
(iv) Never distract the speaker.
(v) Be present in time at the venue.
(vi) Listen not only to the words but also to the feelings of the speaker.
(vii) Never hesitate to ask the questions but at proper time.
(viii) Try to understand the speaker's point of view by being sympathetic, alert and active.
(ix) Follow the trend of discussion.
(x) Avoid thinking too much about a part that has already been covered.
(xi) Don't take too many notes while listening.
(xii) Avoid emotional barriers to listen effectively.

Different Type of Barriers of Communication

Barriers of Communication are of different types. It may be a combination of factors which make the barrier. These are:

(i) Linguistic Barriers
(ii) Psychological Barriers
(iii) Environmental Barriers
(iv) Sender and Receiver Related
(v) Content Related
(vi) Method Related.

Common Barriers to Effective Communication

Overcoming the many barriers to communication is more a matter of common sense, practice and effort than any specific skill. Essentially, being an effective communicator means having the skill to recognize if and when there is a barrier to communication and being able to resolve it.

No matter how good and effective a communicator one may be, yet the fact is that one does face certain barriers, from time to time, which forces him to work on becoming even more effective in his skills to communicate. Given here are the communication barriers that occur while listening, speaking and in the case of non-verbal communications.

Listening Barriers

(i) Interrupting the speaker.
(ii) Not maintaining eye contact with the speaker.
(iii) Rushing the speaker to complete what he has to say.
(iv) Making the speaker feel as though he is wasting the listener's time.
(v) Being distracted by something that is not part of the ongoing communication.
(vi) Getting ahead of the speaker and completing his thoughts.
(vii) Ignoring the speaker's requests.
(viii) Topping the speaker's story with one's own set of examples.
(ix) Forgetting what is being discussed.

Barriers While Speaking

(i) Unclear message.
(ii) Lack of consistency in the communication process.
(iii) Incomplete sentences or mumbling words and sentences.
(iv) Not understanding the receiver/listener.
(v) Poor eye contact with listener/s.

Other Barriers

(i) Assumptions, for instance, assuming others see a situation same as you or have same feelings as yours.

(ii) Patterns/reverting to type.
(iii) Language-different level of meaning.
(iv) Erroneous transition, value judgment.
(v) Use of negative words.
(vi) Perceptions-depending on mood, the receiver may misinterpret the message.

Reducing the Communication Gap

The following steps will help in reducing the communication gap:

(i) Plan ahead of communication.
(ii) Involve others to contribute to planning.
(iii) Listen to the suggestions made by others.
(iv) Speak with purpose and be specific.
(v) Justify your stand without upsetting others.
(vi) Have sense of humour with others.
(vii) Have empathy with others.
(viii) Do not be judgmental.
(ix) Do not underestimate the ability of others to contribute.
(x) Observe the body language or the non-verbal communication of others.
(xi) Be transparent to inform others of the planned activities and get feedback.
(xii) Make modification in the plan to suit the need of time.
(xiii) The words 'yes' and 'no' are very powerful. Learn to use them appropriately.

TIME MANAGEMENT

In the cosmic order time is unlimited and infinite. But in this world, on earth, we have a life span which comprises only a few decades. In this short period we try to do so many things and cannot take life lightly. Of course, we need some time for laughter, fun, entertainment and amusement. But most of the time we have to remain serious as we have to work hard and seriously. It is because only hard, well-planned and serious work can help achieve our goal. We also have to get training in various fields and we should not fight shy of it.

We should do every thing at the right time. We must be punctual and regular in our work. The best way is to chalk out a definite plan for every activity in life. Then we can lead a balanced life which can be alternated between work and rest, activity and amusement.

Major Time Wasters

(i) Telephone & Mobiles
(ii) Visitors & Friends
(iii) Unnecessary Papers
(iv) Lack of Planning & Control
(v) Extra Socializing
(vi) Indecision & Late Decision
(vii) Television & Computer
(viii) Procrastination & Lethargy

Principles of Time Management

(i) Develop a Personal Sense of Time
(ii) Maintain Time Log
(iii) Identify Long-Term Goals
(iv) Concentrate on High Return Activities
(v) Do Daily & Weekly Planning
(vi) Make the Best Use of Your Time
(vii) Organise Your Work
(viii) Organise Paper Work
(ix) Manage Meetings
(x) Delegate Effectively
(xi) Make Use of Committed Time
(xii) Maintain Your Health.

STRESS MANAGEMENT

Stress is our body's reaction to people and events and to our own thoughts. Some level of stress is normal, such as before a test, stage performance or an athletic event. Coping with stress means recognizing the source of stress in our lives, recognizing how this affects us physically and emotionally, and acting in ways that help us control our levels of stress, by changing our environment or lifestyle and learning how to relax.

The best way to cope with unhealthy stress is to recognize when your stress levels are building. While we often think of stress as the result of external events, the events themselves are not necessarily stressful. It is the way we react to an event that causes stress.

Stress Management Techniques

(i) Take Deep Breath
(ii) Talk it Out
(iii) Take a Break
(iv) Create a Quite Place in Your Mind
(v) Pay Attention to Physical Comfort
(vi) Move Your Body
(vii) Take Care of Your Body
(viii) Laugh it Away
(ix) Manage Your Time
(x) Know Your Limits
(xi) Do You Have to Be Right Always
(xii) Have a Good Cry
(xiii) Look for the Good Things around You
(xiv) Talk Less, Listen More

CONFLICTS & RESOLUTION

Conflict : It is a condition that exists when two sets of demands, goals, or motives are incompatible or unmatchable. An important way of resolving conflict is negotiation.

Motives for Conflict

(i) Competition for Limited Resources
(ii) Competing Work and Family Demands
(iii) Culturally Diverse Teams
(iv) Gender Based Harassment
(v) Personality Clashes
(vi) The Generation Gap

Levels of Conflict

Conflict can occur at a number of levels of human functioning. It may be :

(i) Role Conflict
(ii) Interpersonal Conflict
(iii) Intergroup Conflict
(iv) Multi-Party Conflict
(v) International Conflict

Methods of Conflict Resolution

Irrespective of the level of conflict, there are different approaches to deal with the incompatibilities. Given interdependence, three general strategies have been identified that the parties may take toward dealing with their conflict :

(i) The Win-Win Approach
(ii) The Win-Lose Approach
(iii) The Lose-Lose Strategy

Techniques for Resolving Conflicts

(i) Confrontation and Problem Solving
(ii) Disarming the Opposition
(iii) Cognitive Restructuring
(iv) Involving Third Party
(v) The Grievance Procedure

INFLUENCING SKILLS

Influencing others and negotiating for what you need is immensely powerful and rewarding. It is fascinating to have an insight into the reasons behind the success, or otherwise, of someone's tactics and the vital messages they communicate by what they say and how they say it. It is enjoyable working out how to deploy the skills ourselves and sharpen own awareness of the effect the techniques have on what one is trying to achieve.

Types of Influencing Skills

(i) Probing and Listening
(ii) Building Rapport
(iii) Selling own Idea
(iv) Assertiveness

Influencing Principles

(i) Making a Start
(ii) Buying Yourself Thinking Time
(iii) Dealing with Disagreement
(iv) Tackling Difficult Situations with Tact

BODY LANGUAGE

It is a form of mental and physical ability of human non-verbal communication, consisting of body posture, gestures, facial expressions, and eye movements. Humans send and interpret such signals almost entirely subconsciously. Body language may provide clues as to the attitude or state of mind of a person. For example, it may indicate aggression, attentiveness, boredom, relaxed state, pleasure, amusement, etc.

What Speaks the Body Language

The following speak the Body Language :

(i) Posture of the Body
(ii) Eye Contact and Eye Expressions
(iii) Facial and Mouth Expressions
(iv) Movements of Hands/Fingers
(v) Movements of Legs
(vi) Tone of Speech

Personal Space Distances

Every person needs his or her own personal space. Proximity range varies with relation and culture. It may be :

(i) **Intimate Distance :** It is from zero to about 18 inches and is reserved for close family members, friends, and also pet animals.

(ii) **Personal Distance :** It is from 18 inches to 4 feet. This space is used in conversations with friends, to chat with associates, and in group discussions and meetings.

(iii) **Social Distance :** It is from 4 to 8 feet and is reserved for strangers, newly formed groups, and new friends.

(iv) **Public Distance :** It is more than 8 feet, and is used for speeches, lectures, and in theaters between the speaker and audience.

ETIQUETTES AND MANNERISM

Etiquette

It is a code of behaviour that delineates expectations for social behavior according to contemporary conventional norms within a society, social class, or group. Rules of etiquette encompass most aspects of social interaction in any society.

Types of Etiquette

(i) **Social Etiquette :** It is important for an individual as it teaches him how to behave in the society.

(ii) **Eating Etiquette :** Individuals must follow certain decorum while eating. Never make noise while eating and do not leave the table unless and until everyone has finished eating.

(iii) **Washroom Etiquette :** It refers to the set of rules which an individual needs to follow while using public washrooms or office toilets. Make sure you leave the washroom clean and tidy for the other person.

(iv) **Telephone Etiquette :** It refers to the way an individual should speak on the phone. Never put the other person on long holds. Make sure you greet the other person. Take care of your pitch and tone.

(v) **Business Etiquette :** It includes ways to conduct a certain business. Never cheat your customers in any manner.

(vi) **Corporate Etiquette :** It refers to how an individual should behave while he is at work. Each one needs to maintain the decorum of the organization. Never loiter around unnecessarily or peep into other's cubicles.

(vii) **Meeting Etiquette :** It refers to styles one need to adopt when he is attending any meeting, seminar, presentation etc. Listen to what the speaker has to say. Never enter meeting room without a notepad and pen.

(viii) **Party Etiquette :** Everyone should behave sensibly at parties. Never eat, drink or dance uncontrollably.

Need for Etiquette

(i) It makes you a cultured individual.

(ii) It teaches you the way to behave in the society.

(iii) It is essential for an everlasting impression and speaks a lot about your personality and upbringing.

(iv) It enables the individuals to earn respect and appreciation in the society.

(v) Etiquette inculcates a feeling of trust and loyalty in the individuals.

(vi) Etiquette helps individuals to value relationships. One becomes more responsible and mature with etiquette.

Mannerism

Much of the manners we learn from our parents and teachers who tell us the importance of being well-mannered. At some point, our manners are categorized as good or bad depending on the society we live in. But there are some manners which are always considered as Bad Manners everywhere.

Bad Manners

(i) Biting nails.
(ii) Making loud noise.
(iii) Spitting in the public.
(iv) Picking your nose in the public.
(v) Eating with your mouth open and slurping sound while eating.
(vi) Smoking at prohibited places.
(vii) Coughing, sneezing and yawning without covering your mouth.
(viii) Not saying 'excuse me' when required.
(ix) Not saying 'please', 'thank you' and 'sorry'.
(x) Acting rude and telling vulgar jokes.
(xi) Entering someone's room without permission.
(xii) Ridiculing someone for his limitations.
(xiii) Crossing the road wherever you feel like.

The way to gain respect in the society is to learn to respect the society also. All good manners start from home. Having good manners is not just about blending with the best; rather it is more about considering the feelings of others and taking responsibility.

Attitude

Attitude can be defined as a positive or negative evaluation of people, objects, event, activities, ideas, or just about anything in your personal environment.

Types of Attitude

(i) Positive Attitude
(ii) Negative Attitude
(iii) Neutral Attitude
(iv) Rebellious Attitude
(v) Rational and Irrational Attitudes
(vi) Individual and Social Attitudes

SOCIAL SKILLS

It is said, a human being is a social animal, but the question is, does everyone possess social skills? Most of the people do not know the art of speaking. While some are just inept and incompetent, there are others who lack confidence and yet others who do not have mannerism and etiquettes. Having sound social skills is extremely important in the present times, given to the fact that interaction and conversation forms the basis for everything we do. You can improve your social skills by just putting in a little effort yourself.

Improving Social Skills

(i) Be polite (ii) Be aware (iii) Be attentive
(iv) Be cautious (v) Be original (vi) Be responsible
(vii) Be honest (viii) Be open & approachable

GROUP & TEAM WORK

A Group

Two or more people interacting to achieve a common objective are called a group.

Importance of Group

In a group, people come together to achieve some common objectives for which they work in a structured fashion and utilise resources to reach pre-determined goals and targets.

Types of Groups

Classification of group according to evolutions of primary goals is as given below:

1. **Friendship Group** : It evolves informally to meet its members, personal security, esteem and belonging needs.
2. **Task Group** : It is created by the management to accomplish certain organization goals. Task group can further be classified as under :
   (i) **Formal Groups** : They are established by an organization to facilitate the achievement of the organization goals.
   (ii) **Informal Group** : It is one that develops out of the day-to-day activities, interactions and sentiments of the members for the purpose of meeting their social needs.
   (iii) **Effective Group** : An effective group is one which has the following characteristics :
   - Its members know why the group exists; they have shared goals.
   - Its members support agreed upon guidelines and procedures for making decisions.
   - Its members communicate freely among themselves.
   - Its members have learned to receive help from one another and to give help to one another.
   - Its members have learned to deal with conflict within the group.
   - Its members have learned to diagnose individual and group processes and improve their own and the group's functioning.

A Team

Two or more interdependent people who share responsibility for outcomes, who consider themselves and are considered by others as an intact social entity in a larger social system, are called as a team.

Importance of Team

A team is a small number of members with complementary abilities, skills and knowledge who are committed to common performance, goals and working relationship for which they hold themselves mutually accountable. A key aim of teamwork is group synergy, namely the achievement of high quality as a result of combined individual contributions.

In a team, we can establish an agreed set of team guidelines. We know team members, their strengths, and preferred ways of working and preferred roles. We can discuss the task problems to arrive at a shared understanding and summarise this shared understanding of any project.

Types of Teams

(i) **Functional Teams :** They usually represent individuals who work together daily on a cluster of ongoing and independent tasks.

(ii) **Problem-Solving Teams :** They focus on specific issues in their areas of responsibility, develop potential solutions and are often empowered to take actions within defined limits.

(iii) **Cross-Functional Teams :** They bring together the knowledge and skills of people from various work areas to identify and solve mutual problems.

(iv) **Self-Managed Teams :** They normally consist of members who must work together effectively daily to manufacture entire product (or major identifiable component) or service.

Characteristics of a Team

(i) Illusion of invulnerability

(ii) Collective rationalization

(iii) Unquestioned belief

(iv) Stereotypical views

(v) Direct pressure

(vi) Self-censorship

(vii) Shared illusion of unanimity

Teamwork

Teamwork is the fuel that allows common people to attain uncommon results. The opportunity to work with others, rather than on your own, can provide distinct benefits. Groups that work well together can achieve much more than individuals working on their own. A broader range of skills can be applied to practical activities and sharing and discussing ideas can play a pivotal role in deepening your understanding of a particular subject area.

❖ ❖ ❖

CHAPTER 6

Civil Defence & Disaster Management

CIVIL DEFENCE

Civil Defnece are self-help measures adopted by the civilian population, Government, local bodies and voluntary organisations etc. during the war to minimize the effects of enemy action on men and material. In other words, it is the defence of the people by the people.

Civil Defence was first established in India on 24 October, 1941. Two significant events took place after independence which gave a major fillip to Civil Defence in India. The first was the Chinese aggression in November 1962 and the other was the Indo-Pakistan war in September 1965, when, for the first time after Independence, the nation was subjected to enemy air attacks. This led to considerable rethinking about the policy and scope of Civil Defence and as a result the Civil Defence policy, as it exists today, was started.

The Civil Defence Act of India was enacted by Parliament in May 1968. Today, Civil Defence includes any measures, not amounting to actual combat, for affording protection to any person, property, place or thing in India or any part of the territory thereof, against any enemy attack, whether from air, land, sea or other places, or for depriving any such attack of the whole or part of its effect. Vide an amendment to the Civil Defence Act, civil defence also includes any measures taken for the purpose of Disaster Management, before, during or after any kind of natural or man-made disaster.

Civil defence measures consist of the following :

(i) **Preventive Measures :** These are measures which may be taken before an an assault or calamity such as dispersal of population and protecting industries, camouflage, preparation of shelter, warning and training etc.

(ii) **Control Measures :** These are measures taken immediately after an air raid or calamity, such as reconnaissance, reporting of damage and unexploded bombs, rescue of casualties, control of services, extinguishing of fires and clearance of debris.

(iii) **Restorative Measures :** These are measures which become necessary after an air raid or calamity and include feeding, providing shelter and clothing, salvage of property, disposal of dead, disposal of unexploded bombs, control of infection and contamination, repair of damages caused to utility and civil services etc.

Civil Defence is primarily organized on voluntary basis except for a small nucleus of paid staff and establishment which is augmented during emergencies. There are three levels of organisation of Civil Defence:

(i) **National Level :** At the national level, the Home Ministry is responsible for the Civil Defence. It has under its direct control, the Directorate of Civil Defence, headed by a Director General - usually a senior police officer, who is responsible to advise the Home Ministry on all matters relating to Civil Defence. The Civil Defence organization basically comprises of the Home Guards and the Fire-Fighting Units.

(ii) **State Level :** Each State and Union Territory government has, under the overall control of its Director General of Police, a Director General of Home Guards and Civil Defence. As in the case of the central government, he is a senior police officer and is responsible for controlling fire departments as well.

(iii) **District Level :** In a district, the District Magistrate is the highest authority on Civil Defence. He is designated as the Controller of Civil Defence. He is responsible for implementation of all Civil Defence measures by the district departmental heads.

Civil Defence Services: Classification and Duties

Civil Defence is an important activity both, during peace, natural disasters or during war. NCC with its vast trained resource can play an important role and help in the Civil Defence of the country.

Civil defence services can be classified as :

(i) **Headquarters Service :** This service controls all works under civil defence.

(ii) **Warden's Service :** This forms a link between the public and the authorities. This service is responsible for organizing self-help parties, fire parties and to check light restrictions, report damages and guide homeless to the shelters.

(iii) **Fire Fighting Service :** They detect and control small fires.

(iv) **Supply Service :** They plan, organise and procure necessary equipment and ensure proper storage and quick distribution of equipment.

(v) **Welfare Services :** They supply information about missing and dead etc. and provide shelter, food and clothing and also arrange evacuation.

(vi) **Salvage Service :** They recover goods from the damaged buildings and keep it in safe custody.

(vii) **Rescue Services :** They rescue the injured trapped under the debris.

(viii) **Training Services :** They are responsible to train the staff in the Civil Defence duties.

(ix) **Transport Services :** They send various services to the scene of incident and provide necessary transport.

(x) **Communication Services :** This service is responsible for air raid warning and communication between warden posts, control centres through messengers or telephone etc.

(xi) **Casualty Services :** The functions of this service are to render first aid on the spot and to send various casualties for further treatment.

(xii) **Corpse Disposal Service :** They are responsible for collection, identification and disposal of dead bodies.

DISASTERS

A disaster commonly denotes any odd event—natural or man-made that brings about immense misery to the people of a region.

Classification of Disasters

Disasters can be classified as under :

1. *Natural Disasters :*

(i) **Wind Related :** Storm, Cyclone, Tornado, Storm surge and Tidal waves.

(ii) **Water Related:** Flood, Cloudburst, Flash flood, Excessive rains and Drought.

(iii) **Earth Related :** Earthquake, Tsunamis, Avalanches, Landslides and Volcanic eruptions.

2. *Man-Made Disasters :*

(i) **Accidents :** Road, Rail, Air, Sea and Building collapse.

(ii) **Industrial Mishaps :** Gas Leak, Explosion, Sabotage and Safety breach.

(iii) **Fire :** Building, Coal and Oil.

(iv) **Forest Fire :** Most forest fires are man-made.

(v) **Contamination/Poisoning :** Food, Water, Illicit-liquor and Epidemics.

(vi) **Terrorists Activities :** Various kind of destructive activities by terrorists.

(vii) **Ecological :** Pollution (air, water, noise), Soil degradation, Loss of biodiversity, global warming, sea level rise, toxic wastes and nuclear accidents.

(viii) **Warfare :** Conventional, Chemical and Nuclear.

Disaster Management Organisation - NDMA & NDRF

Disasters disrupt progress and destroy the hard-earned fruits of painstaking developmental efforts, often pushing nations, in quest for progress, back by several decades. Thus, efficient management of disasters has, in recent times, received increased attention both, within India and abroad.

- **National Disaster Management Authority (NDMA) :** India is vulnerable, in varying degrees, to a large number of natural as well as man-made disasters. 58.6 per cent of the Indian landmass is prone to earthquakes of moderate to very high intensity. Over 40 million hectares of land (12 per cent of total land mass) is prone to floods and river erosion. Of the 7,516 km long coastline, close to 5,700 km is prone to cyclones and tsunamis. 68 per cent of the cultivable area is vulnerable to drought. Hilly areas are at risk from landslides and avalanches. India also has had a history of natural disasters in recent years. Thus, the importance of Disaster Management in India.

On 23 December 2005, the Government of India took a defining step by enacting the Disaster Management Act of India, which envisaged the creation of the National Disaster Management Authority (NDMA), headed by the Prime Minister.

Organisation of NDMA

- **National Level (NDMA) :** At the national level, the NDMA is the apex body for disaster management, and is headed by the Prime Minister. The NDMA is mandated to deal with all types of disasters; natural or man-made. It is responsible for laying down policies, plans and guidelines for Disaster Management and coordinating their enforcement and implementation for ensuring timely and effective response to disasters.
- **State Disaster Management Authority (SDMA) :** At the State level, the SDMA is headed by the Chief Minister, who lays down policies and plans for Disaster Management in the State. It inter alia approves the State Plan in accordance with the guidelines laid down by the NDMA, coordinate the implementation of the State Plan, recommend provision of funds for mitigation and preparedness measures and reviews the developmental plans of the different Departments of the State to ensure the integration of prevention, preparedness and mitigation measures.
- **District Disaster Management Authority (DDMA) :** The DDMA is headed by the District Collector or Deputy Commissioner or District Magistrate as the case may be, with the elected representative of the local authority as the Co-Chairperson.
- **Local Authorities :** For the purpose of this Policy, local authorities include Panchayati Raj Institutions (PRI), Municipalities, District and Cantonment Boards, and Town Planning Authorities which control and manage civic services. These bodies ensure capacity building of their officers and employees for managing disasters, carry out relief, rehabilitation and reconstruction activities in the affected areas and prepare Disaster Management Plans in consonance with the guidelines of the NDMA, SDMAs and DDMAs.

Disaster management is an important activity both during peace (natural disasters) and during war. NCC with its vast trained resource can play an important role and help in the Disaster management.

FIRE FIGHTING

Enemy may cause maximum damage by bombing during the war. Fire is the major cause of destruction during war, hence everyone should be prepared to fight this evil through training.

Three things or conditions are necessary to start a fire and to sustain it. (i) Fuel (Combustible material), (ii) Oxygen (Air) and (iii) sufficient Heat to raise the temperature of the fuel to its burning point.

Spread of Fire

The fire spreads by the transmission of heat in one or in combination of the following ways :

(i) **Conduction :** It is transfer of heat by the intermediary material. Many materials which do not burn easily, particularly, metals are good conductors for transmitting heat. These materials when heated by the fire may ignite other combustible material in contact.

(ii) **Convection :** It is transfer of heat through gases or smoke. Gases tend to rise until ceiling or roof is reached after which they spread sideways and ignite combustible materials located at higher levels.

(iii) **Radiation :** It is the transfer of heat from the source of fire, without heating the midway media *e.g.* air. The effect of radiation can be countered by forming a 'water curtain' between the fire and the object to be protected.

(iv) **Direct Burning :** It is often due to a combination of the above two or more factors - conduction, convection and radiation.

Fire Extinction

The Fire can be extinguished by :

(i) **Starvation :** It is removal of fuel and combustible material from fire site.

(ii) **Cooling :** It is the removal of heat to lower the temperature of burning material to a point below its ignition point. This is usually achieved by pouring water over a burning material.

(iii) **Smothering :** It means restricting the supply of Oxygen (Air) to the burning material. This is achieved by sealing all the burning material from Oxygen (Air) by covering it with sand/dry earth/foam etc.

House Fire Parties

It consists of four persons who carry stirrup pumps and water buckets. They act as fire watchers and work under the orders of the wardens. They carry one stirrup pump, two buckets, one torch and one hand axe. One steel helmet and one whistle per member is used as personal equipment.

Auxiliary Fire Services

This consists of eight persons with Trailer pump which can throw water at the fire from a distance.

Fire Fighting Equipment

These are :

(i) Fire Extinguishers
(ii) Stirrup Pumps
(iii) Buckets/Tins
(iv) Fire Beaters and Hooks

Fire Extinguishers

(i) **'Soda Acid Extinguishers' :** Fire extinguishers for extinguishing fires involving ordinary combustible material, where the cooling effect is achieved by water or solution containing large percentage of water. Such extinguishers are conical/cylindrical in shape.

(ii) **'Foam Type Extinguishers' and 'Dry Chemical Powder Extinguishers':** Fire Extinguishers with chemicals, solution or dry, exclusively meant for extinguishing fires involving inflammable liquids such as oils, fats, grease, etc. where blanketing the fire to isolate it from Oxygen (Air) is required.

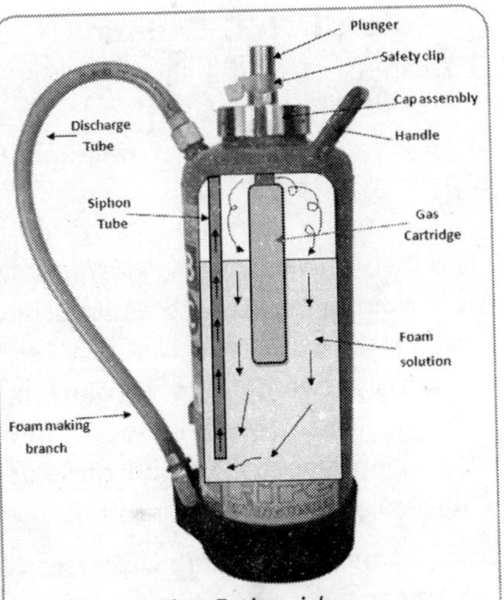

Fire Extinguisher

(iii) **CTC Carbon dioxide and Dry Chemical Extinguishers :** Fire extinguishers with chemicals either liquid, gas or dry, mainly to fight fires involving 'Live' electrical equipment etc. where the use of an electrically non-conductive extinguishing agent is of foremost importance.

ESSENTIAL SERVICES

'Essential Services' are public utility services, public safety services or the maintenance of infrastructure and services necessary for the life of the community, non-availability of which would result in the infliction of grave hardship to many people.

Essential services primarily include :

(i) Postal, telegraph or telephone service
(ii) Railways, road, air and sea transport service

(iii) Running of airports, stations and sea ports
(iv) Provision of electricity, water and sanitation
(v) Medical services and essential supplies
(vi) Production and supply of essential commodities
(vii) Running of currency mint and security presses.

Essential services are maintained by government at all cost since without them life in country will go out of gear. Each district is required to prepare in advance, contingency plans to tackle the likely disturbances in continuity of these services.

Role of NCC Cadets

The cadets of NCC being qualified in First aid, Home Nursing, Signals and having developed leadership traits and learnt about Social Services and Civil Defence, could assist in maintaining the following essential services and important tasks :

(i) Manning Telephone exchange as operators.
(ii) Help in maintaining hospital discipline and security.
(iii) Help as nurses and as links between patients and hospital staff.
(iv) Establish and run First Aid Centres.
(v) Assist civil defence wardens in carrying out their duties.
(vi) Carry out neighbourhood campaigns by motivating people.
(vii) Counteract gossip and rumours to restore the morale of the people.
(viii) Assist the civil authorities.

Some of the areas where cadets can help are :

(i) Search for and rescue trapped people.
(ii) Salvage destroyed structures and property.
(iii) Distribution of relief material.
(iv) Coordinate the provision of relief stores, food and water.
(v) Repair and restore essential services to enable rescue and relief work.

AIR RAID PROTECTION

Advance warning about the approaching enemy aircraft is very important and crucial for public safety as it provides them time to take shelter.

Warning Messages

(i) **Air Raid Warning–Red** : This message means the enemy aircraft are approaching. On receipt of this message, the sirens (hooters) are sounded for two minutes. A short blast is followed by a long blast repeated at intervals of 3 seconds.

(ii) **Air Message–Green :** This message means that raiding aircrafts have left the towns warned, or no longer appear to threaten these towns. A continuous siren for two minutes is sounded on receiving this message.

Protection Measures

The damage by the enemy aircraft can be controlled by training the public in taking the protection measures. The risk of life can be reduced by taking appropriate cover. Covers in various situations may be :

(i) **Trenches :** Dig eight to ten feet long trenches in a zig-zag manner to hide.

(ii) **Open Grounds :** Lie on the ground with face downward resting on elbows and keep a rolled handkerchief in between jaws.

(iii) **When in a Vehicle :** Quickly park the vehicle in a side lane leaving the key in its place and take cover in the open.

(iv) **When inside the Building :** Hide at places below staircases, archways, doorways, corners and under the beds or tables.

(v) **When in a Train/Bus :** Turn off the lights and crawl under seats.

(vi) **When in a Theatre :** Remain seated on your seats. Do not crowd the doors.

Earthquake Protection Measures

Do not panic: Keep calm and keep others calm.

If you are inside a building: (i) Do not rush to the doors or exits; never use the lifts; keep well away from windows, mirrors, chimneys and furniture. (ii) Protect yourself by staying under the lintel, in the corner of a room, under a table or bed.

If you are in the Street :

(i) Do not run. Walk carefully towards an open space.

(ii) Keep away from buildings, electricity wires, slopes and walls which are likely to collapse.

If you are Driving :

Park the vehicle away from buildings, walls, slopes, electricity wires and cables and stay inside the vehicle.

Measures After an Earthquake :

(i) Switch on the transistor-radio and follow the instructions given.

(ii) Keep away from sea beaches and low banks of rivers. A huge wave may sweep in.

(iii) Stay alert and cautious for aftershocks.

Cyclone Protection Measures

(i) Listen to the radio for advance information and advice.
(ii) Find shelter if you are caught in the open.
(iii) Stay in the strongest part of your house.
(iv) Open windows on the sheltered side of the house if the roof begins to lift.
(v) Do not go outside during a break in the cyclone.
(vi) Take precautions listed for floods also if you live near the sea coast.

Flood Protection Measures

(i) Listen to the radio for advance information and advice.
(ii) Disconnect all electrical appliances and move all valuable goods.
(iii) Move vehicle, animals and movable goods to the highest ground.
(iv) Move all insecticides out of reach of the water.
(v) if you have to leave the house, turn off electricity/gas and lock all outside doors and windows.
(vi) Avoid entering floodwaters on foot.
(vii) Do not wander around a flooded area without reason.

SETTING UP RELIEF CAMP

Relief measures in the aftermath of disasters cover search, rescue and evacuation, relief for livestock, clearance of debris, disposal of dead, control of fires, damage assessment and shelter for victims. Setting up of relief camps encompasses shelter provision as part of emergency relief operations and long-term rehabilitation plans.

Shelter must provide protection from the elements, space to live and store belongings, privacy and emotional security. Housing should meet the cultural and social requirements of a displaced person's home.

NCC cadets as trained and organised youth can contribute immensely for conditioning and preparing the locals in mitigating effects of disasters.

COLLECTION AND DISTRIBUTION OF AID MATERIAL

During a crisis there is an urgent need to create alternate methods of collection and distribution of emergency articles so that they reach the affected persons. NCC cadets can play an important role in the collection and distribution of relief items. Some of the tasks which can be performed by them are as under :

1. *Collection Stage*

(i) Cadets can identify the sources, the areas of importance and the agencies.
(ii) Cadets can help at the time of collection and help in maintaining records.

(iii) Help in sifting of articles and bulk breaking and packaging.
(iv) Help in dispatch of items by various means.
(v) NCC can establish their own collection and distribution centres.

2. *Distribution Stage*

(i) Can be co-opted with the PDS system.
(ii) Work along with NGOs or other organisations.
(iii) Work independently in the chain of NCC collection and distribution system.
(iv) Work alongwith Defence Forces in crisis management.
(v) Operate and man various posts established for escorting and guiding delivery.

REMOVAL OF DEBRIS

Debris that are eligible for clearance and removal include trees, sand/gravel, building, wreckage, vehicles and personal property. Debris removal and emergency protective measures are necessary to eliminate immediate threats to life, public health and safety, damage to public or private property and ensure economic recovery of the affected community to the benefit of the community at large.

NCC cadets can be gainfully employed in spreading public awareness and information about the magnitude of the situation, debris removal, identification and guidelines, disposal areas, environmental standards utilized and associated health risks.

TRAFFIC CONTROL IN DISASTER MANAGEMENT

During disaster times there is chaos and panic among public everywhere. This is aggravated by traffic jams as people run helter-skelter for safety. In such conditions traffic control is a real challenge.

Main objectives of traffic control during disasters are :

(i) To help in smooth handling of a disaster situation.
(ii) To help in providing adequate safety and security.
(iii) To help in securing the property of people affected by a disaster.
(iv) To assist in evacuation of the injured persons to the nearby hospitals.
(v) To ensure crowd control at the affected place.
(vi) To ensure all possible help to the fire service, medical and other personnel.
(vii) To help in ensuring proper access to the fire brigade, ambulances, etc. to carry out the rescue/relief operation.
(viii) To restrict movement of onlookers and other vehicular and pedestrian traffic.

❖ ❖ ❖

CHAPTER

7 Social Service & Awareness

SOCIAL SERVICE

Man is a social animal. A society is a group of people living in an area and who are dependent on each other in one way or the other. There are many problems, big or small, in a society which need to be taken care of by its members for co-existence and growth of the society. The selfless service to the society is known as Social Service. NCC cadets have a great role to play in it.

Aims and Objectives of Social Service in NCC

(i) To teach the cadets the dignity of labour

(ii) To create awareness in them about creative work

(iii) To set an example of selfless service

(iv) To inculcate in them the team spirit

(v) To give a lead in organised work with a view to utilizing the maximum possible extent the available unused time, energy and other resources of our people and direct them in various fields of social and economic activity.

Weaker Sections

The weaker sections are disinherited groups like slum dwellers, urban unorganised labourers, bounded labourers, scavengers, forest dwellers, fisherfolk, traditional artisans and agricultural labourers and particularly, females of all these categories. They are being marginalised by the modern policies of the progress. The largest numbers of these people belong to Scheduled Tribes and Scheduled Castes.

In the past, the weaker sections were never included in the social and economic planning of India. People of the weaker sections were victims of cumulative inequalities. In practice, these persons have little or no experience and are marginalised economically, politically, educationally, culturally and socially.

Basic Social Problems in Our Country

(i) Social inequality

(ii) Communalism

(iii) Lack of housing

(iv) Caste System

(v) Illiteracy and ignorance

(vi) Diseases

(vii) Inequality among men & women

(viii) Overpopulation

Types of Social Services

The various types of social services are as under :

(i) Education
(ii) Employment
(iii) Family welfare, Medical care, Family planning and Nutrition
(iv) Provision of Water and Cooking fuel, Roads, Electricity and Sanitation
(v) Old age support systems
(vi) Social assistance, Social security, Care & protection
(vii) Housing and Rehabilitation
(viii) Recreation, Sports and Social activities

Major Social Activities Done by NCC Cadets

(i) Blood donation
(ii) Adult literacy
(iii) Anti dowry drive
(iv) Anti leprosy drive
(v) Anti drug drive
(vi) Tree Plantation
(vii) Eye donation
(viii) Environmental programme
(ix) Work in Cheshire home
(x) Help in natural calamities such as flood, earthquake etc.

SOCIAL AWARENESS

Family Planning

Family planning is defined as the voluntary, responsible decision made by individuals and couples as to have the desired family size and timing of birth.

Various Family planning methods are :

(i) Vasectomy
(ii) Tubectomy
(iii) Condoms and diaphragms
(iv) Oral pills

HIV

HIV (Human Immuno-deficiency Virus) is a virus that gradually destroys the body's immune system. Anyone who has HIV infection will develop AIDS over a period of time.

AIDS

AIDS (Acquired Immuno-Deficiency Syndrome) is a condition wherein various diseases affect the body because of the body's weak natural defence mechanism or the immunity. AIDS is an acquired condition in which a person may have various diseases that cause similar symptoms, all of which are due to the body's diminished ability to fight diseases.

HIV/AIDS Infection

HIV is present in all body fluids of an infected person, especially in blood, semen and vaginal fluids. HIV infection normally spreads when there is contact with these body fluids through :

(i) Sexual transmission
(ii) Blood transfusion
(iii) Sharing needles and syringes
(iv) Mother-to-child transmission

Prevention of HIV/AIDS

HIV/AIDS can be prevented by :

(i) Being in a mutually faithful sexual relationship.
(ii) Correct and consistent use of condoms for every sexual act.
(iii) Checking all the blood and blood-products for HIV infection before transfusion.
(iv) Avoiding sharing needles and syringes for injecting drugs.
(v) Preventing mother to child transmission of HIV infection.

Role of NCC Cadets Regarding HIV

NCC cadets can educate general public by spreading the information that HIV can not be transmitted by the following modes :

(i) Shaking Hands
(ii) Sharing of Clothes
(iii) Sharing of Food and Utensils
(iv) Sharing of Toilets
(v) Insect Bites
(vi) Hugging or Kissing
(vii) Working in the same office or travelling in the same vehicle
(viii) Playing or swimming with the infected person
(ix) Coughing, sneezing or in routine patient-care activities.

CANCER, ITS CAUSES AND PREVENTIVE MEASURES

There are billions of cells in the human body. Normally they grow in a well-regulated pattern. But when cancer sets in, a group of cells, suddenly starts multiplying and forms a tumour or lump. As the tissue progresses in the degree of malignancy, it invades the original site where it has occurred and through blood vessels or lymphatic channels can reach distant parts of the body and damage them irreversibly.

Types of Cancer

Various types of cancers are :

(i) Blood cancer
(ii) Oral cancer
(iii) Larynx cancer
(iv) Lung cancer
(v) Cervical cancer
(vi) Breast cancer
(vii) Prostate cancer
(viii) Colon cancer
(ix) Skin cancer
(x) Liver cancer

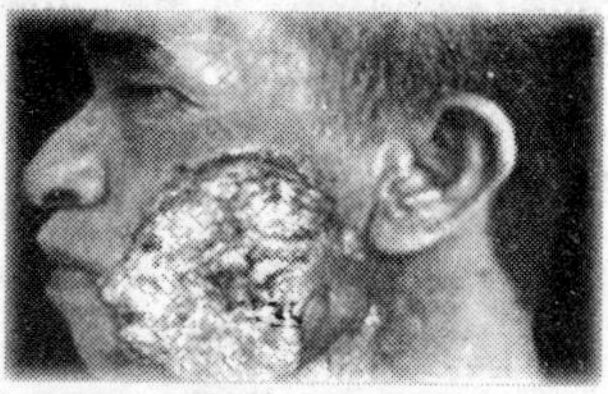

Oral cancer

Causes of Cancer

Main causes of cancer are :

(i) Prolonged chewing of tobacco
(ii) Heavy smoking
(iii) Excessive drinking
(iv) Poor oral hygiene
(v) Air and water pollution
(vi) Deficiency in diet

Signs of Cancer

The signs of cancer are :

(i) A lump in body
(ii) A persistent sore throat
(iii) A change in a mole
(iv) A prominent new spot on the skin
(v) Weight loss
(vi) Frequent difficulty in swallowing
(vii) Persistent indigestion
(viii) Vomiting and coughing of blood
(ix) Loss of appetite
(x) Blood in urine or bowel movement
(xi) A constant cough or hoarseness
(xii) Abnormal vaginal bleeding
(xiii) Persistent diarrhoea or constipation

Early warning signs due to gutka and tobacco chewing are :

(i) Any sore and ulcer on tongue, cheek or gums that does not heal
(ii) Repeated bleeding in the mouth
(iii) Red and white patches on the lips or mouth
(iv) Numbness in the mouth
(v) A lump of swelling anywhere in the mouth or neck
(vi) Difficulty in speech

Warning signs of lung cancer are :

(i) Pain in chest
(ii) Lump in neck
(iii) Change in voice
(iv) Coughing out blood
(v) Increasing cough and breathlessness

Cancer Preventive Measures

To prevent cancer :

(i) Avoid smoking & Wines
(ii) Avoid tobacco & Gutka
(iii) Maintain good oral hygiene
(iv) Avoid diet high in processed and preserved meat
(v) Avoid smoked and salted food
(vi) Avoid obesity
(vii) Handle asbestos and dyes with care
(viii) Go for Regular checkups
(ix) Go for early treatment on detection

Contribution of Youth Towards Social Welfare

Youth may contribute towards social welfare by :

(i) Developing Leadership
(ii) Doing Community Service
(iii) Working for National and Cultural Integration
(iv) Promoting Education and Literacy
(v) Working for Improving & protecting Environment
(vi) Promoting Health Care and Family Welfare
(vii) Involving in Physical Education and Adventure Training
(viii) Contributing in Old Age Care
(ix) Helping in Watershed and Waste Land Development

NON-GOVERNMENT ORGANISATIONS AND THEIR ACTIVITIES

An NGO is a non-profit group or association that acts outside of institutionalised political structures and pursues matters of social interest to its members by persuasion lobbying, or direct action. Their activities are primarily non-commercial.

Types of NGOs

Major types of NGOs are :

	Type		Definition
(i)	INGO	:	International NGOs. Have membership across at least two countries.
(ii)	BINGO	:	Business oriented International NGO
(iii)	ENGO	:	Enviornment NGO
(iv)	GINGO	:	Genuine NGOs – individuals are funded 100% by membership fees.
(v)	GONGO	:	Government oriented NGOs

(vi) QUANGO : Quasi-Autonomous NGO–Allow membership of states but rely on governmental funds.

(vii) Network : Network of NGOs working for same purpose.

(viii) Social Movements : Lack of institutionalization, informal groupings of individuals for change in society.

List of Top Ten NGOs in India

1. **Sammaan Foundation :** Originally established to link the poor to the mainstream through education, training and financial support, the current project of this NGO involves the rickshaw pullers to help them earn a better livelihood. This NGO also has notable contribution in areas like children education, health services and welfare of women.
2. **Goonj :** A recipient of the "NGO of the Year" award in 2007 at the India NGO Awards, this NGO aims at solving the clothing problems of the downtrodden. Goonj also provides relief during floods in West Bengal, Assam and Bihar.
3. **Akshaya Trust :** The sole aim of this NGO is to restore human dignity. Operating in Madurai, this NGO offers rehabilitation, healthy food and care to the street destitute.
4. **Smile Foundation :** The main aim of this NGO is the rehabilitation of the underprivileged by providing them education and healthcare services, thereby converting them into productive assets. It is run by a group of corporate professionals.
5. **Udaan Welfare Foundation :** The main aim of this NGO is to help the destitute, the main area of stress being women, children and senior citizens and also environmental welfare. One of their main projects is a cancer chemotherapy center.
6. **Pratham :** The main aim of this NGO is to provide education to the children living in the huge slums of Mumbai and providing education to those people who are unable to go to school. Their projects have increased enrollment of children in schools thus promising them a better tomorrow.
7. **Lepra Society :** The NGO aims at prevention and control of diseases like AIDS, leprosy and tuberculosis in poor communities.
8. **Deepalaya :** The NGO aims at providing education to the children living in the slums of Delhi. Their projects also include providing healthcare, education, vocational training to the downtrodden and the physically disabled. They have contributed towards significant Rural Development in Haryana and Uttarakhand.
9. **Uday Foundation :** This New Delhi-based NGO provides support to the parents and families of children suffering from congenital disorders and other syndromes. Their projects also include research to open new horizons

of healthcare technologies. They also have health care projects for common people. Their special stress is in the area of protecting childrights.

10. Helpage India : The sole aim of this NGO is to provide resources to the elderly people of our country. Their objective is to make aware the senior citizens of their rights and protect their rights so that they can also play a key role in our society. They also work with the government (both local and national) to implement policies that will be beneficial to the senior citizens of India.

International Red Cross and Red Crescent Movement are the world's largest groups of humanitarian NGOs.

Activities of NGOs

Following activities are mainly undertaken by NGOs :

(i) Child Care
(ii) Polio Eradication drive
(iii) Tree Plantation
(iv) Blood Donation
(v) Anti Dowry Drive
(vi) Adult Literacy
(vii) Anti Drug Drive
(viii) Anti Leprosy Drive
(ix) Human-rights
(x) Awareness Campaign
(xi) Wildlife and Animal Care
(xii) Help during Natural Calamities
(xiii) Family Planning Programmes
(xiv) Community Development Work
(xv) Environmental Programmes
(xvi) Orphanage and Old Age Homes
(xvii) Cottage Industry
(xviii) Educating People about AIDS
(xix) Promotion of Social-equality
(xx) Providing Schooling Facilities
(xxi) Creating and Providing Health and Hygiene Infrastructure.

DRUG ABUSE & TRAFFICKING

A 'Drug' is any substance that, when inhaled, injected, smoked, consumed, absorbed via a patch on the skin, or dissolved under the tongue causes a physiological change in the body.

Drug menace is one of the most serious problems facing the world. Drug trafficking is considered as a greater problem than drug consumption. Drugs affect the central nervous system of the user and adversely affect his thinking, feelings and behaviour. All drugs cause addiction and weaken the body and mind of the consumer.

Drug Abuse : It is consuming the substance which is neither approved nor supervised by medical professionals. The use of steroids for performance enhancement in sports is also called drug abuse. Continuous and prolonged abuse of drugs may make a person an addict.

It was found that all the addicts either take hashish, cannabis or heroin. 72% of addicts are in the age group of 20-24 years. Females comprise only 2% of the addicts. 78% of addicts come from the families which are facing problems such as, loss of one or both parents or separation of the parents.

Reasons for Drug Addiction

Drug addiction does not develop overnight, but have general and genuine reasons. The teen years are often considered the most difficult period of a person's life. It's a vulnerable time of life as teens attempt to navigate the precarious bridge between childhood and adulthood. And one of the most challenging decisions, for an age group that's ill-prepared to make difficult choices, is whether to start using alcohol or drugs. The reasons are as follows:

(i) Peer Pressure
(ii) To look and feel "grown-up"
(iii) Modeling Parents' Behaviour
(iv) Curiosity
(v) Boredom
(vi) Self-medication

Types of Drugs

There are three main types of drugs :

1. Depressants : These are drugs that slow down the function of the central nervous system. They include :

(i) Alcohol
(ii) Cannabis
(iii) Barbiturates
(iv) Benzodiazepines (Tranquilisers)
(v) GHB (Gamma-hydroxybutrate)
(vi) Opiates and Opioids, including Heroin

2. Stimulants : These drugs act on the central nervous system to speed up the messages to and from the brain. Stimulants increase heart rate, body temperature and blood pressure.

They include : (i) Ephedrine (ii) Caffeine (iii) Nicotine

3. Hallucinogens : These drugs affect perception. People who take them may perceive imaginary things.

They includes: (i) Dhatura (ii) Ketamine.

LEGAL DRUGS : Rules and regulations control the availability, quality and price of all legal drugs. For example, tobacco may not be sold to persons below the age of 18 years.

ILLEGAL DRUGS : Many drugs are illegal, there are no fixed prices or quality controls on these illicit drugs such as heroin. A user can never be sure of a drug's strength or purity.

RURAL DEVELOPMENT PROGRAMMES

Our country has a population which is divided into two sections, the urban and the rural. Urban areas are where everything is available, particularly the basic needs like health care, education, water, electricity, telecommunication, roads, transports, railways etc. The areas where such facilities are not available or are not adequate, are known as rural areas. Most villages come under rural area.

Rural Development

Rural development is a process that aims at improving the quality of life and standard of living of the people in the rural areas. It may be defined as overall development of rural areas to improve the quality of life of rural people. It is an integrated and sustainable process of improvement of the rural areas, which includes social, economical, political and spiritual development of the poorer sections of the society.

Rural development encompasses the following :

1. Finding the ways to improve the rural lives, with participation of the rural people themselves, so as to meet the required need of the rural area.
2. It covers the following activities :
   (i) Health
   (ii) Education
   (iii) Employment
   (iv) Roads
   (v) Banking
   (vi) Water and Electricity
   (vii) Rural Tourism
   (viii) Crop, Poultry and Animal Farming
   (ix) Small Scale Industries and Agricultural Products

Need for Rural Development

70% of Indian population lives in rural areas with no or very little facilities. In order to become a global power, we need to develop our rural areas. The need to develop rural areas is :

(i) To empower the rural population.
(ii) To create more job opportunities.
(iii) To bridge the urban–rural divide.
(iv) To have equitable distribution of resources and development activities.
(v) To bridge the economic gap between incomes of rural–urban population.
(vi) To control or reduce mass migration of population from rural to urban areas.

Objectives of Rural Development

Following are the primary objectives of rural development :

(i) To improve the living standards by providing food, shelter, clothing, employment and education.

(ii) To increase productivity in rural areas and reduce poverty.

(iii) To involve people in planning and development through their participation in decision making and through centralization of administration.

(iv) To ensure distributive Justice and equalization of opportunities in the society.

IMPORTANT RURAL DEVELOPMENT PROGRAMMES IN INDIA

Mahatma Gandhi National Rural Employment Guarantee Act (MGNREGA)

- To enhance livelihood security in rural areas by providing at least 100 days of guaranteed demand based wage employment in a financial year to every household whose adult members volunteer to do unskilled manual work.

- Beneficiaries are willing rural population, unskilled manual labourers and seasonally unemployed.
- A 60:40 wage and material ratio has to be maintained.
- No contractors and machinery is allowed.
- Wages are linked to Consumer Price Index (Agriculture labour).
- The central government bears the 100 per cent wage cost of unskilled manual labour and 75 per cent of the material cost including the wages of skilled and semi-skilled workers.
- If work is not provided within 15 days of applying, applicants are entitled to an unemployment allowance.
- MGNREGA is to be implemented mainly by gram panchayats.
- At least one-third beneficiaries shall be women.
- Social audit has to be done by the gram sabha at least once in every 6 months.
- Focuses on creation of durable assets as per local needs.

Deen Dayal Antyodaya Yojana (DAY) - NRLM

- National Rural Livelihood Mission/Aajeevika has been subsumed into Deen Dayal Antyodaya Yojana (DAY).

- The Scheme is assisted by investment from World Bank.
- It aims at creating efficient and effective institutional platforms of the rural poor, enabling them to increase household income through sustainable livelihood enhancements and improved access to financial services.
- At least one woman member from each identified rural poor household, is to be brought under the Self Help Group (SHG) network.
- Target Group is identified through the Participatory Identification of Poor (PIP) method and it is delinked from BPL. The responsibility of identification of poor must be vetted by the Gram Sabha and approved by the Gram Panchayat.
- NRLM provides Revolving Fund (RF) and Community Investment Fund (CIF) as resources in perpetuity to the institutions of the poor to strengthen their institutional and financial management capacity.
- It promotes financial literacy among the poor.
- It also promotes existing livelihood portfolio of the poor through its 3 pillars - 'Vulnerability reduction and livelihoods enhancement', 'employment' and 'enterprises'.
- Partnerships with NGOs and linkages with Panchayat Raj Institutions.

Deen Dayal Upadhyaya Grameen Kaushalya Yojana (DDU-GKY)

- DDU-GKY is tasked with the dual objectives of adding diversity to the incomes of rural poor families and cater to the career aspirations of rural youth.
- It aims at transforming rural poor youth into an economically independent and globally relevant workforce.
- It focuses on rural youth between the ages of 15 and 35 years from poor families.

Special initiatives under DDU-GKY:

- **Himayat:** A special scheme for the youth (rural & urban) of Jammu & Kashmir.
- **Roshni:** A special initiative for the rural youth of poor families in 27 Left-wing Extremist (LWE) districts across 9 states.

Pradhan Mantri Awas Yojana (PMAY) - Gramin

- It replaces Indira Awas Yojana (IAY), which was launched as a subscheme of Jawahar Rozgar Yojana in 1985.

- It aims at helping rural people below the poverty-line (BPL) in construction of dwelling units and upgradation of existing unserviceable kutcha houses by providing assistance in the form of full grant.
- Beneficiaries are people belonging to SC/STs, freed bonded labourers and non-SC/ST categories, widows or next-of-kin of defence personnel killed in action, ex-servicemen and retired members of the paramilitary forces, Disabled persons and minorities.
- It will be implemented in rural areas across the country except Delhi and Chandigarh.
- Government to construct 1 crore pucca (permanent) houses for the rural poor in the next three years.
- The project will be implemented in a span of three years and expected to boost job creation in rural areas.
- Beneficiaries of the rural houses would be chosen according to data taken from the Socio-Economic Caste Census of 2011.
- An allowance of ₹ 120,000 in plain areas and ₹ 130,000 in hilly areas will be provided for construction of homes.
- The unit size will be enhanced from the existing 20 sq.mt. to up to 25 sq.mt. including a dedicated area for hygienic cooking.
- Funds will be transferred electronically directly to the account of the beneficiary.
- The beneficiary would be facilitated to avail loan of up to ₹ 70,000 for construction of the house which is optional.

National Social Assistance Program (NSAP)

- It is a social security and welfare programme to provide support to aged persons, widows, disabled persons and bereaved families on death of primary bread winner, belonging to below poverty line households.
- It comprises of five schemes, namely–
  (i) Indira Gandhi National Old Age Pension Scheme (IGNOAPS),
  (ii) Indira Gandhi National Widow Pension Scheme (IGNWPS),
  (iii) Indira Gandhi National Disability Pension Scheme (IGNDPS),
  (iv) National Family Benefit Scheme (NFBS), and
  (v) Annapurna.
- Under NSAP, 100% Central Assistance is extended to the States/UTs to provide the benefits in accordance with the norms, guidelines and conditions laid down by the Central Government.

Pradhan Mantri Gram Sadak Yojana (PMGSY)

- PMGSY aimed at providing all-weather road connectivity to unconnected habitations.

- A habitation which was earlier provided all-weather connectivity would not be eligible even if the present condition of the road is bad.
- It is a 100% Centrally Sponsored Scheme and 50% of the Cess on High Speed Diesel (HSD) is earmarked for this Programme.
- The target year of achieving 100% rural road connectivity under PMGSY is 2019.
- The unit of this programme is habitation and not revenue villages.
- Major District Roads, State Highways and National Highways cannot be covered under the PMGSY, even if they happen to be in rural areas.
- All habitations with a population of 500 persons and above in the plain areas and 250 persons and above in hill states, the tribal and the desert areas will be connected by PMGSY.

Swarnajayanti Gram Swarojgar Yojana (SGSY)

- SGSY was launched in April, 1999. The objective of SGSY is to provide sustainable income to the rural poor. The programme aims at instituting a large number of small businesses in the rural areas. It is envisaged that every family assisted under SGSY will be brought above the poverty-line within a period of three years. This programme covers families below poverty line in rural areas of the country. Within this, special safeguards for SCs/STs, women and physically handicapped persons are provided.

Jawahar Gram Samriddhi Yojana (JGSY)

- The critical importance of rural infrastructure is the development of village economy. A number of steps have been initiated by the Central as well as the State Governments for building the rural infrastructure. It was launched on 1st April, 1999. The primary objective of the JGSY is the creation of infrastructure including durable assets at the village level, and to increase the opportunities for employment for rural poor. JGSY is implemented entirely at the Village Panchayat level which is the only authority for preparation of the yearly plan and for implementing it.

National Rurban Mission (NRuM)

- NRuM is also called as Shyama Prasad Mukharjee Rurban Mission and aimed at strengthening rural areas by provisioning of economic, social and physical infrastructure facilities
- The objective is to stimulate local economic development, enhance basic services, and create well planned Rurban clusters i.e Smart Villages.
- Smart village is an area which possesses the economic characteristics and lifestyles of an urban area while retaining its essential rural area features.

- It follows cluster based approach and the State Governments would identify geographically contiguous Gram Panchayats with a population of about 25000 to 50000 in plain and coastal areas and a population of 5000 to 15000 in desert, hilly or tribal areas.
- These clusters would be developed by provisioning of economic activities, developing skills & local entrepreneurship and providing infrastructure amenities.
- It provides skill development training, digital literacy, mobile health unit, electronic delivery of citizen-centric services, e-gram connectivity, public transport, inter-village road connectivity etc.
- The funding will be through various schemes of the government through public-private partnerships.
- In addition to it, there will be critical gap funding of 30% of project cost as Central Government share for clusters.

Other Development Projects

- **Sansad Adarsh Gram Yojana :** In this, each Member of Parliament would take out some part of his funds for the development of any one adopted village. The funds would be used for construction and development of that village.
- **Pradhan Mantri Awas Yojana :** It is a credit-linked subsidy scheme by the Government of India to facililate access to affordable housing for the low and moderate-income residents of the country.
- **Jeevan Jyoti Bima Yojana :** It is a life insurance policy in ensuring financial future for the people with lowest cost on yearly basis. Anyone within the age group from 18 to 50 years can get enrolled in it.
- **Krishi Sinchai Yojana :** This scheme is to bloom the agriculture economy of India. Till now only 45 per cent is accessible to irrigation channels, remaining depends on traditional methods of irrigation. This scheme provides required infrastructure arrangements.

It is very important in a large and democratic country like India that all schemes and other administrative benefits reach every citizen. For this to happen, it is important that an effective administration set up is available at every level from Central Government to Gram Panchayat. Of course, honest and corruption free implementation of projects will decide the success of the system. As the future citizens of India, we need to be aware of the system and responsibilities of each official in the administrative set up so that we can contribute in our own way for the development of our society.

TERRORISM AND COUNTER TERRORISM

Terrorism

Terrorism means the process of terrorising others to do or not to do something. A terrorist is one who indulges in such a practice. A terrorist may prefer to belong to a particular religion or country, but actually he has no religion nor he is a real citizen of any country. No religion preaches terrorism; and patriotism also does not mean terrorising the people of any country for the sake of one's own country.

Terrorists are heartless people. They kill or maim unarmed, innocent men, women and children. They are highly immoral and irreligious people as they rape and molest girls and women of all religions and castes whomever they can capture. They can never be regarded as patriotic or religious people. They are enemies of mankind and destroyers of peace. Their only creed is violence.

Most of the terrorists are immature young people who can easily be misled in the name of religion. Unemployment is also one of the major causes of spread of terrorism.

Aims of Terrorist Groups

A terrorist group commits acts of violence mostly to :

(i) Produce widespread fear.

(ii) Satisfy their vengeance.

(iii) Free prisoners of their group from jail.

(iv) Steal or extort money and equipment, especially weapons and ammunition vital to the operation of their group.

(v) Destroy facilities or disrupt lines of communication in order to create doubt that the government can provide for and protect its citizens.

(vi) Discourage foreign investments, tourism, or assistance programs that can affect the target country's economy and support of the government in power.

(vii) Influence government decisions, legislation, or other critical decisions.

(viii) Obtain worldwide, national, or local recognition for their cause by attracting the attention of the media.

(ix) Harass, weaken, or embarrass government security forces so that the government overreacts and appears repressive.

(x) Turn the tide in a guerrilla war by forcing government security forces to concentrate their efforts in urban areas. This allows the terrorist group to establish itself among the local populace in rural areas.

Type of Terrorist Acts

The most common types of terrorist acts include :

(i) Bombings

(ii) Arsons and Fire Bombings

(iii) Armed Attacks and Assassinations
(iv) Hijackings and Skyjackings
(v) Kidnappings and Hostage-takings
(vi) Other Types of Terrorist Acts are :
 (a) Maiming
 (b) Cyber Terrorism
 (c) Robberies and Extortion

Counter Terrorism

Major counter-terrorism strategies involve an increase in standard police and domestic intelligence. The central activities are traditional : interception of communications, and the tracing of persons. New technology has, however, expanded the range of military and law enforcement operations. Domestic intelligence is often directed at specific groups, defined on the basis of origin or religion, which is a source of political controversy most of the time.

Counter Terrorism Strategy :

This includes the following steps :

1. **Preparation :**
   (i) Identification of areas of likely terrorist target and keeping such areas under continuous surveillance / guard and strengthening them by creating multi-tiered layer of security checks / protection / obstacles.
   (ii) Earmarking quick response teams (QRTs) from local police for immediate reaction / cordoning of the area.
   (iii) Earmarking specialist units (like NSG) for tackling of terrorist threats.
   (iv) Preparation of plans for requisition of Army / other agencies like fire deptt, health deptt and bomb disposal units for assistance.
2. **Pre-emptive Action :** This involves a 24 × 7 action plan to track and monitor all activities of terrorist / terrorist groups. This includes the following :
   (i) Collection and Collation of all type of Intelligence of suspected / known terrorist groups / persons especially foreign travel, financial transactions, social media / internet accounts and telephone conversations.
   (ii) Physical Tracking / Surveillance of the suspected persons / groups.
   (iii) Pre-emptive neutralization by apprehension / detention of suspected persons / terrorists.

How can we help Anti Terrorism Operations?

As a responsible citizen, we must assist the Police and other law enforcing agencies to fight this menace. Some of the actions are listed as under:

(i) Be on the lookout of suspicious activities and inform the Police.
(ii) Be alert and active towards emerging situations.
(iii) Be on the guard against unidentified objects while travelling.
(iv) Report any such activities we might come across on the internet.
(v) Take initiative to rescue and assist people in distress.

CORRUPTION

The word 'corrupt' means to abuse or spoil. Corruption can therefore be defined as the abuse of entrusted power for private gains. It hurts everyone who depends on the integrity of people in a position of authority or power.

Types of Corruption

(i) **Petty Corruption :** It occurs at a smaller scale and occurs within established social frameworks and governing norms. Examples include the exchange of small improper gifts or use of personal connections to obtain favours.

(ii) **Grand Corruption :** It is defined as corruption occurring at the highest levels of government in a way that requires significant subversion of the political, legal and economic systems.

(iii) **Systemic Corruption :** It is the corruption which is primarily due to the weaknesses of an organization or process. It can be contrasted with individual officials or agents who act corruptly within the system.

Sectors of Corruption

Corruption can occur in any economic sector whether it be public or private, industry or even NGOs as mentioned below :

(i) Government/Public Sector
(ii) Legislative System (Political)
(iii) Executive System (Police)
(iv) Judiciary System (Courts)
(v) Corporate Sector
(vi) Educational Institutions
(vii) Non-Government Organizations

Methods of Corruption

(i) **Bribery :** It is the most common form of corruption. The types of favours given are diverse and include money, gifts, sexual favours, company shares, entertainment, employment and political benefits. The personal gain that is given can be anything from actively giving preferential treatment to having an indiscretion or crime overlooked.

(ii) **Improper Political Donations :** This is the use of contributions/donations to political parties to secure illicit power, not because one favours their policies.

(iii) **Abuse of Discretion :** Abuse of discretion refers to the misuse of one's powers and decision-making facilities. Examples include a judge improperly dismissing a criminal case.

(iv) **Extortion and Blackmail :** This can be the threat of violence or false imprisonment as well as exposure of an individual's secrets or prior crimes. This also includes such behaviour as an influential person, threatening to go to the media, or threatening a public official with exposure of their secrets, or demanding money in exchange for continued secrecy.

(v) **Embezzlement, Theft and Fraud :** Embezzlement and theft involves someone with access to funds or assets, illegally taking control of them. Fraud involves using deception to convince the owner of funds or assets, to give them up to an unauthorized party.

(vi) **Favouritism, Nepotism and Clientelism :** This involves the favouring of not the perpetrator of corruption, but someone related to them, such as a friend, family member or member of an association.

Prevention of Corruption

Weeding out total corruption from our society is extremely difficult. However, some of the methods by which corruption can be reduced to a great extent are :

(i) Highlighting / Reporting of cases of corruption.

(ii) Never give bribe or favours to any one nor take bribes/favours from any one.

(iii) Speedy trial and exemplary punishment for persons involved in corruption.

(iv) Proper education of all sections of society that corruption in any form is bad and will not be tolerated.

(v) Ensuring transparency in all dealings.

(vi) Dealing with corruption in higher echelons.

(vii) Simplifying routine procedures to prevent corruption.

(viii) Strict implementation of the Prevention of Corruption Act.

(ix) Full freedom to Lok Pal or Lok Ayukt to investigate cases of corruption.

FEMALE FOETICIDE

It is the selective abortion of the girl child in the mother's womb itself, done deliberately after the detection of the child's gender through medical procedure. This is usually done under family pressure.

Causes of Female Foeticide

(i) Preference to have male child

(ii) Unwanted Pregnancy

(iii) Foul Medical Ethics
(iv) Dowry System
(v) Deteriorated Status of Women

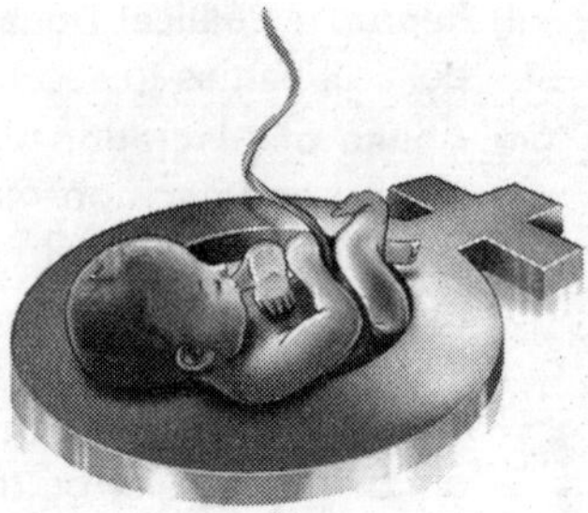

Effects of Female Foeticide

(i) Skewed Sex Ratio
(ii) Women Trafficking
(iii) Increase in Rape and Assault
(iv) Population Decline

Measures to Prevent Female Foeticide

The prominent measures are :

(i) Widespread campaigns about the ill effects of female foeticide.
(ii) Heavy fines and judicial action against people involved.
(iii) Cancellation of the doctor's license who partakes in illegal sex determination and abortion.
(iv) Equal rights for women in the property of parents/spouse.
(v) High incentives for the girl child in education, employment etc.

DOWRY

It is the payment in cash or some kind of gifts given to bridegroom's family along with the bride in marriage. Generally they include cash, jewellery electrical appliances, furniture, bedding, crockery, utensils and other household items that help the newly-wed set up her home. The Dowry prohibition Act 1961 states that : "If any person, gives or takes or abets the giving or taking of dowry, he shall be punishable with imprisonment for a term which shall not be less than five years, and with fine which shall not be less than fifteen thousand rupees or the amount of the value of such dowry, whichever is more."

Causes of Dowry System

(i) **Misconception :** Dowry is one of the most ancient practices of India. Thus, most people think that it is legal as per the vedic rights.

(ii) **Parental Compulsions :** In order to find a good match for their daughter, well to do parents offer huge dowry. This adds fuel to the growing demand for dowry.
(iii) **Growing Economic Inequality :** This fuels the desire to ask for more and more cash or gifts to persue a lavish lifestyle or other ventures.

(iv) **Increasing Unemployment :** In order to prove their status, unemployed males are demanding more and more dowry to fulfill their desires of living a good life.

Effects of Dowry System

(i) Female Foeticide
(ii) Domestic Violence
(iii) False Dowry Allegations
(iv) Female Trafficking
(v) Increase in Mortgage and Loans
(vi) Burning of Brides

Prevention of Dowry

We can do a lot to prevent offences related to dowry by taking the following steps :

(i) Don't demand or accept dowry.
(ii) Educate people that demanding and accepting dowry is an offence.
(iii) Educate people to respect a woman's rights and privileges.
(iv) Encourage women-folk to raise their voice about their rights and to fight against dowry system.

CHILD ABUSE

It is a state of emotional, physical, economic and sexual maltreatment meted out to a person below the age of eighteen and is a globally prevalent phenomenon. Child abuse has serious physical and psycho-social consequences which adversely affect the health and overall well-being of a child.

Forms of Child Abuse

It can be of various forms :

(i) **Physical Abuse :** It is inflicting physical injury upon a child. It may include hitting, shaking, kicking, beating or otherwise physically harming a child.

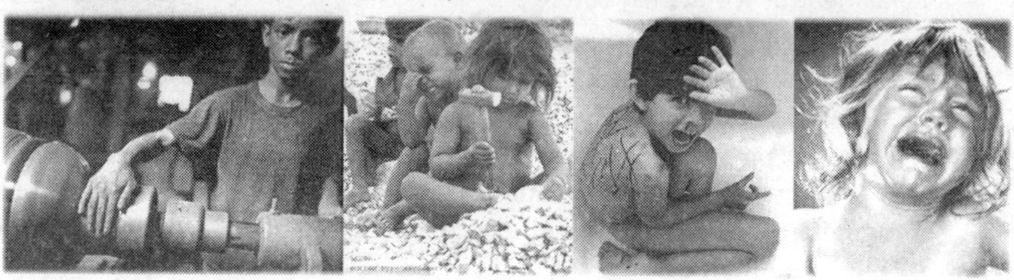

(ii) **Emotional Abuse :** It is also known as mental abuse, verbal abuse, and psychological maltreatment and includes acts or the failure to act by parents and others that have caused or could cause serious behavioural, cognitive, emotional, or mental distress.

(iii) **Sexual Abuse :** It includes fondling a child's genitals, making the child fondle an adult's genitals, sexual assault (intercourse, incest, rape or sodomy), exhibitionism and pornography.

(iv) **Child Neglect :** It is an act of omission or commission leading to the denial of a child's basic needs. Neglect can be physical, educational, emotional or psychological.

(v) **Deprivation :** Unreasonbale deprivation of his/her basic needs for survival such as food and shelter, or failure to give timely medical treatment to an injured child.

(vi) **Other Forms :** Any other act, deed or word which debases, degrades or demeans the intrinsic worth and dignity of a child as a human being.

RIGHT TO INFORMATION (RTI) ACT 2005

The Right to Information Act was notified in the Gazette of India on 21st June, 2005. It became fully operational from 12th October, 2005. This new law empowers Indian citizens to seek any accessible information from a Public Authority and makes the Government and its functionaries more accountable and responsible.

Major Provisions of the Act

(i) RTI Act covers the whole of India. It is applicable to all constitutional authorities, including the executive, legislature and judiciary; any institution or body established or constituted by an act of Parliament or a state legislature.

(ii) In order to promote transparency and accountability in the working of every public authority, the constitution of a Central Information Commission and State Information Commissions are enshrined in the Act.

(iii) It mandates timely response to citizen requests for government information. It is an Act to provide for setting out the practical regime of right to information for citizens to secure access to information under the control of public authorities.

(iv) It is also defined in the Act that bodies or authorities established or constituted by order or notification of appropriate government including bodies owned, controlled or substantially financed by government, or non-Government organizations substantially financed, directly or indirectly by funds provided by the government are also covered in it. Private bodies are not within the Act's ambit directly.

(v) The Act empowers applicant citizens to :

(a) Inspect permissible governmental documents.

(b) Obtain copies of permissible governmental documents.

(c) Inspect permissible Governmental works and obtain samples.

Major Exemptions

The following information is exempt from disclosure under RTI Act :

(i) Information which has been expressly forbidden to be published by any court of law or tribunal or the disclosure of which may constitute contempt of court.

(ii) Information, the disclosure of which would cause a breach of privilege of Parliament or the State Legislature.

(iii) Information, disclosure of which would prejudicially affect the sovereignty and integrity of India, the security, strategic, scientific or economic interests of the State, relation with a Foreign State or lead to incitement of an offense.

RIGHT TO EDUCATION (RTE) ACT 2009

India, on the 1st April 2010, enforced the Right to Education (RTE) act that promises freedom from illiteracy for the country. With this act, India became one of 135 countries to make education a fundamental right of every child.

The Act makes education a fundamental right of every child between the ages of 6 and 14 and specifies minimum norms in elementary schools. It requires all private schools to reserve 25% of seats to children from poor families (to be reimbursed by the state as part of the public-private partnership plan). It also prohibits all unrecognized schools from practice, and makes provisions for no donation or capitation fees and no interview of the child or parent for admission.

The RTE act requires surveys that will monitor all neighbourhoods, identify children requiring education, and set up facilities for providing it. The RTE Act is the first legislation in the world that puts the responsibility of ensuring enrolment, attendance and completion of education on the Government.

Major Points of RTE Act

Following are the main points of the Act :

(i) Free and compulsory education to all children of India in the six to 14 age group.

(ii) No child shall be held back, expelled, or required to pass a board examination until completion of elementary education (up to class eight).

(iii) A child who completes elementary education (upto class 8) shall be awarded a certificate.
(iv) The Act calls for a fixed student-teacher ratio.
(v) The Act applies to all of India.
(vi) The Act provides for 25 per cent reservation for economically disadvantaged communities in all private and minority schools.
(vii) The Act mandates improvement in quality of education.
(viii) School teachers will need adequate professional degree within five years or else will lose job.
(ix) School infrastructure (where required) to be improved in three years, else recognition will be cancelled.
(x) Financial burden will be shared between state and central government on the basis of Sarva Shiksha Abhiyan (Education for All).
(xi) Private schools to face penalty for violating the provisions of RTE.

PROTECTION OF CHILDREN FROM SEXUAL OFFENCES (POCSO) ACT 2012

India has the largest child population in the world, and almost 42 per cent of its total population is under eighteen years of age. The health and security of the country's children is integral to any vision for its progress and development. One of the issues marring the vision for the country's children is the evil of sexual abuse of children.

The Protection of Children from Sexual Offences Bill 2012, was passed by Parliament in May 2012. The Act received the President's assent on 19th June 2012 and was notified in the Gazette of India for public information on 20th June, 2012. It has come into force on the 14th of November, 2012.

General Provisions of the Act

(i) The Act is gender-neutral and defines a child as any person below the age of eighteen years.
(ii) The Act provides precise definitions for different forms of sexual abuse, including penetrative and non-penetrative sexual assault, sexual harassment and pornography.
(iii) The Act provides for stringent punishment graded as per the gravity of the offence, with a maximum term of rigorous imprisonment for life for certain offences, and fine.
(iv) The Act provides for mandatory reporting of sexual offences.
(v) The Act provides for child-friendly procedures for reporting of offences, recording of evidence, investigation and trial.

Punishment for Offences in the Act

(i) **Penetrative Sexual Assault (Section 3) :** Not less than seven years imprisonment, which may extend to imprisonment for life and, fine.

(ii) **Aggravated Penetrative Sexual Assault (Section 5) :** Not less than ten years imprisonment, which may lead to imprisonment for life and, fine.

(iii) **Sexual Assault (Section 7) :** Not less than three years imprisonment, which may extend to five years and, fine.

(iv) **Aggravated Sexual Assault (Section 9) :** Not less than five years imprisonment, which may extend to seven years, and fine.

(v) **Sexual Harassment of the Child (Section 11) :** Three years imprisonment and fine.

(vi) **Use of Child for Pornographic Purposes (Section 13) :** Five years imprisonment and fine, and in the event of subsequent conviction, seven years imprisonment and fine.

CIVIC SENSE & RESPONSIBILITIES

Civic Sense is the sense in an individual which makes him a civilized citizen of a country. It means social ethics, the positive perception, understanding, attitudes, towards society or community. It is the behaviour between individuals and groups, civility and unspoken principles of society. It is not just about keeping the roads clean and avoiding the violation of basic civic rights, it is about respecting one another, abiding by the law and maintaining proper etiquette in public places.

TRAFFIC RULES

To avoid chaos on the roads, there are certain traffic rules and laid down set road signals. These have to be followed strictly for safety of everyone. Some important points are :

Crossing of Roads

Most of the accidents and accidental deaths involving pedestrians are the direct result of their errant behaviour, specially while crossing roads. Pedestrians should keep the following in mind:

(i) **Zebra Crossings :** These are exclusively meant for pedestrians for their safe crossover. They should cross the road by walking over it. Only when the traffic signal for vehicles is green do vehicles drive over zebra crossing.

(ii) **Subways :** It is not only safe to cross roads using a subway, it is fun too. For you can have a leisure walk without any botheration for traffic.

(iii) **Overhead Bridges :** On certain busy roads wherein construction of subway is not feasible overhead bridges are built across road edges to enable pedestrians' safe crossover.

Safety Rules to be Followed, While Walking

(i) Always walk on the footpath only. On roads without footpath, walk on the extreme right hand side of the roads. Do not rush or run on the road.

(ii) Cross only at zebra crossings, traffic signals, subways, foot overbridges. Where such facilities do not exist, look for a safe place to cross.

(iii) At the signal lights, cross only on a clear green signal for pedestrians.

(iv) While crossing between vehicles parked on the side of the road, remember that you are visible to the moving traffic (because the parked vehicles may be higher than you). Stop as you appear from behind the vehicle and look for a safe gap before crossing. Mind it, drivers need enough time to see you and to slow down and stop the vehicle.

(v) While crossing wide road that have central verges, always cross in two stages: Cross to the central verge, stop, and cross when the next section is clear.

(vi) While crossing one-way roads, remember that the traffic will usually be moving in a number of lanes and at higher speeds. Do not cross unless all lanes are clear.

(vii) Never cross a road at a building's corner, as the motorist taking the turn will not be able to see you clearly.

(viii) Running across the road is never safe, as you may slip and fall.

Safety Rules to be Followed, While Going by Bus

(i) Leave home well in time, so that you won't have to run to catch the bus.

(ii) At the bus stand, always follow the queue. Board the bus only after it has come to the proper stop, without rushing in or pushing others.

(iii) While in the bus, shouting or making a noise can distract the driver.

(iv) Do not board or alight at a red light, crossing or unauthorized bus stop.

(v) Always hold onto the hand-rail if standing in a moving bus, especially on sharp turns.

(vi) Do not sit, stand or travel on the footboard of the bus.

(vii) Do not keep any part of the body outside the bus.

Do's & Don'ts: For Road/Rail Safety

1. Do's for Road Safety:

(i) Obey traffic rules.

(ii) Wear helmet and seat belts.

(iii) Give pedestrians the right-of-way in cross-walks.

(iv) Conduct or attend road safety seminars.

(v) Educate general public on traffic rules.

2. Don'ts for Road Safety:

(i) Do not overspeed.

(ii) Do not drink and drive.

(iii) Do not cross the road during the red signal.

(iv) Do not use mobile phones while driving.

(v) Do not engage in other activities while driving.

3. Do's for Rail Safety:

(i) Always use overbridge to cross the track.

(ii) Stop vehicles when the gate is closed at the crossing.

(iii) Carry your Identification Card while travelling.

(iv) Pull the chain, only in emergency if required to stop the train.

(v) Report to the railway police regarding unidentified objects or suspected persons.

4. Don'ts for Rail Safety:

(i) Do not ignore the signal at railway crossing.

(ii) Do not be careless while crossing train tracks.

(iii) Do not try to get in/get down while train is moving.

(iv) Do not sit on the footsteps/footboard while travelling.

(v) Do not use fire while travelling.

(vi) Do not consume alcohol during journey.

(vii) Do not travel on footboards of moving train.

(viii) Do not accept any eatables from unknown persons.

(ix) Do not quarrel with railway staff and fellow passengers.

(x) Do not bunch up to present a large target at railway station.

TRAFFIC CONTROL ORGANISATION

A country's growth is measured by the expansion of its road network. But expansion in the road network, surge in motorization and a rising population of a country contribute towards increasing numbers of road accidents, leading to injuries and fatalities.

Road accidents are a human tragedy, which involve high human suffering. They impose a huge socio-economic cost in terms of untimely deaths, injuries and loss of potential income. The ramifications of road accidents can be colossal and its negative impact is felt, not only on individuals, their health and welfare, but also on the economy. Consequently, road safety has become an issue of national concern in India.

The responsibility to control all traffic in a city or outside it is that of the Traffic Police department which works under the District Police Chief.

Traffic Police Organisation

(i) The entire traffic in any city or town is controlled by the Joint or Deputy Commissioner of Police (Traffic). He is assisted by various Assistant Commissioners of Police (ACPs), Inspectors, Assistant Sub Inspectors (ASIs), Head Constables and Constables. The strength depends on the size of the city or town and the traffic that is to be managed.

(ii) For control of traffic, a city/town is divided into Zones and Divisions. Each Zone is under an ACP and a Division under an Inspector. In addition there is a Control Room, which monitors all Traffic cameras and communications.

The Traffic Police carries out the following tasks :

(i) Management and Regulation of all traffic.

(ii) Opening/closing of roads due to VIP movement, repairs or accidents.

(iii) Checking of vehicles' documents for permits, license and ownership.

(iv) Checking of vehicles for overloading of passengers/load.

(v) Ensuring proper marking and placement of road signs.

(vi) Conduct vehicle based patrolling of roads/highways.

(vii) Manning of road intersections, one way routes and check posts.

(viii) Manning of PCR and recovery vans.

(ix) Investigation of road accidents, making of accident reports and evacuation of injured to hospitals.

(x) Clearing of road blockages due to accidents or any other reason.

(xi) Educating general public on road safety rules.

(xii) Conduct of road safety seminars or training.

(xiii) Speed monitoring checks.

DRUNKEN DRIVING

The statistics say that almost 78% of all road accidents in India are caused due to drivers' fault. Drunk driving is the cause of 39% of all casualties. An act of drunk driving can be described as driving a vehicle under the influence of alcohol. Drunken driving is an offence in India, like many other countries worldwide. The object of making it an offence under law is to improve road safety by seeking to bring down the number of accidents and fatalities caused by drivers' fault.

Law on Drunken Driving : In India, while driving a motor vehicle, if a person has a Blood Alcohol Level (BAC) exceeding 30 mg of intake per 100 ml of blood detected by a Breath analyzer, he or she is booked under 'first offence'. This consists of imprisonment for a term, which may extend up to six months or a fine up to ₹ 10,000 or both. For a second or subsequent offense, if committed within three years of the commission of the previous similar offense, he or she will face an imprisonment of a term, which may extend upto two years, or a fine, which may extend up to ₹ 15,000 or both.

The most common violators of drunken driving have been identified as under :

(i) Most truck drivers.
(ii) Person between 16-25 years of age.
(iii) Most people after new year parties or holi celebrations.
(iv) Most people returning from pubs/parties in cities.

Prevention Measures

The following measures can prevent deaths/accidents due to drunk driving :

(i) Never drive after drinks under any circumstances.
(ii) Report cases of drunken driving to police.
(iii) Strict checking and penalty by police, if found drunk while driving.
(iv) Change of Laws to make drunken driving more serious an offence.

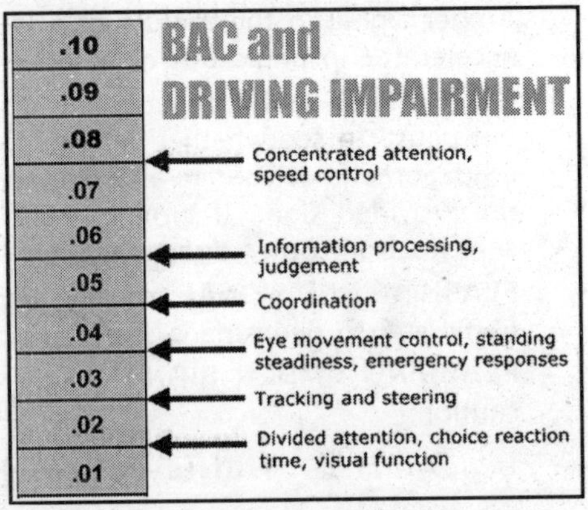

Stringent Penalties for Road Traffic Violations

The revised penalties for road traffic violations are as under :

S.No.	Section	Old Provision/ Penalty	New Provision/ Minimum Penalties
1.	Rules of road regulation violation	₹ 100	₹ 500
2.	Disobedience of orders of authorities	₹ 500	₹ 2000
3.	Unauthorized use of vehicles without license	₹ 1000	₹ 5000
4.	Driving without license	₹ 500	₹ 5000
5.	Driving despite disqualification	₹ 500	₹ 5000
6.	Overspeeding	₹ 400	₹ 2000

7.	Dangerous driving	₹ 1000	₹ 5000
8.	Drunken driving	₹ 2000	₹ 10000
9.	Speeding/Racing	₹ 500	₹ 5000
10.	Vehicle without permit/PUC	₹ 5000	₹ 10000
11.	Without Seat Belt	₹ 100	₹ 1000
12.	Without Helmet	₹ 100	₹ 1000 & Licence disqualification for 3 Months

TRAFFIC SIGNALS AND ROAD SIGNS

- **STOP (Red Signal) :** Stop well before the stop line, and don't crowd the intersection. This not only obstructs a clear view of the intersection for other road users, but also makes the zebra crossing unsafe for pedestrians. You are allowed to turn left at the red signal unless there is a sign specifically forbidding you to do so. When turning, yield the right of way to pedestrians and vehicles from other directions.
- **BE ALERT (Amber Signal) :** The Amber light gives time to vehicles to clear the road when the signal is changing from green to red. If caught in the Amber signal in the middle of a large road crossing do not press your accelerator in panic but do continue with care.
- **GO (Green Signal) :** If first in line, do not go tearing off at the green signal but pause to see whether vehicles from other directions have cleared the road. Sometimes you are allowed to turn left or right too, it all depends on the provided signs. If turning, yield the right of way to pedestrians and vehicles from other directions.
- **FLASHING RED SIGNAL:** You must come to a complete stop, yield to all other traffic and to pedestrians. Proceed only when the way is clear.
- **FLASHING AMBER SIGNAL:** You should slow down and proceed with caution.

Traffic Police Hand Signals

To start one sided vehicles | *To stop vehicles coming from front* | *To stop vehicles approaching from behind* | *To stop vehicles approaching from front and behind*

To stop vehicles approaching from right and left

To start vehicles approaching from left

To start vehicle coming from right

To change sign

To start vehicles on T-point

To manage vehicles on T-point

To give VIP salute

To start one sided vehicles

Mandatory Road Signs

Stop

Give way

No entry

Straight prohibited

One way

One way

Vechicles prohibited in both directions

Horn prohibited

Pedestrians prohibited

Cycle prohibited

Right turn prohibited
Left turn prohibited
U-turn prohibited
Overtaking prohibited
Trucks prohibited
Tonga prohibited
All motor vehicles prohibited
Hand cart prohibited
Bullock cart prohibited
Bullock and hand carts prohibited
50
No parking
No parking NO stopping
Speed limit
4T
Axle load limit
2m
Width limit
3.5m
Height limit
10m
Length limit
5T
Load limit
Restriction ends
Compulsory turn left
Turn right
Ahead or turn left
Ahead or turn right
Ahead
Compulsory keep left
Cycle rickshaw
Slip road ahead (L)
Slip road ahead (R)
Pedestrians only
Buses only

WARNING ROAD SIGNS

INFORMATORY ROAD SIGNS

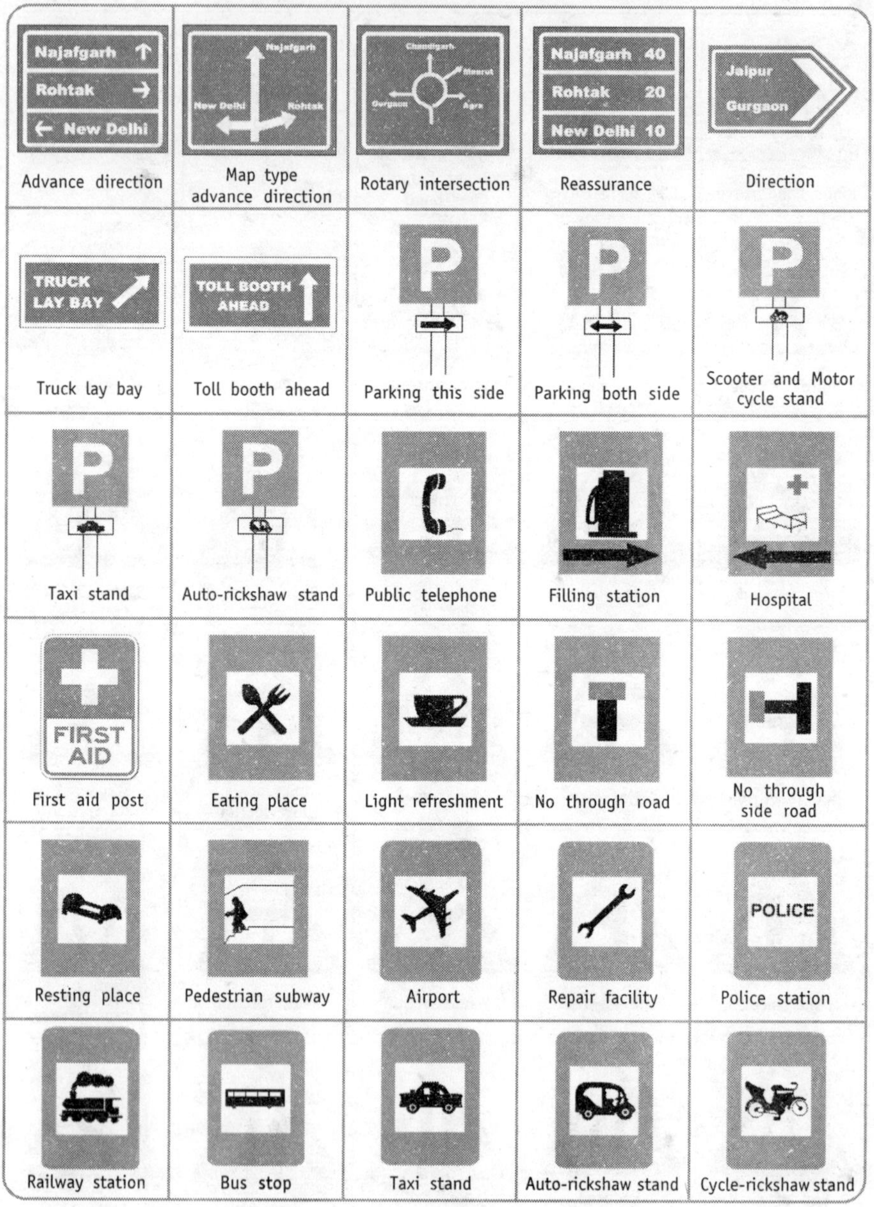

❖ ❖ ❖

CHAPTER

8 Health, Hygiene & Sanitation

THE HUMAN BODY

The human body is the most wonderful machine. To live a healthy life one should have the basic idea of structure and function of every part and organ of human body.

Structure of Human Body

A Human body consists of:

1. Skeleton, 2. Muscles, 3. Blood Circulatory Organs, 4. Respiratory Organs, 5. Digestive Organs, 6. Excretory Organs, 7. Nervous System Organs.

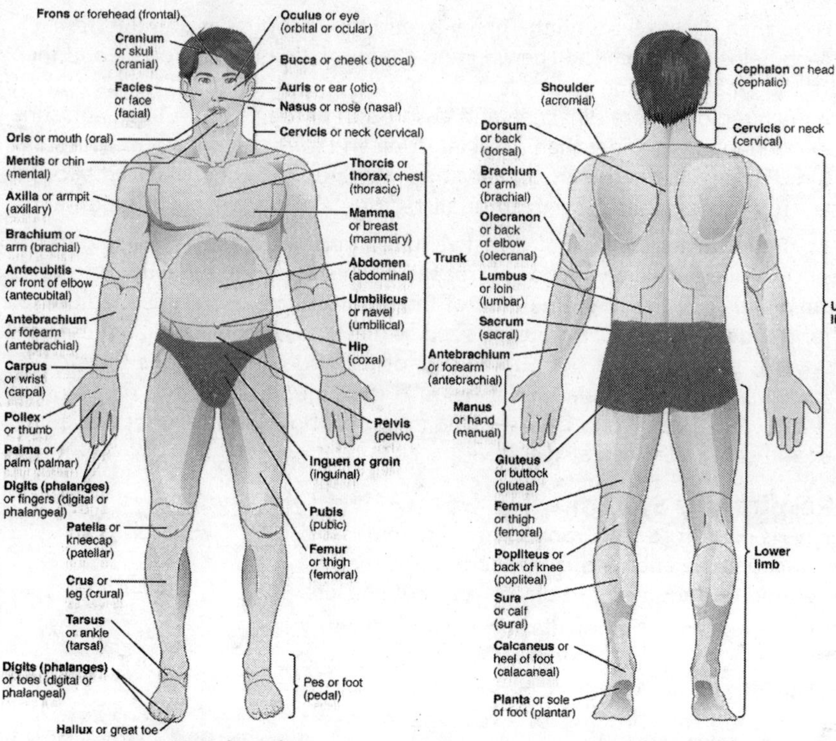

Anterior view **Posterior view**

VARIOUS SYSTEMS OF HUMAN BODY

Digestive System

HUMAN DIGESTIVE SYSTEM

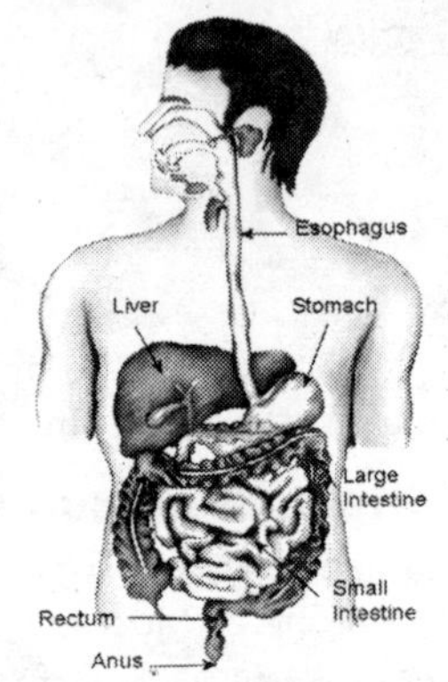

The digestive system consists of alimentary canal and digestive glands. Alimentary canal is about 8-10 metres long tube of varying diameter. Food is taken in through mouth. The tongue helps in ingestion, chewing, tasting and swallowing of food and mixing of food and saliva.

Teeth help in cutting, tearing and grinding the food. Milk teeth start erupting after six months of birth and continue to appear between 6 to 24 months. These temporary teeth are replaced by the permanent teeth between 6 to 12 years. There are 20 temporary teeth while the number of teeth in an adult goes upto 32. Incisors, Canines, Premolars and Molars are the various type of teeth.

Food then passes through the pharynx, and the oesophagus and the stomach. Stomach helps in mechanical chewing and chemical digestion of food. Food then enters the small intestine, which is narrow, tubular and about 20 ft in length. It is the main region where digestion and absorption of food occurs. Large intestine is about 5 ft long but wider than small intestine and forms an arc around the small intestine. It is concerned with conservation of water, minerals and formation of faeces. The faeces after passing through rectum, are thrown out through anus.

As the food travels, several digestive juices get mixed with it, helping in the digestive process. Salivary glands secret saliva which helps in digestion of starch. Gastric glands present in the mucosa of the stomach, provide acidic medium for the food digestion. Liver, the largest sized, reddish brown gland of body, secrets bile. Liver is present in the right upper part of the abdomen. The bile secreted by the liver is stored in gall bladder. It helps in the emulsification and digestion of fats. Pancreas is the second largest gland in human body and secretes pancreatic juices. Intestines also secret digestive juices.

Respiratory System

RESPIRATORY SYSTEM

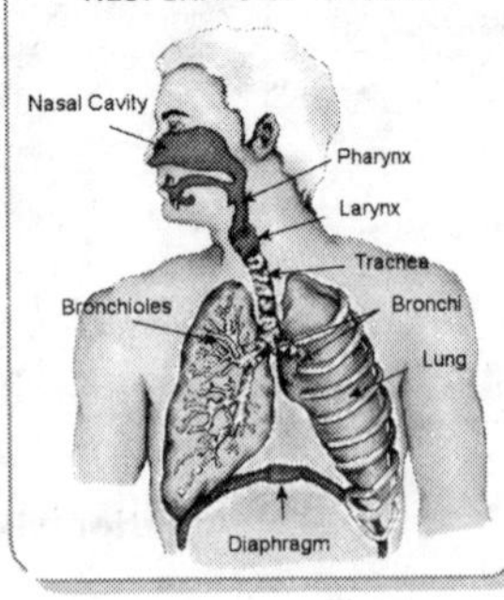

Energy is required for movement, growth and reproduction. The energy thus needed, is obtained by the aerobic oxidation of carbohydrates, proteins, etc.

Glucose + Oxygen $\rightarrow$ Carbon dioxide + Water + Energy

Therefore, oxygen is needed for the oxidation and expelling of carbon dioxide is necessary to avoid its accumulation. This process of exchange of gases between the environment and the body, is called respiration.

In some unicellular organisms like aerobic bacteria, amoeba, hydra, etc. there is direct exchange of gases between the carbon dioxide of the body and oxygen of water. There is no blood for transport of gases. However, in larger and complex form of animals, specialised respiratory organs are developed. Amphibians respire through skin, fishes through gills and mammals, birds and reptiles through lungs.

In human beings, fresh air enters and foul air exits through nostrils. After passing through larynx and trachea (wind pipe), gases enter the primary bronchi which leads them to the lungs.

Lungs are a pair of soft, elastic and spongy organs, present on either side of heart. In the lungs, exchange of gases takes place. A normal adult inspires or expires about 500 ml of gas with each breath and takes about 12 breathes per minute.

Circulatory System

In multicellular organisms, regular supply of oxygen for every cell is needed continuously and constant removal of poisonous products is required. The transport system carrying out these functions is called circulatory system. It helps in transportation of nutrients, respiratory gases, hormones, heat, water and nitrogenous wastes.

HUMAN CIRCULATORY SYSTEM

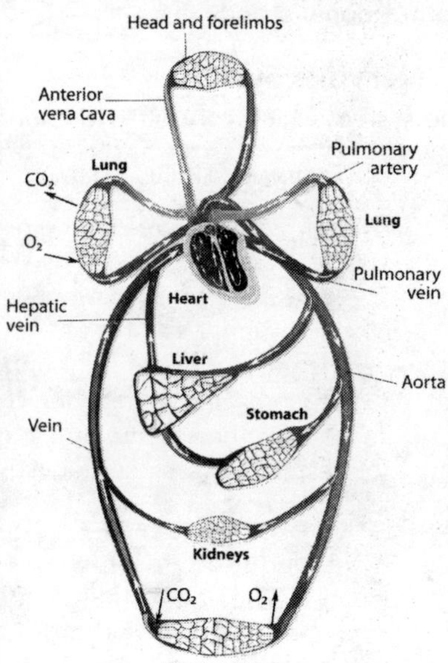

Main components of the circulatory system are heart, blood vessels and blood. Heart is a thick, muscular, contractile and automatic pumping organ. In birds and mammals, heart is divided into four chambers. Arteries are thick walled blood vessels which always carry the blood away from the heart to various body parts. Veins are thin walled blood vessels which always carry the blood from various parts generally to the heart.

Since the heart pumps blood in spurts, the pressure exerted on arteries is different during various stages of the heartbeat. When the heart contracts, there is maximum pressure on the blood vessels. In normal resting adult man, this systolic blood pressure is about 120 mm Hg. When the heart expands, the diastolic blood pressure is measured to be about 80 mm Hg. However, the blood pressure varies with age, elasticity of blood vessels and condition of heart. In an adult healthy person, the normal rate of heart beat at rest is about 70-72 times per minute.

Excretory System

The toxic things that enter our body or are produced during digestion or respiration, must be expelled out of body. Excess of Water is to be expelled out of body to prevent dilution of body fluids. The process of removal of non-gaseous wastes out of body is called excretion.

In men, excretory system is formed of one pair of kidneys, one pair of ureters, a urinary bladder and a urethra. Kidney is about 10 cm long, bean shaped, dark-red and slightly flattened structure. Sweat glands, oil glands, lungs and liver also act as additional excretory organs. In case of kidney failure, a man can be treated by hemodialysis or transplantation of a kidney from a donor's body.

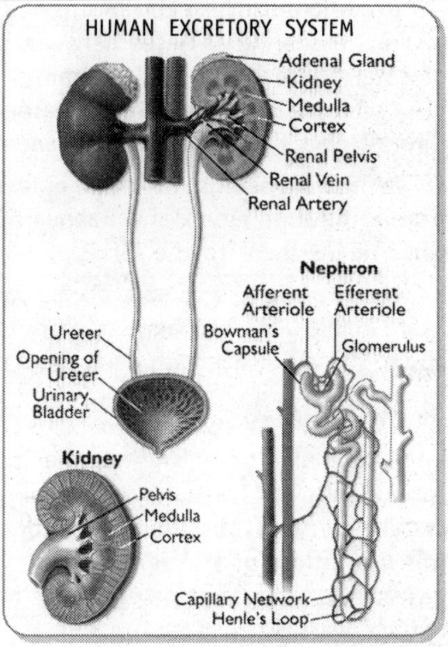

Nervous System

The system which controls and coordinates the body functions, retains memory and receives and sends signals, is called the nervous system. The nervous system comprises brain, spinal cord, nerves and nerve fibres. Human brain weighs about 1200 to 1400 gm. Main parts of the brain are cerebrum, cerebellum and medulla oblongata. Cerebrum controls voluntary functions and is site of intelligence, will power, emotions, etc. Cerebellum controls involuntary functions like heart beat, respiration, etc. Spinal cord is about 45 cm long and about 35 gm in weight. It conducts impulses to and from the brain and controls reflex actions of the body. Various cranial and spinal nerves control smell, vision, movements of body parts, taste and hearing.

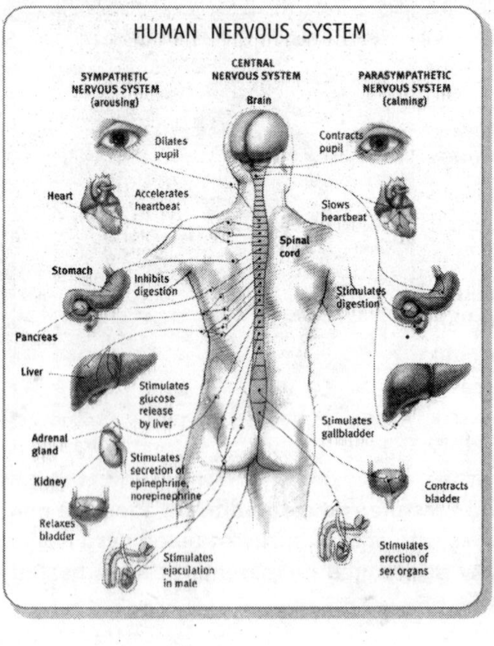

Endocrine System

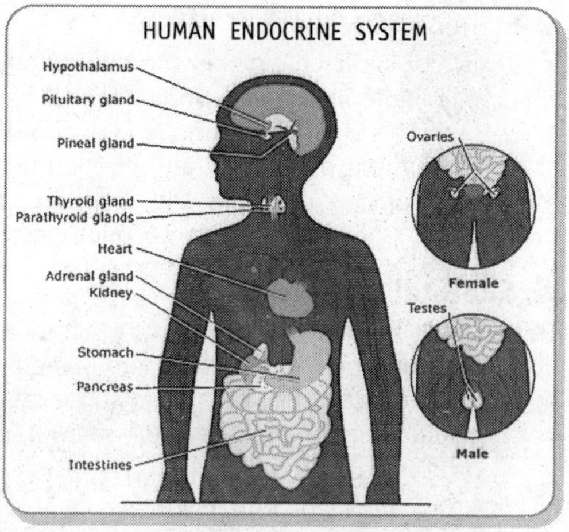

Endocrine glands lack the ducts and generally secrete their secretions into the blood for their transportation to site of action. The secretions are called hormones and stimulate a specific target organ to initiate a specific response. Hormones have slower but widespread physiological effects. Thyroid, parathyroid, adrenal, hypothalamus, pancreas, gonads and pituitary glands are major endocrine glands. Pituitary gland is called the master gland because it controls secretion of hormones from other endocrine glands. The under-secretion and over-secretion of hormones affects the body parts and functioning.

Reproductive System

In sexual reproduction, there is formation and fusion of sex cells, called gametes. Organism develops from the zygote through embryo formation. It generally involves two parents–male and female. The offsprings are different from the parent as variations appear due to new combinations of genes. So, it plays an important role in evolution. All higher plants and animals reproduce sexually.

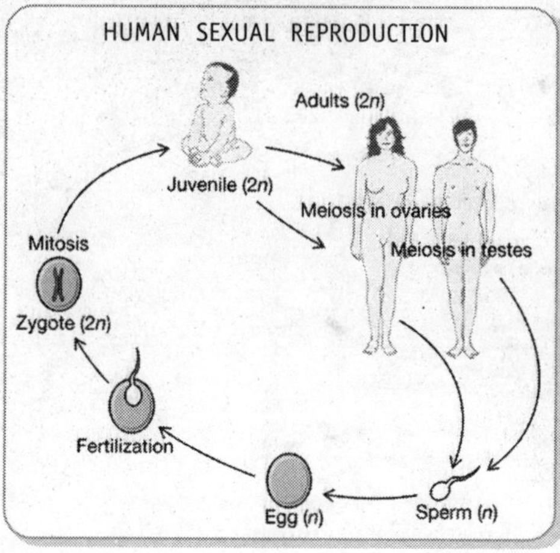

In human beings, primary sex organ of males is a pair of testes. Testes are involved in production of sperms. In females, there is a pair of ovaries, present one on either side of uterus. While millions of sperms are produced at a time, only one egg or ovum is usually produced in about a month. The formation of sperms and ova begin only after a particular age, called puberty. Puberty is attained between 12 and 16 years of age when physiological and hormonal changes take place. The sperms in male are transferred to the vagina of female through penis during copulation. The fertilization may take place, leading to the formation of zygote. The embryo starts developing and around 9 months after the fertilization offspring is born.

Menstrual Cycle

It consists of cyclic changes in the ovaries and the reproductive tracts of females which culminate into the periodic vaginal bleeding. On average, it is completed in 28 days. The bleeding continues for about 4 days. The menstrual cycle begins at the attainment of puberty and continues till the age of 45 to 55 years. When the cycle stops, it indicates the stoppage of egg formation. It is also called menopause. In males, there is no menopause.

Skeletal System

The bony or the skeletal system forms the framework of the body. There are 206 bones in our body. The bones are joined together by fibrous capsules with thickend bands called ligaments. In some cases, bones are fused together and do not have any movement. The skull, sacrum, pelvis etc. are of this type of bones.

HUMAN SKELETAL SYSTEM

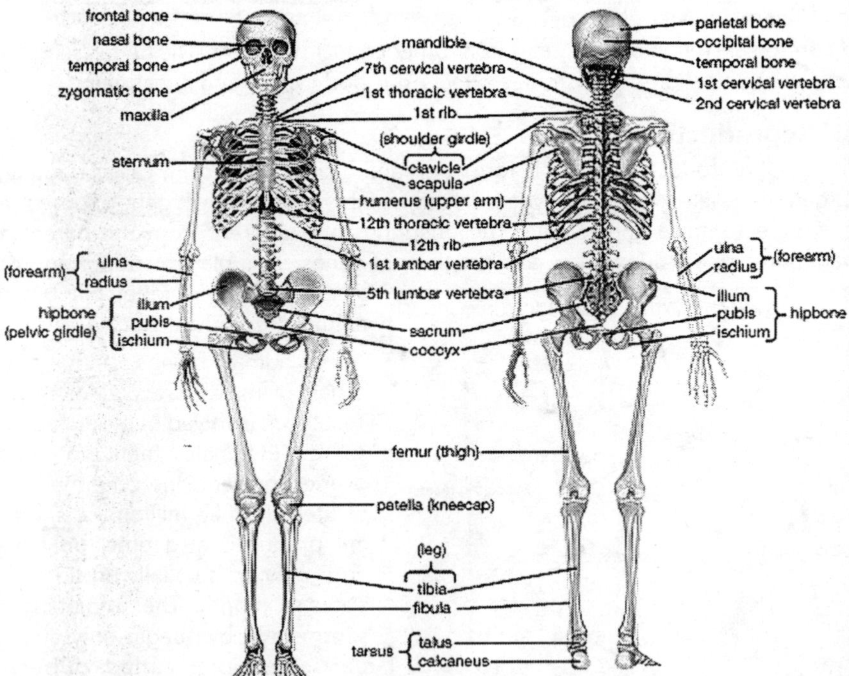

Functions of the Bones

(i) Bones give shape and firmness to the body.
(ii) They protect the delicate organs and soft parts of the body.
(iii) They give attachment to the muscles so that when the muscles contract, the bones move about the joint.

(iv) The bones manufacture red blood cells and some white blood cells.

(v) The skull consists of a large hollow cavity called the cranial cavity. In it lies the brain. Skull is fused mass of bone including the face bones. 32 teeth are fixed in the gums. A tooth has an enamel dentine and the tooth pulp. The tooth enamel is the hardest bone in the body.

(vi) Thorax is the upper portion of the trunk. It consists of a bony cage with 12 vertebrae at the back. The spinal column consists of 33 vertebrae.

Muscular System

There are over 580 muscles in our body. The function of the muscles are:

(i) They give shape to the body.

(ii) Muscles are attached to the bones and when such muscles contract the bones move so that body movement is effected.

(iii) They protect the internal organs. All muscles act in co-ordination. Thus when the extensor muscles contract, the flexor muscles relax, or when the intestinal muscle contracts the intestinal sphincter muscle relaxes.

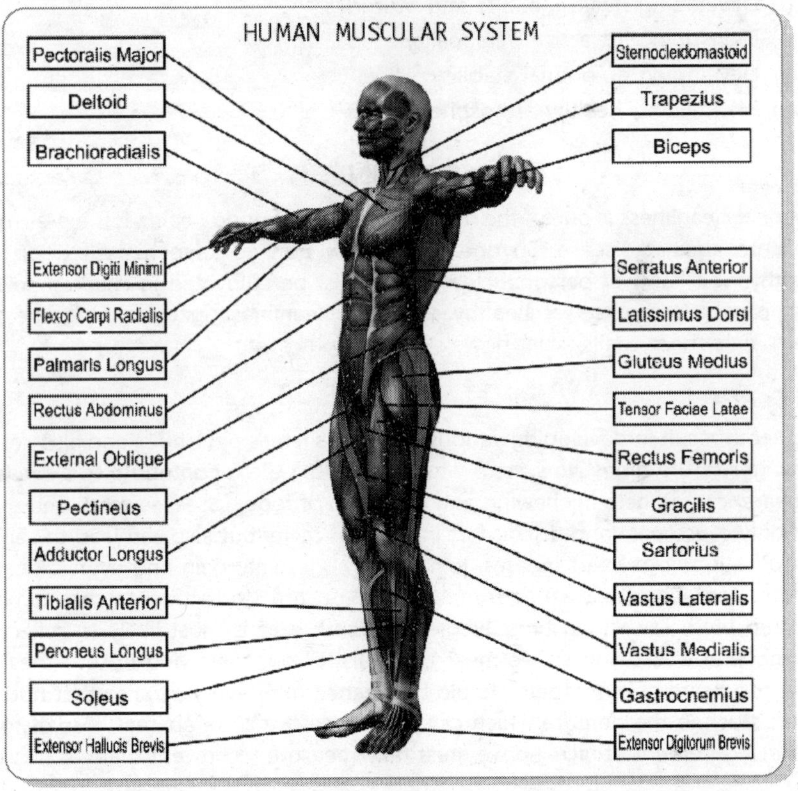

HYGIENE AND SANITATION

The word 'Hygiene' has been derived from Greek word 'Hygienos' which means healthful. However, 'Hygiene is also termed as 'Hygia' in Greek, which means the goddess of health. In the modern times, it means "the art of living". Hygiene is the science which seeks to preserve and improve the health of the individual and of the community as a whole.

Personal Hygiene

It is true that a healthy mind lives in a healthy body. It means that for proper and systematic working of the body it is essential to have proper hygiene, this type of hygiene is called personal hygiene. Good habits serve as an instrument for the promotion of health and long life. Similarly for proper and systematic functioning of the different organs of the body, it is essential to have proper hygiene. Personal hygiene involves all aspects of the health of an individual.

Personal Hygiene helps in:

(i) Developing healthy habits and attitudes
(ii) Developing attractive personality
(iii) Developing emotional stability
(iv) Maintaining healthy atmosphere.

CLEANLINESS

Personal cleanliness is one of the main ingredients of good health. It is a preventive measure against disease. So one must know how to keep himself clean and healthy. The habit of personal cleanliness must be cultivated in children so that they can keep themselves healthy. Personal cleanliness includes: cleanliness of teeth, ears, nose, nails, skin, bowels habit, clothes etc.

Teeth

Bad teeth result in developing various diseases such as pyorrhoea and also causes a danger to the digestive system whereas healthy teeth contribute to a pleasing appearance and help in chewing and digestion of food. Diseased teeth and gums not only cause pain and discomfort in the oral cavity but also can lead to serious complications like heart dieases, joint pain, abdominal pain and even cancer of mouth. Dental health is a matter of life-long concern. Correct dental care can help to keep teeth for a long time. Neglect of teeth care is most likely to reflect on our general well-being so we must take care of our teeth and in turn they will take good care of ours. Teeth should be cleaned after every meal so that nothing is left stuck in the denture which can lead to severe pain, abscess, loss of tooth and disfigurement of face. So we must take measure to prevent them as it is well said, "prevention is better than cure." We must follow such rules regarding healthy teeth:

(i) Brush teeth daily after every meal especially after dinner.
(ii) Brush teeth from up to downward direction and vice-versa.
(iii) Don't eat sweet and sticky food in between meals, children should avoid toffees, candies, chocolates etc.
(iv) Avoid excessive consumption of alcohol, cigarettes, pan chewing to avoid mouth cancer.
(v) Consult dental surgeon regularly. With proper personal and professional care one can keep natural denture throughout life.

Ears

Hygiene of ears is very essential. Ear is a sense organ because we hear things through ears. Good hearing keeps one in active touch with people and events whereas poor hearing makes an individual dull and can lead to serious emotional disturbance. The ear is a delicate organ easily prone to injury. Cadets must learn the precautions to be taken to protect the ear in sports, specifically in swimming and diving. Do not put pins, needles or any sharp thing into the ears. Do not expose ears to loud noise, avoid hitting on ears, don't put hydrogen peroxide in a child's ear. Don't neglect cough or cold. Learn the early signs of deafness. Treat the illness early. If there is discharge or pain in ear, a doctor must be consulted.

Eyes

Eyes are the most important and valuable organs of the body. Every care is essential to retain their sight and keep them healthy. Poor nutrition may cause vision disturbances and inflammatory conditions of eyes and lids, so rich diet is to be taken for better sight. Proper eye hygiene includes good reading habits under lighting conditions and use of glasses when needed. One must practice and learn the following points to protect eyes:

(i) Wash eyes with fresh and clean water.
(ii) Protect the eyes from dust, smoke and bright sunlight and irritating vapours.
(iii) Avoid rubbing eyes with dirty fingers.
(iv) Use clean and separate towel or handkerchief.
(v) If eyes appear red, swollen or watery, consult doctor immediately.
(vi) Playing with bow and arrow, fire crackers, should be discouraged.
(vii) Do not neglect eye strain, consult doctor immediately.
(viii) Disease of diabetes should be effectively treated as early as possible because it can lead to complications related with eyesight.
(ix) Avoid stooping on books, laptops and mobile phones.
(x) Eyesight should be tested regularly.

Nose and Throat

Nose is another important sense organ responsible for giving the idea of smell, and should be kept clean. It is through nose that one breathes and if nose gets stuffed, or disturbed we start breathing through mouth, in such case our respiratory system gets disturbed which can lead to serious lung diseases. Nose should therefore be kept clean, if some problem is experienced in this sense organ, a doctor must be consulted immediately.

Throat is also a vital organ of the body. It is connected with other sense organs like ear, nose, tongue etc. if it is not kept clean, may cause serious disorders. If there is some complaint, one should take medical advice.

Nails and Fingers

The nails are formed by the special horny cells of the epidermis and protect the finger tips of hands and feet. Since hands are used frequently for any work, the nails get dirty very easily and this dirt in the nails becomes a source of infection for food when we touch it with hands. All this dirt may get into our mouth with food and make us sick. It is important to keep the nails of the fingers short, so that no dirt accumulates and chances of infection are reduced. Nails should not be bitten by teeth otherwise dirt of the nails may cause severe ailment of mouth and throat. One must develop the habit of cleaning the hands before cooking, handling and eating food. The nails of the toes be cut straight. The feet should be washed and dried properly before retiring to bed.

Skin

In order to avoid the dangerous effects of polluted atmosphere around us, one has to clean or wash the skin daily. If dirt is allowed to remain over the skin for a long time, it may cause skin diseases. By taking bath the body becomes fresh and remains active. During winter sun-bath may also be practised. Exposure of the body in the sun during winter provides vitamin D and K and improves vitality of the human body, which develops resistance against diseases. The best way to clean the skin or face is with soap and water, dry it with a soft towel by simple patting rather than rubbing. It is advisable to use cold creams in winter particularly when the skin is dry, but care should be taken in case of oily skin and skin with acne. One must avoid over exposure of skin or face to hot weather.

Clothes

One puts on different types of clothes according to various seasons. Clothes should be fit, clean and tidy, as clean dress adds something to one's personality. Preferably clothes should be washed regularly depending on the weather condition and occupation, and then dried in sun. Underclothes which are in direct contact with the body must be cleaned daily because they constantly come in contact with different body secretions and perspiration of skin. They should be made up of cotton as texture synthetic fiber may cause skin allergy. The clothes should be comfortable to the body and must not obstruct breathing and body development. Avoid wearing tight clothes.

Hair

Hair should be brushed or combed with personal brush/comb properly. For healthy hair, these should be washed with a good antiseptic soap or shampoo twice a week and then properly dried up. A gentle massage with oil will improve blood circulation and facilitate proper growth and lustre. The scalp is to be gripped lightly between fingers of both hand and gently moved forward, backward and from side-to-side over the bony skull. If dandruff is there then use anti dandruff shampoo. In case, condition does not improve then consult doctor and follow his instructions carefully. The hair should be free from lice and any other infectious germs.

Bowel

The daily habit of emptying the bowel at regular time should be developed and intentional delay should be avoided. Every child should be given proper training from the very beginning. A good nutritive diet with sufficient amount of roughage, plenty of water intake, regular exercise will help in cleaning the bowel. Frequent intake of junk and fried food should be avoided.

Therefore, one must develop good habit of keeping personal cleanliness up to the mark. Good habits are formed during childhood which last longer. If bad habits are nipped in the bud, it would be very beneficial in the long run for the individual as well as community. As Dr. Fielden said, "Life is like a house, give it good foundation and it shall give you good service for as long as you want it". So if we develop good habits in child to keep him healthy, he will help the society to give his best.

Food & Rest

A balanced diet is essential for a healthy body. Food must be hygienic and cooked properly. It must be taken in sufficient quantity in proper proportion. It should be chewed well. Proper rest, recreation and sleep are also essential for mental and physical health. Clean water is equally important for good health.

Balanced Diet

Our diet usually contains all the nutrients in varying amounts. Rice and bread give us energy. Dal, eggs and meat give us protein, and so on. A diet is balanced if it contains all the nutrients in the correct amount. Carbohydrates and fats provide energy for the body. Proteins provide materials for growth and repair of cellular constituents. Minerals and vitamins are needed to aid vital reactions in cells and tissues and also to regulate body functions. Water plays an important

role in cellular reactions, and other life processes such as digestion, excretion and transport. Alongwith all these, a certain amount of roughage is needed for proper digestion.

FOOD HYGIENE

Food Hygiene is:

1. Protecting food from risk of contamination, including harmful bacteria, poison and other foreign bodies.
2. Preventing any bacteria present multiplying to an extent which would result in the illness of consumers or the early spoilage of the food.
3. Destroying any harmful bacteria in the food by thorough cooking or processing.
4. Discarding unfit or contaminated food.

The Five keys to safe food are:

(i) Keep it clean.
(ii) Separate raw and cooked items.
(iii) Cook thoroughly.
(iv) Keep food at safe temperature.
(v) Use safe water and raw materials.

WATER SUPPLY AND ITS PURIFICATION

Sources of Water

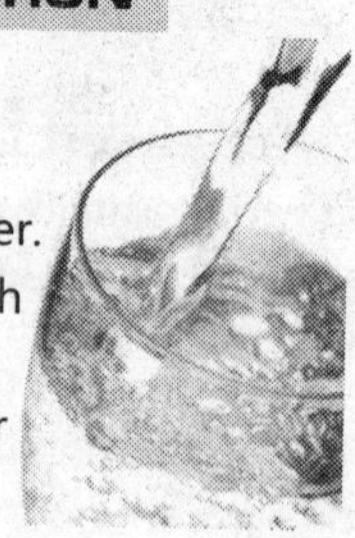

There are three main sources of water:

(i) Rain Water (ii) Surface Water (iii) Underground Water.

* **Rain Water :** It is unfit for drinking as it comes through suspended impurities in the atmosphere.
* **Surface Water :** Lakes and ponds provide good water source only if kept away from pollution.

* **Underground Streams :** Wells are a good source of water supply if protected.

Purification provides good and safe water by eliminating:

(i) Suspended matter (ii) Harmful salts in solution (iii) Disease germs

Method of Purification

The following methods are used for purification of water:

(i) Boiling and Distilling Water : Water is boiled at 100°C for 15-20 minutes.

(ii) Clarification : Removal of suspended matter through filtration by passing it through filters.

(iii) Sterilization : By using chlorine gas or bleaching powder.

(iv) Pinking : By using potassium permangnate for pinking of wells.

(v) Precipitation : By adding alum to water and then passed through a filter.

PHYSICAL AND MENTAL HEALTH

In the past, doctors defined health simply as 'an absence of disease or illness'. However, after the formation of World Health Organization (WHO) in 1948, health is defined as 'a complete state of physical, mental and social well being and not merely the absence of disease or infirmity'.

* **Physical Health :** It is absence of disease and infirmity and is assessed by taking health state measurements of the body.
* **Mental Health :** It refers to the successful performance of mental function, resulting in productive activities, fulfilling relationship with other people, ability to adopt to change and cope up with adversities.

Characteristics of Good Health

Good health is essential condition for a purposeful existence. The main characteristics of good health are:

(i) Absence of all diseases
(ii) Ability to endure strain and stress
(iii) Sense of well-being
(iv) Freedom from anxiety
(v) Cheerfulness
(vi) Sound mental attitude
(vii) Self-confidence and Self-control
(viii) Courageousness
(ix) Ability to work hard with enthusiasm and efficiency

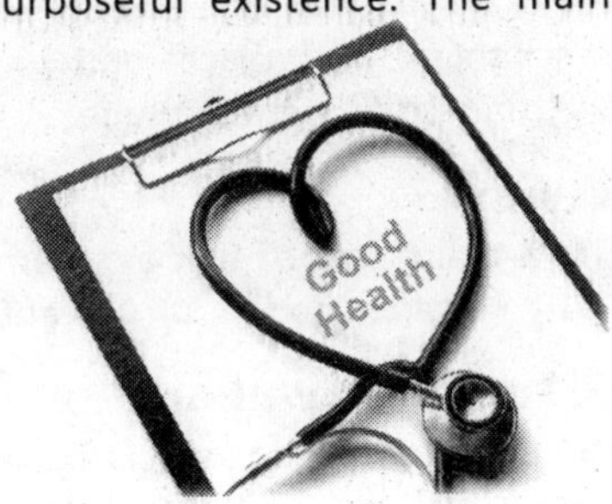

Characteristics of Healthy Mind

(i) Good appetite (ii) Patience

(iii) Cheerful Attitude
(iv) Sweet temper
(v) Good habits
(vi) Good instincts
(vii) Normal physical aptitude
(viii) Acceptance to new ideas
(ix) Sex consciousness

Mental Disorders

Following are some of the indicators of mental disorders:

(i) Bad Temper
(ii) Lack of courage
(iii) Low intelligence
(iv) Depressed and pressimistic outlook
(v) Undue anxiety and Moodiness
(vi) Embarrassment in presence of others

Measures to Improve Mental Health

Following measures will help in improving mental health:

(i) Favorable and stress-free home and school environment.
(ii) Provision of co-curricular activities.
(iii) Provision of educational and vocational guidance/counseling.
(iv) Regular medical examination.

FIRST AID

First Aid is the temporary help given to an injured or a sick person before professional medical treatment can be provided. This timely assistance, comprising of simple medical techniques, is most critical to the victims and is, often, life saving. Any person can be trained to administer first aid, which can be carried out using minimal equipments. Basic training in first aid skills should be taught in school, in work places and, in general, be learnt by all, as it is mandatory to our modern and stressful life.

Aims

The 3 main aims of first aid, commonly referred to as the "3 Ps" are:

(i) Preserve life (ii) Prevent further injury (iii) Promote recovery

First Aid Symbols

Although commonly associated with first aid, the symbol of a red cross is an official protective symbol of the Red Cross. According to the Geneva Convention and other international law, the use of this and similar symbols is reserved for official agencies of the International Red Cross and Red Crescent, and as a protective emblem for medical personnel and facilities in combat situations.

The internationally accepted symbol for first aid is the white cross on a green background.

First Aid Kits

First Aid Kits help in any emergency. If someone is injured, cut, burned, emergency first aid kits come in handy. Few injuries do not require immediate medical attention. Knowing how to treat minor injuries using a first aid kit can make a difference in an emergency. Items for a first-aid kit are as follows:

- Sterile adhesive bandages in assorted sizes
- Small roll of absorbent gauze or gauze pads of different sizes
- Adhesive tape
- Triangular and roller bandages
- Cotton (1 roll)
- Band-aids
- Scissors
- Pen torch
- Latex gloves (2 pair)
- Tweezers
- Needle
- Moistened towels and clean dry cloth pieces
- Antiseptic
- Thermometer
- Tube of petroleum jelly or other lubricant
- Assorted sizes of safety pins
- Cleansing agent/soap

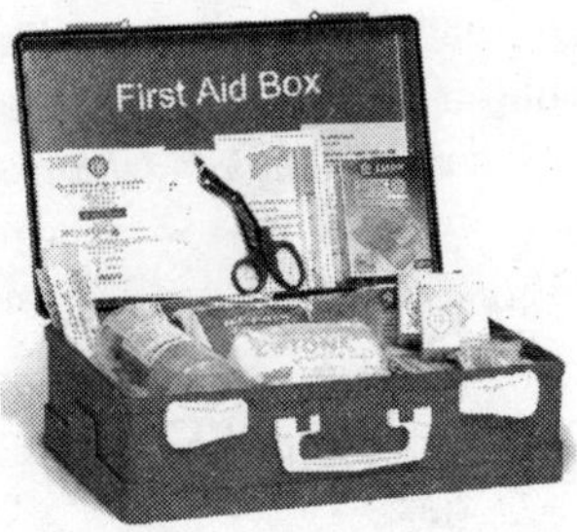

Non-prescription Drugs

- Anti-diarrhoeal medications, tablets
- Potassium Iodide
- Aspirin or non-aspirin pain reliever
- Antacid (for upset stomach)
- Laxatives (for constipation)

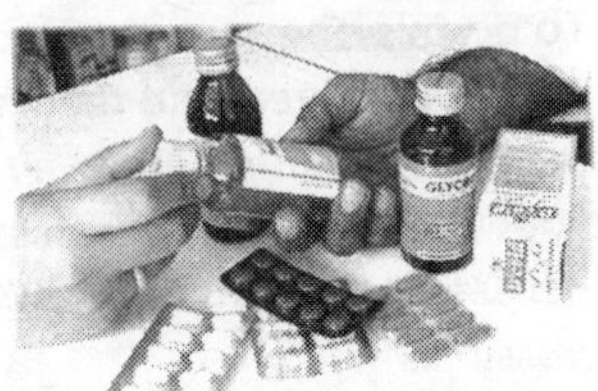

Important Points for First Aid

(i) Move the patient to a safer place.

(ii) Either take-off or loosen his clothes and make him "lie-down" in a convenient position.

(iii) Give "artificial respiration" if required.

(iv) Stop the blood oozing out.

(v) Use proper and regular equipments for First Aid.

(vi) The first-aider should have confidence, common sense, and ability to take a right and prompt decision.

FIRST AID IN COMMON MEDICAL EMERGENCIES

It is very important for all cadets to have knowledge of providing First Aid in common medical emergencies. There will be a number of occasions on which you may be required to provide First Aid to the injured because of an accident or due to a calamity.

Artificial Respiration or Resuscitation

The process of breathing in and breathing out of air is called respiration.

Artificial Respiration is the air provided externally to a living body. It is given at the time, when a person is not able to respire naturally. It is given in different circumstances:

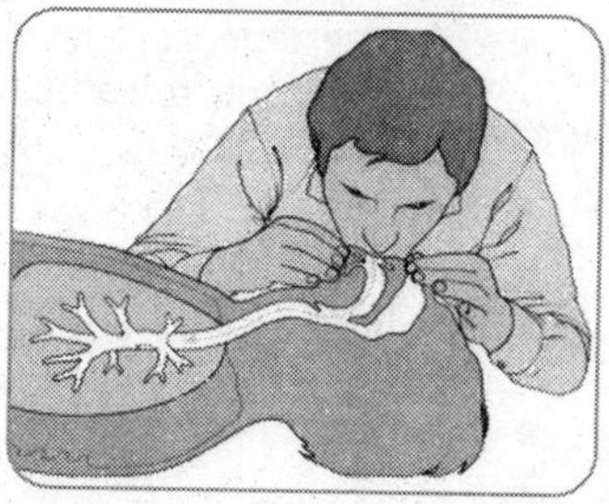

(i) when a person drowns.
(ii) when a person receives an emotional shock.
(iii) when a person receives an electric shock.
(iv) when a person is affected by a poisonous gas.

Treatment

If a person has ceased to breath then immediately place him on his back, and press the top of head backwards so as to extend the head. Pull the chin forward to make a clear airway. If the person is still not breathing, perform mouth-to-mouth resuscitation immediately to save life.

To do this open your mouth and take a deep breath. Close the person's nostrils with your fingers and then seal his mouth with your lips (keeping the head held back all the time). Blow air into his mouth until the chest rises, then remove your mouth and watch his chest deflate. Repeat this operation as long as is necessary at normal breath rate but give the first four blows as rapidly as possible.

Unconsciousness

Head injury, excessive bleeding, cardiac arrest, hysteria, electric shock, intake of sleeping pills, excessive intake of drugs (narcotic), results in unconsciousness. It may be partial or complete (coma).

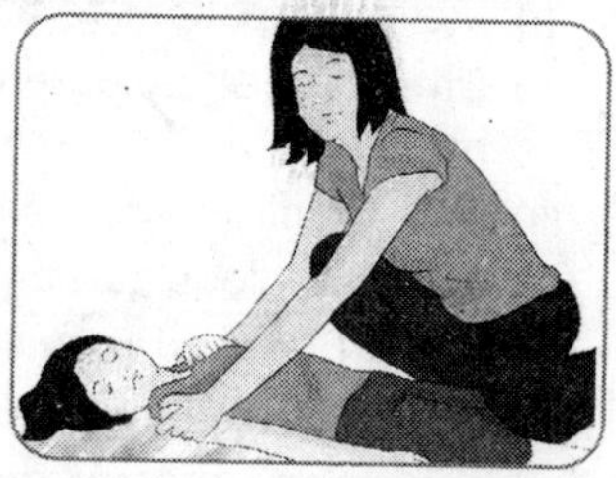

Treatment

(i) Make patient lie flat on his back with head turned to one side, in a convenient position, so that he may breath freely.

(ii) In convulsion, put spoon wrapped in handkerchief between jaws to prevent biting of tongue.
(iii) Loosen the clothes.
(iv) Give artificial respiration if required.
(v) Do not give an oral diet.

Nasal Bleeding

Sometimes, due to excessive heat or injury, nose starts bleeding. This is quite common in children.

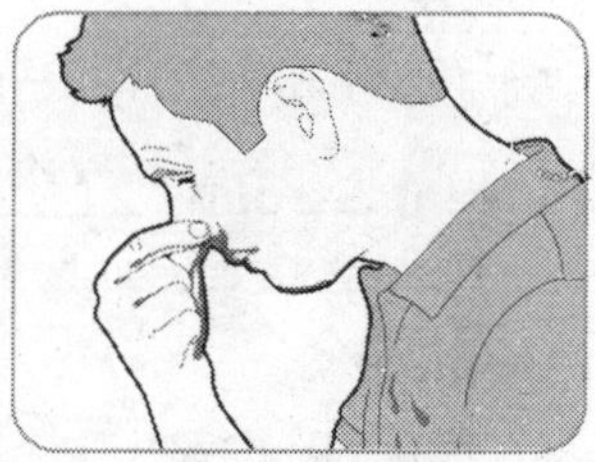

Treatment

(i) Bring the person in open-air.
(ii) Place the head of the patient at the back, to avoid excessive bleeding, by changing the direction of blood flow.
(iii) Loosen the clothes of the patient.
(iv) Give mouth to mouth respiration.
(v) Put ice-bag on the patient's head.
(vi) Make him smell the yellow clay (Multani Mitti).
(vii) Keep the feet of the patient in lukewarm water, so that the blood flows downwards.
(viii) Press the nose gently for few minutes.

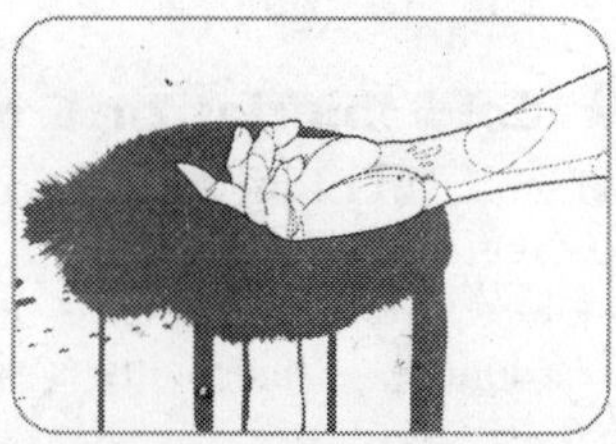

Bleeding

Bleeding from a wound is very common for all.

Treatment

Direct pressure on an open, clean wound will usually control the bleeding. This can be done by pressure by the fingers or hand, but if readily available use a sterile dressing with an adequate pad, and bandage firmly in position. A tourniquet should never be used.

Burns and Scalds

Burns may be produced by heat, scald is produced by steam. If a limb is affected, immerse the part immediately in cold water to relieve the pain. Then cover the part (including any burned clothing) with a dry sterile dressing or freshy laundered material such as tea cloth. If burns are severe, treat for shock and get medical aid as quickly as possible. Do not use ointment or oil dressings.

Treatment

(i) Protect burn area by applying bandage or covering with a clean cloth.

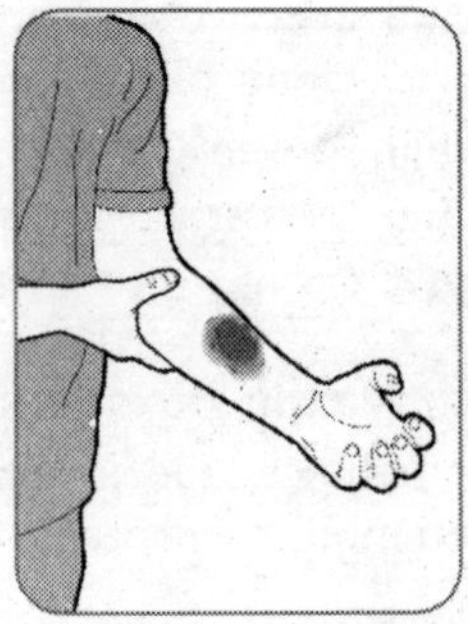

(ii) Keep the patient in lying posture.
(iii) Keep him warm.
(iv) Give plenty of fluids.
(v) Give pain-killer to him, if necessary.
(vi) Do not take-off the clothes of the burnt person.
(vii) Do not rupture the blisters.
(viii) Do not apply anything on the blisters.
(ix) If the burn is due to acid, keep pouring water on the affected part.
(x) Take him quickly, to the hospital.

Heat Stroke

Heat Strokes are caused by high temperature of the atmosphere.

Treatment

(i) Give plenty of saline water to the patient.
(ii) Remove the clothes of the patient and make him lie down in open-air shade.
(iii) Pour cold water on the body.
(iv) Give artificial respiration or take him to the hospital if the need be.

Cold Injuries or Frost Bite

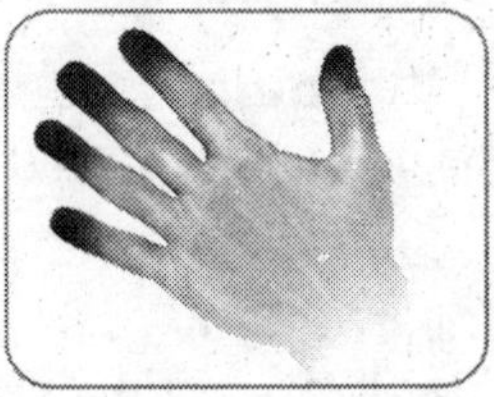

When a part of the body becomes inactive or numb due to excessive exposure of cold, it is called frost bite. There are several other problems that arise due to cold, called cold injuries. Chill Blains is such an example.

Treatment

(i) Quickly warm the affected part with lukewarm water.
(ii) If lukemarm water is not available, cover the affected part with a woolen fabric or keep it in warm hands but do not rub it, and give aspirin as a painkiller.

Drowning

When a person drowns in water his lungs are filled with water.

Treatment

(i) Make patient lie flat on his abdomen and apply pressure on the upper abdominal area to remove water.
(ii) Clean his throat and mouth.

(iii) Give artificial respiration.

(iv) Give a light massage to the heart.

Choking

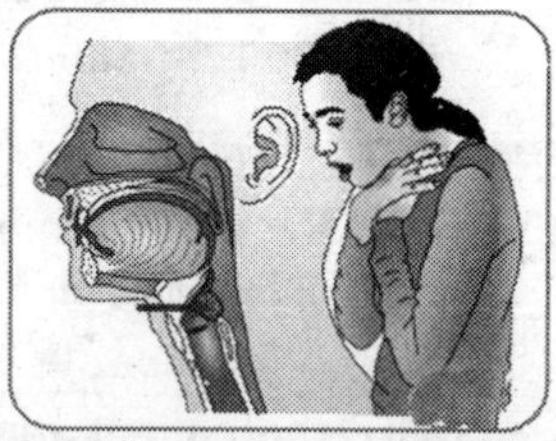

This is usually caused by food or some foreign body, getting into the wind pipe and can often be cured by getting the person to bend over and then thumping with the flat of the hand between the shoulder blades. A small child can be held upside down and thumped. If this does not work, tickle the back of the throat with the finger tips in an attempt to make the person cough or vomit. If neither method succeeds, get medical help at once.

Electric Shock

If the person is still in contact with electrical equipment and you cannot switch off the electricity, do not touch him unless protected by rubber soles or rubber gloves. Apply artificial respiration and treat for burns and shock as necessary.

Poisoning

A substance that causes death or harm when introduced into or absorbed by a living organism, is called Poison. A living body can be poisoned by poisonous food, drink, gas, smoke and alcohol etc.

If someone is believed to have swallowed poison, send for medical help at once, even if no effects have appeared. Have the poison container ready to show to the doctor. Corrosive acid or alkaline poison such as oceosote, ammonia, caustic soda, strong carbolic and oxalic and other acids will all burn or stain the lips and mouth. Give water at once but not an emetic.

If the poison is known to be an acid such as oxalic, nitric or sulphuric acid, rinse the mouth with an alkali such as magnesia, chalk and water or milk and water. If the poison is an alkali such as ammonia or caustic soda, give an acid drink such as vinegar or lemon juice in water. Slow pulse, pallor, sleepiness and in some cases, pin-point pupils are symptoms of an overdose of narcotics such as sleeping pills. Give emetic and try to keep the victim awake. For gas poisoning, give the patient fresh air, artificial respiration and warmth and send for doctor.

Poisons are of various kinds, they affect different parts of the body and have different treatments.

- Intake of "sodium hydroxide", "sulphuric acid" and "potasium hydroxide" results in burning of throat and mouth and severe abdominal pain.
- Intake of "arsenic" and "mercury" leads to vomitting and diarrhoea.
- Intake of morphine and poisoned alcohol results in unconsciousness and weakening of metabolic processes of the body.

Treatment

1. Bring the patient immediately to the hospital.
2. If possible, write down the name of the poison.
3. If the poison-bottle is empty, take it along with the patient.
4. Make the patient vomit.

If the patient is in his senses and the poison has been identified, give the following first aid:

(i) If poison is acidic in nature, give alkaline substances to counter the effect, like—sodawater, chalk, milk of magnesia.
(ii) If poison is alkaline in nature, give acids like—lime water, plenty of water.
(iii) If sleeping pills have been taken, give saline water to the patient.
(iv) If morphine has been taken, give potasium permangnate to the patient and make him vomit.
(v) If the patient is affected with a poisonous gas, make him lie down in open-air and give some tea and milk of magnesia.

Shock

Serious burns or injury always cause shock. The person is pale, his skin is cold and clammy, his breathing quick and irregular and his pulse fast. He should be lying down with head low and hips and legs raised a little, keep him warm and if he is conscious, give him a warm sweet drink but no stimulants. Keep him quiet and reassure him, shock can also occur after quite minor accidents.

Foreign Body in the Eye

Lifting the upper eyelid over the lower will often bring the foreign body on the lower lid from which it can be removed or making the eyes water by rubbing the other eye or blowing the nose will sometimes help. If the object is clearly visible, the torn and moisturised edge of a piece of soft paper can be used to remove it. Never use tweezers and

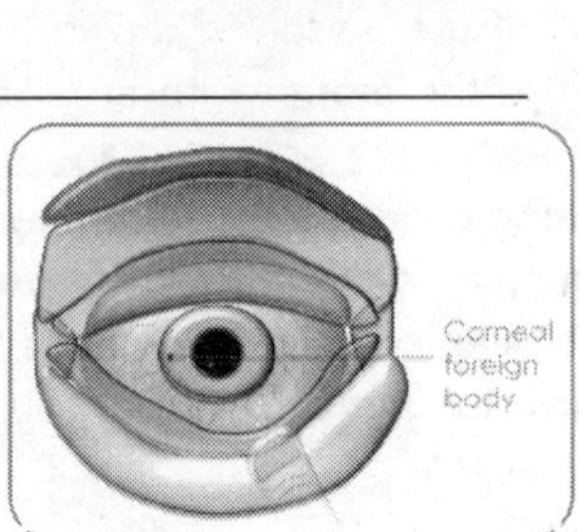

never rub the injured eye. If the object appears to be embedded in the eyeball, leave it for the doctor to remove.

Snake Bite

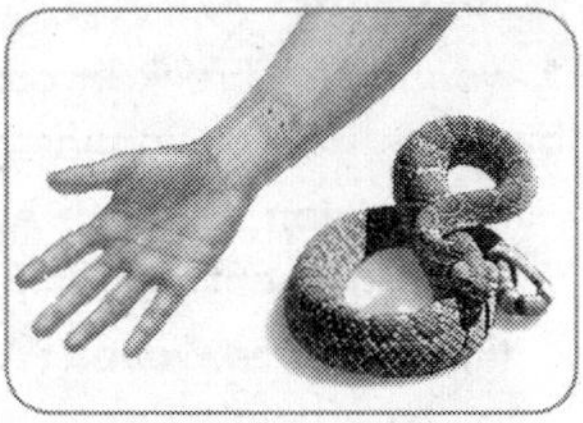

In snake bite, the poison is injected by the snake through a pair of hollow and deeply grooved biting fangs. The majority of bites occur on parts of limbs which are exposed like hands, feet and lower legs.

First Aid

All cases of Snake bite should be treated as being bitten by poisonous snakes. The first aid treatment will be as follows:

(i) Make the victim lie down comfortably.

(ii) Give convincing reassurance against fright and fear of death.

(iii) Apply a light constricting tourniquet with handkerchief, bandage or shoe lace above the knee for a bite on the leg and above the elbow for a bite on the arm so that the poison does not flow to all parts of the body.

(iv) Wash the wound with soap and water. Use water freely.

(v) Suck the blood with a suction pump if available.

(vi) Evacuate the patient quickly to the nearest dispensary or hospital.

(vii) If breathing fails, start artificial respiration immediately.

Scorpion Bite

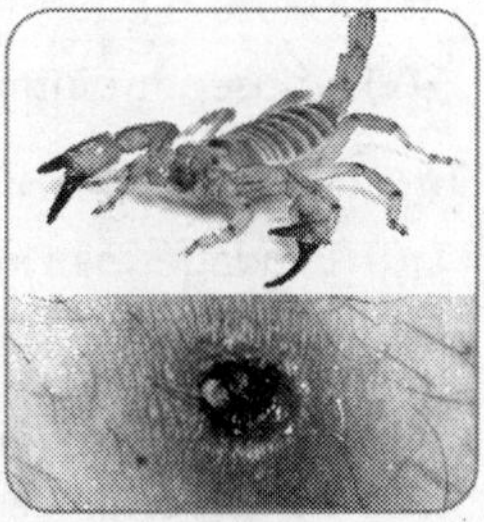

Bite by a scorpion should be treated as a snake bite only.

First Aid

(i) If blood has been drawn, the wound should be cleaned well with antiseptic lotion.

(ii) Evacuate casualty to the nearest dispensary or hospital.

Rabid Dog Bite

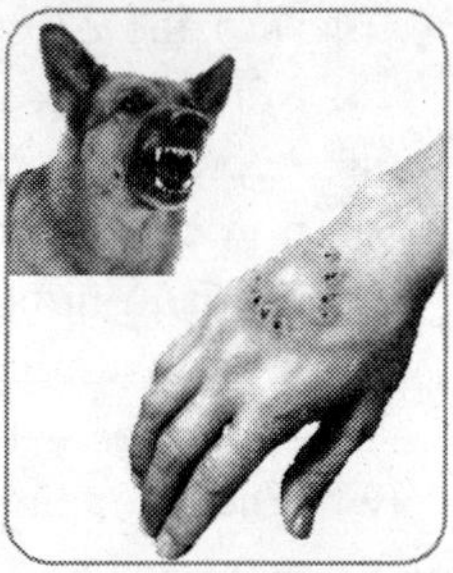

Rabies is a very dangerous disease transmitted by a rabid dog. The disease is preventable by giving anti-rabies vaccine.

First Aid

(i) Immediately wash the wound with soap and water.

(ii) Wound should be cleaned with available antiseptic.

(iii) Patient should be sent to hospital for an anti-rabies injection course.

(iv) Dog and the patient should be kept under observation for at least 10 days.

DRESSING OF WOUNDS

Wound

A wound is a break in continuity of the skin or muscle membrane. It is caused by some injury. Wounds can be classified as below:

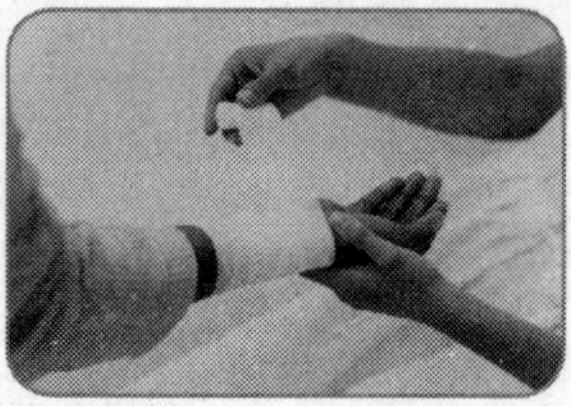

(i) **Incision Wound :** A wound caused by a sharp instrument like knife, razor etc.

(ii) **Punctured Wound :** A deep narrow wound caused by a pointed instrument like knife, bayonet etc.

(iii) **Contusion :** It is an injury or a bruise caused by a blow or blunt instrument.

(iv) **Lacerated Wound :** A wound caused by a blunt instrument. The edges of wound are torn or uneven.

(v) **Gun Shot Wound :** A wound caused by a bullet. It may become complicated with fracture if bullet strikes a bone.

(vi) **Shell Wound :** It is caused by splinters of a shell or grenade.

First Aid of Wounds

Articles Required:

(i) Antiseptic lotion
(ii) Cotton
(iii) Gauze piece
(iv) Bandage of different size and band aid
(v) Antiseptic ointment or powder
(vi) Scissors

The Roller Bandage and its Application: The sizes of various bandages are:

(i) Bandage for Finger – 1" wide
(ii) Bandage for Head and Arm – 2½"
(iii) Bandage for Trunk – 6"
(iv) Bandage for Leg – 3½"

The General Rules of Bandages are:

(i) Face the causality.

(ii) Hold the head of the bandage in the right hand.

(iii) Apply the outer side of the free end to the part, and where possible, lock it in position by a superimposed turn.

(iv) Bandage firmly from below upwards and from within outwards over the front of the limb.

(v) Apply the layer of the bandage so that it covers neither too tight nor too loose.

(vi) When completed, secure the bandage by a safety pin or adhesive strapping.

Procedure:

(i) Reassure and place the patient in a comfortable position.
(ii) Stop the bleeding.
(iii) Remove foreign body, if any.
(iv) Clean the wound with antiseptic lotion and cotton.
(v) Apply antiseptic ointment or powder and cover it with gauze.
(vi) Bandage clockwise from outer aspect to inner aspect.
(vii) Tie the knot away from the wound.
(viii) Bandage should neither be too tight nor too loose.

FRACTURES AND TREATMENT

Fracture

A fracture is a break or discontinuity in a bone resulting in the failure of the supporting framework of the body.

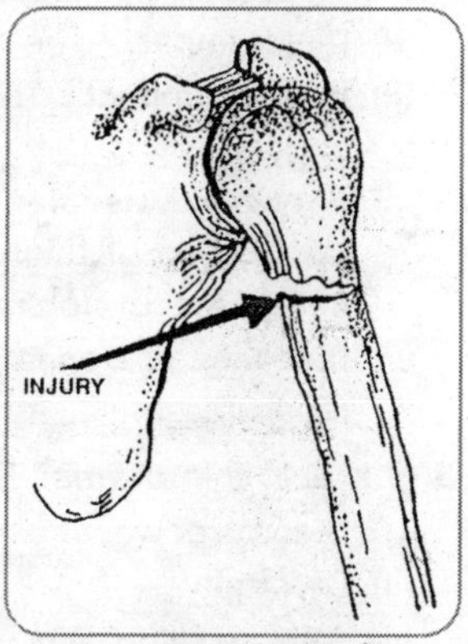

Types of Fractures

There are many kinds of fractures. Common types include simple, compound, multiple, comminuted, greenstick, spiral and stress complicated fractures.

(i) Simple Fracture: In a simple fracture, a bone breaks, but the skin over it does not.

(ii) Compound Fracture: In a compound fracture, both the bone and skin break, and there is danger of infection.

(iii) Multiple Fracture: Multiple fracture means there is more than one fracture in a bone.

(iv) Comminuted Fracture: Comminuted fracture means the bone has splintered, or shattered, usually owing to a crushing injury.

(v) Spiral Fracture: A spiral fracture results when a bone is broken by a twisting force.

(vi) Greenstick Fracture: In a greenstick fracture, the break occurs only part way through the bone.

(vii) Impacted Fracture: When the broken ends of both the bones are driven into one another.

(viii) Communicated Fracture : When the bone is broken into several pieces.

(ix) Stress Fractures : A stress fracture is an overuse injury. It occurs when muscles become fatigued and are unable to absorb added shock. Eventually, the fatigued muscle transfers the overload of stress to the bone causing a tiny crack called a stress fracture.

One can detect a fracture in several ways. Usually, there is pain, soreness, or tenderness in a fracture area. Swelling and discolouration also occur. Sometimes, there is a movement of the bone under the skin and obvious deformity. Crepitus often signals a broken bone. Crepitus is a harsh grating sound caused when the broken ends of the bone rub together. In some cases, only an X-ray reveals a fracture. Fractures require specialized medical treatment. The injured part of the body should be immobilized until skilled help become available.

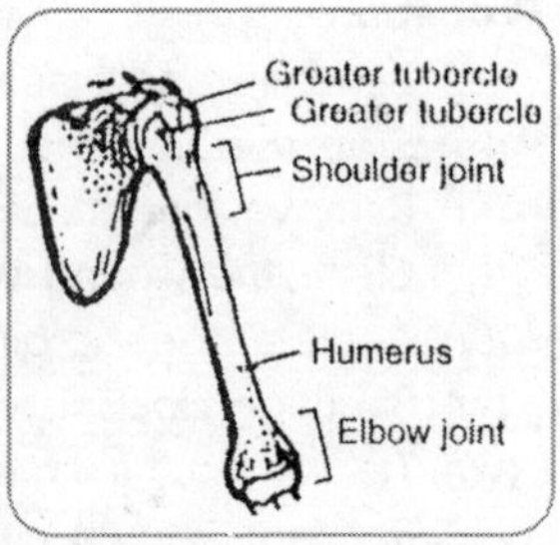

Causes of Fractures

A fracture can be caused by:

- **(i) Direct Impact :** The bone breaks by a direct impact of a kick, blow, bullet etc.
- **(ii) Indirect Impact :** The bone breaks at some distant place from the spot of impact.
- **(iii) Forcible Muscular Contraction :** Fracture like patella (knee cap) by contraction of thigh muscle and fracture of ribs by violent coughing may be caused by forcible musculer contraction.
- **(iv) Diseases of Bones :** Some diseases of bones make them weak and easily breakable.

Signs and Symptoms: The Signs and Symptoms of fractures are:

- (i) Loss of power
- (ii) Abnormal mobility
- (iii) Deformity
- (iv) Grating sound
- (v) Pain, swelling and tenderness

First Aid for Fractures : The first aid measures for fractures are:

- (i) Do not meddle with the fracture.
- (ii) Reassure the patient and make him comfortable.
- (iii) Keep the patient warm.
- (iv) Relieve him of discomfort and pain.
- (v) Apply splints to immobilise the fracture.

First Aid for Compound Fracture : The first aid for Compound Fractures are:

- (i) Do not meddle.
- (ii) Remove foreign objects, if any.
- (iii) Check Bleeding.
- (iv) Cover the wound.
- (v) Apply splints.
- (vi) Shift to the nearest hospital.

Dislocation

A dislocation refers to the displacement of one or more bones at a joint. The joints frequently dislocated are shoulder, elbow, thumb, finger and lower jaw.

Signs and Symptoms

(i) Severe pain
(ii) Swelling at the joint
(iii) Deformity of joint
(iv) Loss of power

First Aid

(i) Do not meddle with the dislocation.
(ii) Apply cold compress.
(iii) Immobilize the joint.
(iv) Take the patient to the nearest hospital.

Sprain

A sprain is the wrenching of the ligaments and tissues around the joint.

Signs and Symptoms

(i) Pain (ii) Swelling (iii) Inability to move

First Aid

(i) Place the joint in a comfortable position and apply a firm bandage.
(ii) Keep the bandage wet with cold water to avoid swelling.
(iii) Gently massage over the muscle and apply a crepe bandage.
(iv) Give pain killers.

Strains

A strain refers to the over-stretching of a muscle.

Signs and Symptoms

(i) Sharp pain.
(ii) Exertion is difficult.
(iii) Swelling or severe cramp.

First Aid

(i) Place the patient in a comfortable position.
(ii) Give cold compress.
(iii) Support the injured part.

Preventive measures for Sprains and Strains

No one is immune to sprains and strains, but here are some tips to help in reducing the injury risk:

1. Daily workout to build muscle strength.
2. Do stretching exercises daily.
3. Always wear properly fitting shoes.
4. Nourish your muscles by eating a well-balanced diet.
5. Warm up before any sports activity including practice.
6. Use or wear-protective equipment appropriate for that sport.

Crepe Bandage

It is a bandage made of elastic material which stretches and binds firmly around the joint and helps in reducing swelling and movements at the affected joint, thus minimising pain and giving it rest. It is used in sprains and strains around joints. It can be washed and used again any number of times.

HAEMORRHAGE

When there is bleeding in the body on getting an injury or a cut with a knife, blade or cutter etc, this condition is called haemorrhage.

It is of two types:

(i) External haemorrhage (ii) Internal haemorrhage

External Haemorrhage

It is visible with the naked eye. Normally, haemorrhage takes place when tissues, arteries or veins are damaged. A very simple method to stop the bleeding is to tie the wound with the help of a bandage.

Arterial Bleeding

Sometimes, a person gets his artery or vein, cut or damaged during accident etc. It is quite essential to stop the bleeding. The colour of this blood is bright red. It flows from the heart with jerks.

Treatment

(i) The person should be made to lie down.
(ii) The affected part should be raised above the heart level and washed with an antiseptic solution.
(iii) Cotton pad should immediately be placed on the wound and then dressed with the help of a bandage.
(iv) The dressing should be done firmly.
(v) Take the patient to the doctor if the bleeding doesn't stop.

Veinal Bleeding

The blood which is flowing in veins, is impure blood. It is dark red or purple in colour, it flows without jerks towards the heart.

Treatment

(i) The affected part should be kept below the heart level, because, veinous blood flows in upward direction towards the heart.
(ii) The "tincture iodine" powder should be sprinkled on the wound, and then dressed with a neat bandage.

(iii) If bleeding does not stop, tie the bandage more firmly.
(iv) Keep the ice or ice-soaked cloth on the wound to stop the bleeding.

Bleeding from the Tissues

When we get some injury or cut by some sharp instrument, our tissues get damaged along with the skin and flesh which leads to bleeding.

Treatment

(i) Hold and press the wound for 4-5 minutes.
(ii) Sprinkle some "Potash alum" powder on the wound and dress the area.

internal Haemorrhage

Many a time a sudden injury does not cause an external wound or cut but, the tissues inside the body get damaged, which leads to internal bleeding. Internal haemorrhage occurs inside the body and is not visible from outside. This can be treated by a doctor only. Victim should be moved to hospital immediately in this case.

Symptoms

(i) Difficulty in breathing
(ii) Uneasiness, nervousness
(iii) Face turns pale
(iv) Palpitation
(v) Lowering of pulse-rate
(vi) Lowering of body temperature
(vii) Sweating, even in winters

Treatment

(i) Rush the patient to the doctor.
(ii) Give ice to suck or chilled water to the patient.
(iii) Do not let the patient eat or drink anything else.
(iv) Recognise the place of bleeding and place ice over there.
(v) Patient must be kept in an open and airy place.

EVACUATION OF CASUALTIES

Natural calamities like earthquake, cyclones, tsunamis, floods, landslides and avalanches occur unannounced leading to large scale casualties. People in large numbers become victim to train, aircraft and road accidents. Advance preparation should be made to combat any such eventuality.

Advance Preparation

Before the casualties begin to arrive

(i) Convert a sheltered place into a first aid post, if no First Aid Post is available.
(ii) Collect First Aid Boxes and sterilized cloth and cotton.

(iii) Collect some blankets, cots and durries.

(iv) Arrange for some clean drinking water.

After a casualty arrives, note:

(i) The details of the accident.

(ii) The signs of the suffering.

(iii) The symptoms of the suffering.

Treat in the following manner:

(i) Reassure the patient.

(ii) Ask on-lookers not to crowd.

(iii) If bleeding, dress the wound.

(iv) If bones are broken, apply splints.

(v) If feeling asphyxia, give artificial respiration.

(vi) It case of burning, cover the wounds with sterile dressing.

(vii) In case of poisoning, try to remove the poison from the body.

A First Aider should make all efforts to revive the patient so that the condition does not get worse. Never perform the functions of a doctor and send the casualty to the nearest hospital.

METHODS OF CARRYING A PATIENT

A patient or victim may be carried in many different ways. It is not necessary that a stretcher or required number of persons for carrying are always available. In such situations following methods can be employed as per the situation:

1. *When One Rescuer*

(i) Human Crutch

(ii) Pick-a-back (reverse)

(iii) Rescue Crawl

(iv) Removal Downstairs

(v) Bowline Drag

(vi) Toe Drag

2. *When Two or more Rescuers*

(i) Firemen's lift

(ii) Two-handed seat

(iii) Three-handed seat

(iv) Four-handed seat

(v) Fore and Aft method

(vi) Two-man human crutch

(vii) Cloth/Blanket lift

3. *With Improvised Stretcher*

A stretcher is prepared by the help of blankets, sheets or rugs and using small poles, bamboos etc.

Methods of CARRYING A PATIENT

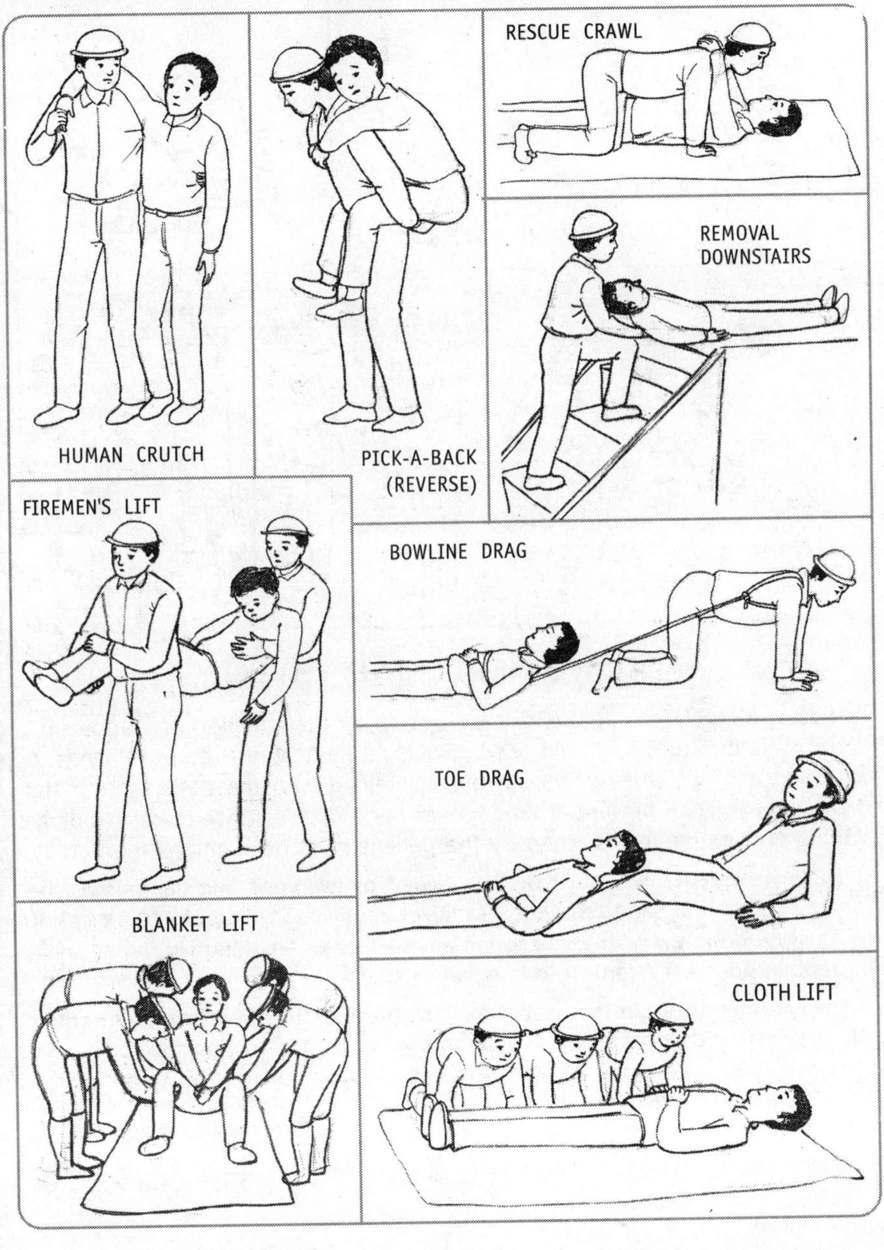

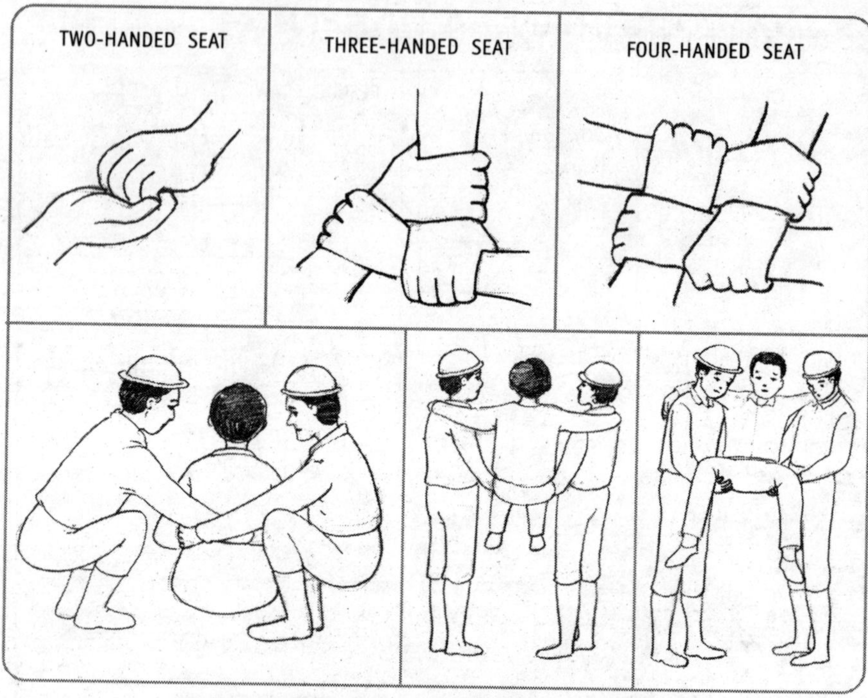

HANDLING A COVID-19 PATIENT

Covid-19 is a highly contagious disease caused by the infection of coronavirus. Anyone suffering from it should not be touched by anyone with bare hands. A safe distance of 1-2 metres should be maintained with the patient. Both the patient and everyone present around him or her must wear face masks properly. Anything and everything touched by the patient must be sanitized thoroughly.

Highest hygiene level must be maintained by everyone and hands must be washed with soap or sanitized with a sanitizer containing minimum 70% alcohol. This must be done everytime you touch any surface or anything like table, chair, pen, mobile phone, TV remote or car keys, etc.

The information about the patient must be given to the appropriate authorities at the earliest so that he or she is quarantined or shifted to hospital for proper care. The patient is attended by highly trained medical professionals wearing high quality face masks and PPE kits.

❖ ❖ ❖

CHAPTER

9 Yoga & Asanas

YOGA

Yoga is as old as Indian civilization. Early Upanishads, the Bhagavadgita and the Yoga Sutras of Patanjali are universally accepted as constituting the verbal foundation of the yoga tradition. Among these, the Yoga Sutras provides the basis and inspiration for most of today's tradition of yoga.

In Sanskrit, 'yoga' means 'to unite'. Primarily an exercise is moral and mental cultivation of poses and practices that aim towards harmonising your mind, body and soul to achieve a state of oneness with the universe. It's a spiritual practice that does not subscribe nor promote any particular faith; hence it can be practiced by all. A lifestyle choice by many, the universally timeless philosophies of yoga can be incorporated into any belief system. Stress, anxiety, ill-health, unhappiness and anger can be transformed into peacefulness, vibrant health, service and love towards all creation. The techniques are important in this process but the goal should be kept firmly in mind. The three main aspects of yoga are :

(i) Asanas or Poses (ii) Pranayama or Breathing (iii) Meditation

Regular practice of yoga helps in cultivating a strict discipline in food habits, cleanliness, sex and character, thus enabling one to become a better person. The therapeutic use of yoga is widely known. In fact, today, yoga is considered a global phenomenon and an essential part of modern civilisation. However, yoga, when practiced in the wrong manner, and without professional guidance, can do more harm than good.

Equally important are the proper time, place, dress and the right diet. Yoga has to be practiced in a quiet, secluded place, where fresh air is easily available - like a verandah, terrace, garden, etc. Ideally, yoga should be practiced in the early hours of either morning or evening (on a relatively empty stomach).

However, it can be practiced after four hours of a heavy meal, or after 20 minutes of having a glass of juice or a cup of skimmed milk. On completion, one can have a meal after half-an-hour. Avoid tea, coffee, smoking, alcohol and spices. The duration of practice should also be fixed according to one's capacity. Most importantly, yoga should be practiced at a fixed time every day; in two sessions if one feels able. One may feel an initial stiffness of the limbs and muscles. This will ease with regular practice. During yoga, the attire has to be clean, light and loose fitting to allow free movement; preferably light cotton garments.

In cold climate, a shirt or thin sweater can also be used. To avoid discomfort, jewellry or accessories need to be taken off. One must always practice barefoot to ensure contact with the ground. Further, since the body has to be stretched in various directions, yogic practice has to be done on a clean mat, rug, carpet or a blanket. The seat should be firm and comfortable.

During Yogasana, one should breathe through the nostrils and not through the mouth, except in the case of Sheetali and Sheetakari pranayama. While bathing is not directly related to yogasana, a shower before and after yogasana can refresh the body and mind.

Eight Limbs of Yoga

Compiled by Maharishi Patanjali in the Yoga Sutras, the Eight Limbs of Yoga are a progressive series of steps or disciplines which purify the body and mind, ultimately leading the yogi (one who practices yoga) to enlightenment. While the physical part of yoga is certainly of significance, it is only one of the eight conventional limbs of yoga practice, all of which have meditation of God as their rationale. These are the eight limbs of the complete yoga system as they are found in the famous Yoga Sutras of Patanjali.

- (i) **Yama** : Moral observances for interactions with others
- (ii) **Niyama** : Moral observances for interactions with yourself
- (iii) **Asana** : Postures
- (iv) **Pranayama** : Breathing
- (v) **Pratyahara** : Sensory inhibition
- (vi) **Dharana** : Focus
- (vii) **Dhyana** : Meditation
- (viii) **Samadhi** : Blissful absorption of one's individual consciousness in the essence of God.

ASANAS

Asana is one of the eight limbs of yoga. Asana means staying or abiding. It is through asanas that an individual achieves the unity of body and mind. The Sanskrit word 'asana' means 'to sit' or 'to be present,' and, in context of the yoga tradition, means 'to be established in a particular posture.'

Characteristics of Yoga

The characteristics of Yoga are given below :

(i) The Yogic system of health involves the exercise of skeletal as well as the deep-seated smooth muscles of the body.

(ii) The intra-thoracic and intra-abdominal pressure may be mentioned as special characteristics of the yoga system of health.

(iii) Every school of Yoga emphasized specific practices, but their aim always remained the same; the highest level of integration through the control of the modification of mind.

(iv) The nature of Yogic practices is psycho-neuro-physical.

(v) All yogic practices are complementary.

(vi) Little expenditure of energy and money is involved in the Yoga practices.

(vii) The rich as well as poor, and men and women of all ages can practise Yogic practices.

Potential Benefits of Yoga for Adults

Yoga as Exercise or Alternative Medicine :

(i) Many yoga practitioners have reported musculoskeletal and mental health improvements, as well as reduced symptoms of asthma in asthmatics.

(ii) The three main focuses of yoga (exercise, breathing, and meditation) make it beneficial to those suffering from heart disease.

(iii) For chronic low back pain, specialist Yoga for Healthy Lower Backs has been found 30% more beneficial.

(iv) A study found that after seven weeks the group treated with yoga reported significantly less mood disturbance and reduced stress compared to the control group. Another study found positive effects on sleep anxiety, quality of life, and spiritual growth.

(v) Yoga has also been studied as a treatment for schizophrenia. It is found to improve cognitive functions and reduce stress in schizophrenia, a condition associated with cognitive deficits and stress-related relapse.

(vi) The practice of yoga in Indian tradition also has psychological benefits, allowing one to develop control over one's mind and body.

Physical Benefits

The physical benefits of the ancient practice are too many to count; each body part gains something from every asana and every breath. Better posture, strength, balance, endurance, coordination, flexibility, steadiness and increased lung capacity are the basic gems one finds when beginning to engage with yoga.

Mental and Emotional Benefits

Continuous practice of yoga enables a person to have greater mind control or control over his/her emotions. It increases concentration and focus and fosters a healthier body-image. Regular practitioners of yoga are happier and more peaceful due to the release of Endorphin or the happiness hormone. It helps in getting better sleep and better digestive health and improves intuitive ability.

Spiritual Benefits

Yoga leads to an overall sense of fulfillment and a deeper sense of gratitude in general. It inculcates a greater sense of appreciation and fosters the ability to truly live the positive experiences of daily life. Yoga allows spending time with ourselves leading to introspection about our limitations: physically, mentally and emotionally. It can lead to the one thing we are constantly looking for: discovery of one's sense of purpose and meaning in life.

IMPORTANT ASANAS

Bakasana

Steps :

1. Put your hands flat on the ground. Lift your heels and shift your weight to your hands.
2. Lift your feet and keep your balance on your hands. Try stretching your back in order to keep your chest free. Breathe in and out quietly and concentrate on a spot in front of you. As you progress, try to keep up this exercise longer and longer and to work out the stretching of the back further and further.

Benefits :

* This posture helps to tone arm and hand muscles. It also strengthens the abdominal muscles and organs. Some people feel that the bowel pressure is eased by the constant practice of this posture.

Balasana

Steps :

1. Kneel and sit on your feet with your heels pointing outward. Your knees should be separated, about the width of your hips.

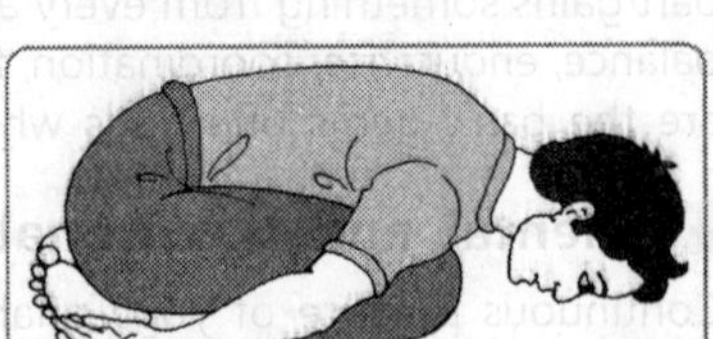

2. Place your forehead on the floor, then swing your arms forward.
3. Rest your forehead on the floor, then bring your arms around and to your sides, palms facing upward.

Benefits :

* Balasana gently stretches and relaxes the shoulders, neck, back muscles, hips, thighs, and ankles. It calms the brain and helps relieve stress and fatigue. It relieves back and neck pain when done with head and torso supported.

Bhujangasana

Steps :

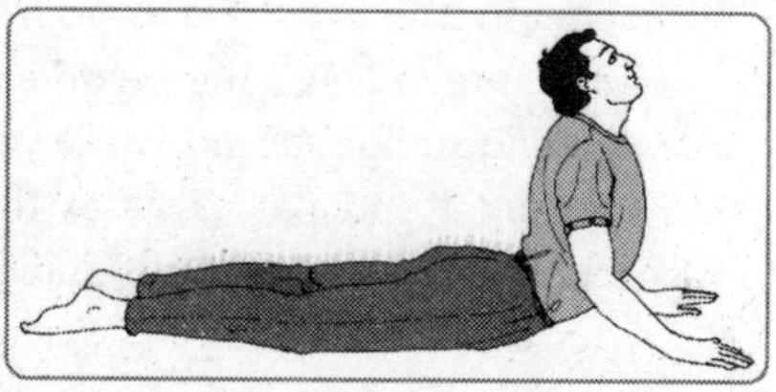

1. This is the relaxation position before and after each of the next few asanas. As you relax on your abdomen, breathe as deeply as you did on your back in the Corpse pose.
2. Bring the legs together and the forehead to the ground. Place the hands, palms downwards on the ground directly beneath the shoulders.
3. Begin with the head bent downwards and the forehead touching the ground.
4. As you inhale, slowly raise the forehead and bring the nose to the ground.
5. Roll the head upwards, raising the nose and brushing the chin on the floor.
6. Pushing the chin forwards, slowly roll the body up and back. When you have come up as far as is comfortable, breathe as you hold the position for at least 10 seconds. Gradually increase to 1 minute. To come down, unroll the body from the base of the spine, vertebra by vertebra, keeping the head back until last. End in the position shown in Step 2, with the forehead on the ground. Repeat 3-6 times.

Benefits :

* Affects the adrenal glands, sending them a richer supply of blood.
* Tones ovaries, uterus and liver.
* Muscles of the back, abdomen and entire upper body are strengthened by the practice of the Cobra Pose.
* Aids in relief and elimination of menstrual irregularities.
* Relieves constipation.

- ✳ Limbers spine.
- ✳ People suffering from gas after meals will find this pose very useful.
- ✳ Excellent for slipped discs. It adjusts displacements in the spinal column and tones the sympathetic nerves.
- ✳ Beneficial for backache due to overwork or long hours of standing.

Bidalasana

Steps :

1. Stand on your hands and knees. Position your hands directly beneath your shoulders and your knees directly beneath the hips. Have your fingers fully spread with the middle fingers pointing straight ahead. Make your back horizontal and flat. Gaze at the floor. This is your 'neutral' positioning. When your pelvis is in neutral, your spine will be at full extension, with both the front and back sides equally long.

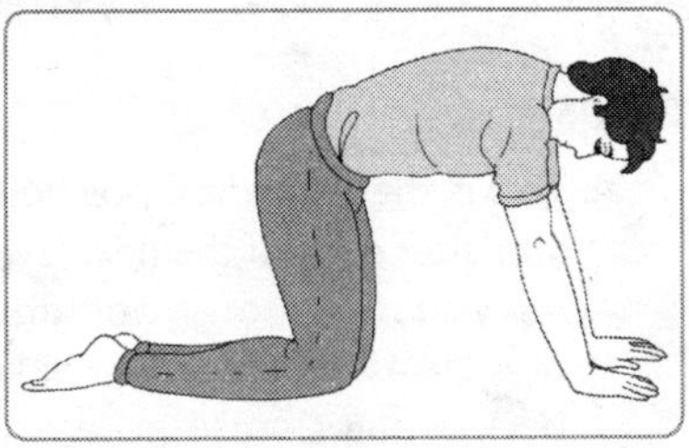

2. As you wait for the inner cue, do not sag into your shoulders. Instead, create a line of energy through each arm by pressing downward into your hands and lifting upward out of your shoulders.

   Go back and forth like this several times to make sure you understand the movement. As you exhale, sag into your shoulders and do the correct action; as you inhale, lengthen the arms, lift out of the shoulders and do the correct action.

3. When you are ready to begin, breathe in deeply. As you exhale, turn your hips into Cat Tilt. Do this by gently pulling the abdominal muscles backward towards the spine, tucking the tailbone (coccyx) down and under, and gently contracting the buttocks. Press firmly downward with your hands in order to stay lifted out of the shoulders, and press the middle of your back towards the ceiling, rounding your spine upward. Curl your head inward. Gaze at the floor between your knees.

Benefits :

- ✳ Doing the Bidalasana benefits your health by stimulating spinal fluid and the digestive tract, besides improving circulation through the spine and core. It is also beneficial in managing stress.

Chakrasana

Steps :

1. Lie on your back on your yoga mat. Pull in your legs and put your feet, somewhat turned inside, on the mat. However, do not pull them further apart than the distance of one hip end to the other.
2. Move your hands towards your head and spread your palms on the floor beside your head, your fingers placed towards your shoulders.
3. Lift your hips, with your head still on the yoga mat.
4. Keep your feet and knees parallel as you push yourself up until you stand on the ground with the crown of your head.
5. Stand on your feet and stretch out your arms until you have assumed the complete bridge position. The arms are slightly bent inwards. Let your head fall backwards. The bending is brought about by strength from your legs and with force from your arms. Aside from that, you try to achieve the bending through the entire back and not just through a few vertebrae. Look at the floor, and every time you exhale, try to bend the upper back further and further. Keep the knees together, stretch the legs without tightening the buttocks, relax the shoulders and try to keep the angle of your wrists and hands at 90 degrees.

   Get back quietly and repeat the exercise a number of times. In case you suffer from any back problems, it should be performed under the guidance of a yoga teacher.

Benefits :

* Strengthens the liver, pancreas and kidneys.
* Strengthens the muscles of the hands and feet.
* Increases elasticity of the spinal cord.
* Excellent for the heart, as it causes the aorta to stretch.

Dhanurasana

Steps :

1. Lie on your stomach, arms on your sides, and palms sideward adhered to the sides of thighs.

2. Move your legs in the 90° angle upwards.
3. Reach back with your arms and grasp your ankles. Let your weight rest on your stomach and not on your pelvis.
4. Raise your knees further by pulling your ankles with your hands.

Continue breathing regularly and try to increase the stretching in the chest and the backward bend for a relaxed body and mind.

Benefits :

* Though this asana is a combination of both Bhujangasana and Shalabhasana it delivers benefits of both the asanas. It activates all the glands of endocrine system.
* This asana also has good effects on pancreas, adrenal, thyroid, parathyroid, pituitary and the sex glands leading to normal secretion of their respective hormones.
* This has favourable effect on enzyme producing organs, liver, pancreas, small intestine and large intestine. As a result of this the concerned organs become more active and efficient.
* It restores flexibility to the spine. Regular practice will relieve lower back pain and release tension and strain in the upper back and neck area.
* It increases blood flow in abdominal area and aids all sorts of digestive disorders and discomforts. Also the blood circulation in arms and legs is improved.

Garudasana

Steps :

1. Stand with feet together on the floor. Keep hands at your sides, eyes looking forward. Breathe normally. Draw the left foot upward bending the knee and wrap the left foot around your right leg as you rest the back of your left thigh on the right thigh.
2. Cross your arms at the elbows, left over right. Join the palms of your hands together keeping the fingers pointed upward. Inhale and hold the posture for the duration of the inhaled breath. Exhale and return to the tadasana. Repeat the posture on the opposite side, wrapping the right leg over the left and the right arm over left.

Benefits :

* The Garudasana strengthens the legs, knees and ankles, tones muscles of the leg and relieves cramps of the legs.

Halasana

Steps :

1. Lie down with your back with hands lying on the back of the head.
2. Your shoulders should lie on the edge and your head rests on the mat. Your legs are drawn in and stand still on the mat.
3. Lift your hips off the floor and bring your legs up, over and beyond your head.
4. At this point, lift your back and move your legs further beyond your head.
5. Straighten your spine and keep your back straight. Move your hands towards your back.
6. Place your arms against your upper back and try to place your hands as near as possible to the shoulder blades. Try to place your elbows at shoulder-width. If you cannot do this, put them at a somewhat wider distance from each other.

Benefits :

* This is the best posture for making the spine flexible. It stretches the spine as no other exercise can, opening up the spinal discs and stretching most of the spinal muscles and ligaments. This posture is very beneficial if you suffer from back or neck stiffness or arthritis in these areas. It also prevents these conditions. Since this posture rejuvenates the spine, and because the spinal nerves go to all parts of the body, it helps to rejuvenate the whole body.
* It benefits the thyroid gland, liver and spleen, stretches and pulls the vertebrae.
* Good for people suffering from stiffness, obesity, muscular rheumatism, enlarged liver and spleen, constipation, indigestion, and arthritis.

Natarajasana

Steps :

1. Stand with the body facing straight ahead. Bend the right knee, lifting the foot until it is close to the buttock. Grasp the ankle with the right hand. Hold the position for a moment until you feel balanced and ready to proceed.

2. Inhale as you stretch the left arm up. With the elbow straight, bring the arm along side the left ear. Keep the eyes focused on a point in front of you to maintain balance.
3. Without releasing the hold on the ankle, slowly begin to shift the line of the body while breathing normally. Stretch the right foot away from the buttock. Straighten and lift the right knee until the right thigh is parallel to the ground.

4. Focus the eyes on a point on the floor just in front of the body and keep the left arm alongside the ear, and slowly shift the weight forward until the chest and arm are parallel to the ground. Hold the position for as long as long as you feel comfortable. Release and practice on the other side.

Benefits :

* Stretches the shoulders and chest.
* Stretches the thighs, groins, and abdomen.
* Strengthens the legs and ankles.
* Improves balance.

Precautions : Asana is not recommended in the cases of:

* High or low blood pressure.
* Serious lower-back injury.
* Knee injury.

Padmasana

Steps :

1. From the easy sitting position take hold of your right foot with both hands and place it on your left thigh. The foot will turn slightly so that the sole is facing upwards.
2. Next, take hold of the left foot and bring it up onto the right thigh. For meditation, place the hands in Chind Mudra pose or join them in other positions.

Benefits :

* This is an extremely good pose for meditation and concentration.
* It has a calming effect on the mind and the nerves.
* This pose keeps the spine erect.

* Helps develop a good posture.
* Helps keep the joints in flexible condition.

Paschimottanasana

Steps :

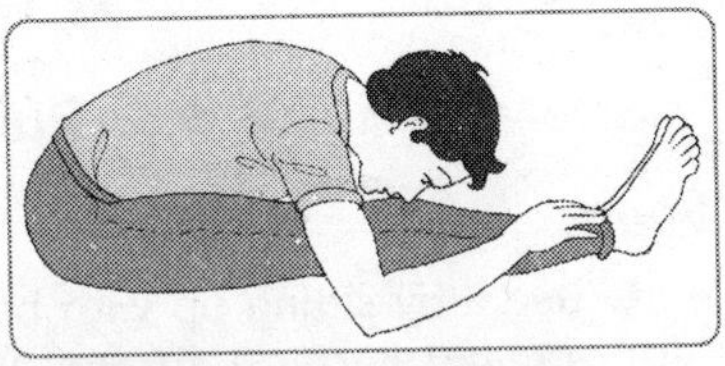

1. Sit down with your legs stretched. The legs lie side by side and the toes point upwards. Stretch your lower back and raise your arms. Look forward, lengthen your back, and keep the chest and your breathing free.
2. Slowly bend forward, stretch your crown upward and try not to lose the supporting dynamism of the lower back. See to it that your legs do not move or tilt up.
3. The moment you notice that you can only bend further by bending the lower back, move your hands to your lower legs, ankles or feet. Lightly pull your legs, ankles or feet and continue stretching.
4. Stretch out your arms forward.
5. Slowly raise your upper body. Keep your legs lying side by side and the toes pointing upwards.
6. Sit straight up again, just like your original position.

Keep your shoulders down. Breathe in deeply and out across the entire length of your spinal column and in a relaxed way. Everytime you exhale, you should bend further towards your legs without losing the length in your back and the dynamism in the lower back. When you lose the dynamism in the lower back, you will notice that you lose a major part of the stretching and you will have a hard time breathing.

Benefits :

* Paschimottanasana is a fine stretching exercise for the back of the whole body, from the heels to the top of the spine. In one continuous movement, almost all the posterior muscles of the body, particularly the hamstring muscles at the back of the thighs and the muscles of the small of the back, are fully stretched and relaxed. The muscles of the neck, chest, shoulders, the spinal column, hips and the recti are also brought into play.
* This asana stretches the spine to its maximum length, which makes it supple and flexible.
* The asana stretches the ribcage and its regular practice will expand the lungs more.

- The practice of this asana improves digestion and the peristaltic action of the bowels.
- The joints of the arms, shoulders, legs, knees, ankles and hips become more elastic.
- It is a good remedy for constipation, dyspepsia, flatulence, belching, hiccoughs and digestive disturbances.

Purvottanasana

Steps :

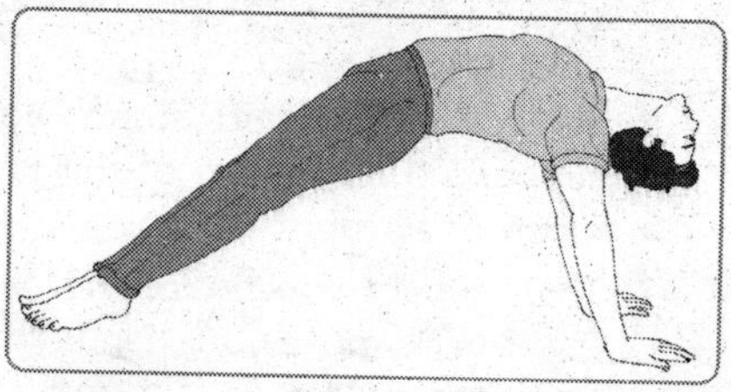

1. Begin by sitting up with both legs straight out in the front. Place the hands flat on the floor behind your back with the finger pointing backwards. Drop your head back and rest on your hands.
2. Inhale as you lift the hips to as much height as possible, trying to bring the feet flat on the floor. Try to hold the pose for at least 10 seconds, gradually increasing to 1 minute. Breathe normally as you hold the position. Lower the hips to the ground, and gently shake out the hands to relax.

Benefits :

- Purvottanasana strengthens and stretches your arms, abdomen, legs and neck. As a balance pose it helps with your sense of balance and calm.

Precautions :

- Don't do this pose if you have any sort of neck or lower back problem.

Sarvangasana

Steps :

1. Lie down with your back on the floor.
2. Your shoulders should lie on the edge and your head rests on the mat. Your legs are drawn in and still stand on the mat.
3. Lift your hips off the floor and bring your legs up, over and beyond your head.
4. At this point, lift your back and move your legs further beyond your head.
5. Straighten your spine and keep your back straight. Move your hands towards your back.

6. Place your arms against your upper back and try to place your hands as near as possible to the shoulder blades. Try to place your elbows at shoulder-width. If you cannot do this, put them at a somewhat wider distance from each other. If you want, you can use a belt to keep the arms together.
7. Push your back upwards with your hands. You will get a force upwards coming from the seventh neck-vertebra. Use your hands to push the back forward with the result that it gets narrower and straighter and there is an increased pressure on your shoulders. At the same time, this requires more power of the muscles of the lower back. Rest your weight on the back side of the shoulders. See to it that you do not bend the upper back and the chest.
8. Lift up your legs, one at a time, and make it sure that the pelvis is placed straight over your back and your hands. Your legs are placed a little forward. Divide the weight of your legs between the hands and the shoulders. Build up strength in the upper lower back and give space to your chest and shoulder muscles.

   A slight bending of the legs sees to it that the back remains straight and that the dynamism from the sacrum and the hip is maintained.

   Wait until your shoulders start to relax more. Try to increase the right dynamism through the angle of the legs and via the hands.
9. After some time, try placing your arms a little lower in the direction of the shoulder blades on your back. See to it that the elbows do not stand too far apart. Breathe in and out quietly and try to find your balance.

   Slowly bring your legs back to the mat, one by one, stretch out your arms (lengthwise), away from you and slowly roll your back downward.

Benefits :

- By doing this asana properly it could help you in curing your ailments related to bronchitis, asthma, heavy breathing and shortness in breath. Digestion is one of the major problems which many people face, due to fast food and other junk we fill in our stomachs. Your digestion would come in terms with your food by this asana as well as your body would be a place of better health. If you happen to be anaemic your conditions could improve by simply doing this asana as well as have daily routine in dietary and exercise habits.
- This asana also helps the sex glands which we all know would be very beneficial for future parents as well as for a good sex life.

Shirshasana

Steps :

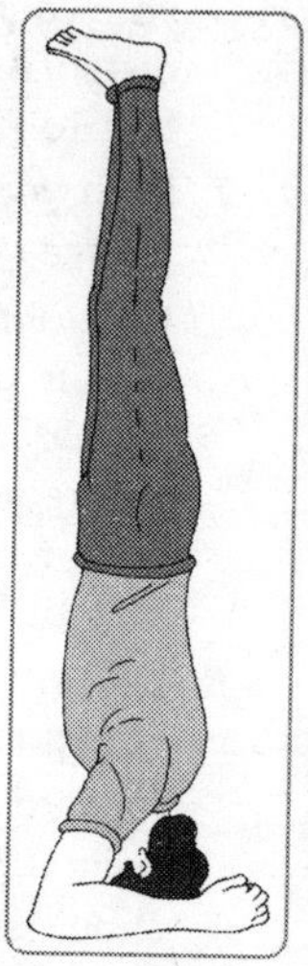

1. Stand on your knees on your yoga mat. Twine your hands together and keep some distance between the hand palms as if you are holding a tennis ball in the basin of both hands.
2. The shoulders will form the basis of Shirsha-asana. Try to let your upper arms 'interlock' with the shoulder blades so that they support the shoulders. Let your upper back sink down and stretch your neck out from the crown. Raise your knees.
3. Support yourself on your lower arms and walk inwards until you have your back straight.
4. Step in with one leg and bring your crown to the floor and jump up one leg at a time. Push your wrists against the floor. There is hardly any weight on your elbows and as much weight as possible on your crown.
5. Stand perpendicular on your head and try to place your hips, chest and legs in such a way that your upper back does not form a bump and your neck does not get sunken. Also, see to it that you do not let the centre of gravity fall in your lower back instead of upper back with the result that you clench the muscles of your lower back.
6. Focus on a point in front of you. Breathe in and out quietly and try to get completely still and experience the exercise in a meditative way.

Benefits :

- It stimulates four of the most important endocrine glands - the pituitary, the pineal, the thyroid, and the parathyroid glands. It has a very beneficial effect on the whole body.
- It improves many ailments, such as nervousness, tension, fatigue, sleeplessness, dullness, fear, poor blood circulation, bad memory, asthma, headaches, constipation, congested throat, liver or spleen, female disorders, the initial stages of eye and nose troubles, and general lack of energy, vitality or self confidence.
- It promotes hair growth by increasing circulation to the scalp, improves brain function (intelligence and memory) and increases vitality and confidence.
- It keeps the spine into correct alignment.
- It restores the position of vital organs by reversing gravity.
- It improves sleep.

Surya Namaskar

Steps :

1. As you exhale, bring your palms together at the chest in the prayer position. This is a powerful physical, mental, and psychic way of centring the body.
2. Inhale and stretch your arms up over your head. Arch your body backwards, keeping the arms alongside the ears, and the knees straight.
3. Exhale as you bend forwards and bring the hands down to the floor next to the feet. If you cannot put your hands on the floor with the knees straight, bend the knees slightly.
4. Without moving your hands, inhale and stretch the right leg back as far as possible. Drop the right knee to the floor and then stretch the head up.
5. Retaining the breath, bring the left leg back and place the left foot next to the right, with the toes pointing forwards. Your body should now be in a straight push-up position.
6. Exhaling, drop the knees straight down to the floor. Keep the hips up. Without rocking the body backwards, bring the chest straight down to the floor between the hands. Bring the forehead to the floor; beginners may place the chin on the ground if this is difficult to do.
7. Inhale as you slide the body forwards until the groin touches the ground. Arch the chest up and bring the head back into the cobra pose. Do not move the hands. The elbows are slightly bent, with the shoulders down and back, so that there is no tension in the neck or shoulder area.
8. Exhale as you tuck the toes under. Without allowing the hands or feet to move from their positions, bring the hips up. Push the heels towards the floor and keep the knees straight. Drop the head down between the arms. This is often referred to as the Inverted 'V' pose.
9. Inhale and bring the right foot forwards between the hands so that the fingers and toes form a straight line. Drop the left knee to the floor and stretch the head up. This is the same as the postion in step 4.
10. Without moving the hands, exhale as you bring the left foot forwards next to the right foot. The forehead is down towards the knees. This is the same position as that shown in step 3.
11. Inhale as you slowly reach the arms forwards and then stretch them up over the head. With the arms alongside the ears, and the weight centred on the balls of the feet, give a complete backward bend to the body. This is the same position as in step 2.
12. Stand facing the direction of the sun with both feet touching. Bring the hands together, palm-to-palm, at the heart.

Benefits :

- Tones up the digestive system by the alternate stretching and compression of abdominal organs. It activates digestion and gets rid of constipation and dyspepsia.
- Strengthens abdominal muscles.
- Thoroughly ventilates the lungs, and oxygenates the blood.
- Acts as detoxifying agent by getting rid of enormous quantity of carbon dioxide and other toxic gases.
- Tones up the nervous system and improves memory.
- Promotes sleep and calms anxiety.
- Normalizes the activity of the endocrine glands - especially the thyroid gland.
- Refreshes the skin. Prevents skin disorders.
- Improves muscle flexibility.

* In women, stimulates the breasts to help firmness normally. Restores any lost elasticity, through stimulation of glands and the strengthening of pectoral muscles.
* Suppresses menstrual irregularity and assists in easy childbirth.
* Prevents loss of hair and graying.
* Helps reduce fat.
* Reduces abnormal prominence of the Adam's apple.
* Eliminates unpleasant smells from the body.
* Lends grace and ease of movements to the body.
* Revives and maintains the spirit of youthfulness.
* Broadens chest and beautifies arms.
* Makes the spine and waist flexible.
* Produces health, strength, efficiency and longevity.

Caution :

* Pregnant women should not practice this after third month of pregnancy.
* Patients of Hernia and high blood pressure are warned against this practice.
* People suffering from back conditions should seek proper advice before commencing Surya Namaskar.
* Women should avoid Surya Namaskar during menses.

Trikonasana

Steps :

1. To come into the position, stand erect facing directly forwards. Place the feet slightly more than shoulder width apart. Balance the weight of the body evenly between the feet.
2. Inhale as you bring the right arm up alongside the right ear. Stretch the arm up as high as possible, and feel the stretch along the entire right side.
3. Exhale as you bend to the left. Slide the left hand down the left leg as far as possible. Breathing regularly, hold the position for at least 30 seconds, and gradually increase to 1 minute. Return to the centre and repeat the same on the other side. Perform this basic asana 2-5 times on each side.

Benefits :

* It removes tension from the neck and the side muscles and opens up the chest and expands it.

- It exercises the hips and the buttocks.
- This asana reduces excess fat in the abdomen, waist and hips and massages that area of the flank where fat accumulates. It, thus, gives the body a graceful form with minimum effort.
- It increases the flexibility of the waist and the hip joints.
- It benefits women by slimming the waistline and giving shape and grace to the hipline besides exercising the pectoral muscles which hold the breasts in position.
- This is an excellent exercise for correcting a faulty posture and for making the body well-proportioned.
- Persons who have to sit for long periods at the workplace will find this posture invigorating, if it is practiced during the period of work.
- Practising Trikonasana regularly improves the appetite. It also helps improve digestion and assimilation of food.
- It relieves constipation by invigorating the peristaltic action of the bowels.
- It will help a person attain full stature.

Ushtrasana

Steps :

1. Sit up on the heels with the feet, knees, and legs together. This is Vajrasana, which stimulates digestion. Try sitting like this while eating, or after a meal.
2. From Vajrasana, inhale as you lift the hips and trunk, standing up on the knees to prepare for the camel pose. The hips and body rise, but the legs and feet do not change position.
3. With the right hand, clasp hold of the right heel. If you find it difficult to reach the heel, place the right hand flat on the floor behind the right foot.
4. Allowing the head to drop back, reach down with the left hand to grasp the left heel (or place the left hand flat on the ground parallel to the right hand). Breathing gently, hold for at least 10 seconds, gradually increasing to 1 minute. Sit back on the heels and relax in the child's pose.

Benefits :

- For the asthmatics Ushtrasana brings a good effect upon the whole of respiratory system. This asana activates the facial tissues, the nasal passages, the pharynx, the lungs and the whole of respiratory organs and the nerves. Because of internal as well as external activation during this asana, the weakened condition of the organs of respiration is corrected and their normal health is restored.

* Ushtrasana has several good benefits for the general practitioners. It corrects any disorders of the neck, shoulders and the spine. It cures various types of visionary defects of the eyes and strengthens all the sense organs. People suffering from throat trouble, tonsil, voice defect and chronic headache will find this asana very beneficial. It has also a good conditioning effect upon the muscles of the chest and in making the chest area proportionate in size. It is not a difficult asana. With a little practice any person can do it.
* This asana belongs to the category of Vajrasana. It should be practiced after practising Vajrasana. 'Ushtra' means a camel. In this asana almost all the limbs of the body are arched like those of a camel. So it is called Ushtrasana.

Uttanasana

Steps :

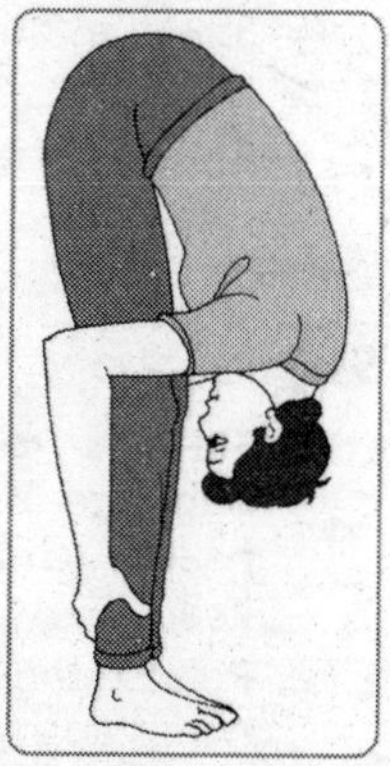

1. Start with the mountain pose.
2. Bend your knees, support your upper body with a straight lower back, and slowly bend forward so that your belly touches your upper legs. Maintain the position of your lower back or else your chest will sink. Move your pelvis, taking the back as the starting point, relax your groins, and keep your weight on the front parts of your heels.
3. Keep breathing correctly through your belly and slowly stretch your chest to the knees without losing the support of your lower back. Stretch your legs everytime you exhale. Your pelvis moves upward from the back until your legs are eventually stretched. Touch the ground or grab your ankles. Stretch downward from your crown and when you have grabbed your ankles, use a slight stretching force to lengthen the body. If you lose the supportive power of the lower back during the exercise, you lose a major part of its effect. As a result, your chest will sink, making your breathing irregular. Also, stretching will not be effective. Now, stand up straight again and jump back to Tadasana.

Benefits :

* Bear in mind that you perform this forward bend through relaxation and not through force by pulling your feet with physical strength. When you pull too hard, the body stiffens, your thinking and breathing will be affected and worst of all, you run a risk of injuring yourself.

Vrikshasana

Steps :

1. Start with the mountain pose.
2. As you exhale, place your left foot on the inside part of your right leg, close to the groin area, with the toes pointing downward.
3. As you inhale, stretch your arms sideways to form a T, palms facing down.
4. As you exhale, bring your palms together in prayer position.
5. Raise your arms overhead, keeping your palms in prayer position. To maintain balance, it helps to focus your eyes on one point in front of you and keep on breathing through the belly.

Benefits :

* This improves body-mind co-ordination.
* Thigh and calf muscles, ankles and the spine are made strong.
* Stretches the groins and inner thighs, chest and shoulders
* Improves sense of balance.
* Relieves sciatica and reduces flat feet.

Vrishchikasana

Steps :

1. Starting from the headstand, bend the knees and begin to bring the feet slowly down towards the head. Arch the entire body backwards, being sure to keep the weight of the body on the elbows.
2. Release the inter-locked fingers slowly, and move your hands apart, bringing them to lie flat on the ground on either side of the head. Feel confident in this position before continuing. Inhale deeply as you pause before trying the next step.
3. Keep the back arched, lift the head as you bring the shoulders back into a position directly above the elbows. You are now in the scorpion position. It requires a good deal of concentration, strength, and upper back flexibility. Hold the position only for as long as you feel comfortable.

Benefits :

* This posture will provide maximum stretch to the neck, spine and chest. It combines many of the benefits of the Chakrasana (the wheel posture) and the Shirshasana (standing on head).

❖ ❖ ❖

CHAPTER

10 Home Nursing

Nurse is a person trained to care for the sick and infirm persons. When nursing care is provided at home it is called Home Nursing.

CHARACTERISTICS OF A GOOD NURSE

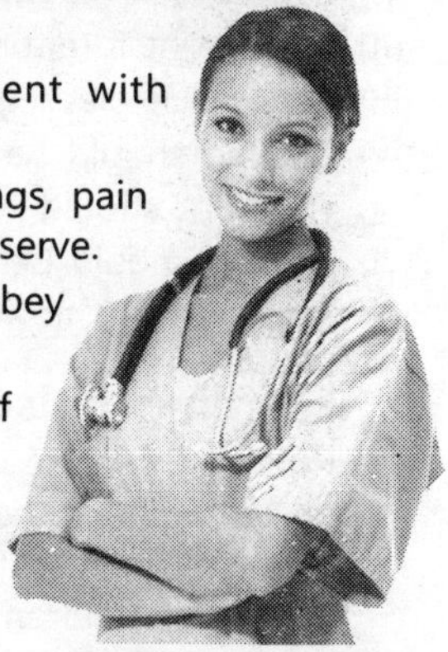

(i) A good nurse should be honest and truthful.

(ii) A good nurse should take care of the patient with understanding and compassion.

(iii) A cheerful and gentle nurse reduces the sufferings, pain and discomfort of the patients with willingness to serve.

(iv) A good nurse should observe self-discipline and obey the orders of doctors without arguing.

(v) A good nurse should observe the minutest detail of patients' condition.

(vi) A good nurse should deal with irritable patients with tact and sense of humour.

Duties of a Nurse

(i) To note the basic details of patient such as—Name, Age, Sex, Address, Medical History etc.

(ii) Maintaining proper account of the patient's condition.

(iii) To take care of the sick-room.

(iv) To clean and feed the patient.

(v) To change patient's clothes and bedsheets.

(vi) Regularly taking pulse rate, temperature etc.

(vii) To collect samples for testing.

(viii) Dressing of the wounds.

(ix) Administration of Medicines.

Sick Room

A sick room should be away from all noise and disturbance. It should have a bathroom and toilet close by. It should be well-prepared, clean with proper lighting and ventilation. Heating and cooling equipments as per the requirement of the patient should be available. If the sunlight and clean air through a window is available, it is better for the patient.

Necessary Items for Sick-room

(i) Proper bed	(ii) Small table & Two chairs
(iii) A stool	(iv) Wash Basin
(v) Mug, Soap & Bucket	(vi) Dust bin
(vii) Towel & Curtains	(viii) Newspaper & Television

Cleaning Sick-room

The points to be borne in mind while cleaning the sick room:

(i) Clean the room without disturbing the patient.
(ii) Move light furniture before the room is swept and dusted.
(iii) Wipe each piece clean with a weak solution of disinfectant.
(iv) Dusting should be done with a damp cloth.
(v) The floor should be cleaned carefully so that dust does not rise.
(vi) Flowers should be removed from the vases at night.
(vii) Arrange fresh flowers in the morning.

Recording Pulse, Respiration and Temperature

- **Pulse :** The pulse is the heart beat and is most commonly felt at the radial on the point of the wrist. The average pulse rate of a normal person is 72 beats per minute. In case of infants, it is 100 to 140 beats per minute and in case of children 90 to 100 beats per minute.
- **Respiration :** The inhalation and exhalation of a person is called respiration. The respiration rate of various ages is :
  (i) Infants 30-40 per minutes
  (ii) Children 24-28 per minute
  (iii) Adults 15-20 per minute.
- **Body Temperature :** The normal body temperature of a person is 98.6° F or 37°C. Fahrenheit is converted to centigrade by the formula : °F − 32° × 5/9 = °C.
- **Taking Temperature :** Place the bulb of the thermometer gently under the armpit or beneath the tongue or in the groin of the patient for 2 minutes.

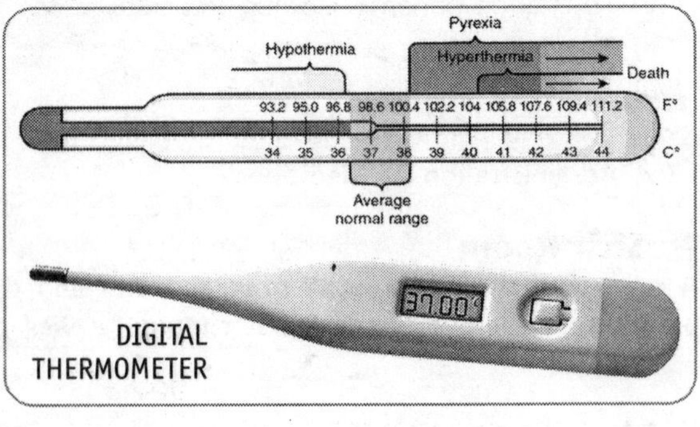

Observation of The Sick

Important points to be observed in a patient for proper treatment :

(i) ***Appearance of the Patient :*** The colour of the skin, rashes, swelling, oedema etc.

(ii) ***Temperature, Pulse and Respiration :*** Temperature, pulse and respiration should be taken twice or four times a day as desired by the doctor.

(iii) ***Stools :*** Frequency and type of stools, colour, composition such as presence of abnormal material as blood, pus, gall stones, worms, undigested food etc. Preserve sample for testing.

(iv) ***Urine :*** Observe frequency, quantity, colour abnormalities, and deposits etc. Preserve sample for testing.

(v) ***Cough and Sputum :*** Note the amount, colour, whether coughed out easily or with difficulty. Preserve sample for testing.

(vi) ***Vomit :*** Note the quantity, time in relation to food, frequency, presence of blood etc. Preserve sample for testing.

Feeding a Patient

Important precautions to be taken while feeding a patient with liquid diet :

(i) The mouth of the patient should be gently washed and wiped clean.

(ii) Liquids can be given in a cup or glass.

(iii) If a straw is required, arrange one.

(iv) Use a feeding cup or a feeder if the patient can not sit up.

(v) Place a clean napkin beneath the patient's mouth.

(vi) Place your left arm under the pillow to raise the patient's head slightly.

(vii) Regulate the flow of liquid like water, milk or juice so that too much of it does not flow into the patient's mouth at once.

(viii) Give one mouthful at one time.

(ix) Feeding can be done with a teaspoon easily.

(x) Mouth should be gently wiped with a clean towel after feeding the patient.

The important precautions to be taken while feeding a patient with solid food :

(i) Serve food properly on a side table.

(ii) Serve one dish at one time.

(iii) Serve the food hot unless advised otherwise.

(iv) Put the food in a plate in the kitchen before bringing to the patient.

(v) Feed the patient with a spoon.

(vi) Remove the plate as soon as food is finished.

(vii) Clean the mouth of patient.

MEDICINE ADMINISTRATION

Precautions while Administering Liquid Medicines

Precautions to be taken while administering liquid medicines to patient :

(i) Check the label of medicine with the prescription and read the instructions carefully.
(ii) Shake the bottle of liquid medicine well.
(iii) Pour the accurate dosage on the medicine glass and replace the cap immediately.
(iv) Bring the medicine on a tray with a glass of water and spoon in case the medicine requires dilution.
(v) If the medicine has a bitter taste, give the patient some sweet drink (Never to diabetics).
(vi) Put the medicine bottle at its right place.
(vii) Never pour back the unused medicine in bottle, just throw it away in the wash-basin.

Abbreviations of Medical Prescriptions

Abbreviation	Derivation (Latin)	Meaning in English
a.c.	ante cibum	before meals
aq	aqua	water
bis	bis	twice
b.i.d.	bis in die	twice daily
b.d.s.	bis die sumendum	twice daily
$\overline{c}$	cum	with (usually written with a bar on top of the "c")
cc	cum cibos	with food, (but also cubic centimetre)
ex aq	ex aqua	in water
h.s.	hora somni	at bedtime
noct.	nocte	at night
o.d.	omne in die	once daily
p.c.	post cibum	after meals
q.h.	quaque hora	every hour
q.h.s.	quaque hora somni	every night at bedtime
q.d.	quaque die	every day
q.i.d.	quater in die	four times a day
q.s.	quantum sufficiat	a sufficient quantity
s.o.s.	si opus sit	if there is a need
t.i.d.	ter in die	three times a day
t.d.s.	ter die sumendum	three times a day
tbsp		tablespoon
tsp		teaspoon

Precautions while Administering Other Medicines

(i) Pills, tablets, capsules and powders should be given with fresh and clean water.

(ii) Tablets and capsules should be put on the back of the tongue for swallowing.

(iii) Powder should be poured at the back of the patient's tongue and water poured in his/her mouth.

(iv) Iron mixture should be given with a straw to avoid staining of teeth.

(v) The patient should be helped to clean his/her teeth after taking such medicine.

FEVER, INFECTION AND DISEASES

Fever

The normal temperature of human body is between 97° F to 99° F. The temperature above 99° causes pain, restlessness, headache and body ache. The state of more than normal temperature is called 'Fever'.

Various types of fevers as per severity are :

(i) **Constant Fever :** In this type of fever the temperature remains the same all the time as in pneumonia and scarlet fever.

(ii) **Intermittent Fever :** In this type of fever the temperature rises very high and falls very low. It appears due to severe infection.

(iii) **Remittent Fever :** This is a very high type of fever. The body temperature rises more than 1° during 24 hours as in case of tuberculosis and sepsis.

(iv) **Irregular Fever :** This type of fever has no set pattern of rise and fall of body temperature.

Infection

The spread of germs from a sick person to a healthy person is called infection. An infection may spread mainly through :

(i) **Air :** Germs spread from a sick person to a healthy person by air when the sick person breathes out foul germs and fit person inhales it. Diseases like tuberculosis and influenza spread in this manner by air.

(ii) **Water :** Germs contaminate water when patients of a disease wash into it their faeces, urine, sputum or vomit. When this water is used by a healthy person, the germs enter his body and he falls victim to diseases. Cholera, enteric fever, dysentery, typhoid and jaundice spread in this manner by water.

(iii) **Insects :** Germs of various diseases are carried by insects like anopheline female mosquito, house fly, sand fly, fleas and ticks. When they bite a healthy man he also starts showing signs of the disease. Malaria, plague and dengue spread in this manner by insects.

Disinfection

Disinfection is destroying the disease germs through various methods. It is done by breaking the chain of infection. The following are major types of disinfectants :

1. **Physical Agents :** (i) Light, (ii) Heat - both dry and moist. e.g., sunlight.
2. **Chemical Agents :** (i) Gases, (ii) Liquids, (iii) Solids. e.g., mosquito sprays, Antiseptics, Antibiotics, Sanitisers etc.

DISEASES IN HUMANS

* **Human Viral Diseases :** Covid-19 (Coronavirus), Chickenpox, Measles, Polio, Rabies, Mumps, Influenza, Hepatitis, Herpes, AIDS, Trachoma (of Cornea).
* **Human Protozoans Deseases :** Amoebiasis, Malaria, Sleeping Sickness, Kalazar, Diarrhoea, Pyorrhoea.
* **Human Bacterial Diseases :** Cholera, Diptheria, Tuberculosis, Leprosy, Tetanus, Typhoid, Plague, Whooping Cough, Sore Throat, Pneumonia, Gonorrhoea, Syphilis, Botulism.
* **Human Fungal Diseases :** Ringworm, Athlete's foot, Dhobie itch.

COVID-19

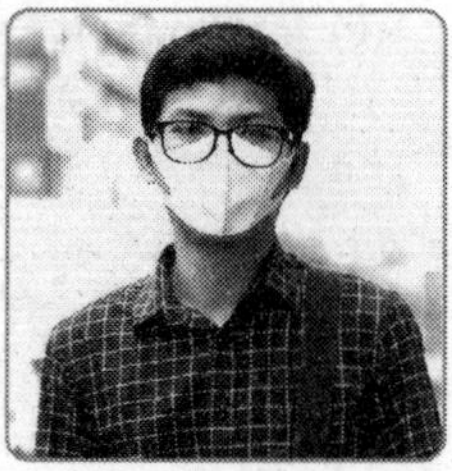

The main symptoms of Covid-19 are fever and dry-cough with difficulty in breathing in severe cases. Coronavirus is a deadly virus which can attack anyone and especially those with weak immunity or maintaining poor hygiene. The patients of any chronic ailment like hypertension or diabetes are especially vulnerable to this disease, hence need to be protected more.

The best way to escape the disease is to wear face mask and stay indoors as much as possible, and avoid crowded places like weekly bazars, shopping malls, ceremonial gatherings and places of worship. Physical contact like shaking hands, kissing, patting, hugging etc should be avoided. Sharing food and especially having street food must be avoided to prevent the spread of the disease. Never eat anything without washing or sanitizing your hands properly for 20 seconds. Special care should be taken while handling currency notes, files and papers as they go in several hands. While travelling in public transport social distance must be maintained.

In places like schools, colleges, offices, libraries and parks maintaining social distance is a must. Mouth, nose and eyes must not be touched by hands to prevent the infection of coronavirus. Drinking hot water is recommended as a preventive measure. All the fruits and vegetables procured from the market must be cleaned thoroughly with water and vinegar or sodium carbonate (Meetha Soda). Steps to raise the immunity levels must be taken. These include - good hygiene, nutritious food, yoga and exercise, and intake of vitamins C and D.

There are some herbal 'Kadhas' and Tulsi drops available which boost the immunity. Ayurvedic chayvanprash also helps boost the immunity as it contains lot of amla and other herbs beneficial for human body.

Some Important Facts about Human Body

* **Length of Alimentary Canal**	Approximately 8 metres
* **Number of Cells in Body**	75 trillion
* **Longest Bone**	Femur (Thigh bone)
* **Smallest Bone**	Ear ossicle, stapes
* **Weight of Brain**	1400 gms
* **Blood Volume**	6.8 litres (in 70 kg body)
* **Normal B.P**	120/80 mm Hg
* **Number of R.B.C**	(*a*) In Male : 4.5-5.0 million/cubic mm. (*b*) In Female : 4.0-4.5 million/cubic mm
* **Life Span of R.B.C**	120 days
* **Normal W.B.C Count**	5000-10000/cubic mm
* **Life Span of W.B.C**	3-4 days
* **D.L.C. (Differential Leucocyte Count)**	(*a*) Basophils : 0.5-1% (*b*) Eosinophils : 1-3% (*c*) Monocytes : 3-8% (*d*) Neutrophils : 40-70% (*e*) Lymphocytes : 2-25%
* **Blood Platelets Count**	2,00,000-4,00,000/cubic mm
* **Haemoglobin**	(*a*) In Male: 14-15.6 gm/100 c.c. of blood (*b*) In Female: 11-14 gm/100 c.c. of blood
* **Hb Content in Body**	500-700 gm
* **Universal Blood Donor**	O Group Blood
* **Universal Blood Recipient**	AB Group Blood
* **Blood Clotting Time**	2-5 minutes
* **Average Adult Body Weight**	70 kg
* **Normal Body Temperature**	98.6° F or 37°C
* **Breathing Rate**	16-20/minute
* **Dental Formula**	Adult : 2123 / 2123 = 32; Child : 2120 / 2120 = 22 Milk Teeth
* **Number of Cranial Nerves**	12 pairs
* **Number of Spinal Nerves**	31 pairs

* **Largest Endocrine Gland**	Thyroid
* **Gestation Period**	9 months (253-266 days)
* **Normal Heart Beat**	72-75/minute
* **Largest Gland**	Liver
* **Largest Muscle**	Gluteus maximus (Buttock Muscle)
* **Smallest Muscle**	Stapedius
* **Largest Artery**	Abdominal Aorta
* **Largest Vein**	Inferior Venacava
* **Greatest Regeneration Power**	In liver
* **Longest Nerve**	Sciatic
* **Longest Cell**	Neuron (Nerve Cell)
* **Minimum Regeneration Power**	In Brain Cells
* **pH of Gastric Juice**	1.5-2.5
* **pH of Urine**	6.0
* **pH of Blood**	7.35-7.45
* **Total Number of Muscles**	639
* **Total Number of Bones**	206

Medical Inventions and Discoveries

Name	Medical Invention
Ronald Ross	Malaria Parasite
Jonas E. Salk	Anti-Polio Vaccine
Frederick G. Banting	Insulin
Christian Barnard	Replacing the human heart
Alexander Fleming	Penicillin (in 1929)
William Harvey	Circulation of Blood
Edward Jenner	Smallpox Vaccination
Robert Koch	Tubercle Bacillus
Lord Joseph Lister	Antiseptic Treatment
Louis Pasteur	Treatment of Rabies; Cure of Hydrophobia

❖ ❖ ❖

CHAPTER 11

Posture Training

POSTURE

Posture means the position of our body segments or the way we carry our body as a whole. Grace and poise are hallmark of an individual's personality. The personality and efficiency of a person depends upon the posture.

Good Posture

A good posture is attained when body segments are held one upon another in the best possible manner and when they are moved in poised and unstrained manner, the body moves efficiently. The segments of the body act, if held in one line and ensure economy of effort, strength, balance and proper support to the body.

An incorrect body posture causes more fatigue as more energy is required to maintain the physical equilibrium. An improperly aligned body structure is generally due to a wrong postural habit of an individual.

Importance of a Good Posture

Nobody can deny the significance and importance of a good posture in our daily life. Good appearance and good posture of an individual conveys good impression of his well being. It reflects the alertness, activeness, agility and wholesomeness of an individual's personality. Good posture allows the minimum or economical use of energy, effort and time whereas poor posture results in excessive utilisation of energy. There is a definite relationship between good posture and good health. Good posture enables an individual to follow good health habits so as to lead a healthy life.

Bad or poor posture may casue psychological problems, emotional disturbances and generate feelings of inferiority in an individual. By attaining good posture one can avoid such psychological problems. A person having good posture is able to draw attention towards him and is able to gain social acceptability, recognition and social efficacy easily. The aesthetic appeal of erect posture and poise cannot be denied. Good posture also improves his economic efficiency as he is full of confidence and is able to properly interact with people. He is also able to perform his duties more effectively and efficiently, thereby improving his employment prospects.

TYPES OF A GOOD POSTURE

Broadly there are two types of postures :

(i) **Inactive Posture :** when a person is sleeping or having rest and body requires minimum muscular efforts, and

(ii) **Active Posture :** where integrated muscular activity is required.

Active posture may be static or dynamic. Static posture is one where the body is passive, not active or changing stance and forces are acting in equilibrium. Dynamic posture is one where the body is in motion, active and changing its stance. Postural positions whether inactive or active (static and dynamic), can be broadly classified in four categories :

1. Standing position or posture
2. Sitting position or posture
3. Lying position or posture
4. Walking posture

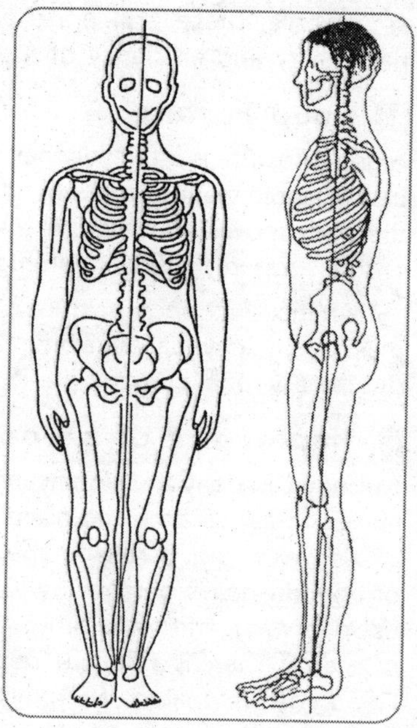

1. Standing Position or Posture

Standing position of an individual is generally considered as the basic posture from which all his other postures stem. Erect standing posture is literally static, it in reality is movement upon a stationary base. The application of the principles of stability to a standing position *i.e.,* balanced and free from muscular and ligamentous strain, would be that the line of gravity of the centre of the head, chest, abdomen (trunk) and pelvis fall in a straight line. In standing position, weight should be equally distributed between the ball of the foot and the heel.

Good standing posture is a position of extension of weight-bearing joints. This should be an easy extension and should not be accompanied by stress or strain of any kind.

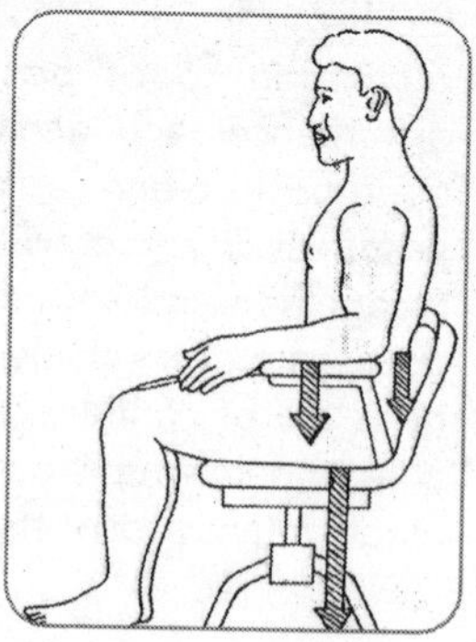

2. Sitting Position or Posture

There are three types of sitting posture

(i) Simple Sitting,

(ii) Reading, While Sitting, and

(iii) Writing, While Sitting.

(i) Simple Sitting : The simple sitting position is one in which a person occupies a position wherein the muscles involved in the process experience minimum stress and strain.

In simple sitting position, the parts of the body, head, shoulder and hips should be well placed in proper alignment with each other. The trunk, including the head and shoulders, should be in a natural, upright and relaxed position. Specially, kyphosis (outward curvature) of the lumbar spine should be avoided by maintaining the natural curves of the spine. The thighs should be placed horizontally, legs placed vertically and the feet resting on the ground in flat position. The hands flexed a little at the elbow, should rest on the thighs.

(ii) Reading, While Sitting: The reading posture is almost similar to the simple sitting position. The only point to be kept in mind is the distance of the reading material and its angle from the eyes. Generally, the distance between the eyes and the reading material should be about 30 centimetres and the angle of the reading material should be of 45 horizontally. The back should be a little more erect as compared to simple sitting position.

Efforts should be made to have proper lighting arrangement so that the light falls on the reading material from the back of the person reading. Appropriate furniture should be used for sitting, it should not be too high or too low, nor too inclined. Hands should be placed on the table holding the reading material comfortably. It is being generally observed that while reading, people assume faulty reading postures which may lead to various posture deformities as well as eyesight problems.

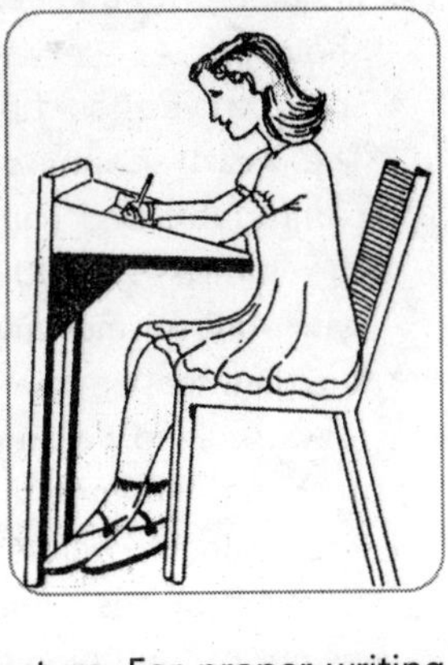

(iii) Writing, While Sitting: In writing posture, the chair should be drawn under the table so that the elbows are resting on the table comfortably and the forearms should be approximately horizontal. The thighs should be horizontally placed with legs placed vertically, and feet resting on the ground in flat position. It has to be kept in mind that the height of the table should be according to that of the person and the chair. There should be a slight slope in the surface of the table towards the person to facilitate the writing process.

In this posture, the person has to have a little forward inclination as compared to the reading pcsture. For proper writing posture, undue bending of the neck, forward or sideways should be avoided.

3. Lying Position or Posture

The best lying posture is one in which all the body segments are placed in such a position so as to exert minimum stress and strain. As one generally lies down to have rest or to relax, the best posture for this purpose is to lie down flat, keeping back on the floor or the bed, with legs fully stretched forward, feet a little apart in a comfortable position, arms straight to the side of the body. This posture is almost similar to one in shavasana in Yoga and is considered best for relaxation. The bedding should be firm if not hard. Spring and sponge mattresses are highly undesirable as they make the body sink out of alignment. High pillows cause tension in the muscles of the neck and impede proper circulation of the blood to the head. While sleeping it is not good to sleep on one's back, nor it is proper to sleep always on the same side, whether right or left. It has been observed that sleeping on one's side with knees drawn up a little, in a comfortable position, is considered as a good lying position while sleeping.

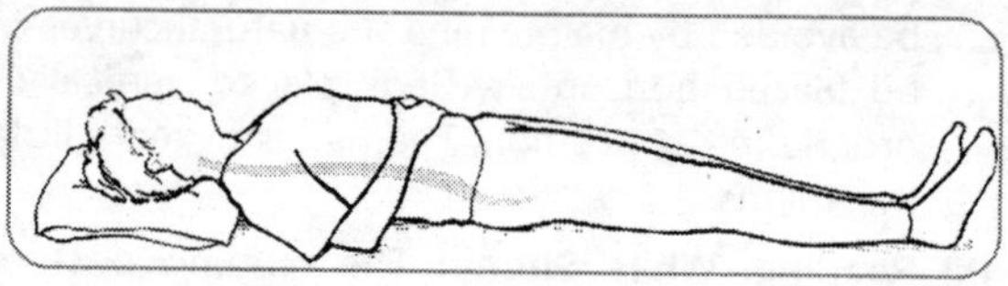

4. Walking Posture

In a dynamic movement like walking, the force should be directed, as much as possible, in a straight line, intersecting the major joints, the foot, knee, hip and the shoulders. At the same time, the spinal curve should be minimized. The head should be held in a comfortable and natural position, the hands should move in a synchronized movement with the legs, in a tension free movement. It is advisable to walk with rhythmical pace in the manner in which one experience minimum stress and strain. The leg moving forward should be in the line of direction, with heel touching first followed by toe pointing towards the direction of the movement, and the weight of the body will be shifted to the toes along with the outer edge of the foot.

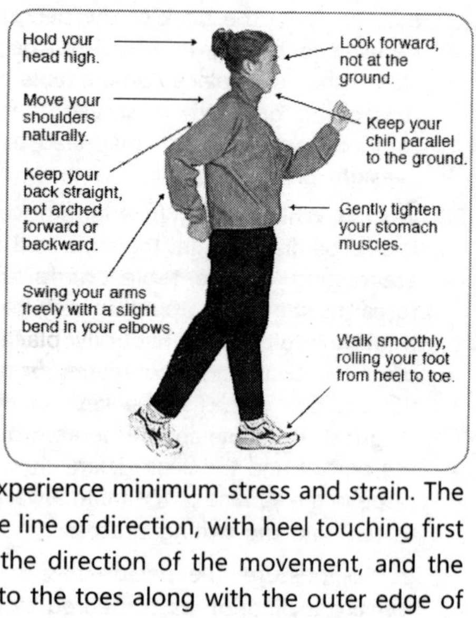

CAUSES OF A POOR POSTURE

The causes of poor posture can broadly be classified into two categories :

(i) Acquired - due to some accident or disease

(ii) Congenital - present at birth or hereditary

The deformities caused due to poor posture can be of two types :

(i) Functional divergence, and

(ii) Structural divergence.

The main causes of poor posture are listed below :

1. **Injury:** When a bone, ligament, or muscle is injured, it is likely to weaken the support at that point and throw the framework out of balance. When such condition exists, it is not possible to have a perfect posture. Even after the injury has fully healed, the habit developed during the injury may still persist, and the faulty posture may continue for a long time.
2. **Disease:** Posture is greatly affected by the disease that weaken the bones or the muscles or cause the joints to lose their strength or mobility. The example of this kind of disease are, rickets caused due to faulty nutrition of bone, and tubercular disease of joints or vertebrae. Poliomyelitis may cause weakening or distorting of motor nerve cells in the spinal cord, and thereby causing partial or complete loss of function in certain muscle groups. This type of loss of power in muscle groups upsets the body control and balance and also cause other kinds of defects.
3. **Habit:** Habits of posture, whether good or bad, are acquired in the same way as the habits of walking, speaking or sitting *i.e.,* by practising a certain type of coordination so many times that the act becomes unconscious and habitual. In case of school and college students though the bones, joints, ligaments and muscles are in normal condition, but due to faulty and wrong habits, their coordination is disturbed, causing poor posture. Wrong habits of posture are also caused by occupation and environment as well.
4. **Weakness:** It is not possible to assume and maintain erect posture without expenditure of some energy. Such efforts, therefore, require some strength and endurance. Experiments have shown that slumped or slouched position of body can be maintained with quite less metabolic energy as compared to the erect position. The muscular weakness and lack of viability is thus responsible for such faulty postures.
5. **Mental attitude:** The posture is the manner is which we carry or hold our body and it is bound to reflect our mental attitude. Feelings of happiness, confidence and satisfaction help in maintaining a balanced and erect posture, whereas depression and feeling of sadness pose hurdles in maintaining proper posture.
6. **Heredity:** Heredity is another factor which is responsible for poor or defective posture. Hereditary defects like kyphosis and other genetic defects may cause poor posture.

7. **Improper clothing:** The type of dress one wears also has impact on individual's posture. For example, wearing tight fitted dress, tight shoes, high heel shoes etc. will result in adopting poor posture. Such improper clothing makes one uncomfortable and may lead to faulty posture.
8. **Improper diet or malnourishment:** Improper diet or malnourishment may result in various diseases due to deficiencies of vitamins and minerals *e.g.* rickets etc. which result in adopting faulty and poor posture.
9. **Chronic fatigue:** Due to continuous work, lack of rest and sound sleep, body tends to develop fatigue, and such condition becomes chronic with persistence of such condition. Without proper relaxation, rest and sleep the body and the mind become overworked and inefficient. Such conditions put undue stress upon muscles thereby causing postural deviations.
10. **Overload:** One may develop round shoulders and deformities of spine like kyphosis and scoliosis by continuously lifting and carrying heavy weight on shoulders and the upper back. Everyday example of overloading can be observed as we find school children carrying heavy school bags on their backs.
11. **Imitation:** Due to over exposure of the children to the popular media like TV, network etc. there is general tendency among children to imitate their favourite heroes, models, stars, teachers, friends etc. Such imitation may distort their natural posture and may cause postural deviations.
12. **Unhygienic conditions:** It is very common to find crowded classrooms with improper sitting arrangements, improper furniture, improper and insufficient lighting arrangements etc. in our country. Such unhygienic conditions result in postural deviations.
13. **Inappropriate time tables:** Improperly planned school curriculum puts extra stress upon the children, *e.g.* during long practical hours they have to maintain a static and most of the time bent posture which may be a factor causing postural defects.
14. **Lack of exercise:** Exercises tone up the spinal nerves and abdominal organs, improves appetite and digestion, promotes flexibility and co-ordination, reduces mental strain, provides energy, improves the physical ability and efficiency. Lack of exercise has several adverse effects which may lead to postural deformities and defects.
15. **Lack of awareness:** Many people are unaware regarding the concept of proper posture and continue to follow wrong or faulty postures. This becomes their permanent habit and a lifestyle which leads to postural defects and deformities.
16. **Obesity:** Obesity or undue body overweight puts extra stress and strain on the muscular as well as skeletal structure of the body which may result in postural deviations.
17. **Poverty:** Lack of essential and basic facilities due to poverty is another important factor which may lead an individual to adopt bad or faulty posture.

18. **Occupation:** Certain occupations require sitting, standing or working in an imbalanced or improper posture constantly for long hours, which may result in postural defects and deviations.

PREVENTIVE AND REMEDIAL MEASURES

The appropriate remedial action should be started as soon as possible. Immediate attention is required as bad posture exerts unusual and atypical stress on the soft tissues, muscles and ligaments of the body segment. Time-to-time screening of body posture will go a long way in preventing postural defects. It must be remembered that the means of correcting postural deviations must be based upon medical diagnosis and recommendations. As ignorance regarding the basic concept of posture is one of the major causes for postural divergencies, proper knowledge regarding the importance of posture and appropriate guidance for correcting the same is necessary so as to develop a postural sense regarding body mechanics in the mind of an individual.

Balance Exercise in Posture Training

Maintaining the correct balance is important in posture training. All remedial exercises should be carried on from basically correct positions due to the prevalence of faulty foot and leg position. Walking on a straight line, narrow beam or even on the flat floor places undue stress on groups of balance muscles that are not developed symmetrically. For this reason, a tilted board balance is devised in which the treads are started outwards at about 15 degrees. Standing on these treads, the leg is rotated outwards and the feet are thrown into a wild universion state which corrects the position. In this position, there is a taking up of a slack of the stretched muscles and a lengthening of the shortened muscles every time one foot is lifted. The effort to keep the balance, or to maintain stability is being done by the opposite leg, body or arm. Something else, gives a powerful stimulus to all the muscles.

Control of Postural Defects

Postural defects can be controlled by various measures like–brisk walking, jogging, running, yogasans, physical exercises, taking balanced diets, wearing well-fitted clothes & shoes, controlling body weight and following good rest and sleep habits.

❖ ❖ ❖

CHAPTER 12

Obstacles Training & Adventure Activities

OBSTACLES TRAINING

The obstacles training is a very important part of NCC training. This training not only makes the cadets physically tough but also develops a very high degree of confidence in them, and inculcates the qualities of courage and patience to face challenges in life.

The obstacle training is imparted to NCC cadets to ensure physical fitness, agility of body, mental robustness, coordination and balance of body and mind. It also improves the risk taking ability, problem solving skills and inculcates the overall team spirit in the cadets. It is also a precursor to SSB Tests.

The cadets are trained on the obstacle course in uniform. The cadets are trained both individually and as members of teams. A competition on obstacles course begins at unit level and finalises at RD camp in New Delhi. The competition is a team-event and all the cadets of a team compete with other teams to cross the 10 obstacles course in minimum time without breaking any rules. For a team to win all its members must cross all the obstacles clearly in minimum time without any break or stop in between the obstacles.

The Obstacles Course

The obstacles course consists of ten obstacles. The obstacles are constructed of wood, bricks, concrete and mud. Each obstacle is placed at a distance of about 25-30 feet from each other.

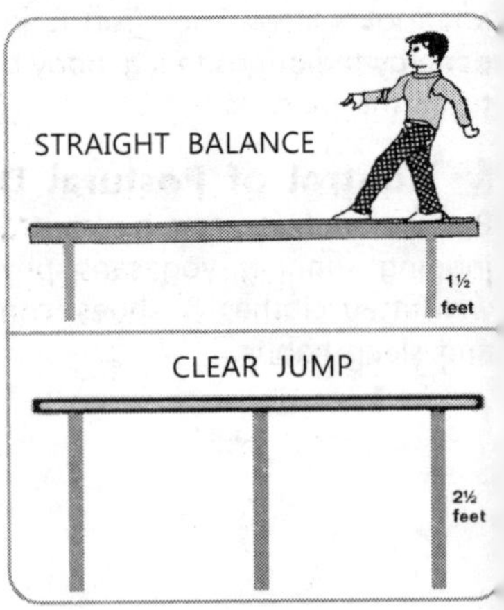

1. **Straight Balance :** This obstacle consists of a wooden plank of 3 inches thickness, 4 inches width and 12 ft in length, placed 1½ feet above ground level. A cadet has to cross it running, keeping his arms open and balancing his body throughout the obstacle.
2. **Clear Jump :** This obstacle is a straight wooden beam fixed 2–2½ feet from the ground. A cadet has to cross it by jumping over it without touching it.

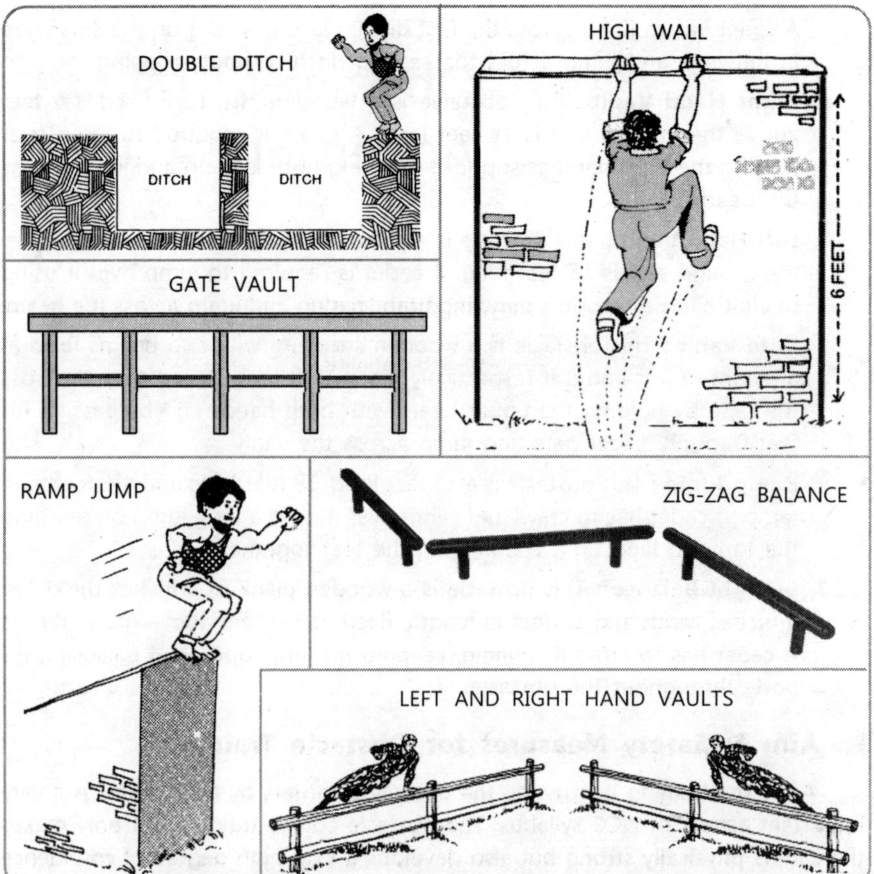

3. **Zig-Zag Balance :** This obstacle is a structure of wooden beam which is 18 feet in length, 3 inch in width and fixed 1½ feet above the ground in a zig-zag manner. Its height gradually increases to 3½ feet in the end. A cadet has to cross it lengthwise with open hands, balancing the body throughout the obstacle.
4. **High Wall :** This obstacle is a 6 feet high and 12 feet long plastered wall. A cadet has to run, jump, kick the wall with one leg and take a leap putting both hands on the wall and pushing his body upwards to jump over to the other side of the wall.
5. **Double Ditch :** This obstacle consists of two ditches each of 6-8 feet in length, 4-6 feet wide and 3-4 feet deep separated by a small gap of 3-4 feet.

A cadet has to jump across the first ditch, place one foot on the small gap in between and jump across the second ditch without stopping.

6. **Right Hand Vault :** This obstacle is a wooden structure fixed 3½ feet above the ground and is 18 feet long. A cadet is required to jump over it using the right hand as support, swinging both legs up and jump across the beam.
7. **Left Hand Vault :** This obstacle is a wooden structure fixed 3½ feet above the ground and is 18 feet long. A cadet is required to jump over it using the left hand as support throwing both legs up and jump across the beam.
8. **Gate Vault :** This obstacle is a wooden structure with two beams fixed at a height of 3 ft and 5 ft respectively, both 18 ft long. A cadet has to cross the gate by holding the upper beam with both hands and by passing his feet through 3 feet gate and jump across the vault.
9. **Ramp Jump :** This obstacle is a 15 feet long, 18 feet wide and 4½ feet high ramp. A cadet has to crawl and climb over it, take a long jump on reaching the top and land on a pit on both the feet together.
10. **Straight Balance :** This obstacle is a wooden plank of 3 inches thickness, 4 inches width and 12 feet in length, fixed at 1½ feet above ground level. A cadet has to cross it running, keeping his arms open and balancing his body throughout the obstacle.

Aim & Safety Measures for Obstacle Training

Aim: The training in crossing the obstacles/barriers by NCC cadets is a very important aspect of NCC syllabus. The obstacle course training not only makes the cadets physically strong but also develops a very high degree of confidence and develops the qualities of patience and courage to face all type of challenges and barriers in life.

Safety Measures: Following safety measures must be ensured during the conduct of Obstacle Course training for cadets:

- Suitable and physically fit cadets only to be selected.
- Training to be given first in PT dress, later on with packs and weapon.
- Emphasis to be given on closing of individual timings and later team timings.
- Wet and slippery obstacles and area to be avoided.
- Obstacles to be done under supervision of qualified instructors and correct techniques only to be used.
- Arrangement of first aid to be ensured.

Types of ADVENTURE ACTIVITIES

PARASAILING

HORSE RIDING

SLITHERING

RAFTING

MOUNTAINEERING

CYCLE EXPEDITION

SAILING

SCUBA DIVING

ROCK CLIMBING

KAYAKING

TREKKING

ADVENTURE ACTIVITIES

It is the training given to the cadets/youth by the NCC to develop the quality of leadership, self-confidence, determination and feelings of team spirit. NCC conducts the adventure activities to inculcate the quality of leadership and determination in the cadets.

Various Land based Adventure Activities :

(i) Mountaineering
(ii) Mountaineering Expeditions
(iii) Trekking
(iv) Cycle and Motorcycle Expedition

Various Naval Activities :

(i) Sailing Expedition
(ii) Scuba Diving
(iii) Boat Pulling
(iv) Wind Surfing
(v) Kayaking

Various Air based Activities :

(i) Parasailing
(ii) Slithering
(iii) Parajumps

Aims of Adventure Activities

The aims of adventure activities are :

(i) To inculcate the spirit of adventure, exploration, inquisitiveness and practical investigation.
(ii) To develop stamina, endurance, self-confidence, team spirit and esprit-de-corps.
(iii) To develop love for nature and concern for environmental cleanliness.
(iv) To promote National Integration.

Important Destinations for Expeditions

The important destinations for expeditions are :

(i) The places of natural beauty
(ii) The places outside the state
(iii) The places of historical and religious importance
(iv) Distant countryside & remote places

❖ ❖ ❖

CHAPTER 13

A Career in Defence Services

A career in Defence Services as a commissioned officer has always had a place of dignity and respect amongst the youth. A student finishing plus two examination can opt for a career in Defence Services through National Defence Academy or Naval Academy after a UPSC written exam. NDA provides world class training facilities which include graduation from JNU whereas Naval Academy candidates go through four years B.Tech program. Air Force also conducts the Common Aptitude Test (AFCAT). Defence Services give one innumerable opportunities to develop one's personality and cultivate new interests. In fact one can choose from over thirty different extra-curricular activities like aero-modeling, golf, gliding, sailing, wind surfing, astronomy and many more. Complete expenses are borne by the government and cadets are paid monthly stipend also.

A graduate can join through the Combined Defence Services examination as a regular/short service commissioned officer. Training for regular commissioned officers is carried out at Indian Military Academy, Dehradun, known as the cradle of Military leadership. Those desirous of joining the Short Service Commission get trained at Officers' Training Academy at Chennai and serve for a period of five years. On completion of this term they can either resign or opt for an extension of five years or a permanent commission.

Engineering graduates can join in the pre-final or final year through the University Entry Scheme or after completion of graduation through Technical Graduate Scheme without any written examination, by appearing before the Services Selection Board. In both the cases the candidate gets an antedate seniority of two years and gets commissioned as a captain.

NCC 'C' certificate holders are eligible to join directly without going through UPSC entrance examination. They have to clear the test and interview at SSB.

Women's entry at graduate, post graduate or an engineering graduate level has been very popular and competitive. A woman officer now gets to serve up to fourteen years after being trained at OTA, Chennai. Entry is based on selection by the Services Selection Board. Women officers have performed well in all spheres with their male counterparts even under field conditions.

There is a confusion that Defence doesn't pay you well. It is a misconception, because payments are of two types, cash and kind. Defence pays you in both cash and kind. In cash, it gives you a handsome salary to begin with, which increases with time and it also gives you incomparable facilities with benefits like medical facilities, insurance and canteen facilities for you and your family as well, and schooling facility for your children.

Defence offers you a way of life which you can't get in any other job. Exposing you to a number of adventure sports, giving you a chance to live in different parts of India. You can travel to foreign countries as well. You are entitled to free rationing and fully furnished houses when you get commissioned.

Defence trainings are the most important part. You are grilled mentally and physically to a level that if you are mentally fit for the job then only you'll be able to sustain. There is nothing bad in training; it only makes you physically fit and mentally strong. The academies that train defence personnel are the best academies of the world. Your physical fitness is raised to a great level. Your personality is enhanced from every side, one can easily distinguish between a defence personnel and a civilian.

While corporate jobs give you chances to be a part of big MNCs and travel to a number of foreign places, defence jobs offer you a chance to be a part of the most elite institutions of India, and work for your motherland. You get a great uniform; you get a chance to work for India directly. There is huge exposure in defence jobs, you can associate with people in the clubs and participate in different types of events which are organized time to time. In fact, a career in defence is not merely a job, it is entirely a way of life. Love for the country and adventure are the driving forces behind defence jobs.

CAREER OPTIONS IN DEFENCE SERVICES : ARMY, NAVY AND AIR FORCE

Indian Army

	Type of Entry	Month of Starting of Course	Age at the Time of Joining	Educational Qualification	Mode of Selection	How to Apply
1.	**National Defence Academy**					
(*a*)	National Defence Academy, Pune	Jan & July	16½ 19 yrs	12th standard of 10+2 System of Education or equl	NDA Exam by UPSC & SSB interview	Apply in response to advertisement in March/April & Oct/Nov
2.	**Indian Military Academy**					
(*a*)	Direct Entry	Jan & July	19-24 yrs	Degree or equilvalent	CDS Exam conducted by UPSC and SSB interview	Apply in response to advertisement in March/April & Oct/Nov
(*b*)	Engineering Graduate	Jan & July	20-27 yrs	Engineering Degree in notified disciplines	Direct SSB interview	Apply to Dte. Gen of Recruiting (TGC Entry), Army HQ, West Block III, R.K. Puram, New Delhi-66 in response to advertisement in March/April & Oct/Nov.

	Type of Entry	Month of Starting of Course	Age at the Time of Joining	Educational Qualification	Mode of Selection	How to Apply
(c)	University Entry Scheme	July	19-25 yrs 18-24 yrs	Final and Pre-final year students of an Engineering degree course	Campus interview and SSB interview	Apply in response to detailed advertisement in July.
(d)	10+2 TES	Jan & July	16½ -19½ yrs	10+2 Pass with 70% aggreagate in PCM	Apply directly to the Recruiting Directorate	Apply in response to advertisement in May and November
3.	**Officers Training Academy, Chennai**					
(a)	Short Service Commission (Non-Tech)	May & Oct/Nov	19-25 yrs	Degree or equivalent	CDSE Exam conducted by UPSC and SSB interview	Apply in response to advertisement in March/April & Oct/Nov
(b)	Short Service Commission (Technical)	May & Oct/Nov	20-27 yrs	Engineering Degree in Notified discipline	Direct SSB interview	Apply in response to advertisement in Mar/April and Oct/Nov.
(c)	Short Service Commission (NCC Special Entry Scheme)	May & Oct/Nov	19-25 yrs	Graduate with 50% aggregate marks with NCC 'C' Certificate	Direct SSB interview	Apply in response to advertisement in Oct/Nov.
(d)	Women Special Entry Scheme (Officers)	March & Sep	19-27 yrs	Graduate/Post Graduate/LLB/ Professional Engineering Graduate	Direct SSB Interview	Apply in response to advertisement in June/Dec.

Indian Navy

	Type of Entry	Educational Qualification	Age Limit (Yrs)	Remarks
(a)	Cadet Entry (10+2) Naval Academy, Goa (Through UPSC)	10+2 or equivalent with Physics & Maths	16½-19	For Men only
(b)	Cadet Entry (NDA) (Through UPSC)	10+2 or equivalent with Physics & Maths	16½-19	For Men only
(c)	Graduate Special Entry, Naval Academy, Goa (Through CDSE)	B.Sc (Physics & Maths) or BE	19-22	For Men only
(d)	NCC Special Entry Naval Academy, Goa	B.Sc (Physics & Maths) or BE, with Naval Wing Senior Div NCC 'C' Certificate	19-24	For Men only
(e)	Direct Entry Naval Armament Inspection Cadre	A Degree in Electronics/Elect/ Mech Engg or Post Graduate Degree in Electronics or Physics	19½-25	For Men only
(f)	Direct Entry Law Cadre	A Degree in Law Qualifying for enrolment as an Advocates under the Advotaes Act, 1961 with minimum 55% marks	22-27	For Men only

Short Service Commission

	Type of Entry	Educational Qualification	Age Limit (Years)	Remarks
(a)	Law Cadre	A Degree in Law qualifying for enrolment as an advocate under the Advocates Act, 1961 with minimum 55% marks	22-27	For Men & Women
(b)	Logistics Cadre	BA (Economics) II Div. Or B.Com II Div, or B.Sc (Physics and Maths) II Div. or B.Tech/BE or Graduation in any subject with Degree/ Diploma in Material/Financial Management	19½-25	For Men & Women
(c)	ATC (Air Traffic Control)	B.Sc I Div or M.Sc II Div	19½-25	For Men & Women
(d)	Hydro Cadre	B.Sc I Div or M.Sc II Div or BE	19½-25	For Men only
(e)	General Service	B.Sc. I Div or M.Sc II Div or BE	19½-25	For Men only
(f)	Logistic (Catering)	Degree in Hotel Management or equivalent with minimum 50% marks in aggregate	19½-25	For Men & Women

Indian Air Force

	Branch/Type of Entry	Educational Qualification	Age Limit (Yrs)	Advertisement Schedule
FLYING BRANCH				
(a)	National Defence Academy (For Men only)	10+2 with Physics & Maths	16½-19	Mar/Oct
(b)	Combined Defence Services Examination (For Men only)	Graduate with Physics & Maths at 10+2 or BE	19-23	Apr/Sep
(c)	NCC Special Entry (Through CO Unit/DG NCC) (For Men only)	Graduate with Physics & Maths at 10+2 or BE & NCC Air Wing Sr. Div. 'C' Certificate	19-23	Apr/Sep
(d)	Short Service Commission (For Women only)	Graduate with Physics & Maths at 10+2 or BE	19-23*	May/Nov
*Upper age limit relaxed to 25 years for holders of Commerical Pilots Licence (CPL)				
TECHNICAL BRANCH				
(PC for Men / SSC for Women)**				
(a)	Aeronautical Engineering (Electronics)	First Class degree in Engineering Electronics/Mechanical/Allied subjects as per advertisement	18-28	Apr/Oct
(b)	Aeronautical Engineering (Mech.)			
SSC for Women				
(c)	Same as above			October
GROUND DUTIES BRANCH				
(PC for Men/SSC for Women)**				
(a)	Administration	First Class Graduate or PG in subjects as per advertisement	20-23	May/Nov

(b)	Logistics		
(c)	Accounts		20-25
(d)	Education	PG in subjects as per adverstisement	20-25

** PC Permanent Commission/SSC Short Service Commission

SELECTION PROCESS : WTLOs

Selection process for the Whole Time Lady Officers (WLTOs)

The Direct Entry Whole Time Lady Officers are selected through an open competition by the Union Public Service Commission as and when vacancies arise. A limited percentage of vacancies is also reserved for 'C' Certificate holders of NCC, subject to fulfilling other conditions.

Eligibility Conditions – Direct Entry

(i) Age – 21-25 years.

(ii) Qualification – Degree of a University or equivalent.

(iii) Must be medically fit for active service.

(iv) Must fulfil the following physical standards :

* Heights – 145 cms
* Relaxation in Height Standards – For Gorkha/Garhwali/Kumaoni/ Dogra/Maratha Ladies 2 cms, Adivasis - 3 cms
* Weight – According to height but not less than 42 Kgs
* Should not have knock-knee or a flat foot.
* Eyesight (with or without glasses).
  Distant Vision–6/6 in one eye and 0.8 in other eye.
  Near Vision–0.6 in one eye and 0.8 in other eye.

(v) Desirable

* 2 years experience as ANO or GCI in NCC or equivalent rank in Police Force.
* NCC 'C' Certificate holder.

JOB APPLICATION & CURRICULUM VITAE

The application carries the burden of attracting attention, creating interest, and doing a substantial part of the job of selling you to your prospective employer.

The resume gives the essential facts about yourself, your education, experience, personal qualities, and what you have actually accomplished.

The Sample Format of a Covering Letter for Writing an Application for a Job.

Date : ....

Full Office Address of the Receiver

Kind Attention : ....

Respected Sir/Madam,

Sub : Application for the post of ....

This application is in reference to your advertisement in (*newspaper*) dated (*date*) regarding the appointment of (post's full name) in your esteemed organisation. I offer my candidature for this post and append the following particulars:

I am (Full Name). I am a resident of (City). I have earned my Graduation degree (name of the degree) from (institute). After completing my education, I joined (firm's name). I joined it on (date) and have been working there since then. My field of specialisation is (exact field of specialisation). I have a total experience of (no. of years) years in this field. I am a part of the technical/supervisory/managerial/senior managerial cadre of my company. I am satisfied by my present assignment. However, I would like to shift to a better job for the sake of job enrichment. I feel that the job offered by you would enable me to have complete professional satisfaction.

If I am given an opportunity, I shall leave no stone unturned to deliver concrete results in your organisation. A copy of my curriculum vitae has been attached with this letter. If you need any other set of information, please do let me know.

Thanking you,

Your's Faithfully

....

Encl : a/a

A Sample Format of a Curriculum Vitae/Resume

FULL NAME : ....

HOME ADDRESS : ....

TELEPHONE & MOBILE NO. : ....

E-MAIL ID : ....

ACADEMIC RECORD :

S.N.	Class	Board/ University	Year of passing	Subjects	Percentage
1.	Matriculation (10th)				
2.	Senior Secondary/ SSC (10+2)				
3.	Graduation				
4.	Post-Graduation				
5.	Diplomas or Professional Courses				

CURRENT ASSIGNMENT

Working for (Firm's full name) as (Full Designation) since (date). Job responsibilities include : (a) ....

(b) ....

(c) ....

I am stationed at (city).

FAMILY DETAILS

1. Father's Name : ....
2. Occupation : ....
3. Mother's Name : ....
4. Occupation : ....
5. Brother's & Sister's (Name and Occupation) :
   (a) ....
   (b) ....
   (c) ....

PERSONAL DETAILS

1. Date of Birth : .... 2. Place of Birth : ....
3. Nationality : .... 4. Marital Status : ....
5. No. of dependents : .... 6. Height : ....
7. Weight : .... 8. Health : ....
9. Achievements (Medals/Certificates) ....
10. Skills : (Fluency in Languages) : ....
11. Interests (Hobbies) ....
12. Other Details : (Anything worth mentioning) ....

Signature

Date : ....

❖ ❖ ❖

CHAPTER 14

Services Tests & Interviews

SSB TESTS AND INTERVIEWS

The candidates of Defence Services when clear their written exams of NDA, CDS or AFCAT are just half-way through, for, not everyone of them becomes a defence officer. They still have to clear several rounds of tests, group discussions and interviews conducted by the Services Selection Board (SSB).

It must be borne in mind that these are not tests of some crammed material or any matter collected or memorized. These are hard and genuine tests of one's personality, though the role of knowledge of various facts and figures regarding multifarious aspects of life and fields of knowledge cannot be altogether ruled out.

Every human being has a distinct personality. As such every person differs from every other person in various ways including physical features, mental make-up, moral and spiritual beliefs and convictions, etc.

Every establishment lays stress on certain basic human traits which are considered part and parcel of a person's personality and which, though they may not vary in kind, vary in degree considerably. The interviewers at SSB often try to measure the extent of such personality traits in each candidate in various ways.

At SSB, in addition to the interview, the candidates are put to Intelligence Tests, both verbal and non-verbal, designed to access their basic intelligence. They are also put to Group Tests such as group discussions, group planning, outdoor group tasks, and asked to give brief lectures on specified subjects. All these tests are intended to judge the mental and physical calibre of candidates. In broad terms, this is really an assessment of not only the intellectual qualities but also one's social traits and interests in current affairs alongwith the test of his mental and physical endurance and stamina.

The right approach to a test or interview is a balanced, non-impassioned approach based on reason and with a clear understanding and realization of the paramountcy of test, interview or task at hand.

There is no denying the fact that getting through a test or interview is an art but you have to cultivate it with care and effort. Remember that a successful SSB interview means a glorious career with Defence Services.

Therefore, irrespective of your academic or family background, if you can prepare well and perform on the expected lines and standards, you can surely be selected for a defence officer's training course at SSB.

It is a common phenomenon observed that candidates believe that they can get through the SSB tests and Interview by just reading text books or by doing a crash-course at the local coaching centre. Unfortunately, this is not true as there is no short-cut to success at SSB. It needs systematic and consistent approach to prepare for it. The selectors are not interested in the mugged up knowledge, data and statistics from the text books, what they want is the application of knowledge and general awareness with clear-thinking and expression, and a sound mind and body as well. Reading daily newspapers, newsmagazines, watching TV news, practice of English conversation, discussions, lectures, physical exercises and sports activities are essential for this.

A defence service officer is no less than an engineer or doctor or an administrative or bank officer in respect of his cadre, pay, perks, or social status. The job satisfaction and service conditions are supreme apart from sense of achievement and serving the country with highest honours and glory. While others just work to earn money for fulfiling the requirements of their families, a defence service officer works truly for the honour and safety of the country and to save the lives of his fellow countrymen. This not only pays back handsomely in return but also brings immense sense of patriotism, glory and achievement, making his work and life truly meaningful for him, his family back home, fellow-countryman and the whole country. The life of a defence service officer is the most complete, vibrant and meaningful in all respects and that is why this is the most sought-after profession of our youth.

WHAT THE INTERVIEWERS EXPECT FROM YOU

The interviewer, tries to find out, through the medium of the tests and interview, how far and how best you can fill the bill for the job in view. Now, put yourself for a moment in his shoes. If you are an interviewer what things you would like to find out about the individual whom you wish to select. What personality and character traits of the individual you would be interested to discover? Here is a checklist:

Appearance and Bearing

What is his first impression like? Is he able to make a favourable impression? Does he create an impact? How are his dressing habits and grooming? Is he cheerful and bright? Does he smile? Is he neat and clean? Does he reveal pleasant and good manners? Does he observe the rules of etiquette?

Level of Intelligence

Is he intelligent as well as sensible? Does he show good awareness? Has he a quick and good grasp? Is he well read? Has he got good general knowledge and sound common sense? What is the extent and depth of his knowledge in regard to the job he has applied for? What are his qualifications and experience? How has he acquainted himself in his studies? Can he learn quickly and improve by training? Does he reveal imagination and foresight? Is he mentally alert?

Power of Expression

Can he talk? Does he speak fluently or does he prove to be a tongue-tied? Is he capable of communicating his thoughts clearly, crisply, coherently and effectively? Does he put across ideas freely, convincingly and powerfully? Is he able to reason out in a logical and rational manner? Does he sound convincing? Does he speak with enthusiasm and interest to impress others? Is he able to command and hold the attention of his audience? Is he practical and accurate in his talk or does he resort to waffle? How does he react to criticism? Is he good at selling his ideas and winning over others to his way of thinking?

Organisation

Is he resourceful? Has he tackled any difficult problems with success? Is he capable of producing workable solutions in practical situations? Is he industrious, painstaking and thorough? Does he display the required concentration? Is he able to stick to his objective and avoid going after red-herrings? Does he know his own mind? Has he the ability to work to time, method and situation? Does he go about a job in a planned, methodical and systematic manner? Is he steady and consistent or does he do things by fits and starts? Can he combine his resources judiciously with an eye for economy? Is he able to exercise control and coordination while effecting decentralization of authority and responsibility?

Physical Fitness

Does he enjoy sound health? Is he physically tough and fit? What efforts does he make to keep himself physically fit? Does he play games or take exercise regularly? How good is his stamina? Does he get tired easily or is he able to carry on and withstand fatigue effectively? Does his physical movements and activities reveal vitality and strength?

Dynamic Qualities

Has he rousing enthusiasm, urge and interest? Is he active, energetic and lively? Does he reveal dash, speed and push? Has he enough self-confidence and courage to act boldly and decisively? Will he take plunge without hesitation? Is he enterprising? Can he take decisions? Does he display initiative? Has he got determination and tenacity? Is he able to grasp and make good use of the opportunities that come his way? Is he willing to take reasonable risks? Can he preserve and hold on with patience and faith in the face of difficulties? Can he get over his defeats and setbacks and succeed in spite of them?

Social Aspects

Is he warm, friendly and cooperative? Does he display the attitude of give and take? Is he ready to make sacrifices for the sake of others or his organization? Does he prove to be flexible, accommodative and easy to approach? Does he enjoy the company of others? Is he reserved, aloof, dull and gloomy or does he prove to be hearty, sociable, cheerful and a ready mixer? Has he been able to get along well with his superiors, equals and subordinates? Is he able to adjust himself readily or does he complain, bicker, bind and moan about all the time? Has he been utilizing his spare time? Has he many friends? Is he willing to help? Can he conduct himself in a cordial and pleasant manner at a social gathering? Is he fond of travelling, seeing new places and meeting new faces? Can he feel relaxed and comfortable in others' presence. Does he display adequate tact? Is he considerate and sympathetic towards the feeling and sentiments of others? Does he keep pace with changing ideas? Is he progressive in his outlook? Has he a good sense of humour?

Character and Integrity

Is he honest, loyal and trustworthy? How is his financial moral rectitude? Does he prove to be responsible while talking about or commenting on others? Does he refrain from speaking ill of others? Has he got national pride and a sense of patriotism? Are his habits temperate and praiseworthy? Has he the moral strength to withstand temptations? Is he well-disciplined and capable of good self-control? Has he self-respect and the courage to stand by his noble ideals? Does he display a sense of duty?

Leadership Qualities

Does he reveal esprit de corps or team spirit? Can he get along well with others? Is he able to create a strong impact on a group? Has he the ability to bind the group into a well-knit and harmonious team? Is he capable of encouraging others and bringing out the best in them? Can he exercise effective command without giving rise to frictions and complaints? Does he place the interests of his men, group or organization before his own? Can he judge others with reasonable accuracy? Is he a bully or a democratic leader? Can he successfully motivate and influence others? Has he been able to get things done smoothly and efficiently? Does he set an example for others to follow? Is he able to inspire others with confidence and enthusiasm?

Optimistic Outlook

Does he display optimism, positive attitude and constructive approach in his undertakings? Has he clear objectives, definite goals and laudable ambitions? Is he confident of success? Does he look forward to a bright, prosperous and happy future? Is he determined to win? Do his words, thoughts, attitudes, approach, behaviour and action always reflect his unanswering faith in ultimate success?

OFFICERS LIKE QUALITIES (OLQs)

The most important and essential qualities of a service officer which SSB look for in the prospective candidates, are given as under. The candidates are strongly advised to inculcate and cultivate these "OLQ (Officers' Like Qualities) Factors".

1. **Planning and Organisation** : The OLQ has the following factors of the mental aspect of a candidate:
   - (i) **Effective Intelligence** : Capability to deal with practical situation and act as per requirement of the situation.
   - (ii) **Reasoning Ability** : Ability to grasp and uptake the situation and arrive at conclusion, by rational thinking.
   - (iii) **Organising Ability** : Ability to plan and organise resources and to make their best use, capacity to finish the given task in a systematic manner within the stipulated period.
   - (iv) **Power of Expression** : Ability to put across one's point/idea clearly and vividly with ease. One should be a good orator and also a good listener. Candidate should speak fluently with confidence.
2. **Social Adjustment** : This OLQ has the following factors of the heart/ concience of a candidate:
   - (i) **Social Adaptability** : To adapt to changing environment and also to adjust accordingly.
   - (ii) **Co-operation** : Participation in working together. Harmony and helping each other.
   - (iii) **Sense of Responsibility** : Willing to discharge responsibility and given duty.
3. **Social Effectiveness** : This OLQ has the following factors of the dynamic interaction of the mind and concience of a candidate:
   - (i) **Initiative** : Ability to initiate (start) and sustain an act.
   - (ii) **Self-Confidence** : Faith in one's ability to meet critical situation and event.

(iii) **Speed of Decision :** Capability to arrive at workable situation judiciously and expeditiously.

(iv) **Ability to Influence Group :** Ability to bring about willing effect from the group.

(v) **Liveliness (Cheerfulness) :** Capacity to keep one buoyant.

(vi) **Resourcefulness :** Capability of the leader to deal with the situation without normally available means and material.

4. Dynamism : This OLQ has the following factors of the coordination of mind and body of a candidate:

(i) **Determination :** A firm resolution. It implies fixedness of purpose, concentration and will-power.

(ii) **Courage :** Ability to take bold preposed risks.

(iii) **Stamina :** Capacity to withstand physical and mental stress and strain to undergo prolonged endurance.

INTERVIEW TIPS

Now you know what your interviewer is interested to find out about yourself. Naturally, he cannot ask you direct questions on such factors or expect to get correct and truthful answers for them. Therefore, he will try to get these details by making you talk about yourself, your activities, achievements and dealing with others. Since you know his mind, and are aware of his requirements, why not take the initiative and present them yourself. It means that you should be ready to talk and touch on such favourable incidents of your life and experience when the opportunity presents itself.

Do not keep on saying 'Yes' or 'No' monotonously all the time when questions are put to you. First understand the question fully and determine what all or what exactly he wants to know. When he asks about your educational qualifications, sports activities, hobbies, domestic background, friendships and association, travel experiences, job experiences, reading habits, life's ambitions and so on, you will have all the opportunities you need. Since you are going to blow your own trumpet, it has to be done in discreet, subtle, diplomatic and expert manner. It should not be too loud, blaring or jarring.

Interview, after all, is nothing but face to face conversation with a purpose. If you make the conversation interesting and enjoyable, your purpose is achieved. To make it interesting, you have to listen and talk as the occasion demands. You must listen with interest and talk with purpose. In both cases you must exercise initiative to say the right things at the right time. Imaginative use of initiative in the interview will thus ensure you sure success.

GROUP DISCUSSIONS

Group discussion is nothing but a discussion on any topic in a group. It is a sort of public speaking in which several candidates in a group take part. Each member expresses his opinions on the subject/topic given by the GTO on the spot. It is thus a spontaneous conversation and not a pre-planned one. The topics for discussion are normally given from 'current affairs' and 'social topics'.

This exercise facilitates the assessment of certain traits of candidates' personality. It depicts his quality of leadership, and social adaptability. Since the group is leaderless, this vacuum is filled by the candidate who demonstrates officers like qualities. He must show tremendous self-confidence and determination. When confronted with odds and stiff opposition he should contain the best of brightest ideas within the time limit.

You must examine the subject in a cool and calm atmosphere. You must shed shyness. Any member, who possesses initiative, tact, self-confidence and drive grabs the opportunity and hence assumes the role of leader.

Every member in a group is expected to express his ideas, and opinion on a given topic. Don't offend any member of your team. Even if you disagree with his point of view, simply say "I beg to differ from you". Don't show-off and avoid being selfish. Avoid undesirable gestures and mannerism. Be cheerful and positive. When your turn comes, speak emphatically, logically and convincingly, use correct accent and pronunciation. Be brief and to the point. Don't beat about the bush.

LECTURETTES

Lecturette is a short lecture. It is a sort of short speech test, imparting knowledge and passing information. SSB lays emphasis on the power of speech. It is a means through which a candidate can impress other aspirant candidates by his expression, fluency, manners, elasticity of thoughts and delivery.

Remember: "Spoken words rule the world".

The GTO gives each candidate a card on which 3 or 4 topics are printed relating to current-affairs, political events or topics on social, economic environment and technology. Each candidate is called by turn to pick up a card. He is asked to select anyone of the topics given therein. He is then allowed to go a little away from the group and prepare his speech or lecturette for about 3 minutes. Then he is asked to make a short speech not exceeding 3 to 5 minutes time. This is an extempore lecture whereby one can impress others by his eloquency and delivery of speech. It is of great importance that a candidate should choose such a subject about which he has sufficient knowledge.

❖ ❖ ❖

CHAPTER

15 Self-Defence

Everyone, including girls, must learn the techniques of self-defence to counter incidences of any misbehaviour or crime. Self defence can be of two type—Moral and Physical self defence.

MORAL SELF-DEFENCE

As is the old saying 'Prevention is better than cure'; one must guard against undesirable incidents. In doing so, not only do we help ourselves or others but can also help in making our society a better place to live. As NCC cadets, with a built-in sense of responsibility, it is necessary that prevention of untoward incidents is ensured by all boy and girl cadets.

Some of the untoward incidents that one can sometimes come across are :

(i) Road Accidents,

(ii) Pick-pocketing, Hooliganism, Theft and Robbery,

(iii) Molestation, Eve-Teasing and Sexual-Harassment,

(iv) Smoking, Drugs and Alcoholism.

The above incidents can be avoided if every person of society knows his/her responsibility towards society and measures to prevent these untoward incidents :

Road Accidents

To avoid road accidents one should :

(i) Drive/walk carefully on the roads and streets.

(ii) Follow all road-safety rules and traffic signals.

(iii) Begin early to reach in time and never overspeed.

(iv) Never mix drinking and driving.

(v) Always cross roads through zebra crossing, foot overbridge or subway.

(vi) All children should be taught the road safety rules.

Pick-pocketing, Hooliganism, Theft and Robbery

(i) One should avoid travelling in crowded places, and should try to carry little cash and valuables to prevent pick-pocketing.

(ii) One should never indulge in hooliganism and if hooligans are seen indulging in such activities, should try for a peaceful dispersion.

(iii) If the incident cannot be controlled, one should report the same to nearest police station.

(iv) One must ensure prevention of robbery and theft and report any such incidents to police if it happens.

Eve-Teasing, Molestation and Sexual Harassment

(i) Boys must understand that eve-teasing, molestation and sexual harassment are criminal offences.

(ii) Girls should not dress in such a way which can attract degrading remarks, glances or action.

(iii) Boys must learn to respect girls' dignity and girls should avoid travelling in darkness alone.

(iv) Working with the opposite sex in a healthy environment must be ensured.

Smoking, Drugs and Alcoholism

(i) They must spread positive thinking and awareness amongst the society.

(ii) They should spend time with their families and should introduce their friends to them to build up confidence of parents that they are in good company.

(iii) They must understand that drug addiction, smoking and alcoholism are health hazards and social evils.

(iv) They must understand that laws are implemented severely to penalize those found guilty of selling drugs or encouraging people to take drugs.

PHYSICAL SELF-DEFENCE

Physical self-defence or unarmed combat is a collection of offensive as well as defensive techniques derived from martial arts and combat sports.

An unarmed combat is a formidable weapon which in many circumstances, is a more effective weapon, against an armed enemy.

Principles of Physical Self-Defence

(i) A brutal method of attack must be used without any hesitation.

(ii) Attack must be aimed and carried out in a fierce, ruthless and determined manner.

(iii) Attack the most vulnerable points of the opponent's body.

(iv) The initial attack must be aimed at disabling, followed quickly by a hold, lock or throw.

(v) A defensive move followed by a rapid counter attack, must be aimed to catch the enemy by surprise.

(vi) Surprise, speed, strength, smoothness of execution, gaining and retention of initiative, are essential to overpower the enemy.

VULNERABLE PARTS OF BODY

The human body has various sensitive or vulnerable spots, which in unarmed combat are considered as vital spots. The degree of pain or injury from a blow to these spots will be graver and more serious than to the other parts of the body. Some of these are :

- **Body front :** Eyes, ears, temples, nose, mouth, chin, front and sides of throat, solar plexus, abdomen, testicles, knees, and insteps etc.
- **Behind the body :** Base of skull, spine, kidneys, testicles etc.

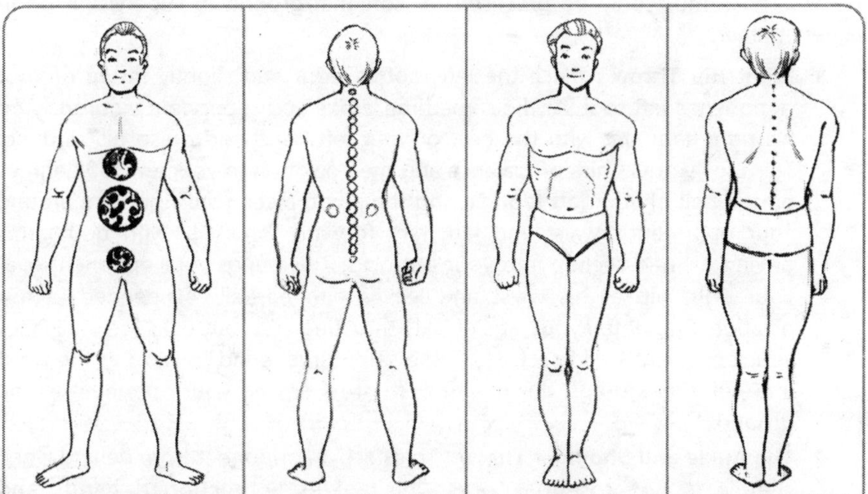

VULNERABLE PARTS OF HUMAN BODY | VITAL SPOTS OF HUMAN BODY

A cadet, therefore, must familiarize himself with the vulnerability of vital spots and the body weapons to select the proper target to achieve the aimed injury and also to be able to defend effectively.

Basics of Training

(i) Learning to use both hands for attacks and defences.
(ii) Practice should be realistic but within safety limits.
(iii) Practice on punching bags, or on a plank of thin wood.
(iv) Attacks must be all out and followed up quickly.
(v) Learn, master and practice each move for speed and coordination.
(vi) Follow all defensive moves with attack.
(vii) Seize initiative at first opportunity available.
(viii) The opponent should be bluffed into thinking that you are not going to attack or are injured.

(ix) Practise in pulling and tripping enemy off-balance.

(x) Surprise and unexpected attacks are important factors.

(xi) Strength is an important factor in physical self-defence.

THROWS & ATTACKS

Throws

Various throwing and attacking techniques important for self-defence are described below. These must only be practised on soft mat/ground in supervision of an expert trainer.

1. **Right Hip Throw :** Place the left foot in front and slightly inside of your opponent's left foot. At the same time, strike your opponent vigorously on his right shoulder with the heel of your left hand and grasp his clothing. This blow knocks him off balance and then pivot on to your left 180 degrees on the ball of your left foot. During the pivot, place your right arm around your opponent's waist and jerk him forward forcefully with both arms driving his mid section into your buttocks. This bends your opponent over your right hip at his waist and leaves him partially suspended in this position. Straighten your legs quickly thrusting your buttocks forcefully into your opponent's mid section. At the same time, bend forward at the waist and pull forward and down with both arms driving your opponent to the ground.
2. **The Ankle and Shoulder Throw :** To attack an opponent from behind when silence is not essential, grasp his ankles with cupped hands and simultaneously force your shoulders into his buttocks. Pull his legs outward and backward as you come to the standing position. This will throw him forward on to his face and you should then follow through with a disabling kick to the fork.
3. **Over Shoulder Throw :** The first movement is identical to the right hip throw. Pivot to the left 180 degrees on the ball of your left foot. Keep your right arm in position to protect your head and neck region until you near the completion of the pivot. Then reach up and grasp your opponent's clothing at his right shoulder with your right hand, gripping him with a double hand hold. As you complete your pivot. Pull your opponent forward and drive his mid section into your buttocks. Your buttocks are directly in front of your opponent's hips. Your right foot is in front of and slightly outside of your opponent's right foot, your elbows are as close to your body as possible. And your knees are bent. Straighten your legs, bend at the waist and pull downward with both hands. This action will catapult him over your shoulder.

Techniques of THROWS

4. **The Rugby Tackle :** A rugby tackle from the rear consists of a swift dive on opponent's legs. As he starts to fall you must be prepared to deal with a disabling blow. This movement can be practised either on a dummy, *e.g.* a weight sack suspended just clear of the ground or on a stationary/running man who has been taught how to fall.
5. **Reverse Hip Throw :** Stand closer to your opponent than in the previous throws. Take a long step forward with your left foot and place it slightly outside of and a few inches beyond your opponent's right foot. Most of your weight is supported on your foot. At the same time, strike your opponent forcefully on his right upper arm and with your left hand grasp his arm at this point with that hand. This blow causes him to lose his balance to the rear, immediately step around your opponent with your right foot and place it directly behind him. At the same time encircle his waist with your right arm. Push your hips to your right as far as possible to gain buttock-to-buttock contact and pull your opponent in position on your right hip. At this time lock your opponent's right arm into your left elbow. Straighten your legs, use your right hip as lever and throw your opponent over your hip, not over the side of your right leg.
6. **Arm Throw :** Face your opponent and seize his right wrist with both hands, right above left, swing his arm up quickly forward and pass under it by turning right-about maintaining a firm grip with your hands, and thus twisting his arm. Bend slightly forward over your left knee straightening and bracing your leg. Pull sharply down on your opponent's arm by bending your leg. Pull sharply down on your opponent's arm by bending forward at the waist and throw him on to his back. In practice, after you have secured your grip and turned, the remaining movements must be done gradually, otherwise you will dislocate your opponent's shoulder or cause him to strike the back of his head on the ground.
7. **Stomach Throw :** Grasp opponent's right and left side collars, disturb his balance by pushing him to his direct rear. In return when the opponent pushes you, place your right foot on his lower abdomen and retaining your firm hand grip on your opponent's lapel, slide to the ground with your buttocks enabling your opponent to fly over your head to the ground beyond, describing an arc in light through space. Sit on his chest and press his neck with both hands.

Attacks

- **Chin Jab :** This is a sharp forward and upward blow delivered with the heel of your hand bent arm under an opponent's chin with full force of the body.
- **The Knee Blow :** This is a blow with your bent knee to opponent's fork or face.

Techniques of ATTACKS

(12) Counter Attack to Front Strangle Hold

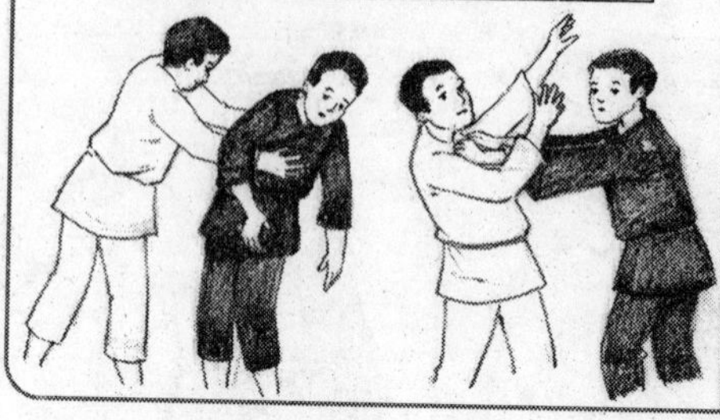

(13) Counter Attack to Rear Strangle Hold

- **The Stamp :** Do it when caught from behind or front, use your boot sharply on the opponent's shin followed by more disabling blow.
- **Full Nelson :** Do it with both arms under the opponent's armpit, place your hands at the back of his head. Apply downward pressure on his head and upward pressure pressing under his arms.
- **The Wrist Lock :** Lock your wrists around opponent's hand, wrist or fingers and bend them. This will cause him extreme pain.
- **The Kick :** Lift your leg and kick the opponent's knee with full force.
- **The Defence Against Kick :** Avoid the kick, catch hold of the kicking leg and twist it.
- **Rear Strangle Hold :** Put your both hands around opponent's neck from behind and hold him.
- **Front Strangle Hold :** Put your both hands around opponent's neck from the front and firmly hold him.
- **Cross Collar Strangle Hold :** Hold the opponent with both hands firmly across the collar.
- **Japanese Strangle Hold :** Hold the neck of the opponent with your right hand from behind and push his head by your left hand.
- **Counter Attack to Front Strangle Hold :** Turn and attack the enemy with cross collar strangle hold.
- **Counter Attack to Rear Strangle Hold :** Lean to your front and throw the opponent to the ground.

❖ ❖ ❖

CHAPTER

16 Environment and Ecology

WHAT IS ENVIRONMENT

The conditions in which an organism exists make up its environment. The physical components of the environment include materials such as rocks, soil, water and air.

The earth is the only planet in the solar system that supports life. Life on earth exists in the biosphere, a narrow zone made up of land, water and air extending up to a few kilometres above and below the earth's surface.

Environmental Factors that Influence Human Beings

1. **Physical Factors :** Earth, water, mountains and climatic conditions
2. **Biological Factors :** Plants, animals, micro-organisms and man himself
3. **Cultural Factors :** Economic, social and political factors.

Human Activities and the Environmental Degradation

To meet his various needs, man alters his natural surroundings. Sometimes such changes disturb natural processes and worsen the living conditions of human beings and other organisms. For example, untreated wastes are often dumped into the rivers. This affects the health of all organisms such as fish, that live in the water and man who drinks that water. This amounts to environmental degradation.

Depletion and Deterioration of Environment

Environmental degradation takes mainly two forms. One is resource depletion *i.e.,* a decline in the quantity of resources. The other is resource deterioration or pollution *i.e.,* decline in the quality of resources. Overuse and wastage are the main reasons for the depletion of resources. In India, forests are rapidly being cleared to provide firewood and agricultural land for the large population.

Deforestation

Large scale felling without planting new trees has led to deforestation or the complete removal of forests. Deforestation also disturbs the balance of gases in the atmosphere, which causes global warming, reduces rainfall and increases soil erosion. Such changes in the environment directly or indirectly harm living organisms.

Forest and Wildlife

Presently, forests cover about one-third of the worlds land area. But at one time, they covered about double the area that they cover now. The land is denuded of forests largely as a result of human activities, although natural occurrences such as volcanoes and forest fires also destroy forests. As the human population is growing, the need for more crop fields, pastures, settlements, mines and so on, is causing more trees to be felled and more forests to be cleared. Like deforestation and environmental damage, reckless hunting by humans is also a threat to the world's wildlife. The Indian tiger, hunted for its hide is near extinct. Whales have been hunted to near its extinction for their meat and fat. Wildlife forms an important link in the balance of ecology and must be protected.

Water Resources

We use water in agriculture and industries and for transportation, power generation and domestic purposes. Agriculture accounts for most of the water used. The groundwater level is sinking because people are pumping out water faster than nature can replace it. The dams built in rapid successions to provide facilities for irrigation, flood control and power generation disrupt the natural flow of water and harm the life forms that thrive in flowing water.

Environmental Problems

Since ages man is related with the environment. He resides in the surroundings alongwith different plants, trees and animals. Long ago he lived with the environment without disturbing its components. But now man has started extensively changing the surroundings, thus transforming the environment and consequently affecting the delicate balance of the ecosystem which is so essential for life on this planet, due to his ever expanding needs. People need food, water and space to live, air to breathe and energy to drive their machines. Increase in number of people, thus causes increase in consumption of food, water and space, and leaves less and less space for other animals and plants which means that many environmental problems have been caused by people. Global warming, acid rain and holes in the ozone layer are just three such examples.

Role of the NCC Cadets Towards Environment

Every one is aware of the environmental problems. NCC cadets are well organized to carry out environmental awareness campaign which is the need of the hour. NCC cadets can conduct tree plantation drives in order to curb the menace of environmental degradation. They should be the motivating and guiding force to friends and family members. As responsible citizens every one should plant trees and not cut them. Water conservation and proper disposal of waste also leads to the safeguarding of the environment. Therefore, it should be the duty of every NCC cadet to educate others towards this grave problem.

OZONE LAYER

The air around us consists mainly of nitrogen and oxygen. It also contains small amounts of other gases, including carbon dioxide (which we breathe out and green plants absorb), hydrogen and ozone.

Some people wrongly think that ozone is the refreshing air we breathe in at the seaside. It is, in fact, a poisonous kind of oxygen. At ground level, the air contains very little ozone. But, 24 kms above the earth, there is a thin layer of it. This ozone layer blocks out most of the ultraviolet rays from the sun. If these rays reached the ground, they would harm all land animals and plants.

Gases called chlorofluorocarbons (CFCs), used in refrigerators, air conditioners, and many aerosol sprays, are rapidly destroying the ozone layer. Satellites have already detected a large 'hole' in it over the North pole. Many countries are passing laws to stop the production and use of CFCs.

In these conditions chlorine and other gases accumulate in the environment. The ultraviolet rays of the spring sun initiate the reactions and chlorine and other gases become active resulting in a hole in the ozone layer. The production of CFCs needs to be cut drastically if the ozone layer is to continue to shield the ozone. If the ozone layer is depleted completely, the following effects may be realised:

* The size of eyes will be small, and may cause cataract.
* The size of nose will be longer.
* The human height will be smaller.
* It may cause skin cancer.
* It may cause low yield of crops.

WHAT IS ECOLOGY

Ecology is the study of organisms and the inter-relationship among organisms and the environment. The destruction of our forests has led to the disturbance of the delicate balance in the entire ecosystem. It has given rise to grave risks for the very survival of life on earth. Only recently we have started correcting this dangerous situation. The concern for ecological conservation has come to dominate the world scene.

Ecosystem

Ecosystem is the basic functional unit which includes both the organisms and non-living environment, each influencing the properties of the other and each one is necessary for maintenance of life on the earth.

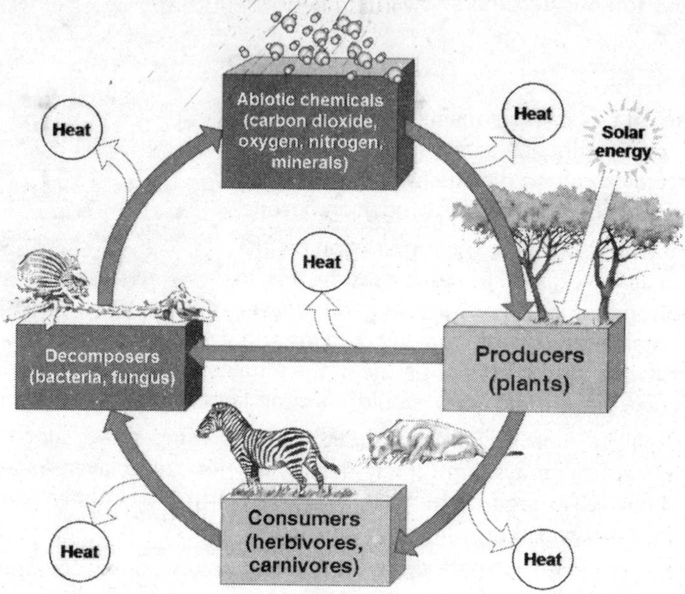

Components of Ecological System

Each ecosystem has two main components :

1. **Abiotic :** Heat, light, water, wind, soil, rocks, organic matter etc.
2. **Biotic :** The biotic components of ecosystems are of the following order :
   (i) **Producers :** They are autotrophic green plants and some photosynthetic bacteria. They produce radiant energy and with the help of minerals derived from water, they manufacture complex organic substances as carbohydrates, proteins, lipids etc.
   (ii) **Consumers :** They are heterotrophic which depend for their nutrition on the organic food manufactured by producers, the green plants. They are of three types :
   - **Primary Consumers :** These are herbivores feeding directly on living plant residues *e.g.* Benthos, Zooplanktons, Cow, Deer etc.
   - **Secondary Consumers :** They are the carnivores which feed on the primary consumers. These are chiefly insects, fish, wolves, snakes etc.
   - **Tertiary Consumers :** They are some large fish or animals that feed on the smaller fish or animals.

(iii) **Decomposers :** They are chiefly bacteria, fungi and actinomycetes. They bring about the decomposition of complex dead organic matter of both producers (plants) as well as macro consumers (animals) to simple forms. Thus they play an important role in the return of minerals and elements again to the soil.

Food Chain

The transfer of food energy from the producers, through a series of organisms (herbivores to carnivores to decomposers) with repeated eating and being eaten is known as a food chain. A food chain in a grassland ecosystem that starts with grasses and goes through grasshoppers, frogs, snakes, hawks and so on.

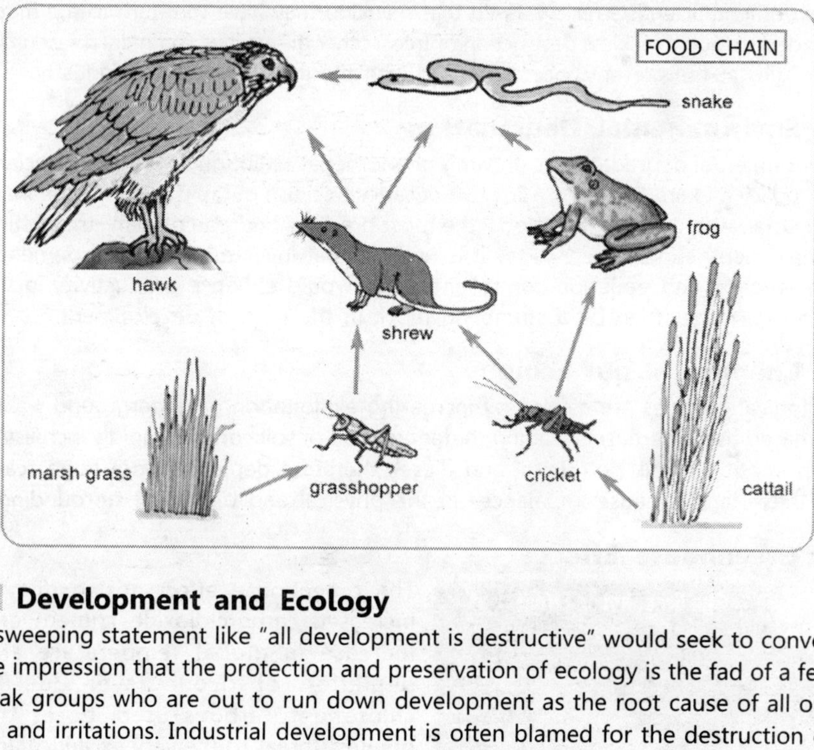

Development and Ecology

A sweeping statement like "all development is destructive" would seek to convey the impression that the protection and preservation of ecology is the fad of a few freak groups who are out to run down development as the root cause of all our ills and irritations. Industrial development is often blamed for the destruction of ecology as it causes pollution, whether through the smoke being belched out by chimneys in the various factories etc or through effluents being constantly dumped into rivers. We need not forget the fact that our civilisation has traversed through several stages to reach its present position. However, progress has not been achieved only at the cost of ecology. There have been several other factors contributing to the modern scientific civilisation.

Pure Environment

Our long term survival depends on environment. We must not, therefore, ignore this fact. Mass poverty and ecological degradation are mutually harming our environment. Environment and economic developmental goals must consequently go hand in hand. After all it is the biosphere *i.e.* the air and the water encasing our earth, besides the green cover and the wildlife, that sustain life on this planet.

Struggle for Preservation

The struggle is now on for preservation and adequate renewal of these resources. Attempts are being made to check the reckless destruction of our precious environment. Scientists have warned that mankind may have to return to the much dreaded ice age if reckless destruction of trees, other greenways and natural resources continues at the present pace associated with progress, especially in industry.

Environmental Degradation

Environmental degradation is drawing phenomenal attention of the academicians and policy makers. During the last two decades because of rapid and indiscriminate industrialisation all over the globe, the most precious heritage of man–the natural environment is in danger. Today it is realised that investments in environmental conservation and pollution control measures would enhance productivity in the long run, rather than be a stumbling block in the path of development.

Changes in our Ecology

Ecological changes are caused by increasing exploitation of underground water, increased use of fertilizers leading to degradation of soil content, rapidly increasing consumption of oil, petroleum and diesel, therefore depletion on a huge scale. All these factors cause imbalances in the physical and biological surroundings.

Greenhouse Effect

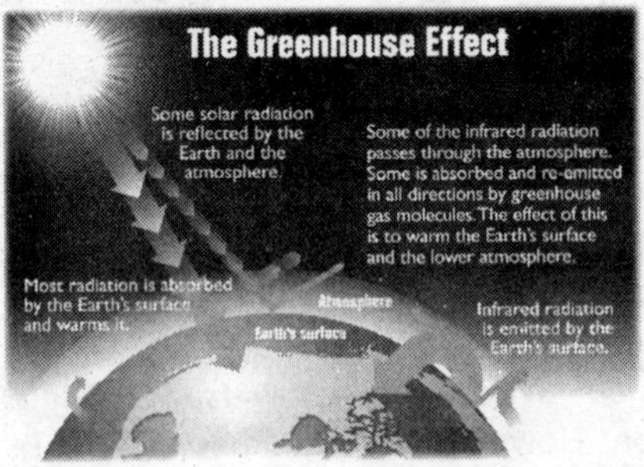

The greenhouse effect arising due to increased carbon dioxide content and increase in global temperature and depletion of ozone layer due to chlorofluorocarbons used, poses the greatest threat to the very existence and survival of human beings and flora and fauna around the globe. The greenhouse effect, acid rain, ozone depletion and nuclear winter all these reflect human interference in the environment and all have become synonymous with catastrophe. Respect for ecology is, therefore, a vital part of any responsible strategy. Investment in conservation and pollution control measures would be beneficial in the long run.

CONSERVATION OF ENVIRONMENT AND ECOLOGY

Conservation Measures

Protection of natural wealth and conservation of nature and life in all forms is a matter of great concern. Checking environmental degradation is a crying need. While degradation is affecting the entire planet and conservation has the attention of all countries, each person has personal responsibilities in this. Following are some of the measures that must be co-ordinated or taken by each one as the case may be, for survival of life on earth :

1. Keeping air, land, rivers, and water-bodies clean and natural.
2. Tree plantation and stopping indiscriminate felling of trees.
3. Prevention of wastage and over-use of all natural resources.
4. Re-cycling industrial wastes.
5. By using renewable resources as far as possible.
6. Employing modern sewage disposal techniques.
7. Imposing restrictions on using chemical substances and toxins harmful to soil, water and air.
8. Fumes, smoke and exhaust gases to be rendered harmless by innovative design of machinery and technology.
9. Proper treatment of effluents.
10. Observing strict emission levels.
11. Elimination of nuclear waste.
12. Ensuring all waste to be biodegradable.
13. Non-biodegradable waste to be recycled.
14. Water bodies to be kept chaste.
15. Conservation of nature in all forms.
16. Protection of all life-forms.
17. Strict policies, regulations and incentives for protection and conservation of nature and life-forms.
18. Impetus to Research and Development for environment-friendly technology.
19. All development involving the biosphere to be environment-friendly with ecological harmony or "Economic Development on Ecological Principles".
20. Management of environmental pollution, at all levels including homes, such as smoke, use of sprays, garbage disposal, non-biodegradable waste, and water pollution.
21. Protection of wildlife.
22. Checking human population explosion.
23. Cleanliness drives for rivers, water-bodies and soil (to remove non-biodegradable waste.
24. Ensuring environmentally rational behaviour in oneself and others.
25. Developing environmental consciousness amongst common people through classroom instructions, posters and hoardings, public and media campaigns.

RAIN WATER HARVESTING

Rainwater harvesting means capturing the runoff rainwater in our own house, village, town or city. It basically means accumulation and storage of rainwater for reuse, before it reaches the aquifer. Utilization includes water for garden, livestock, irrigation, etc. In many places, the water collected is just redirected to a deep pit with percolation. The harvested water can be used as drinking water also, if the storage is a tank that can be accessed and cleaned when needed.

Why Harvest Rainwater?

(i) To conserve surface water runoff during monsoon.

(ii) To beneficiate water quality in aquifers.

(iii) To arrest ground water decline and augment ground water table.

(iv) To reduce soil erosion.

(v) To inculcate a culture of water conservation.

POLLUTION

Pollution means imbalance in the atmosphere caused by pollutants. Air gets polluted with the smoke from homes, factories and vehicles. Water gets polluted by city and factory wastes. Loud noises cause sound pollution. Pollution in fact spreads diseases and makes life uncomfortable on earth.

Man has played a very crucial role in destroying the very essence of life *i.e.* destruction of forests due to excessive urbanization. Due to increase in population and industrialization, the forests have been exploited for wood from trees and land space. Unscrupulous felling of trees has led to the destruction of the forest cover. Hence the air purifier *i.e.* the trees which give us oxygen to survive have been depleted. Depletion of greenery and forests and the pollution of the earth's atmosphere have led to reduction of the protective ozone layer and increase in global warming.

TYPES OF POLLUTION

1. Land Pollution

Today's industrialised society produces a huge amount of garbage, the disposal of such wastes is a major problem, especially in the urban centres. Non-biodegradable wastes such as polythene bags, which cannot be decomposed by natural agents like bacteria have become a menace to the environment besides being health hazards. Use of chemical fertilizers and pesticides containing harmful substances contaminates the soil. Soil may become deficient in nutrients due to excessive cultivation or if the same crop is grown repeatedly on the same field.

2. Water Pollution

Waste from our homes, hospitals and factories is usually discharged into the water-bodies. Such water contains excreta, disease-causing micro-organisms and harmful chemicals. It makes water unfit for drinking and may even kill aquatic plants and animals. Harmful substances seeping through earth rainwater contaminate groundwater. Plant nutrients derived from fertilizers and organic wastes, like dead bodies, thrown into water sometimes cause excessive growth of weeds. Many aquatic organisms die as a result of oil spills from tankers. Leaking pipelines also pollute water organisms. Many species of birds and fish die from contact with oil as it makes their feathers and gills inactive.

3. Air Pollution

Air pollution is caused mainly by harmful substances emitted into the atmosphere by industries and automobiles. It causes respiratory diseases and affects the skin and eyes. Some of the gases emitted by industries dissolve in rainwater to produce acid rain, which can damage vegetation. Atmospheric ozone which protects us from harmful ultraviolet rays is depleted due to release of certain carbon compounds called chlorofluorocarbons (CFCs) into the atmosphere. This also increases the risk of skin cancer and eye damage in humans.

4. Sound Pollution

Sound produced from motor vehicles, trains, aeroplanes, factories, loudspeakers during religious and political public meetings, noise produced by the masses and other living creatures also plays an important role in producing sound pollution. It also affects the health of human beings. Loud sound affects the human heart; create auditory problems and causes mental stress.

Measures to Control Pollution

(i) To develop consciousness among common people to control pollution, plant more and more trees.

(ii) The use of loud horns or mindless blowing of horns by motor vehicles should be banned.

(iii) The water-bodies should not be used as waste reservoirs.

(iv) Various sources of drinking water, and water resources should be well protected so that dirty water does not enter these water-bodies.

(v) Environmental education should be made compulsory in all educational institutions.

(vi) Excessive use of pesticides and insecticides should be avoided.

(vii) In all towns and cities, there should be proper arrangement of dustbins to collect garbage being produced in the houses.

(viii) In the factories, strict precaution should be instituted to avoid pollution of various types.

(ix) Running of old and pollution emitting vehicles should be banned.

(x) The pollution control Administrative Authorities must have independent powers to implement their decisions.

WASTE MANAGEMENT

Waste Management refers to the collection, transport, processing or disposal, managing and monitoring of waste materials. The term normally relates to all kinds of waste, whether generated during the extraction of raw materials, the processing of raw materials into intermediate and final products, the consumption of final products, or other human activities, including municipal (residential, institutional, commercial), agricultural, and social (health care, household, hazardous waste, sewage, sludge etc.).

Waste Segregation

Waste segregation means dividing waste into dry and wet. Dry waste includes wood and related products, metals and glass. Wet waste, typically refers to organic waste usually generated by eating establishments and are heavy in weight due to dampness. Liquid and solid types of waste can also be grouped into organic, re-usable and recyclable waste.

Type of Wastes:

(i) Solid Waste
(ii) Liquid Waste
(iii) Radioactive Waste
(iv) Municipal Solid Waste
(v) Hospital or Bio-Medical Waste
(vi) Electronic Waste
(vii) Organic Waste
(viii) Agricultural Waste
(ix) Industrial Waste
(x) Construction/Demolition Waste
(xi) Hazardous Waste: It can be of four types:
(a) Ignitable (b) Reactive (c) Toxic (d) Corrosive

Disposal and Management of Waste

Action By Individuals : Some steps which all individuals can take while contributing to the waste management includes the following :

(i) Separation of household waste into bio-degradable and non-biodegradable.

(ii) Reduce use of plastic bags and replace them with paper or jute/cloth bags.

(iii) Recyclable waste such as paper, glass, cloth etc could be segregated and disposed off accordingly.

(iv) Keep the surroundings of your house and around the house clean. Do not dump waste just outside the house on the road.

(v) Colonies could start vermin-composting and natural composting.

(vi) What is waste for one is wealth for somebody else. There has been a tradition in India of finding an innovative use for everything - tyres, battery cases, plastic bins and what not. Think of reuse of the thing you would like to discard.

Actions by Civic Bodies : The major functions of civic body may include the following :

(i) Prohibiting littering of street.

(ii) Organizing house to house waste collection.

(iii) Conducting awareness programs to spread information to public.

(iv) Providing sufficient community storage facilities.

(v) Use of colour code bins and promotion of waste separation.

(vi) Transportation of wastes in covered vehicles.

(vii) Processing of wastes by adopting suitable combination of composting, anaerobic digestion, palletization etc.

(viii) Upgradation of the existing dump sites and disposal of inert wastes in sanitary landfills.

ENERGY CONSERVATION

Energy conservation refers to various ways and methods of reducing energy consumption by economizing on the use of a particular source of energy.

Reasons for Increase in Energy Consumption

Over the years, the rate of energy consumption has been increasing at an alarming rate, leading to various environmental problems, besides putting extra pressure on the already insufficient resources. The major causes for increase in higher energy consumption can be attributed to the following :

(i) Population Explosion : Exponential population growth has had a direct bearing on the energy consumption. More people mean - more requirement of energy per person.

(ii) Migration of Rural Population to Urban Areas : Large numbers of rural populations have migrated to urban centre's including Tier II and Tier III cities in India. This population needs housing, electricity, transport etc. which have put a heavy toll on energy consumption.

(iii) Increased Manufacturing : Increased manufacturing is the need of the day. However, more energy is required for the same.

(iv) Increased Number of Vehicles : As the per capita income of people all over the world is increasing especially in India, there has been a great growth in production of vehicles, thus needing increased amount of fuel.

(v) Transmission Losses : Poor infrastructure across the country leads to higher energy losses due to transmission or pilferage.

(vi) Poor Usage Habits of Individuals : This is one of the most significant reasons for high energy consumption in India. Insufficient knowledge and poor habits cause massive energy wastage.

(vii) Poor Building Designs : Buildings made with scant consideration to efficient energy usage were built all over the country thus increasing the consumption.

Energy Conservation Measures

An Energy conservation measure (ECM) is any type of project conducted, or technology implemented, to reduce the consumption of energy in a building. The types of projects implemented can be in a variety of forms but usually are designed to reduce utility costs: water, electricity and gas being the main three for industrial and commercial enterprises. The aim of an ECM should be to achieve a savings, reducing the amount of energy used by a particular process, technology or facility. ECM can be through:

(i) Energy Saving Building Designs
(ii) Use of Energy Efficient Equipment/Implements
(iii) Energy Saving Public Lighting
(iv) Product Usage Habits
(v) Efficient Public Transport System
(vi) Energy Efficient Infrastructure
(vii) Preventing Pilferage
(viii) Use of non-conventional Sources of Energy, like
(a) Solar Energy (b) Wind Energy (c) Biogas

FOREST ECOLOGY

Forests are our natural resources. They have a vital role in maintaining a balanced ecological system. Forests help in global recycling of water, oxygen, carbon dioxide and nitrogen in a balanced way. In controlling the environment and to maintain a healthy ecosystem, forests have greater role to play.

Importance of Forests

Forests are a great national wealth. They provide fuel, wood, and timber for construction and pulp for paper, gums, resins, turpentine and allied materials as well as a variety of medicines. The loss of forest areas has resulted in the persistent loss of these valuable materials.

Forests have great role in maintaining ecological balance on the earth. Forest ecology is responsible for maintaining an adequate balance of carbon dioxide and oxygen in the environment. Forests also stop floods. Forest control humidity of the environment and regulate the weather conditions. All wild animals, including those which are our national pride, get their food and, shelter from the forests. The forests protect the disappearing species of many wild animals and birds and keep the nature balanced.

In order to maintain a pollution-free environment, forests have a greater role. There is an effective need to conserve our natural heritage of forest resources not only to derive timber, fuel and other resources but to protect the ecosystem, to ensure a balanced level of oxygen and carbon dioxide to prevent soil erosion, to regulate the weather conditions, to rescue the environment from toxic pollutants and last but not the least to improve the quality of the environment in order to maintain a healthy ecosystem.

WILDLIFE

Wildlife comprises of nature and its inhabitants form–the flora and fauna. With the increase in the population, more villages are merging into towns and cities at the cost of forests and wildlife and as a result the environment and biological equilibrium is disturbed.

Importance of Wildlife

India is a land with rich and varied wildlife. Wildlife in our forests, plains, hills and valleys includes such majestic animals as the tiger, the elephant, the lion, the cheetah, the wild buffalo and the rhinoceros. Wildlife is indeed our national-wealth and the Government has set up several bird sanctuaries and national parks where birds and wild animals can live in peace in their own natural environment.

The Government of India has declared big areas as bio-reserves. They will help preserve both wildlife and rare varieties of plants. They are distributed in different climatic and vegetation zones such as the high Himalayas, the Rann of Kutch and the coastal waters of the Andaman and Nicobar islands, etc. Some species of plants and animals have already become extinct and there are many facing danger of extinction. The basic reasons for extinction are as follows :

(i) Destruction of their natural habitats
(ii) Over-grazing by domestic animals
(iii) Poaching for meat, skin, fur, ivory, rhino horn etc.
(iv) Export and smuggling of some species

In India, nearly 450 plant species have been identified as endangered or threatened. Similarly, there are a large number of mammals, birds and reptiles which are endangered.

Wildlife Management in India

Due to continuous increase in the number of endangered species of flora and fauna in wildlife, steps have been taken to protect and manage wildlife in our country with an aim to :

(i) Protection of natural habitats through control of exploitation.
(ii) Maintenance of protected areas like parks, sanctuaries, reserve forests.
(iii) Protection through legislation.
(iv) Imposing restrictions on export of rare plants and animals.
(v) Encouraging Non-Government Organisations to participate in protection of wildlife.
(vi) Creating General awareness among the public.

Wildlife Sanctuaries and National Parks

- **Andhra Pradesh:** Kolleru Pelicanry; Nagarjunasagar Srisailam Sanctuary.
- **Assam:** Kaziranga National Park (known for one-horn Rhinoceroses); Manas National Park.
- **Bihar:** Hazaribagh Wildlife Sanctuary; Dalma Wildlife Sanctuary; Palamau Wildlife Sanctuary.
- **Goa, Daman and Diu:** Mollem Wildlife Sanctuary
- **Gujarat:** Valvadar National Park, Bhavnagar; Marine National Park, Gulf of Kutch; Gir National Park, Indian Wild Ass Wildlife Sanctuary.
- **Himachal Pradesh:** The Great Himalayan National Park; Motichur Sanctuary.
- **Jammu & Kashmir:** Dachigam Sanctuary, Kishtwar.
- **Jharkhand:** Hazaribagh National Park; Palamau Reserve.
- **Karnataka:** Bandipur National Park; Bannargheta National Park, Bangalore; Nagorhole National Park, Coorg; Ranganthitto Bird Sanctuary.

- **Kerala:** Eravikulam Rajmallay National Park, Idduki; Periyar National Park.
- **Madhya Pradesh:** Kanha National Park; Bandhavgarh National Park, Shahdol; Shivpuri National Park.
- **Maharashtra:** Tadoba National Park, Chandrapur; Panch National Park, Nagpur; Borivali National Park, Mumbai; Nawagaon National Park, Bandara; Melghat National Park.
- **Manipur:** Keibul Lamjao National Park; Dampa Wildlife Sanctuary.
- **Odisha:** Satkosia Gorge Wildlife Sanctuary; Bhitarkanika Wildlife Sanctuary; Chilka Wildlife Sanctuary; Simlipal National Park.
- **Punjab:** Harike Headworks Sanctuary
- **Rajasthan:** Ranthambore National Park; Sariska National Park; Desert Sanctuary.
- **Sikkim:** Kanchendzonga National Park, Gangtok.
- **Tamil Nadu:** Vedanthangal Bird Sanctuary; Guindy National Park, Chennai; Mudumalai Sanctuary; Kalakkadu Wildlife Sanctuary.
- **Uttar Pradesh:** Chandraprabha Sanctuary; Dudhwa National Park, Lakhimpur.
- **Uttarakhand:** Jim Corbett National Park; Rampur, Nainital
- **West Bengal:** Jaldapara Wildlife Sanctuary; Sunderbans National Park.

Ranthambhore National Park

Kaziranga National Park

Sariska National Park

Jim Corbett Tiger Reserve

Jaldapara Wildlife Sanctuary

Guindy National Park

❖ ❖ ❖

CHAPTER 17

Famous Leaders of India

MAHATMA GANDHI

Mohandas Karamchand Gandhi, also known as Mahatma Gandhi, was an Indian nationalist leader, who established India's freedom from British rule through a non-violent revolution.

M.K. Gandhi was born on October 2, 1869, in the town of Porbandar in the state of Gujarat. He did his schooling in nearby Rajkot, where his father served as a Diwan to the local ruler. Gandhi went to London, to study law, after his university degree. He returned to India in 1891, and then accepted a job at an Indian law firm in South Africa.

There he witnessed, how the non-Whites were ill-treated by the Whites. He was thrown out of a train compartment and was barred from hotels. Many a times, he was even beaten up badly. Facing all the injustices, he became more assertive, and began educating the fellow Indians in South Africa of their rights. In 1894, he opposed a bill that would deprive Indians of their right to vote, and rapidly became a proficient political activist. While unable to stop the bill, he succeeded in attracting widespread attention to his cause.

Gandhi developed the satyagraha, a new non-violent way to redress wrongs. The campaign lasted for over seven years, and in 1913, hundreds of people went to jail—and thousands of striking Indian miners faced imprisonment and injury—for the cause. Eventually, the South African government, agreed to a compromising solution, under the British and Indian pressure, and thus peace was restored.

In 1914, he returned to India. Then in 1919, the British plans to intern people suspected of sedition prompted him to announce a new satyagraha. The result shook the subcontinent, and indirectly led to the Jallianwala Bagh Massacre, in which nearly 400 Indians were killed by the British forces.

Mahatma Gandhi dominated Indian politics, by the year 1920. He transformed the Indian National Congress, and his programme of peaceful non-co-operation with the British included boycott of British goods and institutions, leading to arrests of thousands of satyagrahis—all cheerfully lining up for prison, for defying the British laws.

After the Chauri-Chaura incident in March 1922, he was sent to jail for six years, but was released after two years. By then, the political landscape of India had changed completely. The Congress Party had split and Hindu-Muslim unity had disintegrated.

For some years, Mahatma Gandhi's political influence was minimal, until the Calcutta Congress in December 1928, where he demanded a dominion status for India, and threatened a nationwide campaign for complete independence. In 1931, the Round Table Conference took place in London. Gandhiji attended it as the sole representative of the Indian National Congress. In 1942, Gandhiji made a call for Quit India Movement which was a great success.

The new Labour Government in Britain from 1945 brought negotiations, and these culminated in the Mountbatten Plan of June 1947, and the formation of free India and Pakistan in mid-August 1947.

However, the country was divided and killings and riots between the Hindus and Muslims took place all over the country. Mahatma Gandhi's appeals for peace were ignored, and so he began fasting. This stopped the riots but only days later, he was shot dead in Delhi on January 30, 1948. He will always be remembered as an apostle of peace, love, truth and non-violence in the world.

BHAGAT SINGH

Bhagat Singh was an Indian revolutionary, considered to be one of the most famous martyrs of the Indian freedom struggle.

Bhagat Singh was born in a Sikh family on September 28, 1907 in village Banga in Layalpur district of Punjab. He was the third son of Sardar Kishan Singh and Vidyavati. Bhagat Singh's family was actively involved in freedom struggle. His father Kishan Singh and uncle Ajit Singh were members of Ghadr Party founded in the United States to oust British rule from India. Family atmosphere had a great effect on the mind of young Bhagat Singh and patriotism flowed in his veins from childhood.

While studying at the local DAV School in Lahore, in 1916, young Bhagat Singh came into contact with some well-known political leaders like Lala Lajpat Rai and Rash Bihari Bose. Punjab was politically very charged in those days. In 1919, when the Jallianwala Bagh massacre took place in Amritsar, Bhagat Singh was only 12 years old. The massacre deeply disturbed him. On the next day of the massacre, Bhagat Singh went to the Jallianwala Bagh and collected soil from the spot. He kept it as a memento for the rest of his life. The massacre strengthened his resolve to drive the British out from India.

In response to Mahatma Gandhi's call for the non-cooperation against the British rule in 1921, Bhagat Singh left his school and actively participated in the movement. In 1922, when Mahatma Gandhi suspended the Non-cooperation Movement against the violence at Chauri-Chaura in Gorakhpur, Bhagat was greatly disappointed. His faith in non-violence weakened and he came to the conclusion that armed revolution was the only practical way of winning freedom.

To continue his studies, Bhagat Singh joined the National College in Lahore, founded by Lala Lajpat Rai. At this college, which was a centre of revolutionary activities, he came into contact with revolutionaries such as Bhagwati Charan, Sukhdev and others.

In 1928, he attended a meeting of revolutionaries in Delhi and came into contact with Chandrashekhar Azad. The two, along with other revolutionaries, formed the 'Hindustan Socialist Republican Association (HSRA).

In February 1928, a committee from England, called Simon Commission visited India. The purpose of its visit was to decide how much freedom and responsibility could be given to the people of India. But there was no Indian on the committee. This angered the Indians and they decided to boycott the Simon Commission.

While protesting against the Simon Commission in Lahore, Lala Lajpat Rai was brutally beaten who succumbed to injuries. Bhagat Singh vowed to avenge Lajpat Rai's death by shooting the British official responsible for killing, General Scott. He shot down Saunders instead, mistaking him for Scott. Bhagat Singh had to flee from Lahore to escape the police investigation.

The British government took repressive measures. Under the Defence of India Act, it gave more power to the police to arrest persons to stop processions with suspicious movements and actions. Bhagat Singh who was in hiding all this while, volunteered to throw a bomb in the Central Legislative Assembly at New Delhi where the meeting to pass the ordinance was being held.

On April 8, 1929, Bhagat Singh and Batukeshwar Dutt threw bombs in the Central Assembly Hall while the assembly was in session. The bombs did not hurt anyone. Bhagat Singh and Batukeshwar Dutt deliberately courted arrest by refusing to run away from the scene. Meanwhile, the killers of Saunders were also identified by the treachery of Bhagat Singh's friends who became "Approvers".

In jail, Bhagat Singh along with his friends, went on hunger strike for several days to protest the inhuman treatment of fellow-political prisoners by jail authorities. On October 7, 1930, Bhagat Singh, Sukh Dev and Raj Guru were awarded death sentence by a special tribunal for terrorist activities.

Despite great popular pressure and numerous appeals, Bhagat Singh and his associates were hanged in the early hours of March 23, 1931. His supporters, who had been protesting against the hanging, declared him a shaheed (martyr). Bhagat Singh, along with Sukh Dev and Raj Guru, was cremated at Hussainiwala on the banks of the Sutlej River in Lahore.

LAL BAHADUR SHASTRI

Lal Bahadur Shastri was the second Prime Minister of independent India. He succeeded Jawaharlal Nehru as Prime Minister of India in 1964. He was a significant figure in the struggle for independence.

Lal Bahadur was born in Moghalsarai in Varanasi, Uttar Pradesh on October 2, 1904. His parents were Sharada Prasad and Ramdulari Devi. Though his parents were Srivastavas, Shastri dropped his caste identity in his early years. His father died when he was only a year old. His mother with the help of her father took care of the children.

He acquired virtues like boldness, love of adventure, patience, self-control, courtesy, and selflessness in his childhood.

He abandoned his studies to take part in the Non-Cooperation movement started by Mahatma Gandhi in 1921. He was given the title 'Shastri' at Kashi Vidyapeeth in 1926. During his four years' stay there, he was very much influenced by the lectures of Dr. Bhagawandas on philosophy. In his later life, Shastri displayed poise in the midst of conflict and confusion which he learnt from his teacher, Bhagawandas.

After coming out from Kashi Vidyapeeth, he became the life-member of 'The Servants of the People Society' which was started by Lala Lajpat Rai in 1921. The aim of the society was to train youth who were prepared to dedicate their lives to the service of the country. Shastri earned the love and affection of Lajpat Rai by his earnestness and hard work. Later, he became the President of the society. In 1927, he married Lalita Devi who was from Mirzapur.

Shastri took a leading role in 'Salt Satyagraha' which was intensified by 1930. He also advised people not to pay land revenue and taxes to the British government. He was sent to prison for two and half years for doing so. From this time onwards, prison became his second home. He was sent to prison seven times and was forced to spend nine long years in various prisons on different occasions.

Going to prison became a blessing in disguise for him. He spent time reading a number of books. He became familiar with the works of western philosophers, revolutionaries, and social reformers. Shastri translated the autobiography of Madam Curie, a French scientist who discovered Radium, into Hindi. He was an ideal prisoner. The greatness of Shastri was that he maintained his self-respect even in prison.

After Independence, he became the Minister of Police in the ministry of Govind Vallabh Pant in Uttar Pradesh. In 1951, he was appointed as the General

Secretary of Lok Sabha before regaining a ministerial post as Railways Minister. He resigned following a rail disaster near Ariyalur. He returned to the Union Cabinet following the general elections, first as Minister of Transport, and then in 1961, he became the Home Minister.

PM Jawaharlal Nehru died in office on May 27, 1964, and left something of a vacuum. Though eclipsed by such stalwarts of the Congress Party as Kamaraj, and Morarji Desai, the Finance Minister in Nehru's government, Shastri emerged as the concensus candidate in the midst of the party warfare. The ruling Congress Party unanimously elected Shastri as its leader. He became the Prime Minister on June 9, 1964 at a very crucial time in the Indian history.

The first problem he had to face after becoming the Prime Minister was the one caused by Pakistan. After the Chinese aggression in 1962, when India's confidence in her strength had been shaken, Pakistan was creating trouble along the borders. But Shastriji would not yield to the wickedness of Pakistan. He first tried to earn the goodwill and support from the other nations for India. He attended a meeting of the non-aligned nations and explained India's position.

Pakistan was awaiting to swallow Kashmir into its territory. She pushed her forces across the eastern border into the Rann of Kutch in Gujarat in 1965. Shastri faced the problem with great tact. But later there was a large scale invasion of the territory by Pakistani soldiers which led to the break out of war along the ceasefire line on the Kashmir border. Addressing the nation on August 13, 1965, Shastri referred to Pakistan's threats and said, "Force will be met with force".

Some big nations feared that if India won a total victory over Pakistan, it would lower their prestige. The Security Council of the United Nations Organisation called on India and Pakistan to stop fighting. On the invitation of Kosygin, the Premier of Soviet Russia, Shastri and Ayub Khan met in Tashkent on January 4, 1966. Shastri wished to give one more chance to Pakistan to live in peace and friendship with India. So he signed the treaty of friendship.

Shastriji had suffered heart attacks twice before and during the period of Pakistan war and the following days, his body had to bear a very heavy strain. He signed the Joint Declaration on January 10, 1966, and died the same night. Though his family members and followers had cast some doubt over his untimely death but it was never seriously probed by any central agency.

Gone was the war hero and the messenger of peace, gone was the great statesman who restored to India her honour and self-respect in the assembly of nations. A soul that had lived in perfect purity of thought, word, and deed. Such was this man who had lived in our midst. He belonged to the race of heroes of India.

He was posthumously awarded the Bharat Ratna and a memorial was built for him in Delhi. The slogan, 'Jai Jawan, Jai Kisan' is attributed to Shastri. He was a star of great brightness in the history of India.

SUBHASH CHANDRA BOSE

Subhash Chandra Bose was one of the most influential and charismatic leader of pre-Independence India. His life was full of mystery and adventure and indeed, his death has been a major issue, and creates controversy from time-to-time. Later, the world came to know him as Netaji.

Subhash was born on January 23, 1897. His father was Rai Bahadur Janakinath Bose, a prominent lawyer of Cuttack, Orissa. His mother was Prabhavati Bose, a remarkable example of Indian womanhood. After completing his early studies at the European Protestant Collegiate School in Cuttack, he came to Calcutta (presently, Kolkata) to study at the Presidency College in 1913. Upon completing his graduation, he left India for England to appear at the Indian Civil Service Examination. He cleared the ICS exam but opted out to serve the motherland.

Subhash felt that young militant groups could be molded into a military arm of the freedom movement and used to further the cause. Gandhiji opposed this ideology because it directly conflicted with his policy of Ahimsa (non-violence). The British Government in India perceived Subhash as a potential source of danger and had arrested him without any charge on October 25, 1924. He was sent to Alipore Jail, Calcutta, and on January 25, 1925 transferred to Mandalay, Burma (now Myanmar). He was released from Mandalay in May 1927 due to his ill health. Upon his return to Calcutta, Subhash was elected president of the Bengal Congress Committee on October 27, 1927.

Subhash was one of the few politicians who sought and worked towards Hindu-Muslim unity on the basis of respect of each community's rights. He, being a man of ideals, believed in independence from the social evil of religious discord.

In January 1930, Subhash was arrested while leading a procession condemning imprisonment of revolutionaries. He was offered bail on condition that he signs a bond to refrain from all political activities which, he refused. As a result, he was sentenced to a year's imprisonment.

On his release from jail, Subhash was sworn in as 'Mayor of the Calcutta Corporation'. In 1931, the split between Gandhiji and Subhash crystallised. Although the two never saw eye-to-eye on their view of freedom and the movement itself, Subhash felt that Gandhiji had done a great disservice to the movement by agreeing to take part in the 'Second Round Table Conference'. He viewed freedom as an absolute necessity, unlike the freedom which Gandhiji was "negotiating" with the British.

Subhash was arrested again while returning from Bombay to Calcutta, and imprisoned in several jails outside West Bengal in fear of an uprising. His health once again deteriorated and the medical facilities diagnosed him with tuberculosis. It was recommended that he be sent to Switzerland for treatment.

Realising that his avenues abroad were greater with the restrictions of the British, Subhash set sail for Europe on February 23, 1933. He stayed in various parts of Europe from March 1933 to 1936 making contacts with Indian revolutionaries and European socialists supporting India's Struggle for Independence. Subhash met Mussolini in Italy and made Vienna his headquarters. He was opposed to the racial theory of Nazism but appreciated its organisational strength and discipline. On March 27, 1936, he sailed for Bombay, but was escorted to jail immediately after disembarkation.

After lying low for a year, he was able to work actively. He attended the 'All India Congress Committee Session' in Calcutta, the first one he attended after a lapse of nearly six years. Time had healed the tensions between Subhash and Gandhiji. Now, Gandhiji supported Subhash in his efforts to become the president of the next Congress session in 1938.

He went to England for a month in 1938 and rallied for the Indian freedom cause amongst Indian students and made British labour leaders sympathetic towards India's cause. It was a bold move since he was constantly under the British surveillance. Upon his return to India in February 1938, Subhash was elected president of the Indian National Congress.

Despite opposition from the Congress, Subhash Chandra Bose was a favourite amongst the majority as he was re-elected for a second term in March 1939 but he resigned from Congress due to differences with Mahatma Gandhi.

Subhash Chandra Bose was believed to have died in a plane crash over Taiwan, while flying to Tokyo on August 18, 1945. However, his body was never recovered, and theories concerning his possible survival abound.

In 2021, the Government of India declared 23 January as Parakram Divas to commemorate the birth anniversary of Subhas Chandra Bose. To mark his 125th birth anniversary a holographic statue of Bose was installed at the India Gate. Later, on September 8, 2022 PM Narendra Modi inaugurated a permanent granite statue of Bose replacing the holographic statue.

SWAMI VIVEKANANDA

Swami Vivekananda was one of the most famous and influential spiritual leaders of the Vedanta philosophy. He was the chief disciple of Ramakrishna Paramahansa and was the founder of the Ramakrishna Math and Ramakrishna Mission. Many consider him an icon for his fearless courage, his positive exhortations to the youth, his broad outlook on social problems, and countless lectures and discourses on Vedanta philosophy.

Narendranath Datta (Vivekananda) was born into a prominent Calcutta family on January 12, 1863. His father was a well-known lawyer and his mother was a cultured and aristocratic woman. As a child, he was uncontrollably boisterous and high spirited. As a boy, he was an excellent athlete and superlative student. He read everything ravenously and retained everything he read. Never content to believe what he was told, he always demanded incontrovertible proof or experiential certainty before he would believe anything.

Vivekananda was deeply religious and this same integrity coloured his quest for God. He went from one religious man to another and asked them if they had seen God. Finally, he met Sri Ramakrishna Paramhansa who was the only one to tell him, "Yes, I have seen God and can show you, too". Thus began the discipleship of this highly educated and cultured boy to the mostly illiterate rustic temple priest saint.

After five years of training, his teacher Sri Ramakrishna died. Before his death he had named Narendranath, the leader of all of his disciples. Young Narendra took the monastic name, Swami Vivekananda and founded a monastery where he and his brother disciples could carry on their spiritual practices. Following Indian monastic tradition, he and the other monastics divided their time between the monastery and travelling as itinerant monks. Swami Vivekananda spent many years travelling through all parts of the Indian subcontinent.

In May of 1893, a group of his disciples sent the Swami to the United States to attend the Parliament of World Religions that was being conducted in conjunction with the World's Fair in Chicago. His speeches at the Parliament so impressed listeners that Swami Vivekananda was invited to speak all around Chicago, and then all through the eastern United States. Everywhere he went, he inspired people with his master's message: "Each soul is divine and the goal of life is for each of us to realise that divinity for ourselves".

After four years of strenous teaching in America, the Swami returned to India to win the accolades of the entire country. In India, Swamiji's message was a fiercely patriotic one. Because in his travels throughout India, he had felt such a compassion for the poor and uneducated, that when he returned to India, he exhorted his brother monks to serve the poor and the needy, to serve God as he manifests in man. He said, "In addition to realising your own inherent divinity, you must see that same divinity in others and serve them." Thus, was born the Ramakrishna Mission, the purpose of which is to help alleviate the sufferrings of the poor on the Indian subcontinent.

His books on the four Yogas (Raja Yoga, Karma Yoga, Bhakti Yoga, Jnana Yoga) are very influential and still seen as fundamental texts for anyone interested in the Hindu practice of Yoga. His letters are of great literary and spiritual value.

Swamiji returned to the United States and taught for a short time, primarily on the west coast before returning to his homeland. He died on July 4, 1902 just at the age of 39 at the monastery he founded in the village of Belur which is on the Ganges north of Kolkata.

In the ten years in which he preached Strength, Freedom, Manliness, and that every soul is Divine, he touched the hearts and minds, and changed the lives of thousands of men and women around the world.

SARDAR VALLABHBHAI PATEL

Vallabhbhai Jhaverbhai Patel, popularly referred to as Sardar Patel, was an Indian statesman, an important leader of the Indian National Congress and the Deputy Prime Minister of India in the first cabinet of Independent India.

Vallabhbhai Patel, the iron-man of India was born on October 31, 1875 in a small village, Karamsadh of Bombay region. His father, Jhaverbhai Patel was a simple farmer and mother, Laad Bai was a housewife.

From his childhood itself, Patel was a very hard-working individual. He used to help his father in farming and studied in a school at Petlad. He passed his high-school examination in 1896. Throughout school, he was a very wise and intelligent student. Around three years, he stayed at home, worked hard and prepared for the District Pleader's examination, hence passing with very good percentage.

Sardar Patel did not like to work for anyone, especially the Britishers. He was a person of independent nature. He began his own practice of law in a place called Godhara. Soon the practice flourished. Vallabhbhai sent his elder brother Vithalbhai to England for higher studies in law.

In 1909, his wife became seriously ill and was taken to Bombay for treatment. When his wife died he was arguing for an important case in the court. He received the news but continued with the argument. Such was his determination.

Later, he admitted his children in St. Mary's school Bombay, and left for England. He became a barrister and retuned to India in 1913.

Then, he started his practice in Ahmedabad. Around 1915, he came across Mahatma Gandhi. The Swadeshi Movement was at its peak at the time. Gandhiji gave a lecture at a place in Ahmedabad where Patel heard him and was very impressed. He started actively participating in the freedom movement. The British government's atrocities were increasing. The government declared to confiscate all the lands of farmers. He forced the British government to amend the rules, and brought together the farmers encouraging them to rebel against the tyrannical rule of the British. This is how he got the title of 'Sardar' and thus, became famous.

The British government considered him as a threat and his lectures were considered anti-government. Sardar Patel was imprisoned several times. In 1942, he took part in the Quit India Movement under the leadership of Mahatma Gandhi. He was arrested along with other leaders and was sent to Ahmednagar jail. In spite of the British Rule, rulers of the small kingdoms were spending a lot of public money, and were having a nice time. Sardar Patel opposed this.

After the Independence of India, as the first Home Minister, with great wisdom and political foresight, he consolidated about 600 small kingdoms. He tackled the Nizam of Hyderabad and the Nawab of Junagarh who initially did not want to join India. There were a lot of problems connected with the reunion of the numerous states into India. Sardar Patel's untiring efforts towards the unity of the country brought success. Due to the achievement of this massive task, Sardar Patel got the title of 'Iron Man'. He became immortal by uniting a scattered nation without any bloodshed.

On December 15, 1950, Sardar Patel died of a cardiac arrest. A grateful nation paid a tearful homage to its beloved leader. In 1991, he was honoured with the highest civilian award of 'Bharat Ratna'. The 'Statue of Unity' has been built in his memory in Gujarat which is world's tallest statue.

DR. BHIMRAO AMBEDKAR

Dr. Bhimrao Ambedkar, popularly known as Babasaheb Ambedkar, was the Chief architect of the Indian Constitution. He was a well-known politician and an eminent jurist. His efforts to eradicate the social evils like untouchablity and caste restrictions were remarkable. He, throughout his life, fought for the rights of the dalits and other socially backward classes. He was appointed as the nation's first Law Minister in the Cabinet of Jawaharlal Nehru. He was posthumously awarded the Bharat Ratna, India's highest civilian honour, in 1990.

Bhimrao Ambedkar was born on April 14, 1891 to Bhimabai and Ramji Maloji Sakpal Ambavedekar. His father Ramji was an army Subedar posted at Mhow in Madhya Pradesh.

Bhimrao was a victim of caste discrimination. His parents hailed from the Hindu Mahar caste, which was then viewed as 'untouchable' by the upper class. Due to this, he had to face severe discriminations from every corner of the society. The discrimination and humiliation haunted him even at the Army school, run by British government. Discrimination followed wherever he went. In 1908, he got the opportunity to study at the Elphinstone College, Bombay. Besides clearing all the exams successfully he also obtained a scholarship from the Gayakwad ruler of

Baroda, Sayaji Rao III. He graduated from the Bombay University in 1912 with Political Science and Economics subjects. He was sponsored by Sayaji Rao to go for higher studies in America and England.

After returning from there, he was appointed as the Defence secretary to the King of Baroda. Even, there also he had to face the humiliation for being an 'Untouchable'. With the help of the former Bombay Governor Lord Sydenham, he obtained the job of a professor of political economy at the Sydenham College of Commerce and Economics in Bombay. In order to continue his further studies, in 1920, he went to England again on his own expenses. There he was awarded honour of D.Sc by the London University. He also spent few months at the University of Bonn, Germany, to study Economics. On 8 June, 1927, he was awarded a Doctorate by the University of Columbia.

After coming back to India, Dr. Bhimrao Ambedkar decided to fight against the caste discrimination that almost fragmented the nation. Ambedkar opined that there should be separate electoral system for the untouchables and lower caste people. He also favoured the concept of providing reservations for Dalits and other religious communities.

Dr. Ambedkar objected to the decision of Congress and Mahatma Gandhi to call the untouchable community as Harijans. He said that even the members of untouchable community were same as the other members of the society. Ambedkar was appointed on the Defence Advisory Committee and the Viceroy's Executive Council as Minister for Labour. His reputation as a scholar led to his appointment as free India's first Law Minister and Chairman of the committee responsible to draft a constitution.

Dr. Bhimrao Ambedkar was appointed as the chairman of the constitution drafting committee. He was also a noted scholar and eminent jurist. Ambedkar emphasized on the construction of a virtual bridge between the classes of the society. According to him, it would be difficult to maintain the unity of the country if the difference among the classes were not met.

Dr. Ambedkar traveled to Sri Lanka in 1950 to attend a convention of Buddhist scholars and monks. After his return, he decided to write a book on Buddhism and soon, converted himself to Buddhism. In his speeches, Ambedkar lambasted the Hindu rituals and caste division. In 1955, Ambedkar founded the "Bharatiya Bauddha Mahasabha". His book "The Buddha and His Dhamma" was published posthumously.

Dr. Ambedkar died at his home in Delhi on 6 December, 1956. He was the greatest sons of India. He experienced the suffering and the cruelty, overcame and awakened millions of India's oppressed to their human rights and stand on an equal footing. His role in forming modern India through its constitution is immensely laudable.

NARENDRA MODI

Narendra Damodardas Modi was born on September 17, 1950 in Vadnagar, a small village in Mehsana district of Gujarat. He was the third of the six children of Damodardas and Hiraba Modi. Modi's father was a tea stall owner and quite often Narendra would accompany his father to work. However, at 17, he made the exceptional decision of leaving home and travelling the country. His family was shocked by the decision, but let him go. He travelled to the Himalayas, to West Bengal and even the North-east.

Inspired by his various travel experiences, Narendra joined the RSS. His first job at the organisation was to mop the floor at the RSS headquarters in Ahmedabad. He then met Laxmanrao Inamdar, who soon became his greatest inspiration. Modi was enamoured by his oratory skills.

Modi was married young but the marriage remained unconsummated. He kept the wedding a secret as he imbibed the spirit of selflessness, social responsibility, dedication and nationalism. In 1972, Modi became a pracharak, dedicating his entire life to the organisation and service. He worked hard, waking at 5 a.m. and accomplishing difficult tasks late into the night. In 1973, he also got the opportunity to meet senior Jan Sangh members.

In 1971, Indira Gandhi swept to power. However, the euphoria soon died away and dreams fizzled out owing to the rampant corruption. Amid all the discontent, Indira Gandhi in 1975 promulgated the Emergency. Democracy was under attack, freedom of the press was muzzled. Senior opposition leaders such as L K Advani and Atal Behari Vajpayee were arrested.

Modi was at the core of the anti-Emergency movement. He became the general secretary of the Gujarat Lok Sangharsh Samiti and his primary role was to coordinate between activists in the state. It is said that to avoid arrests and the government's ire, Modi began disguising himself—dressed as a Sikh one day, and an elderly man another day.

After Emergency, the Indira Gandhi government was routed in the polls and the new Janata Party government ascended to power. At the same time, Modi was promoted to sambhaag pracharak, the equivalent of a regional organiser, and soon, he began travelling far and wide, spreading the RSS word.

Even as he embraced politics, Modi graduated in political science from Delhi University and went on to do his Masters from Gujarat University. Modi won the admiration of seniors for his hard work and efficiency. In 1987-88, he was deputed to the BJP's Gujarat unit as organizing secretary, marking his formal launch in mainstream politics.

Narendra Modi as NCC Cadet

Recognised as a master strategist, Modi was trusted with the municipal elections in Ahmedabad. Taking on the challenge head-on, Modi began touring the entire state, campaigning and spreading the BJP's word and worked tirelessly to ensure a victory. His result bore fruit when the party won the elections.

It was in the late 1990s when Modi started to emerge as a key player when he became the general secretary of the party in Delhi. It was then that he was handed over the responsibility of carrying out national yatras. He was tasked with ensuring that L K Advani's Somnath to Ayodhya yatra went off without any hitch. The task was not easy, but Modi carried it off to perfection.

In 2001, Modi received his huge break as chief minister of Gujarat. Successful with his development model, he became the Chief Minister of Gujarat for four successive terms. Finally he received a huge majority in Lok Sabha elections and sworn in as the 15th Prime Minister of India on May 26, 2014.

After becoming the Prime Minister, Modi embarked on his journey for the all-round development of India. He rebuilt friendly relations with almost all the countries of the world. He started many ambitious programmes for the development of India, such as, Prime Minister Jan Dhan Yojana, Shramev Jayate, Make in India, Digital India, Swachch Bharat Mission and Ujjwala Yojana.

The demonetisation of ₹ 500 and ₹ 1000 notes is his masterstroke to curb the black money and corruption in India.

Modi effectively tamed Pakistan by giving a befitting reply for the Pulwama attack by conducting surgical strikes on terror launchpads in POK. He contested the 2019 general election on the theme of 'Nationalism' and received a massive mandate for his second innings as the Prime Minister of India.

Triple Talaq Law, Abrogation of Article 370, Resolving the Ram Mandir – Babri Masjid Issue, and Citizenship Amendment Act have added new feathers to his cap.

In 2020, Modi was among eight world leaders awarded the parodic Ig Nobel Prize in Medical Education "for using the COVID-19 viral pandemic to teach the world that politicians can have a more immediate effect on life and death than scientists and doctors can". On 24 February 2021, the largest cricket stadium in the world at Ahmedabad was renamed Narendra Modi Stadium by the Gujarat Cricket Association.

In 2024 general election, Modi became the Prime Minister for the third consecutive term, second only to do so after the first Prime Minister Pt. Jawaharlal Nehru. Till date, he has been bestowed with so many highest national honours by different countries alongwith so many other awards.

ATAL BEHARI VAJPAYEE

Atal Behari Vajpayee was an iconic leader of the Bharatiya Janata Party (BJP), known for his cultural moderation, liberalism and political reasonableness. He became the Prime Minister of India thrice. Atal Behari Vajpayee was born in a middle-class Brahmin family to Krishna Devi and Krishna Behari Vajpayee on 25 December, 1924 in Gwalior (Madhya Pradesh). His father was a poet and a school teacher. Joining as the Rashtriya Swayamsevak Sangh (RSS) worker in 1939, Vajpayee became a pracharak (full-time worker) in 1947. Vajpayee chose to stay bachelor for entire life however, he adopted two daughters of a friend.

Atal Behari Vajpayee began his career in politics as a freedom fighter. Later, he joined the Bharatiya Jana Sangh (BJS), a Hindu right-wing political party, under the leadership of Dr Syama Prasad Mookerjee. He became national secretary of BJS in charge of the Northern region.

As the new leader of BJS, Vajpayee was elected to the Lok Sabha for the first time in 1957 from Balrampur. He rose to become the national president of the Jana Sangh in 1968 and took it to greater glory.

Atal Behari Vajpayee participated in the Total Revolution movement launched by Jayaprakash Narayan (JP) against the Internal Emergency imposed by then prime minister Indira Gandhi in 1975. In 1977, Jana Sangh became a part of the Janata Party, the grand-alliance against the Indira Gandhi government.

Atal Behari Vajpayee became a Union Minister in 1977 when Morarji Desai-led Janata Party coalition came to power for the first time. He became the Minister of External Affairs in cabinet of Morarji Desai. As foreign minister, Vajpayee became the first person to deliver a speech at the UN General Assembly in Hindi.

Vajpayee along with Lal Krishna Advani, Bhairon Singh Shekhawat and others from the BJS and Rashtriya Swyamsevak Sangh (RSS) formed the Bharatiya Janata Party in 1980. The BJP won two parliamentary seats in the 1984 elections. Vajpayee functioned as BJP President and Leader of the Opposition in the Parliament.

Vajpayee was sworn in as the 10th Prime Minister of India following the 1996 General Elections, where the BJP emerged as the single largest party in the Lok Sabha. However, the government collapsed after only 13 days after his government could not gather support from other parties to obtain a majority.

The BJP-led coalition government came back to power as the National Democratic Alliance (NDA) in 1998. Vajpayee was again sworn in as the Prime Minister. Vajpayee's second term as PM is known for Nuclear tests conducted at Pokhran desert in Rajasthan, in May 1998. Vajpayee also pushed for peace process with Pakistan. He inaugurated the historic Delhi-Lahore bus service in February 1999. He also pitched for resolving the Kashmir dispute and other conflicts with Pakistan. But Pakistan ditched India by launching Kargil War, wherein Pakistani soldiers infiltrated into the Kashmir Valley and captured border hilltops around the town of Kargil.

Indian army units, under Operation Vijay, fought Pakistani intruders and ultimately emerged victorious. However, Vajpayee's government lasted 13 months when the AIADMK withdrew its support to the government in mid-1999.

In the following election, however, the NDA came back with full majority and Vajpayee was able to complete five years (1999-2004) in office as a non-Congress PM for the first time.

Vajpayee government introduced many economic and infrastructural reforms, including encouraging the private sector and foreign investments. It also undertook National Highway Development Projects and Pradhan Mantri Gram Sadak Yojana. Vajpayee adopted pro-business, free-market reforms approach to boost India's economic development.

Vajpayee had major health issues after suffering a stroke in 2009 which impaired his speech abilities. Since then his health became a major issue of concern. He died on 16th August 2018 at New Delhi due to prolonged illness. He was conferred Bharat Ratna, India's highest civilian honour in 2015.

CDS BIPIN RAWAT

General Bipin Rawat was a four-star general of the Indian Army who was appointed as the first CDS of India on 30 December, 2019. He assumed office on 1 January, 2020. He was born in Pauri, Uttarakhand on 16 March, 1958. His father, Laxman Singh Rawat, served the Indian Army and rose to the rank of Lieutenant-General. His mother was the daughter of an ex-MLA from Uttarakhand's Uttarkashi.

He received his formal education at Cambrian Hall School in Dehradun and the St. Edward's School, Shimla and went on to join the National Defence Academy, Khadakwasla and the Indian Military Academy, Dehradun, where he was honoured with the 'Sword of Honour'. He was also a graduate of the Defence Services Staff College (DSSC), Wellington and the Higher Command Course at the United States Army Command and General Staff College at Fort Leavenworth, Kansas. He also held an M.Phil. degree in Defence Studies as well as a diploma in Management and Computer Studies from the University of Madras. For his research on military media strategic studies, he was honoured with a Doctorate of Philosophy by Chaudhary Charan Singh University, Meerut.

On 16 December 1978, CDS Bipin Rawat was commissioned into the 5th battalion of the 11 Gorkha Rifles, the same unit as his father Laxman Singh Rawat. He spent 10 years conducting counter-insurgency operations and served on various ranging from Major to current CDS. He commanded his battalion along the LAC at Kibithu as a Colonel. After getting promoted to the rank of Brigadier, he commanded 5 Sector of Rashtriya Rifles in Sopore and multinational Brigade in a Chapter VII mission in the Democratic Republic of the Congo (MONUSCO), where he was honoured twice with the Force Commander's Commendation.

He assumed the post of General Officer Commanding-in-Chief (GOC-in-C) Southern Command after being promoted to the Army Commander grade. After a short stint, he was promoted to the post of Vice Chief of Army Staff. He was appointed as the 27th Chief of Army Staff (COAS) by the Government of India on 17 December, 2016 and assumed office on 31 December, 2016. He also served as 57th and last Chairman of the Chiefs of Staff Committee of the Indian Army. He was appointed as the first CDS on 30 December, 2019 and assumed office on 1 January, 2020.

Under the leadership of Rawat, the Indian Army took some of the most stringent steps against Pakistan. It was under his tenure that the army provided stronger defences along the border with Pakistan, when the Indian Air Force carried out the Balakot strikes in February 2019. Incidentally, he also ensured strong retaliation to unprovoked ceasefire violations by the Pakistan Army along the Line of Control. Besides Pakistan, he also managed military affairs along the border with China, following the Doklam standoff in 2017 that went on for over two months. He also facilitated better relations between the armies of India and China through regular border meetings, interactions and joint exercises. General Rawat was a brigadier when he was sent to the Congo in August 2008 to command the Indian Army's, then as now, largest deployment on foreign soil, under the United Nations' peacekeeping mission, known by its French acronym MONUC. He is credited with providing dynamic leadership under the UN banner.

He was instrumental in reducing the militancy in the Northeast, with one of the highlights of his career being the 2015 cross-border operation into Myanmar in which the Indian Army successfully responded to an ambush by NSCN-K militants. The mission was conducted from the operation command of Dimapur-based III Corps under Rawat's supervision. He was also part of the planning for the 2016 surgical strikes, in which the Indian Army went across the Line of Control into Pakistan-occupied Kashmir.

During his career that spanned over 40 years, CDS General Bipin Rawat received many medals and honours for gallantry and distinguished service that includes: ✦ Param Vishisht Seva Medal; ✦ Uttam Yudh Seva Medal ✦ Ati Vishisht Seva Medal ✦ Yudh Seva Medal ✦ Sena Medal ✦ Vishisht Seva Medal ✦ Operation Parakram Medal ✦ Sainya Seva Medal ✦ High Altitude Service Medal ✦ Videsh Seva Medal ✦ MONUSCO and others.

CDS Bipin Rawat passed away on 08 December, 2021 in an unfortunate air accident in Tamil Nadu when he alongwith his wife Mrs Madhulika Rawat, President DWWA and 11 other military personnel were aboard IAF Mi 175 V5 helicopter that crashed near Coonoor on way to Wellington, Tamil Nadu.

General Bipin Rawat, India's first CDS, was a visionary who initiated far reaching reforms in the Indian military's higher defence organisation. He was instrumental in creating the foundation of India's joint theatre commands and giving impetus to the increased indigenisation of military equipment, a legacy which will be carried on and strengthened by successive generations.

❖ ❖ ❖

CHAPTER

18 History of India

SOME FACTS

1. The discovery of the Indus Valley Civilisation was made in 1921.
2. The main centres of the Indus Valley Civilisation were—Harappa, Mohenjodaro, Kali Bangan, Lothal, etc.
3. The Aryans came into India from Central Asia and settled first in *Sapta Sindhu.*
4. The Indus Valley Civilisation was urban whereas the Aryan Civilisation was rural.
5. The Vedas are four: (i) Rig Ved, (ii) Yajur Ved, (iii) Sam Ved, and (iv) Atharva Ved.
6. Of the four Vedas, Rig Ved is the oldest.
7. Jainism and Buddhism were founded during the 6th century B.C.
8. Jainism was founded by Lord Mahavir whereas Buddhism was founded by Lord Buddha.
9. Buddha was born at Lumbini.
10. Buddhism got maximum state patronage from Ashoka.
11. Buddha delivered his first sermon at Sarnath (near Varanasi).
12. Megasthenese was the Greek ambassador to the Court of Chandragupta Maurya.
13. The capital of the Mauryan Empire was Pataliputra.
14. Kanishka was the most important Kushana ruler who ruled from Purushpur (Peshawar).
15. Gupta Period is known as the Golden Age of ancient India.
16. Ashoka vowed never to wage a war (after his victory in Kalinga War) and converted himself to Buddhism.
17. Chinese Buddhist monk Hiuen Tsang visited India during the reign of Harshavardhana.
18. Sind (in India) was the first victim of Arab invasion.
19. Mahmud Ghaznavi plundered Somnath temple in 1026.
20. Mohammad Ghori defeated Prithviraj Chauhan in the second battle of Tarain.
21. Qutb-ud-din Aibak was the first Muslim ruler of India.
22. Razia Begum was the first woman who sat on the throne of Delhi Sultanate.
23. The founder of the Mughal Empire in India was Babar.
24. First battle of Panipat (1526) laid the foundation of Mughal rule in India.
25. Akbar was the greatest of the conquerors, administrators and empire builders amongst the Mughal rulers.

26. *Din-e-Ilahi* was a religious sect founded by Akbar.
27. Akbar founded Fatehpur Sikri and constructed beautiful buildings there.
28. Shahjehan died as a prisoner in the jail.
29. Aurangzeb had to face a great challenge from the Marathas.
30. The English established their first factory at Surat in 1615.
31. Portuguese were the first European traders to come to India.
32. Robert Clive was the real founder of British power in India.
33. It was Robert Clive who set up double government in Bengal.
34. Lord Wellesley followed the policy of Subsidiary Alliance to make Indian rulers as subordinate allies of the British power in India.
35. Lord William Bentinck abolished the *Sati* system.
36. During the tenure of William Bentinck English was made medium of instruction in India.
37. The last Governor General of British India was Lord Canning.
38. Lord Dalhousie sowed the seeds of 1857 Sepoy Mutiny.
39. Doctrine of Lapse was used against the Indian rulers by Lord Dalhousie.
40. Warren Hastings introduced the Permanent Settlement of land revenue in Bengal.
41. Lord Curzon partitioned Bengal in 1905.
42. The Sepoy Mutiny of 1857 started from Meerut on May 10, 1857.
43. The glorious leaders of the Revolt of 1857 were–Nana Saheb, Rani Lakshmi Bai of Jhansi, Mughal Emperor Bahadur Shah II Zafar, Kunwar Singh and Tantia Tope.
44. Indian National Congress was founded by A.O. Hume in 1885.
45. Netaji Subhash Chandra Bose founded the Indian National Army (INA) at Singapore.
46. Jallianwala Bagh massacre took place at Amritsar in 1919.
47. Indian National Congress put forth the demand of Complete Independence in 1929.
48. Swadeshi movement became very popular during mass agitation against Partition of Bengal (1905).
49. Gandhiji's Dandi March is associated with the salt law.
50. 'Quit India' slogan was given by the Indian National Congress in 1942.
51. Indian Muslim League was founded in 1906.
52. India achieved Independence in 1947 during the tenure of Lord Mountbatten.
53. With the Partition of India the British Rule ended; two "Independent States" India and Pakistan were created; Mountbatten became the first Governor-General of Free India in 1947.
54. Assassination of Mahatma Gandhi (January 30, 1948) by Nathu Ram Godse; Kashmir acceded to India; C. Rajgopalachari took over as the first Indian Governor-General (1948).
55. Integration of the Princely States into the Indian Union (1948-50).
56. Indian Constitution was signed and adopted on November 26, 1949.
57. India became Sovereign Republic (January 26, 1950). Sardar Patel died (December 15, 1950); Dr. Rajendra Prasad became the first President of India (1950).

PREHISTORIC INDIA

Prehistoric man, according to the materials used in making tools and utensils has passed through four stages: (1) the Palaeolithic or Old Stone Age; (2) the Neolithic or New Stone Age; (3) the Copper Age; and (4) the Iron Age.

In the Palaeolithic Age, the implements were of roughly hewn stone. Thousands of years thereafter man reached the Neolithic Age. The Stone was ground against some hard material and shaped into weapons and utensils, sharply pointed and decently executed. Gradually, man came to learn about the use of metals in the Copper Age. The next and the last stage was the Iron Age when man learnt to use iron.

INDIAN CIVILIZATION

Indian civilization is one of the oldest civilizations in the world. It is a very colourful country with a rich history starting from ancient civilizations, dating back to 5000 years. In the past, people belonging to different races and religions came and settled here. They brought along their distinctive languages, culture and life styles. Different tribes with their distinct languages intermingled with various tribes of our country.

The Indus Valley Civilization : On the basis of archaeological discoveries at Mohenjodaro in Sind, India along with Egypt and Babylonia can claim to be one of the earliest sites of civilization. The site contains the ruins of an ancient city, of which seven strata, one built upon the other, have been found. The date of the upper strata has been fixed at 2700 B.C.

It was largely an urban civilization. The excavations show the existence of : (i) building made up of bricks, pillared halls, a series of halls and baths, long halls probably used as granaries; (ii) the street and roads were well-planned, well laid out with pucca drains; (iii) crafts like tool-making, toys, pottery and jewellery had flourished; (iv) farming and trade were their main occupations (wheat, barley, field peas, melon seeds and cotton were grown) and (v) domesticated animals like dogs, cats, humped cattle, buffaloes, camels, horses and asses. The decline of this civilization was due to wars, climate, racial degeneration, violent geographical changes and the arrival of the Aryans.

THE ANCIENT PERIOD

The Entry of Aryans : The Aryans entered India from the north and northwest and their first settlement in India was established in the Punjab region between B.C. 2500 and B.C. 2000 and then, they spread eastwards and occupied the whole of northern India. In the course of time, they penetrated into South India as well. At first, there were conflicts between the invading Aryans and the natives, believed to be the Dravidians. But gradually, the two intermingled. The Aryans were pastoral people and patriarchal family was their unit.

The tribal chief, known as the Rajan, ruled on the advice of a popular assembly. The early Aryans were a strong race and their main occupations were cattle-rearing and war. After settling down in India, they adopted agriculture as their principal occupation. In the beginning, there were no social divisions among the Aryans. Later, they grouped the society into four divisions–Brahmins, Kshatriyas, Vaishyas and Shudras and this developed later into a rigid caste-system.

Comparison of the Indus and Vedic (Aryan) Civilizations : In both the civilizations, people domesticated animals and were engaged in hunting. In both, men and women decorated their bodies with ornaments though there was difference in the types of ornaments. The Vedic people were warlike, raided their neighbourhood for conquest or plunder. The Indus people had no armour or weapons. The Indus civilization was urban, but the Vedic civilization was rural. The people in the Indus Valley worshipped gods–Rudra and Bhagwati (goddess). The Aryans on the other hand were polytheists who worshipped Nature-gods, preferred outdoor entertainments and used "Som Rasa" as an intoxicant.

Alexander's Invasion : Alexander, the great (son of King Phillip of Macedonia in Greece) crossed the river Indus in B.C. 327 as the head of a large army. After conquering small kingdoms in the northwest, he confronted Puru, ruler of one of the States between Jhelum and Chenab in Punjab. Puru was defeated in the Battle of Hydaspes (Jhelum). Alexander advanced up to Beas when his forces refused to go further. On his way back, he died at Babylon in B.C. 323. Alexander's campaign opened up four distinct routes by land and sea.

The Mauryan Empire : Chandragupta Maurya (322-298 B.C.) : In 322 B.C., he was made the king of Magadh. He came into conflict with Seleucas, the king of western Asia. As Seleucas was defeated, he handed over Berat, Kandhar, Baluchistan, Kabul and also gave his daughter in marriage to Chandragupta.

Ashoka (273-232 B.C.) : He ascended the throne in 273 B.C. Ashoka attacked and captured Kalinga in 261 B.C. and renounced war during that very year. His empire extended up to Mysore in south, Assam in east and Kandhar in the northwest. After renouncing war, he became a Buddhist and propagated "Law of Piety" or "Dharma".

The Kushans (120-162 A.D.) : Kanishka : He became a convert to Buddhism and summoned a Buddhist council at Peshawar to settle the differences among the Buddhists. He built a great stupa at Peshawar and his court was adorned by Buddhist teacher Vasumitra, the Buddhist poet and philosopher Ashvaghosha, the reputed philosopher Nagarjuna and the great authority on

Ayurved, Charak. Two schools of art flourished during his time. They were: (i) the Gandhar school of art (which dealt with stories connected with Ashoka's life); and (ii) the Mathura School of art.

Gupta Dynasty (320-540 A.D.) : The rise of the Guptas is of extraordinary significance for Hinduism. The great rulers in this dynasty are : (1) Chandra Gupta I. (2) Samudra Gupta, (330-375 A.D.) Also Known as Napoleon of India, (3) Chandra Gupta II. (375-413 A.D.) (Vikramaditya), and (4) Skanda Gupta (455-477 A.D.). The Gupta period is described as the golden period in the history of ancient India.

Pushyabhuti/Vardhan Dynasty : Harshavardhan (606-47 A.D.): It was in 606 that Kannauj was ruled by Harshavardhan. He fought many wars to establish an empire but he was not successful. During his time, Chinese traveller Hiuen Tsang visited many provinces of India and was on friendly terms with Harsha. He left a detailed account about the famous Buddhist conference held at Kannauj.

THE MEDIEVAL PERIOD

Mahmud Ghaznavi (999-1030 A.D.) : He carried out seventeen invasions on India. His chief invasions were against the rulers of Punjab, Nagarkot and Thaneswar.

A Great Patron : Many scholars were in his court, like: (i) famous historian Alberuni who is also called Mohammed-bin-Ahmed (he wrote Kitab-ul-Hind (Tehkikat-i-Hind) and Alkanun-al-Masudi); (ii) the famous poet Firdausi composed his Shahnama; and (iii) Utbi (historian), who wrote his Tarikh-i-Yamini.

The Conquests of Mohammed Ghori : He was a great commander but he suffered defeat at the hands of Mulraj II, the Chalukya king of Anhilwara (Gujarat) in 1178 A.D. and in the first battle of Tarain in 1191 A.D. at the hands of Prithvi Raj Chauhan. But later on, he won the second battle of Tarain in 1192 A.D. He established the Muslim Empire in India and is considered to be the real founder of Muslim rule in India. Farishta, the famous historian, has greatly praised Mohammed Ghori's love for art and literature though he did not construct beautiful buildings like Mahmud Ghazni nor did he give patronage to as many scholars.

The Slave Dynasty (1206-1290 A.D.) : Qutubuddin Aibak (1206-1210 A.D.) : Qutubuddin Aibak was the founder of the Slave Dynasty. He commenced the building of the Qutub Minar which was later completed by Iltutmish (1210-1236). Razia Sultan (1236-1239) and Balban were the other great rulers in this dynasty.

The Khilji Dynasty (1290-1320 A.D.) : Alauddin Khilji (1296-1316 A.D.) : He was the first Muslim ruler to invade southern India. It was Alauddin Khilji, who introduced famous market regulations to maintain correct prices and also punished merchants for using false weights.

The Tughlak Dynasty (1320-1414 A.D.) : Ghyasuddin Tughlak (1320-25 A.D.) was the founder of Tughlak dynasty. Mohammed bin Tughlak (1325-1351) was the most distinguished ruler of this dynasty. He was a mixture of opposites. His transfer of capital from Delhi to Daulatabad has been described by historians as an act of madness.

Timur's Invasion : Timur invaded India in 1398. He massacred his prisoners, totalling 1,00,000 in number. He plundered many a city in north India and looted wealth from Delhi and elsewhere. He did not prefer to establish an empire in India and returned.

The Lodi Dynasty (1451-1526 A.D.) : Bahlol Lodi (1451-89 A.D.) : He established his control over Delhi and defeated powerful Sharqi Sultan of Jaunpur and the Rajputs of Doab.

Sikander Lodi (1489-1517 A.D.) : He worked impartially and delivered justice according to Islamic principles. He got land measured and re-fixed land revenue. He built Agra Fort and tomb of his father Bahlol Lodi in Delhi. He could not conquer Gwalior and Ranthambor but successfully suppressed many Afghan chiefs.

Ibrahim Lodi (1517-1526 A.D.) : He was the last and an incapable ruler of this dynasty. He fought the first battle of Panipat and lost it to Babur.

Babur (1526-30 A.D.) : He was the founder of the Mughal empire. In 1526, he defeated Ibrahim Lodi. In 1527, he defeated Rana Sangram Singh. In the Battle of Gogra, he destroyed the Afghans. His biography, known as the Tuzuk-i-Babri is written in chaste Turkish.

Humayun (1530-40 & 1552-56 A.D.) : Humayun was not a strong ruler and was ousted by Sher Shah. After having lost the battles at Chausa and Kannauj, he had to flee to Iran. He waited for his turn and attacked India again in 1552. He defeated the successor of Sher Shah Suri and regained control over his lost kingdom.

Sher Shah Suri (1540-45 A.D.) : Sher Shah's rule is of tremendous significance because the beginnings that he made during his life were carried to their logical conclusions by Akbar. He introduced a system of survey and assessment of land. He built his own mausoleum at Sasaram–the first example of Hindu-Muslim synthesis of architecture. After five years of rule, Sher Shah died.

Maharana Pratap (1540-1597 A.D.) : He is counted in top 10 strongest warriors ever born in India. He was the king of Mewar in Rajasthan. He was very patriotic and brave warrior. He fought several wars against the Mughal army and never surrendered or caught by the enemy. He had one very strong, loyal and clever horse called Chetak who died while saving his life. Pratap died after an accident during hunting in a jungle.

Akbar (1556-1605 A.D.) : Akbar defeated the Afghans in the second Battle of Panipat in 1556. Akbar introduced a very successful revenue administration with the guidance of Todarmal, a former employee of Sher Shah. Because of Akbar's personal interest in administration, every aspect of it functioned well. He showed a receptive interest in Hinduism and Christianity.

Jehangir (1605-27 A.D.) : After Akbar, Jehangir succeeded him. He was an easy-going and luxury oriented ruler. He is remembered for his romance with Nurjahan, who, to a great extent, dominated politics, and so, his eldest son Khurram rebelled. Mahabat Khan, a general, was also a suspect in the eyes of Nurjahan and so, he too rebelled. Jehangir is known for his exemplary justice and love for the gardens.

Shahjahan (1627-58 A.D.) : During his reign, India was at the peak of prosperity and the country was known as the golden bird. In fact, Shahjahan's reign is known as the golden era of medieval history. Shahjahan was a great builder. He founded Shahjahanabad (Delhi) and built the world famous Taj Mahal at Agra along with Red Fort and Jama Masjid at Delhi. There was a war of succession among his sons.

Aurangzeb (1658-1707 A.D.) : Aurangzeb was a strong ruler and a great general but his reign witnessed a lot of turbulence. He devoted almost half of his time in Deccan. During Aurangzeb's rule, the mughal empire was extended to almost whole of India and included Afghanistan also. He was intolerant towards other religions. He re-imposed Jazia on Hindus. He alienated the sympathies of Rajputs also. These resulted in a series of wrangles. After a long rule, Aurangzeb left the vast empire without any able successor.

Chhatrapati Shivaji Maharaj : Chhatrapati Shivaji Maharaj, who founded the Maratha Kingdom was the son of Shahji who served the Bijapur state. His mother, Jijabai and teacher, Dadaji Konddev enthused him with religious spirit since his childhood. Shaista Khan, sent by Aurangzeb was disgraced by him. Once he was captured and imprisoned by Aurangzeb. Luckily, he escaped, re-conquered the territory and was crowned as Chhatrapati in 1674 at Raigarh. Shivaji Maharaj was not only a good soldier, but also an able administrator. He organised civil and military systems. During his time, Marathas came to be recognised as a separate entity. The war waged by Aurangzeb against them was of no use as even after Shivaji's death, Marathas maintained themselves as a military power and gave a lot of trouble to Mughal empire.

Onslaught from Northwest

Nadir Shah's Invasion (1739) : In 1739, the famous invasion of Nadir Shah occurred who entered the capital of Mughals and ordered a general massacre. He carried away with him the diamond of Kohinoor and the peacock throne of Shahjahan. However, he didn't stay in Delhi for long and handed the empire back to the Mughal ruler, Mohammed Shah.

Abdali's Attacks : Ahmed Shah Abdali also invaded India five times. In 1761, he won the famous third battle of Panipat wherein he routed the Marathas completely. This disabled the Marathas to exploit the political vacuum created by the displacement of Mughal empire and the English extended their authority over India.

ARRIVAL OF THE BRITISH

In 1600, East India Company was granted the right to trade with East Indies by Queen Elizabeth-I. By one Sanad, the English established a factory at Surat and later, factories at Madras and Calcutta followed. By this time, the Portuguese were a power in India. From 1505, they acquired a few areas like Goa, Daman and Dieu. But their power declined very soon as they carried sword in one hand and the Bible in the other. Albuquerque, who captured Goa was an important governor. Portuguese rule, though short-lived, was significant. The famous Saint Xavier visited India. They introduced Bengaluru-type architecture, established missionary schools and translated some Indian books on medicine.

Carnatic Wars : There was a trial of strength between the French and the English in Carnatic Wars and the French were defeated due to various reasons; like Duplex, their general, was too hot headed and he could not foresee that the English too could participate in internal affairs of the princes and thus, check French domination. The home government did not help them much. They lacked resources. The French generals were of divided opinion and thus, their ambitions were foiled in the battlefields.

Battle of Plassey : The English won a victory over Siraj-ud-Daula, the Nawab of Bengal, at the battle of Plassey in 1757. After this, the English won the battle of Buxar in 1764 against the Mughal Emperor, the Nawab of Awadh and Mir Kasim, the new Nawab of Bengal. In 1765, the Mughal emperor granted to the English the Diwani of Bengal, Bihar and Orissa (now Odisha). The revenue administration was in the hands of the English Company while responsibility for law and order was that of the native Nawabs. This notorious experiment caused much harm to Bengal.

Pitt's India Act, 1784 : In 1784, Pitt's India Act was passed. By this Act, the control of the Home Government was increased as a member of the British Cabinet began to look after Indian affairs.

Lord Hastings (1807-13 A.D.) : Lord Hastings completed the rout of Marathas in 1818. He was also responsible for the suppression of certain lawless elements like pindaris and the thugs.

The Role of Lord Macaulay : During his reign Lord Bentick decided the educational fate of India through his doctrine of 1835. According to this, English became the medium of instruction. This step resulted in important consequences as Indians came into contact with the ideas and beliefs of western civilization through English language. The liberal ideas of Bentham and Mill, radical ideas of Tom Paine and Rousseau, the literary products of Shakespeare and Milton influenced the intelligentsia of the country of that time.

The Revolt of 1857 : The people of India, right from the beginning of the British conquest never acquiesced in their political exploitation. Not a year passed without an armed resistance to British rule in one part of the country or the other. The greatest of these revolts, which shook the very foundations of the British rule, occurred in 1857. The revolt began at Meerut on 10th May 1857, with the uprising of Indian sepoys of the British armies in India. It was the result of accumulated resentment which had been growing since the beginning of British conquest, but was triggered off by the greased cartridges incident. Dalhousie, who came to India as the Governor-General, annexed eight new states in the course of the eight years of his stay in office. The revolt soon spread all over northern and eastern India and in the Deccan. The rebels declared Bahadur Shah-II the nominal Mughal King, the Emperor of Hindustan. Hindus and Muslims fought shoulder-to-shoulder against the British. The deeds of valour of revolutionaries, like the Rani of Jhansi, Begum Hazrat Mahal, Kanwar Singh, Bakht Khan and Tantia Tope, have become proud legends and have inspired the posterity. The revolt was suppressed after bitter fighting for over a year, though peace was not restored until 1859. The British rulers followed a ruthless and indiscriminate policy of vengeance. The revolt marked a turning point in the history of India. The rule of the East India Company passed to the British Crown.

India Under the Crown : Rule of the East India Company came to an end and administration was transferred to the British Crown. Secretary of state for India was appointed with a Council of fifteen members to assist him. Proclamation of Queen Victoria was issued. The first step after 1857 was the Indian Council Act of 1861. It provided that the Legislative Council should confine itself strictly to legislation.

NATIONAL MOVEMENT

The National Movement or the movement of independence was a part of a larger spectrum of national resurgence which covered almost all the aspects of national life–religious, social, educational, cultural and economic. While the progress in different spheres differed in degree and in kind from region-to-region, one common desire animated all regions–namely independence.

Origin : The origin of the national movement can be traced back to the revolt of 1857. In the summer of 1857, the masses revolted and the entire British dominion of India shook to its foundations. The British historians dubbed the revolt of 1857 as the sepoy-mutiny while the Indian historians termed it as the first war of Independence. True, it began as a mutiny of Indian soldiers against their British Commanders, but it soon changed its character and became a fight against British rule as such. However, Indian nationalism was quite weak in 1857. For 23 years more, it could not succeed in finding a regular expression. The national movement really began in 1885 with the birth of the Indian National Congress. It is sometimes said that the history of the Indian National Congress is the history of Indian Nationalism.

Indian National Congress : The birth of the Indian National Congress was an unprecedented phenomenon in the political history of India. It marked the entry of the newly-educated middle class into national politics. This middle class, a by-product of the British Raj, was mainly composed of three classes: agricultural, industrial and professional. Each class had its own interests but a growing sense of nationality, often extolled as patriotism, united them in a common programme of action. From 1885 onwards, the Indian National Congress met every year. Its influence spread rapidly among the middle class. Three main topics engaged its attention: (i) representative government and expansion of the number of functions of legislative councils both in the provinces and at the centre; (ii) Indianisation of higher services; and (iii) poverty in the country.

The Partition of Bengal : As the 19th century drew to a close–on December 30, 1899–Lord Curzon came down to India as Viceroy. The growing ambition of Curzon was to destroy the political influence of the educated middle class, among whom the Bengali intelligentsia were most prominent. So his first attention was directed to Bengal. By a Royal proclamation of 16th October 1905, Bengal province was reduced in size and population and a new province called East Bengal was created. The Indian National Congress, unanimously condemned the partition.

The Swadeshi Movement : The constitutional agitation so far pursued had not made an impact. The Swadeshi movement and boycott of foreign goods, became the mainstay of the freedom movement. Besides, open defiance of government order, refusal to pay taxes and bandhs and hartals followed one after the other. The Swadeshi movement gave a fillip to indigenous products, especially textiles.

An Aggressive Approach : Lord Minto, who succeeded Curzon, followed a judicious policy of admixture of the carrot and the stick. The 1905 session of the Congress at Banaras was in a sense, a turning point in the history of the Congress. The President, Gopalkrishna Gokhale, though a moderate himself, approved of aggressive agitation. From 1905, the Congress started functioning as a permanent organisation.

Rift Between Hindus and Muslims : The seeds of distrust and suspicion between Hindus and Muslims, which Minto had sown sprouted. The Muslims formed a political organization, tentatively named Muslim League. Communal riots on bigger scale occurred in 1907 at Comilla in Tripura district and in Jamalpur taluk of Mymensingh district. In future, these riots were to become almost a daily occurrence everywhere in British India.

Differences in Opinions : Differences of opinion regarding attitudes and policies to be adopted in the National Movement were discussed in 1907 when the Congress met at Surat. The moderates (doves) in the Congress were against the extremist programme of action lest it should strengthen the anti-Indian stances of the British public. Leaders of the extremist section wanted to "capture the Congress and make it an instrument of revolutionary action." The moderates retained control of the Congress. They met immediately after and drafted the new creed of Congress. The moderates, left alone, kept the Congress going as best they could.

The First World War : The First World War brought Britain into conflict with Turkey, whose Sultan was also the Khalifa of all the Muslims. That the Khilafat was in danger shook the passivity of the Indian Muslims and made them restive and thirsting for some sort of action. The change in leadership helped to bring the Congress and League together. With Turkey joining Germany against the allies in the first World War, loyalty of the Indian Muslims to the British crown became suspect. The Muslim newspapers, which supported Turkey, were suppressed and repression was let loose on the Muslims.

Demand for Home Rule : Annie Beasant, who had joined the Congress joined hands with Tilak in demanding Home Rule for India. With the defeat of Turkey and the abolition of the Sultanate, the Khilafat ceased to exist. This agitated all Muslims in India as the Muslims of the world had no religious head.

All India Khilafat Committee : In 1919, a conference at Lucknow, sponsored by Muslim leaders, the Ali brothers, Mohammed Ali and Shaukat Ali and Maulana Abul Kalam Azad decided to form an All India Khilafat Committee. Rowlatt Act roused the ire of all Indians, Hindus and Muslims alike. Mohammed Ali Jinnah, later to become the president of the Muslim League and the founder of Pakistan, resigned from his seat in the Council.

The Khilafat Movement : The Khilafat movement was organised by the famous Ali brothers, Mohammed Ali and Shaukat Ali, in protest against the injustice done to Turkey after the war. In fact, it became a part of the Indian national movement. The Congress leaders joined the Khilafat agitation and helped in organising it throughout the country.

Massacre at Jallianwala Bagh : Punjab saw the worst manifestation of British power. When the news of Gandhiji's arrest reached Lahore, the students took out a protest procession. The police opened fire on the un-offending processionists. Worse was the fate of Amritsar. Mounted police fired upon the crowd, killing some and wounding many. A protest meeting against this outrage was arranged at Jallianwala Bagh on 13th April, 1919. The government, in anticipation of trouble, handed over Amritsar to the army under the command of General O'Dyer. Jallianwala Bagh turned out to be a deadly trap. As the crowd filled the enclosure, O'Dyer and his troops appeared at the main entrance and rained bullets on the crowd. Men died in hundreds. The massacre at Jallianwala Bagh was an act of unprovoked savagery, unequalled in history. It shook the country from end-to-end.

Swaraj Party : Swaraj Party, founded by C.R. Das and Moti Lal Nehru in 1923, consisted of Moderates and Liberals. They contested the 1920 elections and some of them were elected. They formed a type of opposition and succeeded in defeating many government motions and abolishing certain obnoxious acts like the Press Act of 1910.

Non-cooperation Movement : In 1920, the Congress adopted the new programme of non-cooperation under the leadership of Gandhiji and Moti Lal Nehru. The aims of the non-cooperation movement were to redress the wrongs done to Punjab and Turkey and to help the attainment of Swaraj. It was to proceed in stages, beginning with the renunciation of titles, to be followed by the boycott of the legislatures, law courts and educational institutions and the campaign of non-payment of taxes. The non-cooperation movement was a great success. In the elections to the legislatures, about two-thirds of voters did not vote. Educational institutions were deserted.

A New Programme of National Education : A new programme of national education was started. Such institutions as the Jamia Millia Islamia and the Kashi Vidya Peeth were established. Many Indians resigned their government jobs. Foreign clothes were burnt in bonfires. There were strikes in schools, colleges and commercial establishments all over the country at the height of the non-cooperation movement and against the repressive measures of the British government.

The Congress Session : The annual session of the Congress was held at Ahmedabad in December, 1921. The Congress, under the Presidentship of Hakim Ajmal Khan decided to continue the movement until Punjab and Khilafat grievances were redressed and Swaraj was attained. Early in February, Gandhiji decided to launch a no-tax campaign in Bardoli district in Gujarat.

The Chauri Chaura Incident : In Chauri Chaura (in Uttar Pradesh) people turned violent and set fire to a police station causing the death of 22 policemen. When the news reached Gandhiji, he decided to call off the non-cooperation movement. Gandhiji was arrested and sent to jail.

Stress on Hindu-Muslim Unity : The Working committee of the Congress met on 12th February, 1922 and decided to concentrate on the popularisation of Charkha, the promotion of Hindu-Muslim unity and combating untouchability.

Parliamentary Commission : In 1927, a Parliamentary Commission was appointed to look into the question of Constitutional Reforms for India and make suitable recommendations. The Commission was headed by Sir John Simon, a leading constitutional lawyer of Britain and a member of parliament. The Commission visited India in 1928. The Congress boycotted the Commission.

Satyagraha (1930) : Gandhiji decided to launch satyagraha and informed the Viceroy about his decision. His first act was to go to Dandi and make salt which was then a government monopoly. He set out on the march and reached Dandi with his followers on April 5, 1930. He walked into the sea waters and on return, took a lump of salt from the salt fields and thus violated the Salt law.

Repressive Measures : All repressive laws were soon brought into force. The repealed Press Act of 1910 was revised. Gandhiji and many other outstanding leaders were arrested.

First Round Table Conference (1930) : The Government of England summoned the First Round Table Conference in London but it was not attended by Mahatma Gandhi. Civil Disobedience Movement was started. At the conference representatives of major political groups of India, representatives of the rulers of India, princely states and representatives from three political parties of England participated.

Gandhi-Irwin Pact (1931) : A pact was agreed upon between Mahatma Gandhi and Lord Irwin, the Viceroy. The Gandhi-Irwin pact was ratified by the Congress at its Karachi Session presided over by Vallabhbhai Patel on March 29, 1934. The Congress had not attended the first Round Table Conference. However, the Second Round Table Conference, which opened on 7th September, 1931, was distinguished by the fact that the Congress participated in it and was represented by Gandhiji as the sole delegate of the Congress.

Matters Complicated : By this time, a National Government by Ramsay MacDonald was formed in Britain. It was dominated by the Conservative party. Sir Samuel Hoare succeeded Wedgewood Benn as the Secretary of State for India while Lord Willingdon replaced Irwin as Viceroy.

The White Paper : The Third Round Table Conference met in London on November 17, 1932 and continued its deliberations till December 24. After the end of the conference the British Government published a white paper which practically reproduced the recommendations of Simon Commission but added a scheme for a Federal Government if the Princely States agreed. The white paper, in due course, became the Government of India Act, 1935.

Government of India Act, 1935 : For soothing the Indian people, the British government promulgated the Government of India Act on 2nd August, 1935. This Act envisaged an All India Federation of Provinces and Indian States and the establishment of provincial autonomy in the federating provinces. At the centre, a central legislative assembly and a council of states were to be formed.

The Indian princes were to be given disproportionately high representation in the two houses at the Centre. The provision regarding the formation of the federation never came into operation and the new constitution was introduced only in the provinces.

Khudai Khidmatgars : In the North-West Frontier Province, Khan Abdul Ghaffar Khan (known as the Frontier Gandhi) raised a volunteer corps of one lakh Pathans, called the Servants of God and affiliated it to the Congress.

First Elections : The Act of 1935 provided two alternate constitutions for the Central Government. Firstly, a Federal Government consisting of British provinces and Indian States, provided a majority of Indian States were willing to accede to the Federation. This never happened. Secondly, there was an alternative to work under the 1919 Act with some modifications. This alternative was finally accepted. In the elections, the congress won with a huge majority, in the provinces of Madras, Bombay, Bihar, Central province, United province and Orissa. In other Provinces, Congress acquired a sizeable number of seats. In 1937, the Congress took charge of the governments in seven provinces. In the remaining four provinces–Punjab, Bengal, Assam and Sindh–non-Congress parties took office.

The Second World War : The outbreak of the second Word War, which commenced with Hitler's invasion of Poland on September 1, 1939, called for a complete change of policy on both sides–the British Indian Government and the Indian National Congress. India was declared a belligerent nation by Britain on September 3, 1939 and the British Indian administration was executed on a war footing. The war lasted for 6 years, till September 1945. The Congress asked all provincial Congress ministries to resign.

Demand for Freedom : In March 1940, at its annual session in Ramgarh, the Congress demanded complete independence and a Constituent Assembly to draft a constitution for free India. In the same month, the Muslim League at its Lahore session demanded a separate state for the Muslims of India.

Quit India Movement : In March 1942, the British Government sent Sir Stafford Cripps to India with proposals for a constitution. The Cripps' proposals were found unsatisfactory and were rejected both by the Congress and the League. In May 1942, Gandhiji called Britain to "leave India to God. If this is too much, then leave her to anarchy". In August 1942, the Congress committee considered Gandhiji's call to Britain and passed the famous 'Quit India' resolution.

Shimla Conference : In 1945, Lord Wavell, the Viceroy, announced that he was holding a conference in Shimla to consider the steps necessary to advance self-government for India in the near future. All the leaders in prison, were released. The Shimla conference (June-July 1945) turned out to be a fiasco. But by that time, (July), a Labour Government came into power in Britain. The Labour Government took serious notice of the Indian situation.

Cabinet Mission : The Labour Secretary of State for India, Lord Lawrence announced that a parliamentary commission would be visiting India to negotiate the question of India's independence. This delegation, which later became famous as the Cabinet Mission, announced its constitutional scheme which simply recognised the right of the Muslims to have a state of their own. While the Muslim League accepted the proposal, the Congress rejected it.

The Communal Riots : This was followed by riots. The great Calcutta killings of August 16-18, 1946, were the first of the riots. Then followed the killings in Punjab. The Congress, in desperation, accepted the partition of the country.

The Partition (1947) : In June 1947, Lord Mountbatten declared the partition of India including the partition of Bengal, Assam and Punjab.

Indian Independence Act (1947) : In July, 1947 the British Parliament passed the Indian Independence Act, providing for the independence of two dominions. On 15th August, 1947, the British Rule ended in India and two Dominions of India and Pakistan came into being. Jawaharlal Nehru became the first Prime Minister of India. Lord Mountbatten was the first Governor-General of free India from 15th August, 1947 to 2nd May, 1948. C. Rajagopalachari took over from him as Governor-General. India became a Republic on 26 January, 1950 and Dr. Rajendra Prasad became the first President of India.

RELIGIONS OF INDIA

India is a multi-religious democratic country. There are six major religions in India with percentage of population as under :

	Religion		Percentage
(i)	Hindus	—	79.8%
(ii)	Muslims	—	14.2%
(iii)	Christians	—	2.3%
(iv)	Sikhs	—	1.7%
(v)	Buddhists	—	0.7%
(vi)	Jains	—	0.4%
(vii)	Others	—	0.9%

The following are brief details about major religions of India :

Hinduism

Unlike many other religions, Hinduism does not have any founder. Its sacred writings, beliefs and practices came from widely different places and era. It is more of a way of life. Despite several attempts at forced and organised conversions, Hinduism is one of the few surviving religions with a large following in South Asia. The Hindus have multiple Gods and Goddesses, with Vishnu, Brahma, Mahesh and

Shakti being prominent ones. They are prayed by different names and picturised differently all over. The scriptures of Hinduism are many in number, with the important ones being from Vedas, Gita and Ramayana.

Hinduism teaches the existence of one supreme universal spirit but allows the followers to worship him in any form. It believes in the doctrines of Karma and re-births. Soul within the body is believed to be immortal. It considers Dharma, or virtue, Artha or material well-being and Karma or gratification of the senses as three main aims of human life. Moksha or salvation is the ultimate aim of life, according to Hinduism. Another characteristic of Hinduism is Varnashrama. According to it, there are four Varnas as per the occupation and four ashramas as per different stages of life. The religion has never been static or uniform and has adopted itself to the changing circumstances and conditions of life. Different sects of Hinduism have various doctrines, principles, philosophies and rituals but all of them have co-existed, respecting each other. Since Hinduism did not have any central authority and permitted individuals to think and act on their own, it never developed as an organised religion like others.

Islam

Prophet Muhammad founded in sixth century AD, the religion of Islam, literally meaning submission to God. A Muslim is one who submits. Muhammad was born in Mecca in 570 AD. At the age of 40, he had visions of truth and became a prophet. Due to opposition to his preachings, Prophet fled to Medina in 622 AD (Hejira or Mohammedan calendar begins from this date). He came back to capture Mecca with the help of his supporters. Prophet died in 632 AD.

Islam believes in a single God as supreme lord of the universe, arbiter of man's fate, all-powerful, all-knowing and all-pervading. Man is powerless before Allah and must, therefore, submit to his will. Muslims pray and bow before the God only. They recognize earlier prophets before Muhammad as well but believe that he was the last and the greatest. Islam speaks of a life after death and of a last judgement when all men shall receive the reward for their actions on earth. Muslims all over the world regard themselves as brothers and equals. A muslim must (1) proclaim the unity of God and the prophethood of Muhammad; (2) pray five times in a day; (3) give alms to the poor; (4) keep fast during the days of Ramazan month; and (5) make pilgrimage to Mecca. Islam lays down some observation and forbids some practices. Muslims are forbidden from worshipping an Idol, eating pork and lending money on interest. Islam's emphasis on a life of virtue and benevolence made it one of the great humanitarian religions. Quran is their holy book which is believed to have the word of God, received by Muhammad. Islam's followers got divided into Shiites and Sunnis, but both believe in Quran and Prophet Muhammad.

Christianity

Jesus founded the Christianity religion. He was born as a Jew at Bethlehem near Jerusalem in 4 BC. He went about preaching his message in simple words and come to be known as a great leader. His simple life, magnetic personality and outstanding love and compassion for all made large followers of him. His fearlessness in criticizing the evil made Jewish priests and noble men his enemy. He was crucified but according to legends he rose on the third day after crucifixion. All the years in history are compared in Christian era with the birth of Jesus. BC means Before Christ, and AD means Anno Domini or "in the year of the lord".

Jesus said the authority of God was the Supreme power on earth. He referred to God as father and called himself son of the God. He loved his followers and taught people to love their neighbours. Christians believe that Jesus came to earth and died to redeem from sin and restore him to communion with God. After worldwide preaching of the gospel by his followers, he would reveal himself at the last judgement and reign as universal king. The holy book of Christianity is the Bible, containing two parts–Old Testament has religious beliefs of the Jews while New Testament contains the biography and teachings of Jesus Christ. Jerusalem is the most sacred place for Christians.

Christianity has three major sects: (1) Roman Catholics are the followers of Roman Church, with Pope as the representative of God; (2) Protestants are the followers of Martin Luther and have separate churches (3) Orthodox are Catholics but recognise the authority of a Patriarchate.

Sikhism

The founder of Sikhism, Guru Nanak stressed unity of God and condemned idolatory, ritualism and caste system. He emphasised the necessity of worshipping God through love. He assimilated good features of Hinduism and Islam. His teachings were compiled in a book called Adi-Granth or Guru Granth. The tenth Guru of Sikhism Govind Singh instituted the institution of "Panj Piaras" and five customs–Kesh (hairs of head and beard to be grown), Kaccha (underwear), Kara (bracelet), Kangha (comb) and Kirpan (sword). Guru Govind Singh was the last Guru of Sikhs. Sikhs pray in Gurudwara and their sacred places are Amritsar, Nanakana Sahib and Anandpur Sahib.

Buddhism

Gautama Buddha founded Buddhism in the 6th century BC. He was born as Siddarth in a royal family but sorrows and sufferings of the world bothered him so much that he left earthly world for forests. He got enlightenment at Bodh Gaya and gave his first sermon at Sarnath. He dedicated the rest of his life to teaching. He did not claim to be God but after his death, his followers formed a new religion called Buddhism to worship him and to spread his ideas.

Buddha taught four noble truths–there is suffering in the world; this suffering has a cause; the cause is desire; and it is possible to put an end to suffering if desire is removed. To attain freedom from birth and rebirth or nirvana, eight fold path should be adopted which includes Right view, Right resolution, Right words, Right action, Right living, Right effort, Right thinking and Right concentration. The religion stresses the importance of the middle path, avoiding the extremes of strict asceticism or too much indulgence in worldly pleasures. Buddha also preached non-violence. He rejected the authority of the Vedas and caste-system. The Buddhist monks lived a strict disciplined life. They had to renounce most of their possessions, keeping only a robe, a needle, water strainer and a begging bowl.

A few centuries later, Buddhism divided into two sects–the Hinayana and the Mahayana. The Hinayana (Lesser Vehicle) sect lays emphasis on the salvation of the individual by directly observing the eight fold path, *i.e.,* teachings of Buddha in original form. It is prevalent in Myanmar, Sri Lanka, Cambodia and Vietnam. The followers of Mahayana (Greater Vehicle) worshipped the Buddha as a god and stressed that salvation is open to all. This sect is popular in China, Tibet, Korea and Mongolia.

Jainism

Jainism derives its name from Jaina (the conqueror), the surname of Vardhamana Mahavir who lived in the 6th century BC. Mahavira was the last of the 24 Tirthankars or great religious leaders. The Jains believe that every object, living or non-living, has a soul. So, they lay great emphasis on ahimsa or non-injury. Mahavir denied the authority of the Vedas. He laid emphasis on good conduct and taught right belief, right knowledge and right conduct for attaining salvation. Jainism believes in the doctrine of Karma and rebirth but shunned rituals.

Jainism later on split in two sects–the Digambaras (who wear no clothes) and the Shvetambaras (who wear white clothes).

CUSTOMS OF INDIA

India is a multiracial, multilingual civilization with rich culture heritage and has provided peaceful atmosphere for the development of many religions. Indian culture and customs are influenced by these religions. The customs of India depict very colourful panorama. There are certain customs which are prevalent in a particular religion and some are common to all religions of the country.

Indian festivals are famous in the world. Most of the festivals are related to the change of weather and crop harvesting since India is an agro based economy. The most famous Indian festivals are Diwali, Holi, Dussehra and Eid, etc. There are certain festivals which are prevalent in particular regions only like Bihu in Assam, Baisakhi in Punjab, etc. The customs are of various types in relation to local customs, caste customs and family customs. There are different customs of Hindu marriage as compared to a Muslim marriage or a Sikh marriage. Similarly, there are different customs of celebrations. All these customs have been protected by law.

There are certain religious customs which pertain to particular religion only like Mundan ceremony in Hindus and Naming ceremony in Sikhs. These customs have religious value and are a means of entertainment also.

There are certain customs regarding dresses and ornaments of women. These are associated with particular regions which give a very colourful dimension to Indian customs and traditions, Similarly, all regions have their distinctive ornaments.

India being a big country with different races and religions has rich customs related to festivals, religious ceremonies, dresses, marriage, architecture, painting, song, dance and food habits. The customs and traditions of India, though varied, have a binding force in them which ultimately serves as a unifying factor of United India.

LITERATURE OF INDIA

It is known fact that certain beliefs and inner attitudes are more conducive to spiritual growth than others. Our ancient literature and scriptures teach us to lead a pure and virtuous life.

The following are the major ancient literatures and scriptures of India and the world:

Vedic Literature : The whole Vedic literature, according to an orthodox view, was revealed to a favoured few "the rishis" or the "seers" who uttered the hymns and was communicated down to their descendants. The word "Ved" means knowledge.

The Vedas : These are four in number–the Rig Veda, the Sam Veda, the Yajur Veda and the Atharva Veda. They are written in Sanskrit. The Rig Veda is believed to be the oldest. The Rig Veda has a great literary merit, apart from being a philosophical treatise. The parts which constitute the Vedas are: (1) the Samhitas of the four Vedas; (2) the Brahmans attached to each of the Samhitas; (3) the Aranyakas and (4) the Upanishads, mostly attached to the Brahmans, but in reality forming separate and unconnected treatise.

The Upanishadas : The Upanishadas deal with spiritual topics and are mostly appended to the Aranyakas. These are 108 in number. The philosophy contained in the Upanishadas is called Vedanta (end of the Veda). The essence of this philosophy is "the world is God and God is my soul". This universal philosophy cuts across the frontiers of all religions.

The Puranas : They are 18 in number. They are a mixture of history, religion, mythology and tradition. They deal with primary creation, secondary creation, genealogies of gods and patriarchs, laws of Manu and the history of various dynasties.

The Sutras : The Sutra literature consists of manuals of instructions on various subjects. The Sutras are composed in the most compressed form of prose to ensure brevity and easy memorisation.

The Jatakas : The Jatakas form part of the Buddhist Tripitaka. These give accounts of some of the lives which the Buddha had lived before he attained Buddhahood in his final life as Siddhartha. In reality, however, these are merely folklore and popular stories which have been forcibly given a Buddhistic air and made to suit the Buddhist doctrines.

The Epics : There are two epics–The Ramayana and the Mahabharata, originally written in Sanskrit. These took shape before the 6th Century B.C. The epics present a pantheon of new gods in place of Vedic culture. They reflect a complex social and political set up to replace the simple life of the early Aryans.

Ramayana : The Ramayana is one of the largest ancient epics in world literature. It consists of nearly 24,000 verses. In Hindu tradition, it is considered to be the adi-kavya (first poem). It depicts the duties of relationships, portraying ideal characters like the ideal father, the ideal servant, the ideal brother, the ideal wife and the ideal king. The Ramayana was an important influence on later Sanskrit poetry and Hindu life and culture. Like the Mahabharata, the Ramayana is not just a story: it presents the teachings of ancient Hindu sages in narrative allegory, interspersing philosophical and ethical elements. The characters Ram, Sita, Lakshman, Bharat, Hanuman and Ravan are all fundamental to the cultural consciousness of India.

Bhagwat Gita : The Bhagwat Gita often referred to as simply the Gita, is a 700-verse Hindu scripture in Sanskrit that is part of the Hindu epic. The Gita is set in a narrative framework of a dialogue between Pandava prince Arjun and his guide and charioteer Lord Krishna. Facing the duty as a warrior to fight the Dharma Yudhha or righteous war between Pandavas and Kauravas, Arjun is counselled by Lord Krishna to "fulfill his Kshatriya (warrior) duty as a warrior and establish Dharma. Inserted in this appeal to kshatriya dharma is a dialogue between diverging attitudes concerning methods toward the attainment of liberation (moksha).

Quran : The Quran is the central religious text of Islam, which Muslims believe to be a revelation from God (Allah). It is widely regarded as the finest work in classical Arabic literature.

Guru Granth Sahib : Guru Granth Sahib is the central religious scripture of Sikhism, regarded by Sikhs as the final, sovereign and eternal living Guru following the lineage of the ten human Gurus of the religion.

Bible : The Bible is a collection of sacred texts or scriptures that Jews and Christians consider to be a product of divine inspiration and a record of the relationship between God and humans.

❖ ❖ ❖

CHAPTER

19 The Armed Forces & Military History

Defence Policy

India's defence policy aims at promoting and sustaining durable peace in the subcontinent by means of negotiations and cooperation with various countries in the region and at the same time, equipping the defence forces with modern weapons as a safeguard against aggressions.

Armed Forces

The supreme command of the Armed Forces is vested in the President of India. The responsibility for national defence, however, rests with the Cabinet. All important questions, having a bearing on defence, are decided by the Cabinet Committee on Political Affairs, which is presided over by the Prime Minister. The Defence Minister is responsible to Parliament for all matters concerning the Defence Services.

The administrative and operational control of the Armed Forces is exercised by the Ministry of Defence and the three Services Headquarters of the Army, Navy and Air Force. The three Services–Army, Navy and Air Force–function through their respective Services Headquarters, headed by Chiefs of Staff who work under Chief of Defence Staff (CDS). The first CDS of India was General Bipin Rawat.

INDIAN ARMY

The Indian Army is the land-based branch and the largest component of the Indian Armed Forces. The President of India serves as the de-jure Commander-in-Chief of the army while the de-facto leadership lies with Minister of Defence, and it is commanded by the Chief of Army Staff (COAS), who is a four-star general. Two officers have been conferred the rank of Field Marshal, a five-star ranked general, which is a ceremonial position of great honour.

The Indian Army originated from the armies of the East India Company, which eventually became the British Indian Army and finally the national army after independence. The units and regiments of the Indian Army have diverse histories and have participated in a number of battles and campaigns across the world, earning a large number of battle and theatre honours before and after Independence.

The Chief of Army Staff (COAS) is the head of the Indian Army and is responsible for all army activities. Officers who assist him are:

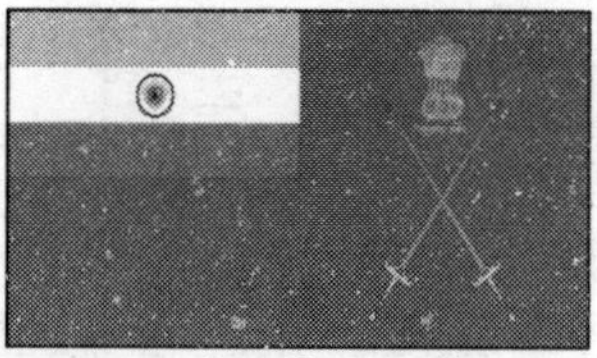

(i) Vice Chief of Army Staff
(ii) Two Deputy Chiefs of Army Staff
(iii) Principle Staff Officers (PSOs)
(iv) Heads of Arms and Services
(v) Field Army (Commands)

The primary mission of the Indian Army is to ensure national security and unity, defending the nation from external aggression, and threats, and maintaining peace and security within its borders. It conducts humanitarian rescue operations during natural calamities and other disturbances and can also be requisitioned by the government to cope with internal threats. It is a major component of national power alongside the Indian Navy and the Indian Air Force.

The army has been involved in four wars with neighbouring Pakistan and one with China. Other major operations undertaken by the army include Operation Vijay, Operation Meghdoot and Operation Cactus. Apart from conflicts, the army has conducted large peace time exercises like Operation Brasstacks and Exercise Shoorveer, and it has also been an active participant in numerous United Nations peacekeeping missions including the ones in Cyprus, Lebanon, Congo, Angola, Cambodia, Vietnam, Namibia, El Salvador, Liberia, Mozambique and Somalia.

The Indian Army has a regimental system, but is operationally and geographically divided into seven commands, with the basic field formation being a division. It is a professional force and comprises more than 80% of the country's active defence personnel. It is one of the largest standing armies in the world, with 11,85,146 active troops and 9,60,000 reserve troops. The army has embarked on an infantry modernization program known as Futuristic Infantry Soldier As a System (F-INSAS), and is also upgrading and acquiring new assets for its armoured, artillery and aviation branches.

Commissioned Ranks in Defence Services

Army	Navy	Air Force
* Field Marshal	Admiral of the Fleet	Marshal of the Air Force
* General	Admiral	Air Chief Marshal
* Lieutenant-General	Vice-Admiral	Air Marshal
* Major-General	Rear-Admiral	Air Vice-Marshal
* Brigadier	Commodore	Air Commodore
* Colonel	Captain	Group Captain
* Lieutenant-Colonel	Commander	Wing Commander
* Major	Lt. Commander	Squadron Leader
* Captain	Lieutenant	Flight Lieutenant
* Lieutenant	Sub-Lieutenant	Flying Officer

Non-Commissioned and Junior Commissioned Ranks

Army	Navy	Air Force
✱ Subedar Major	Master Chief Petty Officer I	Master Warrant Officer
✱ Subedar	Master Chief Petty Officer II	Warrant Officer
✱ Naib Subedar	Chief Petty Officer	Junior Warrant Officer
✱ Subedar	Petty Officer	Sergeant
✱ Havaldar Naik	Leading Sailor I	Corporal
✱ Lance Naik	Leading Sailor II	Leading Aircraftsman
✱ Jawan/Sepoy	Sailor	Aircraftsman/Airman

Regiments in Order of Seniority within the Indian Army are:

- Brigade of the Guards
- Mechanised Infantry Regiment
- The Madras Regiment
- Maratha Light Infantry
- Rajput Regiment
- Sikh Regiment
- Dogra Regiment
- Kumaon Regiment
- Bihar Regiment
- Jammu & Kashmir Rifles
- Naga Regiment
- 3 Gorkha Rifles
- 5 Gorkha Rifles (Frontier Force)
- 9 Gorkha Rifles
- The Ladakh Scouts
- Arunachal Scouts
- The Parachute Regiment
- Punjab Regiment
- The Grenadiers
- Rajputana Rifles
- Jat Regiment
- Sikh Light Infantry
- The Garhwal Rifles
- Assam Regiment
- Mahar Regiment
- Jammu & Kashmir Light Infantry
- 1 Gorkha Rifles (The Malaun Regiment)
- 4 Gorkha Rifles
- 8 Gorkha Rifles
- 11 Gorkha Rifles
- Rashtriya Rifles

Artillery Regiments

The Regiment of Artillery constitutes a formidable operational arm of Indian Army. Historically it takes its lineage from Moghul Emperor Babur who is popularly credited with introduction of Artillery in India, in the Battle of Panipat in 1526. However evidence of earlier use of gun by Bahmani Kings in the Battle of Adoni in 1368 and King Mohammed Shah of Gujarat in fifteenth century have been recorded.

Armoured Regiments

There are 63 armoured regiments in the Indian Army. These include the following historic regiments dating back to the nineteenth century or earlier: 1st (Skinner's)

Horse, the 2nd Lancers (Gardner's Horse), 3rd Cavalry, 4th (Hodson's) Horse, 7th Light Cavalry, 8th Light Cavalry, 9th (Deccan) Horse, 14th (Scinde) Horse, 17th (Poona) Horse, 15th Lancers, 16th Light Cavalry, 18th Cavalry, 20th Lancers, and the 21st (Central India) Horse. A substantial number of additional units designated as either "Cavalry" or "Armoured" Regiments have been raised since Independence.

Formation and Structure

The army has a strength of about a million troops and fields 34 divisions. Its headquarters is located in New Delhi and it is under the overall command of the Chief of Army Staff (COAS). Initially, the army's main objective was to defend the nation's frontiers. However, over the years, the army has also taken up the responsibility of providing internal security, especially in insurgent-hit Kashmir and the Northeast.

Below are the basic field formations of the Indian Army:

- **Corps:** A corps is an army field formation responsible for a zone within a command theatre. There are three types of corps in the Indian Army: Strike, Holding and Mixed. A command generally consists of two or more corps. A corps has Army divisions under its command. The Corps HQ is the highest field formation in the army.
- **Division:** Each Division is headed by General Officer Commanding (GOC) in the rank of Major General. It usually consists of 15,000 combat troops and 8,000 support elements. Currently, the Indian Army has 37 Divisions including; 4 RAPID's (Re-organised Army Plains Infantry Division), 18 Infantry Divisions, 10 Mountain Divisions, 3 Armoured Divisions and 2 Artillery Divisions. Each Division composes of several Brigades.
- **Brigade:** A Brigade generally consists of around 3,000 combat troops with supporting elements. An Infantry Brigade usually has 3 Infantry Battalions along with various Support Arms & Services. It is headed by a Brigadier, equivalent to a Brigadier General in some armies. In addition to the Brigades in various Army Divisions, the Indian Army also has 5 Independent Armoured Brigades, 15 Independent Artillery Brigades, 7 Independent Infantry Brigades, 1 Independent Parachute Brigade, 3 Independent Air Defence Brigades, 2 Independent Air Defence Groups and 4 Independent Engineer Brigades. These Independent Brigades operate directly under the Corps Commander (GOC Corps).
- **Battalion:** A Battalion is commanded by a Colonel and is the Infantry's main fighting unit. It consists of more than 900 combat personnel.
- **Company:** Headed by the Major or Captain, a company comprises 120 soldiers.

- **Platoon:** An intermediate between a company and section, a platoon is headed by a Captain or Lieutenant, or depending on the availability of commissioned officers, even a junior commissioned officer (Subedar). It has a total strength of about 32 troops.
- **Section:** Smallest military outfit with a strength of 10 personnel. Commanded by a non-commissioned officer of the rank of Havildar or Sergeant.

Commands

The army operates 7 operational commands. Each command is headed by General Officer Commanding-in-Chief with the rank of Lieutenant General. Each command is directly affiliated to the Army HQ in New Delhi. There is also the Army Training Command abbreviated as ARTRAC. The staff in each Command HQ is headed by Chief of Staff (COS) who is also an officer of Lieutenant General rank. Besides these, army officers may head tri-service commands such as the Strategic Forces Command, Integrated Defence Staff (IDS) and the Andaman and Nicobar Command.

Command Headquarters

Command Headquarters is commanded by an officer of the rank of Lieutenant General who is called Army Commander or GOC - in - C. The whole country is divided into Seven theatre Commands who have subordinate formations under them. These are:

Command Insignia	Command Name	Headquarters
	Headquarters Indian Army	New Delhi
	Central Command	Lucknow
	Eastern Command	Kolkata
	Northern Command	Udhampur
	Southern Command	Pune
	South Western Command	Jaipur
	Western Command	Chandimandir
	Army Training Command	Shimla

Regimental Organisation

These are the functional divisions entrusted with specific pan-Army tasks. The Indian Territorial Army has battalions affiliated to different infantry regiments and some department units which are either from the Corps of Engineers, Army Medical Corps or the Army Service Corps. They serve as a part-time reserve.

Regimental Arms

* Indian Infantry Regiments
* Armoured Corps Regiments - The Armoured Corps Centre and School is at Ahmednagar
* Regiment of Artillery - The School of Artillery is at Devlali near Nasik
* Corps of Signals - Military College of Telecommunication Engineering (MCTE), Mhow is a premiere training institute for the officers of the Corps of Signals. The corps also has two Signal Training Centres at Jabalpur and Goa
* Corps of Engineers - The College of Military Engineering is at Dapodi, Pune. The centers are located as follows - Madras Engineer Group at Bangalore, Bengal Engineer Group at Roorkee and Bombay Engineer Group at Khadki, Pune
* Corps of Army Air Defence - Center at Gopalpur in Orissa State
* Mechanised Infantry - Regimental Center at Ahmednagar
* Army Aviation Corps (India) - Their training establishment, Combat Army Aviation Training School, is based in Nasik

Military Training Centres

* Indian Infantry Regiments
* National Defence Academy, Khadakvasla
* Indian Military Academy, Dehra Dun
* Rashtriya Indian Military College, Dehra Dun
* National Defence College, New Delhi
* Defence Services Staff College, Wellington
* Armed Forces Medical College, Pune
* Officer's Training School, Chennai
* College of Combat, Mhow
* Armoured Corps Centre and School, Ahmednagar
* Infantry Schools, Mhow and Belgaum
* School of Artillery, Deolali
* College of Military Engineering, Kirkee
* Military College of Telecommunication Engineering, Mhow
* College of Defence Management, Secunderabad

* Army Cadet College, Dehra Dun
* Army Ordnance Corps School, Jabalpur
* Other Army Training Centres and Schools
* High Altitude Warfare School, Gulmarg
* Army Service Corps School, Bareilly
* EME School, Vadodara
* Military College of Electronics and Mechanical Engineering, Secunderabad
* Remount and Veterinary Corps Centre School, Meerut
* Army Education Corps Training College and Centre, Pachmarhi
* Army School of Physical Training, Pune
* Army/Air Transport Support School, Agra
* Army Clerks Training School, Aurangabad
* Military Intelligence Training School and Depot, Pune
* Army School of Mechanical Transport, Bengaluru
* Corps of Military Police Centre and School, Bengaluru
* Counter Insurgency and Jungle Warfare School, Vairengte
* Institute of National Integration, Pune
* Army Medical Corps Centre and School, Lucknow

Services

Name	Center
* Army Dental Corps	Lucknow
* Army Education Corps	Pachmarhi
* Army Medical Corps	Lucknow/Pune
* Army Ordnance Corps	Jabalpur and Secunderabad (HQ)
* Army Postal Service Corps	Kamptee near Nagpur
* Army Service Corps	Bengaluru
* Corps of Electronics & Mechanical Engineers	Secunderabad
* Corps of Military Police	Bengaluru
* Intelligence Corps	Pune
* Judge Advocate General's Department	Institute of Military Law Kamptee, Nagpur
* Military Farms Service	Military Farms School & Center, Meerut Cantt.
* Military Nursing Service	Pune and Lucknow
* Remount and Veterinary Corps	Meerut
* Pioneer Corps	Bengaluru

Task and Role of Fighting Army

Indian Army is the organisation which is mainly divided into two categories the Arms & the Services. The Artillery, Engineers, Signals, Air Defence Corps, and Aviation Corps are called Supporting Arms, as they support the Fighting Arms in the battle field.

ORGANISATION OF INFANTRY BATTALION

Infantry battalion is the basic and the most important organisation of the army. It is equipped, trained and motivated to fight a decisive battle. The importance of an infantry battalion can be judged by the fact that no military operation can start or finish without the participation of infantry.

The infantry battalion is the most important organisation of the army. It is trained and equipped to face any adverse situation. It can fight an enemy independently or as part of a larger force. It has the sustenance power and motivation to fight till the end.

A well trained and motivated Army can defeat enemy by relentless and offensive action of its Armour coupled with Mechanised Infantry, however the overrun enemy can be said to be actually defeated only when his territory is physically captured and is completely destroyed.

Defeat of the enemy implies the destruction of his fighting forces and his war waging potential. It is infantry that captures and occupies the ground.

Role of Infantry

Infantry is essential arm of close combat. Its role in attack is to close in with the enemy and destroy or capture him; in defence it is to hold ground against all forms of attacks by the enemy.

Capabilities

The capabilities of Infantry Battalion are as under:

(i) **Self Reliance:** The Infantry is equipped, trained and organized to fight with the enemy without any outside support. It can fight itself for a long time.

(ii) **Ability to Hold Ground:** The Infantry Battalion can hold ground effectively with or without outside support.

(iii) **Adaptability:** An infantry battalion is highly adaptable and can operate over any type of ground, by day or by night and under any difficult climatic conditions. The infantry battalion can be readily shifted by land, sea or air to the battle field.

(iv) **Mobility:** Infantry battalion has a high degree of mobility. It can go through almost all kinds of obstacles.

(v) **Vulnerability:** In battle, an infantry battalion becomes weak in front of tanks, artillery, small arms, air attack and antipersonnel mines. The infantry battalion overcomes this weakness by careful sighting, hiding, spreading out digging, skillful use of ground, making itself invisible by smoke, utilizing times of poor visibility and darkness and by igniting fire and causing smoke. An infantry battalion is capable of defending itself against tanks with its anti-tank weapons.

Employment and Tactics

* **Employment:** Infantry can be employed in any operation of war. However, the basic role remains the same i.e, close in with the enemy to destroy or capture them and to hold the ground.
* **Tactics:** Fire and movement is the basis of all infantry tactics. It means while one part moves the other gives fire support.
* **Infantry Weapons:** The basic infantry weapons are the rifle and bayonet, the light machine gun and grenades. In addition, certain personnel are armed with carbine and pistol.
* **Training:** The training of Infantry include skill at Arms, endurance, initiative, adaptability, and skillful use of ground.

Armour

The basic role of infantry battalion is to close in with and destroy or capture the enemy and to hold ground. Fire and movement is the basis of infantry tactics. Infantry battalion from section upwards is based on this principle. Infantry battalion and its sub-units are trained to operate in the face of the enemy opposition without entirely depending on support from other arms, by skillful use of ground, weapons, and above all the infantrymen with their sheer courage, determination and valour.

The basic personnel weapons in infantry battalion are pistols, carbines, rifles and bayonets. The fire power is greatly increased by supporting weapons. These are anti-tank guided missiles, 81mm mortars, light machine guns, medium machine guns, automatic grenade launchers, flame throwers, and sniper rifles etc.

Infantry Company Support Weapons

The comapny support weapons are 7.62 mm Dragunov Sniper Rifle, 7.62 mm Medium Machine Gun, 30 mm Medium Grenade Launcher and 84 mm Rocket Launcher. They are used both in defensive and offensive operations. They are discussed in detail in Chapter-3 : Weapon Training & Infantry Weapons.

Infantry Battalion Support Weapons

The Infantry Battalion is a balanced force which can withstand any difficult situation both in offensive, defensive, as well as in special operations against the enemy. The support weapons available with the Battalion can contain the plan of the enemy by causing maximum damage both in fortified fire positions and Armoured protected tanks/personal carriers. Infantry battalion has inherent fire power capability at long ranges in terms of battalion support weapons. The two important infantry battalion support weapons are 81mm Mortar and Anti Tank Guided Missile (ATGM). They are discussed in detail in Chapter-3.

Role of Armour

To destroy the enemy by relentless mobile and offensive action in both offensive as well as defensive operations.

Principles of Employment

* **Offensive Action:** The tasks given to Armour should be offensive in nature and concept. Armour must be employed as aggressively as possible.
* **Concentration.** Armour is concentrated to produce decisive results. For maximum shock effect it should be used in mass in depth.
* **Surprise:** Armour achieves surprise mainly by weight, violence, and direction of its attack combined with the speed with which the operation is executed. This is achieved by skilful use of ground and overcoming of obstacles.
* **Flexibility:** Sound organization, good physical mobility and excellent means of command and control allow a high degree of flexibility.
* **Cooperation:** The full potential of armour can only be developed when it is organised into combined battle groups which should include tanks, mechanised infantry, self-propelled artillery, assault engineers, attack helicopters and is provided with close air support.
* **Speed:** In mobile warfare speed is of great importance. It involves the following:
  - (a) Speed in decision.
  - (b) Speed in issue of orders.
  - (c) Speed in execution.

THE MECHANISED INFANTRY

The concept of mechanised infantry is based on the need to provide protection with added mobility, radio communications and firepower to enable the infantry to operate effectively in mobile operations with armour.

Role of the Mechanized Infantry

* **Primary Role:** The primary role of the mechanised infantry is to close with the enemy in coordination with armour and destroy or capture the enemy.
* **Secondary Role:**
  - (i) Destroy the enemy overrun by armour.
  - (ii) Hold ground temporarily.
  - (iii) Reconnaissance.
  - (iv) For counter infiltration and against parachute and heliborne landings.

Characteristics of Mechanized Infantry

* **Mobility:** It has the capability to move across the country and because of the amphibious capability (capable of operating on both land and water) help infantry to move across the water obstacle.
* **Protection:** The light armour of the armoured personnel carrier provides protection against small arms fire and shell splinters.
* **Fire Power:** Mechanized infantry is able to bring together considerable firepower due to the machine guns mounted on the armoured personnel carriers. Though mechanized infantry will normally operate with armour, they have been provided with their own organic anti-tank weapons to make them self-reliant.
* **Communication:** Radio is the primary means of communication in a mechanized infantry unit. Radio communication facilitates receiving and passing orders quickly while on the move and for close and intimate cooperation with Armour.
* **Flexibility:** Mechanized Infantry units and subunits can quickly form composite groups with Armour for a variety of missions and can be rapidly switched over from one mission to another.
* **Shock Action:** Mechanised infantry can produce shock effect much greater than an equivalent or even a larger quantity of infantry attacking on foot.

TASKS AND ROLES OF SUPPORTING ARMS AND SERVICES

Army is mainly divided into two categories the Arms & the Services. Arms can be further classified into Armoured Corps, Infantry, Artillery, Engineers, Signals, Air Defence Corps and Aviation Corps. The Armoured Corps and Infantry are called Fighting Arms. The Artillery, Engineers, Signals, Air Defence Corps, and Aviation Corps are called Supporting Arms, as they support the Fighting Arms in the battle field. Army Service Corps (ASC), Army Ordnance Corps (AOC), Corps of Electrical and Mechanical Engineers (EME) and Army Medical Corps (AMC) are called Services as they provide logistical support to Fighting Arms.

Supporting Arms

Supporting Arms are those arms who give support to Fighting Arms from behind to enable them to accomplish the assigned task effectively. Armour, Infantry and Mechanised Infantry are known as "Fighting Arms". The supporting arms which help the Fighting Arms to accomplish the task are:

* **Artillery:** The role of Artillery is to provide such fire power in the battle area that enemy neither interferes with our operations, nor develops his own effectively. It comprises of light, medium and field guns, howitzers, mortars, multi barrel rocket launchers and missiles.

Tasks: The tasks of Artillery are as follows:

(i) To provide heavy volume of fire at long ranges

(ii) To provide fire power to advancing Infantry in offensive operations and defensive support to keep enemy head down with shocking firepower.

(iii) To provide fire power to fighting arms.

* **Corps of Army Air Defence:** Army Air Defence is equipped with air defence guns and Short and Medium range surface to air missile systems. Along with Air Force it provides air defence to mobile forces, Vulnerable Areas and Vulnerable Points.

Tasks: The tasks of Air Defence are:

(i) To safeguard against hostile aircrafts, helicopters and drones attacking high values targets including Fighting Arms.

(ii) To ensure early detection and destruction of enemy aircrafts.

* **Army Aviation Corps:** The role of Army Aviation corps is to carry out recce and observation and also to provide commanders and staff, rapid means of communication for liaison visits and reconnaissance. It is ideally suited for evacuation of battle casualties.

* **Corps of Engineers:** It is one of the oldest supporting arms of the Indian army. The role of Engineers in War is to provide support for offensive and defensive operations in mine warfare, bridging, demolition, constructions of field fortifications and operational roads/tracks.

Tasks: The task of Engineers are as follows:

(i) To provide mobility to own forces by constructing bridges, tracks and helipads; on the other hand the Corps denies the same to the enemy by creating obstacles such as laying mine-fields and demolition of bridges.

(ii) To lay mine fields during War and also removing the mines and maintenance of records thereof.

(iii) To create water sources during operations.

(iv) To help in transportation of explosives and undertake bomb disposal activities during peace and war.

* **Corps of Signals:** They are the communicators of Indian Army and provide Radio, Radio Relay, Data and Line communication and establish Signal Centres during war and peace. It also monitors enemy's communication systems.

* **Intelligence Corps:** The main task of Intelligence Corps is to gather intelligence of the enemy and prevent the leakage of own information to the enemy.

Supporting Services

The following Arms are called Services as they provide logistical support to fighting Arms:

* **Corps of Electrical and Mechanical Engineering (EME):** The major role of EME is repair, recovery and maintenance of all vehicles, arms, electrical, electronic and mechanical equipment.
* **Army Service Corps (ASC):** ASC is responsible for:
  (i) The supply and provision of ration to the Army during peace and war.
  (ii) To provide fuel oil and lubricants to the entire Army.
  (iii) To provide transport for conveyance of troops during movement.
  (iv) Transportation of heavy equipment and machineries including ammunition during war.
* **Army Medical Corps:** It provides medical facilities during war as well as in peace stations to troops and their families.
* **Army Dental Corps:** The Corps provides dental hygiene and treatment to the soldiers.
* **Military Nursing Service:** They provide nursing and care to the sick and wounded army personnel.
* **Army Ordinance Crops:** It is responsible to provide equipment support to the Army during war & peace which are not the responsibility of ASC, AMC and that of engineers.
* **Remount and Veterinary Corps:** It deals with caring and training of animals.
* **Military Farms:** They provide the Indian Army with dairy products and fodder for the animals maintained by the Army.
* **Army Education Corps (AEC):** AEC is responsible for imparting Military & Civil education to troops which helps them in passing promotion exams required in their career and profession. They impart high education to JCOs and NCOs.
* **Corps of Military Police:** Its role is to provide security to Army personnel and their families and maintain law and order in the Army area. It also helps in movement of men, material and vehicles during peace or war.
* **Judge Advocate General Branch:** Deals with legal matters relating to all branches of the Armed Forces.
* **Military Engineering Services:** They are responsible for the design, construction and maintenance of all works, buildings, airfields, dock installations and also with accessory services for the Army.
* **Border Roads Organisation:** Their main purpose is to create national highways, airfields, buildings and bridges.

* **Army Pioneer Corps:** Civilian labour is either not available or it is not required for security reasons. The Pioneer Corps provides disciplined and well trained manpower for load carriage. They are mostly committed in operational areas during war.

INDIAN NAVY

The Indian Navy is the naval branch of the armed forces of India. The President of India serves as the Commander-in-Chief of the Navy. The Chief of Naval Staff (CNS), usually a four-star officer in the rank of admiral, commands the navy. The Indian Navy can trace its lineage back to the 17th-century East India Company's Marine; it succeeded the Royal Indian Navy, which was renamed in 1950. The 17th-century Maratha emperor Chhatrapati Shivaji Bhosle is considered as the 'Father of the Indian Navy'.

Though the primary objective of the navy is to secure the nation's maritime borders, India also uses its navy to enhance its international relations through joint exercises, port visits and humanitarian missions, including disaster relief. In recent years, the Indian Navy has undergone rapid modernisation to replace its ageing equipment currently in service, this is often seen as part of "India's drive" to develop blue-water capabilities and enhance its position in the Indian Ocean region.

As of March 2018, the operational fleet consists of one aircraft carrier, one amphibious transport dock, eight landing ship tanks, eleven destroyers, fourteen frigates, one nuclear-powered attack submarine, one ballistic missile submarine, fifteen conventionally-powered attack submarines, twenty-two corvettes, one mine countermeasure vessel, four fleet tankers and various other auxiliary vessels.

As of June 2019, Indian Navy has 67,252 personnel in service and has a fleet of 137 warships and 235 aircraft.

Command and Organisation

The Indian Navy operates three Commands. Each Command is headed by a Flag Officer Commanding-in-Chief of the rank of Vice Admiral. The Eastern and Western Commands each have a Fleet commanded by a rear admiral, and each also have a Commodore Commanding Submarines. The Southern Naval Command is home to the Flag Officer, Sea Training.

Organisation and Administration

Chief of Naval Staff commands Indian Navy. Integrated Headquarters of the Ministry of Defence (Navy) is located in New Delhi. The Navy is divided into three commands:

Commands	Headquarters
Western Naval Command	Mumbai
Eastern Naval Command	Vishakhapatnam
Southern Naval Command	Kochi

The Andaman and Nicobar Command, a Unified Indian Navy, Indian Army, Indian Air Force and Coast Guard Command was set up in the Andaman and Nicobar Islands in 2001. It is headquartered at Port Blair, and is a Unified Tri-services Command under the Commander in Chief Andaman and Nicobar (CINCAN) who reports to the Chairman Chiefs of Staff Committee (COSC) and is provided staff support by the Chief of Integrated Staff to the Chiefs of Staff Committee (CISC) in New Delhi.

Current Role

Currently the principal roles of Indian Navy are:

- In conjunction with other Armed Forces of the union, act to deter or defeat any threats or aggression against the territory, people or maritime interests of India, both in war and peace;
- Project influence in India's maritime area of interest, to further the nation's political, economic and security objectives;
- In co-operation with the Indian Coast Guard, ensure good order and stability in India's maritime zones of responsibility.
- Provide maritime assistance (including disaster relief) in India's maritime neighbourhood.

Naval Training Centres

The Principal training units or establishments for the general service officers and men of the Navy are located at Kochi. These units impart training in gunnery, navigation, anti-submarine warfare, communications, aviation, etc. Other major training establishments are:

- Naval Academy, Goa - basic training for Naval cadets and Direct Entry Officers of all branches.
- INS Chilka, Orissa - basic training for sailors and artificers.
- INS Shivaji, Lonavala - basic engineering training of technical officers, specialised training for all engineering branch offices, sailors and artificers.
- INS Valsure, Jamnagar - specialised training for electrical branch offices and sailors.
- INS Satavahana, Vishakhapatnam - submarine training for all officers and sailors of submarine cadre.
- INS Hamla, Marve, Malad, Mumbai - training of officers and sailors of S and S Branch.
- INS Kunjali, Mumbai - regulating branch training.

* INS Asvini (INM), Mumbai - medical assistance training.
* INS Agrani, Coimbatore - management and leadership training for senior sailors.

INDIAN AIR FORCE

The Indian Air Force is the air arm of the Indian armed forces. Its primary responsibility is to secure Indian airspace and to conduct aerial warfare during a conflict. It was officially established on 8 October 1932 as an auxiliary air force of the British Empire and the prefix Royal was added in 1945 in recognition of its services during World War II. After India achieved independence from the United Kingdom in 1947, the Royal Indian Air Force served the Dominion of India, with the prefix being dropped when India became a republic in 1950.

Since independence, the IAF has been involved in four wars with neighbouring Pakistan and one with the People's Republic of China. Other major operations undertaken by the IAF include Operation Vijay—the annexation of Goa, Operation Meghdoot, Operation Cactus and Operation Poomalai. Apart from conflicts, the IAF has been an active participant in United Nations peacekeeping missions.

Structure

The President of India is the Supreme Commander of all Indian armed forces and by virtue of that fact is the notional Commander-in-chief of the Air Force. Chief of the Air Staff with the rank of Air Chief Marshal is the Commander of the Indian Air Force. He is assisted by six officers, all with the rank of Air Marshal, namely:

* Vice Chief of the Air Staff
* Deputy Chief of the Air Staff
* Air Officer in Charge of Administration
* Air Officer in Charge of Personnel
* Air Officer in Charge of Maintenance
* Director General of Inspection and Safety.

Air Headquarters

Indian Air Force is commanded by Chief of the Air Staff. The staff of Air Headquarters consists of three branches:

(i) Air Staff Branch (ii) Administrative Branch (iii) Maintenance Branch

Commands

The Indian Air Force is divided into five operational and two functional commands. Each Command is headed by an Air Officer Commanding-in-Chief with the rank of Air Marshal. The purpose of an operational command is to conduct military operations using aircraft within its area of responsibility, whereas the responsibility of functional commands is to maintain combat readiness.

Aside from the Training Command at Bangalore, the centre for primary flight training is located at the Air Force Academy in Hyderabad, Andhra Pradesh, followed by operational training at various other schools. Advanced officer training for command positions is also conducted at the Defence Services Staff College; specialised advanced flight training schools are located at Bidar, Karnataka, and Hakimpet, Andhra Pradesh (also the location for helicopter training). Technical schools are located at a number of other locations.

Operational Commands

- Central Air Command (CAC), headquartered at Allahabad, Uttar Pradesh
- Eastern Air Command (EAC), headquartered at Shillong, Meghalaya
- Southern Air Command (SAC), headquartered at Thiruvananthapuram, Kerala
- South Western Air Command (SWAC), headquartered at Gandhinagar, Gujarat
- Western Air Command (WAC), headquartered at Subroto Park, New Delhi

Functional Commands

- Training Command (TC), headquartered at Bangalore, Karnataka
- Maintenance Command (MC), headquartered at Nagpur, Maharashtra

Wings

A Wing is a formation intermediate between a Command and a Squadron. It generally consists of two or three IAF Squadrons and Helicopter Units, along with Forward Base Support Units (FBSU). FBSUs do not have or host any Squadrons or Helicopter units but act as transit airbases for routine operations. In times of war, they can become full-fledged air bases playing host to various Squadrons. In all, about 47 Wings and 19 FBSUs make up the IAF. Wings are typically commanded by a Group Captain.

Squadrons

Squadrons are the field units and formations attached to static locations. Thus, a Flying Squadron is a sub-unit of an air force station which carries out the primary task of the IAF. All fighter squadrons are headed by a Commanding Officer with the rank of Wing Commander. Some Transport squadrons and Helicopter Units are headed by a Commanding Officer with the rank of Group Captain.

Flights

Flights are sub-divisions of Squadrons, commanded by a Squadron Leader.

Within this formation structure, IAF has several service branches for day-to-day operations. They are:

Flying Branch	Technical Branch	Ground Branch
* Flying * Administration * Medical & Dental	* Engineering * Accounts * Meteorological	* Logistics * Education

Personnel

The rank structure of the Indian Air Force is based on that of the Royal Air Force. The highest rank attainable in the IAF is Marshal of the Indian Air Force, conferred by the President of India after exceptional service during wartime. MIAF Arjan Singh is the only officer to have achieved this rank. The head of the Indian Air Force is the Chief of the Air Staff, who holds the rank of Air Chief Marshal.

Airmen (Agniveer Vayu)

The duty of an airman (Agniveer Vayu) in the Indian Air Force is to make sure that all the air and ground operations run smoothly. From operating Air Defence systems to fitting missiles, they are involved in all activities of an air base and give support to various technical and non-technical jobs.

Honorary Officers

Sachin Tendulkar is the first sportsperson and the first civilian without aviation background to be awarded the honorary rank of Group Captain by the Indian Air Force.

Air Force Training Centres

* Air Force Administrative College, Coimbatore
* Air Force Academy, Hyderabad
* Air Force Technical College, Jalahalli
* Air Force School, Sambra, Belgaum
* Flying Instructors School, Tambaram
* Air Force Station, Bidar
* Air Force Station, Hakimpet
* Air Force Station, Yelahanka
* Helicopter Training School, Avadi
* Ground Training School, Avadi
* Ground Training Institute, Vadodara and Barrackpore
* Institute of Aviation Medicine, Bangaluru
* Paratroops Training School, Agra
* Navigation and Signals School, Hyderabad
* College of Air Warfare, Secunderabad

MILITARY HISTORY & WAR HEROES

Military History

Military History is a very important and inspiring subject. By studying the military history of a war, we learn many details about the causes, political decisions, strategies, tatics, weapons and results of wars. What we observe from them is, what led to the war and what brought the ultimate victory or defeat. We learn about the strengths & weaknesses of the forces at war. This study and experience of past wars enlightens us to overcome our weaknesses and prepare better to defend ourselves in future. Let us now learn about two great Generals and some Indian Army war heroes.

WAR HEROES

Field Marshal Kodandera Madappa Cariappa, OBE

Kodandera Madappa Cariappa was born on 28 January 1899 at Shanivarsanthe in erstwhile Coorg, Karnataka. He had his formal education in the Central High School at Madikeri and pursued college education at Presidency College, Madras.

Cariappa grew up equally attached to books and plays under the guidance of renowned academicians. He was an active sportsman and played with vigour and brilliance, games like hockey and tennis.

He joined the first batch of KCIOs (King's Commissioned Indian Officers) in 1919 at Daly Cadet College at Indore and was commissioned as a temporary Second Lieutenant. He received a permanent commission in 1922 and was promoted as Lieutenant in 1923, and as Captain in 1927. He saw active service with the 37 (Prince of Wales) Dogra in Mesopotamia (present-day Iraq) and was later posted to the 2nd Rajput Light Infantry (Queen Victoria's Own) which became his permanent regimental home. He was the first Indian officer to undergo the course at Staff College, Quetta in 1933. He was promoted as Major in 1938.

Cariappa served in Iraq, Syria and Iran from 1941-1942 and then in Burma in 1943-1944. He spent many of his soldiering years in Waziristan. He earned his 'Mentioned-in-Despatches' as DAA and QMG of General (later Field Marshal) Slim's 10th Division. He was the first Indian Officer to be given command of a unit in 1942. After command, he volunteered to serve in 26 Division engaged in clearing the Japanese from Burma, where he was awarded the Order of the British Empire (OBE).

In 1946, he was promoted as the Brigadier of the Frontier Brigade Group. It was during this time that Colonel Ayub Khan - later Field Marshal and President of Pakistan, 1962-1969 - served under him.

Cariappa was the first Indian who was selected to undergo a training course in 1947 at Imperial Defence College, Camberly, UK on the higher directions of war. During the traumatic period of partition, he handled the division of the Indian Army and sharing of its assets between Pakistan and India, in a most amicable, just and orderly manner. He was then the Indian officer in-charge to oversee the transition process.

In independent India, Cariappa was appointed as the Deputy Chief of General Staff with the rank of Major General. On promotion to Lieutenant General he became the Eastern Army Commander. On outbreak of war with Pakistan in 1947, he was moved as General Officer Commanding-in-Chief, Western Command and directed operations for the recapture of Zojila, Drass and Kargil and re-established a linkup with Leh. In all this, he showed tremendous energy in moving troops against heavy odds and finally ensuring success for India.

When he was appointed as the first Commander-in-Chief of an independent Indian Army on 15 January 1949, he was instrumental in—Integration of troops and turning an imperial army into a national army; Raised the Brigade of the Guards and the Parachute Regiments on an all-India caste composition; and Raised the National Cadet Corps (NCC) and Territorial Army (TA) using troops from the Regular Army.

Carippa's career in the Army during which he had the rare distinction of being first in many spheres is a continuous tale of upward progress; he was the :

- First Indian to be commissioned at the age of 19.
- First Indian cadet to be commissioned from Daly Cadet College, Indore.
- First Indian Brigadier.
- First Indian to enter Imperial Defence College in England.
- First Indian Officer to enter Staff College, Quetta.
- First Indian Major General in 1947.
- First Indian Chief of Staff.

His association with the Indian Army is spread over an unbroken period of more than 29 years, during which he had wide experience of staff and command work. After his retirement from Indian Army in 1953, he served as the High Commissioner to Australia and New Zealand till 1956.

After his retirement from public service, Cariappa lived a life of simplicity and dignity, which was the hallmark of a man. He spent a lot of his leisure time educating people about cleanliness, pollution control and other essential issues. During the 1962, 1965 and 1971 wars, he visited the front lines to talk to the troops and keep their morale up.

Cariappa took active part in the reorganisation of armed forces in many foreign countries. He was a much traveled man and visited parts of China, Japan,

United States, Great Britain, Canada and most of the European countries. He was conferred with 'Order of the Chief Commander of the Legion of Merit' by US President, Harry S. Truman. As a token of gratitude of the nation for the exemplary service rendered by him, the Government of India conferred the rank of Field Marshal on Cariappa in 1983.

Field Marshal K.M. Cariappa breathed his last at Bangalore at a ripe age of 94, on 15 May 1993.

Field Marshal Sam Hormusji Framji Jamshedji Manekshaw

Popularly known as "Sam Bahadur", Sam Hormusji Framji Jamshedji Manekshaw was born in Amritsar, Punjab on 03 April 1914, he completed his education in Amritsar and Sherwood College, Nainital. He then joined the first batch of 40 cadets at Indian Military Academy (IMA), Dehra Dun on 01 October 1932. He passed out of the IMA in December 1934 and was commissioned as a Second Lieutenant in the Indian Army.

He held several regimental assignments and was first attached to the Royal Scouts and later to the 12 Frontier Force Rifles. During World War II, he saw action in the Burma campaign on Sittang river and has the rare distinction of being honoured for his bravery on the battle front itself.

During World War II, he was leading a counter-offensive against the invading Japanese Army in Burma. As he charged forward with his men, a Japanese soldier suddenly emerged from the bushes and fired at him, wounding him seriously in the stomach. Fortunately, Major General D.T. Cowan spotted Manekshaw holding on to life and was aware of his valour in face of stiff resistance from the Japanese. Fearing the worst, Major General Cowan quickly pinned his own Military Cross ribbon on to Manekshaw saying, "A dead person cannot be awarded a Military Cross."

When he recovered from those near-fatal wounds in Burma, he went for a course at Staff College, Quetta and later also served there as an instructor before being sent to join 12 Frontier Force Rifles in Burma under General (later Field Marshal) Slim's 14th Army. He was once again involved in a fierce battle with the Japanese, and was wounded for a second time.

Towards the close of World War II, Manekshaw was sent as Staff Officer to General Daisy in Indo-China where, after the Japanese surrender, he helped rehabilitate over 10,000 POWs. He, then, went on a six-month lecture tour to Australia in 1946, and after his return served as a First Grade Staff Officer in the Military Operations Directorate at Army HQ in New Delhi.

Sam Manekshaw showed great acumen for planning and administration while handling the issues related to partition in 1947, and later put to use his battle skills during the 1947-48 Jammu & Kashmir Operations. After command of an Infantry Brigade, he was posted as the Commandant of the Infantry School and also became the Colonel of 8 Gorkha Rifles (his regimental home) and 61 Cavalry. He commanded a Division in Jammu & Kashmir and a Corps in the North East, with a tenure as Commandant of Defence Services Staff College (DSSC) in between.

As GOC-in-C Eastern Command, he handled the tricky problem of insurgency in Nagaland, and the grateful nation in 1968 honoured him with a Padma Bhushan —India's third highest civilian honour.

Gen. AAK Niazi Signing the Instrument of Surrender

Sam Manekshaw succeeded General Kumaramangalam as Chief of Army Staff (COAS) on 07 June 1969. His years of military experience were soon put to the test as thousands of refugees from the erstwhile East Pakistan started crossing over to India as a result of oppression unleashed from West Pakistan. The volatile situation got worse, and soon erupted into a full-scale war in December 1971. During the military campaign, Manekshaw showed uncommon ability to motivate the forces, coupling it with a mature war strategy. The war ended with Pakistan's unconditional surrender, and the formation of Bangladesh.

Sam Manekshaw's achievements as COAS are :

- He prepared the Army for a well-planned and a well executed operation against Pakistan in 1971, leading to the creation of Bangladesh.
- As Chairman of Chiefs of Staff Committee, he welded the Army, Navy and Air Force into a well-knit team.
- Taking of over 90,000 Pakistan POWs, thereby paving the way for favourable negotiations.

For his selfless service to the nation, he was awarded the Padma Vibhushan in 1972 and was conferred with the honorary rank of Field Marshal on 01 January 1973. He retired a fortnight later, on 15 January 1973, after completing nearly four decades of glorious military service.

Sam Manekshaw died at Wellington, Tamil Nadu on 27 June 2008 at the age of 94.

Major Som Nath Sharma, PVC

Major Som Nath Sharma was the first recipient of the Param Vir Chakra, the highest Indian gallantry award. He belonged to the 4th Kumaon Regiment. He was awarded the medal posthumously for his bravery in the Kashmir operations in November 1947. He martyred while evicting Pakistani infiltrators and raiders from Srinagar Airport during the Indo-Pak war of 1947-48 in Kashmir.

Som Nath was born on 31 January 1923 in a Brahmin family at Dadh, in Kangra Himachal Pradesh. He came from a well-known military family, his father, Major General Amar Nath Sharma, was also a military officer (retired as Director, Medical Services (Army)) as were his brothers Lt. General Surindar Nath Sharma (retired as Engineer-in-chief) and General Vishwa Nath Sharma (retired as Chief of Army Staff, 1988-1990), and his sister Major (Doctor) Kamla Tewari.

After completing his education and selection in army, he was commissioned into the 8th Battalion, 19th Hyderabad Regiment (later 4th Battalion, Kumaon Regiment) of the Indian Army (then British Indian Army) on 22 February 1942. He also saw combat during the second World War in the Arakan Operations.

Som Nath Sharma's 'D' company of 4 Kumaon was airlifted to Srinagar on 31 October 1947. On 3 November 1947, his company was ordered on a fighting patrol to Badgam Village in the Kashmir Valley. A tribal "lashkar" of 700 Pak-raiders approached Badgam from the direction of Gulmarg. The company was soon surrounded by the enemy from three sides and sustained heavy casualties from the ensuing mortar bombardment. Sharma realized the importance of holding onto his position as both the city of Srinagar and the airport would be vulnerable if it were lost. Under heavy fire and outnumbered seven to one, he urged his company to fight bravely, often exposing himself to danger as he ran from post to post.

When heavy casualties adversely affected the firing power of his company, Major Sharma, with his right hand in plaster, took upon himself the task of filling the magazines and issuing them to men operating light machine guns. While he was busy fighting the enemy, a mortar shell exploded on the ammunition kept near him injuring him grievously.

His last message to Brigade HQ received a few moments before he martyred was: "The enemies are only 50 yards from us. We are heavily outnumbered. We are under devastating fire. I shall not withdraw an inch but will fight to our last man and our last round."

In this manner, Major Sharma prevented the fall of Srinagar and arguably the Kashmir Valley to Pakistan by sacrifying his life with great bravery.

2nd Lieutenant Arun Khetrapal, PVC

Second Lieutenant Arun Khetrapal was born on 14 October 1950 in Pune, Maharashtra. He martyred in the Battle of Basantar during the 1971 Indo-pak war, where his actions earned him much-deserved Param Vir Chakra.

Arun Khetrapal's father Brigadier ML Khetrapal was serving in the Indian Army and his family traced a long history of military service. Khetrapal joined the National Defence Academy in 1967. In June 1971, Khetrapal was commissioned from IMA Dehradun in the 17 Poona Horse.

During the war, 17 Poona Horse was assigned to the command of the 47th Infantry Brigade of the Indian Army. Among the tasks set for the 47th Brigade was to establish a bridgehead across the River Basantar. By 15 December, the brigade had captured its objectives. However, the place was extensively mined. With some help from Engineers, 17 Poona Horse decided to push through the mine-field. The regiment was able to establish a link-up between the armour and the infantry at the bridge-head by first light the next day.

On December 16, Pakistani 13 Lancers equipped with the then state of the art US made 50 ton Patton tanks launched the first of their counter-attacks under the cover of a smokescreen at 'B' squadron of the Poona Horse at Jarpal. Its squadron commander urgently called for reinforcements.

Arun Khetrapal, who was in 'A' squadron and was stationed close by with his Centurion tank troop, responded with alacrity as did the rest of his regiment. The first counter attack was decimated by accurate gunnery, coolness by our tank troop and individual tank commanders from the iconic CO, Lt Col (later Lt Gen) Hanut Singh, MVC downwards to its dashing troop leader, Arun Khetrapal.

Khetrapal leading his troop was able to thwart the enemy advance with his tanks and even captured some of the enemy infantry and weapon crews at gunpoint. However, Pakistani forces regrouped and counter-attacked. In the ensuing tank battle, ten enemy tanks were hit and destroyed, of which Khetrapal accounted for four.

The skirmish however took its toll on Lt. Arun as he was hit by enemy fire. His final words over the radio to a superior officer who had ordered him to abandon his burning tank were, "No Sir, I will not abandon my tank. My gun is still working and I will get these bastards." But soon his tank received a second hit and he was mortally injured. The officer met his death denying the Pakistani Army the intended breakthrough, setting an example of supreme sacrifice.

Major Shaitan Singh, PVC

Major Shaitan Singh was born on December 1, 1924 at Jodhpur in Rajasthan. He was the son of Lt. Col Hem Singh Bhati.

Major Shaitan Singh was commanding a company of an infantry battalion deployed at Rezang La in the Chushul sector at a height of about 17,000 feet. The locality was isolated from the main defended sector and consisted of five platoon-defended positions. On 18 November 1962, the Chinese forces subjected the company position to heavy artillery, mortar and small arms fire and attacked it in overwhelming strength in several successive waves. Against heavy odds, our troops beat back successive waves of enemy attack.

During the action, Major Shaitan Singh dominated the scene of operations and moved at great personal risk from one platoon post to another, sustaining the morale of his hard-pressed platoon posts. While doing so he was seriously wounded but continued to encourage and lead his men who, following his brave example, fought gallantly and inflicted heavy casualties on the enemy. For every man lost to us, the enemy lost four or five.

When Major Shaitan Singh fell disabled by wounds in his arms and abdomen, his men tried to evacuate him but they came under heavy machine-gun fire. He then ordered his men to leave him to his fate in order to save their lives.

They placed him behind a boulder on the slopes of a hill, as ordered by him. The Chinese announced a unilateral ceasefire on November 21, 1962. In this action, 109 Kumaonis out of a total of 123 were killed. Of the 14 survivors, 9 were severely injured. The Chinese suffered more than a thousand casualties.

After the war was over, the body of Major Shaitan Singh was found at the same place, dead from the bullet wounds and the freezing cold. It was flown to Jodhpur and cremated with full military honours. Major Shaitan Singh was awarded Param Vir Chakra, the highest wartime gallantry medal, posthumously, for his leadership and devotion to duty.

CHM Piru Singh, PVC

Company Havildar Major Piru Singh Shekhawat was an Indian Army soldier, who was awarded the Param Vir Chakra (PVC), India's highest military decoration.

Piru Singh was born on 20 May 1918, in village Beri, Jhunjhunu, Rajasthan. He was the son of Lal Singh. His family consisted of seven children–three brothers and four sisters–with Singh being the youngest son. As a young boy, Singh always hated school, as he was unable to cope with the restricted environment.

One day, after being scolded by his class teacher for quarreling with one of his classmates, Singh ran away, and never returned to school. After that, Singh continued to help his parents in their farm, and grew up to be well-built and handsome youth. Shikar, a local Indian sport, was his favourite game. Though Singh wanted to join the army from his childhood, he was rejected twice, as he was too young, before he was accepted at the age of eighteen.

Singh enrolled in the British Indian Army on 20 May 1936, and was assigned to the 1st Punjab Regiment. Between 1940 and 1945, he served on the North-West Frontier and as an instructor, before deploying to Japan as part of the British Commonwealth Occupation Force. After independence, he took part in the Indo-Pakistani War of 1947, serving with the Indian Army's 6th Rajputana Rifles. During the battle, Singh was part of the leading section of a company that was assigned to capture a Pakistani post at Tithwal, in Jammu and Kashmir.

Following tensions between the newly independent nations of India and Pakistan, war broke out over control of the princely state of Jammu and Kashmir in October 1947, shortly after Singh returned from Japan. In July 1948, Pakistan launched offensive strikes in the Tithwal sector of Jammu and Kashmir, and captured a ring contour on 8 July. This forced the Indian troops stationed in the forward positions across river Kishanganga to retreat. In an attempt to reverse the situation, Singh's unit, the 6th Battalion of the Rajputana Rifles, was moved from Uri to Tithwal, and was assigned to the 163rd Brigade. The troops took position on the Tithwal bridge.

On 11 July, the Indian troops commenced their attack. These strikes continued for another four days. But reports regarding the situation suggested that the Pakistanis were still in command of a strategically important position and the Indian commanders decided that these had to be captured before the advance could continue. Apart from this position, another position was also to be captured by the Indians. The task of capturing these two positions was assigned to the 6th Rajputana Rifles. Two companies were assigned to the operation, with the battalion's 'C' Company securing the second position after the first was captured by 'D' Company.

On 18 July, the 'D' Company launched it first attack at 01:30 hours. The path to the position held by the Pakistani troops was just 1 metre (3 ft 3 in) wide, and deep ravines lay on either side. This narrow path was overlooked by hidden Pakistani bunkers that allowed both observation and clear fields of fire for the defending troops. As they advanced, the Indian company was subjected to heavy shelling from the Pakistanis, and within half an hour the company had recorded fifty-one casualties.

During the battle, Singh's section, leading the company, was sheared down to half strength due to heavy casualties. Singh rushed towards a Pakistani medium machine gun post, which was causing most of the casualties, during which he suffered multiple shrapnel wounds over his body as the Pakistani defenders began rolling grenades down from the heights. Undeterred, Singh continued to advance adopting the battle cry, "Raja Ramchandra Ki Jai". Soon he occupied the post killing the men on guard with his bayonet and sten gun.

But by the time he captured the position, the rest of his company lay dead or wounded. Singh was left alone to achieve the objective assigned. He advanced towards the second Pakistani medium machine gun post. At this juncture, he was almost blinded by a grenade that blast at his face. His sten gun ammunition had run out. Singh moved out of the trench and lobbed grenades at the next Pakistani post. Then, he jumped into another trench, and killed two Pakistani soldiers with his bayonet. Hardly was he able to move out of the trench, when he was hit by a bullet in his head. Before he succumbed to his wounds, Singh hurled a grenade into a nearby Pakistani trench, destroying that.

In July 1948, Company Havildar Major Piru Singh was posthumously awarded India's highest military decoration, the Param Vir Chakra.

Captain Vikram Batra, PVC

Captain Vikram Batra, was an officer of the Indian Army, posthumously awarded with the Param Vir Chakra, India's highest and prestigious award for valour, for his actions during the 1999 Kargil War in Kashmir between India and Pakistan. He led one of the toughest operations in mountain warfare in Indian history. He was often called as "Sher Shah" in the intercepted messages of the Pakistan army.

Vikram Batra was born on 9 September 1974 in Ghuggar village near Palampur, Himachal Pradesh, to GL Batra and Jai Kamal Batra. He got his primary education from his mother, who herself was a teacher. He received his education up to Middle Standard at the DAV Public School in Palampur and up to senior secondary stage in Central School, Palampur. After passing his 10+2 in 1992 from Central School Palampur, he got admitted in DAV College, Chandigarh in B.Sc where he was adjudged the best NCC Cadet (Air Wing) in two zones.

Later, he was selected to join the Indian Military Academy in Dehradun in 1996 in Kesspre company of Manekshaw battalion, and was commissioned in the Indian Army as a Lieutenant of the 13 Jammu & Kashmir Rifles at Sopore, in Jammu and Kashmir. He soon rose to the rank of Captain.

During the Kargil invasion of 1999 by Pakistan, Lt. Batra (at the time), 13 J&K Rifles, and his Delta Company were ordered to recapture peak 5140 on June 19, 1999 five weeks after the war began. Nicknamed Sher Shah (Lion King) for his courage which also doubled as his call sign, he decided to approach the hill from the rear, aiming to surprise the Pakistani defenders. He and his men ascended the sheer rock-cliff, but as the group neared the top, the enemy pinned them on the face of the bare cliff with machine gun fire.

Captain Batra, along with five of his men, climbed up regardless and after reaching the top, hurled two grenades at the machine gun post. He single-handedly killed three enemy soldiers in close combat. He was seriously injured in the process, but insisted on regrouping his men to continue with the mission. Inspired by the courage displayed by Captain Batra, the soldiers of 13 J&K Rifles charged the enemy position and captured Point 5140 at 3:30 a.m. on 20 June 1999. His company is credited with killing at least eight Pakistani intruders and recovering a heavy machine gun.

The capture of Point 5140 set in motion a string of successes, such as Point 5100, Point 4700, Junction Peak and Three Pimples. Along with fellow Captain Anuj Nayyar, Batra led his men to victory with the recapture of Point 4750 and Point 4875. This led to the fall of Tiger Hill and India's eventual hold on the valley was strengthened.

Nine days later, Vikram Batra was assigned to an urgent mission to recapture peak 4875. This was one of the most difficult peaks to capture as the Pakistani troops sat above the peak at 16,000 feet and the climb gradient was 80 degrees. The fog made matters worse for Batra and his team.

In the early morning hours of 7 July 1999, he commanded a mission to rescue an injured officer during a Pakistani counterattack against Point 4875. During the rescue attempt, he pushed aside his Subedar, saying "Tu baal-bacche dar hai, hat ja peeche."(You have children, step aside) and was killed in action while clearing enemy positions. His last words were, "Jai Mata Di."

Captain Anuj Nayyar
17th Battalion,
Jat Regiment
(MVC)

Captain Manoj Kumar Pandey
1st Battalion,
11th Gorkha Rifles
(PVC)

Grndr. Yogendra Singh Yadav
18th Battalion,
The Grenadiers
(PVC)

Rifleman Sanjay Kumar
13th Battalion,
J&K Rifles
(PVC)

IMPORTANT BATTLES & WARS

B.C.

* **Battle of Hydaspes (Jhelum)–326 :** Alexander's invasion of India, Porus was defeated.
* **War against Seleucas–305 :** Seleucas Nikator invaded India but was defeated by Chandragupta Maurya. Seleucas had to cede four states–Berat, Kandhar, Kabul and Baluchistan to Chandragupta.
* **Battle of Kalinga–261 :** Ashoka defeated the King of Kalinga after a bloody battle. The terrible loss of human lives caused by this war moved the conqueror so much that he renounced all wars in future.

A.D.

* **Battle of Thaneswar–1014 :** Mahmud of Ghazni defeated Anangpal, the ruler of Thaneswar. Mahmud destroyed many temples and took away hundreds of slaves.
* **First Battle of Tarain–1191 :** Prithvi Raj Chauhan, the Rajput ruler of Delhi and Ajmer, defeated Mohammed Ghori, the Sultan of Ghor.
* **Second Battle of Tarain–1192 :** Mohammed Ghori, the Sultan of Ghor, defeated Prithvi Raj Chauhan, the Rajput ruler of Ajmer and Delhi. It was a big blow to the Rajput power.
* **First Battle of Panipat–1526 :** Babur defeated Ibrahim Lodi and founded Mughal Empire in India.
* **Battle of Khanwah–1527 :** Babur defeated Rana Sanga, the Rajput Raja and consolidated his rule in north India.
* **Battle of Chausa–1539 :** Sher Khan, who later became Sher Shah Suri, defeated Humayun, the Mughal Emperor of Delhi. Humayun defeated the successor of Sher Shah and regained his lost kingdom in 1552.
* **Second Battle of Panipat–1556 :** Akbar and his general, Bairam Khan, defeated Hemu Banya, the Hindu General of Mohammed Adil Shah. Akbar consolidated his position and the Mughals once again became the mighty rulers of India.
* **Battle of Talikota–1565 :** Ram Rai, the ruler of Vijayanagar, was defeated by the forces of Ahmednagar, Golkunda and Bidar. It started the disintegration of the Vijayanagar Empire in the south.
* **Battle of Haldighati–1576 :** The Battle of Haldighati was fought between Rana Pratap of Mewar and Mughal army led by Man Singh and Asif Khan. Some historian say that this battle was indecisive but some say that Rana Pratap was defeated.

* **Invasion of Nadir Shah–1739 :** Nadir Shah, the ruler of Iran, invaded India and defeated the forces of Mughal emperor Mohammed Shah. It was followed by massacre of the citizens of Delhi by his forces.
* **Battle of Plassey–1757 :** The British led by Clive defeated Siraj-ud-Daula, the Nawab of Bengal. It laid the foundation of British power in Bengal.
* **Battle of Wandiwash-1760 :** Count Lally, the Governor of the French company in India was defeated by Sir Coote, the commander of English forces. The dream of the French to establish their rule in India was finally shattered.
* **Third Battle of Panipat–1761 :** Ahmed Shah Abdali defeated the Marathas on January 14. The dream of Marathas to become a paramount power in India came to a naught with this battle.
* **Battle of Buxar–1764 :** The English forces led by Munro defeated both Mir Kasim and Nawab Wazir of Awadh. The Company's rule was consolidated in Bengal.
* **The Fourth Mysore War–1799 :** The British forces led by Arthur Wellesley defeated Tipu Sultan who died fighting. A part of his kingdom, consisting of Kanara and Coimbatore, was annexed and the rest restored to the old Hindu dynasty.
* **Third Maratha War–1817-18 :** The British forces defeated Peshwa Baji Rao, Appa Sahib Bhonsle and Holkar, the Maratha rulers, in different battles. Power of the Marathas was completely crushed and the British became indisputably the supreme power in the whole of India.
* **The First Sikh War–1845-46 :** The British forces defeated the Sikh armies of Punjab in the battles of Mudhki, Feroze Shah, Aliwal and Sobraon. The defeat of the Sikh armies was largely due to the betrayal of the leaders. The territory between Sutlej and Beas was annexed by the British.
* **The Second Sikh War–1848-49 :** The battle of Ramnagar and Chilianwala between the British forces and the Sikhs was indecisive. However, the Sikhs were defeated by the British in the battle of Gujarat. Punjab was annexed by the East India Company,
* **Indo-China War–1962 :** China attacked India on October 20, 1962. India faced the aggression bravely, but lost sizable land in this war to China.

Our Army has been involved in four wars with neighbouring Pakistan and one with China. Other major operations undertaken by the army include Operation Vijay, Operation Meghdoot and Operation Cactus. Apart from conflicts, the army has also been an active participant in United Nations peacekeeping missions.

BATTLES OF INDO-PAK WAR

The partition of the Indian subcontinent came into effect on 15 August 1947, when India gained independence. Pakistan declared independence a day earlier. At the time of independence the old Indian Army stood divided between Pakistan and India.

Instead of large scale celebrations, riots and mass killing between Hindus and Muslims in Punjab and Bengal intensified. It also led to acute suffering and misery of the displaced people, apart from colossal loss of precious human lives and destruction of property due to communal riots and retribution.

Taking advantage of communal strife, in October 1947 Pakistani troops soon crossed over into Kashmir to precipitate an undeclared war with India. The tribal 'volunteers' along with Pakistani regulars had by then overrun large tracts of Jammu province and the Valley, which shared a porous border with Pakistan. It was when they had reached Badgaon, on the suburbs of Srinagar, that the Maharaja of J&K signed the Instrument of Accession and put in a bid for India's military assistance. Indian Army then swung into action to save J&K state.

Despite the accession of the state, a part of Kashmir, known as Pakistan Occupied Kashmir (POK), remains under the illegal control of Pakistan, and this has remained a contentious issue between both nations.

Since 1947-1948 war India and Pakistan have fought the following wars :

(i) 1965 War
(ii) 1971 War
(iii) 1999 Kargil War
(iv) Proxy War in J & K state since 1988 till date.

Indo-Pakistan War (1965)

A second confrontation with Pakistan took place in 1965, largely over Kashmir. Pakistani President Ayub Khan launched Operation Gibraltar in August 1965, during which several Pakistani paramilitary troops infiltrated into Indian-administered Kashmir and attempted to ignite an anti-India agitation in Jammu and Kashmir.

Pakistani leaders believed that India, which was still recovering from the disastrous Sino-Indian War, would be unable to deal with a military thrust and a Kashmiri rebellion. Pakistan launched Operation Grand Slam on 1 September, 1965 invading India's Chamb-Jaurian sector. In retaliation, India reacted swiftly and launched a counter-offensive on Pakistan.

Initially, the Indian Army met with considerable success in the northern sector. After launching prolonged artillery barrages against Pakistan, India was able to capture three important mountain positions in Kashmir.

By 9 September, the Indian Army had made considerable in-roads into Pakistan. India had its largest haul of Pakistani tanks when the offensive of Pakistan's 1st Armoured Division was blunted at the Battle of Asal Uttar, which took place on 10 September near Khemkaran in Punjab.

Another tank battle of the war came in the form of the Battle of Chawinda, the largest tank battle in history after World War II. Pakistan's defeat at the Battle of Asal Uttar and Dograi hastened the end of the conflict.

To relieve pressure at Chamb-Jaurian Sector in J&K, 15 Infantry Division launched offensive in Lahore sector. On 23 September, 3 JAT of 54 Infantry Brigade crossed Ichogil canal and captured the township of Dograi which was just 13 miles from Lahore.

On 23 September 1965 ceasefire was announced. A decision to return to pre-war positions was taken following the Tashkent Declaration.

Indo-Pakistan War (1971)

An independence movement broke out in East Pakistan in late sixties which was brutally crushed by Pakistani forces. Due to large-scale atrocities against them, thousands of Bengalis took refuge in India causing a major refugee crisis here.

In early 1971, India declared its full-support for the Bengali rebels, known as Mukti Bahini, and Indian agents were extensively involved in covert operations to aid them. Wary of India's growing involvement in the Bengali rebellion, the Pakistan Air Force (PAF) launched a pre-emptive strike on 10 Indian air bases at Srinagar, Jammu, Pathankot, Amritsar, Agra, Adampur, Jodhpur, Jaisalmer, Uttarlai and Sirsa at 17:45 hours on 3 December, 1971.

This aerial offensive, however, failed to accomplish its stated objectives and gave India its excuse to declare a full-scale war against Pakistan the same day. By midnight, the Indian Army, accompanied by Indian Air Force, launched a major three-pronged assault into East Pakistan. The Indian Army won several battles on the eastern front including the decisive Battle of Hilli, which was the only front where the Pakistani Army was able to build up considerable resistance. India's massive early gains were largely attributed to the speed and flexibility with which Indian armoured divisions moved across East Pakistan.

Pakistan launched a counter-attack against India on the western front. On 4 December 1971, the 'A' company of the 23rd Battalion of India's Punjab Regiment detected and intercepted the movement of the 51st Infantry Brigade of the Pakistani Army near Ramgarh, Rajasthan. The battle of Longewala ensued during which the 'A' company, though being outnumbered, thwarted the Pakistani advance until the Indian Air Force directed its fighters to engage the Pakistani tanks.

By the time the battle had ended, 38 Pakistani tanks and 100 armoured vehicles were either destroyed or abandoned. About 200 Pakistani troops were killed in action during the battle while only 2 Indian soldiers lost their lives.

Pakistan suffered another major defeat on the western front during the battle of Basantar which was fought from 4th to 16th December. By the end of the battle, about 66 Pakistani tanks were destroyed and 40 more were captured. In return, Pakistani forces were able to destroy only 11 Indian tanks. By 16 December, Pakistan had lost sizeable territory on both eastern and western fronts.

Under the command of Lt. General J.S. Arora, the three corps of the Indian Army, which had invaded East Pakistan, entered Dhaka and forced Pakistani forces to surrender on 16 December 1971, one day after the conclusion of the battle of Basantar. After Pakistan's Lt. General A.A.K. Niazi signed the Instrument of Surrender, India took more than 90,000 Pakistani prisoners of war.

Kargil War (1999)

Kargil War was fought on the heights of Kargil and Drass in 1999. In mid-1999 Pakistani paramilitary forces and Kashmiri insurgents captured deserted, but strategic, Himalayan heights in the Kargil district of India. Indian forces painstakingly recaptured all posts one after another in a bloody conflict. Operation Vijay was declared success on 26 July, 1999.

KARGIL WAR MEMORIAL

In 1998, India had carried out nuclear tests and a few days later, Pakistan responded by more nuclear tests giving both countries nuclear deterrence capability, although India had exploded three hydrogen bombs which Pakistan lacks.

Diplomatic tensions eased after the Lahore Summit was held in 1999. The sense of optimism was short-lived, however, since in mid-1999 Pakistani paramilitary forces and Kashmiri insurgents captured deserted, but strategic, Himalayan heights in the Kargil district of India. These had been vacated by the Indian army during the onset of the inhospitable winter and were supposed to be reoccupied in spring.

Once the scale of the Pakistani incursion was realised, the Indian Army quickly mobilised about 200,000 troops and Operation Meghdoot was launched.

However, since the heights were under Pakistani control, India was in a clear strategic disadvantage. From their observation posts, the Pakistani forces had a clear line-of-sight to lay down indirect artillery fire on NH1A, inflicting heavy casualties on the Indians.

Thus, the Indian Army's first priority was to recapture peaks that were in the immediate vicinity of NH1A. This resulted in Indian troops first targeting the Tiger Hill and Tololing complex in Drass.

The Battle of Tololing, among other assaults, slowly tilted the combat in India's favour. Nevertheless, some of the posts put up a stiff resistance, including Tiger Hill (Point 5140) that fell only later in the war.

The Indian Army mounted some direct frontal ground assaults which were slow and took a heavy toll given the steep ascent that had to be made on peaks as high as 18,000 feet (5,500 m). Two months into the conflict, Indian troops had slowly retaken most of the ridges they had lost; according to official count, an estimated 75%-80% of the intruded area and nearly all high ground was back under Indian control.

Following the Washington accord on 4 July, 1999 where Pakistan's Prime Minister Nawaz Sharief agreed to withdraw Pakistani troops, most of the fighting came to a gradual halt, but some Pakistani forces cunningly remained in positions on the Indian side of the LOC.

The Indian Army launched its final attacks in the last week of July; as soon as the Drass subsector had been cleared of Pakistani forces, the fighting ceased on 26 July, 1999. 26 July has since been marked as Kargil Vijay Diwas in India. By the end of the war, India had resumed control of all territory south and east of the Line of Control, as was established in July 1972 per the Shimla Accord.

Captain Vikram Batra, Captain Manoj Kumar Pandey, Grenedier Yogendra Singh Yadav and Riflemen Sanjay Kumar have been awarded the Param Vir Chakra for their gallantry services during the Kargil War. Both Captain Batra and Captain Pandey have been awarded posthumously for their supreme sacrifice.

In addition to these three conventional Indo-Pakistan wars, India has been fighting a Proxy war launched by Pakistan since 1988 in Jammu & Kashmir.

Since 1984 both Armies have fought numerous battles on the Siachen Glacier, also known as the highest battle field in the world.

The sacrifices of the Indian Army to safeguard the sovereignty and unity of India have been great for which the whole nation is proud of its achievements.

HONOURS AND AWARDS

The Armed Forces of India are awarded many military decorations, honours and awards. The awards and honours are awarded for extraordinary bravery and courage, as well as for distinguished service during times of war and peace. For the purpose of classification, Indian Armed Forces honours and awards can be divided into two categories:

(a) Gallantry Awards

(b) Non-Gallantry Awards/Distinguished Service Awards

Gallantry Awards : Gallantry awards are further divided into two categories:

1. **Gallantry in the Face of Enemy (War Time) :** These are:
   - (i) Param Vir Chakra
   - (ii) Maha Vir Chakra
   - (iii) Vir Chakra
   - (iv) Sena Medal
   - (v) Nao Sena Medal
   - (vi) Vayu Sena Medal
   - (vii) Mention in Despatches
   - (viii) Chiefs of Staff Commendation Card
2. **Gallantry other than in the Face of Enemy (Peace Time) :** These are:
   - (i) Ashok Chakra
   - (ii) Kirti Chakra
   - (iii) Shaurya Chakra

Non-Gallantry/Distinguished Service Awards : These are:

- (i) Sarvottam Yudh Seva Medal
- (ii) Param Vishist Seva Medal
- (iii) Uttam Yudh Seva Medal
- (iv) Ati Vishisht Seva Medal
- (v) Yuddh Seva Medal
- (vi) Vishisht Seva Medal

Note: Award like Sena Medal is given for all three catagories i.e., during War, Peace and also as a Distinguished Service Award.

Honours and Awards are ultimate recognition by the nation for unmatched act of bravery and selfless service, dedication and supreme sacrifice by soldiers/ civilian/or any professional.

PARAM VIR CHAKRA

Soldiers face the dangers and vagaries of war and sacrifice their lives for their motherland. The Indian Nation also honours its bravest of the brave soldiers by conferring on them the highest gallantry award "Param Vir Chakra" as recognition of their bravery and sacrifice.

Param Vir Chakra

The Param Vir Chakra (PVC) is India's highest military decoration awarded for the highest degree of valour or self-sacrifice in the presence of the enemy.

The PVC was established on 26 January 1950 by the President of India, with effect from 15 August 1947. It can be awarded to officers or enlisted personnel from all branches of the Indian Armed Forces. It is the second highest award of the Government of India after Bharat Ratna. It replaced the former British colonial Victoria Cross (VC).

Param Vir Chakra has been awarded 21 times out of which 20 recipients were from the Indian Army, one from Indian Air Force and none from Indian Navy till October 2020.

Recipients of Param Vir Chakra

Name	Regiment/Squadron	Date & Place of Action
✦ Major Som Nath Sharma (P)	4th Battalion, Kumaon Regiment	November 3, 1947 (Badgam, Kashmir)
✦ Naik Jadu Nath Singh (P)	1st Battalion, Rajput Regiment	February 6, 1948 (Naushera, Kashmir)
✦ Second Lieutenant Rama Raghoba Rane*	Bombay Corps of Engineers	April 8, 1948 (Naushera, Kashmir)
✦ Company Havildar Major Piru Singh Shekhawat (P)	6th Battalion, Rajputana Rifles	18 July, 1948 (Tithwal, Kashmir)
✦ Lance Naik Karam Singh*	1st Battalion, Sikh Regiment	October 13, 1948 (Tithwal, Kashmir)
✦ Captain Gurbachan Singh Salaria*	3rd Battalion, 1st Gorkha Rifles (The Malaun Regiment)	December 5, 1961 (Elizabethville, Congo Katanga)
✦ Major Dhan Singh Thapa*	1st Battalion, 8th Gorkha Rifles	October 21, 1962 (Ladakh, India)
✦ Subedar Joginder Singh (P)	1st Battalion, Sikh Regiment	October 23, 1962 (Tongpen La, Northeast Frontier Agency, India)
✦ Major Shaitan Singh (P)	13th Battalion, Kumaon Regiment	November 18, 1962 (Rezang La)
✦ Company Quartermaster Havildar Abdul Hamid (P)	4th Battalion, The Grenadiers	September 10, 1965 (Pakistan, Khem Karan Sector)
✦ Lieutenant-Colonel Ardeshir Burzorji Tarapore (P)	17th Poona Horse	September 11, 1965 (Phillora, Sialkot Sector, Pakistan)
✦ Lance Naik Albert Ekka (P)	14th Battalion, Brigade of the Guards	December 4, 1971 (Gangasagar, Agartala Sector)
✦ Flying Officer Nirmal Jit Singh Sekhon (P)	No.18 Squadron, *Indian Air Force*	December 14, 1971 (Srinagar, Kashmir)
✦ 2nd Lieutenant Arun Khetrapal (P)	17th Poona Horse	December 16, 1971 (Barapind-Jarpal, Shakargarh Sector)
✦ Major Hoshiar Singh*	3rd Battalion, The Grenadiers	December 17, 1971 (Basantar River, Shakargarh Sector)
✦ Naib Subedar Bana Singh*	8th Battalion, J&K Light Infantry	May 23, 1987 (Siachen Glacier, J&K)
✦ Maj. Ramaswamy Parameshwaran (P)	8th Battalion, Mahar Regiment	November 25, 1987 (Sri Lanka)
✦ Captain Manoj Kumar Pandey (P)	1st Battalion, 11th Gorkha Rifles	July 3, 1999 (Khaluber/Juber Top, Batalik sector, Kargil area, J&K)
✦ Grndr. Yogendra Singh Yadav*	18th Battalion, The Grenadiers	July 4, 1999 (Tiger Hill, Kargil area)
✦ Rifleman Sanjay Kumar*	13th Battalion, J&K Rifles	July 4, 1999 (Area Flat Top, Kargil Area)
✦ Captain Vikram Batra (P)	13th Battalion, J&K Rifles	July 7, 1999 (Point 5140, Point 4875, Kargil Area, J&K)

(P) Awarded Posthumously
*Awarded while serving.

❖ ❖ ❖

CHAPTER

20 Map Reading

MAP

It is a proportionate, graphical representation of the surface of the earth on a plain surface. In Defence Services, map-reading is of great significance. It enables a soldier to form a complete view of a part of Earth's surface. The successful execution of war-related matters depends completely on maps.

A Map :

1. helps locate one's winning position on land.
2. helps locates enemy's position on land.
3. tells the distance and direction of one place from another.
4. helps locate various features of ground.
5. helps plan movements especially during war.
6. tells the constant visibility of two different places.

Types of Maps

1. Relief Map
2. Geographical Map
3. Political Map
4. Historical Map
5. Statistical Map
6. Economical Map
7. Military Map

Limitations of a Map

1. It is only a sketch, not a photograph, and as such can not depict everything on the earth's surface. It is subject to change and is never up-to-date.
2. As it is drafted on a paper, hence, giving all the details of earth on it, is impossible.

Structure of a Map

A map is broadly divided into three parts:

1. The northern margin or top of the map
2. The southern margin or bottom of the map
3. Internal margin

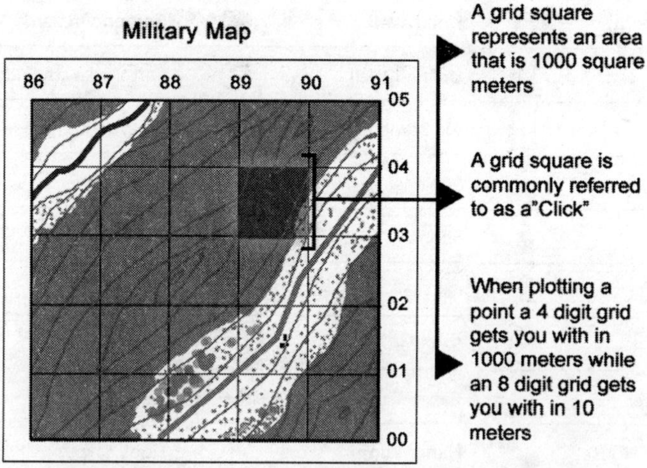

The **Northern Margin**, includes:

1. Subject of the Map
2. Name of the District
3. Security classification
4. Year of Survey
5. Edition of the Map
6. Context of the Map
7. Sheet number

The **Southern Margin**, includes:

8. Year of publication
9. List of conventional signs
10. Picture list of map sheet
11. Name of the publisher
12. Unit and unit-line
13. The relative distance of the contours
14. Context of the Grids
15. Index of the administrative areas

The **Internal Margin**, includes:

1. No. of grid lines
2. No. of lines of Longitude and lines of Latitudes, on all the four corners
3. No. of contours
4. No. of various Tehsils

CONVENTIONAL SIGNS

Broad guage double Railway line	
Broad guage single Railway line	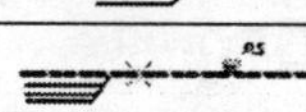
Broad guage under construction	
Narrow guage single Railway line	
Narrow guage double Railway line	
Narrow guage under construction	

Sign	Symbol	Sign	Symbol	Sign	Symbol
Temple		Lined Well		Garden/Orchard	
Mosque		Unlined Well		Cart track with Bridge	
Idgah		Air Bombing Target		Footpath with Bridge	
Tomb		Streams		Tram Way	
Church		Spring		Road Cutting	
Pagoda		Oil Well		Metalled Road	
Chhatri		Salt Pan		Level Crossing	
Watch Tower		Canal Tunnel		Railway Station	RS
Permanent House		Hand Pump		Light Ship	
Temprory House		Helipad		Light House	
Village		Wind Turbine		Telephone Line	
Walled Village		Anchorage		Electric Power Line	
Deserted Village		Tube Well		Viaduct	
Fort		Ferry or Ford	Ford (Mar to July) / Ferry (July to November)	Rifle Range	
Circuit House	□ CH	Marsh		Water Piple line	
Dak Bungalow	□ DB	Dam		Camping Ground	CG
Rest House	□ RH	Graves		Metro Railway	
Inspection Bungalow	□ IB	Battle field		Surveyed Boundary Piller	■
Police Station	□ PS	Cave		Unsurveyed Boundary Piller	□
Post Office	□ PO	Tree		Tehsil Boundary	
Quarry		Palm Tree		Village Boundary	
Contours		Vegetable Garden		State Boundary	
Glacier		Grass High/Low		International Boundary	
Road over Railway		Road under Railway		Bridge carrying Railway	

MILITARY SYMBOLS

1.	Section	•
2.	Platoon	• •
3.	Company or Battery or Squadron	I
4.	Battalion or Regiment	II
5.	Brigade	X
6.	Division	XX
7.	Corps	XXX
8.	Army Group	XXXXX
9.	Infantry	
10.	Infantry Section	
11.	Infantry Platoon	
12.	Infantry Company	
13.	Infantry Battalion	
14.	Infantry Brigade	
15.	Infantry Division 12th corps	
16.	Field Battery	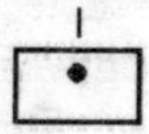

WEAPON SIGNS

Name of the Weapon	Basic Symbol
✦ Machine Gun	
✦ A/A Machine Gun (Anti Aircraft Machine Gun)	
✦ Mortar	
✦ Artillery-Gun	
✦ Artillery-Howitzer	
✦ A/Tank Weapon (Anti tank weapon)	
✦ Artillery-Anti Tank	
✦ Tank	

SCALE

The proportion of distances between two places on the map and the actual distance between those places on surface of the earth is called Scale.

Scales help us work out distance to out destination and therefore how long it will take us to get there. The smaller the area a map covers, the larger the scale will be. So if we have a map on a square meter of paper and the scale of the map is 1:50,000 and another map on the same size paper with a scale of 1:25,000, the area covered by the first map will be 4 times the area covered by the second map. Every map will carry a scale, not just the value of say 1:50,000, but also a depiction of that scale.

Scale can be represented on maps in three ways:

1. By Stating in Words
2. By Representation Fraction (RF)
3. By Graphic Lines

In the "Words" method, scale is expressed in words. For example : 1 cm = 1 km i.e., if the distance between the two places on map is 1 cm, then the distance between the same two places on land will be 1 km.

This is an easy scale to use.

In the "Respresentation Fraction" method, a scale is always represented in the form of a fraction.

$$\text{Representation Fraction} = \frac{\text{Distance on the map}}{\text{Actual distance}}$$

In the "Graphic Lines" method the scale is divided into an equally divided line. This line can be drawn in the desirable length. The numbers are alloted to the division points of line.

SIMPLE SCALE

The common scales used in Survey of India maps are :

(i) 16 inches to 1 mile*	1/3970
(ii) 4 inches to 1 mile	1/15840
(iii) 2.53 inches to 1 mile	1/25000
(iv) 1 inch to 1 mile	1/63360
(v) ½ inch to 1 mile	1/126720
(vi) ¼ inch to 1 mile	1/253440
(vii) 1 inch to 16 miles (Approx)	1/1000000
(viii) 1 inch to 32 miles (Approx)	1/2000000

* 1 mile = 1760 yards; 1 yard = 3 ft; 1 ft = 12 inches; 1 mile = 1760 × 3 × 12 = 63360 inches.

Some Examples

Q.1. Convert 16 inches to 1 mile scale in RF scale.

Ans. **Distance on Map** **Distance on Ground**

16 inches = 1 mile

16 inches = 1 × 1760 × 3 × 12 inches

$$1 \text{ inch} = \frac{63360}{16} = 3960 \text{ inches}$$

$$\therefore \quad RF = \frac{1}{3960}$$

Q.2. Convert 1/253440 into word statement in miles/inches.

Ans. **Distance on Map** **Distance on Ground**

1 inch = 253440 inches

We know, 1 mile = 1760 × 3 × 12 = 63360 inches

∴ 253440 ÷ 63360 = 4 miles/inch

Hence 1 inch on Map represents 4 miles on Ground.

Q.3. Convert 1/5000000 RF scale into word statement in km/cm.

Ans. **Distance on Map** **Distance on Ground**

1 cm = 5000000 cm

We know, 1 km = 1000 m = 1000 × 100 cm = 100000 cm

∴ 5000000 ÷ 100000 = 50 km/cm

Hence 1 cm on Map represents 50 km on ground.

Q.4. Draw a simple scale for the statement of words 1 cm = 1 km.

Ans. Draw a line of 10 cm length of depict a distance of 10 km. Divide the line in 10 equal parts of 1 cm each to represent 1 km distance. Now divide the left-most part into two equal parts which will represent 0.5 km or 5 Hectometer length.

SIMPLE SCALE

Q.5. Draw a simple scale for 1/63360 on RF Scale showing miles and furlong.

Ans. According to question,

1 inch on map = 63360 inches on Ground

$$= \frac{63360}{1760 \times 3 \times 12} = 1 \text{ mile}$$

∴ 4 inches = 4 miles

Draw a 4-inch line and divide it into 4 equal parts of 1 inch each. Each part represents 1 mile distance. Now divide the left-most part in eight equal parts. Each of these eight parts represents 1 furlong distance.

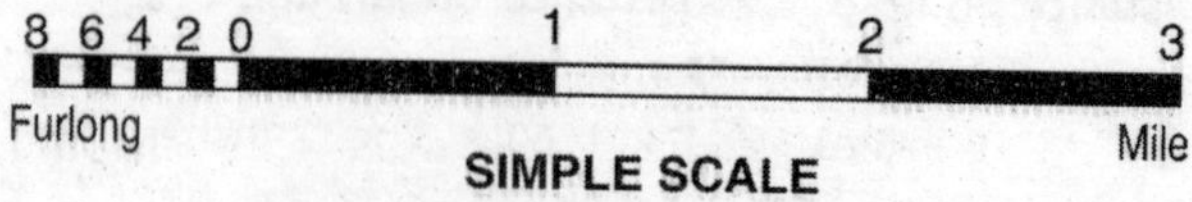

SIMPLE SCALE

TECHNICAL TERMS

Important technical terms used in map reading are:

1. Bearing – The angle formed by a line joining two points and the North and South line. Bearings are always measured clockwise.
2. Bench Mark – A permanent mark usually cut into a wall recording exact height for future reference, marked BM with the height on Ordnance Survey Maps.
3. Contours – A line drawn on the map joining up all points of equal height above sea level.
4. Gradient – The slope of a hill expressed as a fraction.
5. Grid Lines – Lines running parallel to and at right angles to a North and South line through approximately the centre of the area covered by the grid system.
6. Grid North – Except through the origin, grid lines do not lie true North and South or East and West, Grid North is the direction of the North South grid lines on a map.
7. Magnetic Variation – The difference between true North & Magnetic North.
8. Setting – Placing a map so that North on the map points toward the North so that the objects on the map are placed in relationship to the same objects on the ground.
9. Trig Point – A point fixed during the triangulation at the beginning of a survey, marked on Ordance Survey Maps by a small triangle with the height.
10. True North – The direction of the North Pole from the point.

RELIEF

The surface of the Earth is not even throughout. It has various physical aspects like – mountains, rocks, plateaues, hills, rivers, slopes etc. The study of rise and fall of the earth surface is called Relief. Relief can be described on map through the methods mentioned below :

1. **By Contour Line :** The imaginary line joining places of equal vertical heights.
2. **By Spot Height :** Shows the exact height of a point above sea level.

3. **By Trigonometrical Height :** A triangle is drawn and "Point of height" (trigpoint) is written.
4. **By Form Lines :** Lines used to show the form of the land.
5. **By Relative Height :** In this method, the height of a place on earth is compared to the height of another place, and that relative height is represented in the form of "broken lines". That place is highlighted with a number and a letter like '5000 r'.
6. **Bench Mark :** These are stones on which the heights (in ft) of spots are highlighted as BM. BM is carved on stones at railway stations, canals, roads etc. BM 5500 means 5500 ft higher from the sea level.
7. **By Hachures :** These are used to show minor formations omitted by contours, *e.g.*, cuts at ravines, etc.
8. **Hill Shading :** These are used to supplement contours by the pattern of relief features at a glance. The relief features are mentioned through colours. The light slopes are shown in light shades and deep slopes are shown in dark shades.
9. **By Layertint :** In this method, different heights are shown in different shapes (image) of one colour, like – light, soft, moderate, dark, exterme dark, etc. Sometimes, different colours are also used.

SLOPE

The natural rise and fall between two permanent places on the surface of the Earth is called slope:

It is of two types :

1. Regular slope
2. Irregular slope

In regular slope the pattern of rise and fall of land is equal. It is further of two types:

1. Uniform gentle slope
2. Uniform steep slope

In irregular slope, the pattern of rise and fall of land is not equal. It is also of two types :

1. **Concave slope :** When the slope of the bottom part of the hill is broad and gentle and the slope of the top of the hill is comparatively narrow and steep, it is called concave slope.
2. **Convex slope :** When the slope of the bottom of the hill is narrow and steep and slope of the top of the hill is comparatively broad and gentle, it is called convex slope.

MEASURING SLOPES

The slope between two places and the elevation between the two can be measured in two ways:

1. through gradient 2. through degree of slope

The fraction, which is produced by the ratio of the vertical interval and horizontal equivalent of the two points on a slope is called a gradient.

$$\text{Gradient} = \frac{VI}{HE} \rightarrow g = \frac{VI}{HE} \quad ...(1)$$

$$g \times HE = VI \quad ...(2)$$

$$HE = \frac{VI}{g} \quad ...(3)$$

$$\text{Gradient} = \frac{\text{Slope (in degree)}}{60} \qquad VI = HE \times g \quad ...(4)$$

Slope (in degree) = Gradient × 60

SOME EXAMPLES

Q.1. The driver of a lorry after covering a distance of 4000 meters on a hill is at 400 metres height from his point of start. Find the slope of the hill.

Ans. HE = 4000 metres

VI = 400 metres

$$\text{Gradient} = g = \frac{VI}{HE} = \frac{400}{4000} = \frac{1}{10}$$

$$\text{Slope} = \text{Gradient} \times 60° = \frac{1}{10} \times 60° = 6°$$

Q.2. A hill has a slope of 5° and height 500 metres. Find the horizontal equivalent (HE) of the hill.

Ans. $\text{Gradient} = g = \frac{\text{Slope}}{60°} = \frac{5°}{60°} = \frac{1}{12}$

Given VI = 500 metres

$$He = \frac{VI}{g} = \frac{500}{1/12} = 500 \times 12 = 6000 \text{ metres.}$$

TOPOGRAPHY

The study of arrangement of the natural and artificial physical features of an area is called topology. A detailed description or representation of such features on a map is called topography.

The different shapes of the surface of earth (land) is called topographical forms. These are :

1. **Mountain :** The surface of the earth, of excessive height and vast area is called a mountain.
2. **Hill :** The higher surface of the earth with compact/narrow area is called a hill.
3. **Plateau :** The even surface over the mountain is called a plateau.
4. **Knoll :** An isolated hill adjacent to the series of hill with less height and area is called a knoll.
5. **Spur :** The protruding mountaneous part of a plain is called a spur.
6. **Re-entrant :** The land between two spurs is called Re-entrant.
7. **Col and Saddle :** The land of even surface between the peaks of a hill is called a Col, when the depth of this land is quite less than the peaks, it is called a saddle.
8. **Pass and defile :** The path between the two hills is called a Pass. Sometimes, this path becomes so narrow that the soldiers make a "queue" for crossing it, this way, it is called a defile.
9. **Cliff :** An erect mountaineous elevation is called a cliff.
10. **Gorge :** The very narrow hills, which have excessive depth and almost straight slopes are called gorges.
11. **Escarpment :** The excessive steep slope of a hill is called escarpment.
12. **Dune :** The big heep, produced by the accumulation of sand, soil, mud etc by the blowing air, is called a dune. Basically, it is accumulation of sand on a place, forming a three dimensional structure.
13. **Dead ground :** The surface of obscure land under hill etc, is called dead ground. Soldiers at the time of war use dead ground.
14. **Undulating ground :** The piece of land with excessive uneven surface is called undulating ground.
15. **Crest :** The peak of a hill or mountain range is called crest.
16. **Basin :** An area of fairly level ground surrounded by hills or the area drained by a river and its distributaries.
17. **Ridge :** The line along a hill or range of hills or mountains from which water flows in opposite directions, a divide, sometimes and the crest of a line of hills as it appears along the horizon.
18. **Watershed :** The line separating the water flowing into two different river systems, the edge of a river basin.
19. **Vertical Interval (VI) :** The rise between successive contour lines is known as the vertical interval. On map scale 1 inch to 1 mile, the VI of each contour line is 50 feet while on the ¼ inch to a mile it is 250 feet.
20. **Horizontal Equivalent (HE) :** The distance measured flat on the map between adjacent contour lines is horizontal equivalent.
21. **Gradient :** A gradient is a slope expressed as a fraction. If we say that a slope has a gradient of 1 inch to 10 we mean for every 10 feet of horizontal distance the slope rises or falls 1 foot vertically. Simple Formula is VI/HE = Gradient.

Grid and Grid Lines

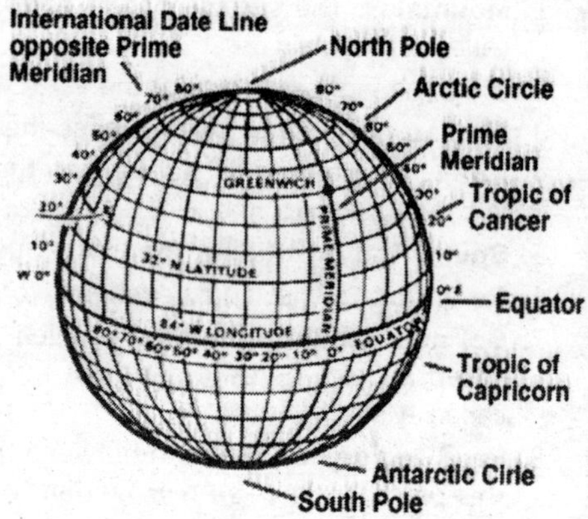

The Grid is a systematic pattern on Earth by laying a vertical and horizontal grid over the Earth's layout. The vertical lines are called the longitude and the horizontal lines are known as the latitude. Combinations of these lines are know as Grid Lines.

The purpose of Grid Lines is to make possible giving and reading Grid References and to facilitate measurement of bearings.

The basic rules for giving grid reference:

(i) A reference must always contain an even number of figures. In the normal method, it will contain six figures.

(ii) Always count along the Easting lines first from West to East and then from South to North, along Northings.

(iii) For the six figures reference, the third and the sixth figure represent the divisions of 1000 yards square to the nearest 10th part, so they have to be estimated and for these figures a slight latitude is allowed.

(iv) If a general grid reference is to be given or there is only one such object in one square *e.g.* bridge, temple, road, junction, then a four figure grid reference would suffice.

Cardinal Points and Finding North

CARDINAL POINTS : East, West, North and South are known as cardinal points while North-East, North-West, South-East and South-West are called small cardinal points. When 0° is considered as North then East will be at 90°, South at 180° and West will lie at 270° to the North.

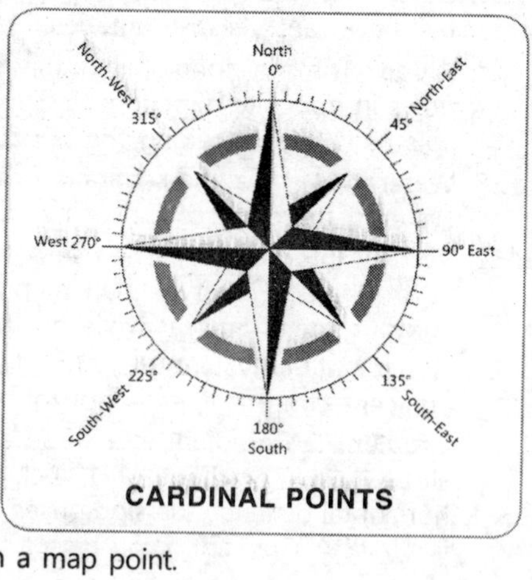

CARDINAL POINTS

Various types of North are :

(i) **True North :** The direction of North pole from the observer.

(ii) **Magnetic North :** It is the point to which an accurate compass needle points, when freely suspended.

(iii) **Grid North :** It is the direction to which the North South grid lines on a map point.

Service Protractor

The service protractor "A" Mark IV is an instrument used for plotting and measuring bearing on the map. It is an essential link between the compass and the map. With the help of the protractor the magnetic bearings have been converted to grid bearing and transferred to the map.

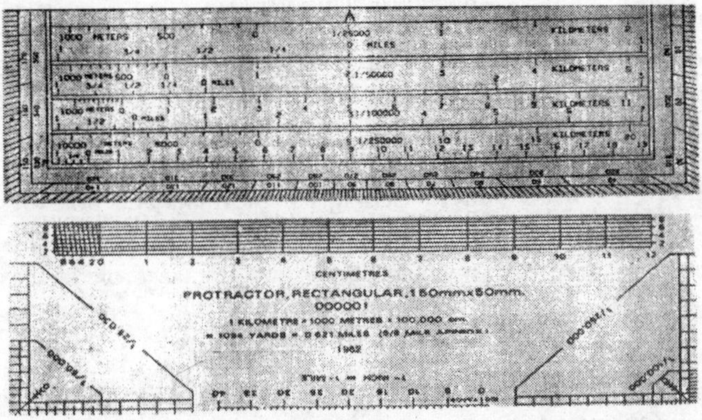

The protractor is made of cardboard or ivories (flexible material) and it measures 6 inches long and 2 inches wide.

Scale of Protractor

The main purpose of the protractor is to measure angles and bearings. The protractor also shows on both its faces a number of the more common map scales. The respective scale lines are drawn out and divided into primary and secondary divisions in exactly the same way as at the bottom of the map.

Uses of Service Protractor

The service protractor is an essential item of Map Reading. With its help we can:

(i) Plot and measure bearing on paper or on a map. For bearing between 0 and 180 degrees their Zero edge must be on the LEFT and for 180 degrees -360 degrees it must be on the RIGHT.

(ii) Measure distance in inches/cm correct up to 1/100th.

(iii) Measure distance in yards, meters or miles on a map by using the appropriate scale.

(iv) For using the diagonal scale we must use an intermediate agent. Mark off the distance to be measured on the straight edge of a paper or by means of a divider and then put the paper or divider on the diagonal scale and measure.

Bearings and Use of Service Protractor

(i) **Bearing :** The clockwise angle formed by a straight line joining two points and direction of North, is called the bearing between the two points. A bearing is always measured clockwise.

(ii) **Grid Bearing :** Measured on the map from the Grid North by the help of a protractor.

(iii) **Magnetic Bearing :** Measured from Magnetic North by the compass.

(iv) **True Bearing :** Calculated by finding out the relation of true North and Grid North or Magnetic North.

MAGNETIC POLE : According to Geologists, the magnetic pole of the earth completes one round of north pole in 100 years. There is a variation in the magnetic bearings due to this, which may slightly increase or decrease.

SOME EXAMPLES

Q.1. A soldier had given 2° magnetic variation to East on map during the year 1985. If the magnetic variation decreases every year by 2 minutes. What will be its magnetic variation in the year 2015?

Ans. No. of years = 2015 - 1985 = 30 years

Decrease in magnetic variation in 30 years $= 30 \times 2°$

$= 60$ minutes or 1°

So magnetic variation in 2015 will be $= 2° - 1°$

$= 1°$ East

Q.2. A soldier had given a 2° magnetic variation on a 1955 map. If the magnetic variation is increasing. 5 minutes every year, what will be its magnetic variation in the year 2015?

Ans. No. of years = 2015 - 1955 = 60 years

Increase in magnetic variation in 60 years $= 60 \times 5$

$= 300$ minutes

$= \frac{300}{60} = 5°$

So magnetic variation in 2015 will be $= 2° + 5°$

$= 7°$

Forward and Back Bearing

(i) Forward Bearing : It is the bearing of the object's position from the observer.

(ii) Back Bearing : It is the bearing of the observer's position from the object.

(iii) Conversion of Forward Bearing to Back Bearing : The difference between the forward bearing and back bearing is always 180°. If forward bearing is $\leq$ 180°, add 180° to get the back bearing. If it is $\geq$ 180°, subtract 180° from it to get the back bearing.

Q.1. Forward bearings of P and Q points are measured to be 50° and 220° respectively. Find out their back bearings.

Ans. Back bearing of P = 50° + 180° = 230°

Back bearing of Q = 220° − 180° = 40°

Conversion of Magnetic Bearing to a True Bearing

Suppose the bearing of a certain point P is measured with a compass and is found to be 160 Degrees. To convert this magnetic bearing to a true bearing, draw a diagram as given in figure.

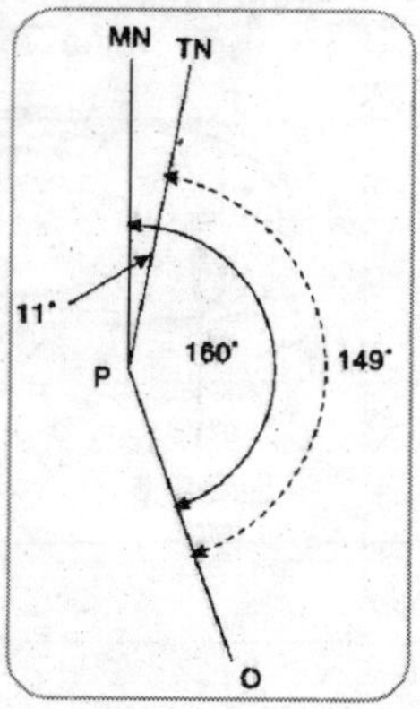

First draw a vertical line to represent Magnetic North (because it is a magnetic bearing which is being considered). Next draw a line to P at an angle of 160 degrees. It is only a rough diagram, and the angle can be judged by eye. Thirdly, draw in the true North line approximately 11 degrees East of Magnetic North, with this diagram, it becomes clear that true bearing (marked with a dotted line) is smaller by 11 degrees. Therefore, the true bearing of P is 149 degrees.

Conversion of Grid Bearing to a Magnetic Bearing

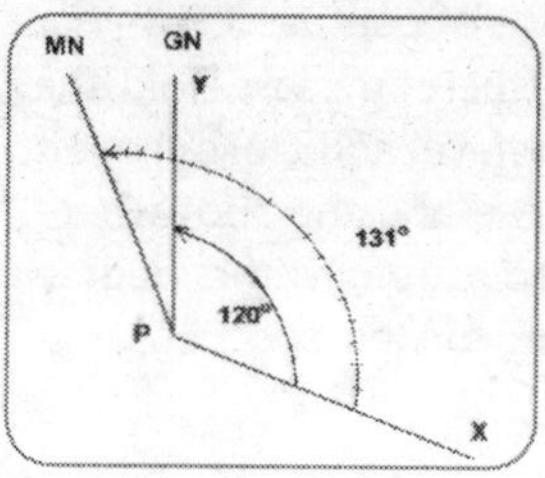

Measuring with a protractor on the map, the bearing of a Wind Mill at Y from a Church at X is found to be 120 degrees. To convert this grid bearing to a magnetic bearing, draw a diagram as under, this time starting with the Grid North line. Since the magnetic bearing is larger than the grid bearing by 11 degrees and it is therefore 131 degrees.

PRISMATIC COMPASS

It is a circular box type instrument. Its pointer always shows the magnetic north. It is of two types :

1. Dry prismatic compass
2. Liquid prismatic compass

In defence forces, usually liquid prismatic compass is used.

Applications

(i) It determines the magnetic north direction.
(ii) It does map setting.
(iii) It helps to move (soldiers, at march) in a particular direction.
(iv) It determines the directional value of different places.
(v) It determines the position of different features of map.

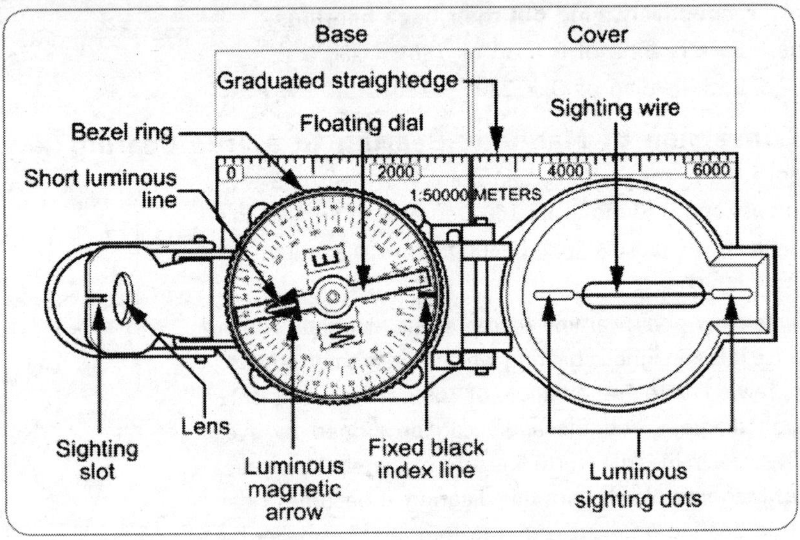

Taking Bearing with a Prismatic Compass

Hold the compass carefully in one hand and open the lid with other hand. Turn over the prism casing so as as to make it lie flat on the face of compass. Put your thumb through the ring and your forefinger underneath the compass. Hold the compass at horizontal level. Bring the prism upto right eye level and close the left eye. Now view hairline through the prism and keep the eye and the spot where bearing is to be taken in straight alignment. Now read carefully the degree measurement on the outer of the dial. This is the bearing of the spot.

Setting Degree with Compass

To set the compass on a particular angle, say 150°, for marching or any other purpose, do as follows. Hold the compass carefully and loosen the clamping screw. Now rotate the milled vane until number 15 at index line (luberline). Now tighten the clamping screw gently. Thus the compass is set at 150°.

Keep holding the compass horizontally on the palm of your hand, let the prism rotate till the arrow on the dial comes in arrow-head direction. The straight direction of the luminous strip marked before hairline on the compass dial is the correct direction of the move. Always keep the tongue of the compass in the front side while keeping it in your palm for use.

Compass Error

Sometimes due to the presence of impurities in the material of which a compass is made or for other reasons, the magnetic needle may not point toward the magnetic NORTH but a little to the EAST or WEST of it. This deviation of the magnetic needle in the compass from the magnetic NORTH is termed compass error.

Global Positioning System (GPS)

Global Positioning System (GPS) refers to a system of satellites and receivers that allows people and devices to pin point their precise location on the earth. The first GPS satellite was launched in 1974. GPS is funded and controlled by the United States, Department of Defence. Present technology provides very handy and accurate navigation.

Usage of GPS:

(i) Used by defense aircrafts, ships and specialized vehicles.
(ii) Used in defense in battle fields and insurgency-affected areas.
(iii) Used by civilian & para military vehicles to navigate their route.
(iv) It assists troops to navigate in thick jungles, mountains and deserts.
(v) Used by fishermen and hikers.
(vi) GPS is also used to guide missiles to pre-specified targets.

Setting A Map, Finding Own Position and North

A map is said to be set or oriented when it is placed such that it corresponds directly with the ground *i.e.* when true NORTH on the map points to true north on the ground.

Finding North

The various methods to find North are :

(i) Watch Method	(ii) From Sun	(iii) By Stars
(iv) From Idgah & Mosque	(v) GPS	(vi) Compass

(i) **Watch Method :** Set the hour needle towards sun and minute needle on 12 in your watch. The line bisecting the angle between the two needles indicates south and just opposite will be north. This method is useful for north pole only and when the angle formed is $< 180°$.

(ii) **Sun Method :** When you face the rising sun you face the east, west is on your back. South on the right and North on the left side. At the time of

12 noon if you stand erect your shadow indicates true north direction. At the time of sunset if you face the sun, you face west, east will be on your back, north on the right and south will be on the left side.

(iii) **Stars Method :** Watch the Pole star which indicates the position of true north within 2°. This is a bright star which can be easily found by observation. This can also be found by drawing a line from the Great Bear. The star is slightly off from this line.

(iv) **Idgah & Mosque Method :** The porch of the Idgah & mosque face the west. The north will be towards right and south on the left while you face the porch.

(v) **GPS & Compass :** Both GPS and compass effortlessly indicate the north and are quite easy to use.

FINDING OWN POSITION ON MAP

On a map own position may be found by :

(i) Inspection Method (ii) Compass (iii) Continuous Map Reading

(i) **Inspection Method :** We can easily find own position by tallying the ground features to map features. Permanent structures and buildings like Railway Stations, Bus Stands, Bridges, Rivers, Roads and Milestones are very helpful in this.

(ii) **Compass :** Mark 2 or 3 features which are common on both map and gound. Take the bearings on these features by compass. Convert this magnetic bearing into grid bearing and find out the back bearing of it. Now draw lines with the help of service protractor. The intersection of these lines on the map indicates your own position. This method is also called the Resection method.

(iii) **Continuous Map Reading :** Keep reading and observing the map when you start your journey. Follow progress on the map by measuring bearings and distance. Also compare other physical features common to both map and ground to know your position on map.

MAP TO GROUND

The methods used to identify objects from map to ground are :

1. **Bearing and Distance Method :** With the help of bearing and distance, find out own position. Find out the distance of the object to be identified on ground with the help of a scale on the map. Using service protractor, find out the bearing of the object and convert it into magnetic bearing. Set the magnetic bearing on compass and look for the object in the given bearing. Estimating the distance on ground, the object will be identified.
2. **Direction and Distance Method :** Draw a line on the map between own position and object to be identified. Calculate its distance and using any of the following methods find the direction of the object :

(i) With the help of a slide rule find the ground direction of the object.
(ii) With the help of two points on the map estimate the ground direction.
(iii) Place a foot ruler/pencil at own position and align it with line of the map.
(iv) Place a pin each at own position and at the object on the map. Align both pins and find general direction.

3. **By Estimation Method :** In this method measuring bearing, distance and direction, object is identified with the help of other details in the proximity of the object.

GROUND TO MAP

The method of identifying objects from ground to map is :

Intersection Method : To find out the objects which are at a larger distance or in hilly terrain, intersection method is used. In this method, help of minimum two prominent objects are taken which can be easily identified on the ground. Lines are drawn from the prominent objects to the object to be identified on map. This method is used when we cannot estimate exact distance. Intersection is done :

By Compass Bearing : Take the bearing of the object from two known prominent objects. Draw the lines on the map. The object will be in the proximity of the intersection of the two lines. Magnetic bearing is found by two methods:

(i) **By Compass :** Take the forward bearing from known object.
(ii) **By Back Bearing :** In war, in case we intercept the enemy's transmission, with the help of the fall of the shot we can find out the location by working out back bearing.

NAVIGATION PARTY

The group of soldiers or party that march at night is called navigation party. The soldier who leads the group is called the guide.

When a navigation party moves at night with the help of compass and night march chart, the items required by the navigation party are:

(i) White cloth
(ii) Frosted torch
(iii) Marching chart
(iv) Luminous stick
(v) White lime/chalk
(vi) Set compass as per bounds
(vii) Stone pebbles for measuring steps

The composition of navigation party :

(i) **Guide :** He carries a luminous stick and a compass set to a given bearing.
(ii) **Assistant Guide :** He has a white piece of cloth at his back for identification and a stick to measure depth of nala/pits.
(iii) **Recorder :** He carries additional compass already set on given bearing, night march chart and stone pebbles. He measures the distance.

(iv) **Scouts :** Number of scouts could be from 2 to 4 depending upon the route and tasks.

The points to be kept in mind by all members of a navigation party :

(i) Party must ensure safety and security.

(ii) To read night march chart use frosted torch.

(iii) While marching keep interperson distance in mind.

(iv) Smoking or using any kind of light is strictly prohibited.

(v) While marching do not cough, talk or make any noise.

NIGHT MARCH CHART

A navigational party also possesses a chart for assistance. It basically shows the initial and destination points of a march. The points mentioned below should be taken care of while making a night march chart:

S.No.	Object	Conventional Sign	Distance	Degree
1.	Temple			
2.	Well		250 M	60
3.	Bridge	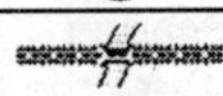	300 M	30
4.	Track Junction		400 M	15
5.	Start Point (Survey Tree)	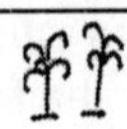	500 M	25

(i) Chart should be made on blank, clean paper.

(ii) Soft lead pencil should be used while preparing a night march chart.

(iii) The distances should be written in yards or meters.

(iv) The symbols, signs, numerals, words etc. should be drawn or written in thick line and good shading, so that these can be read in dim light even.

(v) The directional angle should always be mentioned in magnetic directional value.

(vi) The initial point should be written at the bottom and destination point must be written at the top of the chart.

Point To Point March

Navigation During Day: The methods used for navigation during day are:

1. **With Map Only:** In this method set the map and find your own position. Then, find out the position of the object. Note important landmarks in the vicinity of the object. Also find out the distance of the object. Finally find out the best route to reach the object. While marching, keep comparing the major landmarks en route. Distance can be measured with the help of steps. 100 metre corresponds to 120 steps approximately. On reaching the object, confirm its correctness with help of other details in the proximity.

2. **Marching without Map:** There are two methods of marching without map:
   (i) **With Compass:** In order to use compass for marching point to point, there is a necessity to set the bearing on the compass.
   (ii) **Without Compass:** In this method you are required to march based on your memory power. Points to be kept in mind are:
   - Before marching, recognize the object carefully and take note of other landmarks in the proximity.
   - Choose best route to the object and convert distance into steps/ paces.
   - Take note of all the intermediate landmarks and their distances.
   - En route, ensure you are marching correctly.
   - Be careful while measuring distance in steps.
   - If you deviate while crossing an obstacle, choose a mark across the obstacle. After crossing the obstacle come in line of the mark and recommence marching.
   - If you reach a wrong place, come back to the start point.

Navigation During Night: When a navigation party moves at night with the help of compass and night march chart, this is called night march. It can be:

1. **During Moonlit Night:** If you have a compass, you can select two important land marks on the given bearing in a line and March on the same bearing and line. Repeat this, till you reach the object.
2. **Starlit Night:** Select a prominent star at 30 degree on the horizon on the given bearing. Select a landmark in line of the star. March in line of the star and the land mark for approximately 15 minutes. Then select another star in the same bearing and repeat till you reach the object.
3. **Cloudy Night:** Make a person march on the given bearing to a distance where he can be seen. Then the person holding compass marches, measuring the distance. First person is made to march again in the given bearing and the process is repeated till he reaches the object.

VISIBILITY

To see two different places simultaneously is called the visibility.

Line of Sight

The straight imaginary line which connects points whose visibility is to be found out, is called the line of sight.

Methods to Find out the Visibility

1. By inspection 2. By calculation 3. By calculating gradient

By applying inspection method one can find out the visibility, with the help of inspecting the map. Connect both these points, by drawing a line.

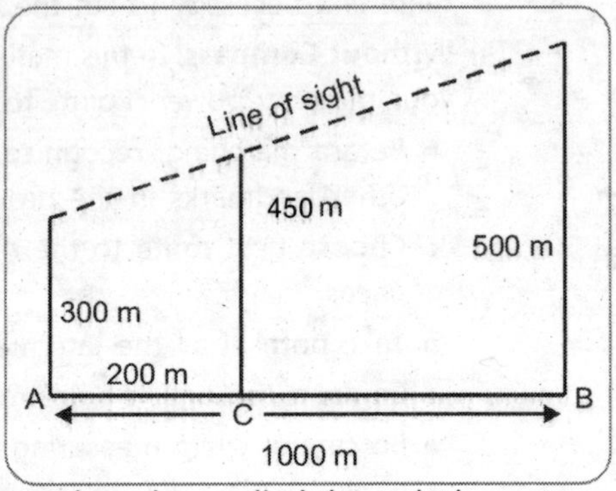

If the contour lines between the two places on map symbolises either the concave slope or uniform slope, then both the places will be simultanuously visible. Hence, the visibility can be traced out.

The calculation method is the easiest method to find out the visibility and can be applied through these steps:

1. Connect the two places with the help of a line and find out its distance from the sea level.
2. Find out the height of the place in between the two places (whose visibility is to be traced) on the line of sight.

The calculating gradiant method compares the gradients of all the places with the gradient of 'line of sight'. If the gradient of the 'line of sight' has more slopes than the gradients of all the places, then both the places will be visible, otherwise not.

❖ ❖ ❖

CHAPTER

21 Field Craft & Battle Craft

FIELD CRAFT

Field Craft is an art of making the best use of the available ground and the weapon. While applying field craft soldiers can attack the enemies in a smarter way.

The Advantages of Field Craft : Useful in tackling minor tactical problems without confusion but the basic knowledge of field signals, section & platoon formations is essential.

Essential Parts of Field Craft

1. Judging distances
2. Covers
3. Camouflage and Concealment
4. Indication and recognition of targets
5. Fire and movement
6. Field signals

JUDGING DISTANCES

As we know, every weapon has a shooting range and impact of its own. Therefore, it is essential to determine the distance between the weapon (or shooter) and its target for appropriate firing. The distance can be found out by the following methods:

1. **Unit of Measurment Method:** In this method, we take any of the simple and convenient unit (say 100 yards) and determine the distance between the target and the shooter in multiples of 100 yards.
2. **Appearance Method:** Same object may appear differently at different distances. A human being may appear :
   - (i) at a distance of 200 yds – the full human picture with all parts visible.
   - (ii) at a distance of 250 yds – a person at a kneeling position is covered by the foresight blade.
   - (iii) at a distance of 300 yds – face turns diminished (hazy)
   - (iv) at a distance of 400 yds – face can not be recognised, the foresight blade covers a standing person.

(v) at a distance of 500 yds – the body over the shoulders looks comparatively taper. The body movements can be noticed.

(vi) at a distance of 600 yds – the human head appears like a point and body below the shoulders looks taper.

3. **Bracketing:** In this method, we take the maximum and minimum estimation of distance and then take its average.
4. **Section Average Method:** In this method, distance is judged by each soldier. These distances are summed up and then divided by the total number of soldiers to get the average.
5. **Key Range Method:** In this method, anything whose distance is known, is taken for help, to determine the distance, like—milestones, telephone poles, etc.
6. **Halving Method:** In this method, the "half" distance of an object is guessed and then it is made "double" to find the desired distance.

There may arise certain problems in measuring the distance:

1. When distances are overestimated, the reasons are—
   (i) Non-availability of proper light.
   (ii) Sun, just before the eyes
   (iii) Judging through a valley
   (iv) Observer, in a lying position
   (v) Small size of the object (target) as compared to rest of the objects around
2. When distances are underestimated, the reasons are—
   (i) Bright light
   (ii) Sun behind the observer
   (iii) Looking in upward direction from lying down the hill
   (iv) Big size of the object (target) as compared to rest of the objects around.

COVERS

A cover symbolizes a place where a soldier can hide himself and attack the enemy easily, without being captured. This is the place, where movements are easily conducted and which is an ideal destination for rest and relaxation "for a long time". In a cover, an enemy can not watch or attack its counter (rival).

Covers are of two types:

1. **Cover from view:** Hiding oneself behind bushes, plants and broken grounds, is the cover from view.
2. **Cover from fire:** Hiding oneself behind a wall or huge tree.

The proper manners to use cover are:

(i) Whenever possible look through the cover and not over it.

(ii) If it is not possible to look through the cover, look round it rather than over it.

(iii) If it is necessary to look over the cover, avoid breaking skyline.

(iv) The skyline is the worst background you could choose, but if you cannot avoid observing over the cover and against the skyline, use something to break your silhouette.

(v) When firing from inside a building, keep well back making use of the shadow.

(vi) A rough, dark and irregular background which matches your clothing, provides considerable cover from view.

(vii) Isolated cover is dangerous because it will attract attention of the enemy and can be easily indicated in a fire order.

CAMOUFLAGE AND CONCEALMENT

Camouflage is the art of making use of artificial articles to achieve concealment.

Concealment is hiding oneself from enemy's view and fire, with the help of natural background.

The various factors which aid recognition are :

(a) Shape, (b) Shadow, (c) Silhouette, (d) Surface, (e) Spacing, (f) Movement, (g) Shine, (h) Position, (i) Contrast, and (j) Noise, sound and activity.

The fundamental ways of concealing activities:

(i) **Hiding :** It is complete concealment of an object by placing a screen between the object and the observer.

(ii) **Blending :** It is the arrangement of camouflage materials on, over and around the object so that it appears to be part of the surroundings. The aim is to prevent detection of the object by a change in natural appearance of the position.

(iii) **Deceiving :** Deceiving simulates an object or disguises it so that it appears to be different.

Principles of Good Camouflage and Concealment

1. Conceal shine & shape
2. Make use of shadow
3. Avoid skyline
4. Slow movement
5. Merge with natural colour and surroundings
6. Avoid unnecessary movements

7. Avoid reflections in water
8. Change the camouflage articles according to the suitability of time and circumstances.

INDICATION AND RECOGNITION OF TARGETS

In the battle field, it is essential to make aware the soldiers about the surface symbols and other marks of indications, so that the soldier may fire on the appropriate target.

But, sometimes it becomes difficult because there can be many things of similar shape, which makes the indication really tough. Before indicating the target, a soldier is made aware about the types of ground, limits of section and the famous landmark of the place.

The ground is divided into three parts :

1. Foreground - upto 300 yds
2. Middle distance - 300 to 500 yds
3. Distance - more than 500 yds

Types of Ground

1. Broken ground – affords good cover but slow movement
2. Dead ground – not visible to the firer because of depth
3. Open ground – flat observation, easier and quicker movement
4. High ground – provides good movement, observation and field of fire
5. Low ground – not as deep as dead ground
6. Slopy ground – which has a slope for the required movement

The common mistakes in the use of ground are that :

(i) Carelessness by troops while making a reconnaissance, such as unfolding a map in the open or not using a covered approach.
(ii) Unnecessary movement in a position overlooked by the enemy.
(iii) Using conspicuous landmarks such as isolated trees, bushes or cottages.
(iv) Halting troops near road or track junctions or other mapped features which are always registered as targets by the enemy.
(v) Bad track discipline.
(vi) Failure to guard against enemy air observation.

INDICATION OF SIMPLE TARGETS

1. By simple naming
   e.g., No. 1 Section-300-factory
2. By General line of direction
   e.g., No. 1 Section-3-half left-hut

3. By last target
   e.g., No. 1 Section-30 last target slightly right-lane tree
4. Indication by description-simple famous targets are spoken streight away
   e.g., Section bridge
5. Indication by direction or range of both
   e.g., By direction - No. 1 Section, half right, mosque
   By range - No. 1 Section, 300 mosque
   By both - No. 1 Section, half right 300, mosque

INDICATION OF DIFFICULT TARGETS

1. **The Reference Point Method**
   e.g., No. 1 Section, 300, half left, temple, name of the temple (help mark) Slightly right, Banyan tree
2. **By General line of direction**
   e.g., No. 1 Section, 500, look forward, single tree, name of the tree, slightly-left, three trees.
3. **The Clock Ray Method**
   Here, the "help mark" is considered 12 o'clock and then target is indicated.
   e.g., No. 1 Section, 600, half left, bridge 3 o'clock enemy's post.
4. **The Degree Method**
   The 'Degree' is taken as a help factor to simplify the target.
   e.g., No. 1 Section, 400, half right, bridge, 4 o'clock, 5° tree, enemy's post.

Hand Angles

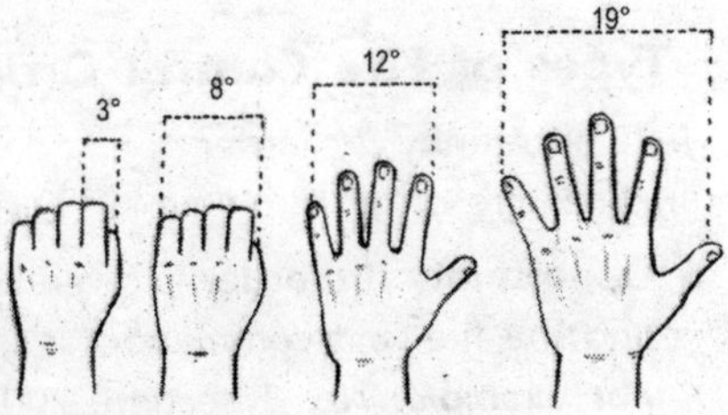

This is a rough method which is sufficiently accurate for practical purposes. The various degree measure-ments are given in the diagrams. Remember to keep the left hand fully stretched and tilt it in the required direction. As the size of hand varies considerably the figures given are approximate only. Each cadet, with the help of a degree scale should check his hand for degrees.

FIRE AND MOVEMENTS

The objective behind fire discipline is to produce an efficient and wise fire unit commander, so that he may achieve the target. Fire discipline asks for more results in less time.

- **Fire Unit**

It is a small body of men, usually a section firing under the command of a man.

- **Fire Unit Commander**

The man who commands the men or section to fire, is called the "fire unit commander".

- **Fire Control**

Its object is to enable commander of a fire unit to direct fire of his unit to the enemy, to achieve maximum effect.

- **Fire Order**

It is a sort of command given in three different ways:

1. **Plan order** includes the command given by higher officials.
2. **Fire direction order** includes the command received by the fire unit commander by his higher officials (seniors).
3. **Fire control order** includes the command given by "fire unit commander" to his men to regulate the fire of his group or section.

- ***Arc of Fire***

The area within which the fire unit will engage the enemy is called "arc of fire".

SEQUENCE OF FIRE CONTROL ORDER

1. G - Group i.e., rifle or LMG group.
2. R - Range i.e., distance of target
3. I - Indication of target (description of target)
4. T - Type of fire (single shot OR burst)

Types of Fire Control Orders

(i) Opportunity fire order
(ii) Preparatory fire order
(iii) Brief fire order
(iv) Full fire order

- **Opportunity fire order** is given on such a time, when the enemy is hidden and the fire unit commander is unable to locate him.
  For example: No. 3 section, 200, enemy is hidden behind the collapsed building, whosoever see, fire.
- **Preparatory fire order** is commanded on seeing the activities of the enemy.
  For example: No. 2 section, look ahead, enemy is approaching, wait for orders.
- **Brief fire order** is commanded when enemy either runs from left or right, or attacks through any of the sides.
  For example: Bren group, sight up, right enemy, fire.
- **Full fire order** is commanded at the time, when enemy approaches in our range.
  For example: Bren group, 200 half left, enemy near the temple, burst fire.

Precautions, while giving "fire control order"

These commands (orders) should be :

1. brief and clear (clarity of words)
2. this much loud that each and every soldier may hear it properly
3. in the form of "order"
4. given, one after another, with a little pause, so that everybody (soldiers) may follow them easily and appropriately.

The ideal points for selection of Fire positions are that:

(i) Provide cover from fire.
(ii) Provide cover from view.
(iii) Afford a good view of the ground to be watched or target to be engaged.
(iv) Provide room in which to use the weapon freely.
(v) Have a covered approach.
(vi) Be easy to advance from.

Fire and Movement

The primary aim of infantry is to close in with the enemy and destroy him. The aim of getting close is achieved by making skilful use of ground. A clever enemy will however, deny you the use of such ground which you may need. When such a cover is denied by the enemy, we may have to make movement in open.

Once we are forced to make movement in open, a part of our force will have to fire on enemy position and force him to keep his head down. This would render the enemy incapable of bringing down aimed fire at us while we are on the movement. This process of keeping one element on the ground to give covering fire, while the other element is on movement, is called fire and movement. This is the basic tactics of all infantry and mechanised operations.

When To Use Fire And Movement Tactics: Fire and movement tactics may be used in following circumstances:

(i) The enemy has opened SA fire which is effective.
(ii) When own troops have seen the enemy first - within 400 to 700 meters.
(iii) When the enemy is known or suspected to be in a certain area, then fire and movement tactics may be adopted when the troops reach within the effective range of enemy weapons/observation.
(iv) To cross obstacles by day or by night, e.g. nullahs/rivers.

Basic Considerations: There are five basic considerations for fire and movement. These are as under:

(i) **No movement on exposed ground without covering fire:** The Advantages of covering fire are obvious, but this does not mean that fire will be brought down continuously when you are moving. Whenever you have ground providing you cover, you must use it. Whenever you have to move in open, fire must be brought down on the enemy in small bursts to keep his head down.

(ii) **Control by the Commander:** The section can remain a viable force only when it is under the control of its commander. Otherwise, it is likely that the required fire support will not be brought down at the required place and time. In a section, control is exercised by voice command and hand signals. As a rule, section commander must keep his section within range of voice or visible control.

(iii) **Wide Angle of Fire:** The angle of covering fire from direct firing weapons should be as wide as possible without loss of control or time. It is to ensure that own troops are not coming under effective fire of own fire spell. It also ensures that the fire support is provided till as late as possible so that assault troops are able to close in with the enemy.

(iv) **Full use of Available Cover:** Full use should be made of cover provided by the ground. Various types of cover have already been taught to the cadets.

(v) **Optimum use of all Available Weapons:** All available weapons should be used for producing covering fire.

Movements

At the time of war, soldiers use variety of movements to escape from the vigil of enemy. A knowledge of how to move correctly and how to use ground is important to enable soldiers and group of soldiers to close in with the enemy. The movement is of two kinds :

(a) Movement without arms	(b) Movement with arms
(i) The monkey run	(i) The ghost walk
(ii) The leopard crawl	(ii) The monkey run
(iii) The walk	(iii) The leopard crawl
(iv) The roll	(iv) The moderate walk
(v) Crawl through abdomen	(v) The roll
(vi) The kitten crawl	
(vii) The cat walk	

Points to be remembered while making movements :

(i) Move from cover-to-cover and make use of natural camouflage. Stop, observe and listen from bound-to-bound and do not keep moving forward the whole time.

(ii) Watch your front and flanks.

(iii) Crawl slows the movement and hinders observation, therefore crawl only when you must. After crawling for some distance stop, listen and observe and then crawl further.

(iv) Weapons must always be kept ready for use.

(v) Look carefully and all round for enemy.

(vi) Double across small gaps.

(vii) If shot at, drop and crawl away to a side.
(viii) Check equipment for noise.
(ix) Always consider an alternative route.
(x) Do not disturb the birds, if this can be helped.

Common Mistakes

The wrong use of ground may lead to casualties and loss of surprise; some common mistakes are:

(i) Carelessness by troops while making a reconnaissance, such as unfolding a map in the open or not using a covered approach to an Observation Post.
(ii) Unnecessary movement in a position overlooked by the enemy.
(iii) Using conspicuous landmarks such as isolated trees, bushes or cottages.
(iv) Halting troops near road or track junctions or other mapped features which are always registered as targets by the enemy.
(v) Bad track discipline.
(vi) Failure to guard against enemy air observation.

BATTLE CRAFT

Battle craft is nothing but set of drills which are essential for conduct of successful operations in the battle field. These battle drills are very useful in tackling minor tactical problems. They save time, ensure rapid action and avoid confusion. Knowledge of field signals and section and platoon formations, however, is essential in the execution of various battle drills. Battle Craft includes the following subjects:

(i) Field Signals
(ii) Section Formations
(iii) Fire control orders
(iv) Fire and move
(v) Section battle drills

FIELD SIGNALS

Sometimes in the battle field, there needs a complete silence, then "signals" are applied in place of verbal communication. These signals are thrown with the help of hands, rifles and "whistling sound" etc.

Hand Signals

1. **Deploy:** Right arm fully extended above head and waved from side to side, palm open.
2. **Advance:** Stretch the right arm fully backward, palm facing the front and then move forward below the shoulder.

3. **Halt:** The right arm is raised to the full extent above the head.
4. **Follow me:** Raise the right arm and move the arm back to front to lowering a bit in front.
5. **Double march:** Bend the right arm from the side towards the shoulder and move it away from and towards the shoulder quickly, many times.
6. **About turn:** The arm is bent and circles above the head and drop the hand down.
7. **Turn About:** Right arm raised and bent above head.
8. **Close:** Take the right hand (fingers closed) on the head and then drop the hand in the direction of the place where you want to close your men.
9. **Change Direction:** Right arm raised to front in line with shoulder. Body then turned in required direction.
10. **Right turn:** Extend the left arm forward parellel to ground, move body and arm to the right at an angle of 90°, then drop the arm and join the left foot with right.
11. **Quick march:** Extend the right arm forward parallel to the ground, elbow adjacent and plam open.
12. **Run:** Close the palm of right hand (punch) and move it in upward and downward direction again and again.
13. **Spread:** Stretch the full right arm above the head and move it in "to and fro" motion and circular motion, keep palm open.
14. **Enemy is approaching:** Open both the hands, keep both the palms on the waist line.
15. **Enemy LMG firing:** Right hand thumb down signal.
16. **Attack:** Indicate the punch in the direction of attack.
17. **Understood signal:** Salute.
18. **Accumulate on meeting place:** Symbolise the plus-sign (+) by keeping hands on the waist line.
19. **Closed to Rendezvous:** Close sign followed by both hands clasped in front of body at waist level.
20. **Infantry obstacle ahead:** Both hands crossed in front of body at the waist, palm open downwards.
21. **Single file formation:** Stretch one arm behind the body.
22. **File formation:** Strech both the arms at the back.
23. **Arrow head formation:** Stretch both the arms at the back at an angle of 45°.
24. **Diamond formation:** Keep the crossed fingers on the head.
25. **Spear head formation:** Extend the left arm forward and right arm backward.
26. **Extended line formation:** Stretch both the arms in sideways direction.

Positions of FIELD SIGNALS

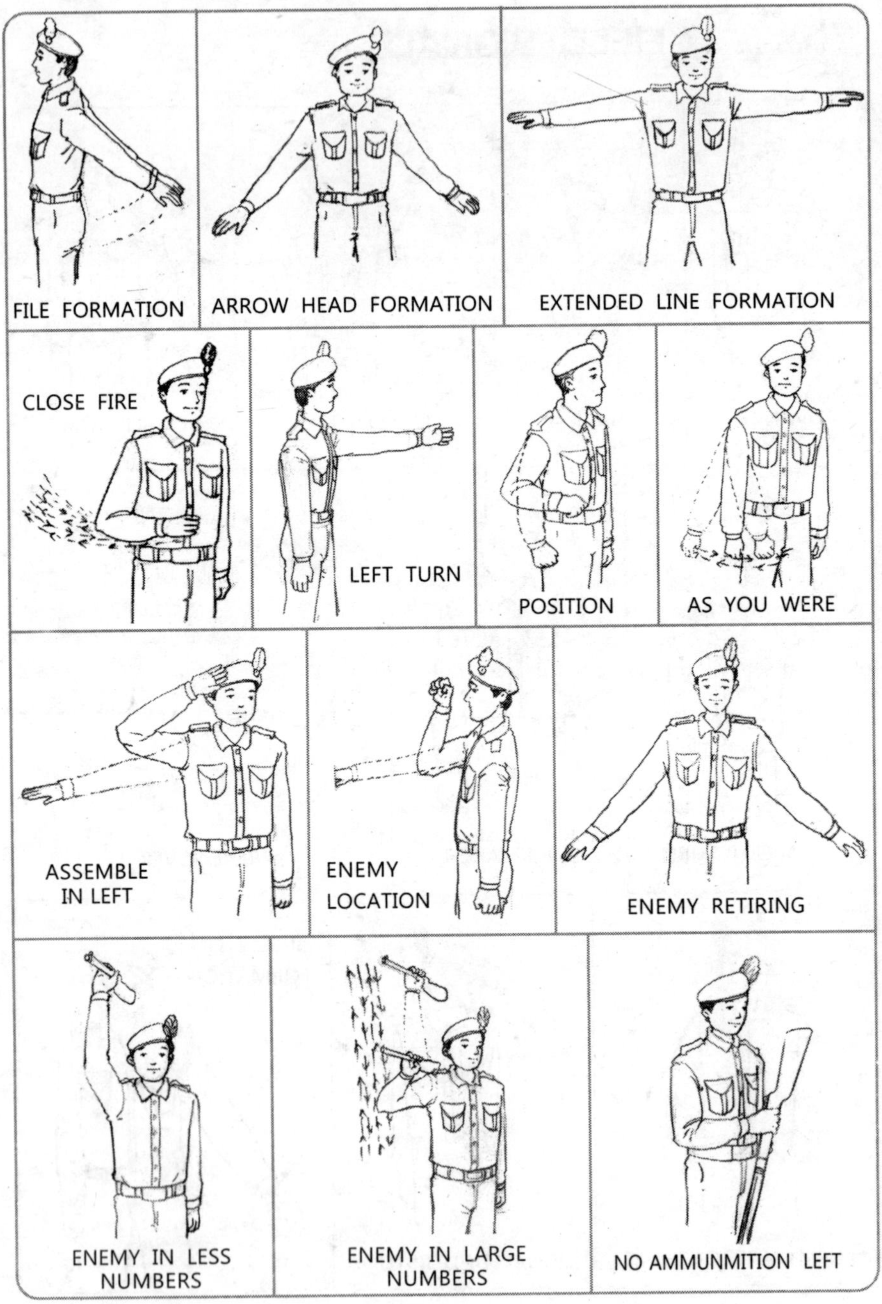
FILE FORMATION
ARROW HEAD FORMATION
EXTENDED LINE FORMATION
CLOSE FIRE
LEFT TURN
POSITION
AS YOU WERE
ASSEMBLE IN LEFT
ENEMY LOCATION
ENEMY RETIRING
ENEMY IN LESS NUMBERS
ENEMY IN LARGE NUMBERS
NO AMMUNMITION LEFT

Arm Signals

1. **Enemy in Sight:** Rifle held above the head parallel to the small number muzzle in the direction of the enemy.
2. **Enemy in less strength:** Raise the rifle over the head and keep the barrel towards the direction of enemy coming.
3. **Enemy in huge strength:** Raise the rifle above the head and keep the barrel towards the direction of enemy approaching. Move the rifle up and down.
4. **Enemy can not be seen:** Keep the rifle straight (vertical) over the shoulder.
5. **No Ammunition:** Keep the barrel of the gun, down towards the earth.
6. **Advance:** Raise both the arms above, making a letter "U".

Whistle Signals

1. **For danger:** Give long and short whistles, alternatively with pauses.
2. **For alertness:** Give a short whistle.
3. **Enemy aircraft:** Give very short whistles, after pauses.
4. **Aircraft gone:** Give two long whistles after the interval of 5 seconds.

Field Signals as Means of Giving Orders

Field signals are alternate means of giving orders and to control troops when voice control is not possible. Control over troops deployed can be done better by field signals than by voice control. There are various occasions when voice control is not possible. They are:

1. Battle noises
2. Need for silence
3. Intervening distances are too large.

Field Signals by Day

Some of the visual signals used during the day are flags and mercury coated mirrors. Flags are very effectively used by Navy on board a ship.

1. Flags: (Red, Green and White flags)
2. Mercury coated mirrors
3. Smoke
4. Miscellaneous: Various signals can be improvised and pre-arranged as under:
   - (i) Clothes superficially hung out to dry.
   - (ii) Hurricane lamp, kept in the window.
   - (iii) Flashing of torch is used as Morse Code.
   - (iv) Applying various colours/signs on forehead and arms.

Field Signals by Night

Some of the field signals that can be used at night are:

1. Pre decided signals on a walkie talkie
2. Click by fingers
3. Clicks by using tongue
4. Whistle by the mouth
5. Use of rope
6. Use of colour light
7. Use of blacked out torch
8. Firing of weapon

SECTION FORMATION

The different sections have to be divided into several formations or shapes in certain conditions.

It basically depends upon the conditions of soldiers on land, firing from the enemy's side, excessive firing from the counter part, and the control of section commander over the section, etc.

In a Section Formation, the distance between the two soldiers should at least be 15-25 yds. They should not move in a line but should spread in a zig-zag manner.

The common formations are mentioned below:

1. **Single File :** It has a good control, good speed and suitable for fighting through pass and defile. The frontal firing leads to more damage.

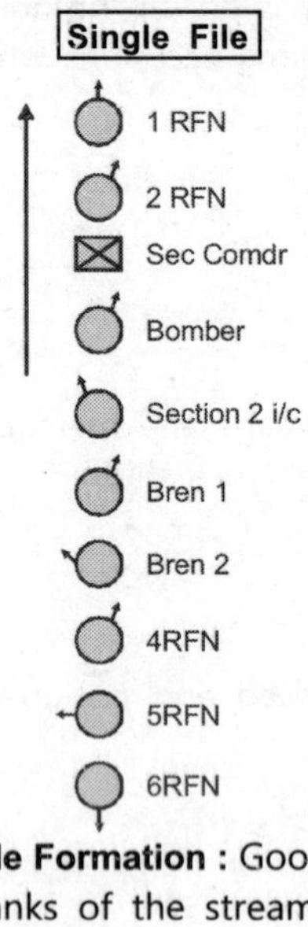

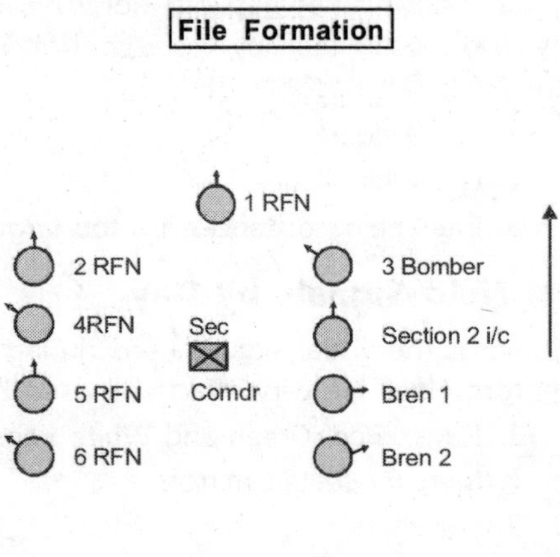

2. **File Formation :** Good control and good for moving through the roads and banks of the streams. Frontal firing leads to excessive destruction. Not suitable to fire on the enemy.

3. **Diamond Formation :** Good control, proper security, easy to fire.

Diamond Formation

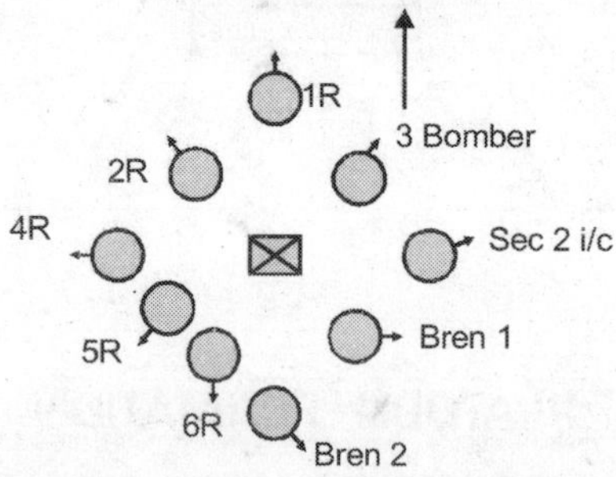

4. **Arrow Head Formation :** Good to move in open space, good depth, suitable to fire on enemy. Less destruction from the frontal firing. Control lesser than in Diamond formation.

Arrow Head formation

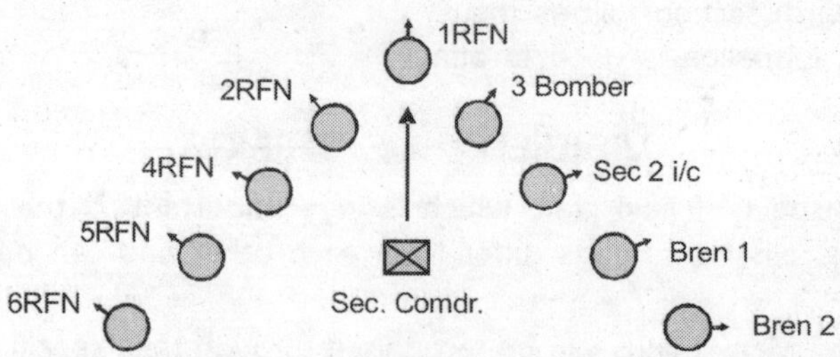

5. **Spear Head Formation :** Good depth, difficult control, less vulnerable.

Spear Head Formation

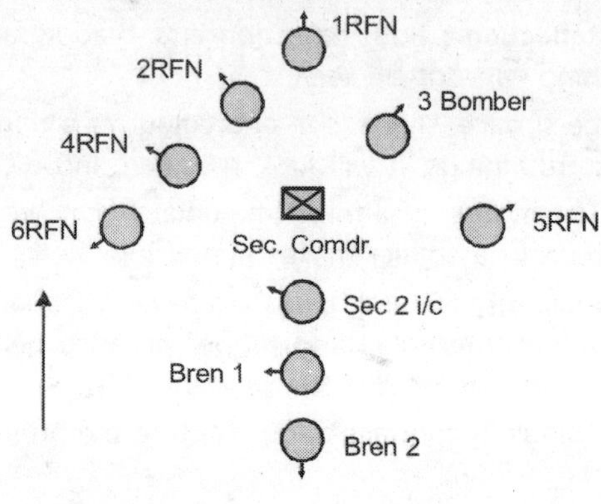

6. **Extended Line Formation :** Used in final attack, good for severe war, difficult control, less depth and more damage in case of side firing.

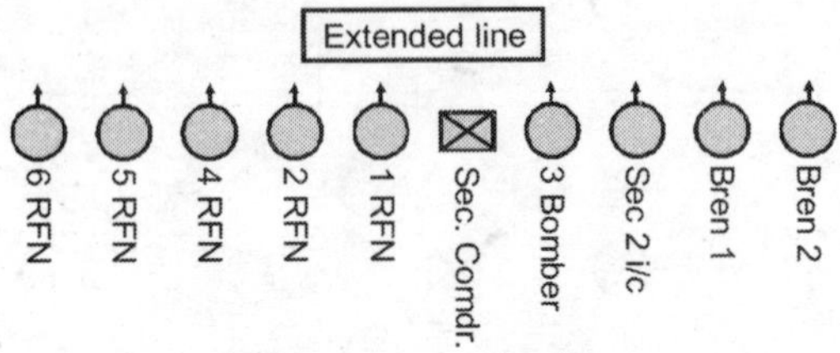

PLATOON FORMATION

A platoon may have the following formations:

1. **One up Formation :** In this formation, one of the sections of platoon moves ahead while two sections move behind this. This formation is good for field signal - Advance.
2. **Two up Formation :** In this formation, two sections move ahead and one (the third) section follows them.

   This formation is good to attack.

VISIBILITY OF THINGS

One more aspect of field craft, which is very important, is the "visibility of things". This tells how things differ from each other and can be recognised well.

1. **Shape :** Many things can be recognised through their specific shapes and sizes and when these articles are particularly different from the things of our own surroundings.
2. **Shine :** Eyes are very much sensetive towards the shine of anything.
3. **Shadow or Reflection :** Both reflection and shadow attract at the most, even if the thing can not be seen.
4. **Texture :** If the surface, shade, size and colour of a thing is different from the normal surroundings, it will look specified and distinct.
5. **Movement :** The motion of a thing immediately catches the attention. The slight movement of a soldier makes him visible.
6. **Alignment (Spacing) :** Natural things are never at equal distance from one another. Therefore, the equal and proper distance between the vehicles, soldiers or aircrafts etc. attract the senses.
7. **Silhouette :** Things in contrast colour capture the attention, *e.g.* diamond in coal or ants in flour.

PROCESS OF BATTLING

The battle procedure is the method of preparation of war. In this regard, a commander makes plans, give commands and makes a list of the "functions" of the war.

The forces are sent to him, for fullfilling this objective. His aim is to:

1. Prepare (physically and mentally) each individual (soldier).
2. Control, minimise or eradicate the nervousness or anxiety of the crew.
3. Save time.
4. Encourage the soldiers by inspiring them.

BATTLE DRILL

In Battle Drill, a soldier is intimated about the nature of work, he is supposed to handle. The battle drill is divided into four sections for maintaining the pace of work, during the warfare:

1. **R** (recce) group
2. **O** (order) group
3. **F** (fighting) group
4. **T** (transport) group

Significance of Battle Drill

A. Thorough Information (Appreciation)

A huge success at war depends on this factor. Appreciation includes several kinds of investigation, inspection and criticism, etc. This factor should follow this procedure :

1. **Aim** to destroy the place (unit) of enemy.
2. **Factors** to collect information on several factors.

   For example: complete information on own unit and rival unit (enemy), types of ground, time, hiding places, staying places, food, weather, etc.
3. **Paths** or the roads and ways to be followed by own unit and enemy.
4. **Plan of action** or a layout for the attack and defence is prepared.

B. Fire and Movement

This factor has a significant role to play in 'Army' exploring war-skills. It means, when a unit moves ahead, then the other unit provides 'covering fire'.

Principles of 'Fire'

1. One bullet, one enemy
2. Target 'covering fire' on enemy's head
3. The time slot between the termination of covering fire and attack should be very-very less.

Principles of 'Movement'

1. Move in organised groups.
2. Move in appropriate formations.
3. Move in such a way that only one foot touches the ground at one time.

The basic considerations for fire and movement are :

(i) There should be no exposed ground without covering fire.
(ii) Control by the commander.
(iii) The angle of covering fire from direct firing weapons should be as wide as possible without loss of control or time.
(iv) Full use should be made of all available cover. When cover is lacking the use of smoke (smoke grenade) should be considered.
(v) Full use should be made of all available weapons for covering fire.

It should be appreciated under the following headings :

(i) Fire positions (ii) Observation positions (iii) Cover from fire
(iv) Cover from view (v) Obstacles

C. Verbal Commands

The orders which are orally given by the commander to his junior are called verbal commands. A platoon commander commands the platoon and section commander commands his section during the warfare.

The verbal orders make the following series :

1. **Landmarks** – Helping marks
2. **Information** – Details, regarding the weapons of enemy
3. **Intention** – Modus operandi or execution of action
4. **Method** – Procedure to follow the intention
5. **Administration** – Responsible for the complete functioning of the unit
6. **Intercommunication** – Regarding the 'field signals'

The following points must be kept in mind while conveying verbal orders :

1. Commands must be conveyed in a clear-cut manner.
2. Orders should follow their chronology.
3. The commands should be given with complete patience and courage.
4. Unnecessary things (actions) should not be added in orders.
5. None of the soldiers should interrupt in between the orders.

SECTION BATTLE DRILL

In the battle field a section can be divided into four parts. The section battle drill is divided into four stages :

1. Action on coming under fire
2. Locate and neutralise enemy
3. Attack
4. Reorganisation.

***Drill to be followed for locating and neutralizing the enemy* :**

By Observation

Look in the area from which the 'thump' came. The time between the 'crack' and the 'thump' gives an indication of the range. If nothing is seen after about 30 seconds or so, it is very unlikely that enemy will be located by looking.

By Fire

The section commander will give a fire control order to a couple of rifleman to fire two shots each into likely cover. The rest of the section will observe their area of observation carefully. If there is no answer to fire, then the section commander should try another couple of rifleman at some other target. If there is still no enemy fire, either they are well trained or they have withdrawn.

By Movement

The section commander will order one or two men to get up and double forward about 10 yards to a different cover. He might do this again if it draws no fire. If the enemy troops are there, they must be extremely well trained not to fall for these tricks and start firing at such poor targets. (A man getting up and moving fast for about 10 yards is a very difficult target to hit). If there is still no enemy reaction then the section commander must continue the advance.

FIELD DEFENCE

The basic aim behind field defence is to organise the soldiers and weapons in such a way, that can terminate or control the movement and attack of enemy in a constructive manner. Defence has following two aspects :

1. Quick defence
2. Deliberate defence

Requirements of Good Defence

1. Selection of a good defence place
2. Depth
3. Concealment
4. Complete protection
5. Centralised power
6. Counter attack
7. Communication
8. Capture of deserted place

Defence Divisions

1. Covering troops
2. Covering patrols
3. Main defence
4. Mobile troops

Defence Obstacles

The following obstacles are used while taking deliberate defence :

1. Road blocks
2. Booby traps
3. Mines
4. Wire obstacles
5. Natural obstacles

Points to be borne in mind while constructing field defences :

1. Fire trenches should be close enough for the section commanders orders to be heard during battle.
2. Reverse slopes are a great aid to concealment and surprise, provided the field of fire is sufficient.
3. With the increasing efficiency of airburst missiles, overhead protection is important but needs good concealment and sound construction.
4. In open country, crawl trenches may have to be dug to allow movement between fire trenches.

The various field fortifications are :

(i) Bunker, (ii) Communication Trench, (iii) Fire Trench, (iv) Pill Box,

(v) Shelter Trench, (vi) Slit Trench, and (vi) Weapon Pit.

SENTRY

Sentry is a soldier to keep guard or to control access to a place. The sentry has a very important role to play in a war unit. During day time, a sentry guards alone and a couple of sentries are on-duty at night.

A sentry must know the following points :

1. Time to report (arrival) and time to leave (departure)
2. Complete information of the own unit and counter part (enemy) unit
3. Time of patrolling
4. Area watch and common (famous) landmarks of the area
5. A password (if given)

If a stranger approaches towards the sentry box—the sentry should inform the section commander. It he comes quite closer, the sentry can interrogate him, if he does not answer and tries to escape, the sentry can fire. If he raises his hands as ordered by sentry, he will interrogate him and inform the section commander. He (commander) will order the whole section. The soldiers will take their position and wait for the further action to be taken according to the commands.

PATROLLING

Patrolling is, to keep watch over an area by regularly walking or travelling around it. It is done to gain information about enemy and to protect own troops against enemy patrolling.

A patrol is a person or group sent to keep a watch over an area.

A successful patrolling depends on good leading, proper preparation, arrangements (management), determination of patrols, courage and bold approach.

Types of Patrolling

1. Recce Patrol
2. Protective Patrol

Recce Patrol Includes:

(i) Gaining information about enemy's position, disposition and intention.
(ii) Obtaining identification about enemy's position, disposition and intention.
(iii) Obtaining identification, topographical and technical information.
(iv) Denying information to enemy (if captured).
(v) Capturing "No Man's land".
(vi) Getting information about the habits and nature of enemy.

Protective Patrol includes:

(i) Preventing enemy patrols from getting information
(ii) Giving early warning of enemy approach and may even fight
(iii) Capturing "No Man's Land"

Stages of Patrolling

1. Preparation
2. Conduct
3. Debriefing (Conclusion)

Preparation

In preparation stage, the Patrol Master appoints the Patrol Commander and gives him the following details :

(i) Task
(ii) Wage of patrol
(iii) Information of own unit and counter (enemy) unit
(iv) Time to move for and come back from patrolling
(v) Paths for patrolling
(vi) Information regarding weapons and fire
(vii) Arrangements
(viii) Password

After receiving the above information, the men for patrolling are selected by the Patrol Commander. He provides them the required weapons, clothes, food etc., along with the necessary instructions.

All men selected for patrolling should be young, agile, healthy, courageous, daring and intelligent.

Then, the patrol-group is brought to the 'sand model' for grasping more about:

(i) Landmarks
(ii) Situation (of the enemy and own troop)
(iii) Mission (objective)
(iv) Wage of Patrol
(v) Time to go and come back
(vi) Paths to be followed
(vii) Bounds (leaping strides)
(viii) Formations
(ix) Halts
(x) Action while facing 'ambush'
(xi) Signals for patrolling
(xii) Passwords

The patrol party practices patrolling for at least thrice. The patrol master observes and inspects the group.

Conduct

In second stage, conduct gives details of, how patrolling is done:

(i) Walk on lower lands during night and on upper lands during day.
(ii) Move bound-to-bound (leaping strides)
(iii) Whatever is seen on the way during patrolling, must be memorised or written.
(iv) Do not smoke, speak or cough during patrolling.
(v) If meet enemy on the way, fire first and dominate them.
(vi) Avoid fighting on the way back.

When patrolling is over, relax for sometime. After some time, discuss the process of patrolling by putting queries and experience. Interrogate and bring conclusions (results).

Debrifing

Debrifing includes the following points:

(i) Patrol commander has the liberty to say or ask anything.
(ii) All patrols must be informed of something really important and even of the small details of patrolling.
(iii) The exhausted patrols must be given tea or coffee.
(iv) The interrogation of the patrols must be very sympathetic and humble.
(v) The patrolling reports can be multi-opinionated, but do not create arguments over them.
(vi) The patrol information must be clearly analysed.

The important points to be remembered by scouts are :

(i) Scouts should move from cover-to-cover using the correct methods of observation around cover.
(ii) Scouts should move by short bound in area where enemy is suspected.
(iii) A pair of scouts should move one behind another and should keep each other within easy voice control. The leading scout should often look over his shoulder to ensure that he has the second scout in visual contact. However, it is for the second scout to keep up.
(iv) Scouts must always be alert.
(v) Scouts must protect each other by placing themselves in such a way that they can cover each other by fire.
(vi) Scouts move as individuals making use of ground and cover.
(vii) Scouts must always remain in contact with the unit through the sub-units commander.
(viii) Communication are from front to rear. Contact is visual.
(ix) Scouts must so move on ground and take cover in such a way that they do not give away each others position.
(x) Scouts must not bunch together on bounds.

AMBUSH

An ambush is a surprise attack from a concealed position upon an unsuspecting moving or temporarily halted enemy. It is an operation that includes attack and run (escape). The best method of ambush is to confuse the enemy and attack him.

Objective

1. Obtain information of intelligence value
2. Destroy a number of enemies
3. Trouble the enemy up to such an extent that they apply majority of their troops

Types of Ambush

1. Opportunity ambush - without detailed planning
2. Deliberate ambush - laid on a pre-selected ground

Conduct of Ambush includes

(a) Composition (b) Execution

Composition

(i) **Scouts :** They are the men sent ahead of a section on the move. They are the eyes and ears of a sections. They give the information of arrival of enemy.
- They work in pair
- They move bound to bound
- They conduct all round observation
- They maintain distance

(ii) **Covering Party :** This is called the "firing party". Its main function is to harass the enemy and confuse them by firing on being ordered by the commander.

(iii) **Stops :** They prevent the enemy stuck in ambush from escaping.

(iv) **Reserve Party :** Its main function is to attack the enemy, search and seal their belongings etc, after the covering party's firing.

Execution

(i) Rehearse ambush plan
(ii) Use concealed approach
(iii) Men so positioned, can fire in killing area
(iv) Reserve to be correctly positioned
(v) A rendezvous for ambush party after action

FIELD ENGINEERING

Field engineering is the study of field fortification, obstacle planning including minefields, mine warfare, and stores and equipment relating to the same.

The various tasks performed by Field Engineers are :

(i) Laying of mine fields
(ii) Breaching of mine fields
(iii) Construction of field defences
(iv) Construction of tracks in mountains
(v) Construction/maintenance of border roads
(vi) Water supply to troops in the field, especially in deserts
(vii) Construction of Helipads where ever required
(viii) In Counter Insurgency Operation : 1. Detection, neutralisation and removal of IEDs and explosives. 2. Road opening etc for all type of traffic
(ix) Maintenance of essential services

To ensure the safety of their soldiers and weapons the defence forces have to fortify their defences. Field engineering is an essential part of it. Each and every soldier must learn about the various tools and techniques of field engineering.

Tools

The various types of digging tools used in field engineering are :

(i) Axe pick (ii) Shovel (iii) Entrenching Tool
(iv) Hammer (v) Crow Bar

Tools Drill

When the tools are issued from the store room the cadets move in a line and pick axe with the left hand and shovel with right hand.

Cadets should practise picking and keeping tools, 'Savdhan' and 'Vishram', and turn and march with tools. A regular rhythm should be maintained during the tools drill. The word of command in Axe Pick Drill are : Ready (Taiyar), Raise (Uthao), Strike (Maro), Break (Toro), Rake & Raise (Uthao). The word of command in Shovel Drill are : Ready (Taiyar), Strike & Fill (Maro aur Bharo), Swing & Throw (Ghumao aur Phenko).

KNOTS AND LASHES

The Purpose of Knots : Knots, bends and hitches are used to join two lashings together, to form a loop in a lashing, to make a stop on a lashing or to secure a lashing to a spar, or to make a hook.

The characteristics of Knots :

(i) Knot should be strong so that it does not open due to pull and pressure.
(ii) Knot should be in conformity to work and simple to use.
(iii) Knot should be easy to open.

Types of KNOTS

The diagrams self explain how the knot is tied. The letter "1" means the standing or secured end, and letter "2" means the free or untied end of the rope.

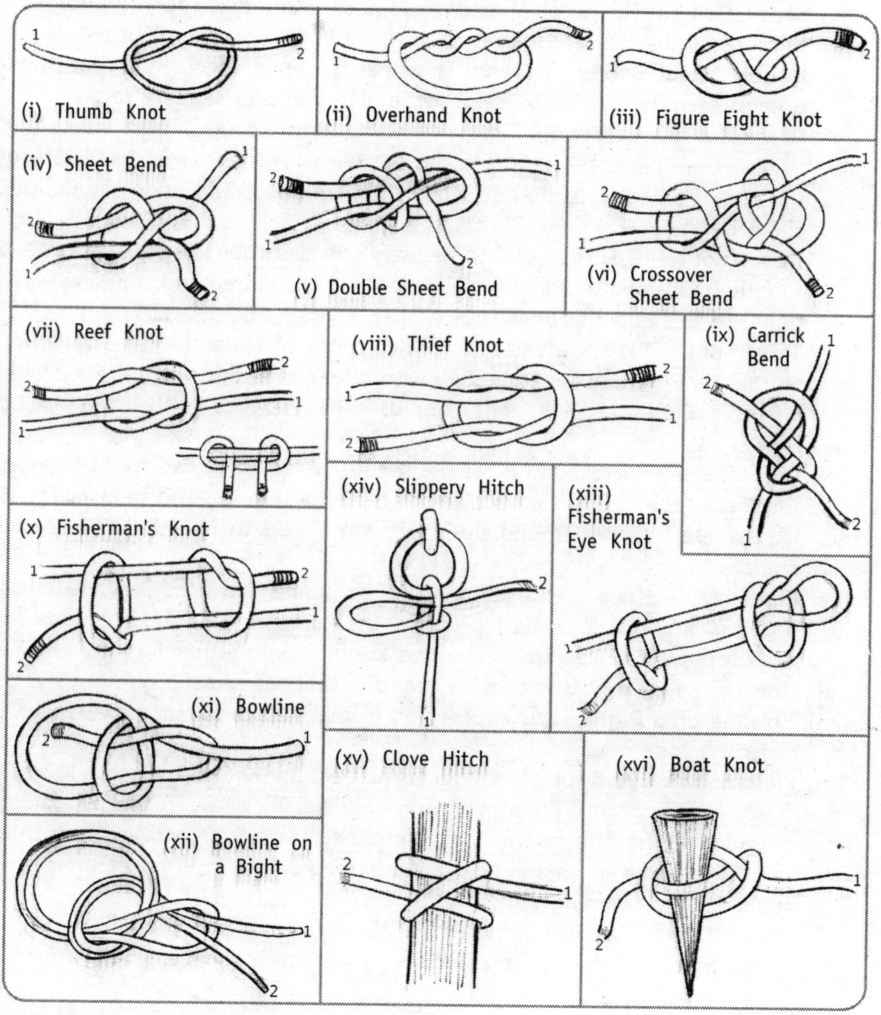

The various types of knots are :

(i) **Thumb Knot :** This knot is tied to make a stop on a rope end, to prevent the end from fraying or to stop the rope slipping through a sheave (wheel or pulley).

(ii) **Overhand Knot :** The overhand knot may be put to the same use as the thumb knot. It makes a better grip knot, and is easy to untie.

(iii) **Figure Eight Knot :** This knot is also used as the thumb knot. It is easy to untie, and more good looking.

(iv) **Sheet Bend :** This knot is tied to join or bend two ropes of unequal thickness together. The thicker rope is the bend on other rope.

(v) **Double Sheet Bend :** This knot is similar to single sheet bend, but gives greater security, It is also useful for joining wet and slippery ropes.

(vi) **Crossover Sheet Bend :** This knot holds more securely than either the single or double sheet bend and has occasional real uses such as fastening the eye of a flag to its halyard where the flapping might undo the double sheet bend.

(vii) **Reef Knot :** This knot is tied to securely join two ropes of equal thickness together. Observe the difference in position of the free and standing ends between this and the thief knot.

(viii) **Thief Knot :** This knot is tied to tie two ropes of equal thickness together so that they will appear to be tied with a reef knot, and will be retied with a true reef knot. This knot was often used by sailors to tie their sea chests, hence the name.

(ix) **Carrick Bend :** This bend is for the secure fastening of two ropes of even thickness together. It is particularly suitable for hawsers and steel cables. It can be readily undone and does not jam, as do many other bends and knots.

(x) **Fisherman's Knot :** This knot is tied for joining two springy materials together; suitable for wire, fishing gut or vines. Two thumb knots (one on each rope) are pulled tight. The two knots lock together firmly.

(xi) **Bowline :** This knot is tied to form a loop that will not slip on a rope end.

(xii) **Bowline on a Bight :** This knot is tied to make a double loop that will not slip on a rope end.

(xiii) **Fisherman's Eye Knot :** This knot is the best method of making a loop or eye in a fishing line. The strain is divided equally between the two knots.

(xiv) **Slippery Hitch :** This knot is very useful because of the ease with which it can be released in emergency. It holds securely for so long as there is a strain on the standing end.

(xv) **Clove Hitch :** This knot is tied for securing a rope to a spar. The hitch, if pulled taut, will not slip up or down on a smooth surface. This is a useful start for lashings.

(xvi) **Boat Knot :** This knot is a method of securing a rope to a hole pin or other small piece of wood on a boat. It is quickly released with ease.

(xvii) **Double Boat Knot :** In this knot a bight is simply passed through the ring and a marlin spike or other round piece of wood is put between the bight or the rope. Withdrawal of the spike quickly releases the knot easily.

Types of LASHES

These are the methods employed to tie poles with ropes, or any rope to a stationary object to securely hold it in its place.

The various types of lashes are :

(i) Square Lashing (ii) Frapping Turns
(iii) Short Splicing (iv) Long Splicing

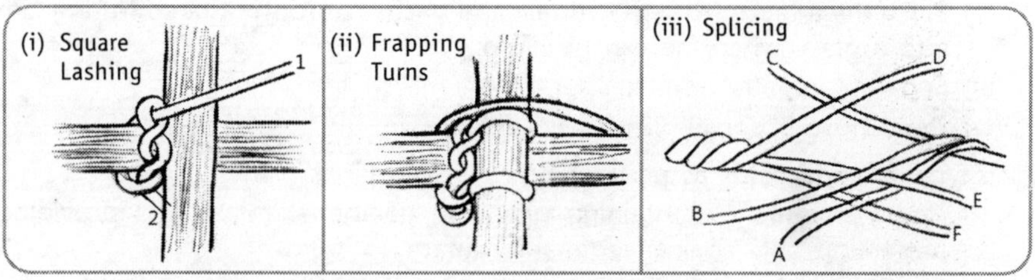

(i) **Square Lashing :** It is used to join poles at right angles. Begin with a timber hitch or a clove hitch below cross bar. If using a timber hitch, see that the pull is straight through the eye and not back from it. Pulling back will cut the lashing material. Put lashing material tightly around upright and cross bar four times for sure.

(ii) **Frapping Turns :** You must make about two or three frapping turns that go round the lashing and pull it taut. Secured end of frapping turns either by half-hitches or by passing between lashing at the crossover and secure with a half hitch. Diagonal Lashing is done for bracing or joining spars at irregular angles securely.

(iii) **Short Splicing :** You should unlay the strands and marry them together; butt hard up to each other. The strand D first goes under the standing end of A, but over strand B and over C on the standing end. Thus each strand at either end goes over one strand of the standing and on the opposite side and under the next strand, so that there is a strand of the standing end between each short side of the splice. Continue working the free strand of each end four or five times into the strands of the standing end to make it stronger.

(iv) **Long Splicing :** In this the strands are unlaid for a considerable length and then married as for the short splice. Then the one strand is unlaid and its married counterpart is laid along its place in the rope. The two centres are simply held with a crossover knot, and the strands thinned down and spliced as for a short splice. The end strands are finished with a crossover knot and again the strands are thinned down and finished as for a short splice. This long splice does not appreciably thicken a rope which may be thus spliced to go through a sheave (wheel or pulley).

MINES & OBSTACLES

Mines

A mine is a weapon to be used cunningly and with the constant aim of catching the enemy unawares.

The main functions of mine fields are :

(i) Delay and disorganize enemy attack and discourage his entering into our defended positions.
(ii) Force the attacker to select certain approaches or routes thereby luring him into a place where he can be killed.
(iii) Separate infantry from tanks.
(iv) Deny close observation of main defences.

The type of mine fields as per technical considerations :

(i) **Anti Personnel :** Containing only anti personnel mines and providing protection only against an infantry attack.
(ii) **Anti Tank :** Containing only anti tank mines and providing protection only against an armoured attack.
(iii) **Mixed :** Containing both anti tank and anti personnel mines and providing protection against both infantry and armoured attack.

The tactical classification of the mine fields are :

(i) Protective, (ii) Defensive, (iii) Tactical, (iv) Nuisance, (v) Dummy.

Obstacles

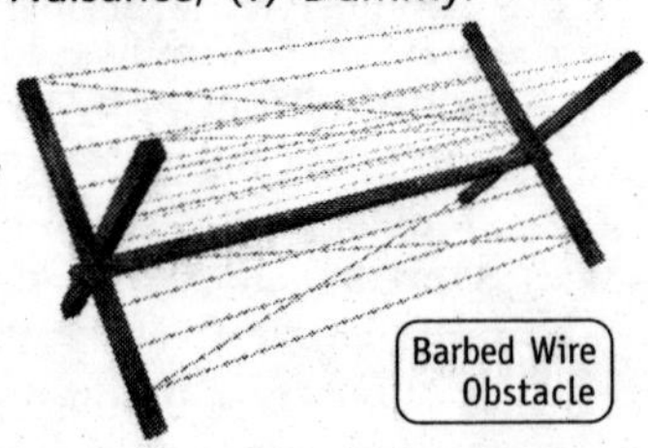

Barbed Wire Obstacle

Obstacles are the problems created for the enemy to hinder their movements and plans.

The purpose of obstacles are :

(i) Lowering his morale.
(ii) Disorganizing his plan of attack.
(iii) Delaying and disorganizing enemy under fire.
(iv) Denying him the opportunity of surprise attack.
(v) Restricting his power of manoeuvre thereby canalizing him into a pre-selected killing ground.
(vi) Making him waste time, labour and equipment in forcing a passage.

The essential characteristics of obstacles are:

1. It must be strong and of sufficient depth to impose maximum delay to enemy.
2. It is sited to fit in with coordinated plan; covered by fire and concealed to achieve surprise.
3. It is constructed outside the hand grenade range.

4. It must not;
   (i) Obscure the fire or observation of the defender,
   (ii) Afford cover to enemy,
   (iii) Reveal the exact position of the defence,
   (iv) Hinder the mobility of the defender,
   (v) Permit the enemy reconnaissance without interference by the defender.

The various types of infantry obstacles are:

1. **Artificial Obstacles :**
   (i) Wire obstacles, (ii) Anti-personnel minefields, (iii) Thorn fences, (iv) Panji fields, (v) Walls, (vi) Ditches with or without water.
2. **Natural Obstacles :**
   (i) Marshes, (ii) Rivers, nullahs and canals, (iii) Unscalable cliffs, escarpments and steep slopes, (iv) Dense growth like tea or rhodendrous bushes.

The various types of vehicles and anti-tank obstacles are:

1. **Anti-tank Minefields :** Mines designed primarily against tanks.
2. **Physical Obstacles :**
   (i) **Steep Slopes :** Slopes of 50 degrees can stop tanks under normal conditions. If the slopes are of loose slippery surface, even lesser angel is sufficient. However the slops must be of sufficient length.
   (ii) **Vertical Steps :** A vertical step of 6 feet can be an effective obstacle against all types of tanks.
   (iii) **Ditches :** A ditch, which is sufficiently wide and deep to make the nose of the tank tilt down so much that it loses hold on the ground, is an effective obstacle.
   (iv) **Water :** For a river or canal to be an obstacle against tanks it must have depth more than tanks' heights and length more than ¾ of tanks' length.

Water Crossing

The various kinds of improvised water crossing equipment are:

(i) Groundsheet Water Belt
(ii) Tin Float
(iii) Two Men's Equipment and Groundsheet
(iv) Bamboo Pole
(v) Chattis Water Wings
(vi) Water Bottle Belt
(vii) Drum Rafts
(viii) Bundle of Logs
(ix) Bamboo Mat Raft
(x) Hay Bundle Raft
(xi) Charpoy Raft

Use of Explosives and Improvised Explosive Device (Ied)

The main components of IED (improvised explosive device) are:

1. Explosive, 2. Detonator, 3. Initiating Mechanism, 4. Power Source.

The IED can be planted by the enemy in/at :

(i) Public areas (railway stations, bus stands and airports)
(ii) Public Transport (bus, train, aeroplane and ship)
(iii) Public Utilities (library, offices and industries)
(iv) Military Installations (ammunition dump, fuel oil and lubrication dump and supply depot)
(v) VIP vehicles
(vi) Along road/tracks, where VIP/security forces are likely to move
(vii) Places where large congregations are likely to take place
(viii) Places of religious worship
(ix) Important buildings *e.g.* schools, colleges, hospitals and business centre, government offices etc
(x) Important bridges
(xi) Historical monuments

The indications of IED :

(i) Any unattended item
(ii) Unclaimed attractive items like cell phones, transistor, tape recorder etc
(iii) Any object out of place
(iv) Loose electric wire
(v) Any antenna wire
(vi) Freshly dug earth
(vii) Dry grass/leaves, cow dung/garbage etc for camouflage
(viii) Broken road or freshly repaired road
(ix) Fresh plaster or painting

The Do's with IED :

(i) Remain away from suspected object.
(ii) Be aware of booby traps.
(iii) Warn the people about the suspected objects.
(iv) Inform police/bomb disposal squad.
(v) Help police in crowd management and traffic control.
(vi) Evacuate local population to a safe place.

The Don'ts with IED :

(i) Do not believe unattended object to be safe.
(ii) Do not handle suspected object.
(iii) Do not panic on detection of IED.
(iv) Do not think only one IED has been placed.
(v) Do not immerse suspected object in water.
(vi) Do not spread rumours.
(vii) Do not bunch up near the suspected object.
(viii) Do not cut any wire.
(ix) Do not make loud sounds near the IED.
(x) Do not light a fire near IED.
(xi) Do not be in a hurry and try to become a dead hero.

COMMUNICATION

When two or more persons share some idea or information via some media, it is called communication. It has great importance in Defence Forces.

The word, 'Communication' has been made up from Latin word 'Communis' which means 'to make common'. Communication is the art of transmitting information, ideas and attitudes from one person to another.

Elements of Communication

All communications consist of a few elements, understanding them can help explain what happens when one person tries to express an idea to others.

- **Sender :** The communication process begins with a sender, the person who transmits a message.
- **Message :** A message is any signal that triggers the response of a receiver.
- **Encoding :** The sender chooses certain words or non-verbal methods to send an intentional message. This is called encoding.
- **Channel :** The channel (medium) is the mode used to deliver a message.
- **Receiver :** The receiver is any person who notices and attaches some meaning to a message.
- **Decoding :** The receiver decodes the message by attaching meaning to the words or symbols.
- **Feedback :** The response of a receiver to sender's message is called feedback.

Effective Communication

Communication is a two-way process. A transmitted message should be completely understood by the person who is at the receiving end. The message should be kept as brief as possible.

Inter-Personnel Communication

It has many forms. There may be one-to-one meetings, either scheduled or at the spur of the moment. Some may involve small groups of people, gathering spontaneously or in scheduled meeting. It may also occur in a large group, where one or more speakers speak to an audience or gathering.

- **Verbal-Communication :** It is the oral expression of knowledge, viewpoint, and emotions through words.
- **Non-Verbal Communication :** A non-verbal communication may be– (a) Voice; (b) Appearance; (c) The Face and Eyes; or (d) Posture and Movement.
- **Written Communication :** Written Communication may be in the form of Letters, memos, bulletins and reports.
- **Telephone :** Telephones are a useful tool for communication for people at distant places.

* **Teleconferencing** : Personal meetings are good, but distances often make them difficult. Teleconferencing is the next best thing to face-to-face meeting.

Importance of Communication in Defence Forces

The efficient signal; communication is important for the Defence Forces:

(i) Communicating between deployed troops and commanders.
(ii) Convey the details of enemy troop movements and their activities.
(iii) To change the mode of battle activities.
(iv) To implement emergency instruction in battle field.
(v) To convey specific orders in terrain and snow bound area.
(vi) For effective operational changes in battle field.
(vii) To acquire and decipher the information and misinformation of enemy.
(viii) To prepare the troops for further operational activities.
(ix) To assess ground level effect of operational activities.
(x) To improve infrastructure facilities in battle field.
(xi) To carry out secure and effective communications with precaution and privacy.
(xii) Communication supply of food and evacuation of casualties.

Methods of Communication

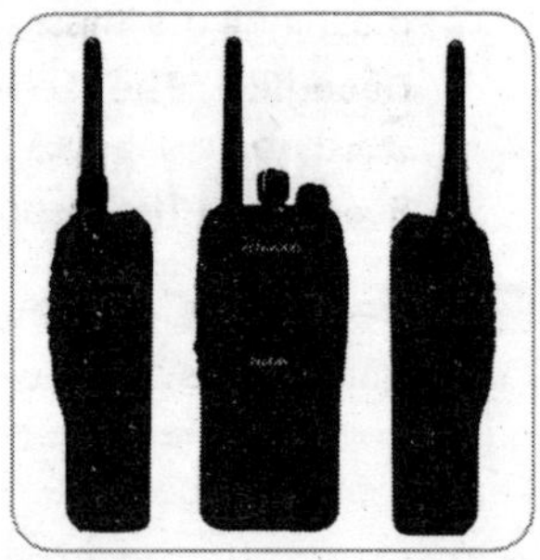

The various methods of communication are:

(i) Sign Language
(ii) Voice Medium
(iii) Written Script
(iv) Runners and Message Bearers
(v) Line and Cable (Line Communication)
(vi) Wireless (Radio Communication)

While (i) to (iv) are easy to understand by itself, we will discuss the methods at (v) and (vi) i.e. Line communication and Radio communication.

LINE COMMUNICATION : It is the basic means of signal communications for a force which is static. A telephone is by far the best means of signal communication between individual officers, and data is the best means of clearing/passing messages. Line communication is provided using of field cable, permanent lines, underground or submarine cables and now optical fiber is being used extensively. Use of multiplexing/demultiplexing equipment provides multiple channels for voice, data and video.

RADIO COMMUNICATION : It is the wireless transmission of signals through free space by electromagnetic radiation of a frequency significantly below that of visible light, in the radio frequency range, from about 30 kHz to 300 GHz. These waves are called radio waves. Electromagnetic radiation travels by means of oscillating electromagnetic fields that pass through the air and the vacuum of space. Information, such as sound, is carried by systematically changing (modulating) some property of the radiated waves, such as their amplitude, freqeuncy, phase, or pulse width. When radio waves strike an electrical conductor, the oscillating fields induce an alternating current in the conductor. The information in the waves can be extracted and transformed back into its original form. Radio communication involves Net Radio and Radio Relay.

NET RADIO : Net radio is the basic means of signal communication for any mobile force. It provides facilities for the following :

(i) Radio Telephony – Simplex, depending on the type of equipment available.

(ii) Radio telegraphy for transmission of message and key conversations.

(iii) Use of the printers over radio transmission.

Efficiency of net radio communication is appreciably affected by factors such as weather, terrain, power output of the set, state of training of operators and equipment maintenance. This can be operated in the High Frequency (HF) or Very High Frequency (VHF). VHF band is the most common form of field radio equipment in use with most of armies today.

RADIO RELAY : Radio relay implies that a series of radio transmitters and receivers normally spaced between 20-35 KMs apart and are used to provide point signal communication. Radio relay transmission and reception at each terminal take place on separate frequencies and therefore no send/receive switching is necessary. It is duplex link and can therefore be connected to link ordinary line circuits to telephone or telegraph exchanges.

Advantages/Disadvantages of Various Modes of Communications

1. The advantages and disadvantages of Line communication are :

Advantages :

(i) Reliable and practically free from electrical interference.

(ii) Relatively secure.

(iii) Number of circuits and message carrying capacity is more.

Disadvantages :

(i) Expensive in men and material.

(ii) Takes time to construct.

(iii) Inflexible once it is laid.

(iv) Vulnerable to physical interference and enemy interception along the entire length of the route.

2. The advantages and disadvantages of Net Radio are :

Advantages :

(i) It is rapid in establishing communication.

(ii) It is economical in personnel and equipment.

(iii) It is very flexible, can be rapidly re-arranged in the event of regrouping.

(iv) It can work on the move although range obtained will be much less than when stationary.

(v) It is vulnerable only at terminal and is therefore reasonably protected from enemy action except by a direct hit.

Disadvantages :

(i) Net radio being inherently insecure demands a considerable degree of security consciousness on the part of the users. This means adherence to standard procedure and security codes.

(ii) It is inherently insecure and susceptible to enemy interception which necessitates the use of codes and ciphers with a consequent delay in clearing traffic and overall increase in operating personnel.

3. The advantages and disadvantages of Radio Relay are :

Advantages :

(i) It provides greater flexibility than line.

(ii) It is vulnerable physically only at terminal.

(iii) It is quick to set up and move except in mountainous country.

(iv) Replace line with considerable economy of manpower and stores.

(v) It can be operated over area where for reasons of ground or enemy activity use of line may not be possible.

(vi) By its ability to employ multichannel equipment radio relay provides more teleprinter circuits over one link than can normally be provided over the average field cable. Thus it has much greater traffic handling capacity.

Disadvantage :

(i) It needs critical siting.

(ii) It cannot work on the move.

(iii) Slightly more expensive in men and material than in the case of net radio.

(iv) Location of terminal and intermediate stations may not suit tactical layout and may, therefore, create additional protection requirements.

(v) It is liable to interference from enemy jamming although not as much as in the case of net radio.

(vi) It is liable to interception and hence insecure. Has relatively greater security than net radio, depending upon the siting and direction of the beams.

(vii) Terrain between stations must be reasonably suitable to get a 'quasi optical path', this presents difficulty in siting.

Communication Media

The various communication transmission lines are: 1. Parallel Wire type, 2. Coaxial type, 3. Wave Guide type. Transmission is done through propagation of waves.

The various types of propagation of waves are:

(i) **Ground Wave Propagation** : Used for long and medium waves, limited range is 30 Kms.

(ii) **Sky Wave Propagation** : Used for HF range up to 30 MHz communication, range is 100 Km to 1000 Kms. These make use of ionosphere layer existing to a height of 150-200 Kms from the surface of earth.

(iii) **Space Wave Propagation** : The propagation of VHF and UHF frequency takes place in straight lines. The range is limited by curvature of earth and so distance between two neighbouring stations is approx 50 Kms.

(iv) **Tropospheric Scatter Propagation** : Also known as tropo scatter or forward scatter propagation, extended height up to 8-10 Kms from the surface of earth.

Characteristics of Wireless Technology (Wi-Fi)

Wi-Fi Technology provides its users with the liberty of connecting to the Internet from any place such as their home, office or a public place without the hassles of plugging in the wires. Wi-Fi is quicker than the conventional modem for accessing information over a large network. With the help of different amplifiers, the users can easily change their location without disruption in their network access. Wi-Fi devices are compliant with each other to grant efficient access of information to the user. Wi-Fi location where the users can connect to the wireless network is called a Wi-Fi hotspot.

Features of Wi-Fi

Wireless operations permit services, such as long-range communications, which are impossible or impractical to implement with the use of wires. Information is transferred in this manner over both short and long distances.

The following list summarizes some of the benefits of a Wi-Fi network:

(i) **Unmatched mobility and elasticity:** Wi-Fi is allowing the new intensity of connectivity without giving up functions. Wi-Fi has introduced various types of utilities such as music streamers that transmit music to speakers without any wire. You can also play music from the remote computer or any other device attached to the network. The most important thing is that now you can play online radio. Wi-Fi technology system is rather remarkable, you can download songs, send an email and transfer files expediently at sky-scraping speed and you can move your computer easily because your Wi-Fi network has no cable to disrupt your work so it is quite easy, helpful and most of all expedient.

(ii) **Fortress Technology:** Wi-Fi providing secure wireless solutions support the growth and release of a prototype mobile ad hoc wireless network for use in the wireless strategic skirmish.

(iii) **Supports an Entire Age Bracket:** Wi-Fi technology has several advantages, it supports an entire age bracket and creates a connection between components on the same network and has the ability to transfer data between the devices and enable different kinds of devices such as game console, MP3 player, PDA's and much more.

(iv) **Convenient and Available Everywhere:** Wi-Fi is a convenient technology and where the network range station exists you are online during travel; you can equip with a Wi-Fi network and get connected. You will automatically connect to the internet if you are near a hotspot. These days Wi-Fi exists everywhere with all its wonders.

(v) **Faster and Secure:** With Wi-Fi, you can get a high speed of internet because it is faster than DSL and Cable connection. You can establish a Wi-Fi network in small space now. You don't need any professional installation– just connect to a power outlet with an Ethernet cord, and start browsing. Wi-Fi security system for Threats makes it more renewable and its tool protect your VPN and secure web page. You can easily configure the device to take better performance. The standard devices, embedded systems, and network security make it more powerful.

(vi) **No limitation:** You can use a "Wi-Fi" network with no limitation because it can connect you worldwide. You can easily cater to your requirements with Wi-Fi networking applications because the power consumption is not very high as compared to another bandwidth networks. The future of wireless internet network communications is bright.

(vii) **Extension of Technology:** It is because of this wireless technology that so many other advancements could take place. There are smart TVs in the market which connect to the internet. Having the internet on TV makes it possible to watch Youtube videos, Net Flix and so much more.

(viii) **Cost Reduction:** As mentioned above, the absence of wires and cables brings down cost of networking to a great extent.

(ix) **Flexibility:** Extended access, cost reductions, and mobility create opportunities for new applications as well as the possibility of creative new solutions for legacy applications.

Wireless Data Communications

Wireless data communications is an essential component of mobile computing. The various available technologies differ in local availability, coverage range and performance, and in some circumstances, users must be able to employ multiple connection types and switch between them.

Flows of Wi-Fi Technology: Wi-Fi technology is not perfect and has many flaws that limit its use as follows:

(i) **Security:** Wireless transmissions can pass through walls hence security is an issue.

(ii) **Wireless Reception**: It varies from area to area, even within your own apartment. It's not always guaranteed that you'll have a connection to the Internet.

(iii) **Interference:** Call quality is greatly influenced by the environment. It is particularly sensitive to electromagnetic radiation generated by other household appliances.

(iv) **Compatibility Issue:** Despite the global standardization, many devices from different manufacturers are not fully compatible, which in turn affects the speed of communication.

The environment is flooded with various Wi-Fi software tools. Each of these tools is specifically designed for different types of networks, operating systems and usage types. It is imperative for users to have a good detailed knowledge about this latest technology and pick out a Wi-Fi software tool that is compatible with their computer and its dynamics. Through the Wi-Fi hotspot, the users can even enhance their home business, as accessing information through Wi-Fi is quite simple.

Characteristics of Walkie/Talkie

A walkie-talkie is a hand-held, portable, two-way radio transceiver. Major characteristics include a half-duplex channel (only one radio transmits at a time, though any number can listen) and a "push-to-talk" (PTT) switch that starts transmission. Typical walkie-talkies resemble a telephone handset, possibly slightly larger but still a single unit, with an antenna mounted on the top of the unit. Where a phone's earpiece is only loud enough to be heard by the user, a walkie-talkie's built-in speaker can be heard by the user and those in the user's immediate vicinity. Hand-held transceivers may be used to communicate between each other, or to vehicle-mounted or base station.

Radio set GP338 Motorola: Defence organizations use hand-held radios for a variety of purposes. Radio Set GP338 Motorola can do communication on a variety of bands and modulation schemes.

Facilities:

(i) It is portable and light weight.

(ii) It can be operated easily.

(iii) It can be operated in VHF/UHF and 2 way simplex mode.

(iv) 128 channels of this radio set can be preset into 8 zones.

(v) Option of selective call facilities available.

(vi) Call alert can be given to receiver station.

(vii) Can select required zone.

(viii) Start/stop facilities of scan operation available.

(ix) Add/Delete from scan list facilities available.

BASIC RADIO TELEPHONY PROCEDURE

The procedure laid out to communicate on the Radio, so as to make the conversation secure and successful, is referred to as "Radio Telephony". This procedure is very important to avoid utter confusion over radio and is generally used by Defence Forces, air traffic controllers, maritime operations and amateur radio operators. In army RT procedure follows a set of rules. Various advantages/disadvantages of RT procedure and radio communications are as under :

Advantages :

(i) It is easy to establish.

(ii) It is flexible.

(iii) Transmissions to more than one station.

Disadvantages :

(i) It is easier to intercept.

(ii) It is liable to atmospheric interference and interference from other stations.

(iii) It is liable to be jammed.

(iv) Skilled operators are required.

Need for Standard Procedure

Standard procedure in RT needed to attain Speed, Uniformity, Security and prevents misunderstanding & confusion by use of code signs; link signs etc, which hides identity of an operator and that of a unit. RT procedure needs to be practiced for attaining strict discipline.

Principles of RT Procedure: BASS defines the principles of RT procedure.

(i) **B** - Brevity
(ii) **A** - Accuracy
(iii) **S** - Security
(iv) **S** - Speed

Types of RT Communication

- **RT Conversation:** This is normal conversation between radio operators, which is not registered.
- **Unregistered (UR) Message:** The only record taken will be in radio operator's logs of the sender and receiver.
- **Formal Message:** It is written down and signed by the originator and will be written on a message form (IAFU-4009).
- **Radio Net:** Stations working on same frequency in order to communicate with each other comprise a Radio Net.

- **Control Station:** Station serving as the senior HQ in the Radio Net. It is responsible for establishment of communications and maintains radio discipline on the net.
- **Link Sign:** It is secret group of letters or combination of letters and figures, allotted to a station on radio net, for concealing the identity of the communicating station. Link signs are changed daily or even earlier if required.
- **Code Sign:** It is three-letter group allotted to HQ/formation or unit to conceal their identity. These are changed daily.
- **Long Message:** Message that lasts for more than half a minute generally consists of more than thirty groups.
- **Short Message:** A short message lasts for half a minute or less.
- **Phonetic Alphabet:** Alpha, Bravo, Charlie... etc.
- **Standard Phrases:** Use of standard procedure ensures that exact meaning of a sender is conveyed to the receiver in minimum time.
- **Code Word:** A code word is single word used to provide security cover for reference to a classified matter.
- **Nicknames:** A nick name consists of two separate words that do not bear any relationship to each other i.e., PAHAD SHER. Nicknames have very little security value and are used for convenience.

RT Procedure

- **Standard Phrases:** Standard phrases used in RT procedure are as under:
  - (i) **Over:** My transmission has ended and I expect to hear a further transmission from you on this subject. Other stations will not transmit.
  - (ii) **Out:** My transmission has ended and I do not expect you to make a further transmission on the subject. Other stations may transmit.
  - (iii) **Wait Out:** I have finished for the time being and will call you later. Other stations may transmit.
  - (iv) **Wait:** Pause for a few seconds follows. Other stations will not transmit.
  - (v) **Out to You:** I have finished with you and am about to call another station. No reply is expected from you. Other stations will not transmit.
  - (vi) **Roger:** Message received and understood.
  - (vii) **Wilco:** Message received, understood and will be complied with.
- **Type of Calls:** Calls can be categorised as under:
  - (i) **Single Call:** A call when only one station on a net is addressed by any one station of the net.
  - (ii) **Mutliple Call:** A call when two or more but not all stations on the net are addressed. The pro word "and" will be inserted between the last two calls signs e.g, 'A1 for A2 and A3'.

(iii) **Net Call:** A call used to address all stations on a net e.g., "All stations Alpha".

(iv) **Net Call with Exceptions:** A call used to address all stations on the net except a few. Here a net call is made and stations not called are specified e.g., "all stations Alpha except ABC 3".

- **Establishment of Communication:** Preliminary instructions are issued by Control. They are not sent by radio unless in dire emergency. On establishment of communications, signal strength will always be confirmed. Link signs will not be abbreviated in bad weather conditions. If a station has not come up during establishment of communication but comes up little later, communication will be again established. Signal communication will always be established in the following situations:
  (i) After change of frequency
  (ii) Bad weather
  (iii) After move
  (iv) After lifting of radio silence
  (v) After change of link sign
- **Documentation:** Documentation forms a very important aspect of RT procedure. All events need to be documented for future reference in case of a query.
- **Rules on Security:** Security over radio is an important issue in defence forces hence there is a need to adopt these procedures and follow certain golden rules.
  (i) Think before you speak.
  (ii) Use correct procedure.
  (iii) Avoid use of jargon.
  (iv) Use official codes only.
  (v) Substitute clear names by code signs.
  (vi) Be brief.

Proper Radio Telephony procedure is essential to estabilsh communication both during war and peace time. There are certain advantages and disadvantages of RT procedure. The messages can be intercepted by enemy and the complete information can be retrieved especially during field conditions. Considering the same one must follow all the rules of security while communicating.

LATEST TRENDS AND DEVELOPMENTS IN COMMUNICATIONS

Necessity being the mother of invention, changes drove the evolution and adoption of modern technologies. The field of communication has seen rapid growth during the last century; beginning with the discovery of radio telephony by

Marconi and Graham Bells the development has been speedy. Various forms of communication media have been discovered. The medium of space has acquired special importance in communications.

The latest trends in communication are :

1. Troposcatter,
2. Modem,
3. Fax,
4. Telex,
5. Satellite,
6. Fiber optic communications,
7. Computer system,
8. Internet,
9. Cell phone,
10. Multimedia, and
11. Videophone.

1. **Troposcatter :** The troposphere is lower layer of the atmosphere below the height of 15 Kms. Communication carried out in this layer use the principle of troposcatter. In this system microwaves are transmitted in the UHF and SHF Band to achieve radio communication over the horizon covering a range between 70 to 1000 KMs. The digital mobile troposcatter systems are operated by specialized signal groups.

   Application of Troposcatter

   (i) Ideal for rugged terrain of deserts, mountains, sea, etc.

   (ii) It is used for long range point to point communication.

   (iii) It has the following channel capacities :

   - Data : 03
   - Voice : 24
   - Telegraph/Telex : 32

2. **MODEM :** A modem is used to translate information transferred through telephone lines, cable, satellite or line-of-sight wireless.

   The term stands for modulate and demodulate which changes the signal from digital, which computers use, to analog, which telephones use and then back again. Digital modems transfer digital information directly without changing to analog.

   Modems are measured by the speed that the information is transferred. The measuring tool is called the baud rate. Originally modems worked at speeds below 2400 baud but today analog speeds of 56,000 baud are standard. Cable, wireless or digital subscriber lines can transfer information much faster with rates of 300,000 baud and up.

3. **FAX :** Fax or facsimile, is the telephonic transmission of scanned printed material (both text and images), normally to a telephone number connected to a printer or other output device. Some of the advantages of Fax are as under :

(i) It can transmit graphics as well as alphanumeric information.
(ii) It reduces time and eliminates transmission error.
(iii) It can transmit information in any vernacular language.
(iv) It can use any transmission medium e.g., telephone, line, micro radio wave.
(v) It can receive the document like a photocopy.

4. **SATELLITE :** A satellite is an object which revolves around another larger object whose motion is primarily and permanently determined by the force of attraction of the body. Before the space age, planets and moons were the only known satellites. On 4th October 1957 the first man made satellite called the SPUTNIK was launched by the erstwhile USSR since then satellites have brought about a revolution in the field of communications.

Type of Satellites

(i) Communication Satellite (ii) Weather Satellite (iii) Scientific Satellite
(iv) Military Satellite (v) Navigational Satellite

- **Communication Satellite:** A communication satellite is an artificial satellite that relays and amplifies radio telecommunication signals via a transponder; it creates a communication channel between a source transmitter and a receiver at different locations on Earth. Communication satellites are used for television, telephone, radio, internet, and military applications. There are over 2,000 communications satellites in Earth's orbit, used by both private and government organizations.
- **Weather Satellite:** The weather satellite is a type of satellite that is primarily used to monitor the weather and climate of the Earth. A satellite can be polar orbiting, covering the entire Earth asynchronously, or geostationary, hovering over the same spot on the equator.
- **Scientific Satellite:** Scientific research satellites provide meteorological information, land survey data (e.g. remote sensing), Amateur (HAM) Radio, and other different scientific research applications such as earth science, marine science, and atmospheric research.
- **Military Satellite:** A military satellite is an artificial satellite used for a military purpose. The most common missions are intelligence gathering, navigation and military communications. The first military satellites were photographic reconnaissance missions.
- **Navigational Satellite:** A satellite navigation or satnav system is a system that uses satellites to provide autonomous geo-spatial positioning. It allows small electronic receivers to determine their location (longitude, latitude, and altitude/elevation) to high precision

Latest Trends in COMMUNICATIONS

(within a few metres) using time signals transmitted along a line of sight by radio from satellites. A satellite navigation system with global coverage may be termed a global navigation satellite system (GNSS).

5. **FIBRE OPTICS COMMUNICATION :** It is a method of transmitting information from one place to another by sending pulses of light through an optical fiber. The light forms an electromagnetic carrier wave that is modulated to carry information. Optical fibers are hollow tubes made of corning glass with an outer protective coating of rubber/plastic etc. and are very delicate and small in diameter.

Advantages :

(i) It has wide band width carrying different types of information.
(ii) Small cable size.
(iii) Low power consumption.
(iv) Not susceptible to electromagnetic interference.
(v) Provides inherent secrecy, as it is difficult to decipher bulk signals.
(vi) Repeater station at long ranges and can be unmanned.

Disadvantages :

(i) More expensive
(ii) Jointing problem
(iii) Channel dropping not possible at will.

6 **COMPUTER SYSTEM :** The term computer is derived from the Latin word *compute*, which means to calculate. A computer is an electronic machine, devised for performing calculations and controlling operations that can be expressed either in logical or numerical terms. In simple terms, a computer is an electronic device that performs diverse operations with the help of instructions to process the information in order to achieve the desired results. A Computer application extends to cover huge area including education, industries, government, medicine, scientific research etc.

Advantages :

(i) Ability to handle large volume of data.
(ii) High speed of computation and multiple processing features.
(iii) Accuracy of process and calculation once the programme is proved.
(iv) Mass storage of data along with auto backups.
(v) It will continue on the same job, always working in the same way, persistently.

Disadvantages :

(i) Constant power source is required.
(ii) Manpower expertise is mandatory.
(iii) Back up of data still required to be maintained.
(iv) Data loss if machine malfunctions because of virus or cyber attacks.

7. **INTERNET :** Internet is a communication network which bridges all the small computer networks worldwide as a whole. Internet is based upon Internet technology, in particular World Wide Web (WWW), to build Information System within organization or enterprise to accomplish standardization and automation. Fundamentally, it means network computing environments which let the users share the information through the Internet and Web browsers. The Internet has grown from a small project to today's biggest network of computers. Due to this colossal growth, the Internet has become the biggest domain of information. Now-a-days, an Internet user has access to a wide variety of services such as electronic mail, file transfer, vast information resources, interest group membership, interactive collaboration, multimedia displays, real-time broadcasting, shopping opportunities, and much more.

8. **CELL PHONE :** A cell phone (also known as a mobile phone) is a device that can make and receive telephone calls over a radio link while moving around a wide geographic area. It does so by connecting to a cellular network provided by a mobile phone operator, allowing access to the public telephone network. Apart from telephony, modern mobile phones also support a wide variety of other services such as text messaging, MMS, email, Internet access, GPS, Television, weather forecasts, short-range wireless communications (infrared, Bluetooth), business applications, gaming and photography. Mobile phones that offer these and more general computing capabilities are called as smartphones.

   Advantages :

   (i) Better quality of service.
   (ii) Higher speed of data exchange.
   (iii) High density of subscribers and large traffic handling capability.
   (iv) Can be used in an integrated mode with computer network.
   (v) Not perceptible between mobile and fixed subscribers.
   (vi) Miniaturization using very large scale integration (VLSI) technology.

   Disadvantages :

   (i) Open source. It can be jammed if required.
   (ii) Repeated charging of battery.
   (iii) Security related issues.
   (iv) Works on the capability and commercial interests of service provider.
   (v) Health hazards due to excessive radiations.

9. **MULTIMEDIA :** There are software programs that combine text and graphics with sound, video, and animation. A multimedia PC contains the hardware to support these capabilities. Multimedia is usually recorded and played, displayed or accessed by information content processing devices, such as computerized and electronic devices, but can also be part of a live performance. Multimedia devices are electronic media devices used to store and experience multimedia content. Multimedia is distinguished from mixed

media in fine art; by including audio, for example, it has a broader scope now-a-days.

10 **VIDEO CONFERENCING :** A remote "face-to-face chat," when two or more people using a webcam and an Internet telephone connection chat online. The webcam enables both live voice and video. With the introduction of relatively low cost, high capacity broadband telecommunication services, coupled with powerful computing processors and video compression techniques videoconferencing usage has made significant inroads in business, education, medicine, defence forces and media. Like all long distance communication technologies (such as phone and Internet), by reducing the need to travel to bring people together the technology also contributes to reduction in carbon emissions, thereby helping to reduce global warming.

11. **VIDEO PHONE :** It is a terminal equipment that enables us to transmit an image via digital communication network, making visual contact possible over great distances, apart from transferring speech.

Advantages :

(i) Called subscriber is seen on the monitor.
(ii) Can transmit speech as well as video.
(iii) Conduct of videoconferences.
(iv) High quality of voice.
(v) Map overlays can be transmitted.
(vi) Speed of sending/receiving can be adjusted by the user.

12. **INFORMATION TECHNOLOGY :** IT refers to the creation, gathering, processing, storage, presentation and dissemination of information, and also the processes and devices that enable all this to be done. IT stands firmly on the hardware and software of a computer and the telecommunications infrastructure. Computers have been primarily used for information processing but now they are becoming more and more powerful both in terms of their computational speeds and high capacities for storage of data.

What has made the high difference in recent years is not the fact that individual computers have dramatically improved in their capabilities, but that all those information islands are being connected by digital highways made possible through the use of the telecommunications infrastructure by the computers, which largely explains why the internet and the WWW have begun to play such a significant role in our daily life. Information technology is being used in education, business, agriculture, banking, hotel industry, marketing and the defence forces.

❖ ❖ ❖

CHAPTER

22 Solved Questions for Practice

IMPORTANT QUESTIONS & ANSWERS

Q.1. What is the rank of DG NCC?

Ans. Lt General.

Q.2. What is the rank of Dy Director General of NCC Directorate?

Ans. Brigadier OR Equivalent.

Q.3. How many Directorates are there in NCC?

Ans. 17.

Q.4. What are the ranks of SD/SW ANOs?

Ans. Lieutenant, Captain and Major.

Q.5. What are the ranks of JD/JW ANOs?

Ans. 3rd Officer, 2nd Officer, First Officer and Chief Officer.

Q.6. Name the social service and community development activities.

Ans. These are as under :

(i) Tree Plantation, (ii) Blood Donation,
(iii) Old Age Homes, (iv) Adult Education,
(v) Community work, (vi) Disaster relief,
(vii) AIDS and Cancer awareness programmes.

Q.7. What are the fundamentals of national unity?

Ans. These are as under :

(i) Language, (ii) Casteism, (iii) Education,
(iv) Communalism, (v) Regionalism.

Q.8. Write the aims of National Integration Camp.

Ans. The aims of National Integration Camp are :

(i) Create awareness amongst the youth of diverse cultural heritage of our country.

(ii) To foster national integration despite cultural, religious, geographical and environmental barriers.

(iii) To gain experience, to live, co-operate and work in harmony with cadets of other states who they have not known before.

(iv) To help in personal growth of cadets.

Q.9. What are the major Indian religious groups?

Ans. (i) Hindus, (ii) Muslims, (iii) Christians, (iv) Sikhs, (v) Buddhists, (vi) Jains.

Q.10. What is the importance of national unity?

Ans. National unity is essential for social well-being, peace and harmony. People can enjoy peace and security, if there is a mutual trust and goodwill among all sections of society. No progress can be made in the field of art & literature, science & cultural advancement and economic well-being, if the disruptive tendencies and divisive forces are present in the country. Nation can play an effective role in the international field if our own house is in order.

Q.11. What are the geographical factors which influence the defence of India?

Ans. The geographical factors are :

(i) Himalaya in the North of India
(ii) Deserts on western borders
(iii) Arabian sea in the west coast of India
(iv) South Indian Ocean
(v) Bay of Bengal in the east
(vi) Plains of Punjab

Q.12. Name the following :

(i) Nightingale of India
(ii) First Home Minister of India
(iii) First Indian Astronaut
(iv) First Indian who swam across English Channel
(v) First Field Marshal of Indian Army.

Ans. (i) Sarojini Naidu, (ii) Sardar Patel, (iii) Sqn. Ldr. Rakesh Sharma, (iv) Mihir Sen, (v) Sam Manekshaw.

Q.13. How many parts does a word of command consist of?

Ans. The word of command is divided into two parts: (i) Cautionary, (ii) Executive.

Q.14. Write the paces in a minute to the following :

Ans. (i) Slow Time ....
(ii) Quick Time ....
(iii) Double Time ....

Ans. (i) 70 (ii) 120 (iii) 180

Q.15. What is the aim of Drill?

Ans. (i) To inculcate a sense of discipline,
(ii) Improve bearing, smartness in appearance and turn out,
(iii) Create self confidence, and
(iv) To develop the quality of immediate and implicit obedience to orders.

Q.16. What are the factors which led to the growth of Indian Nationalism?

Ans. The factors which led to the growth of Indian Nationalism are :

(i) Religions, social and cultural renaissance.
(ii) Influence of western education and literature.
(iii) Influence of modern means of transport and communication.
(iv) Influence of Indian press and literature.

Q.17. Fill in the blanks.

(i) In Vishram left foot is taken .... high.
(ii) .... is a straight line formed by a few persons standing side-by-side.
(iii) The strength of Guard of honour for the President is .... cadets stand in three rows.
(iv) General salute is given to ....
(v) The number of persons detailed for guard mounting in quarter guard is ....

Ans. (i) 6″, (ii) Rank, (iii) 150, (iv) Maj Gen & above, (v) 2+6.

Q.18. What points must be kept in mind while assembling Rif .22?

Ans. (i) Bolt head to be fully tight.
(ii) Bolt head and guide rib as well as cocking piece and steel lug to be in a line.
(iii) Number of the bolt should tally with that of the rifle.
(iv) Safety catch should be applied.

Q.19. Define the terms:

(i) Trajectory (ii) Line of Sight (iii) Angle of descent
(iv) First Catch (v) First Graze

Ans. (i) **Trajectory :** Parabolic path traced by the bullet during its flight.
(ii) **Line of Sight :** Imaginary line formed between eye of the firer and point of aim through the sight.
(iii) **Angle of descent :** Angle formed between trajectory and the line of sight before bullet hits target.
(iv) **First Catch :** The point where bullet hits the target.
(v) **First Graze :** The point where bullet hits the ground passing through the target.

Q.20. Expand the following :

(i) MPI (ii) SMC (iii) LMG (iv) SLR (v) DP

Ans. **(i) MPI** : Mean Point of Impact
(ii) SMC : Sten Machine Carbine
(iii) LMG : Light Machine Gun
(iv) SLR : Self Loading Rifle
(v) DP : Drill Practice

Q.21. What is Group in Shooting? What are the methods of finding MPI?

Ans. The pattern formed by three or more than three bullets fired by a single firer, at a single target, with same hold and aim under same weather conditions and with same arm is called a Group.

Methods :

(i) Graphical Method, (ii) Axis of departure method, (iii) Calculation method.

Q.22. Fill in the blanks:

(i) The discriminatory feelings of an individual against other on the basis of caste and religion is called ....

(ii) Quit India Movement was launched on ....

(iii) Army day is celebrated on ....

(iv) Highest Military Honour is ....

(v) Highest civilian award is ....

(vi) .... is called land of five rivers.

(vii) Arabian sea is along .... coast of India.

(viii) .... is awarded for outstanding contribution to promotion of adult literacy.

(ix) Kaziranga National park is in ....

(x) NCC Song is written by ....

Ans. (i) Communalism, (ii) July 14, 1942, (iii) 15th January, (iv) Param Vir Chakra, (v) Bharat Ratna, (vi) Punjab, (vii) West, (viii) Nehru literarcy award, (ix) Assam, (x) Sri Mudgalaya.

Q.23. What materials are used for cleaning .22 Rifle?

Ans. (i) Pull through

(ii) Wire gauge (2.5" × 1.5")

(iii) Oil

(iv) Flannel for cleaning (4" x 2") and for oiling (4"x1½")

Q.24. What parts of a rifle are stripped and cleaned?

Ans. The various parts of a rifle are stripped and cleaned in the following sequence :

(i) Barrel, (ii) Bolt, (iii) Bayonet and Scabbard, (iv) Chamber, (v) Magazine.

Q.25. Fill in the blanks :

(i) The 7.62mm rifle can fire effectively up to .... yards.

(ii) The basic weapon of an infantry soldier was 7.62mm SLR and now it is .... mm rifle.

(iii) The magazine capacity of 7.62mm SLR is .... rounds.

(iv) The muzzle velocity of 7.62mm SLR is .... ft/sec.

Ans. (i) 300 (ii) 5.56 (iii) 20 (iv) 27

Q.26. Fill in the blanks :

(i) The weight of LMG with bipod is ....

(ii) The length of 0.22" Deluxe rifle is ....

(iii) Effective range of 7.62 mm Bolt action rifle is ....

(iv) The chindi size of SMC for oiling is ....

(v) The muzzle velocity of SLR is .... ft/second.

(vi) The Basic weapon used by NCC Cadets for firing is ....

(vii) The effective range of .22 Rifle is ....

Ans. (i) 9.2 kg (ii) 43 inches (iii) 275 mtr (iv) 4"×2"
(v) 2700 (vi) .22 Rifle (vii) 25 yards

Q.27. Write any 10 parts common to all firing weapons.

Ans. (i) Barrel, (ii) Foresight knobs, (iii) Bayonet, (iv) Magazine, (v) Trigger and Trigger guard, (vi) Backsight, (vii) Butt, (viii) Piston grip, (ix) Cocking handle, (x) Safety catch/change lever.

Q.28. What are the basic essentials for good shooting?

Ans. Essentials for good shooting are :
Good-Holding, Aiming and Trigger operation.

Q.29. What is MPI?

Ans. Mean Point of Impact is the central point of area covered by the group of rounds fired with consistent aim and held at the same aiming mark.

Q.30. When the rifle will be half cocked?

Ans. On pressing the trigger, when the bolt lever is not fully down OR when the safety catch is not fully forward.

Q.31. What is the battle effective range of LMG (caliber-7.6mm)?

Ans. With Bipod-500 yards, With Tripod-1000 yards.

Q.32. Fill in the blanks:

(i) One can not be a good citizen of more than .... at a time.

(ii) A good citizen is one who knows his ....

(iii) Customs helps in developing the .... in one's service.

(iv) It is customary to salute the ...., when it is being hoisted or hauled down at Reveille and Retreat.

(v) When the National Anthem is being played, all will stand in ....

(vi) .... are symbolic of the .... of a regiment.

(vii) It is a matter of .... that the regiment would not let their colours fall.

(viii) All infantry regiments, with the exception of .... carry colours.

(ix) The colours are awarded to a regiment by the ....

Ans. (i) One Country, (ii) Rights & Duties, (iii) Esprit-de-Corps and Pride, (iv) National Flag, (v) Attention, (vi) Colours, Spirit (vii) Honour, (viii) Rifle Regiments, (ix) President.

Q.33. What is the assistance required during flood/cyclone?

Ans. (i) Flood/Cyclone Warning
(ii) Shelter Management
(iii) Evacuation & Rescue
(iv) First aid & Medical
(v) Sanitation
(vi) Relief
(vii) Carcass Disposal
(viii) Patrolling and Liaison

Q.34. What is the effective method to contact NCC cadets to be available for any assistance during calamities?

Ans. (i) Radio/TV
(ii) Contact telephone numbers
(iii) Jeep with loudhailer
(iv) By word of mouth

Q.35. How NCC cadets can help the local authorities during war/ emergency?

Ans. (i) Cadets can boost morale of population by contradicting various rumours that keep on spreading.
(ii) Cadets can assist the medical team by doing first aid.
(iii) Cadets can manage and control communication by doing signals.
(iv) Cadets can supply food, ration etc.

Q.36. Give types of services, which cadets can provide to maintain essential services?

Ans. (i) Operation of telephone exchange
(ii) Traffic control
(iii) To give first aid & help to hospital staff
(iv) Maintain various records
(v) Cadets belonging to ITI can provide skilled hand help

Q.37. How do NCC cadets help local authority during National Calamities such as earthquake, flood etc?

Ans. (i) First aid
(ii) Evacuation of casualties
(iii) Food & clothes distribution
(iv) Maintenance of electrical lines and communication
(v) Disposal of wounded & dead
(vi) Arrangement of shelters
(vii) Maintenance of various data

Q.38. How does HIV/AIDS spread?

Ans. (i) Sexual transmission
(ii) Blood transfusion
(iii) Sharing needles and syringes for intravenous drug use
(iv) Mother-to-child transmission during pregnancy, delivery or breastfeeding

Q.39. Define 'citizen'.

Ans. A member of the community who owes allegiance to the state and who enjoys protection and the rights granted by the constitution of the country is called as a 'citizen'.

Q.40. What are the main reasons for not practising family planning in India?

Ans. The main reasons are :

(i) Mainly old customs and beliefs
(ii) Thinking children are the gift of the god
(iii) Thinking the number of children are determined by god
(iv) Thinking every Hindu must have a son
(v) Thinking children are wealth

Q.41. What does family welfare refer to?

Ans. It refers to the practice that help individuals or couples to gain following objectives :

(i) To avoid unwanted births.
(ii) To bring about wanted births.
(iii) To regulate intervals between pregnancies.
(iv) To control the time at which birth occurs.
(v) To determine the number of children in the family.

Q.42. What is the modern concept of family welfare?

Ans. Family welfare is not merely birth control, it includes :

(i) Proper spacing and limitation of births
(ii) Advice on sterility
(iii) Education for parenthood
(iv) Screening for diseases related to the reproductive system
(v) Parental counselling
(vi) Marriage counselling
(vii) Pregnancy tests
(viii) Services for unmarried mother
(ix) Service of adoption

Q.43. How to ensure proper personal hygiene?

Ans. It is as under :

(i) 7-8 hours of Sleep
(ii) Regular Bathing
(iii) Eating and Drinking
(iv) Care and Cleanliness of Skin, Hands, Hair and Teeth
(v) Healthy food and proper rest
(vi) Exercise

Q.44. Is there any risk of HIV/AIDS infection due to blood donation?

Ans. Blood donation has no risk of getting HIV infection because the needles and other equipment used for collecting blood are safe.

Q.45. How do NCC cadets establish rapport for getting participation of people in welfare work?

Ans. (i) NCC unit should identify a village preferably within the environment.

(ii) The unit to study problems of people and then motivate to solve their problems.

(iii) People must be convinced about the benefit of welfare work.

Q.46. What are the various methods of water purification?

Ans. These are as under :

(i) Boiling and distilling (ii) Filtration (iii) Sterilization

(iv) Pinking (v) Precipitation

Q.47. Define the term Health.

Ans. Health is defined as a state of complete physical, mental and social well-being and not merely absence of disease. The basic factors that keep a person healthy are :

(i) Good Sleep (ii) Bathing (iii) Cleanliness

(iv) Eating & Drinking (v) Exercises

Q.48. What are the sources of water? How is water purified?

Ans. The sources of water are :

(i) Rain water, (ii) Surface water, (iii) Underground water.

Methods of Purification :

(i) **Clarification :** Removal of suspended matters

(ii) **Sterilisation :** By chlorine

Methods of Clarification :

(i) **Sedimentation** : By use of chemicals

(ii) **Filtration** : Using filters

(iii) **Sterilisation** : By boiling water/bleaching powder

Q.49. What are the two important aspects of health of an individual?

Ans. The two important aspects of health of an individual are Hygiene and Sanitation.

Q.50. What are the arrangement required to maintain sanitation in the camp?

Ans. The arrangement required to maintain sanitation in the camp are :

(i) Sufficient water should be made available.

(ii) Food cleanliness and security till distribution.

(iii) Garbage should be thrown far away.

(iv) Area around camp should be clean.

(v) Latrine should be kept far away from the camp.

Q.51. Explain the general rules for the treatment of burns & scalds.

Ans. The general rules for the treatment of burns & scalds are :

(i) Avoid handling affected area more than necessary.

(ii) Do not apply lotions of any kind.

(iii) Do not remove burned clothing and do not rupture blisters.

(iv) Cover the area with a sterile dressing if possible, otherwise cover it with clean cloth.

(v) Bandage firmly if there are no blisters.

Q.52. What method will you adopt as NCC cadet to improve ecology in your village?

Ans. The methods to improve ecology in the village are :

(i) Using organic manure instead of chemical fertilizers and pesticides.

(ii) Recycling solid waste.

(iii) Afforestation.

(iv) Restrict washing, bathing in rivers/near wells.

(v) Promote gas cooking.

(vi) Using pollution free vehicle.

(vii) Educating the people.

(viii) Purify water before use.

(ix) Sanitary land fillings.

(x) Waste control through management.

(xi) Water harvesting.

(xii) Enforce laws on waste disposal.

Q.53. What measures can be taken to control pollution?

Ans. (i) To develop consciousness among common people to control all pollution plant more and more trees.

(ii) The use of loud horns or mindless blowing of horns by motor vehicles should be banned.

(iii) The water bodies should not be used as waste reservoirs.

(iv) Various sources of drinking water, and water resources should be well protected so that dirty water does not enter these water bodies.

(v) Environmental education should be made compulsory in all educational institutions.

(vi) Excessive use of pesticides and insecticides should be avoided.

(vii) In all towns and cities there should be proper arrangement of dustbins to collect garbage being produced in the houses.

(viii) In the factories strict precaution should be instituted to avoid pollution of various types.

(ix) Running of old and pollution emitting vehicle should be banned.

(x) The pollution control Administrative Authorities must have independent powers to implement their decisions.

Q.54. How to prevent Pick-pocketing, Hooliganism, Theft and Robbery?

Ans. Following measures must be taken :

(i) To prevent pick-pocketing, one should avoid travelling in crowded places, and should try to carry little cash and valuables.

(ii) One should not indulge in hooliganism.

(iii) If cadets see hooligans indulging in such activities, and if it is a small and manageable group and cadets are in a large number, they can try for a peaceful dispersion.

(iv) If the incident cannot be controlled, cadets should report the same to nearest police station or to any law & order authority.

(v) Cadets must ensure prevention of robbery & theft and report any such incidents to law and order authority.

(vi) Cadets must make good contribution in prevention of such incidents in their neighbourhood.

Q.55. How to manage and protect the wildlife in India?

Ans. (i) Protection of natural habitats through control of exploitation.

(ii) Maintenance of protected areas like parks, sanctuaries, reserve forests.

(iii) Protection through legislation.

(iv) Impose restrictions on export of rare plants and animals.

(v) Encourage Non-Government Organisations to participate in protection of wildlife.

(vi) Spread general awareness among the masses.

Q.56. What is First aid? What are the equipment or items present in first aid kit?

Ans. First aid is the immediate help given to an injured person until expert medical attention is received. The First Aid box contains :

(i) Sterile gauze dressing
(ii) 2″ roll of bandage
(iii) 1″ one roll adhesive tape
(iv) A roll of absorbent cotton
(v) Ice bag
(vi) Mild antiseptic
(vii) Sunburn lotion
(viii) Clove oil
(ix) Pair of scissors
(x) One pack of needles
(xi) Thermometer
(xii) Iodine bottle or Tincture
(xiii) Triangular bandage
(xiv) Snake bite kit

Q.57. What are various untoward incidents plaguing the society which must be prevented by cadets?

Ans. These are as under :

(i) Road Accidents.

(ii) Pick-pocketing, Hooliganism, Theft and Robbery.

(iii) Eve-Teasing, Molestation and Sexual-Harassment.

(iv) Smoking and Alcoholism.

Q.58. How to avert road accidents?

Ans. (i) Walk carefully on the roads.

(ii) Follow all safety rules.

(iii) Take into account all signals.

(iv) Start early to reach in time.

(v) Do not overspeed.

(vi) Do not mix drinking and driving.

(vii) Cross roads at zebra crossing.

(viii) Where there is no zebra crossing, one should look towards both sides and then cross.

(ix) Hold children's hands, when they are going to cross roads.

(x) Children must be taught all the road safety rules.

Q.59. How to discourage Eve Teasing, Molestation and Sexual-Harassment?

Ans. (i) People must abide by moral values right from young age.

(ii) They must learn to respect dignity of opposite sex.

(iii) Work together with the opposite sex in a healthy environment.

(iv) People must understand that eve-teasing, molestation and sexual harassment are criminal offences.

Q.60. How to discourage Drugs, Smoking and Alcoholism?

Ans. It must be ensured that :

(i) One should spend time with their families and should introduce their friends to them.

(ii) One must understand that drug addiction, smoking and alcoholism are health hazards, and social evils and these are to be avoided.

(iii) One must spread awareness and positive thinking in the society.

(iv) One must remember that laws are implemented severely to penalize those found guilty of selling drugs or encouraging people to take drugs.

Q.61. What is the objective of posture training for NCC cadets?

Ans. (i) To develop the personality of cadets.

(ii) To build their physique and teach them correct postures.

(iii) To make them more self-reliant.

(iv) To coordinate body movements.

Q.62. How is water pollution caused?

Ans. It is caused by following means :

(i) Discharge of domestic waste

(ii) Discharge of industrial waste

(iii) Discharge of agricultural waste

Q.63. Name some forms of attacks in self defence.

Ans. Chin Jab, Knee blow, The kick, Full Nelson, Wrist locks, Strangle holds.

Q.64. How to attain the correct posture?

Ans. It can be attained by ensuring:

(i) The individual possesses sufficient strength and tone of the opposing muscle groups.

(ii) There is adequate organic vigour and the body is free from infection.

(iii) There is sufficient strength of ligaments and muscles to permit correct body position without undue strain on these ligaments or muscles.

(iv) The individual knows what correct body mechanics is.

(v) The individual has had sufficient practice in the correct position. The muscle sense of the correct position must be fully developed.

(vi) The external conditions for maintaining correct body mechanics are conducive to correct posture *i.e.,* chairs must fit the body.

Q.65. Fill in the blanks.

(i) .... and ..... are the hallmark of one's personality.

(ii) The function of Bending, Straightening and extending are of .... Joint.

(iii) Bending and straightening are the functions of .... and .... Joints.

(iv) The functions of rotation is of .... Joint.

(v) Fore arm, head and neck are examples of ...... type of Joint.

(vi) Elbow, Knee, Ankle, fingers are examples of .... type of Joint.

(vii) Hip, Shoulder and trunk are examples of .... Joints.

(viii) Head, Neck, Wrist, Fingers and Toes are of .... Joints.

(ix) When muscles are continuously stretched by habitually .... they lengthen and their tone diminishes.

(x) We constantly adjust to .... segments of the body.

(xi) When the eight segments of the body are held one upon another in the best possible manner the .... is good.

(xii) The incorrect body posture is more .... as more energy is required to maintain the physical equilibrium.

(xiii) Correct standing means that the weight of the body should be on ...., knees should be relaxed line of abdomen should be almost straight, pelvis should held .... over the base of the support, chest over ...., shoulders resting easily over the rib cage. Head over shoulder and chin should be .... to the feet.

Ans. (i) Grace, Poise, (ii) Ball and socket, (iii) Condyloid, Hinge, (iv) Pivot, (v) Pivot, (vi) Hinge, (vii) Ball and socket, (viii) Condyloid, (ix) poor posture, (x) eight, (xi) posture, (xii) fatiguing, (xiii) both feet, squarely, pelvis, parallel.

Q.66. What are the various types of Joints of the human body?

Ans. The various types of Joints in the human body are :

(i) Ball and socket (ii) Condyloid (iii) Hinge
(iv) Pivot (v) Irregular

Q.67. What are the causes of bad posture?

Ans. The following are the causes of bad posture :

(i) Due to muscular and organic defects.
(ii) Lack of nourishment.
(iii) Fatigue due to overwork.
(iv) Due to illness and infections.
(v) Due to bad habits.
(vi) Due to poor hygiene.

Q.68. What are the various causes of incorrect walking?

Ans. (i) Fatigue
(ii) Poor health
(iii) Disturbed state of mind
(v) Lack of knowledge of correct way of walking.

Q.69. Describe the standing exercise for correct walking and standing.

Ans. (i) Stand with back against the wall.
(ii) Stretch up tall.
(iii) Contact abdominal muscles and place pelvis under the abdomen.
(iv) Relax and repeat.

Q.70. Describe the walking exercise for correct standing and walking.

Ans. (i) Walk on toes with hands stretched upwards without letting the body slump.
(ii) Lower the heels and hands gradually.
(iii) Ensure that trunk and head are held in fully extended position while walking.

Q.71. Describe the correct walking.

Ans. (i) Heels in contact with the ground first.
(ii) Weight of the body transferred to the balls of the feet.
(iii) Toes used in definite push of action at each step.
(iv) Legs swinging forward and parallel.
(v) Feet swinging forward and parallel.
(vi) Relaxed arm swing.
(vii) Good body alignment.

Q.72. Name some types of throws in self defence.

Ans. Right hip throw, Ankle and shoulder throw, Overshoulder throw, Rugby tackle, Reserve hip throw, Arm throw.

Q.73. Describe the correct standing exercise for strengthening of lower back.

Ans. (i) Back lying knee pulled to chest and held.

(ii) Roll forward and back and from side-to-side.

(iii) Repeat.

Q.74. Describe the exercise "Standing with hands on hips" for developing balance and muscle strength.

Ans. (i) Raise heels.

(ii) Bend knees keeping trunk erect.

(iii) Stretch and stand

(iv) Lower heels and repeat.

Q.75. What is the highest rank in Indian Army? Name two officers to secure it.

Ans. The highest rank in Indian army is 'Field Marshal'. The officers who have been decorated with the rank of Field Marshal are:

(1) Gen. Sam Manekshaw (2) Gen. K.M. Cariappa.

Q.76. Where is the Headquarters of Armed Forces located?

Ans. New Delhi.

Q.77. Where is the NCC headquarters located?

Ans. New Delhi.

Q.78. When and where were the first atom bombs used?

Ans. The first atom bombs were used by America against Japan during the Second World War.

1. Hiroshima–6th August, 1945. 2. Nagasaki–9th August, 1945.

Q.79. Who were the first chiefs of staffs of Independent India?

Ans. The first chiefs of staffs were :

1. Army Chief : Gen. K.M. Cariappa.
2. Naval Chief : Vice Admiral R.D. Katari.
3. Air Chief Marshal : S. Mukherjee.

Q.80. When was the first atom bomb exploded by India?

Ans. India exploded the first atom bomb on May 18, 1974 at Pokhran in Rajastan. India tested the nuclear devices for the second time on May 11 and May 13, 1998, again at Pokhran.

Q.81. What is biological warfare?

Ans. Use of disease producing germs, bacteria and viruses by air burst in enemy country causing damage, disability and death to the enemy, animals and his crops is called biological warfare.

Q.82. What is NBC warfare?

Ans. NBC warfare means the use of Nuclear, Biological and Chemical Weapons.

Q.83. What is meant by 'No Man's land'?

Ans. It is the common land between the LOC of two countries. It does not belong to any country.

Q.84. What is psychological warfare?

Ans. Psychological warfare means spreading rumour amongst the enemies so as to create panic, lower their morale and disrupt their discipline, team spirit and mutual cooperative endeavour.

Q.85. When was NCC started in India?

Ans. NCC was started on 16 July, 1948.

Q.86. What is NCC Motto?

Ans. Unity & Discipline.

Q.87. What are the aims of NCC?

Ans. (i) To develop character, comradeship, discipline, leadership, secular outlook, spirit of adventure, sportsmanship and ideals of selfless service among the youth of the country.

(ii) To create a human resource of organized, trained and motivated youth, to provide leadership in all walks of life and always be available for the service of the nation.

(iii) To provide a suitable environment to motivate the youth to take up a career in the Armed Forces.

Q.88. How to prioritize casualties for treatment?

Ans. (i) Priority I - cases requiring resuscitation and urgent surgery.

(ii) Priority II - cases requiring early surgery and possibly resuscitation.

(iii) Priority III - All other casualties who require minor treatment.

Q.89. Describe balanced position when standing.

Ans. These are as under :

(i) Your knees will be free and easy, neither bent nor thrust back.

(ii) Your hips will be under you neither leading nor thrust back.

(iii) Your abdomen will be up and in, neither relaxed nor protruding.

(iv) Your chest will be held up and easy, neither sagging nor too high and leading.

(v) Your shoulder blades will be drawn down and flat on your back.

(vi) Your arms will hang naturally and relaxed at your sides, neither rigid nor too relaxed.

(vii) Your trunk will be within normal limits of curves, neither too straight and flat nor too rounded and hollow and you will stretch your back straight upward towards the crown of your head. Your head and chin will be easy and centre over your trunk with chin held at right angles to front of your neck.

Q.90. Why is national integration important for progress of any nation?

Ans. It is important for the following reasons :

(i) Maintenance of sovereignty and territorial integrity of the nation.
(ii) Maintenance of peace and harmony.
(iii) Growth and development of the nation.
(iv) Eradication of poverty and illiteracy.
(v) Internal security and law and order.
(vi) Culture and religious development.
(vii) Economic and industrial growth.
(viii) Attract foreign investment and increase import and export.
(ix) Exchange of technological know-how and culture.
(x) Dignity and self-respect as a nation.
(xi) Welfare and well-being of the people.
(xii) Foreign relations and better standing among the nations of the world.

Q.91. When a map is considered to be set?

Ans. A map is said to be set or oriented when it is placed such that it corresponds directly with the ground *i.e.,* when true North on the map points to true North on the ground.

Q.92. How the ground should be appreciated?

Ans. It should be appreciated under the following headings :

(i) Fire positions
(ii) Observation positions
(iii) Cover from fire
(iv) Cover from view
(v) Obstacles

Q.93. Why the efficient signal communication is important for the Defence Forces?

Ans. Efficient signal communication is important for :

(i) Communicating between deployed troops and commanders.
(ii) Convey the details of enemy troop movements and their activities.
(iii) To change the mode of battle activities.
(iv) To implement emergency instruction in battle field.
(v) To convey specific orders in terrain and snow-bound area.
(vi) For effective operational changes in battle field.
(vii) To acquire and decipher the information and misinformation of enemy.
(viii) To prepare the troops for further operational activities.
(ix) To assess ground level effect of operational activities.
(x) To improve infrastructure facilities in battle field.
(xi) To carry out secure and effective communications with precaution and privacy.
(xii) Communication, supply of food and evacuation of casualties.

Q.94. What is the calibre of Rif 7.62 mm SLR?
Ans. 7.62 mm.

Q.95. What is the weight of Rif 7.62 mm SLR?
Ans. 5.1 Kg.

Q.96. What is the effective range of Rif 7.62 mm SLR?
Ans. 275 metres.

Q.97. How many round are filled in Rif 7.62 mm SLR?
Ans. 20 Rds.

Q.98. What is the full name of Rif 7.62 mm SLR?
Ans. 7.62 mm self loading rifle.

Q.99. How many fires per minute can be fired by Rif 7.62 mm SLR?
Ans. 05 rounds.

Q.100. What are the cleaning materials of Rif 7.62 mm SLR?
Ans. (i) Pull through (ii) Oil bottle
(iii) Combination tool (iv) Gas regulator key screw driver
(v) Cylinder/Chamber cleaning brush (vi) Rifle cleaning brush
(vii) Graphite grease tube (viii) Chindi

Q.101. What is the position of trigger at Ready position?
Ans. At 'R'.

Q.102. What kinds of firing is done by Rif 7.62 mm SLR?
Ans. (i) Deliberate (ii) Snap shooting (iii) Rapid fire.

Q.103. What is the full name of INSAS 5.56 mm Rifle?
Ans. Rifle 5.56 mm Indian Small Arms System.

Q.104. What is the calibre of Rifle 5.56 mm?
Ans. 5.56 mm.

Q.105. What is the weight of Rifle 5.56 mm?
Ans. 3.6 Kg.

Q.106. What is the effective range of Rifle 5.56 mm?
Ans. 400 metres.

Q.107. What is the rate of fire of Rifle 5.56 mm?
Ans. (i) Normal - 60 rds/min.
(ii) TRB (Three Round Burst) - 90 rds/min.
(iii) Intense - 150 rds /min.
(iv) Cyclic - 600 to 650 rds/min.

Q.108. What is the full name of 7.62 mm LMG?
Ans. 7.62 mm Light Machine Gun.

Q.109. What is the effective range of 7.62 mm LMG?

Ans. (i) On bipod - 500 yds.

(ii) On tripod - 1000 yds.

Q.110. What is the rate of fire of 7.62 mm LMG?

Ans. (i) Normal - 28 rds (One mag) per min.

(ii) Rapid - 112 rds (four mag) per min.

(iii) Cyclic - 450 - 500 rds per min.

Q.111. How many rounds are loaded in the magzaine of 7.62 mm LMG?

Ans. 30 Rds.

Q.112. 7.62 mm LMG works on which principle?

Ans. Gas.

Q.113. How many positions are there of the change lever of 7.62 mm LMG?

Ans. 3.

Q.114. What is the caliber of Rocket Launcher 84?

Ans. 84 mm.

Q.115. What is the weight of 84 mm Rocket Launcher?

Ans. 16.100 Kg.

Q.116. How many types of ammunitions can be fired by 84 mm RL?

Ans. 06.

Q.117. How many types of ammunition can be fired by 81 mm Mortar?

Ans. Three.

Q.118. What is the killing area of Hand Grenade No 36?

Ans. 8 Mtr radius

Q.119. How many seconds fuse is of Hand grenade No. 36?

Ans. 4 second.

Q.120. What is the rate of fire of 7.62 mm?

Ans. (i) Normal - 100 rounds per minute.

(ii) Rapid - 200 rounds per minute.

(iii) Cyclic - 600-1000 rounds per minute.

Q.121. Define role of youth in nation building.

Ans. Youth is the backbone, hope of the future, potent tools of national integration and reckonable force to shape the destiny of the nation. Youth can play a leading role in bringing together the people of different states and religions with a view to integrating them emotionally, culturally and geographically.

Q.122. Name various camps conducted in NCC.

Ans. Basically there are two types of camps as under :

1. Annual Training Camps
2. Centrally Organised Camps, some of which are as under:
   (i) Leadership Camps–Advance & Basic leadership camps.
   (ii) Thal Sainik Camps.
   (iii) Vayu Sainik Camps.
   (iv) Rock Climbing Camps.
   (v) National Integration Camps.
   (vi) Republic Day Camp and Prime Minister's Rally.

Q.123. What is the relevance of NCC in unifying India and what are the important ingredients of national unity?

Ans. NCC creates awareness amongst youth about the diverse heritage of our country and fosters national integration despite linguistic, cultural, religious and geographical barriers. It helps cadets to gain experience to live together, co-operate with each other and work in harmony amongst cadets of various states, thus strengthening unity. Important ingredients of national unity are as under:

(i) Ethics and social values
(ii) Cultural and traditional values
(iii) Discipline and patriotism

Q.124. What is National Integration? What are the methods to remove the factors hindering National Integration in India?

Ans. The process of creating and strengthening the feeling of national unity is called National Integration. The methods to remove hindrances are :

(i) The education system should be improved and the students should be taught the lesson of secularism, toleration and mutual respect.
(ii) The illiteracy should be eradicated as early as possible.
(iii) The economic disparity should be narrowed.
(iv) The political parties should not be formed on the basis of religion.
(v) Every citizen should be taught to respect the National language, the National Flag, the National song and participate in National festivals.
(vi) We should keep the neighbourhood clean and beautiful.

Q.125. Write the details of Guard of Honour.

Ans. The strength of the Guard of Honour will be as follows:

(i) 150 rank and file for the President (will be formed up in 3 equal division).
(ii) 100 rank and file for the Vice President and Prime Minister (will be formed up in two equal division).

Q.126. What are the various factors that affect duty and discipline in NCC?

Ans. (i) Individual's own state of mind
(ii) Ambition
(iii) Self respect
(iv) School and college atmosphere
(v) NCC COY/BN atmosphere
(vi) Less emphasis on NCC by institutions/parents
(vii) COY commander's/senior's attitude
(viii) State/quality of training imparted
(ix) Peer pressure
(x) Communication problems

Q.127. What is likely to be the impact of earthquakes?

Ans. (i) Loss of Life
(ii) Injury
(iii) Damage to or destruction of property including crops
(iv) Disruption of production
(v) Disruption of lifestyle
(vi) Loss of livelihood
(vii) Disruption to essential services
(viii) Damage to national infrastructure and disruption to administrative and organisational systems
(ix) Sociological and psychological after-effects

Q.128. Define major joints, their location, direction of their movements and their functions.

Ans. These are as under :

S.No.	Type	Where Joined	Directions of movements	Functions
(i)	Ball & Socket	Hip, Shoulder Trunk	Forward Backward and rotation sideways	Bending, Straightening, extending
(ii)	Condyloid	Head, Neck, Wrist Fingers, Toes	Forward Backward sideways	Bending and straightening
(iii)	Hinge	Elbow, Knee Ankle, Fingers	Forward Backward	Bending and straightening
(iv)	Pivot	Fore-arm, Head, Neck	Around	Rotation, right, lift, in and out
(v)	Irregular	Foot, Hand	Gliding	In and out movement

Q.129. How can youth contribute individually for nation building?

Ans. (i) Be good human being by imbibing oriental value system.

(ii) Help the friends & colleagues from unprivileged section of society.

(iii) Improve personal talent, innovate and enhance usefulness for society and nation.

(iv) Discourage corruption in every form and manifestation in society.

(v) Participate in sports, yoga and improve personal health.

(vi) Use national/natural resources like, energy in all forms, communication spectrum, water resources etc with due austerity and discourage its misuse by others.

(vii) Develop secular outlook and tolerance for all sections of society.

(viii) Extend willing help to civil administration during natural and man-made disasters.

(ix) Learn healthy politics during college days.

Q.130. 'Right Turn' is of what degree and given on which foot?

Ans. 90° and given on left foot.

Q.131. 'About Turn' is of what degree and given on which foot?

Ans. 180° and given on left foot.

Q.132. 'Left Turn' is of what degree and given on which foot?

Ans. 90° and given on right foot.

Q.133. How many types of salutes are there?

Ans. Salutes are of three types :

(i) Salute to the front

(ii) Salute to the right

(iii) Salute to the left

Q.134. Salute to the front is given on which foot?

Ans. On the left foot.

Q.135. Salute to the right is given on which foot?

Ans. On the left foot.

Q.136. Salute to the front is given by which hand?

Ans. Right hand.

Q.137. There are .... steps per minute in normal march.

Ans. 120.

Q.138. There are .... steps per minute is slow march.

Ans. 70.

Q.139. On the command 'Quick March' first step is of .... inches.

Ans. 30

Q.140. Who all are eligible of salute?
Ans. Naib Subedar and above ranks.

Q.141. Who are eligible of National Salute?
Ans. President and Governors of States.

Q.142. Who are eligible of General Salute?
Ans. Major General and above ranks.

Q.143. Write any four factors which make things visible.
Ans. Shape, Shine, Shadow, Movement.

Q.144. What are the various types of patrols?
Ans. Recce, Protective patrols.

Q.145. What are the types of section formation?
Ans. Single File, Arrow head, Spear, Diamond & Extended line formation.

Q.146. What are the various types of grounds?
Ans. Broken, Open, High, Dead and Low ground.

Q.147. Which are the methods of conveying signals?
Ans. By hand, with rifle and whistle signals.

Q.148. What are scouts?
Ans. Scouts are eyes and ears of a section. They are men sent ahead of a section on move to gather information.

Q.149. Which are various groups in Infantry section?
Ans. Rifle and Bren group.

Q.150. In which year did the following events took place?
(i) Indo-China War (ii) Indo-Pak War-I
(iii) Indo Pak War-II (iv) Kargil War
Ans. (i) 1962 (ii) 1965 (iii) 1971 (iv) 1999

Q.151. How are Combat formations grouped? Who commands these formations.
Ans. Combat formations are grouped as Corps, Divisions and Brigades. These are commanded by an officer of the rank of Lt General, Major General and Brigadier respectively.

Q.152. What are Grid Lines? Mention any three rules of Grid Reference.
Ans. A map is covered with a network of purple lines, some running North and South and others West and East. These form a series of small squares all over the map. These lines are known as Grid Lines.

Rule of Grid Reference:

(i) A reference must always contain an even number of figures. Normally it contains six figures.

(ii) Always count along the EASTING lines first from the WEST to EAST and then from SOUTH to NORTH along NORTHINGS.

(iii) For six figure Grid Reference the third and the sixth figure represent the divisions of 1000 meters square to the nearest 10th part, so they have to be estimated and for these figures a slight latitude is allowed.

(iv) If a general Grid Reference is to be given or there is only one such object in one square e.g., bridge, temple, road junction then its identity and four figure grid reference would suffice.

Q.153. Explain major types of knots for joining ropes.

Ans. **(i) Sheet Bend:** To join or bend two ropes of unequal thickness together. The thicker rope is the bend.

(ii) Double Sheet Bend: Similar to single sheet bend, but gives greater security, also useful for joining wet ropes.

(iii) Crossover Sheet Bend: This holds more securely than either the single or double sheet bend and has occasional real uses such as fastening the eye of a flag to its halyard where the flapping might undo the double sheet bend.

(iv) Reef Knot: To securely join two ropes of equal thickness together. Notice the difference in position of the free and standing ends between this and the thief knot.

(v) Thief Knot: To tie two ropes of equal thickness together so that they will appear to be tied with a reef knot, and will be retied with a true reef knot. This knot was often used by sailors to tie their sea chests, hence the name.

(vi) Carrick Bend: This bend is for the secure fastening of two ropes of even thickness together. It is particularly suitable for hawsers and steel cables. It can be readily undone and does not jam, as do many other bends and knots.

(vii) Fisherman's Knot: For joining two springy materials together; suitable for wire, fishing gut or vines. Two thumb knots (one on each rope) pulled tight. The knots lock together.

Q.154. What are the disadvantages of line (Wires/ Cables) communication?

Ans. Disadvantages of Line Communication:

(i) Vulnerable to physical intereference and enemy interception along the entire length of the route.

(ii) Takes time to construct.

(iii) Inflexible once it is laid.

(iv) Expensive in men and material.

Q.155. Give meaning of the following terms:

(i) Knoll **(ii) Spur** **(iii) Spot Height** **(iv) Bearing**

Ans. **(i) Knoll:** A small isolated hill.

(ii) Spur: A piece of high ground jutting out from a range of hills into lower ground.

(iii) Spot Height: A point on a map whose height has been determined by Survey method. This height is printed alongside the point.

(iv) Bearing: The angle formed by a line joining two points and the North and South line. Bearings are always measured clockwise.

Q.156. How are the following signals made by the use of hand.

(i) Deploy (ii) Halt (iii) Close (iv) Follow me

Ans. **(i) Deploy:** Right arm fully extended above head and waved from side to side, palm open.

(ii) Halt: Right arm raised to full extent above head.

(iii) Close: Right hand place on top of head, elbow to the right.

(iv) Follow me: Right arm swung from rear to front above the shoulder, in "over arm bowling" fashion.

Q.157. Which is the youngest of the three services? When did it come into existence?

Ans. Indian Air Force is the youngest of the three Services. It was in 1932 that an Act was passed in Indian Legislature for establishing the Indian Air Force on the recommendations of Skeen Committee.

Q.158. Write any three relevant points related to 'appearance method' of judging distance.

Ans. **Appearance Method:** The distance can be judged by noting the detailed appearance of man at various ranges. This is the best method under service conditions. The following is a guide to distance:

(i) At 200 yards, all parts of the body are distinct.

(ii) At 250 yards, blade of the foresight covers a kneeling man.

(iii) At 300 yards the face becomes blurred.

Q.159. What facilities are provided by videophone?

Ans. (i) High quality of voice.

(ii) Called subscriber is seen on the monitor.

(iii) Can transmit speech as well as colour video.

(iv) Conduct of video conferences.

(v) Speed of sending/receiving can be adjusted by the user.

(vi) Map overlays can be transmitted.

Q.160. Write about any five characterisitics of contours.

Ans. (i) Contour lines vary in appearance.

(ii) Contours are shown generally in brown.

(iii) Height is marked on every fifth contour.

(iv) These lines never touch or cross each other.

(v) Contours accurately show height, shape and slope of the ground.

Q.161. Write about the subjects that are included in field craft.

Ans. Field Craft includes the following subjects:

(i) Judging distance.

(ii) Movement with and without arms.

(iii) Personal camouflage and concealment.

(iv) Recognition and description of targets.

Q.162. Write about the subjects that are included in battle craft.

Ans. Battle Craft includes the following subjects:

(i) Field Signals (ii) Fire and movement

(iii) Section Formations (iv) Section battle drills

Q.163. What are the advantages of Net radio?

Ans. Advantages of Net Radio:

(i) Fast in establishing communication.

(ii) Flexible as it involves no lying & wires/cables. Any radio set can speak to any troops/commander by putting his frequency.

(iii) Vulnerable only at terminal and is therefore reasonably protected from enemy action except by a direct hit.

Q.164. What is the full form of GPS? What does it refer to and who funds and controls GPS?

Ans. Global Positioning System (GPS): Global Positioning System refers to a system of satellites and receivers that allows people and devices to pin point their precise location on the earth. GPS is funded and controlled by the United States, Department of Defence.

Q.165. Under what circumstances fire and movement tactics are used?

Ans. (i) To cross obstacles.

(ii) When own troops have seen the enemy first.

(iii) The enemy has opened Small Arm fire which is effective.

(iv) When the enemy is known or suspected to be in a certain area.

Q.166. With regard to 5.56 INSAS rifle provide the following information :

(i) Who makes it? (ii) Who uses it?

(iii) What is its intense rate of fire?

Ans. (i) Indian Ordnance Factory Board.

(ii) It is being used by the Indian army.

(iii) 150 rds/min.

Q.167. What are the basic considerations for fire and movement?

Ans. The basic considerations for fire and movement are as under:

(i) No movement on exposed ground without covering fire: The advantages of covering fire are obvious, but this does not mean that fire will be brought down continuously when you are moving.

Whenever you have ground providing you cover, you must use it. Whenever you have to move in open, fire must be brought down on the enemy in small bursts to keep his head down.

(ii) Control by the Commander: The section can remain a viable force only when it is under the control of its commander. Otherwise, it is likely that the required fire support will not be brought down at the required place and time. In a section, control is executed by voice command and hand signals. As a rule, section commander must keep his section within range of voice or visible control.

(iii) The angle of covering fire from direct firing weapons: It should be as wide as possible without loss of control or time. It is to ensure that own troops are not coming under effective fire of own fire spell. It also ensures that the fire support is provided till as late as possible so that assault troops are able to close in with the enemy.

(iv) Full use of Available Cover: Full use should be made of cover provided by the ground. Various types of covers may be used.

(v) Optimum use of all Available Weapons: All available weapons should be used for producing covering fire.

Q.168. What is 'Radio Telephony'?

Ans. Radio Telephony is the procedure laid out to communicate on the Radio so as to make the conversation secure and successful.

Q.169. Write some differences between Code Sign and Link Sign.

Ans.

Code Sign	Link Sign
(i) Identifies a unit.	(i) Identifies a radio link.
(ii) Issued down to unit level.	(ii) Issued to all radio stations.
(iii) Cannot be abbreviated.	(iii) Can be abbreviated.
(iv) Can be changed to link sign.	(iv) Cannot be changed to code sign.
(v) Not issued to branches of a HQ.	(v) Issued to branches of a HQ.

Q.170. What is webbing with regard to rock climbing? What are its uses?

Ans. Webbing or "Tape" made of nylon. When webbing is sewn or tied together at the ends, it becomes a sling or runner. Webbing has many uses such as:

(i) Extending the distance between protection and a tie-in point.
(ii) An anchor around a tree or rock or an anchor extension or equalization.
(iii) Makeshift harnesses.
(iv) Carrying equipment (clipped to a sling worn over the shoulder).
(v) Protecting a rope that hangs over a sharp edge (tubular webbing).

❖ ❖ ❖

CHAPTER

23 Test Your Knowledge

UNSOLVED QUESTIONS FOR PRACTICE

1. Name the Nobel prize winners of India.
2. Name the capitals and the classical dances of the following states :

   (i) Tamil Nadu, (ii) Odisha, (iii) Andhra Pradesh, (iv) Kerala, (v) Manipur, (vi) Uttar Pradesh.
3. Name the four important mountain ranges of our country.
4. India is the ____ largest in the world (Military).
5. Name any four neighbours of our country.
6. Who was the Indian Army chief during Bangladesh war?
7. India tested its Nuclear explosion at ________.
8. The name given to Indian troops who moved to Sri lanka is _____.
9. Where are the following located : (i) NDA (ii) OTA (iii) IMA (iv) RIMC.
10. Name the North-Eastern states of India and their capitals.
11. Name the main religions of India, their major festivals and holy places.
12. National Integration includes : (any five points)
13. Name any five factors which enhance National Integration.
14. First battle of Panipat was fought in the year ___________.
15. Second battle of Panipat was fought in the year ___________.
16. What are the basic commonalities in all our major religions?
17. Name any five Gallantry awards given in India.
18. Name any five Army personnel who have won the highest Gallantry Award in our country.
19. Briefly explain the factors that hinder National Integration.
20. Hinduism is also known as _______________.
21. Islam has two major sects called ________ and ________ .
22. The major religious places of Islam are ________ and ________ .

23. The religious scripture of the Sikhs is ______________ and the golden temple is located at ________.

24. The ______________ is the holy book of the Christians.

25. Nightingale of India is ______________.

26. Iron man of India is ______________.

27. The first Indian woman who scaled Mount Everest is ______________.

28. The first Indian Astronaut is ______________.

29. The first Indian who swam across English Channel is ________ .

30. Majors rivers in the country are ________, ________, ________, ________, ________, _______ .

31. Name the five Bravery Awards given to the defence personnel.

32. Holy book of Muslims is ____________, Hindus is ____________, Christians is ______________.

33. The sepoy mutiny against British rule took place in the year ________.

34. The three major wars fought between India and Pakistan were in the years ________, ________, _______.

35. India became a Republic on ________________.

36. The new year festival in Punjab is known as ______________ and in Kerala it is known as ____________.

37. Bhangra is the dance form popular in the state ____________ & Bihu dance in the state ___________.

38. What is the aim of drill?

39. What are the essentials of a good word of command?

40. What is the length of pace and number of pace per minute for :

(i) Tez chal (ii) Dhire chal.

41. What is the difference between 'Visarjan' and 'Line Tor'?

42. How many parts, word of command consist of? What are they?

43. Give the length of pace in minutes :

(i) Slow time (ii) Quick time (iii) Double time.

44. The strength of guard of honour for the following will be :

(i) President (ii) Vice President (iii) Others.

45. Translate in Hindi :

(i) Stand at ease, (ii) About turn, (iii) Eyes right, (iv) Right-turn, (v) Stand easy.

46. The distance between heel-to-heel in 'Vishram' position is ________.

47. In 'Tej chal' the length of one pace is __________.

48. While on 'Tej chal' there are three types of saluting. They are ________, __________, _________.

49. The word of command for temporary rest is _________.

50. 'Bagal Shastra' is completed in ________ movements.

51. In 'Tej chal', the number of steps taken per minute is _________.

52. The distance between two persons when forming in rank is _______.

53. In 'Dahine Mur' you turn to _______ degrees to _________ (Left/Right).

54. In 'Vishram' position, the distance between the toe-to-toe (Feet) is ________.

55. The angle formed by the feet in 'Savdhan' position is ___________ degree.

56. Word of command 'Tham' is given on __________ foot.

57. The strength of guard during guard mounting is ___________.

58. In 'Adha Dahine Mud' the squad turns __________ degrees.

59. In 'Tej chal' the distance between the cadets is _______.

60. In 'Dahine saj', the squad takes a step forward by ____________ inches.

61. What are the characteristics of word of command?

62. ______________ is the basic movement of drill.

63. Basic essentials of a good firing or shooting are?

64. Write the full form of the following :

(i) MPI (ii) SMC (iii) LMG (iv) SLR (v) DPBF (vi) MMG (vii) RCL (viii) CQBW.

65. Write sequence of action for stripping a rifle.

66. Write in point form why a group is formed in firing and why bullets do not pass through the same hole?

67. What are the major parts in which an LMG can be stripped?

68. What are the materials required for cleaning a rifle?

69. What are the points do you ensure for correct lying position?

70. The five major factors affecting the bullet inside the barrel are?

71. Name any five parts of Sten Machine Carbine.

72. The LMG can be stripped into five major groups. Name them.

73. What is half cock? How is it caused and remedied?

74. Name various parts of the .22 Rifle.

75. Explain briefly : (a) Aiming (b) Half cock.

76. What are the major characteristics of Rifle No. 1 MK III?

77. The battle effective range of SMC is ________.

78. The barrel of Rifle is cleaned with patch of flannelette (Chindi) measuring 6" x 4" (True/False)

79. The barrel of Rifle is oiled using 4" x 5" patch of flannelette. (True/False)

80. SMC fires only one round at a time. (True/False)

81. The change lever of LMG has three positions. (True/False)

82. Name any five parts of a .22 Rifle.

83. Effective range of LMG on tripod is ________.

84. ____________ rounds are filled in the LMG Magazine.

85. The weight of Rifle (without Bayonet) is ________.

86. Grouping Fire is carried out from ____________ metres.

87. The effective range of 7.62 mm SLR is ________.

88. The muzzle velocity of SLR is ________.

89. Grouping fire is carried from ____________ position.

90. The size of chindi to clean a rifle is ________ and for oiling is ________.

91. The cyclic rate of fire per minute for a LMG is ________ to ________ rounds.

92. The weight of an SMC is approximately __________ Kgs.

93. The magazine capacity of LMG is __________ rounds.

94. Answer in one or two sentences each : (a) Trajectory (b) Axis of Barrel (c) Danger space.

95. Battle effective range of 7.62 mm rifle is ________.

96. The magazine capacity of 7.62 mm rifle is ________ rounds.

97. The battle effective range of 7.62 mm LMG is ____________ yards on bipod.

98. The pull through has ________ loops.

99. In immediate action during firing in LMG what is done?

100. What points do you ensure for correct lying position?

101. The allowance in front of the target given for aiming and firing is termed ____________.

102. What is line of sight?

103. Combination tool is used to ______________.

104. What are the duties of a good citizen?

105. What are the ways of acquiring citizenship?

106. What is Leadership?

107. What are the main traits of a Leader?

108. Define Citizen. Explain the qualities of a good citizen.

109. Define Duty.

110. Define Discipline.

111. What are the cardinals spelt out by DG-NCC.

112. Name any five Customs/Traditions of services being observed by the Army.

113. Discipline is of two types *i.e.,* ________ and ________.

114. In the Army ________ and ________ represent fighting arms and ________ and ________ represent services.

115. Write down the Aims of NCC.

116. Duty may be defined as a ________ obligation and a binding force of what is ________ and ______ towards superiors, colleagues and subordinates.

117. A Leader should be hardworking and courageous. (True/False)

118. A Leader should have plenty of money. (True/False)

119. A Leader should be concerned over the safety of his men/followers. (True/False)

120. A Leader need not set an example. (True/False)

121. A Leader should work without worrying about awards and rewards. (True/False)

122. You are walking to your college and there are just five minutes left. A bus knocks down a cyclist, who is badly hurt. What will you do?

123. On a cold winter night, there are some threatening sounds in your neighbour's house at midnight. There may be thieves. What will you do?

124. What is Civil Defence? What is its aim? Name any six Civil Defence services.

125. What are the various modes of spread of Fire?

126. What is the necessity of Civil Defence?

127. Write short note on restorative measures.

128. What are the measures that are taken to reduce the effects of enemy air-attack?

129. What are the main advantages of portable fire extinguishers?

130. Name the Civil Defence measures. Write short note on any one of them.

131. What are the roles assigned to Home Guards?

132. Name the different types of Fire fighting equipments.

133. What are the elements essentials for combustion?

134. The risk of air-raid casualties could be reduced by taking adequate care such as :
(i) ________, (ii) ________, (iii) ________, (iv) ________,
(v) ________, (vi) ________, (vii) ________, (viii) ________,

135. What are the categories of fire fighting equipment/appliances.

136. The controller of Civil Defence in district is ________.

137. Name any 7 services performed under civil defence task.

138. What is Fire? Write short note on extinguishing a fire.

139. Briefly explain the modes of extinguishing fire.

140. What are the types of Air-Raid messages?

141. List out Major Social problems of our country.

142. How will you plan & organize the social service to be rendered at an 'old age home' by NCC cadets?

143. What is social service?

144. What are the factors to be borne in mind before planning a social activity?

145. Name any five social activities where NCC cadets can take part.

146. Explain what do you understand by Adult literacy.

147. Briefly explain how will you organize Tree plantation in your locality.

148. Briefly discuss the methods undertaken for community development.

149. What are the duties of an individual as per traditions in our country?

150. You are an under officer, you have been tasked by your CO to undertake Adult Education Programme. Enumerate the sequence in which you will proceed with your task.

151. Your Battalion was tasked to collect clothes for cyclone victims. Name five important points to keep in mind while doing so as a senior cadet.

152. What kind of civil activities you can undertake during social service camps?

153. As an NCC cadet what type of social service/community development programmes can you conduct. Briefly explain them.

154. The minimum age limit for Blood donation is ________ years, while minimum weight is ________ Kg.

155. Traffic control by NCC cadets should be in non-peak hours. (True/False)

156. Blood donation makes a person weak. (True/False)

157. Working voluntarily in an 'Old age home' is a social service. (True/False)

158. List out five personal protective measures to prevent malaria.

159. Purification of water on large scale (one line each – any three methods).

160. Purification of water on small scale at home is done by?

161. Name the basic factors which contribute to good health.

162. Write the important aspect on personal hygiene that you would like to follow.

163. What is full form of AIDS? What action will you take to prevent AIDS?

164. Name the preventive measures that can be taken to stop spreading of communicable diseases.

165. How is Obesity checked?

166. Mention the six constituents of food.

167. What is safe water?

168. What are the types in which communicable diseases can be classified?

169. AIDS is spread by __________, __________ & __________.

170. Dental decay is caused by the deficiency of vitamins __________ & __________.

171. Leprosy is caused by a germ called __________.

172. The carrier of malaria, dengue and filaria are __________.

173. The largest component of diet is __________.

174. Describe how to treat a case of snake bite.

175. The two main types of bleedings are __________ and __________.

176. In case of a fracture, the correct action is "__________ them where they lie and as they lie".

177. What is first aid? What are the immediate aims of first aid?

178. What are the first aid treatments given to one with burn injuries.

179. Write the items held in the first aid box.

180. Write the function of the following : (a) Lungs, (b) Skin, (c) Skeleton.

181. Define First Aid.

182. Define Fracture. What are the signs and symptoms of simple fracture?

183. Write down the signs and symptoms of Asphyxia.

184. Write down the types of Artificial respiration.

185. How does a trained first aider proceed to treat a patient?

186. What points will you keep in mind while giving mouth-to-mouth respiration?

187. What are the causes of Ecological Imbalance?

188. What are the aims of adventure training?

189. What are the Adventure activities undertaken by NCC cadets?

190. Write down how you will plan, organize and conduct cycle expedition in which about 100 Kms is to be covered in three days.

191. What are the actions to be taken while planning a trek of NCC cadets? Give your reply in chronological order in point form.

192. What are the aims of Trekking camps?

193. While selecting cadets for Trekking, what points will you bear in mind?

194. What are the various types of Adventure Activities conducted by NCC?

195. How can you protect Wildlife?

196. _________ is our National flower.

197. _________ is our National Bird.

198. _______ is our National Animal.

199. What are the main causes for environmental deterioration?

200. Name any five actions to preserve environment.

201. Bandhabghar National park is located in _________ state.

202. Elephants are poached so as to steal _________ .

203. A fragrant tree which is smuggled out of Karnataka is _________.

204. Sunderban Delta is in ___________ state.

205. What are the hazards of destabilization of environment?

206. Define Environment.

207. What are the causes of atmospheric pollution in cities and how can it be reduced?

208. Name different types of Forests.

209. Lion is found in _____________ forest of _____________state.

210. The Horn-Rhino is found in __________ wildlife sanctuary.

211. Late Dr. Salim Ali was associated with __________ throughout his life.

212. Species content of animals present in any area is ________.

213. World Environment day is ________.

214. The architects of Indus Valley Civilization were ________.

215. ________ is the world's largest Delta.

❖ ❖ ❖

CHAPTER

24 General Awareness

CONSTITUTION OF INDIA

The constitution of India is the supreme law of India. It establishes the structure, powers, procedures and duties of government institutions. It defines fundamental rights, fundamental duties and directive principles. The nation is governed by it. It was created and adopted by the constituent assembly on 26 November, 1949 and came into effect on 26 January, 1950. Dr. B R Ambedkar is known as the architect of Indian constitution.

Preamble to the Constitution of India

The constitution of India begins with a preamble which describes the nature of the Indian state and the objectives it is committed to secure. It is regarded as the political horoscope of the constitution. It is the most precious part and the soul of the constitution. The preamble states the philosophical foundations of the constitution and enumerates the objectives of constitution. It is a part of the basic structure of the constitution. The constitution through its preamble commits itself to democracy, republicanism, socialism, secularism and liberalism.

Fundamental Rights

1. Right of Equality (Article 14-18)
2. Right to Freedom (Article 19 & 358)
3. Right Against Exploitation (Article 23-24)
4. Right to Freedom of Religion (Articles 25-28)
5. Cultural and Educational Rights (Articles 29-30)
6. Right of Constitutional Remedies (Articles 32-35 & 359)

PREAMBLE

'We the people of India, having solemnly resolved to Constitute India into a Sovereign, Socialist, Secular Democratic Republic and to secure to all its citizen: ***Justice:*** Social, economic and political; ***Liberty:*** Of thought, expression, belief, faith and worship; ***Equality:*** Of status and of opportunity, and to promote among them all; ***Fraternity:*** Assuring the dignity of the individual and the unity and integrity of the nation. In our Constituent Assembly, this twenty-sixth day of November, 1949, do hereby adopt, enact and give to ourselves this constitution.'

Fundamental Duties

The following duties need to be adhered to by all citizens :

1. To abide by the constitution and respect its ideal and institutions.
2. To cherish and follow the noble ideals which inspired our national struggle for freedom.
3. To uphold and protect the sovereignty, unity and integrity of India.
4. To defend the country and render national service when called upon to do so.

5. To promote harmony and the spirit of common brotherhood amongst all the people of India transcending religious, linguistic and regional diversities, to renounce practices derogatory to the dignity of women.
6. To value and preserve the rich heritage of our composite culture.
7. To protect and improve the natural environment including forests, lakes, rivers, and wildlife and to have compassion for living creatures.
8. To develop the scientific temper, humanism and the spirit of inquiry and reform.
9. To safeguard public property and to abjure violence.
10. To strive towards excellence in all spheres of individual and collective activity, so that the nation constantly rises to higher levels of endeavour and achievement.
11. Who is a parent or guardian, to provide opportunities for education to his child or as the case may be, ward between the age of six and fourteen years.

Important Features

1. Constitution of India came into force on January 26, 1950.
2. President of India is elected for a term of five years.
3. Sessions of Parliament are summoned by President.
4. Vice-President of India is the ex-officio Chairman of Rajya Sabha.
5. Lok Sabha is elected for a term of five years.
6. Speaker, Lok Sabha is elected by the members of Lok Sabha.
7. Council of Ministers is appointed by the President on the recommendation of the Prime Minister.
8. The Union Council of Ministers is responsible to Lok Sabha.
9. Rajya Sabha is a permanent body and cannot be dissolved.
10. Members of Rajya Sabha have a term of 6 years.
11. Judges of Supreme Court are appointed by the President.
12. State Governors are appointed by the President.

NATIONAL AWARDS AND HONOURS

Civilian Awards

- **Bharat Ratna:** This is India's highest civilian award. It is given for exceptional work in art, literature, science and recognition of public service of the highest order. Government servants are not eligible for it.
- **Padma Vibhushan:** This award is given for exceptional and distinguished service in any field, including service rendered by Government servants.
- **Padma Bhushan:** This award is given for distinguished service of a high order in any field, including service rendered by Government servants.
- **Padma Shri:** This award is given for distinguished service in any field, including service rendered by Government servants.

INDIA

Facts About India

1. **Area :** 32, 87,263 sq. km.
2. **Land Frontier :** 15,200 km
3. **Total Coast line :** 7516.6 km
4. **Population (2011 census) :** 1,21,08,54,977 (623.27 million males and 587.58 million females)
5. **Average Density of Population** : 382 per sq. km.
6. **Total Literacy :** 73.00%
   (i) Male literacy : 80.9%
   (ii) Female literacy : 64.6%
7. **India is :**
   (i) 7th largest country in the world in area.
   (ii) 2nd largest populous country in the world.
   (iii) Home to more than 16 per cent of world population (2011 census) and accounts for 2.42 per cent of the total world area.
8. **India's Neighbours :**
   (i) In the north — China, Nepal and Bhutan
   (ii) In the east — Myanmar (Burma)
   (iii) Bangladesh lies wedged between India's north-eastern States and West Bengal
   (iv) In the west and north-west — Pakistan
   (v) In the south — Sri Lanka

States

1. Largest in population : Uttar Pradesh (about 19.9 crore)
2. Smallest in population : Sikkim (about 6 lakh)
3. Largest in area : Rajasthan (about 3.4 lakh sq. km)
4. Smallest in area : Goa (3702 sq. km)
5. Highest density of population : Bihar (1106)
6. Lowest density of population : Arunachal Pradesh (17)
7. First to achieve 100% rural electrification : Haryana
8. First to achieve total literacy : Kerala
9. Lowest percentage of literacy : Bihar (61.8%)
10. With high number of females than males : Kerala (1084 females for 1000 males)

Union Territories

1. Largest in population : Delhi (over 1.6 crore)
2. Smallest in population : Lakshadweep (over 64 thousand)
3. Highest density of population : Delhi (11,320)
4. Lowest density of population : Andaman & Nicobar Islands (46)
5. Highest percentage of literacy : Lakshadweep (91.8%)
6. Lowest percentage of literacy : Dadar & Nagar Haveli (76.2%)

National Flag

1. It is horizontal tricolour
2. Three equal horizontal stripes:
   (i) Deep saffron at the top
   (ii) White in the middle
   (iii) Dark Green at the bottom.
3. Ratio of width to length : 2 : 3
4. In the centre of the white stripe : A wheel in navy blue.
5. Number of spokes in the wheel : 24
6. The wheel is a replica of the wheel on the capital of the Ashoka Pillar at Sarnath.
7. The National Flag was adopted by the Constituent Assembly of India, on July 22, 1947.
8. Its use and display are regulated by a specific code.

State Emblem

1. State Emblem is an adaptation from the Sarnath Lion Capital of Ashoka.
2. In the adapted form, only three lions are visible, the fourth being hidden from the view.
3. A wheel appears in relief in the centre of the abacus with a bull on the right and a horse on the left.
4. Below the abacus appears *Satyameva Jayate* in the devanagari script.
5. *Satyameva Jayate* has been taken from Mundaka Upanishad.
6. *Satyameva Jayate* means "Truth Alone Triumphs."
7. The State Emblem was adopted by the Government of India on January 26, 1950.

STATES OF INDIA

	State	Capital	Principal Language(s)	Area (sq. km)	Population 2011
1.	Andhra Pradesh	Amravati	Telugu, Urdu	1,60,229	49386799
2.	Arunachal Pradesh#	Itanagar	Monpa, Miji, etc.	83,743	1383727
3.	Assam	Dispur[1]	Assamese, Bengali	78,438	31205576
4.	Bihar	Patna	Hindi	94,163	104099452
5.	Chhattisgarh	Raipur	Hindi	1,36,034	25545198
6.	Goa	Panaji	Konkani, Marathi	3,702	1458545
7.	Gujarat	Gandhi Nagar	Gujarati	1,96,024	60439692
8.	Haryana	Chandigarh	Hindi	44,212	25351462
9.	Himachal Pradesh	Shimla	Hindi, Pahari	55,673	6864602
10.	Jharkhand	Ranchi	Hindi	79,714	32988134
11.	Karnataka	Bengaluru	Kannada	1,91,791	61095297
12.	Kerala	Thiruvananthapuram	Malayalam	38,863	33406061
13.	Madhya Pradesh	Bhopal	Hindi	3,08,000	72626809
14.	Maharashtra	Mumbai	Marathi	3,07,713	112374333
15.	Manipur	Imphal	Manipuri	22,327	2570390
16.	Meghalaya	Shillong	Khasi, Garo, English	22,429	2966889
17.	Mizoram	Aizawl	Mizo, English	21,081	1097206
18.	Nagaland	Kohima	6	16,579	1978502
19.	Odisha	Bhubaneshwar	Odiya	1,55,707	41974218
20.	Punjab	Chandigarh	Punjabi	50,362	27743308
21.	Rajasthan	Jaipur	Hindi, Rajasthani	3,42,239	68548437
22.	Sikkim	Gangtok	7	7,096	610577
23.	Tamil Nadu	Chennai	Tamil	1,30,058	72147030
24.	Telangana	Hyderabad	Telugu, Urdu	1,14,840	35193978
25.	Tripura	Agartala	8	10,491	3673917
26.	Uttarakhand	Dehradun (Provisional)	Hindi	53,484	10086292
27.	Uttar Pradesh	Lucknow	Hindi, Urdu	2,40,928	199812341
28.	West Bengal	Kolkata	Bengali	88,752	91276115
UNION TERRITORIES					
1.	Andaman & Nicobar Islands	Port Blair	9	8,249	380581
2.	Chandigarh	Chandigarh	Hindi, Punjabi, English	114	1055450
3.	Delhi	Delhi	Hindi, Urdu, Punjabi	1,483	16787941
4.	Lakshadweep	Kavaratti	Malayalam	32	64473
5.	Puducherry	Puducherry	Tamil, French, Telugu, English and Malayalam	480	1247953
6.	Jammu & Kashmir[10]	Srinagar[2]	3	2,22,236[4]	12541302[5,11]
7.	Ladakh	Leh	–	–	–
8.	Dadra & Nagar Haveli and Daman & Diu[12]	Daman	Gujarati and Hindi	603	586956

1. Pragjyotishpur will be the new capital of Assam; **2.** In winter the capital shifts to Jammu; **3.** Kashmiri, Dogri, Gujri, Urdu, Balti, Dadri, Pahari, Ladakhi, Punjabi; **4.** Includes 78,114 sq km under illegal occupation of Pakistan, 5,180 sq. km illegaly handed over by Pakistan to China and 37,555 sq km under illegal occupation of China, also includes Ladakh area; **5.** The population figure excludes population of area under unlawful occupation of Pakistan and China. **6.** Angami, Ao, Chang, Konyak, Lotha, Sangtam, Semaand Chakhesang; **7.** Bhutia, Nepali, Lepcha and Limbu; **8.** Bengali, Kakborak and Manipuri, **9.** Hindi, Nicobarese, Bengali, Malayalam, Tamil & Telugu. # This State enjoys special status on traditional and customary laws. **10.** Jammu & Kashmir state has been converted to two Union Territories, namely, Jammu & Kashmir and Ladakh w.e.f. 31 October, 2019. **11.** Also includes population of Ladakh. **12.** Dadra & Nagar Haveli and Daman & Diu have become single UT w.e.f. 26/01/2020.

Note: The figures are based on Final Census of India, 2011.

National Anthem

1. *Jana-gana-mana* composed by Rabindranath Tagore is our national anthem.
2. The Constituent Assembly of India adopted it as the national anthem on January 24, 1950.
3. It was first sung on December 27, 1911 at the Calcutta Session of the Indian National Congress.
4. It was first published under caption 'Bharat Vidhata' in January 1912 in the magazine named *'Tatva Bodhini'.*
5. Playing time of the full version of the national anthem is approximately 52 seconds.

Jana-gana-mana-adhinayka, Jaya he
Bharat-bhagya-vidhata
Punjab-Sindh-Gujarat-Maratha
Dravida-Utkala-Banga
Vindhya-Himachala-Yamuna-Ganga
Uchchala-Jaladhi-taranga
Tava shubha name jage,
Tava shubha ashisha mange,
Gahe tava jaya gatha,
Jana-gana-mangala-dayaka jaya he
Bharata-bhagya-vidhata,
Jaya he, jaya he, jaya he,
Jaya, jaya, jaya, jaye he!

National Song

1. *Vande Mataram* is our national song.
2. It was composed by Bankim Chandra Chatterji.
3. It has an equal status with *Jana-gana-mana.*
4. It was first sung at the 1896 session of the Indian National Congress.
5. This song occurs in the novel *Anand Math,* written by Bankim Chandra Chatterjee.

Vande Mataram!
Sujalam, Suphalam, Malayaja Shitalam,
Shasya shyamalam, Mataram!
Shubhra jyotsana Pulakita yaminim,
Phulla kusmita drumadala Shobhinim
Suhasinim Sumadhura bhashinim
Sukhadam, Varadam, Mataram!

National Symbols

1. National Animal - Tiger
2. National Bird - Peacock
3. National Flower - Lotus
4. National Fruit - Mango
5. National Currency - Rupee (₹)
6. National Tree - Banyan
7. National River - Ganga
8. National Aquatic Animal - Dolphin

National Calendar

1. India's National Calendar is based on *Saka* Era.
2. It was adopted and introduced on March 22, 1957.
3. It has a normal year of 365 days.
4. *Chaitra* is the first month and *Phalguna* is the last month of the year.
5. *Chaitra* 1 falls on March 22 in a normal year and on March 21 in a leap year.

FIRST IN INDIA

✦ The first Indian to get the Nobel Prize	Rabindra Nath Tagore (1913)
✦ First President of Indian Republic	Dr. Rajendra Prasad
✦ First Prime Minister	Pt. Jawaharlal Nehru
✦ First Woman Prime Minister	Smt. Indira Gandhi
✦ First Woman President	Smt. Pratibha Patil
✦ First President of the Indian National Congress	W.C. Banerjee
✦ First Woman Governor of a State	Smt. Sarojini Naidu
✦ First Woman Chief Minister of a State	Smt. Sucheta Kriplani
✦ First Indian President of the International Court of Justice	Dr. Nagendra Singh
✦ First Indian in the British Parliament	Dadabhai Naoroji
✦ First Field Marshal	S.H.F.J. Manekshaw
✦ First Indian to conquer Mt. Everest	Tenzing Norgay
✦ First Indian Cosmonaut	Rakesh Sharma
✦ First Indian to address UN General Assembly in Hindi	Atal Behari Vajpayee
✦ First Indian to get Special Oscar Award	Satyajit Ray
✦ First Indian Satellite	Aryabhatta
✦ First person to get Bharat Ratna	C. Rajagopalachari
✦ First Women to get Bharat Ratna	Smt. Indira Gandhi
✦ First Governor-General of Free India	C. Rajagopalachari
✦ First Woman Defence Minister	Smt. Nirmala Sitharaman
✦ First Chief of Defence Staff (CDS)	General Bipin Rawat

LARGEST, HIGHEST, BIGGEST AND LONGEST IN INDIA

✦ Award for Gallantry, highest	Param Vir Chakra
✦ Award, highest civilian	Bharat Ratna
✦ Cattle Fair, largest	Sonepur Fair (Bihar)
✦ Desert, largest	Thar (Rajasthan)
✦ Dam, largest	Hirakud Dam (Odisha)
✦ Gateway, highest	Buland Darwaja at Fatehpur Sikri (176 ft.)
✦ Lake, largest (Fresh water)	Wular Lake (Jammu & Kashmir)
✦ Literacy, highest	Kerala
✦ Museum, largest	Indian Museum (Kolkata)

✦ Peak, highest*	K-2 (Pak-occupied Kashmir)
✦ River, longest**	The Ganga (2,510 km)
✦ Platform, longest	At Shree Siddharoodha Swamiji Railway Station Hubballi, Karnataka (1507 mtr)
✦ Railway Bridge, longest	Vembanad, Kerala (4.62 km)
✦ Rainfall, highest (mean annual)	Mowsynram near Cherrapunji (1178 cm)
✦ Road, longest	NH-44 (3,745 km)
✦ State, with maximum density of population	Bihar
✦ Minaret, highest	Qutub Minar (Delhi 72.5 m)
✦ Waterfall, highest	Kunchikal Waterfall (Karnataka : 455 mtr)
✦ Zoo, largest	Arignar Anna Zoological Park, Chennai (TN)

PLACES OF CULTURAL IMPORTANCE

Abu, Mount: Hill station in Rajasthan; contains famous Dilwara Jain Temples and Training College for the Central Reserve Police.

Agra: Situated in UP, famous for Taj Mahal, Red Fort and Pearl Mosque. Sikandra, the tomb of Akbar is situated here. It is also a centre of leather industry.

Taj Mahal

Ajanta: Situated in Maharashtra, near Aurangabad, it is famous for its cave temples some of which date back to 2nd century BC. The caves contain magnificient frescoes and sculptures depicting Buddhist Jatakas and teachings of Buddha.

Aligarh (UP): Seat of Muslim University, also manufactures locks, scissors, knives and dairy products.

Amritsar: Situated in Punjab, it is the most important religious centre of the Sikhs. It is famous for Golden Temple, Durgiyana Mandir and Jallianwala Bagh tragedy in 1919.

Golden Temple

Amarnath (J&K): 28 miles from Pahalgam; famous pilgrim centre of Hindus.

Ajmer: Situated in Rajasthan, it is known for Pushkar Lake, Pushkar Temple, Tomb of Muslim Saint Shaikh Moinuddin Chishti, Palace of Akbar and other well-known historical buildings.

Badrinath: Situated in Himalayas in Uttarakhand, it is a famous pilgrim place for Hindus as it is identified as one of the four Dhams.

Badrinath Dham

* Highest peak in the world is Mount Everest, which is in Nepal. K-2 is the second highest peak in the world. It is 8,611 metres high.

** Indus and Brahmaputra (each 2900 km). Both of them, however, cover a long distance outside India.

Varanasi (UP): A holy place of the Hindus, a seat of Hindu University, famous for silk and brocade and wooden toys, brassware, lac bangles and diesel locomotive engines.

Bhubaneshwar: Capital of Odisha; also famous for Lingaraja Temple.

Chidambaram (Tamil Nadu): Famous for Nataraja Temple.

Dakshineswar: Situated near Kolkata, West Bengal, it is known for one of the priest of the Kali temple- Ramakrishna Paramhansa. His famous disciple, Swami Vivekananda spread the message of nationalism, love and devotion.

Ellora: Situated near Aurangabad, Maharashtra, it is famous for its 34 Cave temples, including the one being the largest Rock-cut temple. There are twelve Buddhist, seventeen Hindu and five Jain cave temples. These temples have been declared as world heritage.

Elephanta Caves: Situated in an island, off the coast of Mumbai in Maharashtra, the caves have remarkably well executed sculptures of the Hindu Gods.

Haridwar: In Uttarakhand on the Ganga, an ancient place of Hindus pilgrimage, and Heavy Electricals Industry at Ranipur.

Jagannath (Puri): Situated in Odisha, it is one of the four Hindu Dhams. The Jagannath temple, built in 11th century AD, is a marvellous architectural monument. A large number of tourist flock the place due to nice beaches.

Kedarnath (Uttarakhand): A holy place for the Hindus in Garhwal district.

Rameshwaram (Tamil Nadu): A sacred place of the Hindus in the southern tip of India connected with Lord Rama's invasion of Sri Lanka. It has a huge temple with long corridors. It is situated on a small island.

Chidambaram

Dakshineshwar

Jagannath Temple

Rameshwaram

NICKNAMES OF RIVERS AND CITIES

✦	Bengal's Sorrow	–	Damodar River
✦	City of Palaces	–	Kolkata
✦	Gateway of India	–	Mumbai
✦	Land of Five Rivers	–	Punjab
✦	Pink City	–	Jaipur
✦	Blue Mountains	–	Nilgiri Hills

IMPORTANT ARCHITECTURES, MONUMENTS ETC.

✦ Meenakshi Temple	Madurai (Tamil Nadu)
✦ Khajuraho Temple	Madhya Pradesh
✦ Lingaraja Temple	Bhubaneswar (Odisha)
✦ Jagannath Temple	Puri (Odisha)
✦ Gateway of India	Mumbai (Maharashtra)
✦ Buland Darwaja	Fatehpur Sikri (UP)
✦ Victory Tower	Chittorgarh (Rajasthan)
✦ Gol Gumbaj	Bijapur (Karnataka)
✦ Golden Temple	Amritsar (Punjab)
✦ Dilwara Temples	Mt. Abu (Rajasthan)
✦ Sarnath Temple	Varanasi (UP)
✦ Rameshwaram	Tamil Nadu
✦ Amarnath Temple	Jammu & Kashmir
✦ Sambhar Lake	Rajasthan
✦ Dal Lake	Srinagar (Jammu & Kashmir)
✦ Thumba (Rocket Launching Station)	Kerala
✦ Sriharikota (Satellite Launching Station)	Andhra Pradesh
✦ Ajanta and Ellora Caves	Aurangabad (Maharashtra)
✦ Taj Mahal	Agra (UP)
✦ Char Minar	Hyderabad (Telangana)
✦ Sabarmati	Ahmedabad (Gujarat)
✦ Sanchi (Stupa)	Madhya Pradesh
✦ Vivekanand Rock	Tamil Nadu (near Kanyakumari)

MEMORIALS/SAMADHIS

Name	*Associated with*
✦ Rajghat	Mahatma Gandhi
✦ Shantivan	Jawahar Lal Nehru
✦ Samta Sthal	Jagjivan Ram
✦ Vijayghat	Lal Bahadur Shastri
✦ Shakti Sthal	Indira Gandhi
✦ Vir Bhumi	Rajiv Gandhi
✦ Kisan Ghat	Ch. Charan Singh
✦ Sadaiv Atal	Atal Behari Vajpayee

Rajghat (Gandhi Samadhi)

IMPORTANT DAYS OF INDIA

✦ National Youth Day	January 12
✦ Army Day	January 15
✦ Republic Day	January 26
✦ Martyr's Day	January 30
✦ National Science Day	February 28
✦ Independence Day	August 15
✦ Teacher's Day	September 5
✦ Mahatma Gandhi's Birthday	October 2
✦ Air Force Day	October 8
✦ Energy Conservation Day	October 14
✦ National Integration Day	October 31
✦ Children's Day	November 14
✦ Navy Day	December 4
✦ Flag Day	December 7
✦ Good Governance Day	December 25

POPULAR NAMES

Popular Name	Real Name
✦ Iron Man	Sardar Vallabhbhai Patel
✦ Bapu, Father of Nation	Mahatma Gandhi
✦ Chachaji	Jawaharlal Nehru
✦ Gurudev	Rabindranath Tagore
✦ Lokmanya	Bal Gangadhar Tilak
✦ Netaji	Subhash Chandra Bose
✦ Punjab Kesari	Lala Lajpat Rai
✦ Mahamana	Madan Mohan Malviya
✦ Baba Saheb	Dr. B.R. Ambedkar
✦ Grand Old Man of India	Dada Bhai Naoroji
✦ Lok Nayak	Jay Prakash Narain
✦ Nightingale of India	Sarojini Naidu
✦ Bal, Pal, Lal	Bal Gangadhar Tilak, Bipin Chandra Pal, Lala Lajpat Rai

Sardar Vallabhbhai Patel

IMPORTANT SLOGANS & QUOTATIONS

Slogans

✦ Dilli Chalo	Netaji Subhash Chandra Bose
✦ Jai Jawan Jai Kisan	Lal Bahadur Shastri
✦ Garibi Hatao	Indira Gandhi
✦ Quit India	Mahatma Gandhi

Quotations

✦ Swarajya is my birth right and I shall have it.	Bal Gangadhar Tilak
✦ Give me blood, I shall give you freedom.	Subhash Chandra Bose

REGIONAL FESTIVALS

Festival	*State*
✦ Teej	Rajasthan
✦ Baisakhi	Punjab and Haryana
✦ Ganesh Chaturthi	Maharashtra
✦ Durga Puja	West Bengal
✦ Onam	Kerala
✦ Pongal	Tamil Nadu and Andhra Predesh
✦ Lohri	Punjab & Haryana
✦ Bhageli Bihu	Assam
✦ Ugadi	Karnataka

POPULAR DANCES

Dance	*State*
✦ Bharat Natyam	Tamil Nadu
✦ Kathakali	Kerala
✦ Kathak	North India
✦ Manipuri	Manipur
✦ Odissi	Odisha
✦ Kuchipudi	Andhra Pradesh
✦ Bhangra	Punjab
✦ Bihu	Assam
✦ Garba	Gujarat
✦ Ghoomar	Rajasthan

BOOKS AND AUTHORS

✦ Ain-e-Akbari	Abul Fazl
✦ Anand Math	Bankim Chandra Chatterjee
✦ Arthashastra	Kautilya
✦ Chidambara	Sumitranandan Pant
✦ Devdas	Sarat Chandra Chatterjee
✦ Discovery of India	Jawaharlal Nehru
✦ Geet Govind	Jaya Dev
✦ Geetanjali	Rabindranath Tagore
✦ Godan	Munshi Prem Chand
✦ Idols	Sunil Gavaskar
✦ India Divided	Dr. Rajendra Prasad
✦ India Wins Freedom	Abul Kalam Azad
✦ Kamayani	Jaishankar Prasad
✦ Mahabharat	Ved Vyas
✦ My Experiments with Truth	Mahatma Gandhi
✦ Ramayan	Valmiki
✦ Ram Charit Manas	Tulsidas
✦ Saket	Maithili Sharan Gupta
✦ Pancha Tantra	Vishnu Sharma

WORLD

Facts About UNO

- UNO officially came into existence on October 24, 1945.
- UNO headquaters are located at New York.
- UN Charter was signed on June 26, 1945 by 50 countries at San Francisco.
- Objectives of the UN are:
  (i) Security, (ii) Welfare, (iii) Protection of Human Rights
- UN is financed by the contibution from member countries.
- The six major organs of the UNO are:
  1. General Assembly
  2. Security Council
  3. Economic and Social Council
  4. Trusteeship Council
  5. International Court of Justice
  6. Secretariat
- The Security Council has 15 members–5 permanent members and 10 non-permanent members.
- The permanent members of the Security Council are–USA, UK, Russia, France and China.
- The non-permanent members of the Security Council are elected by the General Assembly for a term of 2 years.
- The right to veto is available to only 5 permanent members of the Security Council.
- At present 193 countries are members of the UNO.

FIRST IN THE WORLD

First Chinese visitor to India	Fahien
First foreign invader of India	Alexander, the Great (Greek)
First person to climb Mt. Everest	Tenzing Norgay (Indian)
First atom bomb dropped at	Hiroshima (Japan)
First man in the space	Yuri Gagarin (former USSR)
First woman in the space	Valentina Tereshkova (former USSR)
First person to land on the moon	Neil Armstrong (USA)
First person to climb Mt. Everest twice	Nawang Gombu
First President of the USA	George Washington
First woman Prime Minister	Sirimavo Bandaranaike (Sri Lanka)
First person to swim across English Channel	Mathew Webb
First woman to swim across English Channel	Gertrude Caroline Ederle
First woman to climb Mt. Everest	Junko Tabei (Japan)

✦ First test-tube Baby	Louise Brown (UK; 1978)
✦ First person to reach South Pole	R. Amundsen (Norway)
✦ First person to reach North Pole	Robert Peary (USA)

HIGHEST, BIGGEST, LARGEST, LONGEST, ETC. IN THE WORLD

✦ Animal, tallest	Giraffe
✦ Bird, largest	Ostrich
✦ Canal, longest	Suez canal
✦ Church, largest	St. Peter's Church (Rome)
✦ Continent, largest smallest	Eurasian Landmass (Europe and Asia) Australia
✦ Country, largest smallest	(i) in population: China (ii) in area: Russia In both population & area: Vatican City
✦ Desert, largest	Sahara (N. Africa)
✦ Gulf, largest	Gulf of Mexico
✦ Island, biggest	Greenland
✦ Lake, largest largest (fresh water)	Caspian Sea Superior Lake (USA-Canada border)
✦ Mountain, highest peak	Mt. Everest
✦ Ocean, largest and deepest	The Pacific Ocean
✦ Place, rainiest	Mowsynram near Cherrapunji (Meghalaya)
✦ Planet, biggest brightest nearest to the sun	Jupiter Venus Mercury
✦ Railway Line, longest	Trans-Siberian Railway
✦ River, longest	(i) Nile (6670 km) (ii) Amazon (6570 km)
✦ Statue, tallest	Statue of Unity (182 m, Gujarat)
✦ Building, tallest	Burj Khalifa, Dubai (2010), 818 m
✦ Museum, Largest	American Museum of Natural History, New York
✦ Waterfall, highest	Salto-Angel (Venezuela)

Geographical Explorations/Discoveries

Place	*Explorer/Discoverers*	*Nationality*	*Year*
America	Christopher Columbus	Italy	1492
Hawaii Islands (Sandwich Islands)	Captain James Cook	England	1778
Newfoundland	John Cabot	England	1497
New Zealand	Abel Janszoon Tasman	Holland	1642
North Pole	Robert Peary	USA	1909
Sea Route to India	Vasco da Gama	Portugal	1498
South Pole	Ronald Amundsen	Norway	1911

IMPORTANT DAYS OF THE WORLD

✦ International Women's Day	March 8
✦ World Consumers' Rights Day	March 15
✦ World Disabled Day	March 15
✦ World Health Day	April 7
✦ World May Day	May 1
✦ World Red Cross Day	May 8
✦ Commonwealth Day	May 24
✦ World No Tobacco Day	May 31
✦ World Environment Day	June 5
✦ International Yoga Day	June 21
✦ Day Against Drug Abuse & Trafficking	June 26
✦ World Population Day	July 11
✦ Hiroshima Day	August 6
✦ World Literacy Day	September 8
✦ World Ozone Day	September 16
✦ World Tourism Day	September 27
✦ World Habitat Day	October 3
✦ World Standards Day	October 14
✦ World Food Day	October 16
✦ World UN Day	October 24
✦ World Human Rights Day	December 10

NICKNAMES OF COUNTRIES, RIVERS AND CITIES

✦ China's Sorrow	Hwang-Ho
✦ Cockpit of Europe	Belgium
✦ Dark Continent	Africa
✦ Empire City	New York
✦ Eternal City/ City of Seven Hills	Rome
✦ Forbidden City	Lhasa (Tibet)
✦ Gift of the Nile	Egypt
✦ Hermit Kingdom	Korea
✦ Holy Land	Jerusalem (Palestine)
✦ Island of Cloves	Zanzibar
✦ Key to the Mediterranean	Gibraltar
✦ Land of Maple Leaf/Lilies	Canada
✦ Land of the Rising Sun	Japan
✦ Land of the Thousand Lakes	Finland
✦ Land of Golden Fleece	Australia
✦ Land of Kangaroo	Australia
✦ Land of Midnight Sun	Norway
✦ Land of the White Elephants	Thailand
✦ Manchester of the Orient	Osaka (Japan)
✦ Playground of Europe	Switzerland
✦ Queen of the Adriatic	Venice (Italy)
✦ Roof of the World	Pamirs
✦ Sickman of Europe	Turkey
✦ Sugar Bowl of the World	Cuba
✦ Venice of the North	Stockholm (Sweden)

ABBREVIATIONS

AD	:	Anno Domini (in the year of our Lord)
AHQ	:	Air Head Quarters: Army Head Quarters
AIDS	:	Acquired Immuno Deficiency Syndrome
AIIMS	:	All India Institute of Medical Sciences
AM	:	Ante Meridiem (before noon), Amplitude Modulation
BC	:	Before Christ, Backward Class
BSF	:	Border Security Force
CBI	:	Central Bureau of Investigation
C-in-C	:	Commander-in-Chief
CTBT	:	Comprehensive Test Ban Treaty
DoT	:	Department of Telecommunication
E&OE	:	Errors and Omission Excepted
FAX	:	Fascimile Exchange
FDI	:	Foreign Direct Investment
FIR	:	First Information Report
GATT	:	General Agreement on Tariffs and Trade
GMT	:	Greenwich Mean Time
HRD	:	Human Resource Development
ICAR	:	Indian Council of Agricultural Research
ILO	:	International Labour Organisation
IMF	:	International Monetary Fund
ISRO	:	Indian Space Research Organisation
LASER	:	Light Amplification by Stimulated Emission of Radiation
NASA	:	National Aeronautics and Space Administration (of USA)
NCERT	:	National Council of Educational Research and Training
NHRC	:	National Human Rights Commission
PIN	:	Postal Index Number, Personal Identification Number
PM	:	Post Meridiem (afternoon); Prime Minister
PSU	:	Public Sector Undertaking
RBC	:	Red Blood Corpuscles
RBI	:	Reserve Bank of India
SOS	:	Save our Souls
TNT	:	Tri Nitro Toulene
UNO	:	United Nations Organisation
UNESCO	:	United Nations Educational, Scientific and Cultural Organisation
VIP	:	Very Important Person
WHO	:	World Health Organisation

❖ ❖ ❖